Psychological Trauma

Edited by
DORA BLACK
MARTIN NEWMAN
JEAN HARRIS-HENDRIKS
GILLIAN MEZEY

Psychological Trauma

A Developmental Approach

GASKELL

Gaskell is an imprint of the Royal College of Psychiatrists,
17 Belgrave Square, London SW1X 8PG

British Library Cataloguing-in-Publication Data
A catalogue record for this book is available from
the British Library.

ISBN 0-902241-98-2

Distributed in North America
by American Psychiatric Press, Inc.
ISBN 0-88048-578-7

Printed by Bell & Bain Ltd, Glasgow

Contents

Contributors   8
Foreword   11

Part I. Human responses to stress: normal and abnormal

1   On the origins of post-traumatic stress disorder
    Alan Beveridge   3
2   Normal and abnormal responses to stress: a
    developmental approach   *Colin Murray Parkes*   10
3   Classification   *Gordon Turnbull*   19
4   The interaction of trauma and grief   *Beverley Raphael*   31
5   Memory and trauma   *Daniel Siegel*   44
6   Theoretical models of post-traumatic stress disorder   54
    A.   Physiological and biological mechanisms
       Ronan McIvor   55
    B.   Psychoanalytical models   *Cleo Van Velsen*   61
    C.   Cognitive–behavioural models of PTSD   *Deborah Lee*
       and Stuart Turner   64

**Part II. Disasters, war, civil conflict, dislocation
and interpersonal violence**

7   A typology of disasters   *Colin Murray Parkes*   81
8   Community disasters   94
    A.   The *Jupiter* disaster   *William Yule*   94
    B.   The *Herald of Free Enterprise* disaster
       William Yule, Ruth Williams and Stephen Joseph   97
    C.   Help-seeking by community residents following the
       Lockerbie air disaster   *Margaret Mitchell*   99
    D.   The *Marchioness* riverboat disaster   *Linda Goldsmith*
       and Janet Haddington   104
    E.   The Kegworth air disaster   *Marion Gibson*   108
    F.   The King's Cross fire: second phase intervention
       Rachel Rosser   111
    G.   The Hungerford massacre   *Elizabeth Capewell*   116

H.   The Piper Alpha oil platform disaster
     David Alexander   121
I.   Psychological consequences of road traffic accidents
     Martin Newman   126
9   The effect of conflict on combatants   *Martin Deahl*   134
10 The effect of conflict on civilian populations   148
A.   The impact of war and atrocity on civilian populations
     Derek Summerfield   148
B.   Civil violence   *Gerard Loughrey*   156
C.   Children and conflict   *Anula Nikapota*   161
D.   Concepts, causes and magnitude of population
     displacement   *William Parry-Jones*   165
11 Psychological responses to interpersonal violence   176
A.   Adults   *Gillian Mezey*   176
B.   Children   *Tony Kaplan*   184
12 Post-traumatic stress disorder in the elderly   *Inge Hyman* 199
13 Torture   *Stuart Turner and Ronan McIvor*   205

Part III. Diagnosis, intervention and treatment

14 Diagnosis and treatment   219
A.   Diagnosis   *Martin Newman and Deborah Lee*   219
B.   Interventions and treatments   *William Parry-Jones*   230
15 Debriefing and crisis intervention   *Walter Busuttil
    and Angela Busuttil*   238
16 Bereavement counselling   *Bill Young and Dora Black*   250
17 Treatment of adults   264
A.   Behavioural and cognitive approaches   *David Richards
     and Karina Lovell*   264
B.   Psychodynamic psychotherapy   *Cleo Van Velsen*   274
C.   Eye movement desensitisation   *Martin Newman*   278
18 Children and adolescents   281
A.   Treatment of children and families   *Dora Black*   281
B.   Psychodynamic psychotherapy   *Ricky Emanuel
     and Annette Mendelsohn*   287
19 Psychopharmacology   *Martin Newman*   294
20 Service provision   305
A.   The role of the police   *Thomas Dickie*   305
B.   Social work in disasters   *Marion Gibson*   309
C.   The school in disasters   *William Yule and Anne Gold*   314
D.   The role of volunteers   *Dora Black*   320
E.   The role of employers   *David Richards*   323
21 Effects of disasters on helpers   *Rachel Rosser*   326

Part IV. Legal aspects: victims as witnesses and claimants

22 Civil law and psychiatric injury   *Michael Napier
    and Kay Wheat*   341

23 Post-traumatic stress reactions and the criminal law
    Gwen Adshead and Gillian Mezey   351
24 Psychiatric assessment of stress disorders for legal purposes
    Nigel Eastman   363
25 Ethical issues in disaster and other extreme situations
    Naomi Richman   374
26 Organising psychosocial responses to disasters   *Dora Black
    and Jean Harris-Hendriks*   383
27 Overview and comment   *Jean Harris-Hendriks,
    Martin Newman, Dora Black and Gillian Mezey*   392

Contributors

Gwen Adshead, MBBS, MRCPsych, MA, Lecturer in Victimology, Department of Forensic Psychiatry, Institute of Psychiatry, London SE5 8AF

David A. Alexander, MA, PhD, FBPsS, Professor, Department of Mental Health, University of Aberdeen, and Honorary Consultant, Grampian Police; Department of Mental Health, University of Aberdeen, Aberdeen AB9 2ZD

Allan Beveridge, MB ChB, MRCPsych, MPhil, Consultant Psychiatrist, Queen Margaret Hospital, Whitefield Road, Dunfermline, Fife KY12 0SU

Dora Black, MB ChB, FRCPsych, DPM, Consultant Child and Adolescent Psychiatrist and Director, Traumatic Stress Clinic, Camden & Islington Community Health NHS Trust, 73 Charlotte Street, London W1P 1LB. Honorary Senior Lecturer, Royal Free Hospital School of Medicine, University College, London and Institute of Child Health. Honorary Consultant, Royal Free Hospital, Great Ormond Street Hospital for Children, and Tavistock Clinic.

Angela Busuttil, BSc, MSc, C.Psychol AFBPsS, Chartered Clinical Psychologist, Department of Clinical Psychology, Victoria Hospital, Swindon

Squadron Leader **Walter Busuttil**, MB ChB, MPhil, MRCGP, MRCPsych, RAF, Consultant Psychiatrist, Department of Community Psychiatry (East Anglia), Royal Air Force Marham, Kings Lynn, Norfolk, PE33 9NP

Elizabeth Capewell, MA, PGCE, Dip HumPsych., Cert Couns, Director, Centre for Crisis Management and Education, Roselyn House, 93 Old Newtown Road, Newbury, Berkshire RG14 7DE

Martin P. Deahl, MA, MB BS, MPhil, MRCPsych, Senior Lecturer in Psychological Medicine, St Bartholomew and Royal London Hospital School of Medicine and Dentistry

Thomas I. Dickie, QPM, Chief Superintendent (Operations), Strathclyde Police, Police Headquarters, 173 Pitt Street, Glasgow G2 4JS

Nigel Eastman, MB BSc, FRCPsych, Barrister at Law, Head, Section of Forensic Psychiatry, St George's Hospital Medical School, London SW17 0RE

Ricky Emanuel, MSc, Head of Child and Adolescent Psychotherapy Services, Department of Child and Adolescent Psychiatry, Royal Free Hospital, London NW3 2QG

Marion C. A. Gibson, MSSc, Dip SW, CQSW, PQSW, Manager, Staff Care Service and Crisis Support Team, South and East Belfast HSS Trust, Trust Headquarters, Knockbracken Healthcare Park, Saintfield Road, Belfast BT8 8BH

Anne Gold, MA, Lecturer in Education Management, Management Development Centre, Institute of Education, University of London, 55 Gordon Square, London WC1H 0NU

Linda Goldsmith, CQSW, Social Services Inspector and Counsellor/Psychotherapist, London West Inspection Group, Social Services Inspectorate, Department of Health, 7th Floor, Hannibal House, Elephant and Castle, London SE1 6TE

Janet Haddington, MA, CQSW, Analytic Psychotherapist (Arbours), Founder, National Association of Bereavement Services, 20 Norton Folgate, London E1 6BD

Jean M. Harris-Hendriks, MB ChB, DPM, FRCPsych, Consultant Child and Adolescent Psychiatrist, Traumatic Stress Clinic, Camden & Islington Community Health NHS Trust, 73 Charlotte Street, London W1P 1LB. Honorary Senior Lecturer, Royal Free Hospital School of Medicine, and University College, London

Inge Hyman, MSc, Chartered Clinical Psychologist, 101 Hampstead Way, London NW11 7LR

Stephen Joseph, BSc, MSc, PhD, Lecturer in Psychology, University of Essex, Wivenhoe Park, Colchester CO4 3SQ, Essex

Tony Kaplan, MB ChB, MRCPsych, Consultant Child and Adolescent Psychiatrist, Service for Adolescents and Families in Enfield, Rownham's Centre, 24 Dryden Road, Enfield EN1 2PP, and Honorary Consultant, Traumatic Stress Clinic, 73 Charlotte Street, London W1P 1LB

Deborah Lee, MSc, Chartered Clinical Psychologist, Deputy Director (Adult Services), Traumatic Stress Clinic, 73 Charlotte Street, London W1P 1LB

Karina Lovell, RMN, MSc, Research Nurse, Institute of Psychiatry, London SE5 8AF

Gerard C. Loughrey, MB, MRCPsych, Consultant Psychiatrist, Downshire Hospital, Ardglass Road, Downpatrick, Co. Down BT30 6RA, Northern Ireland

Ronan J. McIvor, MB BCh, BAO, MRCPsych, Senior Registrar, Bethlem and Maudsley NHS Trust, London

Annette Mendelsohn, MA, MACP, Child Psychotherapist, Department of Child and Adolescent Psychiatry, Royal Free Hospital, London NW3 2QG

Gillian C. Mezey, MB BS, MRCPsych, Senior Lecturer and Consultant, Section of Forensic Psychiatry, St George's Hospital, London SW17 0RE

Margaret Mitchell, MA, PhD, MSc, C. Psychol., Reader in Psychology, Department of Psychology, Glasgow Caledonian University, Cowcaddens Road, Glasgow G4 0BA

Colin Murray Parkes, MD, FRCPsych, OBE, Consultant Psychiatrist, St Christopher's Hospice, Lawrie Park Road, Sydenham, London SE26 6DZ

Michael Napier, LLB, Solicitor, Senior Partner, Irwin Mitchell, St. Peter's House, Hartshead, Sheffield S1 2EL and Visiting Professor of Litigation, Nottingham Trent University

Martin C. Newman, MB ChB, MRCPsych, Senior Registrar in Child and Adolescent Psychiatry, Department of Child and Adolescent Psychiatry, St George's Hospital, London SW17 0RE

Anula Nikapota, MB BS, DPM, FRCPsych, Consultant in Child and Adolescent Psychiatry, Brixton Child Guidance Unit, 19 Brixton Water Lane, London SW2 1NU

William Parry-Jones, MA, MD, FRCPsych, Professor of Child and Adolescent Psychiatry, University of Glasgow, Royal Hospital for Sick Children, Yorkhill, Glasgow G3 8SJ

Beverley Raphael, AM, MB BS, MD, FASSA, FRCPsych, FRANZCP, Director, Centre for Mental Health, NSW Health Department, 73 Miller Street, North Sydney, NSW 2060, Australia

David Richards, BSc Hons, RN, Research and Development Manager, Leeds Community and Mental Health Services NHS Trust, 24 Hyde Terrace, Leeds LS2 9LN

Naomi Richman, BM BCh, FRCPsych, Emeritus Reader in Child Psychiatry, Medical Foundation for Victims of Torture, 96 Grafton Road, London, NW5 3EJ

Rachael Rosser, MA, MB BChir, FRCP, FRCPsych, Professor of Psychiatry and Honorary Consultant, University College London, Department of Psychiatry, Middlesex Hospital, London W1A 8NN

Daniel J. Siegel, MD, Assistant Professor, Acting Director of Training in Child and Adolescent Psychiatry, University of California at Los Angeles, 11980 San Vicente Boulevard, Suite 810, Los Angeles, California 90049, US

Andrew Sims, MA, MD, FRCPsych, FRCP Ed, Professor of Psychiatry, University of Leeds, Division of Psychiatry, St James's University Hospital, Leeds LS9 7TF

Derek A. Summerfield, BSc, MB BS, MRCPsych, Honorary Senior Lecturer in the Section of Community Psychiatry, St George's Hospital Medical School, London SW17 0RE, and Psychiatrist at the Medical Foundation for Care of Victims of Torture, 96–98 Grafton Road, London NW5 3EJ

Gordon J. Turnbull, BSc, FRCP, FRCPsych, Clinical Director, Traumatic Stress Unit, Ticehurst House Hospital, Ticehurst, East Sussex TN5 7HU

Stuart W. Turner, MA, MD, MRCP, FRCPsych, Consultant Psychiatrist, Director, Traumatic Stress Clinic, 73 Charlotte Street, London W1P 1LB; Medical Director, Camden and Islington Community Health Service NHS Trust; and Honorary Senior Lecturer, UCL Medical School

Cleo van Velsen, MB BS, MRCPsych, Consultant Psychotherapist, Psychotherapy Unit and Department of Forensic Psychiatry, The Bethlem and Maudsley NHS Trust, Maudsley Hospital, Denmark Hill, Camberwell, London SE5 8AZ

Kay Wheat, BA, Solicitor, Senior Lecturer in Law, Nottingham Law School, Nottingham Trent University, Nottingham, NG1 4BU

Ruth Williams, MA, Dip Psych, Senior Lecturer in Psychology, Institute of Psychiatry; and Honorary Consultant Clinical Psychologist at the Maudsley Trust, Institute of Psychiatry, London SE5 8AF

Bill Young, MB ChB, DCH, MRCP, MRCPsych, Consultant Child and Adolescent Psychiatrist, Howard House Children's Therapy Centre, Hampstead, London

William Yule, PhD, FBPsS, Professor of Applied Child Psychology, University of London Institute of Psychiatry, and Consultant Clinical Psychologist, Bethlem Maudsley NHS Trust, Institute of Psychiatry, London SE5 8AF

Foreword

This is a book which has been needed for a long time – a comprehensive text dealing with psychological trauma from the standpoint of the practitioner. Psychological trauma is an example of that class of phenomena that we, as human beings, have known over many centuries to be significant, but because we had believed there was so little we could do about it, we had chosen to ignore and deny. This was certainly true as far as the provision of services was concerned. Until very recently, neither the National Health Service in the UK nor employers of individuals in potentially dangerous occupations had made any provision for people who had become the victims of individual or collective disaster from the psychological standpoint, even though there may have been elaborate arrangements for the prevention, treatment and rehabilitation of physical trauma.

This topic, psychological trauma or post-traumatic stress, gained much greater prominence in British psychiatry at the time of the Gulf war as, fortuitously, six months notice was given of the expected onset of hostilities and it was initially anticipated that many injured servicemen would be repatriated to hospitals in the UK. At the same time, early in the 1990s, effective methods of treatment for psychological trauma had been developed both for the victims themselves and those providing help and care. Although, thankfully, the influx of casualties never happened, the Royal College of Psychiatrists responded to a Government request by establishing a network of experts able to provide local services for the management of psychological trauma in district hospitals. The momentum of this initiative has been maintained so that management of the psychological sequelae of disaster is now an accepted task of all psychiatrists and psychiatric services. For this reason, if for no other, detailed and accurate information is urgently needed.

This makes this contribution by Dora Black, Martin Newman, Jean Harris-Hendriks and Gillian Mezey particularly appropriate. This is a comprehensive account of psychological trauma from a predominantly British perspective and deals with major topics of professional interest.

Part I, 'Human responses to stress: normal and abnormal', covers contributions made by different psychological mechanisms and theoretical standpoints to the origins of psychological distress. Part II, 'Disasters, war, civil conflict, dislocation and interpersonal violence', describes a number of the recent community disasters in and around Britain and looks at the effects of trauma upon different groups such as combatants, civilian populations, children, old people and victims of torture. Part III, 'Diagnosis, intervention and treatment', is an account of the range of treatments and management strategies, described both for the individual sufferer and as applied to a defined population, including how to enlist the help of the various professionals and volunteers. Part IV, 'Legal aspects: victims as witnesses and claimants', deals with the interface between the law, psychiatry and the experience of disaster, mostly from a British standpoint.

It has recently been accepted by the courts that psychological trauma is an occupational hazard of certain types of employment and at certain times, and that these employees do indeed suffer from psychological distress and illness as a direct result of trauma. This being so, it behoves employers and the providers of healthcare to be aware of the danger of psychological trauma and make adequate arrangements for its prevention when possible, or to diminish the severity, chronicity and degree of suffering, both of sufferers and their relatives, when it is not. For these reasons this book should not only be prescribed for psychiatrists, clinical psychologists, accident and emergency specialists and other involved health professionals, but also lawyers, employers and those involved in the strategic planning of healthcare.

It is therefore my pleasure to commend this book to fellow practitioners in any of the relevant professions. I have been involved in a professional capacity with several major disasters and with the victims of many individual situations of trauma, and I would have been grateful to have had this work available at that time. It should prove a useful source of information for practitioners in the future.

Andrew Sims
Past President
Royal College of Psychiatrists

Part I. Human responses to stress: normal and abnormal

1 On the origins of post-traumatic stress disorder

ALLAN BEVERIDGE

The reactions of human beings to catastrophic events have been recorded from earliest times, as is evident from sources depicting the Sumerian, Hebrew and Ancient Greek eras (Boehnlein & Kinzie, 1992). Rather more recently, the diaries of Samuel Pepys in the 17th century have described responses to the Great Plague and the Fire of London, while the psychological impact of an avalanche on Italian peasants in the 1750s has been reconstructed from original documents by Parry-Jones & Parry-Jones (1994). However, serious medical interest in the subject began in the 19th century.

Psychiatry has played only a minimal role in the early evolution of the concept. A search of Victorian psychiatric literature finds little discussion of any condition that might be regarded as anticipating post traumatic stress disorder. For example, in the standard psychiatric textbooks of the day, such as Bucknill & Tuke's (1879) *Manual of Psychological Medicine*, George Savage's (1884) *Insanity and Allied Neuroses*, William Sankey's (1884) *Lectures on Mental Diseases* or Thomas Clouston's (1896) *Clinical Lectures on Mental Diseases*, we find scant mention of the topic.

The reason for this lies partly in the nature of Victorian psychiatry. It was overwhelmingly physicalist – or what we might call 'organic' – in its conception of mental disorder. Bucknill & Tuke (1879) had declared that insanity was a disease of the brain, and this was repeated as an article of faith by all leading Victorian alienists. For example, Clouston (1896) maintained "the brain is the man". The historian Michael Clark (1981) has characterised late 19th century British psychiatry by what he calls its "rejection of psychological approaches to mental disorder". Indeed, when one looks at the discussions of Victorian psychiatrists on the causes of insanity, we find that they gave much greater weight to the physical causes rather than the psychological – or what they called "moral" – causes. Shepherd (1977) has shown that, as the century wore on, alienists increasingly emphasised the physical causes of insanity at the cost of psychological ones. Victorian psychiatric textbooks bear out Shepherd's observation. For example, Clouston (1896) in his discussion of the causes of insanity was dismissive of the potential of wars or external events to produce mental disorder. Instead he maintained that if a man's brain was sound, he could withstand any degree of emotional stress. It was only those individuals whose

3

brains were weakened by hereditary taint or by the ravages of a debauched lifestyle, who were tipped into insanity by external events. Such psychiatric thinking would have had little place for a syndrome of psychological distress triggered by outside events.

However, although the contemporary psychiatric literature yields little, the writings of physicians and surgeons – especially those interested in neurology – proves more rewarding. As Trimble (1981) has shown in his valuable book *Post-Traumatic Neurosis*, Victorian doctors were much exercised by railway accidents and the effects on their victims. The Liverpool and Manchester Railway had opened in 1830 and the train became a powerful symbol of the industrial age. It exemplified not only the spirit of progress by virtue of the tremendous feat of engineering that it involved, but it also suggested the dark underside of disorder in society by its alarming capacity for accidents.

In 1865 Charles Dickens travelled by rail from Folkestone to London. Near Staplehurst a foreman who had misread the timetable had given instructions that two rails be taken off and placed at the side of the track. The train approached the broken line at between 20 and 30 m.p.h., jumped the gap and swerved off the track so that central and rear carriages fell from a bridge onto the bed of a river below. Dickens and his companions were in a carriage which hung from the rail across the bridge at an angle. Afterwards, even one of the greatest authors of the day had difficulty in writing or speaking of his experience. He is described as having run with his hat full of water "doing his best to revive and comfort" the dead and dying who lay around. Then Dickens remembered that his manuscript (*Our Mutual Friend*) was still in the railway carriage which swayed on the edge of the drop. He climbed back and retrieved it.

A year later Dickens confessed, "I have sudden vague rushes of terror even when riding in a hansom cab, which are perfectly unreasonable but quite insurmountable". His daughter Mamie recorded:

> "My father's nerves were never really the same again – we have often seen him, when travelling home from London, suddenly fall into a paroxysm of fear, tremble all over, clutch the arms of a railway carriage, large beads of perspiration standing on his face, and suffer agonies of terror. We never spoke to him but would touch his hand gently now and then. He had, however, apparently no idea of our presence; he saw nothing for a time but that most awful scene."

There were times when Dickens was unable to travel, leaving the train and walking home (Ackroyd, 1990).

Doctors observed that there were many victims of railway accidents who appeared to suffer no obvious physical injury, and yet who complained of a variety of symptoms. Such patients complained of headaches, sleeplessness, emotional disturbance and perplexing paralyses of arms and legs. Doctors were divided as to the cause of these symptoms. On one side were those who argued that the symptoms represented damage, albeit in a very subtle form, to the nervous system. On the other were those who argued that the nervous system was structurally unscathed and that the symptoms were nervous in origin. Notable among the organic theorists was John Erichsen (1882), professor of surgery at University College Hospital, who advanced his views in his book *On Concussion of the Spine*. Erichsen maintained that an organic lesion could follow relatively mild trauma and that it could be responsible for a variety of symptoms which could occur long after the actual accident. Erichsen coined the term 'railway spine' and held that post-traumatic symptoms were the result of damage to the nervous system.

Erichsen's views were opposed by Herbert Page (1885), a London surgeon who published a book-length rebuttal. Using evidence from 234 of his own cases, Page insisted that there was no evidence of structural damage and, instead, put forward the thesis that accident victims were suffering from what he called "nervous shock", which he defined as a "functional disturbance of the whole nervous balance or tone rather than structural damage to any organ of the body". Page maintained that extreme fright, such as occurred in response to railway accidents, could produce a functional disturbance of the nervous system which could lead to a wide variety of symptoms, and he described how they might develop after the original trauma:

> "Soon, ... during which the scene of the accident may have been terribly present to him, both in sleep and when awake, repeating the terror ... which originally harmed him, the victim has an attack of acute uncontrollable crying. Attacks recur and also a sense of extreme despondency." (Tuke, 1892)

Page maintained that it was often an advantage to the victim to have actually experienced physical injury because, as he wrote, "the bodily injury . . . satisfies the requirements of the patient himself in seeking an explanation consciously or unconsciously of the symptoms present . . . after the accident" (Tuke, 1892).

As Trimble (1981) showed, these two opposing views had legal implications. Erichsen's organic theory was seized upon by litigants in compensation claims against the railways, while Page's views were quoted by lawyers defending railway companies against damages. Page's more psychological model was to gain greater acceptance in medical circles, and an eminent supporter of his views emerged in the person of Jean-Martin Charcot.

Charcot, the celebrated Parisian neurologist – the "Napoleon of the Neuroses", as he has been dubbed – is currently the subject of much scholarly attention by the likes of Showalter (1985), Micale (1990) and Harris (1991). Charcot's importance in this context lies in his highly influential contention that the so-called syndrome of 'railway spine' was not the result of organic damage but rather a form of hysteria. Furthermore, Charcot suggested a mechanism for the development of post-traumatic symptoms. He likened the post-traumatic state to the hypnotic state. He had shown that ideas could be suggested to a person under hypnosis. For example, the idea of a paralysed limb could be suggested to the hypnotic subject who would later develop this symptom. Charcot argued that in the immediate aftermath of an accident, the victims were also in a suggestible state and that their own idea of the type of physical injury they had sustained would suggest itself to them and that they would later develop symptoms accordingly. Charcot's approach thus allowed for a psychological interpretation of symptom formation, but his theory was nevertheless built on a neurophysiological model that treated symptoms as evidence of a functional disturbance of the brain.

Charcot's work was ground-breaking in his demonstration that hysteria was not exclusively a disorder of females, but that a large number of men suffered hysterical symptoms. In fact, Charcot's detailed case histories of male hysteria served to highlight the extraordinary dangers of the 19th century workplace. The perils of the mines, factories, building sites, and, of course, the railways were all vividly illustrated in Charcot's cases of workmen who had developed hysterical symptoms following accidents at work. In contrast to Page, whose views had been used to dispute compensation claims, Charcot argued in favour of paying compensation to victims because he held that hysterical symptoms were real and painful.

Charcot exercised a seminal influence on the young Sigmund Freud, who attended his demonstrations at the Salpetriere and learned from Charcot that hysterical symptoms were related to ideas, and he developed this concept further. In *Studies in Hysteria* which he co-wrote with Josef Breuer (Freud & Breuer, 1895), Freud suggested that the symptoms of hysteria were due to the repressed memories of traumatic events. These memories were too painful to acknowledge and, instead, they found expression in the form of symptoms. Freudian ideas were largely ignored by Victorian British psychiatrists, although they were to be rediscovered and to some extent rehabilitated during the First World War.

Before considering the Great War, it is useful to examine a publication which appeared at the end of the 19th century because it gives a snapshot of late Victorian British psychiatry. This publication was Tuke's (1892) *Dictionary of Psychological Medicine*, which assembled a 128-strong cast of notable alienists, neurologists and physicians, as well as eminent specialists from Europe, to provide detailed entries on a host of psychiatric subjects. With specific regard to potential forerunners of post-traumatic stress disorder, there are several relevant entries in the *Dictionary*. These include 'traumatic hysteria', 'traumatic neuraesthenia', 'traumatic neuroses', 'shock', 'trauma', and 'hysteria'. Significantly the majority of these entries were written by physicians and surgeons rather than by psychiatrists. In fact, there was only one psychiatric contribution and this was by Julius Mickle, medical superintendent of the Grove Hall Asylum and lecturer in mental diseases at University College, London. Mickle wrote the entry about traumatic neuroses, a diagnostic group which specifically excluded any organic damage. Mickle's account of the symptomatology is comprehensive and has many parallels with today's concept of post-traumatic stress disorder.

> "(There is) . . . melancholy, often of a hypochondriacal type with great irritability, sadness, indifference to friends and family, distress, oppression, sombre feeling rising into fear and culminating perhaps in seizures of terror or in suicidal attempts; despair, often with praecordial pain, oppression and palpitations; variable, fickle and tumultuous emotional change; vivid and terrifying recollections and dreams of the accident or injury. Frequent are self-study as to symptoms and concentration of mind upon them . . ." (Tuke, 1892)

The non-psychiatrists who contributed to the *Dictionary* on this subject included Page who reiterated his views under the entry entitled 'Shock from fright'. Interestingly, Charcot was also invited to contribute and he provided an entry about hysteria, in which he outlined his theory and took space to criticise the German concept of 'traumatic neurosis' which had been advocated by Oppenheim (1911). Charcot felt that this category was just another variety of hysteria and should be subsumed within this diagnostic group, rather than having a separate category of its own. In his entry Charcot also gave his views on male hysteria.

Significantly, the editor felt it advisable to provide a British perspective on hysteria, so as well as Charcot's entry there was an entry by Dr Horatio Donkin, a physician at Westminster Hospital. Donkin maintained that hysteria in men was less common in Britain than was reported to be the case in France. He suggested that this discrepancy was probably due to what he called "racial and social differences" (Tuke, 1892).

Tuke's *Dictionary* is often seen as marking the end of the Victorian psychiatric era, published as it was before the full impact of both Kraepelin and Freud had been felt in psychiatric circles. As we have noted, Freud's ideas gained little support among British psychiatrists in the late 19th century, but the experiences of the First World War led to a re-evaluation of his theories as the country struggled to find an explanation for the phenomenon of 'shell-shock'.

The First World War witnessed a mass epidemic of mental disturbance among soldiers at the Front. By the end of the war, 80 000 soldiers from Britain alone had presented with the emotional and psychological symptoms of shell-shock. According to the historian Martin Stone (1985) who has examined this episode, the experience of shell-shock profoundly undermined the foundations of contemporary British psychiatry, built as it was on the notions of degeneracy and unsound brains. Young men of respectable and proven character were reduced to mental wrecks within a few months at the Front. Individuals with no hint of hereditary taint or debauched lifestyle, and often from the higher echelons of society – or in the words of one contemporary commentator, "England's finest blood" – were struck down with nervous symptoms and became psychiatric casualties. Not only was British psychiatry at a loss to explain shell-shock within its degenerationist and physicalist framework, but it was also unable to offer anything by way of effective treatment for the thousands of mentally disabled casualties returning from the Front.

If asylum doctors had little to offer, however, there were other doctors, mainly from a neurological background, who did prove to be more therapeutically successful. These doctors saw the problems of shell-shock in psychological terms, and as a consequence tried psychological techniques. They felt that it was important for the victims to come to terms with their past experiences at the Front, and they employed such techniques as abreaction and catharsis, as well as letting the person simply talk about their traumas. Prominent among these doctors was William Rivers, who looked after shell-shock casualties including the poets Siegfried Sassoon and Wilfred Owen at the Craiglockart Hospital in Edinburgh. Rivers drew on Freud's work, but instead of seeing his patients' mental symptoms as consequent upon past sexual conflicts, he viewed their symptoms as the result of the conflict between duty and fear – the conflict between a soldier's desire to be brave and obey orders, and his terror of being injured or killed. Rivers (1920) expanded upon his views in his book *Instinct and the Unconscious*. While he rejected the Freudian theory of infantile sexuality, he nevertheless supported the concept of the unconscious and the mechanism of repression. Rivers held that repression explained how an individual suppressed painful and terrifying experiences, and that these later became converted into physical and mental symptoms. Rivers maintained that the Freudian techniques of dream interpretation, hypnosis and transference were useful therapeutic tools. In accounts of shell-shock by, for example, Stone (1985), Showalter (1985), or more recently by Barker (1991), Rivers is portrayed as the hero of the hour, although there were several other clinicians, such as Myers and McDougall, doing similar work.

The experience of shell-shock did much to support Freudian theory that symptoms could arise as a result of emotional conflict, but as Merskey (1991) has pointed out, it also served to refute his theory of infantile sexuality. Shell-shock was seen to be the result of conflict directly caused by the demands of the war, rather than by the events of childhood. Shell-shock also supported Charcot's view that male hysteria was a real phenomenon. No longer could it be dismissed as a continental aberration from which stout British manhood was immune. Showalter (1985), in her book *The Female Malady*, has made much of this episode, and has compared the lot of the First World War soldier in the trenches with the lot of the Victorian woman. Both were in a helpless position, both had feelings of anger and hostility about their situation which they were not allowed to express, and both dealt with their situations by developing hysterical symptoms.

In his recent book *Images of Trauma*, David Healy (1993) has observed that the creation of the category of post-traumatic stress disorder (PTSD) represents the recognition by psychiatry that a psychological illness can be precipitated entirely by external stress, and certainly in this brief survey of the origins of PTSD we can trace the growing emphasis on psychological explanations of symptoms rather than physical ones. However, as Trimble (1981) has advised, both factors should be taken into account in the understanding and treatment of patients with post-traumatic symptoms.

References

Ackroyd, P. (1990) *Dickens*. London: Sinclair-Stevenson.

Barker, P. (1991) *Regeneration*. London: Viking.

Boehnlein, J. K. & Kinzie, J. D. (1992) Commentary. DSM diagnosis of post-traumatic stress disorder and cultural sensitivity: a response. *Journal of Nervous and Mental Disease*, **180**, 597–599.

Bucknill, J. C. & Tuke, D. H. (1879) *A Manual of Psychological Medicine* (4th edn). London: Churchills.

Clark, M. J. (1981) The rejection of psychological approaches to mental disorder in late nineteenth century British psychiatry. In *Madhouses, Mad-doctors and Madmen: The Social History of Psychiatry in the Victorian Era* (ed. A. Scull), pp. 271–312. London: Athlone Press.

Clouston, T. S. (1896) *Clinical Lectures on Mental Diseases.* London: Oliver & Boyd.

Ellenberger, H. F. (1970) *The Discovery of the Unconscious.* New York: Basic Books.

Erichsen, J. E. (1882) *On Concussion of the Spine: Nervous Shock and Other Obscure Injuries of the Nervous System in Their Clinical and Medico-Legal Aspects.* London: Longmans, Green & Co.

Freud, S. & Breuer, J. (1895) *Studies in Hysteria* (trans. J. Hogarth, 1955). London: Hogarth Press.

Harris, R. (1991) *Clinical Lectures on Disease of the Nervous System by J. M. Charcot.* Tavistock Classics in the History of Psychiatry. London: Tavistock/Routledge.

Healy, D. (1993) *Images of Trauma. From Hysteria to Post-Traumatic Stress Disorder.* London: Faber.

Merskey, H. (1991) Shell-shock. In *150 Years of British Psychiatry 1841–1991* (eds G.E. Berrios & H. Freeman), pp. 245–267. London: Gaskell.

Micale, M. S. (1990) Charcot and the idea of hysteria in the male: gender, mental science, and medical diagnosis in late nineteenth century France. *Medical History,* **34,** 363–411.

Oppenheim, H. (1911) *Textbook of Nervous Diseases for Physicians and Students* (trans. A. T. N. Bruce). London: Foulis.

Page, H (1885) *Injuries of the Spine and Spinal Cord Without Apparent Mechanical Lesion* (2nd edn). London: J. & A. Churchill.

Parry-Jones, B. & Parry-Jones, W. L. (1994) Post-traumatic stress disorder: supportive evidence from an eighteenth century natural disaster. *Psychological Medicine,* **24,** 15–28.

Rivers, W. H. R. (1920) *Instinct and the Unconscious.* Cambridge: Cambridge University Press.

Sankey, W. H. O. (1884) *Lectures on Mental Diseases* (2nd edn). London: H. K. Lewis.

Savage, G. H. (1884) *Insanity and Allied Neuroses: Practical and Clinical.* London: Cassells.

Shepherd, M. (1977) Lunacy and labour. *Bulletin of the Society for Study of Labour History,* **34,** 66–69.

Showalter, E. (1985) *The Female Malady. Women, Madness and English Culture, 1830–1980.* London: Virago Press.

Stone, M. (1985) Shell shock and the psychologist. In *The Anatomy of Madness,* vol. 2 (eds W. F. Bynum, R. Porter & M. Shepherd), pp. 242–271. London: Routledge.

Trimble, M. R. (1981) *Post-Traumatic Neurosis. From Railway Spine to the Whiplash.* Chichester: John Wiley.

Tuke, D. H. (1892) *A Dictionary of Psychological Medicine.* London: J. & A. Churchill.

2 Normal and abnormal responses to stress – a developmental approach

COLIN MURRAY PARKES

A response to a specific stimulus or situation may be deemed 'abnormal' because it is infrequent (statistically deviant from the mean for this class of responses), unexpected, excessive, weak, pathological (denoting 'illness'), bad (denoting culpability) or just plain obnoxious (meaning that we do not like it).

Standards of normality are culturally defined. Maoris are expected to cry while mourning, Apache Indians are not; hit a child in Italy and he will cry, hit one in Bali and he will laugh (Rosenblatt *et al*, 1976). Yet our common sense tells us that there are universal tendencies present in all human beings which provide a substrate for human behaviour, however much this may be modified by learning. Responses to stress become problematic when they cause unnecessary suffering, and it is this pragmatic view of the 'abnormal' which is adopted here. Viewed in this way it becomes possible for an entire society to react 'abnormally' and to need help. Some would say that this is the case in many Western societies today where the rituals and beliefs that, in the past, facilitated mourning have been lost or attenuated and unnecessary suffering has resulted.

Reactions to stress, more than other types of reaction, take us straight into the biological roots of human behaviour, the survival of the gene. Major stresses threaten our survival or the survival of those we love (who are likely to carry or protect our genes). It is not surprising to find that the reactions they evoke take priority over most other behavioural systems and that the emotions evoked are powerful.

In this chapter a model will be outlined which the author has found useful in explaining the major reactions to traumatic stress. It does not attempt to be exhaustive and may even appear simplistic. Thus it attempts to demystify and render into ordinary language some of the theories which underlie our thinking, but which are often puffed up by the use of jargon terms which make them appear to be more profound than they really are. The reader should not, however, imagine that there is nothing more to these ideas than the bare outline which follows. Most of the theories will be developed in more detail elsewhere in this book.

Three overlapping behavioural systems together explain much of the overall response to stress – the response to threat, the response to separation and the response to change.

The response to threat

In mammals and many other species, any event that is perceived as a threat to individual or group survival gives rise to a psycho-physiological response which is remarkably uniform and will be described and referenced more fully elsewhere in this volume.

An immediate 'startle' response involves arousal of the central nervous system (CNS). The 'gates' to sensation are opened, reaction time speeds up and attention is directed outwards towards any potential danger. At the same time, pre-existing chains of thought are broken, routine processing of information is postponed and all interests of lesser priority are placed on 'hold'. At the same time the sympathetic nervous system is stimulated and the parasympathetic inhibited. This results in the inhibition of vegetative functions, blood is diverted from the internal organs, the heart rate and stroke volume increases, capillaries in the muscles and skin dilate, perspiration increases and muscle tone becomes greater. The respiratory rate increases to meet an expected increase in the demand for oxygen and to expel a tide of carbon dioxide. This means that the body is primed for instant action – to fight or to flee. The emotions triggered by the perception of danger are powerful but not necessarily unpleasant. Acute excitement predominates and may then be associated with fear, anger or elation as the individual evaluates the likely outcome of the situation.

One might think that this hyper-alert state would increase the perception of pain, but the opposite may be the case and it has been postulated that, during acute emergencies, pain sensation may be diminished as a consequence of the release of endorphins in the brain (Fields & Besson, 1988); hence the reports of many severely injured victims that their injuries did not begin to hurt until several hours had elapsed.

One consequence of the immediate response to threat is the release of noradrenaline and other neuro-endocrine secretions into the blood-stream. These then help to maintain the autonomic response and may explain why many of the symptoms of anxiety persist for some time after the emergency is over and the individual is no longer emotionally disturbed.

However effective (or ineffective) the response may be in helping a person to deal with an emergency when it arises, if the danger is seen to persist, sooner or later the individual must give priority to other demands. Eating, drinking, excreting and other necessities must be attended to despite continued central and autonomic arousal. At the same time, reserves of strength and a second line of defence is mobilised. Glycogen in the liver is converted to glucose in order to provide a rapidly accessible source of increased energy, the immune response system is activated to improve bodily response to infection or tissue damage, and several defensive functions are enhanced by the release of corticoid hormones from the cortex of the adrenal gland.

Together, these responses enable the individual to continue to cope with danger for a considerable length of time. But the time will come when reserves of strength become depleted, available energy flags and the arousal of the CNS diminishes. The individual experiences this as fatigue and is faced with an increasing need to escape from the situation, perhaps by withdrawing or submitting. Failure to find a way out of a continued danger has been postulated as a cause for 'adrenal exhaustion', fainting and a variety of psychological and somatic problems including post-traumatic stress disorder.

The response to separation

Human beings are social animals. This means that we rely on each other for mutual protection and collaborate together to ensure the perpetuation of our genes. The principal mechanisms that facilitate social functioning are attachments. These ensure that we stay close enough to each other to obtain mutual support when it is needed. Attachments can be personal (to an individual) or group (to a family, class, nation, creed, etc.). Attachments are made and continued by a number of behavioural mechanisms. There are those that maintain proximity to the object of the attachment (smiling, clinging, following) and those which facilitate reunion when separated (calling, searching and confronting opposition to reunion).

The responses associated with separation take priority over most other behavioural systems and are accompanied by a distinctive emotion – pining or yearning for the lost person or object (also known as separation anxiety). In primates and humans separations have been shown to be associated with alteration in the neuro-endocrine system and the immune response system. The specificity of these changes has not been established (see Jacobs, 1993).

These responses take place even when the separation is known to be permanent, but in this case the urge to search and to cry aloud is in conflict with the awareness that such behaviour is illogical and antisocial. The outcome of the conflict is very variable and influenced from the outset by cultural and other factors. Following lasting major losses, episodes of separation anxiety (pangs of grief) continue to be evoked by reminders of the loss for a considerable length of time (sometimes for life). Even so, they tend to diminish in intensity and frequency over the years and the increasing feelings of apathy, despair and withdrawal which occupy the early months grow less and usually come to an end. At the same time appetites and interests, which decline during the first few weeks of bereavement, gradually return.

The response to major change

Each one of us carries, within our minds, a complex model of the world which is based on our experience of the world and our interpretation of it. This is the world that we assume to exist and, for this reason, it has been termed the assumptive world (Parkes, 1971). The assumptive world includes everything we know or think we know about everything, including ourselves, and because it is based on our experience of the real world, it is usually an accurate reflection of the world and a reasonable basis for action. It enables us to recognise and order incoming sensations, and to plan and carry out what are mostly appropriate actions.

Certain life change events can render substantial parts of the assumptive world obsolete. Loss of sight, loss of a limb and loss of a partner are each examples of events which face people with the need to review and revise their assumptive world in order to bring it into line with the world which now exists. This process has been termed a 'psychosocial transition' (PST).

Because the provision of an accurate assumptive world is essential for effective planning and action, any major discrepancy between the real world and the assumptive world (between what is and what should be) renders us, to some degree, incapacitated. The widow who has relied on her husband to manage all her financial affairs feels and is incapacitated by his death in much the same way as the blind person or the amputee are incapacitated by loss of sight or loss of a limb. Each of them must now learn new ways of interpreting, ordering and planning their lives. Such new learning takes time.

New situations are arising all the time and most of them do not require a major PST. Hence people faced with a discrepancy between their assumptive world and the real world do not immediately change their basic assumptions. They usually focus attention on the discrepancy and seek for ways to explain it within their existing frame of reference. In fact, most people resist major change until it becomes imperative, and even then the modifications to the assumptive world that are necessary may be carried out in a piecemeal and incomplete manner.

Psychosocial transitions are most likely to take place smoothly and appropriately if they have been anticipated and prepared for. Changes for the better are "looked forward to" and create fewer problems than changes for the worse, perhaps because we prefer not to anticipate and prepare for them. Conversely, massive losses for which we are unprepared often give rise to lasting difficulties in adjustment. Problems in restructuring the assumptive world frequently complicate rehabilitation after physical losses, as well as impairing adjustment to other types of loss. It seems to be necessary for people to grieve for the world they are losing if they are to draw from that world the elements that will help them in the new world which they are now entering. Two defensive alternatives which create problems are: (a) the people who refuse to accept that change is necessary and remain stubbornly locked into an obsolete set of assumptions; and (b) the people who go to the other extreme, turning their back on the past, hiding away anything that reminds them of the old world, and embracing the new in an uncritical and enthusiastic way which attempts to by-pass the painful process of teasing out the remnants of the old. In the first type of reaction, the old world is idealised at the expense of the new, and in the second, the new world is idealised at the expense of the old. Both idealisation and denigration (or 'monsterisation') are dangerous misperceptions that can easily lead to conflicts with others who have different views of the world. These difficulties are obvious and easy to understand in immigrants who have literally exchanged one country for another, but they can occur following any PST.

Developmental aspects

Although the roots of these reactions to stress are innate they are modified by learning from the time of their earliest manifestation. New-born babies show a 'startle response' to any sudden inflow of sensation, be it noise, movement or flash. Some are more reactive than others, and there are, no doubt, genetic factors that account for this.

In order to survive, children must learn what to fear and the people from whom they will learn are usually their parents. Within the first year of life small children become increasingly sensitive to parental cues to danger. In so far as these are realistic the child will develop a realistic set of assumptions about the dangers of the world. If, on the other hand, the parents are excessively fearful or, alternatively, if they are blind to danger or uncaring, the child will develop a distorted assumptive world. Once established, these models of the world are difficult to change, perhaps because they deal with issues of survival or because once one has learned to avoid a danger one may have no means of finding out if the danger continues. In any event, learned fear in childhood is a significant predictor of vulnerability to fear or anxiety in later life.

In order to stay safe in the world a child must recognise danger and cope with it when it arises. In order to cope with danger children have two alternatives – to act themselves or to induce someone else to act on their behalf. To act effectively requires skills and the confidence to use them, while relying on others requires attachments to others who have the necessary skills, and trust in their ability and willingness to use these skills on our behalf. All of this sounds very self-evident, but it is spelt out here to provide a frame of reference for a consideration of the ways in which these factors can be influenced in the course of maturation.

Ainsworth's (1991) seminal studies of small children in her standard Strange Situations Test have shown clearly that the patterns of interaction established between the primary care-giver (usually the mother) and the young child in the first two years of life are powerful predictors of the types of attachments that the child will develop later in life. They also predict how the child will cope with separations and there is retrospective evidence from my own studies of psychiatric patients that they predict the type of psychiatric problems to which that person will be vulnerable in response to bereavements and other stressful life events in adult life (Parkes, 1991).

This is a complex field on which a great deal of research has been conducted in recent years. For a more adequate review of the field the reader is referred to *Attachment Across the Life Cycle*, a volume which contains contributions from many of the principal researchers in this field (Parkes *et al*, 1991). In this chapter there is only space to draw together some of the main findings from this research and to suggest an explanation for them.

Ainsworth (1991) distinguished four patterns of response made by most children during and immediately after brief separation from their mother in a standard strange situation. *Securely attached* babies were not greatly distressed by brief separation; they sometimes cried a little but when the mother returned they readily came to her for a cuddle and soon stopped crying. *Insecurely attached* babies were further subdivided into an anxious–ambivalent group, a detached group and an inconsistent group.

The *anxious–ambivalent* group reacted strongly to the separation, crying intensely and gazing towards the door while ignoring toys and other objects. When mother returned they grabbed hold of her and continued to cry intensely. Many of them kicked and punched her. The *detached* babies showed little sign of distress when mother left the room; they played fitfully with the toys and sometimes ignored her pointedly or turned their backs when she returned. Others would kick and attack her but without any apparent wish to be held. Recent studies have shown that this group have a greater increase in heart rate than any other group during the separation experience. They are certainly not as unaffected as they appear to be. The *inconsistent* babies show responses that are difficult to categorise or to predict. In the original research they were not regarded as of special interest, yet it is this group who had the greatest evidence of emotional disturbance on follow-up ten years later.

Further research has shown that these patterns predict lasting attachment styles, and they are consistent over time and across cultures, although the proportions in each group do vary. Fathers as well as mothers play a part and can mitigate some of the insecurity.

It has become increasingly clear that these patterns of behaviour in the child reflect the parenting style of the primary care-giver. Thus anxious–ambivalent babies have parents who view with alarm their child's attempts to face and explore the world, while rewarding clinging behaviour. The detached babies, on the other hand, have parents who cannot tolerate physical contact and who punish the child's bids for attention and affection.

The parents of inconsistent babies have been found to have experienced personal losses resulting in 'unresolved grief' shortly before or after the birth of the child (Ainsworth & Eichberg, 1991). This seems to make them inconsistent in their parenting, sometimes responding and at other times resisting the child's bids for proximity. The baby has no means of knowing whether or not attachment behaviour will be rewarded or punished.

These patterns of mother–child interaction foreshadow how these children will cope with stress later in life. Anxious–ambivalent babies become clinging and dependent children. They lack confidence in themselves and their intense relationships are tinged with ambivalence. In later life their tendency to cling may lead to repeated rejection. Far from correcting the tendency this tends to aggravate it. When these attachments end they give rise to severe and lasting grief, the so-called 'chronic grief syndrome'.

Detached babies learn to stand on their own feet at an early age; they may even become 'compulsively self-reliant'. They are intolerant of closeness and those relationships that they do make are impaired by distrust. When such relationships come to an end their significance is often denied and grief may be delayed or complicated by anger and guilt. The bereaved person tends to withdraw from social relationships on the grounds that it is safer not to fall in love.

Inconsistent babies are faced with the situation which has been described by Seligman (1975) as "learned helplessness". This constitutes a cognitive basis for depression. Children faced with this predicament grow up with little trust in themselves or others and it is not surprising if, faced with losses and other traumatic stresses in later life, they become depressed and withdrawn.

Secure parenting provides the secure base from which the child can explore the world and, in due time, achieve a reasonable degree of autonomy. Trust in oneself and trust in others are the twin benefits of 'good-enough' parenting, and they improve the child's chances of building up a repertoire of coping strategies that will enable them to cope with most psychosocial transitions and to seek for help when it is needed. Insecurely attached individuals, on the other hand, often show signs of cognitive impairment, they do less well at school than their intelligence leads people to expect, and even those who are 'compulsively self-reliant' are restricted and patchy in their achievements, attaching excessive importance to strategies that enable them to exert control, and ignoring or distrusting collaborative endeavours.

The findings of this research go some way towards integrating the empirical findings of psychologists who study cognitive responses to stress with the clinical observations of psychotherapists who take a developmental approach. They are, of course, only the first fruits of a developing field of study and do not fully account for the complexity of human behaviour. The behaviours described seldom appear in pure culture, and it is quite possible for a person to be 'strong' in some settings and 'weak' in others. Things are not always what they seem, and there are many 'strong/weak' relationships in which the role of the 'weak' partner is to reassure the 'strong' one of his own strength. The true situation becomes very obvious if, for instance, the 'weak' partner dies. The 'strong' one may then be quite unable to cope.

The world of the developing child is constantly changing, and given a secure base children tend to learn rapidly and to be reasonably flexible. By the time adult life is reached, however, our internal models have become firmly established and as we get old they become more difficult to change. It is hard to "teach an old dog new tricks", and in old age inflexibility may become a serious problem. If, in addition, there is some degree of brain damage, the loss of memory for recent events may cause old people to "live in the past", recent bereavements may be forgotten, illnesses denied and current life situations interpreted on the basis of obsolete assumptions.

Practical implications

It follows from the foregoing considerations that lack of preparation and/or insecurity are at the root of most of the abnormal or pathological responses to stress. In order to mitigate or avoid these responses we must attempt to prepare people for the stresses that are to come and reduce insecurity. Preparation for stress can be general or specific. General methods include the teaching of relaxation and other techniques of anxiety management. Specific methods aim to prepare people for particular life events that are likely to occur to them. Thus the relatives of seriously ill patients need information about the likely outcome of the illness and emotional support if they are to take in and make appropriate use of this information.

Insecurity can be reduced by removing danger (where possible), establishing a safe base (i.e. a place with 'home valency'), providing assurance of protection, reassuring people of their existing strengths and skills, of our care for them and of our respect for their worth. Coping skills can be fostered by encouraging people to explore their world and to make the best possible use of the skills that they already possess. Since people are more likely to remember solutions which they have worked out for themselves than solutions which have been reached by others it is more important to encourage them to find their own than to offer ours.

Of course, people also need to be aware of and to accept their own limitations and to know when and how to ask for help. But even here it is better for us to encourage our clients (or patients) to find their own sources of help than to encourage them to rely on us. In this way we avoid the risk of excessive reliance on medical or other caring agencies. In so far as we have anything at all to teach, it is more likely to be in the area of sharing a different point of view than of imparting knowledge. Thus people who see the world as more dangerous than it really is can be encouraged to reconsider these assumptions, and people who see themselves as more weak and helpless than they really are can be encouraged to test their own strength and skills. Assumptions that are both negative and unrealistic need to be challenged, and the challenge is more likely to be accepted if the person understands how their tendency to misperceive the world has arisen. Again, we can do this better by asking the client to explain themselves to us than by ourselves doing the explaining.

The question "Why do you tend to put yourself down?" both challenges the assumption of worthlessness and invites the client to explain it. If they are unable to do this we may be able to offer a clue: "Such misperceptions are often rooted in childhood, did either of your parents tend to criticise or put you down when you were little?" In explaining themselves to us our clients are also explaining themselves to themselves and this can have great therapeutic value.

As we have seen, anxiety and fear give rise to a variety of bodily symptoms and these may then become the source of further anxiety. To break the escalating circle of fear, leading to symptoms which lead to fear about symptoms which, in turn, lead to more symptoms, it is necessary to explain the effects of stress on the body and mind in language which the client will understand. If, in addition, we help clients to regain a feeling of control over their bodies, perhaps by teaching relaxation techniques and imagery, there is every chance that the vicious circle will be broken and the symptoms diminish. Control is all important. We need to know that if painful feelings and fears emerge nothing terrible will happen. We need to know that we are less, not more, likely to be haunted by painful memories if we choose to think about them than we are if we try to force them out of consciousness. We increase control by confronting problems rather than avoiding them, but we do not have to do this all the time. It is all right to take a break from grief. Even when dreaming we have a much greater control than we imagine.

If we go to bed dreading a recurrent nightmare we will surely have one, but if we have worked out an alternative 'happy' ending for the nightmare it will come out the way we want it to, and when we stop worrying about it, it will cease. In a similar way people may be alarmed by the intensity of the grief that threatens to emerge after a loss. Difficulty in maintaining control may cause them to fear that they are suffering a 'nervous breakdown'. Among patients referred to the writer for the treatment of psychiatric problems after bereavement, two-thirds are suffering from "feelings of panic and acute fear". Reassurance of the normality of grief and its symptoms is sometimes all that is needed to break the cycle.

Cross-cultural studies such as those by Burgoine (1988) indicate that those societies that encourage the overt expression of grief are less plagued by lasting problems in adjustment than those that inhibit grieving, and this observation has important implications for all those who are in a position to influence these attitudes.

The overall lesson that emerges from this work is not only that people may need help in expressing grief, but also that they may need help in stopping grieving and getting on with the task of discovering a new place in the world and building a new identity.

References

Ainsworth, M. D. S. (1991) Attachments and other affectional bonds across the life cycle. In *Attachment across the Life Cycle* (eds C. M. Parkes, J. Stevenson-Hinde & P. Marris), pp. 33–51. London: Routledge.

—— & Eichberg, C. (1991) Effects on infant–mother attachment of mother's unresolved loss of an attachment figure, or other traumatic experience. In *Attachment across the Life Cycle* (eds C. M. Parkes, J. Stevenson-Hinde & P. Marris), pp. 160–183. London: Routledge.

Burgoine, E. (1988) A cross-cultural comparison of bereavement among widows in New Providence, Bahamas and London, England. Paper read at International Conference on Grief and Bereavement in Contemporary Society, London, July 12–15.

Fields, H. L. & Besson, J. M. (eds) (1988) Pain Modulation. *Progress in Brain Research*, **77**. Amsterdam: Elsevier.

Jacobs, S. (1993) *Pathologic Grief: Maladaptation to Loss*. Washington, DC: APP.

Parkes, C. M. (1971) Psycho-social transitions: a field for study. *Social Science and Medicine*, **5**, 101–115.

—— (1991) Attachment, bonding and psychiatric problems after bereavement in adult life. In *Attachment across the Life Cycle* (eds C. M. Parkes, J. Stevenson-Hinde & P. Marris), pp. 268–292. London: Routledge.

——, Stevenson-Hinde, J. & Marris, P. (eds) (1991) *Attachment across the Life Cycle*. London: Routledge.

Rosenblatt, P. C., Walsh, R. P. & Jackson, D. A. (1976) *Grief and Mourning in Cross-Cultural Perspective*. Washington, DC: HRAF Press.

Seligman, M. E. P. (1975) *Helplessness*. San Francisco, CA: Freeman.

3 Classification

GORDON J. TURNBULL

Clinicians have come to recognise that many of the symptoms of post-traumatic stress disorder (PTSD) are reflections of adaptive mental processes involved in the assimilation of new information which has an intense survival emphasis (i.e. the trauma) and making repairs to the internal structure of reality (Janoff-Bulman, 1985; Epstein, 1990). It is as if the PTSD represents an unvelling of a normal survival instinct in exposed individuals.

ICD–9

The ninth revision of the *International Classification of Diseases* (ICD–9; World Health Organization, 1978) incorporated the subcategories of "acute reaction to stress" and "adjustment reaction" following exposure to acute stress. "Acute reaction to stress" was described as very transient disorders of any severity and nature which occur in individuals without any apparent mental disorder in response to exceptional physical or mental stress, such as natural catastrophe or battle, and which usually subside within hours or days. Alternative terms were "catastrophic stress", "combat fatigue", and "exhaustion delirium". Adjustment reactions were specifically excluded from this category. The transient nature of this category provided a limiting factor. Some acute stress reactions moved into the territory of longer-term "adjustment reactions". Adjustment reactions described mild or transient disorders lasting longer than acute stress reactions, occurring in individuals of any age without any pre-existing mental disorder. Often circumscribed or situation-specific, generally reversible adjustment reactions were described as usually lasting for only a few months. They were described as being usually closely related in time and content to stresses such as bereavement, migration or separation experiences. It is important to note that adjustment reactions were described as not being associated with significant distortions of personal development, especially in children. Of major significance was the exclusion of "neurotic disorders" under the rubric. Perhaps the most important distinguishing feature between adjustment reactions and neurotic disorders was the specific exclusion of any demonstrable organic quality in the latter. Neuroses had qualities of considerable insight, unimpaired reality testing and non-disorganisation of the personality.

DSM–III: the development of the category of PTSD

The third edition of the *Diagnostic and Statistical Manual of Mental Disorders* (DSM–III; American Psychiatric Association, 1980) was the first to give official recognition to PTSD as a distinct diagnostic classification (Table 3.1). Previous editions of DSM (American Psychiatric Association, 1952, 1968) had included, respectively, "gross stress reactions" and "anxiety neurosis/ transient situational disturbance" with reference to "response to overwhelming environmental stress" (Horowitz & Wilner, 1980; Brett *et al*, 1988; Parry-Jones & Parry-Jones, 1994). "Gross stress reaction" (DSM–I) represented a transient response to severe physical or emotional stress which could evolve into a chronic neurotic reaction in accordance with predisposing character traits. Publication of DSM–I coincided with the Korean War. DSM–II developed during a period of relative global peace and eliminated the diagnostic category of gross stress reaction. DSM–III probably reflected the catastrophic effect of the Vietnam war which added considerable impetus to the rekindling of PTSD as a distinct clinical entity.

In the mid 1970s, when PTSD was being proposed for inclusion within the rubric of DSM–III, a relative lack of literature was available on the subject of 'traumatic neuroses' to guide the creation of a diagnostic classification for PTSD. The DSM–III committee relied mainly on the existing literature, which had focused its attention on traumatised male adults. These included combat veterans (Kardiner, 1941) and holocaust survivors (Krystal, 1968).

Sociological stimuli may be one of the factors that stimulates interest in PTSD. Interest in PTSD or traumatic stress reactions occurs after wars in

TABLE 3.1
Diagnostic criteria for post-traumatic stress disorder (DSM–III)

A. Existence of a recognisable stressor that would evoke significant symptoms of distress in almost everyone.

B. Re-experiencing of the trauma as evidenced by at least one of the following:
 (1) recurrent and intrusive recollections of the event,
 (2) recurrent dreams of the event,
 (3) sudden acting or feeling as if the traumatic event were recurring, because of an association with an environmental or ideational stimulus.

C. Numbing of responsiveness to or reduced involvement with the external world, beginning some time after the trauma, as shown by at least one of the following:
 (1) markedly diminished interest in one or more significant activities,
 (2) feeling of detachment or estrangement from others,
 (3) constricted affect.

D. At least two of the following symptoms that were not present before the trauma:
 (1) hyperalertness or exaggerated startle response,
 (2) sleep disturbance,
 (3) guilt about surviving while others have not, or about behaviour required for survival,
 (4) memory impairment or trouble concentrating,
 (5) avoidance of activities that arouse recollection of the traumatic event,
 (6) intensification of symptoms by exposure to events that symbolise or resemble the traumatic event.

Table reproduced with permission of the American Psychiatric Association.

which the victims are usually men. Only relatively recently has there been an interest in rape victims, in which the victims are usually women, and in domestic and road traffic accidents (Mezey & Taylor, 1988; Mayou *et al*, 1993), which might be regarded as everyday events. This is strange for two reasons. Firstly, more women are raped and more people injured in accidents than men go to war. Secondly, although rape and accidents are eminently suitable as research items there has been little research performed until very recently. Freud's abandonment of the sexual seduction theory (Masson, 1984) might have been a significant manoeuvre to distract attention away from these much more commonplace events, and the high profile given to war-related trauma might have attracted disproportionate attention as a result.

Relying on follow-up studies of Second World War veterans, the DSM–III PTSD committee constructed a 27-item questionnaire in 1975, which was administered to 724 adult male Vietnam veterans. The results of this survey guided the definition of PTSD for the DSM–III (Shatan *et al*, 1977; Scott, 1990). Interestingly, a rapidly-growing research literature, which was expanding even before the publication of DSM–III in 1980, confirmed the relevance of PTSD as a diagnostic classification applicable to a wide variety of traumatised populations such as rape victims, abused children, refugees, and victims of accidents, disasters and domestic violence (van der Kolk, 1987).

DSM–III–R

The definition of PTSD was modified in the revised edition of DSM–III which appeared in 1987 (DSM–III–R; American Psychiatric Association, 1987). This was done to incorporate the evolving research findings. It is important to recognise that the essential features of PTSD remained the same (Table 3.2). There are important differences, however. The most significant was the increased emphasis on avoidance phenomena in DSM–III–R. The criteria for avoidance were listed under section C and included:

(1) deliberate efforts to avoid thoughts or feelings associated with trauma;
(2) deliberate efforts to avoid activities or situations that arouse recollections of the trauma;
(3) inability to recall an important aspect of the trauma.

The inclusion of these criteria reflected the importance of avoidance-related symptoms in the growing understanding of PTSD and their importance in treatment.

There were four main differences between the definition of PTSD in DSM–III and DSM–III–R. The first has been mentioned above and concerns the increased emphasis on avoidance phenomena. The second is an elaboration of the syndrome in children:

TABLE 3.2

Diagnostic criteria for post-traumatic stress disorder (DSM–III–R)

A.   The individual has experienced an event that is outside the range of usual human experience and that would be markedly distressing to almost anyone, e.g., serious threat to one's life or physical integrity; serious threat or harm to one's children, spouse, or other close relatives or friends; sudden destruction of one's home or community; or seeing another person who is being (or has recently been), seriously injured or killed as a result of an accident or physical violence.

B.   The traumatic event is persistently re-experienced in at least one of the following ways:
    (1) recurrent and intrusive distressing recollections of the event (in young children, repetitive play in which themes or aspects of the trauma are expressed);
    (2) recurrent distressing dreams of the event;
    (3) sudden acting or feeling as if the traumatic event were recurring (includes a sense of reliving the experience, illusions, hallucinations, and dissociative (flashback) episodes, even those that occur upon waking or when intoxicated);
    (4) intense psychological distress at exposure to events that symbolise or resemble an aspect of the traumatic event, including anniversaries of trauma.

C.   Persistent avoidance of stimuli associated with the trauma or numbing of general responsiveness (not present before the trauma), as indicated by at least three of the following:
    (1) deliberate efforts to avoid thoughts or feelings associated with the trauma;
    (2) deliberate efforts to avoid activities or situations that arouse recollections of the trauma;
    (3) inability to recall an important aspect of the trauma (psychogenic amnesia);
    (4) markedly diminished interest in significant activities (in young children, loss of recently acquired developmental skills such as toilet training or language skills);
    (5) feeling of detachment or estrangement from others;
    (6) restricted range of affect, e.g. unable to have loving feelings;
    (7) sense of foreshortened future, e.g. child does not expect to have a career, marriage, or children, or a long life.

D.   Persistent symptoms of increased arousal (not present before the trauma) as indicated by at least two of the following:
    (1) difficulty falling or staying asleep;
    (2) irritability or outbursts of anger;
    (3) difficulty concentrating;
    (4) hypervigilance;
    (5) exaggerated startle response;
    (6) physiological reactivity at exposure to events that symbolise or resemble an aspect of the traumatic event (e.g. a woman who was raped in an elevator breaks out in a sweat when entering any elevator).

E.   Duration of the disturbance of at least one month. Specify delayed onset if the onset of symptoms was at least six months after the trauma.

Table reproduced with permission of the American Psychiatric Association.

"Age-specific factors. Occasionally, a child may be mute or refuse to discuss the trauma, but this should not be confused with inability to remember what occurred. In younger children, distressing dreams of the event may, within several weeks, change into generalised nightmares of monsters, of rescuing others, or of threats to self or others. Young children do not have the sense that they are reliving the past; reliving the trauma occurs in action through repetitive play. Diminished interest in significant activities and constrictions of affect both may be difficult for children to report on themselves, and should be carefully evaluated by reports from parents, teachers, and other observers. A symptom of post-traumatic stress disorder in children may be a sense of a

foreshortened future; for example, a child may not expect to have a career or marriage. There may also be 'omen formation', that is, belief in an ability to prophesy future untoward events. Children may exhibit various physical symptoms, such as stomachaches and headaches, in addition to the specific symptoms of increased arousal noted above."
(American Psychiatric Association, 1987)

The new description for symptoms in children includes items B(1) and C(4) in Table 3.2.

The third change was the removal of "survivor guilt" from the list of primary features. It was relegated to the list of associated features. Although "survivor guilt" continued to be considered unique to PTSD, it was not considered to be a sufficiently general term to encompass all of the different types of guilt associated with PTSD. "Guilt" was selected as the overall term. Since "guilt" was seen to be a feature of other disorders in DSM–III–R such as depression, and not exclusive to PTSD, it was relegated to the category of associated features.

The fourth and last change was a reflection of the increased appreciation that cognitions could be legitimately represented in a symbolic way in PTSD (see criteria B(4) and D(6) in Table 3.2).

New classifications

ICD–10

The tenth edition of the International Classification of Diseases (ICD–10; World Health Organization, 1992) offers a much looser description of characteristic symptoms than DSM and positions a range of "reactions to severe stress and adjustment disorders" (F43) (amongst which is included PTSD as F43.1) alongside "dissociative disorders" (F44) and "somatoform disorders" (F45). These are all placed under the rubric of "neurotic, stress-related and somatoform disorders". In addition it recognises a disorder of adult personality, which is termed "enduring personality changes (following catastrophic stress)" (F62). PTSD is itemised as F43.1 in ICD–10. In the category covered by F43 the ICD–10 includes acute stress reaction, PTSD and adjustment disorder. It distinguishes acute stress reaction as a reaction in which the symptoms typically resolve within hours or days of the causative traumatic event, PTSD as a reaction where the symptoms rarely develop after six months have elapsed but frequently persist beyond that period, and adjustment disorders where the emotional distress and functional impairment usually arise within one month of traumatic exposure and rarely exceeds six months.

DSM–IV

Although DSM–III–R modified the definition of PTSD to reflect evolving research findings and theoretical frameworks from a growing world

TABLE 3.3
The ICD–10 classification of post-traumatic stress disorder (F43.1)

Post-traumatic stress disorder arises as a delayed and/or protracted response to a stressful event or situation (either short- or long-lasting) of an exceptionally threatening or catastrophic nature, which is likely to cause pervasive distress in almost anyone (e.g. natural or man-made disaster, combat, serious accident, witnessing the violent death of others, or being the victim of torture, terrorism, rape, or other crime). Predisposing factors such as personality traits (e.g. compulsive, asthenic) or previous history of neurotic illness may lower the threshold for the development of the syndrome or aggravate its course, but they are neither necessary nor sufficient to explain its occurrence.

Typical symptoms include episodes of repeated reliving of the trauma in intrusive memories ("flashbacks") or dreams, occurring against the persisting background of a sense of "numbness" and emotional blunting, detachment from other people, unresponsiveness to surroundings, anhedonia, and avoidance of activities and situations reminiscent of the trauma. Commonly there is fear and avoidance of cues that remind the sufferer of the original trauma. Rarely, there may be dramatic, acute bursts of fear, panic or aggression, triggered by stimuli arousing a sudden recollection and/or re-enactment of the trauma or of the original reaction to it.

There is usually a state of autonomic hyperarousal with hypervigilance, an enhanced startle reaction, and insomnia. Anxiety and depression are commonly associated with the above symptoms and signs, and suicidal ideation is not infrequent. Excessive use of alcohol or drugs may be a complicating factor.

The onset follows the trauma with a latency period which may range from a few weeks to months (but rarely exceeds six months). The course is fluctuating but recovery can be expected in the majority of cases. In a small proportion of patients the condition may show a chronic course over many years and a transition to an enduring personality change.

Diagnostic guidelines: This disorder should not generally be diagnosed unless there is evidence that it arose within six months of a traumatic event of exceptional severity. A "probable" diagnosis might still be possible if the delay between the event and the onset was longer than six months, provided that the clinical manifestations are typical and no alternative identification of the disorder (e.g. as an anxiety or obsessive–compulsive disorder or depressive episode) is plausible. In addition to evidence of trauma, there must be a repetitive, intrusive recollection or re-enactment of the event in memories, daytime imagery, or dreams. Conspicuous emotional detachment, numbing of feeling, and avoidance of stimuli that might arouse recollection of the trauma are often present but are not essential for the diagnosis. The autonomic disturbances, mood disorder, and behavioural abnormalities all contribute to the diagnosis but are not of prime importance.

The late chronic sequelae of devastating stress, i.e. those manifest decades after the stressful experience, should be classified {elsewhere}.

Table reproduced with permission of the World Health Organization, Geneva.

literature, it is now evident that the concept of PTSD captures a limited aspect of post-traumatic psychopathology (Breslau *et al*, 1991; Cole & Putnam, 1992; Herman, 1992). During the post-DSM–III decade a critical evolution has occurred that recognises that the severity and duration of traumatic exposure are not the only factors which affect long-term biological adaptation. The developmental level at which the trauma occurs is also significant (van der Kolk *et al*, 1991). It has become apparent that complex but consistent patterns of psychological disturbances emerge in traumatised children, as well as in adults who have been exposed to chronic and/or severe interpersonal trauma. One of the stated aims of the DSM–IV (American Psychiatric Association, 1994) field trial for PTSD was to study the prevalence of the most commonly reported trauma-related psychological

TABLE 3.4
DSM–IV: diagnostic criteria for 309.81, post-traumatic stress disorder

A. The person has been exposed to a traumatic event in which both of the following were present:
    (1) the person experienced, witnessed, or was confronted with an event or events that involved actual or threatened death or serious injury, or a threat to the physical integrity of self or others;
    (2) the person's response involved intense fear, helplessness, or horror (note: in children, this may be expressed instead by disorganised or agitated behaviour);
B. The traumatic event is persistently re-experienced in one (or more) of the following ways:
    (1) recurrent and intrusive distressing recollections of the event, including images, thoughts or perceptions (note: in young children, repetitive play may occur in which themes or aspects of the trauma are expressed);
    (2) recurrent distressing dreams of the event (note: in children, there may be frightening dreams without recognisable content);
    (3) acting or feeling as if the traumatic event were recurring (includes a sense of reliving the experience, illusions, hallucinations, and dissociative flashback episodes, including those that occur on awakening or when intoxicated). Note: in young children, trauma-specific reenactment may occur;
    (4) intense psychological distress at exposure to internal or external cues that symbolise or resemble an aspect of the traumatic event;
    (5) physiological reactivity on exposure to internal or external cues that symbolise or resemble an aspect of the traumatic event.
C. Persistent avoidance of stimuli associated with the trauma and numbing of general responsiveness (not present before the trauma), as indicated by three (or more) of the following:
    (1) efforts to avoid thoughts, feelings, or conversations associated with the trauma;
    (2) efforts to avoid activities, places, or people that arouse recollections of the trauma;
    (3) inability to recall an important aspect of the trauma;
    (4) markedly diminished interest or participation in significant activities;
    (5) feeling of detachment or estrangement from others;
    (6) restricted range of affect (e.g. unable to have loving feelings);
    (7) sense of a foreshortened future (e.g. does not expect to have a career, marriage, children, or a normal life span).
D. Persistent symptoms of increased arousal (not present before the trauma), as indicated by two (or more) of the following:
    (1) difficulty falling or staying asleep;
    (2) irritability or outbursts of anger;
    (3) difficulty concentrating;
    (4) hypervigilance;
    (5) exaggerated startle response.
E. Duration of the disturbance (symptoms in criteria B, C and D) is more than one month.
F. The disturbance causes clinically significant distress or impairment in social, occupational, or other important areas of functioning.

Specify if: acute (duration of symptoms is less than three months) or chronic (duration of symptoms is three months or more).
Specify if: with delayed onset (onset of symptoms is at least six months after the stressor).

Table reproduced with permission of the American Psychiatric Association.

problems not currently captured by the PTSD diagnostic construction, their relation to each other and to PTSD itself (as defined in DSM–III–R). The work was based on a review of hundreds of published research studies on the effects of chronic physical and sexual abuse of children, and other populations exposed to prolonged and/or severe interpersonal trauma such as concentration camp survivors, battered women, and hostages. Twenty-seven symptoms were identified which were arranged into seven main symptom clusters (Pelcovitz *et al*, 1996). These were: alterations in regulating affective arousal (chronic affect dysregulation, difficulty modulating anger, self-destructive and suicidal behaviour, difficulty modulating sexual involvement, impulsive and risk-taking behaviours); alterations in attention and consciousness (amnesia, dissociation); somatisation; alterations in self-perception (chronic guilt and shame, feelings of self-blame, feelings of ineffectiveness, feelings of being permanently damaged, minimising the importance of the traumatic experience); alterations in perception of the perpetrator (adopting distorted beliefs, idealising the perpetrator); alterations in relations with others (inability to trust or maintain relationships, tendency to be re-victimised, to victimise others); and alterations in systems of meaning (despair, hopelessness, loss of previously sustaining beliefs).

The study data indicated that, for a substantial proportion of traumatised patients, the diagnosis of PTSD alone captures only a limited aspect of their psychopathology. The 'working term' for this syndrome of seven trauma-related psychobehavioural disturbances uncovered by field trials for DSM–IV was 'disorders of extreme stress' (DES). However, the study suggested that since the symptoms of DES are associated with PTSD (only 3.4% of the sample showed DES in isolation), there is no need to establish a new diagnostic category, but merely to broaden the category of stress-related disorders beyond the relatively narrow confines of PTSD. Another advantage might be a greater understanding of the issues of vulnerability and resilience. This might help to formulate effective and specific approaches to treatment. The diagnostic criteria for PTSD in DSM–IV includes two important changes compared with DSM–III–R criteria. The first is in criterion A (the stressor), where being confronted with an event that involved serious injury to others and responding with horror can fulfil criterion A, thus incorporating the concept of vicarious traumatisation. The second is that the symptom of physiological reactivity has been moved from the hyperarousal cluster in DSM–III–R (criterion D) to the re-experiencing cluster in DSM–IV (criterion B).

Acute stress disorder (ASD) was included as a new diagnostic classification in DSM–IV. This is distinguished from PTSD because the symptom pattern in ASD must occur within four weeks of the traumatic event and resolve within that four week period.

Comorbidity

Lillenfield (1994) has observed that the term comorbidity has been used in different ways. In some cases comorbidity denotes diagnostic co-occurrence among diagnoses, a dual diagnosis or the simultaneous presence in the same individual of two diagnoses which are not necessarily correlated to an appreciable extent within the population. Another meaning of comorbidity is diagnostic covariation, which is the tendency of certain diagnoses to co-occur more often than by chance. As will be discussed in the context of PTSD, the question emerges as to whether or not depression and PTSD represent the same psychopathology: a form of co-occurrence or a covariation? Exposure to traumatic events is associated with the development of multiple forms of comorbid psychopathology. These include both Axis I and Axis II disorders. Substance misuse, depression, anxiety states, somatisation, eating disorders, dissociative states, antisocial and aggressive behaviours, marital problems and multiple personality disorder may co-occur with PTSD. In particular, there is a high prevalence of alcoholism, depression, generalised anxiety and panic anxiety with PTSD. Green (1994) revealed that 75% of Vietnam veterans with PTSD also met criteria for at least one other diagnosis; the most common being depression and alcohol misuse. The National Study of Vietnam Veterans (NVVRS) yielded current PTSD comorbidity rates of 15.7% for major depression and 19.8% for generalised anxiety disorder. The NVVRS also found a life-time prevalence of PTSD in Vietnam veterans of 30%, of whom 75% met the criteria for a diagnosis of alcohol misuse or dependence.

Anxiety states

The core difference between PTSD and other anxiety disorders is the specific nature of the cluster of symptoms and the presence of a specific trauma. There seems little point in making the diagnosis of generalised anxiety state coexistent with PTSD because no useful information is made available which would improve the overall understanding of the altered mental state or sponsor specific therapy strategies. This is not the case, however, for panic anxiety disorder where the symptoms may be blocked by the use of medication. The same may be true of phobic anxiety states, which might be regarded as accentuation of the avoidance element in PTSD where medication and behavioural techniques such as exposure/ desensitisation are thought to be of benefit.

The debate continues as to the nature of these specific types of anxiety state within the rubric of post-traumatic stress reactions. There is a general notion that they represent epiphenomena: satellite fragments of the PTSD core which might, however, usefully be treated separately. Falsetti & Resnick (1994) highlighted the comorbidity of panic attacks and PTSD. They reported a high incidence of a history of criminal victimisation in individuals found to be suffering from panic disorder.

Depressive disorders

Depression frequently coexists with PTSD (Sierles *et al*, 1986; Mayou *et al*, 1993). Green (1994) reported a high incidence of comorbidity of PTSD and other diagnoses, usually depression, in studies of natural and technological disasters. For example, studies of survivors of a dam collapse at 14 years post-incident revealed that only 5% of those with a diagnosis of PTSD had that diagnosis alone. A follow-up study of firefighters demonstrated that 77% who had a diagnosis of PTSD also had an additional diagnosis, which was most commonly major depression. The most salient clue that this is the case is the presence of the 'biological' features of depressive illness: early morning wakening, changes in appetite and weight, diurnal variation in mood, fatigue, anhedonia, morbid thoughts and, most importantly, evidence of familial predisposition for depression or previous personal history of depressive episodes, either 'reactive' or 'endogenous'. The real importance of separate recognition of depression in PTSD is the effectiveness of antidepressive medication and the amelioration or resolution of a potentially lethal psychopathology. Further discussion of the use of drugs in the treatment of PTSD is dealt with in another chapter.

Somatisation disorders

Pribor *et al* (1993) supported the observation made by Pierre Janet that approximately a third of female psychiatric out-patients who present with Briquet's syndrome, dissociative and somatoform disorders give a history of having been abused, physically, emotionally or sexually, in childhood. Women who present with chronic pelvic pain are reported to have commonly been sexually assaulted before the age of 14 (Walker *et al*, 1992). There is a strong association between chronic PTSD and physical illness, exaggerated somatic concerns and medical facility use (Shalev *et al*, 1990).

Matsakis (1992) reported an incidence of previous traumatisation of 40–60% of women in recovery programmes for bulimia, anorexia and compulsive overeating, and approximately 50–60% of women and 20% of men in chemical dependency recovery programmes had been the victims of childhood sexual abuse. In the same text he reported that there was evidence of severe trauma in the backgrounds of compulsive gamblers seeking help, among runaway and delinquent children and adolescents, and also among both male and female prostitutes and models in pornographic films and magazines.

Controversy

The role of compensation proceedings in affecting outcome in litigation has been raised (Miller, 1961; Cohen, 1987). Miller found an inverse relationship between accident neurosis and the severity of injury among head injury victims claiming compensation for a variety of neurotic symptoms. Only at follow-up after compensation claims had been settled did the majority of these individuals recover completely. However, a subsequent and larger study of individuals who had suffered a variety of injuries was undertaken using a prospective design (Kelly & Smith, 1981). This subsequent study indicated that most of the patients with a post-traumatic syndrome who were working prior to their accidents did recover and were able to return to work before settlement, but that failure to do so indicated a poor prognosis. A further study by Tarsh & Royston (1985) supported the notion that compensation issues did not affect the outcome in terms of resolution of the affected individual's symptoms, but did affect the attitude of their family members.

In Northern Ireland clinicians have recognised the psychological effects of exposure to terrorist violence and detected PTSD in up to 50% of bomb victims requiring surgical intervention (Hadden *et al*, 1978). Overall, the psychological impact of over 20 years of violence is less considerable than in post-Vietnam studies, possibly because incidents are restricted to a very small proportion of the population with increased cohesion in others (Curran, 1988).

Despite an intense interest on the part of the British media in the aftermath of community disasters such as Piper Alpha, the Hillsborough football stadium disaster and the Hungerford shootings, with an undoubted increase in public awareness of their potential to create psychological as well as physical injury, there remains a public uncertainty about responses to trauma. This was amply shown after the Lockerbie air disaster, when local psychiatric services established an emergency help-line which was not utilised (McCreadie, 1989).

Conclusions

PTSD has grown from its early roots as a varied, descriptive terminology in the field of human reactions to high-magnitude stressors, to become a well-defined entity with a real utility. The major international research effort has pointed the way to new treatments. The evidence is that there is a unique biological dimension which underpins the behavioural phenomena, indicating hope for a multidimensional approach to treatment. Since the problem is very large and the effects highly corrosive to the quality of human life, it seems important to classify and categorise the syndrome as a real aid to its understanding. The tracing of the impact of traumatic exposure on human beings appears to parallel the growth in the understanding of the entire field of psychopathology. In particular, the weaving together of the psychosociobiological strands of PTSD are making a significant contribution to the fabric of modern psychiatry.

References

American Psychiatric Association (1952) *Diagnostic and Statistical Manual.* Washington, DC: APA.
—— (1968) *Diagnostic and Statistical Manual* (2nd edn) (DSM–II). Washington, DC: APA.
—— (1980) *Diagnostic and Statistical Manual of Mental Disorders* (3rd edn) (DSM–III). Washington, DC: APA.
—— (1987) *Diagnostic and Statistical Manual of Mental Disorders* (3rd edn, revised) (DSM–III–R). Washington, DC: APA.
—— (1994) *Diagnostic and Statistical Manual of Mental Disorders* (4th edn) (DSM–IV). Washington, DC: APA.
Brett, E., Spitzer, R. & Williams, J. (1988) DSM–III–R criteria for post-traumatic stress disorder. *American Journal of Psychiatry*, **144**, 1232–1236.
Cohen, R. I. (1987) Post-traumatic stress disorder: does it clear up when the litigation is settled? *British Journal of Hospital Medicine*, **37**, 485.

Curran, P. S. (1988) Psychiatric aspects of terrorist violence 1969–87. *British Journal of Psychiatry*, **153**, 470–475.

Epstein, S. (1990) Beliefs and symptoms in maladaptive resolutions of the traumatic neurosis. In *Perspectives on Personality*, vol. 3 (eds D. Ozer, J. M. Healy & A. J. Stewart), pp. 63–98. London: Jessica Kingsley.

Falsetti, S. A. & Resnick, H. S. (1994) Helping the victims of violent crimes. In *Traumatic Stress: From Theory to Practice* (eds J. R. Freedy & S. E. Hobfall). New York: Plenum.

Green, B. L. (1994) Traumatic stress and disaster: mental health effects and factors influencing adaptation. In *International Review of Psychiatry*, vol. 2 (eds F. Liehmac & C. Nadelson). Washington, DC: APP.

Hadden, W. A., Rutherford, W. H. & Merrett, J. D. (1978) The injuries of terrorist bombing: a study of 1532 consecutive victims. *British Journal of Surgery*, **65**, 525–531.

Horowitz, M. & Wilner, N. (1980) Signs and symptoms of post traumatic stress disorder. *Archives of General Psychiatry*, **37**, 85–92.

Janoff-Bulman, R. (1985) The aftermath of victimisation: rebuilding shattered assumptions. In *Trauma and its Wake: The Study and Treatment of Post-traumatic Stress Disorder*, vol. 1 (ed. C. R. Figley), pp. 15–35. New York: Brunner Mazel.

Kardiner, A. (1941) Traumatic neuroses of war. In *American Handbook of Psychiatry* (ed. S. Arietti). New York: Hoeber.

Kelly, R. & Smith, B. N. (1981) Post-traumatic neurosis: another myth discredited. *Journal of the Royal Society of Medicine*, **74**, 275–277.

Krystal, H. (1968) *Massive Psychic Trauma*. New York: International Universities Press.

Lillenfield (1994) Comorbidity. *Clinical Psychology*, **1**, 70–100.

McCreadie, R. G. (1989) The Lockerbie air disaster: one psychiatrist's experience. *Psychiatric Bulletin of the Royal College of Psychiatrists*, **13**, 120–122, 134.

Masson, J. M. (1984) *The Assault on Truth: Freud's Suppression of the Seduction Theory*. New York: Farrar, Straus & Giroux.

Matsakis, A. (1992) *I Can't Get Over It: A Handbook for Trauma Survivors*. Oakland, CA: New Harbinger Publications.

Mayou, R., Bryant, B. & Duthie, R. (1993) Psychiatric consequences of road traffic accidents. *British Medical Journal*, **307**, 647–651.

Mezey, G. C. & Taylor, P. J. (1988) Psychological reactions of women who have been raped: a descriptive and comparative study. *British Journal of Psychiatry*, **152**, 330–339.

Miller, H. (1961) Accident neurosis. *British Medical Journal*, **1**, 919–925

Parry-Jones, B. & Parry-Jones, W. Ll. (1994) Post-traumatic stress disorder: supportive evidence from an eighteenth century natural disaster. *Psychological Medicine*, **24**, 15–27.

Pelcovitz, D., van der Kolk, B. A., Roth, S., *et al* (1996) Development and validation of the structured interview for measurement of disorders of extreme stress. *Journal of Traumatic Stress*, in press.

Pribor, E. F., Yutzy, S. H., Dean, J. T., *et al* (1993) Briquet's syndrome, dissociation and abuse. *American Journal of Psychiatry*, **150**, 1507–1511.

Scott, W. J. (1990) PTSD in DSM–III: a case in the politics of diagnosis and disease. *Sociological Problems*, **37**, 294–310.

Shalev, A. Y., Bleich, A. & Ursano, R. J. (1990) Post-traumatic stress disorder: somatic comorbidity and effort tolerance. *Psychosomatic Medicine*, **55**, 413–423.

Shatan, C. F., Smith, J. & Haley, S. (1977) Johnny comes marching home: DSM–III and combat stress. Paper presented at the 130th Annual Meeting of APA, Toronto.

Sierles, F. S. & Chen, J.-J. (1986) Concurrent psychiatric illness in non-Hispanic outpatients diagnosed as having post traumatic stress disorder. *Journal of Nervous and Mental Disease*, **174**, 171–173.

Tarsh, M. J. & Royston, C. (1985) A follow-up study of accident neurosis. *British Journal of Psychiatry*, **146**, 18–25.

van der Kolk, B. A. (1987) *Psychological Trauma*. Washington, DC: APP.

——, Perry, J. C. & Herman, J. L. (1991) Childhood origins of self-destructive behaviour. *American Journal of Psychiatry*, **148**, 1665–1671.

Walker, E. A., Katon, W. J., Nerras, K., *et al* (1992) Dissociation in women with chronic pelvic pain. *American Journal of Psychiatry*, **149**, 534–537.

World Health Organization (1978) *Mental Disorders: Glossary and Guide to their Classification in Accordance with the Ninth Revision of the International Classification of Diseases* (ICD–9). Geneva: WHO.

—— (1992) *The ICD–10 Classification of Mental and Behavioural Disorders: Clinical Descriptions and Diagnostic Guidelines*. Geneva: WHO.

4 The interaction of trauma and grief

BEVERLEY RAPHAEL

Bereavement – the response to loss – has long been seen as one of the most stressful of life's experiences, leading to distress and the complex affects referred to as grief. Recovery from, or adjustment to, this common experience is usual for most people, although some are at risk for pathological outcomes. The understanding of the nature of loss as a stressor has been complicated in that Lindemann's classic description of 'acute grief' was derived from a group of people, many of whom had suffered other traumata, apart from loss – for instance had been the victims of a major disaster and had their own lives threatened (Lindemann, 1944). In exploring the traumatic potential of loss, Horowitz (1976) saw it as leading to a stress response syndrome, but did not distinguish the response to loss from the response to other traumatic stimuli, such as threat to the individual's life, combat and so forth. Psychological reactions to loss and bereavement have often been seen as part of the depression spectrum. Stress response syndromes belong in the spectrum of anxiety disorders, and the inconsistencies between these two views have not been adequately addressed. Both the relationship between bereavement reactions and depression, and bereavement reactions and stress response syndromes, need to be further investigated.

On the basis of clinical and scientific evidence it is hypothesised that two different reactive processes occur. In response to a traumatic event such as a shocking encounter with death, a traumatic stress reaction occurs, with phenomena which specifically reflect this and the traumatogenic stimulus. In response to loss, the reactive processes of bereavement encompassing grief and mourning occur, with phenomena that are specific for loss and the lost object. In both situations, non-specific affective and cognitive reactions may also occur in addition to these specific phenomena. Some situations of bereavement also involve a shocking and horrific encounter with death, for instance, witnessing the suicide of a loved one, or being involved in an accident in which the bereaved is injured and nearly dies, and the loved one is killed. In these situations of traumatic or sometimes catastrophic loss, the bereaved person may demonstrate both traumatic stress reaction phenomena and bereavement phenomena, with either predominating or appearing intermittently. Understanding these processes and their different potential outcomes is critical for management of the stressed person and for the prevention of morbidity.

Traumatic stress and disaster studies

The earliest conceptualisation of the psychological impact of traumatic events as external stressors was that of Freud (1966) with his concept of traumatic neurosis. The evolution of the concept of trauma and the impact of extremely stressful experiences in leading to reactive processes and psychological disorder was reviewed by Horowitz (Horowitz, 1976; Horowitz *et al*, 1979) with his description of stress response syndromes. In this account, response to an extremely stressful event leads to alternating intrusive/re-experiencing and avoidance/numbing processes as the individual attempts to master and integrate the experience.

Empirical studies which could add further to findings relevant to these hypotheses came from two main fields: disaster studies and combat studies (especially in relation to Vietnam veterans). Both sets of studies initially saw stress effects as global, but subsequently attempted to clarify the particular stressor components responsible for different reactions.

Disaster studies examining individuals stressed by a tropical cyclone suggested that there was a mortality stressor which explained the early intense distress identified by screening a group of victims, while a later rise in distress constituted a relocation stressor effect (Parker, 1977).

Other disaster studies, for example Weisaeth's (1989) in-depth study of the effects of a paint factory fire and explosion, showed that those exposed to the stressors of shock and life-threat showed traumatic anxiety as the reactive process, the level of anxiety relating directly to the level of exposure. This reactive process developed into post-traumatic stress disorder for a significant group of exposed people (Weisaeth, 1989).

Green *et al* (1983, 1985) followed survivors of the Beverly Hills Supper Club fire and examined them on impact of bereavement, life-threat and extent of personal injury. However, they merged bereaved and rescuers into a 'not at the fire' group of passive victims compared with an 'at the fire' group. One year and two years later, anxiety, depression and overall symptomatology were higher in the 'not at the fire' group. Depressive symptoms were, though, more pronounced, as was overall severity for both groups.

Reporting on psychotherapy with a group of these survivors Lindy *et al* (1983) noted that the traumatic stress and loss effects operated separately, and quite specifically stated that the trauma effects had to be dealt with first so that the bereavement could then be worked with.

McFarlane (1988*a,b*) identified the differing stressor effects, i.e. threat and loss, which potentially contributed to post-traumatic morbidity, and reported on the evolution of post-traumatic stress disorder in a population of volunteer bushfire fighters. Bereavement as a stressor contributed more generally to morbidity, especially bereavement related to the loss of home and all personal belongings, and it seemed likely that personal loss was so profound that the different factors could not be separated out. He showed that while the degree of exposure to threat contributed to the development of PTSD, other factors, such as personal vulnerability (neuroticism, past psychiatric history), often appeared to be more significant.

Wilson *et al* (1985) carried out a comparative analysis of PTSD in a number of different survivor groups, in a questionnaire study. Their findings clearly differentiated loss and life-threat categories of stressor and showed that PTSD phenomena were more intense with the life-threat group, especially with rape and Vietnam combat survivors, and that depressive phenomena were more common with the loss group. This study provided the first systematic evidence of a differential effect with two highly stressed groups, which both differed very significantly from the no stress, no loss group.

It is with Pynoos *et al*'s (1987*a,b*) systematic study of children that the differential effects of threat and loss become clear. This group developed two separate measures, a Grief Reaction Inventory (nine items) and a PTSD Reaction Index (16 items). In a study of the reactions of school-age children (Pynoos *et al*, 1987*b*) following a sniper attack at school, they were able to show that severity of exposure to the threat correlated with a high symptom score (> 12 of 16 symptoms), and that the phenomena of grief, as identified in the Grief Reaction Inventory, related to closeness of acquaintance with the children who died. They were also able to show that sometimes the grief and post-traumatic phenomena manifest themselves independently of one another, while at other times there was an interplay between them. These workers also comment that instruments such as the Impact of Event Scale (Horowitz *et al*, 1979) do not "discriminate between these two sets of phenomena".

Pynoos's group has been able to demonstrate, in their studies of children, the relationship between specific stressor and specific forms of morbidity: life-threat and witnessing injury and death was highly correlated with the onset of PTSD; loss of a significant other with the onset of a single depressive episode or adjustment reaction; and worry about, or sudden separation from a significant other, with persistent anxiety regarding the safety of significant others (Pynoos *et al*, 1987*b*).

Adult studies have not adequately pursued these findings and tested such hypotheses, although the reviews of disaster research provide some support (Raphael, 1986).

Bereavement studies

It is interesting that Freud's classic description of the processes of bereavement in 'Mourning and melancholia' (1917) did not in any way reflect a similarity to his conceptualisation of trauma. Rather he spoke of the "loss of interest in the outside world – in so far as it does not recall the dead one – loss of capacity to adopt any new object of love" and "turning from every active effort that is not connected with thoughts of the dead". He described this process of internalisation, preoccupation with the deceased, the review of memories, and gradual withdrawal, step by step, of bonds to the deceased. He did not consider or describe it as a trauma overwhelming the ego, as he describes response to other stimuli which lead to traumatic neurosis.

Later, more systematic studies describing bereavement phenomena included those of Parkes (1972) and Maddison & Walker (1967). Clayton *et al* (1971, 1972), who carried out a number of systematic studies of bereavement, viewed the phenomena, as did Parkes (1972), as depressive in nature and identified depressive symptomatology patterns occurring in the first year following loss in widowed people. She found, for instance, that depressed mood, sleep disturbance and crying were the main symptoms in the bereaved spouses studied. However, this general depressed mood of grief could be seen to distil specifically into an affective syndrome in the first month for about 35% who were diagnosed as suffering from depression on the basis of a low mood plus five out of eight symptoms of depressive illness. These 'depressed' bereaved differed from non-bereaved people with affective disorder in that a family history of psychiatric illness did not predict outcome, and this 'depression' appeared to be accepted as a part of grief by those experiencing it. Clayton (1990) recently suggested that further research was necessary to clarify the relationship of depression and bereavement. She at no time, however, equated this bereavement reaction with a post-traumatic reaction.

Zisook (1987) and his group (Zisook *et al*, 1987), in a number of studies using the Texas Grief Inventory as well as semistructured interviews, described affective responses including numbness, tearfulness, loneliness, depression, guilt and anger, as well as phenomena implying a continuing relationship with the deceased (preoccupation, sense of presence, clear visual memories, difficulty accepting the loss). Zisook *et al* (1990) also highlighted the occurrence of anxiety phenomena and disorders after bereavement. They reviewed work such as that of Parkes (1972) and highlighted separation anxiety, characterised by yearning and longing, as one of the facets of anxiety in the bereaved. Their own studies showed higher levels of anxiety symptoms and syndromes during the first year of bereavement, compared with control populations. However, in a study of the full group of 350 subjects, general anxiety symptoms, such as nervousness, feeling keyed up and having difficulty remembering and getting things done, occurred in about a quarter of subjects, usually decreasing somewhat over the first seven months, but with considerable persistence. They concluded that anxiety symptoms were prevalent in the bereaved, and that they did not simply represent general distress, nor was anxiety simply a transient manifestation of separation. Rather it reflected a range of anxiety disorders and led bereaved people to take sedatives and anxiolytics to deal with it. The circumstances of the death did not clearly correlate, but early anxiety, depression and grief at intense levels tended to predict persistent anxiety.

Jacobs *et al* (1987) have also reported extensively on bereavement phenomenology. Their measures include dimensions of numbness, disbelief and separation anxiety, measured by a scale developed by this group; despair and depressive symptoms being measured by the Center for Epidemiological Studies of Depression (CESD) depression scale which he calls the mourning dimension. He also reported high levels of depressive disorders and anxiety disorders appearing in the post-bereavement period (Jacobs, 1993).

Depression was found in 32% of bereaved spouses at six months, and in 27% one year after the loss.

From these studies it is clear that while there is evidence of anxiety appearing following bereavement, this has usually been seen specifically as separation anxiety, or as part of an anxiety disorder which has developed at this time. Phenomena such as preoccupation with thoughts of the dead person and intrusive thoughts have been described, but there has been a failure to clarify the nature of the affect associated with these and whether or not they have the re-experiencing content and anxious, ego-dystonic affects typical of post-traumatic intrusions and re-experiencing.

Depressive phenomena have been the more typical and prominent picture. However, there has usually been a failure to distinguish between depression and sadness, and an unwarranted assumption has been made that bereavement phenomena are the same as those of depression. Some early studies of bereaved widows identified traumatic stress type phenomena which appeared to complicate the bereavement where the circumstances of the death had been sudden, unexpected and traumatic, e.g. violent and accidental deaths (Raphael & Maddison, 1976). Although post-traumatic stress disorder had not been identified as a diagnostic entity at that time, the authors suggested that the occurrence of a traumatic neurosis interfered with the capacity of the bereaved to grieve and constituted a risk factor for pathology.

Studies of traumatic bereavement

Studies of traumatic bereavement shed some further light on these issues. For instance, Raphael (1977) identified traumatic circumstances of the death as a risk factor for adverse health outcome following bereavement. Parkes & Weiss (1983) identified the 'traumatic' effects of sudden unanticipated death on the adaptation of the bereaved. Those suffering such unanticipated loss, compared with those with long forewarning, showed greater disbelief initially and more severe disturbance, with anxiety, self-reproach and feelings of abandonment. The long-term outcome for those with anxiety was also worse. It may be that these findings reflected post-traumatic stress effects, although these researchers did not consider this possibility.

Lundin's (1984) studies of sudden and unexpected bereavement found increased morbidity compared with those where bereavement was expected. Unexpected loss resulted in more pronounced psychiatric symptoms, especially anxiety, which was more difficult to resolve. The phenomena identified at long-term follow-up included high levels of numbing and avoidance and could be interpreted as reflecting traumatic stress effects.

Lehman *et al* (1987) studied bereavement after motor vehicle accidents, likely to involve traumatic and unexpected losses, especially when the bereaved had been an occupant of the vehicle and thus involved in and potentially traumatised by the accident. Even 4–7 years later, spouses showed significantly higher levels of phobic anxiety, general anxiety, somatisation, interpersonal sensitivity, obsessive–compulsive symptoms and poorer well-being. There were also high levels of apprehensiveness about bad things happening. It might be hypothesised, although it was not discussed by the authors, that these phenomena reflected parameters of post-traumatic stress disorder related to trauma surrounding the circumstances of the death. For more than 90% of subjects, memories, thoughts or mental pictures of the deceased intruded into the mind frequently; and for more than half of these they were "hurt and pained" by these memories. These phenomena did not appear to be the sad nostalgic memories of someone who has recovered from a loss, but were more like the intrusive re-experiencing of post-traumatic memories. Nevertheless, this study did not purport to distinguish these phenomena, but simply to report on the poor outcome of this type of loss.

Some recent work has addressed the issue of post-traumatic symptomatology in bereaved people quite specifically. Schut *et al* (1991) studied 128 bereaved spouses, mostly women. These workers were interested in the overlap between bereavement and post-traumatic phenomena and believed there were some differences. They assessed 95 self-reported elements of post-traumatic stress disorder in the previous 2–4 weeks, according to DSM–III–R (American Psychiatric Association, 1987) criteria. They found that only 9% met diagnostic criteria for PTSD at 4, 11, 18 and 25 months. Those who showed lasting symptoms typically showed these at four months. The diagnosis of PTSD was made on the simultaneous occurrence of intrusive, avoidance and arousal phenomena, and overall, counting all times and episodes, the rate ranged from 20–31%. They noted that high levels of arousal were quite rare. Factors that correlated with the occurrence of PTSD were: being a younger male; the death being unanticipated; not being able to say farewell or feeling that the farewells were unsatisfactory. Such factors could be related to traumatic effects such as the shock of an unanticipated death, or painful aspects of the death itself but the authors do not take this further, concluding that their findings contribute evidence that 'simple' bereavement should be included as a stressor criterion for PTSD. It should be noted, however, that a detailed examination of the operational definitions of the phenomena they measured indicates that they did not distinguish whether the bereaved person was experiencing intrusion and avoidance symptoms relating to memories of the lost person or to the death itself.

This study highlights a problem in considering whether phenomena of traumatic stress and bereavement are different, in that questionnaires such as Horowitz's Impact of Event Scale, and Schut's, may not adequately specify the nature of the intrusive and other phenomena, such as "thoughts coming into the mind". Such thoughts may be intrusive and highly affectively charged images of horrific scenes of the death; or intruding thoughts and longings that are images of the deceased, or are associated with fond and nostalgic memories. The above study does not make any distinction of this kind. These aspects will be considered further below.

Dyregrov & Mattheisen (1987*a,b,c*) investigated the sudden infant death syndrome (SIDS), stillbirth and neo-natal deaths, with measures of depression, anxiety and the Impact of Event Scale. They found, using the Impact of Event Scale, that high levels of intrusive and avoidant phenomena occurred in SIDS parents compared with the other groups. Evidence of arousal such as sleep disturbance, restlessness, anxiety and irritability was differentially higher in this group, as was anxiety. SIDS parents reported the events of the child's death as "printed" on their minds, with recurring flashbacks and nightmares, and intense distress at reminders of the scene of death and the dead baby.

L'Hoir (1992) specifically studied parents of children who died of SIDS, believing the intense disruptive stress of the infant's death constituted a stressor of the extent indicated in the DSM–III–R description of PTSD. 30.6% of mothers and 19.6% of fathers developed acute or chronic post-traumatic stress disorder. He did not compare grief and PTSD phenomena but noted the need to treat both these phenomena for those so affected.

Raphael (1992) reviewing this and other SIDS studies, including those of Vance *et al* (1991), showed that anxiety phenomena and symptoms relating to the "devastating" scenario of the death were prominent in SIDS parents compared with neonatal death and stillbirth. Thus there is much to suggest that PTSD is common after this shocking type of death and that its phenomena relate to the death scene and event. However, the nature of loss phenomena in these groups has not been further clarified by such studies.

Bereavement after 'unnatural dying' (i.e. traumatic losses such as suicide and homicide) has been described and has some findings relevant to the theme of this chapter. Rynearson (1984) described the presence of intrusive, repetitive and vivid images of the homicide, preoccupying the bereaved. These involved details of the death, the terror and helplessness of the victim, even when they (i.e. the bereaved) had not personally seen these. These unbidden and intrusive images interfered with the bereaved's cognitive processes including concentration and thought sequencing. Nightmares of the murder were also frequent, and often involved the bereaved in trying to save the victim. While affects of sadness, anxiety and guilt were common, there were also pervasive fears related to the violence of the death, to dread of violence to the self, and general and extensive fearfulness about the future. Heightened arousal, hypervigilance and avoidance were also prominent. Retribution themes were common. Rynearson concluded that PTSD according to DSM–III (American Psychiatric Association, 1980) partially described and subsumed the phenomena observed.

Clinical vignettes

Case A

A widow of 38 was intensely distressed and highly aroused, irritable and unable to sleep. She could think only of the circumstances of her husband's death as he died before her eyes, collapsing onto the floor, purple in the face, while she watched helpless. Repeated intrusive images of this scene came into her mind, unbidden, with intense anxiety, and nightmares with similar images and anxiety woke her from her sleep. She tried to avoid all reminders, including the room in which he died. She did not have images of her husband as he had been, or any other thoughts about him coming to her mind. She avoided talking about and reviewing the lost relationship and their shared past. She was preoccupied with the circumstances of the death and talked only of those. She could not feel sad for her husband, only intensely distressed with a sense of great dread and fearfulness. After therapy which helped her discuss and work through her feelings of terror and helplessness about the death itself, those images faded and did not return. Instead she became preoccupied with remembering her past relationship with her husband – anxiety changed from a general dread, to feelings specifically directed towards the recognition of his absence, and fears about life without him. She experienced pangs of distress when his image came to her mind, but as she clearly stated, this "pain" was with the knowledge of how much she had loved him, and that he was gone. Her dreams were no longer nightmares, but dreams of her husband alive and filled with longing. Later she dreamed of him asleep and moving away from her. These dreams did not have the disturbing affect of the earlier dreams.

Case B

A 50-year-old father returned from work to find his 18-year-old son hanging from the rafters in the garage. His mind was filled with images of his son's swollen face, his own shock and horror as he cut him down and tried to revive him, and the taste in his mouth as he attempted mouth-to-mouth resuscitation – the "taste of death". He was intensely distressed, restless and agitated for weeks after the death. Images of the death scene would come to his mind all the time – his heart would race and he would break out into a sweat. He could not go into the garage at all. He tried desperately to shut the images out of his mind but with little success, often drinking heavily in attempts to sleep. He was filled with dread that terrible things would happen to his daughters. After a number of sessions of counselling dealing with the trauma he became far less distressed, started to sleep and began to talk of his son, his love for him, his distress about his disturbance and suicide, his great sadness over the lost future, his attempts to make meaning of what had happened, the many loving images of their times together, as well as their differences. The images he described then were similar to those described by other bereaved people and his affects were sad grieving affects. Some intrusions occurred from time to time, but as the arousal patterns diminished there were far fewer and he felt able to go on with life again. Although still extremely sad he described how different the latter period was from the former: "I was stuck there – I thought I'd never be able to talk of him, remember him or have all those great things we shared there to go back to".

Case C

A young woman of 22 years of age was seen for counselling four months after her boyfriend's death. She said that she was "in a mess" – there was so much happening in her mind. They had had an intense relationship and had intended to marry. He was killed in a motor vehicle accident, where she had been an injured passenger and he was the driver. She remembered and could not get out of her mind the scene of the crash, the feeling that they were "for it", the prayers that he would be alive and the fear while waiting for rescue. While she had nightmares of what had happened, she also at times had mixed dreams of him still beside her in bed and would be very distressed to wake and find he was not there. Sometimes she would think she saw him in familiar places and would feel she should find him, that he wasn't really gone. At other times the horrific images of his dead body beside her and the smell of blood would flash into her mind, "destroying" her. She was torn between longing for him, longing to think and talk of him, and dread at the memories of his death. In her sessions she talked of the death and trauma at some times, and her sadness, regret, longing and loss at others.

It may be suggested that in these 'traumatic' losses the bereaved suffered the stressor effects of both trauma and loss. Each reactive process needed to be worked through after the trauma, just as described by Lindy *et al* (1983). These individuals frequently commented on the different nature of their experiences, which suggests that these could be seen to reflect different processes.

A clinical model for differentiating threat and loss

It is hypothesised (and yet to be established by empirical studies of adults) that following a traumatic encounter with death, particularly where this involves either personal life-threat for the individual, with shock, helplessness, or violence, or the gruesome multiple deaths of others, post-traumatic stress reactive processes will occur, and may continue or recur as an ongoing post-traumatic stress disorder. Where loss occurs (without the above), phenomena of bereavement reactions appear and gradually settle, or may go on or recur as pathology (chronic grief or depression are the likely types of pathology that may result). In certain bereavements where very traumatic circumstances have surrounded the death, and involved the bereaved (e.g. as a victim or witness), both sets of phenomena may occur and one, particularly the post-traumatic, may override the other, producing a block to the grief process.

Furthermore it is suggested that ample evidence exists from the clinical literature in both the fields of traumatic stress and bereavement to provide a basis for viewing bereavement and post-traumatic stress responses as different syndromal areas, even though it is recognised that significant overlap may occur, for instance with the occurrence of depressive type symptomatology (Raphael, 1983; Wilson & Raphael, 1993). Furthermore it is recognised that, in the broad approaches to aetiology of psychiatric syndromes, the role of either stressor in contributing to anxiety and/or depressive disorders must be seen as far from established as specific at this stage.

More refined hypotheses and measures will be necessary to answer some of these questions. Any such research must commence, however, with clarification of the exact nature of the phenomena being assessed. It is clear that items from the Impact of Event Scale do not enquire as to the nature of "thoughts coming into the mind" in such a way as to clarify whether or not these are the same as items such as those from the Texas Grief Inventory (Horowitz *et al*, 1979; Faschingbauer *et al*, 1987). These include "Even now it's painful to recall memories of the person who died" or "I am preoccupied with thoughts about the person who died". Similarly items such as those from Jacobs Separation Anxiety Scale – "Was your mind preoccupied with thoughts of your . . . ?" or "Sometimes experience mental images so vivid that for a moment it was as though your (husband, wife) was there" – do not allow any clarification of intrusive qualities typical of post-traumatic phenomena (Jacobs *et al*, 1987). Studies clarifying the nature of the phenomena, the specificity of the stressors and the quality of outcomes can help address such questions.

Further research is necessary to identify in depth both these separate phenomena and their interweaving in situations of loss where there has also been, for the bereaved, the additional stressor of traumatic encounter with death. Not only should these studies involve human populations, but animal models would also be useful, for instance, such as those suggested for PTSD and those that use separation of primates as a loss model (Laudenslager, 1988; Krystal, 1990; Bremner *et al*, 1991). There is a need to examine in depth:

(a) the specificity of stressors
(b) the cognitive phenomena and their associated response systems
(c) affects – their nature, occurrence and triggers
(d) avoidance phenomena
(e) arousal
(f) pathophysiology
(g) sleep and its architecture
(h) signs.

Outcomes of traumatic stress reactions and bereavement reactions

These reactive processes may or may not go on to be so distressing, or so impair the individual's functioning that they meet the diagnostic criteria for a disorder. In the case of traumatic stress reactions, it is clear that the DSM–IV (American Psychiatric Association, 1994) criteria for acute stress disorder or post-traumatic stress disorder are more related to the nature of the reactive process than to severity and duration. Anxiety syndromes (e.g. generalised anxiety disorder, panic disorder) and depressive syndromes are common in the comorbidity of PTSD, as is substance abuse disorder (Davidson *et al*, 1991).

There is no specific bereavement disorder identified in DSM–IV. Nevertheless common usage accepts that bereavement pathology syndromes exist, such as chronic grief (Middleton *et al*, 1993). This extreme, distressing, prolonged bereavement reaction is a pathological outcome of bereavement, much as PTSD is a pathological outcome of a traumatic stress reaction. Chronic grief is often seen as being the same as depression or PTSD, yet more usually it reflects a pattern of exaggerated and continuing grief, with the loss the central preoccupation, and significant functional impairment. Chronic grief is often associated with depressive and anxiety disorders, and not uncommonly with substance abuse disorder (Raphael, 1983; Jacobs, 1993). This hypothesis is summarised in Fig. 4.1.

Implications for preventive intervention and therapy

Preventive and therapeutic techniques are described in Part III of this book.

Many preventive or therapeutic methods do not take into account the potential double stressor effect, and indeed may not operate on models that allow for the recognition of both stressor components when they occur simultaneously, as in traumatic bereavements. While a few workers address these issues specifically (Lindy *et al*, 1983; Raphael, 1983, 1986; Van de Hart *et al*, 1990), much further work is required to develop models that take into account the delicate balancing of trauma and grieving to achieve optimum outcomes for those suffering this double psychological burden. It should also be noted that this may also be difficult for therapists who may feel overwhelmed by trauma, loss or both, especially if it affects children. It should be noted that Pynoos *et al* (1987 *a,b*) saw that interventions may be preventive and therapeutic with young people as well.

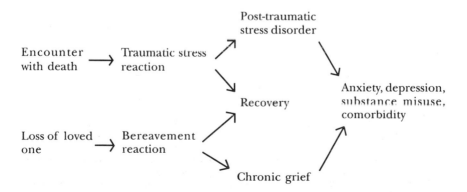

Fig. 4.1 Outcomes of traumatic stress reactions and bereavement reactions.

Conclusions

The detailed exploration and investigation of the phenomena of reactions to trauma and those of reactions to loss has much to offer, both in contributions to clinical understanding and care, and in validating the contributions of these stressors and other variables to the evolution of pathology. If specificity of effects and outcomes is further substantiated, very significant clues to understanding the aetiology of some psychiatric disorders may be found.

References

American Psychiatric Association (1980) *Diagnostic and Statistical Manual of Mental Disorders* (3rd edn) (DSM–III). Washington, DC: APP.
—— (1987) *Diagnostic and Statistical Manual of Mental Disorders* (3rd edn, revised) (DSM–III–R). Washington, DC: APP.
—— (1994) *Diagnostic and Statistical Manual of Mental Disorders* (4th edn) (DSM–IV). Washington, DC: APP.
Bremner, J. D., Southwick, S. M. & Charney, D. S. (1991) Animal models for the neurobiology of trauma. *PTSD Research Quarterly*, **2**, 1–3.
Clayton, P. J. (1990) Bereavement and depression. *Journal of Clinical Psychiatry*, **51** (suppl.), 34–40.
——, Halikas, J. A. & Maurice, W. L. (1971) The bereavement of the widowed. *Diseases of the Nervous System*, **32**, 592–604.
——, —— & —— (1972) The depression of widowhood. *British Journal of Psychiatry*, **120**, 71–78.
Davidson, J. R. T., Hughes, D., Blazer, D. G., *et al* (1991) Post-traumatic stress disorder in the community: an epidemiological study. *Psychological Medicine*, **21**, 713–721.
Dyregrov, A. & Mattheisen, S. B. (1987*a*) Similarities and differences in mothers' and fathers' grief following the death of an infant. *Scandinavian Journal of Psychology*, **28**, 1–15.
—— & —— (1987*b*) Anxiety and vulnerability in parents following the death of an infant. *Scandinavian Journal of Psychology*, **28**, 16–25.
—— & —— (1987*c*) Stillbirth neonatal death and Sudden Infant Death (SIDS): Parental reactions. *Scandinavian Journal of Psychology*, **28**, 104–114.
Faschingbauer, T. R., Zisook, S. & DeVaul, R. A. (1987) The Texas Revised Inventory of Grief. In *Biopsychosocial Aspects of Bereavement* (ed. S. Zisook). New York: APP.
Freud, S. (1917) Mourning and melancholia. In *Sigmund Freud Collected Papers*, vol. 4. New York: Basic Books.
—— (1966) *Introductory Lectures on Psychoanalysis*. New York: Liveright.
Green, B. L., Grace, M. C. & Lindy, J. D. (1983) Levels of functional impairment following a civilian disaster: the Beverly Hills Supper Club fire. *Journal of Consulting and Clinical Psychology*, **51**, 573–580.
——, —— & Gleser G.L. (1985) Identifying survivors at risk: long-term impairment following the Beverly Hills Supper Club fire. *Journal of Consulting and Clinical Psychology*, **53**, 672–678.
Horowitz, M. A. (1976) *Stress Response Syndromes*. New York: Jason Aronson.
——, Wilner, N. & Alvarex, W. (1979) Impact of event scale: a measure of subjective stress. *Psychosomatic Medicine*, **41**, 209–218.
Jacobs, S. C. (1993) *Pathologic Grief: Maladaptation to Loss*. Washington, DC: APP.
——, Kosten, T. R., Kasl, S. V., *et al* (1987) Attachment theory and multiple dimensions of grief. *Omega*, **18**, 41–52.
Krystal, J. H. (1990) Animal models for post traumatic stress disorder. In *Biological Assessment and Treatment of PTSD* (ed. E. L. Giller). Washington, DC: APP.
Laudenslager, M. L. (1988) The psychobiology of loss: lessons from human and non-human primates. *Journal of Social Issues*, **44**, 19–36.

Lehman, D. R., Wortman, C. B. & Williams, A. F. (1987) Long-term effects of losing a spouse or child in a motor vehicle crash. *Journal of Personality and Social Psychology*, 52, 218–231.

L'Hoir, M. (1992) Psychological aspects of SIDS: post-traumatic stress disorders? *Proceedings, Second SIDS Family International Conference*, University of Sydney.

Lindemann, E. (1944) Symptomatology and management of acute grief. *American Journal of Psychiatry*, 101, 141–148.

Lindy, J. D., Green, B. L., Grace, M., *et al* (1983) Psychotherapy with survivors of the Beverly Hills Supper Club fire. *American Journal of Psychotherapy*, 37, 593–610.

Lundin, T. (1984) Morbidity following sudden and unexpected bereavement. *British Journal of Psychiatry*, 144, 84–88.

McFarlane, A. C. (1988a) The aetiology of post-traumatic stress disorders following a national disaster. *British Journal of Psychiatry*, 152, 116–121.

—— (1988b) The longitudinal course of posttraumatic morbidity: the range of outcomes and their predictors. *Journal of Nervous and Mental Disease*, 176, 30–39.

Maddison, D. C. & Walker, W. L. (1967) Factors affecting the outcome of conjugal bereavement. *British Journal of Psychiatry*, 113, 1057–1067.

Middleton, W., Moylan, A., Raphael, B., *et al* (1993) An international perspective on bereavement related concepts. *Australian and New Zealand Journal of Psychiatry*, 27, 457–463.

Parker, G. (1977) Cyclone Tracey and Darwin evacuees: on the restoration of the species. *British Journal of Psychiatry*, 130, 548–555.

Parkes, C. M. (1972) *Bereavement: Studies of Grief in Adult Life*. New York: International Universities Press.

—— & Weiss, R. S. (1983) *Recovery from Bereavement*. New York: Basic Books.

Pynoos, R. S., Frederick, C., Nader, K., *et al* (1987a) Life threat and posttraumatic stress in school-age children. *Archives of General Psychiatry*, 44, 1057–1063.

——, Nader, K., Frederick, C., *et al* (1987b) Grief reactions in school age children following a sniper attack at school. *Israel Journal of Psychiatry and Related Sciences*, 24, 53–63.

Raphael, B. (1977) Preventive intervention with the recently bereaved. *Archives of General Psychiatry*, 34, 1450–1454.

—— (1983) *Anatomy of Bereavement*. New York: Basic Books.

—— (1986) *When Disaster Strikes*. New York: Basic Books.

—— (1992) Traumatic stress and SIDS. *Proceedings, Second SIDS Family International Conference*, University of Sydney.

—— & Maddison, D. C. (1976) The care of bereaved adults. In *Modern Trends in Psychosomatic Medicine* (ed. O. W. Hill). London: Butterworth.

Ryncarson, E. K. (1984) Bereavement after homicide: a descriptive study. *American Journal of Psychiatry*, 141, 1452–1454.

Schut, H. A. W., Keijser, J. D., Van Den Bout, J., *et al* (1991) Post-traumatic stress symptoms in the first years of conjugal bereavement. *Anxiety Research*, 4, 225–234.

Vance, J. C., Foster, W. J., Najman, J. M., *et al* (1991) Early parental responses to sudden infant death, stillbirth or neo-natal death. *Medical Journal of Australia*, 155, 292–297.

Van de Hart, O., Brown, P. & Turco, R. N. (1990) Hypnotherapy for traumatic grief: Janetian and modern approaches integrated. *American Journal of Clinical Hypnosis*, 32, 263–271.

Weisaeth, L. (1989) The stressors and the post-traumatic stress syndrome after an industrial disaster. *Acta Psychiatrica Scandinavica*, 335 (suppl. 80), 25–37.

Wilson, J. P., Smith, W. K. & Johnson, S. K. (1985) A comparative analysis among various survivor groups. In *Trauma and its Wake: The Study and Treatment of Post-Traumatic Stress Disorder* (ed. C. R. Figley). New York: Brunner Mazel.

—— & Raphael, B. (1993) *International Handbook of Traumatic Stress Syndromes*. New York: Plenum Press.

Zisook, S. (1987) Adjustment to widowhood. In *Biopsychosocial Aspects of Grief and Bereavement* (ed. S. Zisook). Washington, DC: APP.

——, Shuchter, S. R. & Lyons, L. E. (1987) Predictors of psychological reactions during the early stages of widowhood. *Psychiatric Clinical of North America*, 10, 355–368.

——, Schneider, D. & Shuchter, S. R. (1990) Anxiety and bereavement. *Psychiatric Medicine*, 8, 83–96.

5   Memory and trauma

DANIEL J. SIEGEL

This chapter on memory and trauma includes, for completeness, a discussion of some therapeutic interventions. Other therapeutic interventions are discussed in Part III.

Normal memory

From the beginning of an infant's life, the mind/brain is organising experiences and stimuli and attempting to 'make sense' out of them (Flavell *et al*, 1993; Siegel, 1995).

Memory refers to a number of processes in which the mind/brain is able to perceive a stimulus, encode elements of it, and then store these for later retrieval. It is reconstructive, not reproductive, and influenced by active mental models or schemata which link together perceptual biases, associated memories, emotions and prior learning.

Implicit and explicit memory

There are at least two forms of memory which depend on different brain structures. Some forms of remembering involve conscious awareness (*explicit* or *declarative memory*), while others are not easily accessible to consciousness but can influence behaviour (*implicit* or *procedural memory*).

Implicit memory is likely to reside in the brain structures that mediated its initial encoding (e.g. basal ganglia and amygdala and possibly motor, somatosensory and sensory cortices) and includes information acquired during skill learning, habit formation, simple classical conditioning, and other knowledge that is expressed through performance rather than recollection (Squire, 1992*a*).

Explicit memory is what people generally think of as 'memory', in which an event can be recalled as if it were from the past and communicated to others as such (Squire *et al*, 1990). Explicit memory requires focal (conscious) attention for processing and is thought to be mediated via the medial temporal lobe system which includes the hippocampal formation and related structures (Squire, 1992*a,b*). Hippocampal processing is dependent on an easily disrupted neurophysiological process called long-term potentiation.

By the separate, subsequent process of cortical consolidation, which takes days to weeks to months, memories are made 'permanent' in the cortex and independent of the hippocampus for retrieval.

Studies of the development of memory (Fivush & Hudson, 1990; Nelson, 1993a) suggest that: (a) children have excellent encoding and retrieval capacities for *implicit* memory from early on; (b) *explicit* memory encoding may be good, but retrieval strategies for young children are immature and this may lead to the observed limitations and inconsistencies in cued and spontaneous recall for personally experienced events; (c) the nature of *post-event dialogue* regarding an experience can influence the manner and probability of recall of aspects of an experience (Ceci & Bruck, 1993); and (d) emotional states bias the interpretation of stimuli, encoding and the retrieval of memories in a process known as *state-dependent learning* (Bower, 1987; Eich & Metcalfe, 1989; MacLeod, 1990).

Narrative, attachment and memory

The development of explicit, autobiographical memory in children has been found to be markedly influenced by 'memory talk', in which adults (usually parents) talk to children about the contents of their memory (Nelson, 1993b). This enhanced recall by social interaction may be due to the reinforcing impact of such talk, the learning about 'how to remember' as well as the co-construction of a 'narrative' about events.

There may be confirmation from attachment theory. For the parents of avoidantly attached children there is a fascinating set of converging findings. One of the characteristics of the parents of avoidantly attached children is that they insist on an inability to recall their childhood experiences. The first year of life of their infants was marked by a mother–child relationship which was emotionally distant and rejecting (Ainsworth *et al*, 1978). On follow-up at ten years of age, Main's sample of avoidantly attached children had a unique paucity in the content of their spontaneous autobiographical narratives (Main, 1991). Perhaps the parents of these avoidantly attached children do not engage them in talking about events which will become their memories (co-construction of narrative), and thus the accessibility of memories for those experiences is greatly diminished.

Metacognition

The capacity to 'think about thinking' is a process termed *metacognition*. In general, sometime between three and nine years of age, children develop the capacity and then ability to express directly their metacognitive functions. Theoretically, the stage of metacognitive development of a child at the time of a trauma may have an important influence on how the child is able to adapt, especially in cases of intrafamilial abuse involving a sense of betrayal and conflictual mental models for the same care-giver (Main, 1991). *Metamemory*, or 'thinking about memory' includes the processing of memory processes. A metamemory process called *source monitoring* is thought to determine the origin of a memory. One form of source monitoring, reality monitoring, is the process by which "people discriminate, when remembering, between information that had a perceptual source and information that was self-generated from thought, imagination, fantasy or dreams" (Johnson, 1991).

Traumatic memory

Processing/encoding and storage

Traumatic experience becomes encoded differently from a non-traumatic event. Only a selected portion of the traumatic experience can be processed with the 'conscious' focal attention required for explicit processing. The need to diminish emotional flooding during trauma may lead to the focusing of attention away from traumatic elements of an experience. Excessive stress, mediated via glucocorticosteroids, may also directly impair hippocampal functioning (Sapolsky *et al*, 1990), leading to greater or sometimes exclusive reliance on non-hippocampal (amygdaloid) memory pathways. Thus the majority of traumatic elements may be primarily processed in parallel without focal attention.

Thus perceptual and emotional flooding, extreme stress and divided attention during trauma may cause *impaired explicit processing* but leave *intact implicit processing*. This configuration may explain numerous findings in post-traumatic stress disorder, for example how specific avoidance behaviours, startle response and somatic symptoms (intact implicit memory) may occur in spite of dissociative amnesia (impaired explicit memory).

The emotional features of the trauma may become integral to the memory trace for that experience. There may be a minimal amount of 'reflective processing' at the time of encoding, which leads the storage of the event to be (primarily) in perceptual form and to include a flood of intense emotions. This configuration is prone to mistaken source monitoring on retrieval, possibly resulting in a 'flashback'.

Research with organic amnesic patients has also suggested a 'consolidating' process over weeks to months, in which explicit memory encoded via the hippocampus becomes embedded in the (associational) cortex and does not require, after consolidation, the hippocampus for retrieval (Squire *et al*, 1990). Dreaming and REM sleep may be important in this long-term memory consolidation (Hartmann, 1982). Commonly, permanent or 'longer term long-term' memory can be intact in certain amnesic patients. The extension of this finding to trauma processing raises the possibility that the unresolved quality of traumatic memory could be explained via the impairment of the consolidation process normally occurring between the hippocampus and associational cortex. Thus, blockade of hippocampal processing during and subsequent to trauma may result in both impaired explicit recall and to lack of subsequent cortical consolidation.

It has been demonstrated that conditioned fear or 'emotional memories' may be mediated primarily through the amygdala, the part of the brain with a central role in emotional behaviour (Le Doux, 1992). The amygdala receives direct sensory input from connections via the thalamus, which then sends projections on to the sensory cortex. In contrast, the hippocampus receives input later on, following processing by the sensory cortex (Davis, 1992). Thus the amygdala may process sensory data and encode fear, independent of any input from the hippocampus. PTSD may be understood to be *pathologically conditioned fear*, with broad generalisations and context-independent responses to trauma-related stimuli. Neural circuits established via the amygdala are tenacious. Behavioural change that may be achieved via various forms of therapy is thought to be due to cognitive override mechanisms rather than elimination of basic learning in the amygdala (Le Doux, 1992). These additional cognitive mechanisms may rely on hippo-campal and cortical processing to override established amygdala circuits. This may involve making fears more specific and context-dependent, thus rendering them less disabling.

In addition, one may see 'dissociations' in the normally associated sensory input, such that different modalities (e.g. sight, hearing, tactile sensation) are segregated in perception and stored (and then retrieved) 'separately'. (This is a significant problem for retrieval in that only one sensory channel may be recalled at a time.) Furthermore, traumatic memories may have dissociations between episodic and semantic memory such that the factual content of an episode may be accessible, but the sense of self, time and interpersonal context may be absent. Thus, a subjective experience of depersonalisation ('non-self'), disorientation and intrusiveness may occur initially when memories of trauma are reinstated.

Retrieval, re-enactment and recall

Traumatic re-enactment, as evidenced by patients' repeated behaviours and children's spontaneous play, can be seen as driven by implicit memory. Even traumatic narratives (retold as fictional stories involving violence and death but devoid of a sense of oneself in the past) can be viewed as implicitly derived, despite being mediated by language (which is often considered expressive of explicit or declarative memory).

Memories of traumatic events that do not fit into prior schemata, and are not stored as narrative and consolidated explicitly in the cortex, may be prone to repeated retrieval. Triggers of this implicit retrieval may be perceptual stimuli (a car backfiring), emotional states (fear, anxiety), interpersonal contexts (separation, illness of a care-giver) and language cues (talk about trauma-specific issues). Implicit retrieval would produce a subjective internal experience of trauma-related emotions, bodily sensations and images which would be sensed as 'self in present' rather than 'self in past'. Implicit retrieval would also produce manifest behaviours such as the telling of fictional narratives, re-enactment of the trauma and abrupt changes in behaviour shifts (in response to sudden intrusions of implicit recall). Abrupt 'state of mind' shifts may not "make sense" and may be attributed to different 'selves' as a dissociative adaptation. Adaptations to these implicit retrievals may include specific avoidance behaviours and chronic distractibility and difficulty with focal attention (as conscious/focal attention is bombarded by internal stimuli).

Adaptations

Childhood trauma may involve several 'intrapsychic' adaptations (defence mechanisms) which may influence memory: suppression/repression, denial, fantasy and dissociation.

Repression

In *repression* an experience is attended focally, encoded explicitly and then stored in an elaborated form. Active intentional suppression may initially inhibit retrieval, limiting further elaborative and organisational processing. Retrieval of these memories is thus actively inhibited and later may become an automatic process called repression. Some authors view suppression and repression as utilising the same cognitive mechanisms (Erdelyi, 1993). Conscious awareness of this latent or potential memory becomes automatically blocked. Retrieval inhibition (Bjork, 1989) is a normal and essential function of memory which makes certain data more accessible than others. In the retrieval of a previously repressed memory, this view predicts that, although the reactivation would be experienced as intrusive, this would not be a flashback, but a more fully processed set of images which may have already to some extent been organised in narrative form.

Dissociation

It is likely that in clinical *dissociation*, the division of attention and/or state of mind during a traumatic experience leads to the inhibition of explicit encoding. Furthermore, the normally associated elements of perceptual modalities, context, emotions and reflections may be differentially processed and thus have segregated associative linkages. Their storage and subsequent reinstatement will reflect this 'dis-association' and be experienced consciously as a set of disjointed perceptual and reflective components. The depersonalisation, time distortion and intrusive subjective experiences in clinically dissociative patients reflect this trauma-specific form of cognitive dissociation in processing. The hypothesis presented here is that repressed memories are explicitly processed more fully than dissociated memories, and thus when retrieved are subjectively experienced as a 'past' form, in contrast to the disjointed nature of recall, with distortions in both self and time and the consequent predisposition towards flashbacks, as found with dissociated memories.

Studies of suppression and other forms of mental control also support the concept of active inhibitory processes which, under stress, may lead to increased retrieval of a 'blocked' item (Wegner & Pennebaker, 1993).

The prohibition against talking openly about traumatic experiences (for example in abusive families) may also play an important role in blocking traumatic events from becoming a part of the child's personal memory.

Implications for psychotherapeutic interventions

Approaches to treatment need careful research evaluation, but generally include the view that the impaired emotional processing of the traumatic event requires the active recollection, in explicit terms, of the details of the experience (Foa & Kozak, 1986; Pennebaker *et al*, 1988; Greenberg & Safran, 1989; Putnam, 1989; Herman, 1992; Harber & Pennebaker, 1993).

Basic principles

The overall goal in the treatment of an individual who has experienced trauma is to allow them to function as fully as possible and to have a subjective experience in life which is characterised by a sense of well-being, choice and dignity. One of the most important principles is that of a therapeutic alliance. Given that many forms of childhood trauma involve mistreatment by adults, the issue of trusting authority/parental figures often becomes a crucial therapeutic area in these individuals. The patient's narratives and manifestations of mental models of the self and others may be revealed in descriptions of present relationships and in the therapeutic relationship itself. The patient's metacognitive knowledge and metacognitive monitoring will become evident in self-reflection during therapy. However, adaptations to trauma may involve the avoidance of "thinking about thinking" in order to have maintained minimal disruptions to the child's capacity to participate in the flow of 'normal' family life. An awareness of and respect for the patient's developing metacognitive capacities, memories, narratives and models of the self is essential.

Effective therapy may catalyse the development of each of these processes, which can thus become more coherent and functional. As this chapter has discussed, memory is reconstructive. There may be an emotional gist or theme (Christianson & Loftus, 1987) of a memory with only vague details accessible to conscious recollection. A therapeutic goal is to enable specific memories to become more complex. This is no simple or painless process, but it may be highly rewarding.

It would be wise, however, for the enthusiastic clinician to be aware of the suggestive nature of human memory (Pettinati, 1988; Schumacher, 1991). Normal human discourse may lead to "filling in of the gaps" as a story is elaborated in order to make sense. The listener's bias can shape the nature of the unfolding story. The therapist's bias may be manifested as subtle non-verbal cues, verbal emphases or repeated questioning around a given topic. Delayed recall of repressed or dissociated memories of childhood trauma is a phenomenon (Terr, 1987, 1994) with a plausible, theoretical, underlying cognitive mechanism. Clinicians need to be aware that partially distorted or wholly false memories of traumatic events are also theoretically plausible and supported by studies on the suggestibility of human memory (Schumacher, 1991; Ceci & Bruck, 1993) and case examples (Terr, 1994).

It is important for clinicians involved in evaluations and treatment to be aware of their own biases and the potential authority/parental role they may play which may make patients particularly vulnerable to suggestive influence. Within the therapeutic relationship, it is important to be supportive, empathic and concerned, without leading. This delicate balance is a challenge to all therapists. The basic principles of clinical interest, compassion and open-mindedness can help to optimise therapeutic progress and minimise iatrogenic distortions.

Specific techniques and helpful tools: working with traumatic memories

Several authors have written about various techniques (Freud, 1958; Pennebaker *et al*, 1988; Spiegel, 1988; Putnam, 1989; Van der Kolk & van der Hart, 1989; Harber & Pennebaker, 1993) in the treatment of traumatised individuals. *Abreaction* is a term referring to the reinstatement of a memory with its concomitant emotional responses from the time of the event. Clinically it has been noted that the symptoms of an 'unresolved trauma' are prone to recur if intervention has not involved some form of therapeutic abreaction. The retrieval of a memory by itself is not therapeutic, nor does it necessarily alter the form in which the memory is stored. A flashback or abreaction which does not involve therapeutic processing exposes the patient to a repeated experience of being overwhelmed, helpless and in pain. A therapeutic abreaction emphasises both cognitive and emotional processing of dissociated elements of a previously inaccessible or only partially accessible memory.

What is different in the recalling from the actual experiencing is that the patient can now reflectively process the experience and co-construct a narrative with the therapist. This processing includes emotionally responding in the present to what happened in the past. By drawing this distinction between remembered pain and the pain of remembering, the patient can begin to gain a sense of mastery in the present by beginning the process of grief which has been impaired for so long.

This process often involves asking the patient at appropriate times and gently about some of the details of the experience (what was seen, felt, heard, etc.) and its interpersonal context. These elements can help focus holistically on the sequence of events, giving the episode of trauma *narrative coherence*. Possible feelings of shame or guilt at having caused the trauma should be explored. Should the patient have flashbacks which may be a fundamental part of abreaction, he/she should be encouraged in the present to process cognitively this newly assembled set of perceptions, emotions and reflections from the past.

Therapeutic tools for psychological distancing, such as those derived from imagery or hypnosis, provide a number of helpful techniques for use during abreactive sessions (Spiegel, 1988). Judicial use of psychopharmacological agents may be helpful at specific times in treatment when autonomic hyperarousal becomes incapacitating (Silver *et al*, 1990; Nagy *et al*, 1993).

Cognitive processing may help to override conditioned fear responses, and make them less broadly generalised and more context-specific and thus less disabling. This explicit processing will also lead to the establishment of hippocampal and cortical circuits and thus the storage of a different form of memory. What is not known is whether newly associated explicit and implicit memory actually replaces prior forms, or merely become a more accessible form, making reinstatement of the original implicit-only form less likely.

Therapeutic interventions that allow implicit memories to be processed in an explicit manner, including desensitisation, self-reflection and narrativisation, will be essential in the resolution process, and self-reflection during an abreactive experience will provide additional reflective components to a previously 'perceptual-rich/reflective-poor' memory profile. This increase in reflective processes will then permit source monitoring to assess accurately the origin of the memory and to reduce the misinterpretation that results in flashbacks.

The emotional sequelae of trauma – essentially the psychological meaning of having been helpless – may have persistent effects. Resolution invariably involves grieving in the advent of the new knowledge which destroys an often idealised sense of a significant other or of the self. Depression as a part of this grief is also common and can be seen as part of the acceptance of what was previously an event unavailable to explicit awareness. The incorporation of the knowledge of the traumatic event(s) into the person's view of the self, others and the world around them can lead to profound changes in their experience of life. This change can itself be disorienting. This is counterbalanced, however, by relief from the torment of flashbacks, intrusive images and nightmares.

The working through of traumatic memories thus enhances the patient's sense of agency, accommodation to their own emotional experience, sense of bodily integrity, and narrative coherence and continuity. The process of grief and healing, like other forms of learning and psychological change, takes time. Although a difficult and often painful process, the rewards for patient and therapist can be deeply gratifying.

Acknowledgements

This chapter has been edited by Tony Kaplan from a longer paper entitled 'Memory, trauma and psychotherapy: a cognitive science view' which was written by Daniel J. Siegel and published by the American Psychiatric Press, Inc. in the *Journal of Psychotherapy Practice and Research* (1995), **4**, 93–122. Extracted with permission from the author.

References

Ainsworth, M. D. S., Blehar, M. C., Waters, E., *et al* (1978) *Patterns of Attachment*. Hillsdale, NJ: Lawrence Erlbaum.

Bjork, R. A. (1989) Retrieval inhibition as an adaptive mechanism in human memory. In *Varieties of Memory and Consciousness: Essays in Honor of Endel Tulving* (eds H. L. Roediger & F. I. M. Craik). Hillsdale, NJ: Lawrence Erlbaum.

Bower. G. H. (1987) Commentary on mood and memory. *Behavior Research and Therapy*, **25**, 443–456.

Ceci, S. & Bruck, M. (1993) Suggestibility of the child witness: a historical review and synthesis. *Psychological Bulletin*, **113**, 403–439.

Christianson, S. A. & Loftus, E. F. (1987) Memory for traumatic events. *Applied Cognitive Psychology*, 1, 225–239.

Davis, M. (1992) The role of the amygdala in fear and anxiety. *Annual Review of Neuroscience*, 15, 353–375.

Eich, E. & Metcalfe, J. (1989) Mood dependent memory for internal vs. external events. *Journal of Experimental Psychology: Learning, Memory and Cognition*, 15, 443–455.

Erdelyi, M. H. (1993) Repression: the mechanism and the defense. In *Handbook of Mental Control* (eds D. M. Wegner & J. W. Pennebaker), pp. 126–146. Englewood Cliffs, NJ: Prentice Hall.

Fivush, R. & Hudson, J. A. (eds) (1990) *Knowing and Remembering in Young Children.* Cambridge: Cambridge University Press.

Flavell, J. H., Miller, P. H. & Miller, S. A. (1993) *Cognitive Development.* Englewood Cliffs, NJ: Prentice Hall.

Foa, E. B. & Kozak, M. J. (1986) Emotional processing of fear: exposure to corrective information. *Psychological Bulletin*, 99, 20–35.

Freud, S. (1958) Remembering, repeating and working through. In *Complete Psychological Works*, Standard Edition vol. 12. London: Hogarth Press.

Greenberg, L. S. & Safran, J. D. (1989) Emotion in psychotherapy. *American Psychologist*, 44, 19–29.

Harber, K. D. & Pennebaker, J. W. (1993) Overcoming traumatic memories. In *Handbook of Emotion and Memory* (ed. S. A. Christianson), pp. 359–387. Hillsdale, NJ: Lawrence Erlbaum.

Hartmann, E. (1982) The functions of sleep and memory processing. In *Sleep, Dreams and Memory* (ed. W. Fishbein), pp. 111–124. New York: Spectrum.

Herman, J. L. (1992) *Trauma and Recovery.* New York: Basic Books.

Johnson, M. K. (1991) Reflection, reality monitoring and the self. In *Mental Imagery* (ed. R. G. Kunzendorf). New York: Plenum.

Le Doux, J. E. (1992) Brain mechanisms of emotion and emotional learning. *Current Opinion in Neurobiology*, 2, 191–197.

MacLeod, C. (1990) Mood disorders and cognition. In *Cognitive Psychology – An International Review* (ed. M. W. Eysenck) pp. 9–56. Chichester: John Wiley.

Main, M. (1991) Metacognitive knowledge, metacognitive monitoring, and singular (coherent) vs. multiple (incoherent) models of attachment: findings and directions for future research. In *Attachment Across the Life Cycle* (eds P. Marris, J. Stevenson-Hinde & C. Parkes). New York: Routledge.

Nagy, L. M., Morgan, C. A., Southwick, S. M., *et al* (1993) Open prospective trial of fluoxetine for posttraumatic stress disorder. *Journal of Clinical Psychopharmacology*, 13, 107–113.

Nelson, K. (1993a) The psychological and social origins of autobiographical memory. *Psychological Science*, 2, 1–8.

—— (1993b) Events, narratives, memory: what develops? In *Minnesota Symposium in Child Development: Memory and Emotion* (ed. C. A. Nelson). Hillsdale, NJ: Lawrence Erlbaum.

Pennebaker, J. W., Kiecolt-Glaser, J. K. & Glaser, R. (1988) Disclosure of traumas and immune function: health implications for psychotherapy. *Journal of Consulting and Clinical Psychology*, 56, 239–245.

Pettinati, H. M. (ed.) (1988) *Hypnosis and Memory.* New York: Guilford.

Putnam, F. (1989) *Multiple Personality Disorder: Diagnosis and Treatment.* New York: Guilford.

Sapolsky, R. M., Uno, H., Rebert, C. S., *et al* (1990) Hippocampal damage associated with prolonged glucocorticoid exposure in primates. *Journal of Neuroscience*, 10, 2897–2902.

Schumacher, J. F. (ed.) (1991) *Human Suggestibility: Advances in Theory, Research and Applications.* New York: Routledge.

Siegel, D. (1995) Cognition and Perception. In *Comprehensive Textbook of Psychiatry* (6th edn) (eds H. I. Kaplan & B. J. Sadock), pp. 277–291. New York: Williams and Wilkins.

Silver, J. M., Sandberg, D. P. & Hales, R. E. (1990) New approaches in the pharmacotherapy of posttraumatic stress disorder. *Journal of Clinical Psychiatry*, 51, 33–38.

Spiegel, D. (1988) Dissociation and hypnosis in post-traumatic stress disorders. *Journal of Traumatic Stress*, 1, 17–33.

Squire, L. R. (1992a) Declarative and non-declarative memory: multiple brain systems supporting learning and memory. *Journal of Cognitive Neuroscience*, 4, 232–243.

—— (1992b) Memory and the hippocampus: a synthesis from findings with rats, monkeys and humans. *Psychological Review*, 99, 195–231.

——, Zola-Morgan, S., Cave, C. B., *et al* (1990) Memory: organization of brain systems and cognition. Cold Spring Harbor Symposia on Quantitative Biology LV, 1007–1023.

Terr, L. (1987) What happens to early memories of trauma? A study of twenty children under age five at the time of documented traumatic events. *Journal of the American Academy of Child and Adolescent Psychiatry*, **27**, 96–104.

—— (1994) *Unchained Memories*. New York: Basic Books.

Van der Kolk, B. A. & van der Hart, O. (1989) Pierre Janet and the breakdown of adaptation in psychological trauma. *American Journal of Psychiatry*, **146**, 1530–1540.

Wegner, D. M. & Pennebaker, J. W. (eds) (1993) *Handbook of Mental Control*. Englewood Cliffs, NJ: Prentice Hall.

6   Theoretical models of post-traumatic stress disorder

The concept of post-traumatic stress disorder (PTSD) has been accompanied by a variety of theoretical models to explain its origins and maintenance in the traumatised individual. These models have their roots in apparently contrasting biological, physiological, cognitive, behavioural and psychodynamic frameworks. However, one of the fascinating features of work in the field of trauma reactions is the way that insights gained within one theoretical approach can help identify important features to be studied within a different model. This chapter will present models from writers with widely differing backgrounds.

In the last ten years, many theories have been put forward to advance our understanding of this complex disorder. None have captured the whole story, and collaboration of workers from different theoretical backgrounds would appear to be the way forward if we are truly going to understand the nature of this complex disorder.

A. Physiological and biological mechanisms

RONAN MCIVOR

In the first comprehensive description of what we now call post-traumatic stress disorder (PTSD) (American Psychiatric Association, 1987, 1994), Kardiner & Spiegel (1947) emphasised the physiological as well as the psychological manifestations of their "physioneurosis". In the past decade there has been increasing interest in the neuropsychiatry of PTSD (Burges Watson *et al*, 1988; Charney *et al*, 1993; Pitman *et al*, 1993) after the long domination of research into the psychological and social aspects of the condition.

A number of psychobiological models of PTSD have been advanced that provide tentative explanations for the neuropathological substrate of symptom clusters, namely intrusive phenomena, arousal and avoidance. These theories provide a rational framework for various treatment methods.

Altered autonomic function

Blanchard's (Blanchard *et al*, 1986) early work showed conditioned autonomic responses, such as tachycardia and increased blood pressure, muscle tension and skin resistance, in veterans exposed to combat sounds. Such work has been repeated and extended using electromyographic measurements (Pitman *et al*, 1989; 1990*a*) and event-related brain potentials (Paige *et al*, 1990; McFarlane *et al*, 1993). It has been suggested that physiological discriminant functions derived from Vietnam veterans can significantly distinguish PTSD from non-PTSD subjects (Orr *et al*, 1993), including those with non-traumatogenic anxiety disorder.

Not surprisingly, such physiological arousal, when exposed to reminders of the trauma, be they auditory or visual, is accompanied by increased levels of noradrenaline and adrenaline (Kosten *et al*, 1987; McFall *et al*, 1990), although baseline levels between patients and controls are not different (McFall *et al*, 1992). Yehuda *et al* (1992) found that dopamine and noradrenaline levels, but not adrenaline, were significantly related to PTSD symptom severity. In addition, Perry *et al* (1987) has reported a reduction in the number of high-affinity alpha2-adrenergic binding sites in the platelets of Vietnam veterans with PTSD, while Lerer *et al* (1987) report a decrease in lymphocyte adenylate cyclase activity. Finally, yohimbine, a noradrenergic agonist which blocks alpha2-adrenergic autoreceptors, increases the severity of the core symptoms in PTSD (Southwick *et al*, 1993). These data, consistent with earlier animal work, are compatible with a down-regulation of receptor activity in response to increased levels of circulating catecholamines secondary to intense stress.

These findings underlie the autonomic conditioning hypothesis of PTSD (Keane *et al*, 1985*c*), where sympathetic hyperarousal occurs to conditioned stimuli which, in turn, elicits elements of the original 'fight or flight' response (the increased arousal symptom group in DSM–IV). In an effort to relieve symptoms, sufferers are more likely to misuse alcohol and drugs. Kolb (1987, 1993) proposed that with excessive noradrenergic activation, lower brain-stem structures, such as the medial hypothalamic nuclei and the locus coeruleus (LC), escape from inhibitory cortical control. He hypothesised that such stimulus overload may lead to structural synaptic changes, leading to reduced capacity for habituation, discriminative perception and learning. Van der Kolk *et al* (1985) saw the LC and its connections with the amygdala, hippocampus (HC) and temporal neo-cortex as a "neurophysiological analogue of memory", and long-term potentiation of these pathways, by massive noradrenergic activity secondary to stress, may be a biological correlate of flashbacks and vivid nightmares. Such a 'kindling' phenomenon may explain why anticonvulsants such as carbamazepine (Lipper *et al*, 1986; Wolf *et al*, 1988; Lipper, 1990) and valproate (Fesler, 1991) may be useful in symptom relief in PTSD.

While the initial neurochemical response is characterised by increased synthesis and utilisation of catecholamines, animal studies have shown that prolonged and repeated exposure to inescapable shock, leading to the clinical state of learned helplessness, may be followed by reduced levels of noradrenaline, dopamine and serotonin (Weiss *et al*, 1975). The learned helplessness model to inescapable shock (Seligman, 1975) has many similarities with the avoidance symptoms of PTSD (van der Kolk *et al*, 1985), and may be related to the depletion of catecholamines in the LC. It is of interest that medications that inhibit LH in animals, such as tricyclic antidepressants and clonidine, are also useful in decreasing the symptoms of PTSD (Saporta & van der Kolk, 1993).

Neuroendocrine abnormalities in PTSD

Hypothalamic–pituitary–adrenal axis

As PTSD represents a major stress reaction, it is not surprising that there are abnormalities in the hypothalamic–pituitary–adrenal (HPA) axis. These abnormalities do not appear to parallel those seen in major depressive disorder (MDD), providing evidence of diagnostic independence. In contrast to the hypercortisolaemia seen in depression, there is evidence that the HPA axis in PTSD may become underactive as a result of chronic and repetitive stress. This attenuated adrenocortical response may reflect a heightened sensitivity in the negative feedback loop at the level of the hypothalamus (HT), hippocampus or pituitary glucocorticoid receptors (Yehuda *et al*, 1991*a*). Such an adaptive mechanism would help prevent the harmful sequelae of chronically raised glucocorticoid levels.

Mason and Yehuda, with their colleagues (Mason *et al*, 1986; Yehuda *et al*, 1990) showed lower levels of urinary free cortisol (UFC) in patients with PTSD when compared with other psychiatric conditions and normal controls. Even in those with comorbid depression, Yehuda *et al* did not find increased UFC typical of that seen in MDD alone. Supporting this, Halbreich *et al* (1989) found that basal plasma cortisol levels in patients with PTSD and coexisting endogenous depression were within the normal range and significantly lower than those with uncomplicated endogenous depression. These findings suggest a lower basal activity of the HPA-axis in PTSD, as an adaptation to chronic stress.

Mason *et al* (1988) suggested that the high urinary noradrenaline/cortisol ratio may be useful in distinguishing PTSD from other diagnostic groups. It may also reflect a dissociation in adrenal medullary and adrenal cortical activity in PTSD. Contrasting with these findings, Pitman & Orr (1990) reported higher mean cortisol excretion in PTSD patients compared with normal combat controls. Yehuda *et al* (1991*a*) noted that the Pitman & Orr (1990) study used combat controls instead of normal volunteers. Combat controls have undergone the stress of combat, and may therefore have a different basal HPA activity than normal volunteers. Yehuda *et al* (1991*a*) recommended further, more detailed studies using all three groups (combat controls carefully evaluated for lifetime diagnosis of PTSD and other psychiatric conditions, individuals with PTSD, and normal volunteers).

Consistent with the decrease in urinary cortisol excretion, Yehuda *et al* (1991*b*), in a preliminary study, reported increased lymphocyte glucocorticoid receptors in 15 PTSD patients versus 11 normal (non-combat) controls, with morning glucocorticoid receptor numbers correlating with symptom severity. These findings contrast with observed changes in glucocorticoid receptors in MDD.

Cortisol response to dexamethasone

The dexamethasone suppression test (DST) has been shown to be a useful marker in psychiatry; 46% of depressed patients show non-suppression of cortisol in response to the synthetic glucocorticoid (Carroll, 1982). In contrast, patients with PTSD but no depression show the normal suppression response to the standard 1 mg dose (Kundler *et al*, 1987; Dinan *et al*, 1990; Kosten *et al*, 1990), although those with co-existing MDD may (Kundler *et al*, 1987; Olivera & Fero, 1990) or may not (Halbreich *et al*, 1989; Kosten *et al*, 1990) show non-suppression. Going one step further, Yehuda *et al* (1993), using low dose (0.5 mg) dexamethasone in 21 male patients with PTSD, found an exaggerated suppression response of cortisol to dexamethasone, a pattern opposite to that seen in depression. Together with the findings of low urinary cortisol excretion, and increased lymphocyte glucocorticoid receptor number, these data suggest an abnormally sensitive negative feedback system in the HPA axis, giving rise to lower than normal HPA activity.

ACTH response to CRF

The normal rise in adrenocorticotrophin hormone (ACTH) in response to corticotropin-releasing factor (CRF) infusion is attenuated in MDD (Gold *et al*, 1986). In a small sample, Smith *et al* (1989) found a blunted ACTH response to CRH in eight PTSD patients compared with a control group of normal volunteers, although this effect may have been due to depressive symptomatology. The blunting was not confirmed in a preliminary study by Hockings *et al* (1993). As well as occurring with depression, a blunted response can also be seen in other psychiatric disorders, such as panic disorder and anorexia nervosa. An enhanced sensitivity of the HPA axis may account for the blunted ACTH response to CRF.

Other neuro-endocrine features of PTSD

Dinan *et al* (1990) examined a number of endocrine parameters in eight women who had experienced violent sexual assaults. As well as finding no differences between patient and control group with respect to the dexamethasone suppression test, they also found no differences using the desipramine/growth hormone test (measuring alpha-2 adrenoreceptor activity) or the buspirone/prolactin test (reputedly measuring serotoninergic activity). They concluded that the results do not support a link between PTSD and depression. Distinction between depression and PTSD has also been observed using the thyroid stimulating hormone response to thyroid releasing hormone (Kosten *et al*, 1990), but more work needs to be carried out in this area to clarify matters. Another area of interest is possible alterations in serum testosterone levels in PTSD patients (Mason *et al*, 1990).

Endogenous opioids and PTSD

Encephalins and β-endorphins have a number of complex functions, including pain control, via their influence on the dorsal grey matter of the spinal cord, the LC, the HT and the limbic system (Burges Watson *et al*, 1988). It is well known that subjective pain sensations are less likely to be experienced in situations of intense stress (Lewis *et al*, 1980). Such stress-induced analgesia (SIA) can be reversed by the opiate antagonist naloxone (Moretti *et al*, 1983).

Exposure to stress-inducing stimuli, as we have seen, can produce self-reported fear and intense autonomic responses. Exercise-induced stress in PTSD patients may produce a greater increase in plasma β-endorphin levels than in controls (Hamner & Hitri, 1992), although baseline levels may be low (Hoffman *et al*, 1989). The inescapable-shock animal model of PTSD predicts that re-exposure to traumatic stimuli will precipitate opiate-mediated SIA in PTSD patients. This hypothesis was confirmed in a pilot study by van der Kolk and associates (van der Kolk *et al*, 1989; Pitman *et al*, 1990*b*) when, in a cross-over design, they found that in eight combat veterans with PTSD, no decrease in pain ratings occurred in subjects who were given naloxone before and during viewing of a combat video, while those who received a placebo treatment experienced a 30% decrease in reported pain intensity after standardised heat stimuli. Control subjects without PTSD, but matched for combat exposure, did not show a decrease in ratings in either condition. The absence of a significant co-existing endocrinological response suggests that the SIA is centrally mediated, an idea which is consistent with the learned helplessness/inescapable shock model of PTSD.

As well as functioning to reduce pain sensation, opiate-mediated analgesia may play a role in symptoms such as numbing of responsiveness (Sapporta & van der Kolk, 1993). Opiates inhibit the LC and decrease the level of hyperarousal, while opiate exhaustion may remove this normal inhibition, leading to noradrenaline excess (Burges Watson *et al*, 1988). Furthermore, although not supported by psychophysiological evidence, PTSD sufferers may become 'addicted' to their condition in order to maintain levels of endogenous opioids through re-exposure (van der Kolk *et al*, 1985). Self-medication with opiates is a preferred drug of misuse in many patients, and opiate withdrawal may cause a worsening of PTSD symptoms. The plasma half-life of methionine-enkephalin in PTSD patients may be longer than in controls (Wolf *et al*, 1991).

Sleep disturbance

Sleep disturbance is common among PTSD sufferers (Ross *et al*, 1989; van Kammen *et al*, 1990). A unique profile is emerging characterised by increased rapid eye movement (REM) latency (the period between sleep onset and the first episode of REM sleep, usually 70–110 minutes), decreased REM sleep duration, decreased Stage 4 sleep and decreased sleep efficiency (Friedman, 1988). In contrast, patients with endogenous depression are more likely to have shortened REM latency and increased REM activity (Rush *et al*, 1986). The LC plays an important role in regulating sleep phenomena. Ross *et al* (1989) regarded sleep disturbance, and its attendant dream mentation, as the central hallmark of PTSD, and that dysfunctional REM circuitry may participate in the control of the exaggerated startle response. Surprisingly, patients with PTSD may have higher non-REM awakening thresholds (Schoen *et al*, 1984; Dagan *et al*, 1991), and sleep disturbance in ex-prisoners of war may be associated with structural brain abnormalities (Peters *et al*, 1990).

Summary

It is possible to draw some tentative conclusions concerning the biological underpinnings of PTSD. The acute traumatic situation is undoubtedly associated with sympathetic hyperarousal and hypercortisolaemia which contribute to the fight or flight reaction. Opioid release produces analgesia and contributes to emotional withdrawal. Such acute reactions help to ensure initial survival in a threatening environment, but in the long-term may give rise to more persistent conditioned neurobiological responses which become maladaptive. Such modifications may become relatively stable through the processes of kindling or structural neural changes. Repetitive and intrusive memories and nightmares, for example, may be associated with long-term potentiation of the locus coeruleus pathways to the HC and the amygdala. The locus coeruleus plays an essential role in autonomic regulation and stress responses, while the amygdala is of importance in conditioning and extinction of memories. Re-exposure to traumatic stimuli may cause fluctuations in endogenous opioid levels, resulting in changes in affective response and alertness. The attenuated adrenocortical response may reflect a heightened sensitivity in the negative feedback loop of the HPA axis, giving rise to lower than normal HPA activity. Such neurobiological changes may impair the survivor's ability to learn from or adapt to familiar or novel situations.

To date there has been a marked preponderance of work concentrating on the role of the noradrenergic system to the relative exclusion of other neurotransmitter systems, such as serotonin, dopamine, N-methyl-D-aspartate and the neurosteroids. Interrelationships between neurotransmitter systems in PTSD require further investigation. Dynamic imaging techniques will help to locate structures implicated in brain pathology, and enable researchers to examine metabolic activity during arousal. More specific neuro-endocrine probes may clarify levels of pathology. The intriguing process of how an external traumatic event can produce such enduring effects on memory and conditioning is still a long way from being answered (Pitman, 1989). Such research will provide a theoretical framework for the rational development of more effective treatments.

B.   Psychoanalytical models

CLEO VAN VELSEN

Freud's (1896) first theory for an aetiology of neurosis postulated the necessity of an external trauma, namely seduction. Although he went on to develop his psychology in terms of infantile conflicts, he remained interested in traumatic neurosis, especially the "war neuroses", for example giving expert evidence to a commission investigating the treatment of soldiers with shell-shock in 1918 (Freud, 1920*a*). This topic also formed the basis for a symposium at the Fifth International Psychoanalytic Congress held in Budapest in 1918, with Freud (1919) writing an introduction to the small book that followed.

The word *trauma* is derived from the Greek, meaning to wound or pierce, and Freud (1920*b*) referred to trauma as involving the breaching of a protective shield or stimulus barrier, which normally functions to prevent the overwhelming of the mind (ego) from internal and external stimuli, by means of managing, or binding, the excitations. A flood of unmanageable impulses would cause "disturbance on a large scale" and set "in motion every defensive measure". Freud drew attention in particular to "repetition compulsion" namely the re-experiencing of a disturbing and catastrophic event in an attempt to master it. This fixation to the trauma alternated with defences aimed at avoiding remembering or repeating the trauma. Thus we have the basis for a distinct 'post-traumatic state' with symptoms that are similar in all those experiencing an external stressor, and which forms the basis for the diagnosis of post-traumatic stress disorder as we know it today.

Freud (1926) later elaborated this theory, suggesting that it was the helplessness of the ego which formed the core of the traumatic situation, and that anxiety could be used as a signal of the possible danger of repeating the earlier experience, thus linking with the phenomenon of increased arousal in PTSD. However, classical Freudian analytical theory, with its emphasis on drives, instincts and regression, meant that for a long time analysts thought that it was not the stressor, in particular, that was traumatic but the recrudescence of a previously repressed infantile conflict. Ferenczi (1931, 1933) was an exception in emphasising the importance of the actual event and the necessity of recovering lost and split-off experience in treatment.

Kardiner (1941) challenged and developed all these ideas, placing much more emphasis on the actual event or stressor, describing what he called ego contraction and disorganisation leading to symptoms of numbing and disintegration as well as intrusion.

During the 1950s, 60s and 70s interest in traumatic stress grew with the examination and treatment, firstly of Holocaust survivors and then of Vietnam veterans who were returning with high levels of stress reactions (Niederland, 1961, 1968; Krystal, 1968; Lifton 1968, 1973; Niederland & Krystal, 1971). Sixty years after Freud, Horowitz (1976) used the language of information processing, but based his model of traumatic stress on the alternation of a tendency to repeat an aspect of the trauma with denial.

During this period, research on external trauma was much more significant in the US than in the UK (apart from isolated examples such as Fairbairn, 1952), one reason possibly being the presence of fewer Holocaust victims and no Vietnam veterans. In the UK the psychotherapeutic treatment of war neuroses as a result of the Second World War was associated with the development of group analytical and therapeutic community theory (Pines, 1983). Overall concern was more with intrapsychic trauma until recent events such as the Falklands and Gulf wars and a string of disasters, for example the Zeebrugge Ferry disaster, the Kings Cross fire and Piper Alpha (see chapter 8).

Thus the debate surrounding dynamic views of the aetiology of trauma has tended to focus on whether individual, as opposed to stressor characteristics, are decisive. Of course, this concern is one which extends to the field of PTSD as a whole with contradictory research findings (for a discussion see McFarlane, 1989; Taylor *et al*, 1993). Sandler *et al* (1991) argued that it is clearer to describe a process of "traumatisation" where the traumatic event causes an "internal adaptation which *may or may not be pathological or pathogenic*" (my emphasis).

Brett (1993) has described two models now prevalent in the psycho-dynamic view of traumatic stress. The first derives from Freud's original description regarding the re-experiencing phenomena as primary, leading to defensive functioning. The second model derives from the work of Kardiner and Krystal and describes the reaction to the stressor as being a "massive adaptive failure", with phenomena such as repetition compulsion being secondary. She argues that the first model, associated with Freud and Horowitz, is more appropriate for those who have suffered less severe stress than the second model, which is developed out of work with Holocaust survivors.

Overall there has been a move away from the idea of regression to early ego processes, towards an interest in the effect of trauma on an adult psychic structure. There may be, as Winnicott (1974) put it, "a release of primitive horrors" and primitive methods of functioning, but not a developmental regression. According to psychoanalytical theory, an individual functions partly by the use of defence mechanisms that exist to defend the ego from anxiety related to internal conflicts, super-ego demands, external situations and emotions. A variety of defensive procedures was first described by Anna Freud in 1937. In response to trauma, these established defences may be fully, or partially, superseded by other defence mechanisms, some of which are associated with the primitive functioning referred to above (these defences will be described in more detail in chapter 17). Such a change may be immediately adaptive and vital for survival, but long-term maladaptive sequelae can be generated. People can be locked into their trauma and become entrenched in their view of themselves as a victim. Thus it is vital to acknowledge, recognise, explore and reintegrate the patient's destructiveness in fact and fantasy.

Common to all dynamic models is a concern with the meaning a person gives to a traumatic event and/or its aftermath. This is particularly relevant in a condition where there is so often a sense of unpreparedness and helplessness. Explaining the effect of a damaging or crushing event on an adult psychic apparatus, in an environmental context, has begun to make use of the theory of object relations (Rayner, 1991; Grotstein & Rinsley, 1994) and attachment (Bowlby, 1969,1988; Holmes, 1993), associated with British psychoanalysts.

Thus Garland (1991) drew on Bion's (1962, 1970) notion of an internal container necessary for the transformation of the unthinkable to the thinkable, as well as on Segal's (1957) theory of symbolism. Impairment of the capacity to symbolise is a common observation in traumatic states of stress in childhood (Piaget, 1962; Terr, 1991) and is of increasing interest to psychodynamic theorists. Garland (1991) gave a vivid example of a woman who, some months after being involved in a fire where several colleagues were killed, experienced fog as if it were smoke: not as a symbol, even though a part of her "knew" it was fog.

Following on from the work with disasters is a concern with the effects of victimisation, namely where there is a victimiser and a relationship with the victim, however brief; this can range from rape to torture. Kilpatrick *et al* (1989) have suggested that the effects of victimisation are worse than the effects of other disasters or crises. This has led to increasing interest in the effect of victimisation in childhood and its relation to vulnerability to PTSD in adulthood, as well as its relationship to diagnoses such as borderline personality disorder (Bremner *et al*, 1993; Gunderson & Sabo, 1993).

The increasing realisation of the complexity and diversity of PTSD is reflected in the way that psychoanalytical psychotherapists, too, are concentrating on various aspects of traumatisation rather than describing an overall, simple and comprehensive theory. I can mention but a few here. De Zulueta (1993), a psychotherapist with a background in biology, used attachment theory and a wide review of empirical research to examine the psychological, biological and social aspects of PTSD, as well as discussing the place of aggression. She argues that violence may be a maladaptive post-traumatic response. Hopper (1991), a psychoanalyst in London, examined in detail the fear of annihilation. This links to studies which demonstrate that the risk of adults developing PTSD after disasters is raised if there is a time when the person believed he or she would die (Green, 1993). Krystal (1968, 1978, 1993) has become particularly interested in the impact of traumatic stress on affects, and Lifton (1968, 1973, 1993) has postulated a "psychoformative approach" which concentrates on the structure of the self and its transformation in very particular ways by trauma. He described ten fundamental principles affecting survivor reactions based on an understanding of death and continuity or the so-called life/death paradigm.

In common to all is a concern with the damage done by a stressor to the important integrative functions of the mind and the necessity of giving meaning to the traumatic instance as a vital part of treatment. In my discussion of treatment (chapter 17A) I describe in more detail some of the psychological mechanisms disrupted and distorted by traumatic stress and how this can be approached using psychodynamic psychotherapy.

C.   Cognitive–behavioural models of PTSD

DEBORAH LEE and STUART TURNER

An individual involved in a traumatic event is faced with the task of dealing with a new and out of the ordinary experience. Bowlby (1969), within a psychodynamic framework, has written of the need to master the extra-ordinary information received from the event. Such mastery would lead to a congruence between the traumatic memories and the individual's inner working models of the mind (in cognitive psychology, these would be termed cognitive schemata). In this way, successful integration of the traumatic event is achieved. Thus by contrast, PTSD can be seen as a result of the failure or inability to integrate successfully the traumatic event into the individual's cognitive schemata.

Rachman (1980), drawing on psychodynamic and behavioural literature, used the concept of "emotional processing" to explain the process of *absorbing* emotional disturbances. Successful emotional processing is associated with a return to normal functioning whereby the emotional events no longer cause distress or disruption. He postulated that a central indicator of unsuccessful emotional processing is the persistence of intrusive activity. He further identified factors relating to the trauma which promote or impede emotional processing of affect-laden events (these include factors such as intensity, uncontrollability, predictability and dangerousness). Other factors relating to the individual include the state of the individual at the time of the event (high arousal, illness, fatigue, relaxation) and personality type (neuroticism, self-efficacy).

Horowitz (1986, 1990), also drawing from psychodynamic theory, deve-loped one of the most comprehensive models to date to offer an explanation of the processes involved in the integration of information from a traumatic event. He suggested that the information received from a traumatic event is stored in the individual's memory and continually brought to the conscious mind or repeated in the mind (Horowitz, 1990). By the very nature of the traumatic event, the individual is inevitably faced with an overwhelming and negative experience, which is associated with a negative emotional response. The individual is faced with the task of integrating huge changes in his/her schemata in order to achieve harmony. This is achieved by the individual working through the event in such a way that this new information from the event is repeated several times into the conscious mind. Such repeated recollection is associated with powerful negative emotional responses.

Furthermore, in order for the individual to avoid being overwhelmed by these negative emotional responses, Horowitz (1986) suggested that various defence mechanisms (inner inhibitory control systems) become operative. Such mechanisms control the presentation of information into the conscious mind and thus allow for gradual assimilation of traumatic information. These mechanisms can operate at a conscious level (suppression) or indeed at a subconscious level (repression).

His model proposed that PTSD is a result of the individual's inability to integrate successfully a traumatic event into his or her cognitive schemata. Thus his model of PTSD is a two-phase model, with alternating intrusion–repetition and denial–numbing. He suggested that the avoidant symptom cluster of PTSD (denial of the event, numbness and avoidance) arises when inner inhibitory control mechanisms predominate over the repetition of information into the conscious mind (the intrusion symptom cluster of PTSD). At other times, intrusion symptoms are dominant over the avoidance state. The cyclical nature of the PTSD symptomatology can be accounted for in this way. Completion of the working-through phase is associated with a cessation of intrusion and denial.

This theory has been of heuristic value in understanding the concept of PTSD. It proffers an explanation of the intrusion-avoidance symptomatology of the disorder. However, other theorists have pointed out that it lacks an adequate exploration of the nature of increased physiological activity, the third cluster of symptomatology associated with PTSD (Foa *et al*, 1989). Furthermore, Foa highlighted the fact that, although the theory refers to the presence of strong and often overwhelming negative emotional responses associated with information from the traumatic event, it offers no full explanation as to why such emotional states as fear, survivor guilt, anxiety and depression are typically associated with PTSD.

Behavioural models of PTSD

Prominent behavioural theories of PTSD have utilised the principles of conditioning theory. In particular, Mowrer's (1947, 1960) two-factor learning theory has been used as a basis for the explanation of the development and maintenance of PTSD (Becker *et al*, 1984; Keane *et al*, 1985a,c; Kilpatrick *et al*, 1985).

Mowrer's theory proposed that two types of learning, classical and instrumental, are present in fear acquisition and avoidance. Via the process of classical conditioning, a previously neutral stimulus becomes associated with an unconditioned stimulus (UCS) that innately evokes fear or discomfort. The neutral stimulus then takes on the aversive properties of the UCS and its presence evokes fear/anxiety as well. The neutral stimulus now becomes a conditioned stimulus (CS) for fear responses. During a traumatic event an individual is exposed to a variety of 'neutral' stimuli (smells, shapes, sounds, words) present at the time of the trauma. Such stimuli are, in turn, associated with fear or discomfort and thus become conditioned. Their presence alone can evoke intense fear and anxiety responses.

Thus when the original CS is subsequently paired with another neutral stimulus, this stimulus may also take on the aversive properties of the CS and evoke anxiety. This process of higher-order conditioning is used to explain why many other stimuli of a previously neutral nature also take on aversive properties and thus elicit anxiety responses. Similarly in stimulus generalisation, stimuli that are similar to the original CS also gain anxiety eliciting properties.

The second stage of Mowrer's theory involved instrumental conditioning. Here the development of behaviours such as escape and avoidance are selectively reinforced by virtue of their quality of reducing exposure to an aversive CS. Thus an alleviation or termination of the discomfort associated with such stimuli is experienced.

An example of Mowrer's theory as an explanation of PTSD can be found in the work of Keane *et al* (1985*c*) with Vietnam veterans. These authors proposed that when an individual is exposed to a life-threatening situation, he/she may become conditioned to a wide variety of stimuli present during the trauma. These stimuli may include certain smells, colours, noises or times of the day. These stimuli (CS) then become associated with the traumatic event; their presence subsequently elicits discomfort or anxiety. Keane postulated that higher-order conditioning and stimulus generalisation account for the wide variety of stimuli, not originally present in the trauma, that are capable of triggering memories of the event and associated physiological arousal. Thus cues originally conditioned during the trauma become associated with similar unconditioned stimuli and eventually come to elicit a similar response. For example, a car backfiring may trigger fear and anxiety.

Keane suggested that these repeated spontaneous exposures to the feared stimuli are incomplete (they do not include all the conditioned stimuli and the exposure is of short duration) and therefore do not result in a reduction of anxiety (Stern & Marks, 1973).

This use of Mowrer's two-factor theory to explain the genesis of PTSD offers an explanation for the attachment of fear to trauma-related cues that were previously neutral and/or not present during the original trauma. Furthermore, it accounts for escape/avoidance behaviours and the presence of such behaviour in seemingly safe situations. Foa *et al* (1989) suggested that the degree of stimulus generalisation (characteristically greater for PTSD than for phobias) could be accounted for by the greater severity and intensity of the original trauma. They draw on evidence from animal experiments which indicates that longer duration and greater intensity of the unconditioned stimulus lead to greater escape and avoidance responses (Kamin, 1969; Baum, 1970). However, Mowrer's theory does not offer an adequate explanation of the mechanisms behind the re-experiencing phenomena central to PTSD (Foa *et al*, 1989).

Cognitive models of PTSD

The importance of cognitive processes in PTSD has not gone unnoticed. Researchers have attempted to explain the role of cognitive factors in the development and maintenance of disorder by drawing on theories of cognitive appraisal, expectancy theory, attributional style and causal attributions (Veronen & Kilpatrick, 1983; Joseph *et al*, 1991, 1993). The theory of learned helplessness has been proposed as an explanation of the numbing of affect and passivity seen in PTSD (Peterson & Seligman, 1983) and, on the face of it, this work may well be more appropriate to PTSD than to depression (as originally proposed). The model incorporates data derived from animal responses to inescapable shocks (Maier & Seligman, 1976). Similarities between learned helplessness and victimisation have been highlighted. Both these situations lead to generalised beliefs about future uncontrollability and the futility of future responses.

Abramson *et al* (1978) added to this model and suggested that people seek to explain uncontrollable events on three dimensions: (a) source (internal–external); (b) temporality (stable–unstable); and (c) situational (global–specific). They propose that individuals who make internal, stable and global attributions suffer more than those who make external, unstable and specific attributions. In support of this hypothesis, Joseph *et al* (1991, 1993) found that the number of internal attributions made for disaster-related events was positively associated with levels of intrusive thoughts, depression and anxiety at follow-up in the survivors of the Herald of Free Enterprise disaster. They further postulated that causal attributions for disaster related events may predict specific emotional states such as guilt and shame, which could in turn exacerbate responses to the disaster. This hypothesis has also been developed by Weiner (1986).

Cognitive appraisal (a process whereby individuals attach meaning to an event) has been examined by several authors (Veronen & Kilpatrick, 1983; Schepple & Bart, 1983; Frank & Stewart, 1984). For example, Frank & Stewart (1984) and Schepple & Bart (1983) have demonstrated that women raped in situations where they believed they were safe were more likely to experience severe reactions than women who were raped in situations they believed to be dangerous. Similarly, people who believe they are invulnerable to crime have more difficulties recovering than those who believed they were as vulnerable as others (Perloff, 1983). Such findings would appear to lend support to the notion that pre-existing cognitive schemata influence the individual's response to that trauma and their ability to process it successfully

This importance of core cognitive functions in trauma response is evidenced above. Highlighting within-person variables and identifying mechanisms involved in the emergence of shame, guilt, poor self-esteem and depression (all frequently observed in association with PTSD) offers insight into the pertinent issue of variability in presentation of the traumatic response observed among traumatised individuals. By placing the emphasis on pre-existing cognitive schemata, the research further sheds light on possible factors that determine why some individuals but not others develop PTSD, and also its severity of presentation. Yet in terms of offering an overall theoretical perspective of PTSD, these approaches lack a convincing means of explaining the core symptoms of PTSD.

Information-processing models of PTSD

Chemtob *et al* (1988) developed an information-processing model which drew on the work of other exponents of cognitive–behavioural theory (Lang,

1977; Beck & Emery, 1985). They suggested that fear structures are made up of hierarchically and interconnected nodes. These nodes represent all elements (i.e. physiological, behavioural, cognitive and affective memories) that may be required for the execution of a specific act. They postulated that the traumatised individual continues to act in the 'survival mode' which was present during the original trauma. This survival mode is considered to represent the activation of the fear structure. Thus, in studies with combat veterans, they suggested that individuals with PTSD have (to some degree) persistently activated threat-related arousal. Such specific arousal increases the likelihood that individuals will search for and identify threatening information.

Further feedback loops may also be operative in the remaining elements of the fear network; for example, threat-related arousal may trigger threat-seeking behaviour. This, in turn, is associated with attentional narrowing and an increased likelihood that ambiguous information will be interpreted as threatening. Once a threat is perceived, threat-related arousal is further increased, and so on. Chemtob suggested that activation of this network inhibits the activation of other more adaptive networks. This model attempts to explain the development and maintenance of re-experiencing phenomena through feedback loops and covers many of the elements of PTSD. It requires further evaluation and development for non-combat-related PTSD.

Foa & Kozak (1986) argued that the concept of meaning (not incorporated into the traditional learning theories) is essential and indeed central to the understanding of the human experience of trauma. They also argue that information-processing theories give a more substantial account of the re-experiencing phenomena and the generalisation of fear (Lang, 1977; Beck & Emery, 1985; Foa & Kozak, 1986; Resick & Schnicke, 1990, 1992).

Foa & Kozak (1986) postulated a model which incorporates both Lang's (1977, 1979) work on fear structures and Rachman's theory of emotional processing (Rachman, 1980). They proposed that fear structures in the memory contain three types of information: (a) information pertaining to the feared stimulus situation; (b) information about verbal, physiological and overt behavioural responses; and (c) interpretative information about the meaning of the stimulus and response elements of the fear structure. Such an information structure is perceived as a programme for escape or avoidance behaviour (Lang, 1977). They have argued that if the fear structure is indeed a programme for escape behaviour, it must purvey a meaning of danger. They illustrated this point by using a case scenario of a delayed reaction of PTSD in a rape victim who only developed symptoms of PTSD when she was given the information that her attacker had killed his next rape victim (Kilpatrick *et al*, 1986). With this additional information, she interpreted the rape situation as life-threatening and developed an information structure which included a 'changed interpretative information' to do with threat. Further evidence to support this essential meaning element is found in the work of Kilpatrick *et al* (1986) who found that rape victims who perceived their situation as life-threatening were more likely to develop

PTSD than those who did not. These violations of safety concepts led to the perception of the world as unpredictable and uncontrollable.

Foa & Kozak (1986) distinguished the fear structure of PTSD from that of a phobia in relation to: (a) the intensity of the response; (b) the size of the structure; and (c) the ready accessibility of the structure. Thus they argued that the change in rules of safety lead to a vast array of stimuli in the fear structure. The pervasiveness of the stimuli, the intensity of the responses (both physiological and behavioural) and the low threshold for activation renders PTSD more disruptive to daily functioning.

In order to change a dysfunctional fear structure, Foa & Kozak (1986) suggested that two steps are required. Firstly, the fear structure has to be activated in its entirety, and secondly, new information needs to be incorporated into the structure which is incompatible with some elements already present. They argued that the common denominator for the feared situation in PTSD is the perceived threat. They suggested that this is a better predictor than objective measures of trauma of the development of PTSD (supported by Kilpatrick *et al*, 1986). Thus, a theoretical position which incorporates the element of meaning is required to explain PTSD.

However, this model of PTSD does not explain all the features of PTSD, for example emotional numbing or delayed onset. Neither does it fully utilise the role of environmental factors such as social support in the development or maintenance of PTSD (Jones & Barlow, 1990).

Cognitive processing theory

More recently a promising theory and therapy, also based on information processing, has been developed – that of cognitive processing therapy (CPT; Resick & Schnicke, 1992, 1993). Although this theory has been developed for victims of rape, its intrinsic interest makes it a valuable contribution to theories of PTSD in general.

Their theory and therapy draws on the work of Foa *et al* (1989) outlined above. Resick & Schnicke (1992) rightly point out that information-processing theories fit the currently popular belief of PTSD as an anxiety disorder. However, they remind readers that PTSD is much more than fearful memories. Intrusive memories may be activated by other strong affects and beliefs. Indeed, within the literature on victimisation, crime victims frequently report experiencing anger, disgust, humiliation, guilt and conflicts between pre-existing schemata and the actual event (Resick & Gerrol, 1988; Resick *et al*, 1990).

Resick & Schnicke (1992) suggested that when a rape experience conflicts with prior beliefs, the victim is less able to reconcile (process) the event and has greater difficulty recovering. Evidence can be found in support of the contention that PTSD is associated with a range of frequently intense emotions (Schepple & Bart, 1983; Frank & Stewart, 1984).

In order to explain how the individual deals with conflicts between new information and prior schemata, Resick & Schnicke (1992) used the concepts of assimilation and accommodation. Hollon & Garber (1988) pointed out that when an individual is exposed to schema-discrepant information, one of two things normally happens. Firstly, the information can be altered to fit into the existing schemata (assimilation), and so an example of assimilation in a rape victim might be, "it must have been something that I did to make this happen to me so it wasn't really rape". Thus Resick & Schnicke (1992) suggested that flashbacks and other intrusive memories may be attempts at integration when assimilation fails. Secondly, existing schemata may be altered to accommodate new incompatible information (accommodation), and an example of this might be, "the world is an unpredictable place and sometimes bad things happen to good people". Hollon & Garber (1988) suggested that assimilation usually happens more readily than accommodation, since it appears easier to alter one's perception of a single event than to change one's view of the world. Resick & Schnicke (1992) proposed that accommodation is a goal of therapy, but pointed out that over-accommodation can occur when accommodation happens without good social support or therapeutic guidance.

In terms of cognitive content, Resick & Schnicke (1992) drew on the work of McCann *et al* (1988), who proposed five areas of major functioning which become disrupted by victimisation: safety, trust, power, esteem and intimacy. Each of these areas are further divided into two loci – schemata relating to self and schemata relating to others. McCann related each of these ten areas of functioning to specific symptoms if pre-existing positive schemata are disrupted or if pre-existing negative schemata are confirmed by victimisation.

Thus in terms of PTSD, Resick & Schnicke (1992) propose that systematic exposure is important in altering the feared memory structures, to the extent that threat cues are restructured and habituated, and indeed, perceptions of fear and danger may be altered (Foa & Kozac, 1986). However, they suggested that such exposure will not necessarily alter other emotional reactions, without *specific* confrontation of conflicts, misattributions and expectations. Thus, victims may still blame themselves, and feel anger and shame. All such emotions may be sufficiently intense to elicit intrusive memories and avoidance reactions. Thus, without elicitation, the individual may still continue to suffer symptoms of PTSD.

CPT assumes that symptoms of intrusion, avoidance and arousal are caused by conflicts between new information received from the trauma and prior schemata. Within CPT, it is proposed that such new information is typically assimilated into prior schemata in such a way that it blocks attempts at integration and is associated with intense emotions; intrusive memories are evidence of failed integration when assimilation fails. It does not assume that the trauma of rape elicits previously existing dysfunctional thinking patterns – as proposed by Beck *et al* (1979) in Beckian cognitive therapy. CPT emphasises the eliciting and expression of frequently intense emotions associated with PTSD (Resick & Schnicke, 1992).

Conclusions

Many models have been described from many different theoretical persuasions. All the models discussed above offer an insight into and further understanding of traumatic stress reactions and PTSD. However, none offer a comprehensive view of the disorder. This undoubtedly reflects the very nature of the disorder, which is multifaceted and associated with a complex and variegated range of symptoms. Furthermore, beneath the large umbrella of PTSD there lies a multitude of traumas that challenge the individual's resources in different ways. Some theories have focused on a specific type of trauma such as combat or rape (Keane *et al*, 1985*a,c*; Resick & Schnicke, 1992, 1993). These theories are interesting and informative, but more research is needed to see if they apply to the whole range of trauma-types.

Other theories have offered explanations of a cluster of symptoms evidenced in PTSD (such as intrusion), but have failed to explain the presence of other central symptoms. Indeed, most of the theories above are mechanistic in that they offer explanations as to why a certain symptom-atology appears. They do not adequately explain why some people develop PTSD and others do not. Recent work on causal attributions and attributional style (Joseph *et al*, 1991, 1993) offers promising insight into the question of variable outcome following trauma.

A wholly persuasive model is required which offers an explanation of the complexity and range of the associated symptomatology. Also such a theory needs to answer why some people develop PTSD and others do not. Furthermore, no theory of PTSD can be complete without empirical data to back up the findings.

Jones & Barlow (1990) attempted to integrate various theoretical positions and proposed an aetiological model of PTSD based on the process and origins of anxiety and panic. They drew on similarities between panic disorder and PTSD. Their conceptualisation included discussion of the role of biological and psychological vulnerabilities, negative life events, fear reactions, perceptions of control, social support and coping strategies. They proposed that the most important function of any aetiological model is to explain the absence of symptoms in some individuals exposed to similar traumatic events. The authors proposed that variables implicated in the aetiology and maintenance of panic disorder are also involved in PTSD. They drew on research of biological vulnerability to certain anxiety disorders (Crowe *et al*, 1980, 1983) and suggested that such a pattern may be relevant to PTSD. Their review extended to examining the role of psychological vulnerability, negative life events and the nature of the stressor in panic disorder and show similarities in PTSD (Frank *et al*, 1981; Frye & Stockton, 1982; Laufer *et al*, 1985; McFarlane, 1988).

Jones & Barlow (1990) also touched on moderating variables which could explain the presence and absence of symptoms and also the variation in presentation. They reviewed research suggesting that emotion-focused coping and distancing techniques are associated with more severe PTSD (Solomon *et al*, 1988). Social support was targeted as another important moderating variable in the development and maintenance of PTSD

(Kilpatrick *et al*, 1982; Keane *et al*, 1985*b*). This aetiological theory, with its emphasis on moderating factors in the development of PTSD, is a most thorough examination and amalgamation of research from many different theoretical backgrounds.

References

Abramson, L. Y., Seligman, M. E. P. & Teasdale, J. D. (1978) Learned helplessness in humans: critique and reformulation. *Journal of Abnormal Psychology*, **87**, 49–94.
Adshead, G. & Van Velsen, C. (1995) Psychotherapeutic work with victims of trauma. In *Textbook of Forensic Psychiatry* (eds M. Cox & C. Cordess). London: Jessica Kingsley.
American Psychiatric Association (1987) *Diagnostic and Statistical Manual of Mental Disorders* (3rd edn, revised) (DSM–III–R). Washington, DC: APP.
American Psychiatric Association (1994) *Diagnostic and Statistical Manual of Mental Disorders* (4th edn) (DSM–IV). Washington, DC: APP.
Baum, M. (1970) Extinction of avoidance responding through response prevention (flooding). *Psychological Bulletin*, **74**, 276–284.
Beck, A. T. & Emery, G. (1985) *Anxiety Disorders and Phobias: A Cognitive Perspective*. New York: Basic Books.
——, Rush, A. J., Shaw, B. F., *et al* (1979) *Cognitive Therapy for Depression*. New York: Guilford Press.
Becker, J. V., Skinner, L. J., Abel, G. G., *et al* (1984) Sexual problems of sexual assault survivors. *Women and Health*, **9**, 5–20.
Bion, W. R. (1962) *Learning from Experience*. London: Heinemann.
—— (1970) *Attention and Interpretation*. London: Tavistock.
Blanchard, E. B., Kolb, L. C., Geraldi, R. J., *et al* (1986) Cardiac response to relevant stimuli as an adjunctive tool for diagnosing post traumatic stress disorder in Vietnam veterans. *Behaviour Therapy*, **17**, 592–606.
Bowlby, J. (1969) *Attachment and Loss*. New York: Basic Books.
—— (1988) *A Secure Base: Clinical Applications of Attachment Theory*. London: Routledge.
Bremner, J. D., Southwick, S., Johnson, D., *et al* (1993) Child physical abuse and combat related PTSD in Vietnam veterans. *American Journal of Psychiatry*, **150**, 235–239.
Brett, E. A. (1993) Psychoanalytic contributions to a theory of traumatic stress. In *International Handbook of Traumatic Stress Syndromes* (eds J. P. Wilson & B. Raphael), pp. 61–68. New York: Plenum.
Burges Watson, I. P., Hoffman, L. & Wilson, G. V. (1988) The neuropsychiatry of post-traumatic stress disorder. *British Journal of Psychiatry*, **152**, 164–173.
Carroll, B. J. (1982) The dexamethasone suppression test for melancholia. *British Journal of Psychiatry*, **140**, 292–304.
Charney, D. S., Deutch, A. Y., Krystal, J. H., *et al* (1993) Psychobiologic mechanisms of posttraumatic stress disorder. *Archives of General Psychiatry*, **50**, 294–305.
Chemtob, C., Roitblat, H. C., Hamada, R. S., *et al* (1988) A cognitive action theory of post traumatic stress disorder. *Journal of Anxiety Disorders*, **2**, 253–275.
Crowe, R. R., Pauls, D. L., Slymen, D. J., *et al* (1980) A family study of anxiety neurosis: morbidity risk in families of patients with mitral valve prolapse. *Archives of General Psychiatry*, **37**, 77–79.
——, Noyes, R., Pauls, D. L., *et al* (1983) A family study of panic disorder. *Archives of General Psychiatry*, **40**, 1065–1069.
Dagan, Y., Lavie, P. & Bleich, A. (1991) Elevated awakening thresholds in sleep stage 3–4 in war-related post-traumatic stress disorder. *Biological Psychiatry*, **30**, 618–622.
de Zulueta, F. (1993) Traumatic origins of violence in adults. In *From Pain to Violence: The Traumatic Roots of Destructiveness*. London: Whurr.
Dinan, T. G., Barry, S., Yatham, L. N., *et al* (1990) A pilot study of a neuroendocrine test battery in posttraumatic stress disorder. *Biological Psychiatry*, **28**, 665–672.
Fairbairn, W. R. D. (1952) *Psychoanalytic Studies of the Personality*. London: Tavistock.
Ferenczi, S. (1931) Child analysis in the analysis of adults. In *Further Contributions to the Problems and Methods of Psychoanalysis* (1955), pp. 126–142. London: Hogarth Press.

—— (1933) Confusion of tongues between adults and the child. In *Further Contributions to the Problems and Methods of Psychoanalysis* (1955), pp. 156–167. London: Hogarth Press.

Fesler, F. A. (1991) Valproate in combat-related posttraumatic stress disorder. *Journal of Clinical Psychiatry*, **52**, 361–364.

Foa, E. B. & Kozak, M. J. (1986) Emotional processing of fear: exposure to corrective information. *Psychological Bulletin*, **99**, 20–35.

——, Steketee, G. & Olasov-Rothbaum, B. (1989) Behavioural/cognitive conceptualisations of post-traumatic stress disorder. *Behaviour Therapy*, **20**, 155–176.

Frank, E. & Stewart, B. D. (1984) Depressive symptoms in rape victims. *Journal of Affective Disorders*, **1**, 269–277.

——, Turner, S. M., Stewart, B. D., *et al* (1981) Past psychiatric symptoms and the response to sexual assault. *Comprehensive Psychiatry*, **22**, 479–487.

Freud, A. (1937) *The Ego and the Mechanisms of Defence.* London: Hogarth Press.

Freud, S. (1896) Studies on hysteria. In *The Complete Psychological Works of Sigmund Freud*, vol. III, pp. 187–221. London: Hogarth Press.

—— (1919) Introduction to psychoanalysis and the war neuroses. In *The Complete Psychological Works of Sigmund Freud*, vol. XVII, pp. 206–210. London: Hogarth Press.

—— (1920*a*) Beyond the pleasure principle. In *The Complete Psychological Works of Sigmund Freud*, vol. XVIII, pp. 7–64. London: Hogarth Press.

—— (1920*b*) Memorandum on the electrical treatment of war neurotics. In *The Complete Psychological Works of Sigmund Freud*, vol. XVII, pp. 211–215. London: Hogarth Press.

—— (1926) Inhibitions, symptoms and anxiety. In *The Complete Psychological Works of Sigmund Freud*, vol. XX, pp. 77–175. London: Hogarth Press.

Friedman, M. J. (1988) Toward rational pharmacotherapy for posttraumatic stress disorder: an interim report. *American Journal of Psychiatry*, **145**, 281–285.

Frye, J. S. & Stockton, R. A. (1982) Discrimination analysis of posttraumatic stress disorder among a group of Vietnam veterans. *American Journal of Psychiatry*, **139**, 52–56.

Garland, C. (1991) External disasters and the internal world: an approach to psychotherapeutic understanding of survivors. In *Textbook of Psychotherapy in Psychiatric Practice* (ed. J. Holmes). London: Churchill Livingstone.

Gold, P. W., Loriaux, D. L. & Roy, A. (1986) Responses to corticotrophin-releasing hormone in the hypercortisolaemia of depression and Cushing's disease. *New England Journal of Medicine*, **314**, 1329–1335.

Green, B. (1993) Identifying survivors at risk. In *International Handbook of Traumatic Stress Syndromes* (eds J. P. Wilson & B. Raphael), pp. 135–144. New York: Plenum.

Grotstein, J. & Rinsley, D. B. (eds) (1994) *Fairbairn and the Origins of Object Relations.* London: Free Association Books.

Gunderson, J. G. & Sabo, A. N. (1993) The phenomenological and conceptual interface between borderline personality disorder and PTSD. *American Journal of Psychiatry*, **150**, 19–27.

Halbreich, U., Olympia, J., Carson, S., *et al* (1989) Hypothalamo–pituitary–adrenal activity in endogenously depressed post-traumatic stress disorder patients. *Psychoneuroendocrinology*, **14**, 365–370.

Hamner, M. B. & Hitri, A. (1992) Plasma beta-endorphin levels in post-traumatic stress disorder: a preliminary report on response to exercise-induced stress. *Journal of Neuropsychiatry and Clinical Neuroscience*, **4**, 59–63.

Hockings, G. I., Grice, J. E., Warren, K. W., *et al* (1993) Hypersensitivity of the hypothalamic–pituitary–adrenal axis to naloxone in post traumatic stress disorder. *Biological Psychiatry*, **33**, 585–593.

Hoffman, L., Burges Watson, P., Wilson, G., *et al* (1989) Low plasma beta-endorphin in post-traumatic stress disorder. *Australian and New Zealand Journal of Psychiatry*, **23**, 269–273.

Hollon, S. D. & Garber, J. (1988) Cognitive therapy. In *Social Cognition and Clinical Psychology: A Synthesis* (ed. L.Y. Abramson), pp. 204–253. New York: Guilford Press.

Holmes, J. (1993) *John Bowlby and Attachment Theory.* London: Routledge.

Hopper, E. (1991) Encapsulation as a defence against the fear of annihilation. *International Journal of Psychoanalysis*, **72**, 607–624.

Horowitz, M. J. (1976) *Stress Response Syndromes.* New York: Jason Aronson.

—— (1986) *Stress Response Syndromes* (2nd edn). Northvale, NJ: Aronson.

—— (1990) Posttraumatic stress disorder: psychotherapy. In *A Handbook of Comparative Treatments for Adult Disorders* (eds A.S. Belleck & M. Herson), pp. 289–301. Chichester: Wiley.

Jones, J. C. & Barlow, D. H. (1990) The aetiology of post-traumatic stress disorder. *Clinical Psychology Review*, **10**, 299–328.

Joseph, S. A., Brewin, C. R., Yule, W., *et al* (1991) Causal attributions and psychiatric symptoms in the survivors of the *Herald of Free Enterprise* disaster. *British Journal of Psychiatry*, **159**, 542–546.

——, Yule, W. & Williams, R. (1993) Post-traumatic stress: attributional aspects. *Journal of Traumatic Stress*, **6**, 501–513.

Kamin, L. J. (1969) Predictability, surprise, attention and conditioning. In *Punishment and Adversive Behaviour* (eds B.A. Campbell & R.M. Church). New York: Appleton-Century-Crofts.

Kardiner, A. (1941) *The Traumatic Neuroses of War*. New York: Hoeber.

—— & Spiegel, H. (1947) *The Traumatic Neurosis of War*. New York: Hoeber.

Keane, T. M., Fairbank, J. A., Caddell, J. M., *et al* (1985*a*) A behavioural approach to assessing and treating post-traumatic stress disorder in Vietnam veterans. In *Trauma and its Wake: The Study and Treatment of Post-traumatic Stress Disorder* (ed. C. R. Figley), pp. 257–294. New York: Brunner/Mazel.

——, Scott, W. O., Chavoya, G. A., *et al* (1985*b*) Social support in Vietnam veterans: a comparative analysis. *Journal of Consulting and Clinical Psychology*, **53**, 95–102.

——, Zimmering, R. T. & Caddell, J. M. (1985*c*) A behavioural formulation of post-traumatic stress disorder in Vietnam veterans. *The Behavior Therapist*, **8**, 9–12.

Kilpatrick, D. G., Veronen, L. J. & Resick, P. A. (1982) The aftermath of rape: factors predicting successful coping at three months post-rape. Paper presented at the 59th Annual Meeting of the American Orthopsychiatric Association, San Francisco, CA.

——, —— & Best, C. L. (1985) Factors predicting psychological distress among rape victims. In *Trauma and Its Wake* (ed. C. R. Figley), pp. 113–141. New York: Brunner/Mazel.

——, Best, C. L., Veronen, L. J., *et al* (1986) Predicting the impact of a stressful life experience: criminal victimisation. Presented at the 7th Annual Meeting of the Society of Behavioral Medicine, San Francisco, CA.

——, Saunders, B. E., Arick McMullen, A., *et al* (1989) Victims and crime factors associated with crime-related PTSD. *Behaviour Therapy*, **20**, 199–214.

Kolb, L. C. (1987) A neuropsychological hypothesis explaining posttraumatic stress disorders. *American Journal of Psychiatry*, **144**, 989–995.

—— (1993) The psychobiology of PTSD: perspectives and reflections on the past, present and future. *Journal of Traumatic Stress*, **6**, 293–304.

Kosten, T. R., Mason, J. W., Giller, E. L., *et al* (1987) Sustained urinary norepinephrine and epinephrine elevation in post-traumatic stress disorder. *Psychoneuroendocrinology*, **12**, 13–20.

——, Wahby, V., Giller, E., *et al* (1990) The dexamethasone suppression test and thyrotrophin-releasing hormone stimulation test in posttraumatic stress disorder. *Biological Psychiatry*, **28**, 657–664.

Krystal, H. (ed.) (1968) *Massive Psychic Trauma*. New York: International Universities Press.

—— (1978) Trauma and affect. *Psychoanalytic Study of the Child*, **33**, 81–116.

—— (1993) Beyond the DSM–III–R: therapeutic considerations in post-traumatic stress disorder. In *International Handbook of Traumatic Stress Syndromes* (eds J. P. Wilson & B. Raphael), pp. 841–854. New York: Plenum.

Kundler, H., Davidson, J., Meador, K., *et al* (1987) The DST and post-traumatic stress disorder. *American Journal of Psychiatry*, **144**, 1068–1071.

Lang, P. J. (1977) Imagery in therapy: an information processing analysis of fear. *Behaviour Therapy*, **8**, 862–886.

—— (1979) A bio-informational theory of emotional imagery. *Psychophysiology*, **16**, 495–512.

Laufer, R. S., Brett, E. & Gallops, M. S. (1985) Traumatic stressors in the Vietnam war and post-traumatic stress disorders. In *Trauma and its Wake: The Study and Treatment of Post-traumatic Stress Disorder* (ed. C. R. Figley), pp. 73–89. New York: Brunner/Mazel.

Lerer, B., Ebstein, R. P., Shestatsky, M., *et al* (1987) Cyclic AMP signal transduction in posttraumatic stress disorder. *American Journal of Psychiatry*, **144**, 1324–1327.

Lewis, J. W., Cannon, J. T. & Liebeskind, J. C. (1980) Opioid and nonopioid mechanisms of stress analgesia. *Science*, **208**, 623–625.

Lifton, R. J. (1968) Observations on Hiroshima survivors. In *Massive Psychic Trauma* (ed. H. Krystal), pp. 168–203. New York: International Universities Press.

—— (1973) *Home from the War*. New York: Simon and Schuster.

—— (1993) From Hiroshima to the Nazi doctors. An evolution of psycho-formative approaches to understanding traumatic stress syndromes. In *International Handbook of Traumatic Stress Syndromes* (eds J. P. Wilson & B. Raphael), pp. 11–23. New York: Plenum.

Lipper, S. (1990) Carbamazepine in the treatment of posttraumatic stress disorder: implications for the kindling hypothesis. In *Posttraumatic Stress Disorder: Etiology, Phenomenology, and Treatment* (eds M. E. Wolf & A. D. Mosnaim), pp. 185–203. Washington, DC: APP.

——, Davidson, J. R., Gradym, T. A., *et al* (1986) Preliminary study of carbamazepine in post-traumatic stress disorder. *Psychosomatics*, **27**, 849–854.

McCann, I. L., Sakheim, D. K. & Abrahamson, D. J. (1988) Trauma and victimisation: a model of psychological adaptation. *Counseling Psychologist*, **16**, 531–594.

McFall, M. E., Murburg, M. M., Ko, G. N., *et al* (1990) Autonomic responses to stress in Vietnam combat veterans with posttraumatic stress disorder. *Biological Psychiatry*, **27**, 1165–1175.

——, Veith, R. C. & Murburg, M. M. (1992) Basal sympathiadrenal function in posttraumatic stress disorder. *Biological Psychiatry*, **31**, 1050–1056.

McFarlane, A. C. (1988) Post traumatic morbidity of a disaster: A study of cases presenting for psychiatric treatment. *Journal of Nervous and Mental Disease*, **174**, 4–14.

—— (1989) The aetiology of post traumatic morbidity: predisposing, precipitating and perpetuating factors. *British Journal of Psychiatry*, **154**, 221–228.

——, Weber, D. L. & Clark, C. R. (1993) Abnormal stimulus processing in posttraumatic stress disorder. *Biological Psychiatry*, **34**, 311–320.

Maier, S. F. & Seligman, M. E. P. (1976) Learned helplessness: theory and evidence. *Journal of Experimental Psychology: General*, **105**, 3–45.

Mason, J. W., Giller, E. L., Kosten, T. R., *et al* (1986) Urinary free cortisol levels in posttraumatic stress disorder patients. *Journal of Nervous and Mental Disease*, **174**, 145–149.

——, ——, ——, *et al* (1988) Elevation of urinary norepinephrine/cortisol ratio in posttraumatic stress disorder. *Journal of Nervous and Mental Disease*, **176**, 498–502.

——, ——, ——, *et al* (1990) Serum testosterone levels in posttraumatic stress disorder inpatients. *Journal of Traumatic Stress*, **3**, 449–457.

Moretti, C., Fabbri, A., Gnessi, L., *et al* (1983) Naloxone inhibits exercise-induced release of PRL and GH in athletes. *Clinical Endocrinology*, **18**, 135–138.

Mowrer, O. H. (1947) On the dual nature of learning: a reinterpretation of "conditioning" and "problem solving". *Harvard Educational Review*, **17**, 102–148.

—— (1960) *Learning Theory and Behavior*. New York: Wiley.

Niederland, W. G. (1961) The problem of the survivor. *Journal of Hillside Hospital*, **10**, 223–247.

—— (1968) Clinical observations on the "survivor syndrome". *International Journal of Psychoanalysis*, **49**, 313–315.

—— & Krystal, H. (eds) (1971) *Psychic Traumatisation*. Boston: Little, Brown.

Olivera, A. A. & Fero, D. (1990) Affective Disorders, DST, and treatment in PTSD patients: clinical observations. *Journal of Traumatic Stress*, **3**, 407–414.

Orr, S. P., Pitman, R. K., Lasko, N. B., *et al* (1993) Psychophysiological assessment of posttraumatic stress disorder imagery in World War II and Korean combat veterans. *Journal of Abnormal Psychology*, **102**, 152–159.

Paige, S. R., Reid, G. M., Allen, M. G., *et al* (1990) Psychological correlates of posttraumatic stress disorder in Vietnam veterans. *Biological Psychiatry*, **27**, 419–430.

Perloff, L. S. (1983) Perceptions of vulnerability to victimisation. *Journal of Social Issues*, **39**, 41–61.

Perry, B. D., Giller, E. L. & Southwick, S. M. (1987) Altered platelet alpha2-adrenergic binding sites in posttraumatic stress disorder. *American Journal of Psychiatry*, **144**, 1511–1512.

Peters, J., van Kammen, D. P., van Kammen, W. B., *et al* (1990) Sleep disturbance and computerized axial tomographic scan findings in former prisoners of war. *Comprehensive Psychiatry*, **31**, 535–539.

Peterson, C. & Seligman, M. E. P. (1983) Learned helplessness and victimisation. *Journal of Social Issues*, **2**, 103–116.

Piaget, J. (1962) *Plays, Dreams and Limitations in Childhood*. New York: W.W. Norton.

Pines, M. (ed.) (1983) *The Evolution of Group Analysis*. London: Routledge & Kegan Paul.

Pitman, R. K. (1989) Post-traumatic stress disorder, hormones and memory. *Biological Psychiatry*, **26**, 221–223.

—— & Orr, S. P. (1990) Twenty-four hour urinary cortisol and catecholamine excretion in combat-related posttraumatic stress disorder. *Biological Psychiatry*, **27**, 245–247.

——, Scott, M. D., Orr, S. P., *et al* (1989) Psychophysiological investigations of posttraumatic stress disorder imagery. *Psychopharmacology Bulletin*, **25**, 426–431.

——, Orr, S. P., Forgue, D. F., *et al* (1990*a*) Psychophysiologic responses to combat imagery of Vietnam veterans with posttraumatic stress disorder versus other anxiety disorders. *Journal of Abnormal Psychology*, **99**, 49–54.

——, Van der Kolk, B. A., Orr, S. P., *et al* (1990*b*) Naloxone-reversible analgesic response to combat-related stimuli in posttraumatic stress disorder. A pilot study. *Archives of General Psychiatry*, **47**, 541–544.

——, Orr, S. P. & Shalev, A. Y. (1993) Once bitten, twice shy: beyond the conditioning model of PTSD. *Biological Psychiatry*, **33**, 145–146.

Rachman, S. (1980) Emotional processing. *Behaviour Research and Therapy*, **18**, 51–60.

Rayner, E. (1991) *The Independent Mind in British Psychoanalysis*. London: Free Association.

Resick, P. A. & Gerrol, R. (1988) The effect of within-assault cognitive appraisals, behavior and emotions on subsequent distress in female victims of crime. In Symposium conducted at the 22nd Annual Convention of the Association for the Advancement of Behavior Therapy, New York, NY.

—— & Schnicke, M. K. (1990) Treating symptoms in adult victims of sexual assault. *Journal of Interpersonal Violence*, **5**, 488–506.

—— & —— (1992) Cognitive processing therapy for sexual assault victims. *Journal of Consulting and Clinical Psychology*, **60**, 748–756.

—— & —— (1993) *Cognitive Processing Therapy For Rape Victims: a Treatment Manual*. London: Sage.

——, Churchill, M. & Falsetti, S. (1990) Assessment of cognitions in trauma victims: a pilot study. Paper presented at the Sixth Annual Meeting of the International Society for Traumatic Stress Studies, New Orleans.

Ross, R. J., Ball, W. A., Sullivan, K. A., *et al* (1989) Sleep disturbance as the hallmark of posttraumatic stress disorder. *American Journal of Psychiatry*, **146**, 697–707.

Rush, J. A., Erman, M. K., Giles, D. E., *et al* (1986) Polysomnographic findings in recently drugfree and clinically remitted depressed patients. *Archives of General Psychiatry*, **43**, 878.

Sandler, J., Dreher, A. U. & Drews, S. (1991) An approach to conceptual research in psychoanalysis illustrated by a consideration of psychic trauma. *International Review of Psychoanalysis*, **18**, 133–141.

Saporta, J. A. & Van der Kolk, B. A. (1993) Psychobiological consequences of severe trauma. In *Torture and its Consequences: Current Treatment Approaches* (ed. M. Basoglu), pp. 151–181. Cambridge: Cambridge University Press.

Schepple, K. L. & Bart, P. B. (1983) Through women's eyes: defining danger in the wake of sexual assault. *Journal of Social Issues*, **39**, 63–81.

Schoen, L., Kramer, M. & Kinney, L. (1984) Auditory thresholds in the dream disturbed. *Sleep Research*, **13**, 102.

Segal, H. (1957) Notes on symbol formulation. In *The Work of Hanna Segal* (1981), pp. 49–65. New York: Jason Aronson.

Seligman, M. E. P. (1975) *Helplessness: On Depression, Development and Death*. San Francisco: W. H. Freeman & Co.

Smith, M. A., Davidson, J., Richie, J. C., *et al* (1989) The corticotrophin-releasing hormone test in patients with posttraumatic stress disorder. *Biological Psychiatry*, **26**, 349–355.

Solomon, Z., Mikulincer, M. & Flum, H. (1988) Negative life events, coping responses and combat-related psychopathology: a prospective study. *Journal of Abnormal Psychology*, **97**, 302–307.

Southwick, S. M., Krystal, J. H., Morgan, C. A., *et al* (1993) Abnormal noradrenergic function in posttraumatic stress disorder. *Archives of General Psychiatry*, **50**, 266–274.

Stern, R. S. & Marks, I. M. (1973) Brief and prolonged flooding: a comparison in agoraphobic patients. *Archives of General Psychiatry*, **28**, 270–276.

Taylor, P. J., Gunn, J. & Mezey, G. (1993) Victims and survivors. In *Forensic Psychiatry: Clinical, Legal and Ethical Issues* (eds J. Gunn & P. Taylor), pp. 885–944. London: Butterworth-Heinemann.

Terr, L. C. (1991) Childhood traumas: An outline and overview. *American Journal of Psychiatry*, **148**, 10–20.

Van der Kolk, B. A., Greenberg, M. S., Boyd, H., *et al* (1985) Inescapable shock, neurotransmitters, and addiction to trauma: toward a psychobiology of posttraumatic stress. *Biological Psychiatry*, **20**, 314–325.

——, ——, Orr, S. P., *et al* (1989) Endogenous opioids, stress induced analgesia, and posttraumatic stress disorder. *Psychopharmacology Bulletin*, **25**, 417–421.

van Kammen, W. B., Cristiansen, C., van Kammen, D. P., *et al* (1990) Sleep and the prisoner-of-war experience – 40 years later. In *Biological Assessment and Treatment of Posttraumatic Stress Disorder* (ed. E. L. Giller), pp. 159–172. Washington, DC: APP.

Veronen, L. J. & Kilpatrick, D. G. (1983) Stress management for rape victims. In *Stress Reduction and Prevention* (eds D. Meichenbaum & M.E. Jaremko). New York: Plenum Press.

Weiner, B. (1986) *An Attributional Theory of Motivation and Emotion.* Berlin: Springer Verlag.

Weiss, J. M., Glazer, H. I., Pohorecky, L. A., *et al* (1975) Effects of chronic exposure to stressors on subsequent avoidance-escape behaviour and on brain norepinephrine. *Psychosomatic Medicine*, **37**, 522–524.

Winnicott, D. W. (1974) Fear of breakdown. *International Review of Psycho-Analysis*, **1**, 103–107.

Wolf, M. E., Alavi, A. & Mosnaim, A. D. (1988) Posttraumatic stress disorder in Vietnam veterans. Clinical and EEG findings: possible therapeutic effects of carbamazepine. *Biological Psychiatry*, **23**, 642–644.

——, Mosnaim, A. D., Puente, J., *et al* (1991) Plasma methionine-encephalin in PTSD (correspondence). *Biological Psychiatry*, **29**, 305–306.

Yehuda, R., Southwick, S., Nussbaum, G., *et al* (1990) Low urinary cortisol excretion in patients with posttraumatic stress disorder. *Journal of Nervous and Mental Disease*, **178**, 366–369.

——, Giller, E. L., Southwick, S. M., *et al* (1991*a*) Hypothalamic–pituitary–adrenal dysfunction in posttraumatic stress disorder. *Biological Psychiatry*, **30**, 1031–1048.

——, Lowy, M. T., Southwick, S. M., *et al* (1991*b*) Lymphocyte glucocorticoid receptor number in posttraumatic stress disorder. *American Journal of Psychiatry*, **148**, 499–504.

——, Southwick, S., Giller, E. L., *et al* (1992) Urinary catecholamine excretion and severity of PTSD symptoms in Vietnam combat veterans. *Journal of Nervous and Mental Diseases*, **180**, 321–325.

——, ——, Krystal, J. H., *et al* (1993) Enhanced suppression of cortisol following dexamethasone administration in posttraumatic stress disorder. *American Journal of Psychiatry*, **150**, 83–86.

Part II. Disasters, war, civil conflict, dislocation and interpersonal violence

7 A typology of disasters

COLIN MURRAY PARKES

Coping with disasters is probably the most daunting task with which members of the caring professions can be faced. We need to be prepared in advance and to have some cognitive models, and ways of approaching these situations, that reduce the awful feelings of helplessness that inevitably arise in both care-givers and the cared-for when we are faced with massive loss.

The scientific justification for intervention comes from three types of research:

1. Evidence that disasters constitute a risk to mental health has been reviewed by Raphael (1986) and Lystad (1988). This research discloses an increased risk of PTSD among survivors, an increased risk of pathological grief among those bereaved by disasters, and an increased risk of depression and other psychiatric disorders among affected people who are already vulnerable.
2. Evidence that people at special risk can be identified soon after a disaster strikes is most adequate for bereaved people (Parkes & Weiss, 1983; Osterweis *et al*, 1984). It is to be hoped that others at special risk will be identified by further research.
3. Persuasive evidence from random-allocation studies of high-risk bereaved people indicates that counselling can substantially reduce the risk (Raphael, 1977; Parkes, 1979).

Few hospital disaster plans take proper account of the psychosocial needs of people affected by disasters. These plans are usually confined to the provision of rescue services and physical treatments.

Studies of the psychological effects of disasters have been somewhat piecemeal. Few investigators have the opportunity to study more than one disaster and there has been a dangerous tendency for them to over-generalise. Some have assumed that the particular psychological problems which they have found following a particular type of disaster are peculiar to that situation and deserve a special diagnostic category. Hence we have descriptions of "disaster syndromes" (Wallace, 1956), "A-bomb neurosis" (Lifton, 1967) and "post-earthquake neurosis" (Cohen, 1976). In recent years, as our knowledge has accumulated, the theoretical base has become more sophisticated. It is now recognised that many of the psychological effects of disasters are no different from the psychological effects of other types of acute psychological trauma. Post-traumatic stress disorder does not differ greatly, whether it is caused by a road traffic accident or an earthquake, and neither do panic syndromes, depressive reactions or morbid grief reactions.

Where disasters do differ from the other traumata of life is in their effects on the social systems in which they occur, and this certainly adds an important dimension which affects how they need to be handled. Survivors of a car crash can reasonably expect to be supported by their family and their community. Medical and other caring services exist to meet their physical and psychological needs, and there is no reason for them to feel that the world itself has become chaotic and uncaring. The same cannot be said following disasters. These not only traumatise individuals, but they also disrupt the families and larger support systems in which we all live and take for granted. Disasters bring home to us, as nothing else can, the frailty of man and his place on the planet. Those who suffer them discover the hard way that nothing can be taken for granted. The world becomes a dangerous place in which we can no longer trust in our own strength or in the strength and goodwill of others to keep us free from harm.

In this chapter we shall first consider a way of classifying disasters according to the social systems affected. This provides a frame of reference for the organisation of a response, and the chapter examines the types of psychosocial problems that are likely to arise in each type of disaster, using examples from actual disasters in recent times. The model employed was described by the writer as a contribution to the work of the Disasters Working Party (see chapter 26; Parkes, 1991).

Social systems

In the environment in which man evolved it was the extended family which was the main source of security to its members. In the world in which we now live this is no longer the case. As the organisation of society grew more complex, local communities took over the ordering of our lives, and the tribe became the unit of organisation and the main source of security for its members. Eventually national and international organisations took over many of the functions of the tribe or local community. Today the provision of food, work, housing, and even the education and care of children, is placed in the hands of these huge units of organisation, and elaborate systems of law and government have become our main sources of security. The family remains important (particularly in childhood) but we are all, to some extent, cogs in a larger social machine and sometimes the machine breaks down. Natural phenomena, accidents or acts of war destroy or disrupt the ordered mechanisms of society and a disaster results.

Operational definitions

For the purposes of discussion let us define a *disaster* as any situation which, over a short space of time, causes ten or more deaths and/or an equivalent amount of destruction of property. This definition is necessary to distinguish disasters from other traumatic stresses. For convenience we shall use the term *survivors* for people who survived a disaster without physical injury, those who are injured and survived we shall term *victims*, those who witnessed the disaster without being personally at risk we term *bystanders* and those who have lost relatives or friends the *bereaved*.

Types of disaster

The two most important variables to be considered in planning a response to a disaster are the *scale* (or magnitude) of the disaster and the *spread* (the size of the geographical area covered by the disaster). These are not one and the same thing, thus it is possible to have many deaths confined to a single locality or a few deaths in a widely scattered population.

Table 7.1 divides disasters into nine types according to the scale (large, medium or small) and the spread (local, national or international) of the disaster. A large-scale disaster is one that gives rise to over a thousand deaths or threatens the lives of a similar number of people and/or causes destruction of property. A medium-scale disaster would involve 100 to 1000 deaths, and a small-scale disaster smaller numbers, given that here too the overall impact will also be affected by the threat to life and amount of destruction of property.

The selection of these orders of magnitude is not entirely arbitrary. In general it should be possible to cope with small-scale disasters by means of existing services within the area(s) in which they occur, although advice from specialists will be of value. Medium-scale disasters will over-stretch existing local services and special services will need to be set up. Although the staff for these can usually be found from within the affected region(s), advice and other support from national organisations are also needed. Large-scale disasters require the mobilisation of national and international resources.

When a disaster only affects one locality, the organised response will be focused on that locality, whereas disasters with national and international spread require a much more complex network of responses.

TABLE 7.1
Spread and scale of types of disaster

Scale	Spread		
	Local	*National*	*International*
Small	Hungerford massacre	Clapham train crash	Cheddar/Axbridge air crash
Medium	Aberfan	Zeebrugge ferry disaster	Lockerbie bombing
Large	Managua earthquake	Armenian earthquake	Falklands War

Let us look in more detail at each of the nine scenarios covered by Table 7.1.

1. Small local disasters

These give rise to considerable distress within the locality in which they occur and may receive wider attention if they are of a dramatic or 'newsworthy' character. While the number of people directly affected is relatively small and should not overtax existing resources, the number indirectly affected may be very much greater. For this reason it is usually wise to set up some kind of *information and referral centre* and/or *help-line* which can meet the needs of a wide range of affected people.

An example is the 1987 Hungerford Massacre, in which a gunman fired indiscriminately at people in the small town of Hungerford in Berkshire (see chapter 8G). The number injured or bereaved by the disaster was relatively small. They were well supported by local social and bereavement services. The impact on the population at large, however, was considerable and fully justifies the term 'disaster'. A large proportion of the community was involved as survivors, bystanders, or as friends and neighbours of bereaved people or victims. Many children and other people whose age, frailty or psychological predisposition made them more vulnerable than others to the effects of the threat to life, suffered lasting anxiety and/or post-traumatic stress disorder.

As often happens in such circumstances, offers of help flooded in. It was important to set up a central body to coordinate and match the helpers to those needing help. Liaison was also needed with the press and other media both to minimise the risk that bereaved people or injured victims would be exploited, and to obtain the collaboration of the media in dispelling rumours and providing accurate information about the facilities available. A *Family Help Unit* was set up to support anyone who needed help. It remained a valued source of support for many months to come (Lane & Stacey, 1988)

2. Small national disasters

Here the bereaved, the survivors and the victims come from a wide area within the same country. Their needs for help can normally be met by existing services, provided a proper link is made. Because the impact of the disaster is spread out over a wide area it is less locally disruptive than it is in the case of local disasters, but special problems may exist in the identification of bodies, in the support of families during the emergency, and in ensuring that all those people who need help actually get it.

An example is the Clapham train crash in 1988. Two commuter trains collided and there was some loss of life. Over 100 people were injured and more survived the crash without physical injury. Some were trapped in upturned carriages and the general experience was very frightening. Most casualties were taken to the same hospital and it was here that psychosocial support was needed not only by victims and survivors, but also by some of the rescuers who had to remove bodies and who worked under great pressure.

The majority of the affected people soon dispersed to their homes and it was difficult for the hospital authorities to provide follow-up over the wide area from which they came. Particular help was given at and after the memorial services that were held on the anniversary of the disaster for several years in succession. The second of these attracted more of the survivors than the first and showed that many people only become able to face the memories of a disaster when a considerable time has elapsed. Again there was evidence that many survivors were haunted by post-traumatic memories and were in need of treatment for PTSD.

3. Small international disasters

Air crashes often affect people from different parts of the world and present special difficulties in ensuring that everyone who needs psychosocial support gets it. Often the crash takes place in one country while the majority of the passengers come from another. On other occasions passengers may come from many different countries. For this reason British Airways have set up a special unit at Heathrow Airport which can act as an information and monitoring centre for air crashes occurring anywhere in the world. Its 500 telephone lines enable the unit to handle a large volume of enquiries from worried relatives and to coordinate support services.

The 1968 Cheddar/Axbridge air crash took place in Switzerland. A party of women from two villages in Britain had chartered a plane which crashed into a mountain. There were no survivors. Support was needed in Basel, Switzerland, and in Cheddar and Axbridge, in Somerset. The team in Basel coordinated the return of the bodies and supported husbands and other relatives who flew out to Switzerland. The team in Britain was initially set up by the Department of Social Services. Special problems existed in the provision of care for the children of the women who had been killed, many of whom were young mothers. Social workers rapidly mobilised surrogate mothers for these children, but it was notable that, within a few weeks, the surrogates from outside the district had all been replaced by women from within the community. Similarly the professional social workers who set up a special office to support bereaved families were little used, villagers preferring to make use of the help of a local counsellor who had been appointed by a voluntary organisation. As a general rule, support systems from within a community are usually preferred to others from outside, no matter how 'expert' the latter may be. In the case of small-scale disasters it is seldom necessary for outsiders to act in anything but an advisory capacity.

4. Medium-scale local disasters

In the UK it is the responsibility of local Directors of Social Services to organise services in support of people affected by disasters. They are expected to do this within their existing budgets unless the cost exceeds that of a 'penny rate' (or its current equivalent). While there are obvious advantages in local people dealing with local disasters, there are also likely to be problems. In a small community everybody is traumatised by disaster.

Social workers, general practitioners and others may have been bereaved or may themselves be survivors. Even if they are not directly affected, they are indirectly affected by the overall level of public anxiety, depression or fear. Most are likely to be busy people at the best of times. They seldom complain of the added burden of care which rests on their shoulders following disasters, but they will soon 'burn out' if they are not properly supported.

This means that resources, human and financial, have to be freed up to enable local care-givers to go on caring for their own communities after a medium-scale disaster. Outside help may have to be brought in to take over routine tasks, and experts have a role to play in training local care-givers in the special skills of disaster management.

An example of a medium-scale local disaster is the 1966 Aberfan disaster. Aberfan is a linear village which was built alongside a coal mine in the Taff Valley in South Wales. Because the sides of the valley are steep, the waste (or slurry) from the mine had been dumped on a series of 'tips' on the hillside above the village. On a rainy morning in October 1966 one of the tips, which had become waterlogged, suddenly began to shift. An avalanche of mud thundered down the hillside to destroy the village primary school and several houses; 116 children and 28 adults were killed.

Although nobody was brought out of the ruin alive after the first hour, digging continued for several days. The news was on everyone's television screen and the road to the village was rapidly blocked with sightseers or would-be helpers who obstructed the rescue operation. Even a week later the scene was still chaotic, local people were in a daze, unable to take in the awful reality of what had happened, and there was no agreed plan of support for bereaved families. When a local psychologist rebuffed a reporter he retaliated by publishing a story that "A team of psychologists will exorcize by Freud the fears of the little children." This put paid to any attempt by outside experts to introduce such a team, but it did not prevent the appointment of a family case worker (Audrey Davey) who worked in the village for the next 18 months and became the focus of a network of care by a mixed bag of social workers, GPs and ministers of various denominations. This team was supported by a psychiatrist (the writer), a child psychotherapist and several sociologists, some from the Tavistock Institute of Human Relations in London and some from the University of Swansea. They acted in an advisory and supportive capacity to the front line of local workers. Because there was no existing structure to support or pay this group, it relied entirely on the goodwill of its members, whose sole aim was to give help. The group evolved slowly during the first year after the disaster and it was a long time before it became fully effective. Tensions between the local departments of Education and Health, distrust between the villagers and the local government officers (who were based in Merthyr Tydfil, five miles up the valley) and the long-standing suspicion with which many local people viewed "the English", all made it difficult to reach agreement on any plan. On the other hand, this community had a tradition of self-help and a number of small mutual support groups soon came into being, some of them with explicit political aims, but others more therapeutic in their objectives.

The numbness of the first few weeks was soon followed by a period of anger and distress. Several public meetings broke up in violence, well-meant decisions led to bitter controversy, and one had the feeling that any attempt at leadership was bound to be opposed. A succession of community leaders burnt their fingers and a paralysis of decision-making resulted, large sums of money in the Disaster Fund remaining unspent (Austin, 1967). When Fyffe Robertson, the television commentator, visited the village a year after the disaster he was shocked at the depression and lack of progress. The programme he made was called "Whatever Happened to Pity?" and reflected the bitter feelings that were prevalent at that time. He did, however, acknowledge that Audrey Davey was "the best thing that has happened to Aberfan".

Her work and that of her colleagues began to bear fruit in the course of the second year. As well as supporting bereaved families the group supported each other, meeting regularly and talking through the many problems they faced. During that year a Community Association was brought into being with the specific aim of drawing together the various factions that had sprung up. Derek Nuttall became its first Secretary and it subsequently played an important part in a community development programme which enabled moneys from the Disaster Fund to be put to good use.

Five years after the disaster, Aberfan acted as host to a series of conferences on 'Community development' which enabled the lessons that had been learned and the progress made to be passed on. (The proceedings were published in Ballard & Jones, 1975.) From being a depressed area before the disaster, and then a much-publicised stricken community, Aberfan finally emerged as an example to others of what can be achieved. This change was reflected in a number of ways: in the rates of absenteeism in the mine which, during the first year after the disaster, was very high but then gradually picked up; in the birth rate in the village, which remained unchanged during 1967 but shot up a year later so that, during the next five years, the number of extra children born in this community exceeded the number lost in the disaster (Williams & Parkes, 1975); and in the part which Aberfan played in supporting other disaster areas. A change in attitude took place in the village which was reflected in a statement by the wife of the former headmaster of the school: "This disaster was caused by apathy, it is up to us to ensure that Aberfan never becomes apathetic again."

It would be misleading to suggest that all the consequences of the Aberfan Disaster were positive; there were people who 'fell through the net' of care and others who may not have benefited. It took far too long to get things organised and many mistakes were made, but a great deal was also achieved and lessons learnt that proved valuable in the succession of disasters which took place in Britain in the years that followed.

5. Medium-scale national disasters

A very different set of problems arise when those affected by a medium-scale disaster come from a wide area. There is a need for immediate action near the site of the disaster itself; there is a need for a central organisation to be set up which should probably be located in the area most affected by the disaster; and there is a need for a network of care to extend across the country to assess the need for counselling and support to affected persons wherever they live.

The site of the disaster is important for several reasons. Firstly, it is the place where the rescue operations are going on. Secondly, it is the place where bad news is broken and bodies identified. Thirdly, it is the focus of traumatic memories for the survivors and of traumatic images in the minds of the bereaved, who may not have been present during the disaster but whose imagined view of what happened may be every bit as vivid and may be more horrific than the actuality. Disasters cause chaos and the site of the disaster is likely to be particularly chaotic. Fearful sights and sounds become etched in the mind and will be recalled with utmost clarity in the years to come. Hence, anything which mitigates some of the horror, and produces order and control out of chaos and loss of control, will be very helpful and will be remembered with gratitude. Even the traditional lady with a cup of tea brings a feeling of normality to the nightmare. The support which survivors and bereaved people give each other, and the help of social workers and others who help them to express grief and to talk through and make sense of what has happened, reduce the level of anxiety and enable people to regain control. The grisly process of identifying or viewing the dead can be made less horrific if it is handled with sensitivity and tact in an environment that is reasonably friendly and unclinical.

The centre of care may well be in a different place, perhaps in the centre of the community from which the greatest number of affected persons comes. It is here that an office needs to be established and a database set up to record details of victims, survivors, bereaved people and those who offer help. It is the nerve-centre of the aftermath plan and the main point of communication between carers. It is also the base from which the carers can reach out more widely to make contact with affected individuals and families over a wide area.

Because national disasters are less likely to disrupt existing organisation than local disasters, they cause less organisational chaos. Unfortunately the current Government policy in Britain, which places responsibility for disaster care firmly in the hands of *local* government, makes it difficult to organise and pay for proper care on a base which crosses local boundaries.

The capsize of the "Herald of Free Enterprise" outside Zeebrugge Harbour in 1987 can be taken as an example of a national disaster, since most of the passengers came from the south of England. Further details are given in chapter 8B. Here, it is sufficient to point out that two support teams were established, each containing a psychologist and several counsellors, many of them trained by Cruse: Bereavement Care. One, the Home Team, ran the office and provided support to families and crew in the vicinity of Dover; the other, the Away Team, travelled widely across England to visit and assess the need for support of survivors and bereaved family members in their homes. Attempts were made to refer those who were thought to be in need to local sources of help, but many refused these offers and preferred to remain in touch with the members of the Away Team despite the difficulties that this entailed.

This was the first time that an outreach of this extent had been attempted and it remains something of a model of what can be achieved. Even so, the delays in setting up the service were unsatisfactory and it was a year before every bereaved family had been visited and assessed. The main problems here were the lack of pre-planning and the lack of rapidly available financial and manpower resources to implement the plan.

6. Medium-scale international disasters

These are further complicated by the need for cooperation across national boundaries and the problems of differences of language and culture. Ships and aircraft now carry large numbers of people from many different nations across the world, and transport disasters can easily reach medium-scale proportions. The problems for families at home when people die overseas, difficulties in obtaining reliable information, and distrust of legal and other authorities in alien countries, make the management of international disasters particularly complicated.

An example of a medium-scale international disaster was the destruction by a bomb of flight PA103 over Lockerbie in Scotland in December 1988. All 270 passengers and crew were killed, plus 11 local residents. The jumbo jet disintegrated in the air and wreckage and bodies were strewn over a wide area. Although the largest number of passengers came from the US, many came from other countries and 33 different nationalities were involved in the aftermath. The recovery and identification of bodies was based in Lockerbie and took several weeks.

The Director of Social Services in the area set up a creditable support service for local people affected by the disaster and for family members who visited the area, and he worked closely with representatives of the airline who also organised support by social workers for families in the US. A well-planned memorial service was held in Lockerbie, and others in London and the US. Most of the crew had been based in London and were well-known to other members of Pan American Airline's staff, who were themselves at risk should the terrorists carry out their threat of further bombs. For this reason a support team of counsellors, all of whom had experience as flight crew, was set up at Heathrow Airport. Crews coming in from distant parts of the world needed to talk about the disaster, about the friends who had died and about their own fears and anger at the event and its implications.

In this instance the international repercussions of the disaster were handled by the international airline who were well qualified to respond. Little help was needed at a governmental level. Further details of the response to the Lockerbie disaster are described elsewhere in this book (chapter 8C).

7. Large-scale local disasters

There have been no large-scale disasters in the UK in recent years, and little account has been taken of the possibility of these in disaster plans which, as already observed, tend to assume that local disasters can be coped with by means of local resources. However, there can be no doubt that a large-scale local disaster would immediately overwhelm any local services and necessitate the rapid mobilisation of help from across the nation. It would no longer be appropriate for outsiders to act solely in an advisory capacity in support of the local care-givers.

An example of a large-scale local disaster was the earthquake in Managua, Nicaragua, in 1972. This had its epicentre in the centre of the city in which few houses were left standing. There were 20 000 injured and 10 000 lost their lives, 50 000 people lost their homes and 250 000 were displaced. The rescue resembled a military operation and was backed by aid from many parts of the world.

In circumstances like these, physical survival is the first priority and it was several months before any attention was paid to the fact that many people in the disaster area were suffering from the effects of psychological stress. Of special concern were the children, many of whom had witnessed the deaths of parents and others.

A team of bilingual psychiatrists, psychologists and psychotherapists, all of them volunteers, was organised by the National Institute of Mental Health in Washington and arrived in Managua three months after the disaster (Cohen, 1976, 1980). They worked closely with Nicaraguan professionals, running treatment programmes for traumatised children and their parents, training psychiatric staff in the techniques of crisis intervention, training and supporting public health nurses, clergy and various other types of counsellor, and setting up demonstration projects. In this way they were able to influence a very large number of care-givers and to make an appreciable impact on the enormous number of traumatised people. They initiated and supported a help-line and information service. Perhaps their most important activity was the support that they were able to give to the professional staff, who had been working under enormous stress.

8. Large-scale national disasters

Events such as earthquakes, floods and typhoons may cause extensive damage with great loss of life across large areas. Their effects may tax the resources of a nation, and help from international agencies will be needed. Because of the extent of the damage, telephone and power lines may be interrupted and communication with the disaster areas affected. Quite apart from the difficulties this presents to the rescuers, it is likely to be experienced by the inhabitants of the disaster area as indicating the loss of the support of the authorities on which they have come to rely; suddenly people are isolated at a time when they are desperately in need of security and support. Anger and distrust are then likely to complicate their relationship with carers.

Wolfenstein (1957) spoke of the "illusion of centrality" which is common in such circumstances. People affected by the disaster imagine themselves to be in the centre, even though they may occupy a peripheral position. Their demands for immediate help may conflict with the greater need of others and add to the problems of those who are trying to organise a response.

The earthquake in Armenia in December 1988, although similar in scale to that in Managua, covered a wider area, destroying several townships and leading to great disruption of services. The 'military' style of leadership which had enabled an effective rescue and rehabilitation plan to be introduced in Managua was missing, and although international aid poured into the country, its distribution was patchy and planning was impaired by the political instability that was already evident in Armenia.

Many months elapsed before any serious attempt was made to provide psychosocial care and this was largely limited to the support of traumatised children. Armenian immigrants to the US and Britain organised a series of teams of psychologists and psychotherapists who visited Armenia for limited periods of time in order to work with local carers and set up support groups in the disaster areas. These were well received by local people who felt that their needs had been forgotten by the outside world.

9. Large-scale international disasters

These are the most difficult and frightening types of disaster. They include the effects of wars, droughts, floods, nuclear accidents and other calamities which cross national boundaries. When conflict exists the warring factions may make it difficult for international agencies such as the United Nations and the International Red Cross to take effective action. As in other large-scale disasters, physical needs tend to take priority over the psychological.

Not all of the effects of war are psychologically damaging. Thus the Second World War undoubtedly caused psychological damage to many individuals, but any overall damage to the health of the British nation was offset by the positive effects of high morale, social cohesiveness and the rationing of food (which ensured a healthier diet for everyone). The mental hospitals that had been set aside for the anticipated psychological casualties were never used. In fact, human beings seem to be well adapted for coping with mild to moderate degrees of danger, which were, after all, very common in the environment in which man evolved. On the other hand, sudden and unanticipated bereavements, lasting threats to life against which people have no defence, and the breakdown of social systems of support can all happen at times of war, and are likely to have damaging effects.

The 1982 Falklands conflict was small by comparison with the two World Wars, but the scale of disruption and the loss of life on both sides puts it in the category of a large-scale disaster. During the course of the war, the main responsibility for psychosocial care of British forces and their families was in the hands of the armed forces welfare services.

One of the problems, in this as in other wars, was the fact that most of the fatalities took place overseas. Bodies were initially interred in the Falkland Islands if they were recovered at all (many of those who were lost at sea were not), and there was no opportunity for families to attend the funeral services. Consequently many family members found it difficult to accept the fact that these young men were truly dead. The whole thing seemed unreal.

The camaraderie and group support which servicemen and their families give each other and the gratitude of the civilian population are important factors enabling service families to tolerate the stresses of war. By the same token the psychological trauma is greater when this comes to an end, as it tends to do once the war is over. The wives of servicemen who have died cease to be service families, they soon lose their entitlement to accommodation on army camps, etc., and consequently they lose the support of the service community. Similarly, the army that is defeated or in which faith in the justice of the cause is lost, as happened in US armed forces after the Vietnam War, is very likely to suffer psychological damage. High rates of depression and drug misuse have been reported (Lifton, 1973).

When the Falklands War came to an end, families were given the opportunity to choose whether the bodies should be disinterred and returned in Britain or should remain in the Falklands. In the latter case bereaved relatives were given an opportunity to visit the Falklands by ship in order to see the graves and visit the place where the death had occurred. Many opted to go and were accompanied on the journey by social workers who encouraged them to share thoughts and feelings with each other. Memorial services were held and wreaths laid. This was the first time that sensitive support of this kind has been given to the bereaved relatives of bereaved servicemen and it was an undoubted success. Those who took part spoke warmly of the help they had received and the difference that this had made to their grief. This confirms Walters' (1993) report on the value of pilgrimages to war graves by the bereaved.

Conclusions

Although the categories listed above are useful, there are many disasters that contain elements of more than one category. Thus, a disaster in which many local people are killed could be regarded as a medium-scale local disaster, but if bystanders came from a much wider area and some of them were traumatised, it may also be considered to have been a medium-scale national disaster. In responding to such a disaster, therefore, it may be necessary to organise resources so as to meet both local needs and wider needs.

References

Austin, T. (1967) *Aberfan: The Story of a Disaster.* London: Hutchinson.

Ballard, P. H. & Jones, E. (1975) *The Valleys Call: A Self-examination of the South Wales Valleys during the 'Year of the Valleys' 1974.* Ferndale: Ron Jones.

Cohen, R. E. (1976) Post-disaster mobilization of a crisis intervention team: the Managua experience. In *Emergency and Disaster Management: A Mental Health Sourcebook* (eds H. G. Parad, H. L. P. Resnik & L. P. Parad). Bowie, MD: Charles Pr.

—— & Ahearn, F. L. (1980) *Handbook for Mental Health Care of Disaster Victims.* Baltimore: John Hopkins University Press.

Lane, S. K. & Stacey, A. (1988) *The Hungerford Family Help Unit.* London: National Institute for Social Work.

Lifton, R. J. (1967) *Death in Life: The Survivors of Hiroshima.* London: Weidenfeld & Nicholson.

—— (1973) *Home from the War: Vietnam Veterans, Neither Victims nor Executioners.* New York: Simon & Schuster.

Lystad, M. (ed.) (1988) *Mental Health Response to Mass Emergencies: Theory and Practice.* New York: Brunner/Mazel.

Osterweis, M., Solomon, F. & Green, M. (eds) (1984) *Bereavement: Reactions, Consequences and Care.* Washington, DC: National Academy Press.

Parkes, C. M. (1979) Evaluation of a bereavement service. In *The Dying Human* (eds A. de Vries & A. Carni), pp. 389–402. Ramat Gan, Israel: Turtledove.

—— (1991) Planning for the aftermath. *Journal of the Royal Society of Medicine,* **84,** 22–25.

—— & Weiss, R. S. (1983) *Recovery from Bereavement.* New York: Basic Books.

Raphael, B. (1977) Preventive intervention with the recently bereaved. *Archives of General Psychiatry,* **34,** 1450–1454.

—— (1986) *When Disaster Strikes: How Individuals and Communities Cope with Catastrophe.* New York: Basic Books.

Wallace, A. F. C. (1956) *Disaster Study No. 1.* Washington, DC: National Research Council.

Walters, T. (1993) War graves pilgrimages. *Bereavement Care,* **12,** 26–28.

Williams, R. M. & Parkes, C. M. (1975) Psychosocial effects of disaster: birth rate in Aberfan. *British Medical Journal,* **2,** 303–304.

Wolfenstein (1957) *Disaster: A Psychological Essay.* Glencoe: Free Press.

8 Community disasters

A. The *Jupiter* disaster

WILLIAM YULE

Twenty-two years to the day after the Aberfan disaster, on 21 October 1988, the cruise ship *Jupiter* sailed from Athens to take a party of around 400 British schoolchildren and their teachers from several schools on an educational cruise of the eastern Mediterranean. Just out of the harbour, the *Jupiter* was struck amidships by an Italian tanker and holed. The ship began listing badly and sank within 45 minutes. Although only one teacher and one pupil were missing presumed drowned, two rescuers were killed and many children saw their bodies. The children were flown home the following day to a barrage of publicity.

This is the sort of brief paragraph that might be used to convey an outline of a nasty incident. It is the job of mental health professionals to get behind this outline and help those involved to articulate what they experienced and how they reacted subsequently. For most of the survivors, it will be the first time they have been overwhelmed with fear and other conflicting emotions. In the aftermath, it will be the first time they come into contact with mental health professionals. How these initial contacts are managed will be crucial to engaging survivors in useful intervention.

The picture painted by the adolescent survivors is both graphic and, at times, painful. Many had been looking forward to the trip and had saved money over a long time. For some it was their first time away from home, let alone their first trip abroad. There had been delays in the flights and so they arrived at the ship as darkness was falling, tired and excited.

The parties were split in two. Half the children went down to the cafeteria to get their evening meal; half went to the lounge-cum-dancefloor to hear a lecture on safety on board. As the vessel reached the harbour entrance, it was hit amidships by an oil tanker. Girls queuing up to fetch their meal felt the bump at water level, and some saw the side of the ship cave in. They heard water trickling in. There was uncertainty and a bit of calling out. An

94

announcement came over the tannoy system, but as it was in Greek it was not much help. A little while later, the children in the dining area were told to make their way to the lounge where the others were assembled. To get there they had to climb winding staircases in a ship that was beginning to list badly. In the lounge there was a terrible crush. People found it difficult to keep their balance on the slippery floor. Glasses were crashing off the bar. Some children feared they would be crushed to death. As the ship listed, they saw the sea rising outside the windows.

They were told to get out on to the top deck. Tugs had come out from Piraeus and pushed against the ship to keep it afloat for as long as possible while children scrambled down the sloping decks and over to the safety of the tugs. Sadly, two of the rescuers slipped between a tug and the ship and were crushed to death. Their bodies were quickly pulled on board and roughly covered, but this meant that when many frightened children reached the tug, they saw, often for the first time in their lives, dead bodies. Some could not believe the men were dead and touched them to make sure. Such was the stuff of nightmares over succeeding months.

The *Jupiter* sank after 45 minutes. As it went under, water entered the engine and there was an explosion. Debris and oil were scattered across the surface of the sea. The last children on board had to jump into the water and they knew enough to swim as far as possible to avoid being sucked under. As they surfaced in the oily scum, some realised that they were alone in the sea with rescue boats searching in the dark. Some children were hit by rescue vessels and received physical injuries.

When they were ferried to shore, those who had been hurt or in the water were taken to hospital, while the others were accommodated overnight in the sister ship tied up in the harbour. Many spent a very uneasy night listening to every creak as the ship moved in the water. Most managed to telephone home, but not all did. There was the inevitable chaos for a number of hours before all children, but one, were accounted for. One teacher described her feelings as she stood on the dock with her list of names, only half of them ticked off. All she could think of was the number of funerals she was going to have to attend.

Following the sinking of the *Jupiter*, my colleague, Orlee Udwin, and I went to one school and met with the adolescent girls and their teachers who had returned from the cruise in a very shaken state. We also met briefly with the parents. In the course of an initial debriefing meeting in a group, we helped the girls to clarify in their own minds what had happened and in what sequence. We helped them to articulate how they had been feeling in the intervening ten days, using this technique to convey to them that the problems with sleep and concentration, the replaying of events in their minds, feeling upset, and so on were reactions shared with their peer group. We told them that what they were experiencing was a normal, understandable reaction to abnormal events, and that they were not going out of their minds. We then gave some simple advice on stress management and offered to see any girl who wanted us to, either individually or in small groups. While I saw the parents, the girls completed a brief screening battery to measure symptoms of PTSD, depression and anxiety (Yule & Udwin, 1991). We found that those girls who scored highest on the scales were most likely to seek help over the subsequent weeks.

Later, solicitors acting for the children asked us to screen most of the survivors and we collected data on 334 of them, mostly aged 14–15 years. These data, gathered around five months after the disaster, showed the children to be scoring highly on the Impact of Event Scale (Horowitz *et al*, 1979) and also to be significantly more depressed and anxious than normal controls. Girls reported significantly higher scores than boys (Yule, 1992). The screening scores were used to prioritise the individual assessment of the children. Two-thirds of 90 children (presumably those at highest risk) were found to meet DSM–III–R criteria for PTSD when individually assessed on average 12–15 months after the accident. Unfortunately, as children were assessed at a number of different centres and by many different professionals, it is not yet possible to compute an estimated prevalence rate for PTSD in this sample.

A number of other questions have been examined using the large data-set developed from this group. We were able to compare our early intervention in one school with the results in another who had refused offers of outside help. We found that the early intervention helped to lower self-reported fears and scores on intrusion and avoidance on the Impact of Event Scale (Yule & Udwin, 1991). We also showed that children were more likely to develop fears of things they had experienced in the disaster, rather than merely develop increased fearfulness (Yule *et al*, 1990). The academic performance of girls in one school plummeted significantly in the year following the disaster (Tsui, 1990).

Individual reactions to treatment have been described elsewhere (Yule & Gold, 1994; Yule, 1994). The need to help schools to cope with such crises was very evident and resulted in a booklet for them (Yule & Gold, 1993; see also chapter 20C). A long-term follow-up of the survivors has been funded by the Medical Research Council and so we will be able to examine in detail the transition of these adolescents into adulthood and examine the risk and protective factors related to their outcome.

B. The *Herald of Free Enterprise* disaster

WILLIAM YULE, RUTH WILLIAMS and STEPHEN JOSEPH

The *Herald of Free Enterprise*, a roll-on/roll-off ferry, capsized in Zeebrugge harbour on 6 March 1987 with the loss of at least 193 lives. Some 260 passengers and crew survived. The ship had capsized without warning and rolled over in 45 seconds. The bow doors had been left open, allowing water to rush across the open car deck, so destabilising the vessel.

As the ship was bound for Dover, Kent Social Services were quickly involved in setting up services to assist the survivors and the bereaved. The Herald Assistance Unit provided advice and counselling almost immediately. The staff were, in turn, supported by an advisory group made up of many leading experts in the field of bereavement care and disasters. A few months later, many adult and most child survivors were referred to the departments of psychology and forensic psychiatry at the University of London Institute of Psychiatry for help and assessment for legal purposes. Thus the survivors became among the most studied survivors of a modern transport disaster.

The Herald Assistance Unit organised two teams to meet with and assess the needs of all survivors. It was quickly established that the levels of psychopathology were very high (Hodgkinson & Stewart, 1991). The team adapted a leaflet first developed following the Australian bush fires and in turn used with survivors of the Bradford fire, and sent this leaflet to all known survivors. Most found it helpful as it put their strange feelings into a normalising context, but a few found receipt of the leaflet distressing. The leaflet, *Coping with a Major Personal Crisis*, is now distributed by the British Red Cross and has won general approval.

Data from those assessed at the Institute of Psychiatry, together with questionnaires filled out by many survivors contacted subsequently, demonstrated that subsequent psychopathology emerges as a result of a complex interaction between the 'objective' level of threat experienced during the disaster and the way the survivor appraises that threat (Joseph *et al*, 1991). More internal and controllable attributions were related to intrusive thoughts, depression and anxiety at 8 and 19 months following the disaster. Attributions may be important in the way survivors cope after a disaster, and this may exacerbate their symptoms.

Cognitive theories of depression suggest that dysfunctional thinking can be activated by stressful life events. Williams *et al* (1995) developed a measure of negative attitudes towards the expression of emotion (i.e. the British "stiff-upper-lip" syndrome) and found that people who showed strongest dysfunctional assumptions also reported the highest psychopathology, including symptoms of PTSD, and lowest levels of received support three years after the disaster.

Seventy-three survivors returned questionnaires three years after the disaster and, of these, over 60% reported feeling guilty at staying alive when others perished (Joseph *et al*, 1993*a*). Even though 'survivor guilt' was dropped as one of the criteria of PTSD by the American Psychiatric Association in 1987, it still clearly characterises many survivors.

There is no doubt that many survivors employ a coping strategy of avoidance for various time periods after a disaster. A major unresolved question is to what extent this is a healthy adaptive strategy and when should it be regarded as interfering with a return to health. Joseph *et al* (1995) reported a tendency for people who showed more avoidance in the first months following the capsize of the *Jupiter* cruise ship to have lower intrusive thinking a year later. Early intrusive thinking was the single best predictor of later anxiety. Unfortunately, parallel studies were not undertaken with survivors of the *Herald*.

Psychometric studies of the Impact of Event Scale (Horowitz *et al*, 1979) by and large confirm that the scale reflects both intrusion and avoidance, but also suggest that avoidance is a multifactorial construct (Joseph *et al*, 1992, 1993*b*). Some forms of avoidance may be more pathological than others.

Social support has been shown to be a buffer against the effects of external stress. Joseph *et al* (1994) found that crisis support measured three years after the event predicted avoidance behaviour as well as levels of depression and anxiety at the five-year follow-up.

Emotional processing has also been studied in *Herald* survivors using techniques such as the Stroop colour interference task (Thrasher *et al*, 1994). In line with predictions, survivors showed greater interference (longer response latencies) when asked to name the colours in which trauma-related words as opposed to neutral words were presented.

It is clear that survivors of mass transport disasters are at very high risk of developing major psychopathology. It is possible to study the course of their recovery and so cast more light on important risk and protective factors relating to traumatic stress reactions.

C. Help-seeking by community residents following the Lockerbie air disaster

MARGARET MITCHELL

The "Lockerbie disaster" or the "Pan Am disaster" was the result of a bomb exploding in the baggage hold of a Boeing 747 aircraft carrying passengers from London to New York. The explosion happened 31 000 feet above the rural community of Lockerbie in Dumfries and Galloway, southwest Scotland, scattering debris and bodies on the town of Lockerbie and over an area of 900 square miles. The 243 passengers and 16 flight crew on board were all killed. Eleven Lockerbie residents were killed by being caught in conflagrations in their homes near where the wings, which were full of aviation fuel, had landed and exploded. The main fuselage and 67 bodies landed between two rows of houses, and the cockpit and a further 20 bodies landed three miles distant on a field out of town.

A criminal investigation started that night and, despite protracted negotiations, the named terrorist suspects have yet to be brought to justice.

This account will focus on the effects on the community and the perceived need by the residents for psychosocial support following the disaster.

Hundreds of people in the US, Britain and throughout the world were bereaved by this disaster. The particular way in which the people were murdered added the burden of an untimely and violent death to the loss, and both factors are known to increase vulnerability to long-term and unresolved grief (Stroebe *et al*, 1993). The effects of the bereavement continue: most of the passengers were American and the organisation representing the US relatives, 'Victims of Pan Am Flight 103', meets every two months, and even now remains extraordinarily active as a political lobby and as a mutual support network. The relatives find participation in the group helpful, although acknowledging that their lives are permanently altered (Coyle, 1994).

At the level of the community where the disaster physically took place, such events have the potential to produce considerable emotional distress in those involved, some of which meets the criteria for post traumatic stress disorder. Estimates of the incidence of PTSD in the Lockerbie community vary (Brooks & McKinlay, 1992), although it is recognised that no-one who was exposed to the disaster was unaffected. In other words, while the symptoms experienced by some in the community fit the criteria for PTSD, many were distressed in other ways and experienced a range of affective disorders for which help and support were needed.

There are many difficulties associated with estimating likely incidence following exposure, which makes research in this area difficult. These include individual variation in the nature of the exposure, in the individual's social context, in the time taken to react and the different ways in which subsequent life events may interact to produce distress. Research to clarify these issues needs to be prospective and longitudinal, which, because of other more pressing practical considerations of recovery after sudden human disasters, is rarely possible. This chapter contributes by providing some insight into the natural course of help-seeking following traumatic exposure, by presenting information from interviews with the Lockerbie (and neighbouring Lochmaben) general practitioners (GPs) conducted almost three years afterwards. The interviews with the seven local GPs are used here to discuss help-seeking in the community and the challenges and sensitivities involved in help provision.

GPs are of particular interest in assessing the impact of disaster, because when community services aimed at providing acute and immediate care are withdrawn, the pre-existing regular services such as a general practice bear the brunt of late onset and longer-lasting responses to trauma. The information achieved from the GPs provides evidence of the duration of emotional disorder following the disaster, as well as of late onset, both of which are pivotal issues for the timing of offers of support. This group of GPs saw over 400 patients presenting with various degrees of emotional difficulty attributable to the disaster. It is regrettable that no systematic longitudinal study was conducted at the time, and the interview data are obviously subject to biased recall. Nevertheless, the doctors' impressions are informed and provide a unique and valuable source of information about help-seeking and the longer-term consequences of trauma.

It is important to explain why the GPs were involved in the particular way they were. Community residents seeking financial compensation for emotional disorder were required to obtain a record of their medical history and a report of their current medical status. This necessitated a visit to their GP. Contrary to conventional wisdom that claiming compensation magnifies symptoms and protracts morbidity (Weighill, 1983), the GPs believe that this logistical requirement was instrumental in bringing to their medical attention those people who were in great distress and who otherwise would not have presented.

Perhaps the most surprising and significant theme which emerged from the interviews, and contrary to their expectation of a rush of patients, was the reluctance of people to seek help. One GP said:

> "I think they felt guilty and didn't want to be bothering the doctors with something they thought they should be coping with themselves. The people were quite reticent about their symptoms because they thought everyone felt the same way and they had no right or need greater than the next person. They only came because they were told to by the lawyer. Some came and were embarrassed because they thought they should be getting over it by that time."

Older men seemed most unwilling and had:

> "particular difficulty coming to terms with what they regarded as their own weakness. They thought they should be able to cope and when eventually they found they couldn't, they came for help in quite a bad state. It was surprising what they accepted as an understandable reaction, like very extreme nightmares, even after having the symptoms for six

months. It worries me because I doubt if they would have come to see me off their own bat." (i.e. without being required to for legal reasons)

Help-seeking by community members appeared to be influenced by social expectations about who 'should' be affected and for whom professional help was appropriate, and those who 'should not'. In such social comparison terms, children were expected to be affected, while men in general and in particular those with training in dealing with death and emergencies, such as police officers, should not. Three broad 'waves' of referrals resulted: mothers brought children whose behaviour had regressed, and who were bed-wetting, or not sleeping or eating, or who were afraid of the dark. Then the women themselves came, acknowledging their inability to overcome the experience as they had expected. The men appeared to be the most reluctant, and in some instances were brought in by a partner complaining of intolerable behaviour and domestic arguments because of inappropriate reactions to the children or increased drinking. For some others, visiting the doctor was legitimised by (albeit stress-related) physical symptoms such as headaches, sleep disturbance or loss of appetite, for which seeking medical attention is seen as appropriate. Social taxonomies of perceived vulnerability are interesting (Mitchell, 1994), particularly as other work (for example, Mitchell *et al*, 1991) confirms that police officers, for instance, are emotionally affected and their training and work experience is not necessarily prophylactic.

In terms of what patients seemed to need and want, the GPs found that simply listening seemed to be essential:

> "A lot of my time was spent listening, and doing nothing else. Often I found myself listening to the same person giving their same story again and again. Possibly they may have needed or received a more structured interview from other people. But for my part just listening seemed to benefit them . . . People suffer catastrophes every week, sudden bereavement, terrible illness, and so on. On a one to one basis the skills which were being asked for were really no different than those required in other situations."

It was also important to the survivors that the GPs had experienced the same trauma, and often checked mutual experiences. The GPs' impressions are resonant of research on the importance of disclosure (Pennebaker, 1988), and the concept that common experience is important for this process is also found in other work (Newman, 1993). As time went on, and as it became evident that some individuals were not improving, or were showing signs of depressive illness, accelerated referral to specialised psychiatric help or drug therapy was considered, but the GPs report that, in practice, these were rarely instigated.

In terms of the reticence of people to come forward, there is a range of possible explanations why people do not seek help and these cannot be overlooked. The most obvious and important of these is that the person is perfectly all right and has coped with their experience. Within the cultural context of southwest Scotland and in other places, however, the media represented this observed reluctance as stoicism, and in this representation there is a clear value judgement. It implies a belief that the people *are* suffering yet are to be admired for not showing it or being weak in seeking help. The potential effects of such a cultural context and expectations on the likelihood that people will seek help obviously is considerable, and there is evidence from these interviews that what looked like coping and resilience simply may have been confused and embarrassed silence.

The damage to the community was of a long-lasting psychological and social nature, and it is because of this that the question of help provision is of such great importance. It is purported that the disaster drew the community together, but there is as much evidence that its aftermath was damaging and divisive to the social fabric of families and of the community. Informal support from family and friends is of tremendous importance to a survivor in his or her recovery, but this can also place great strain on family relationships. Moreover, dependence on informal support may be based on a rather idealised image of the family and its ability to provide the support required. Indeed, if a survivor stoically believes they should be able to cope, there may even be reticence in seeking help from their family.

A further complicating issue is the variation in the way individual family members who have been through the same experience reacted. The GPs found that people from the same family had completely opposite reactions which, in itself, produced additional distress:

> "Some people couldn't go out of the house, and other people in the same family – which made me wonder how they managed to cope – would have the totally opposite reaction and couldn't stay in the house. They really had quite florid symptoms and you wondered how these people could live together. It was very sad, and many marriages went through a lot of stress."

The issues raised here present challenges for how help can be provided in a way which is acceptable to potential users, considering its form, timing and how it is offered without being intrusive. Newman (1993) proposed that a greater number are likely to be reached if services are not merely *available,* but are actively *offered.* This, he argued, requires a sense of purpose, confidence, security and knowledge in those offering help (i.e. professionals), in contrast to that help which may only be available haphazardly from those from whom help is *requested* (family or professionals without specialised training). In other words, those providing help need to be sensitive to a person's desire to regain control over their lives by collecting their own resources to recover, but also be able to respond appropriately when and if additional help is requested. This cannot be left to 'natural' helping or to informal support networks, on the assumption that these exist.

This exploration of issues and review of research on Lockerbie is necessarily limited. Interested readers who wish fuller accounts are directed to other research on the disaster: on community residents (Brooks & McKinlay, 1992; Livingston *et al,* 1992), a more detailed treatment of the police operation (Mitchell, 1993*a*), the psychological impact on police officers (Mitchell *et al,* 1991), and a further account of the work of the GPs (Mitchell, 1993*b*). Detailed reports of organisational and procedural aspects of the disaster and the recovery operation can be found in the official account by Dumfries and Galloway Regional Council (McIntosh, 1989) and in the report by the Fire Service (Stiff, 1989).

In conclusion, while it is argued in many texts that there are typical and recognisable reactions to a traumatic experience, the wide range of individual and specific ways in which survivors may react presents an enormous challenge to those organising and providing sensitive, appropriate and reflective psychosocial care. In Lockerbie, while psychiatric, psychological and social work support was available, there appears to have been a resistance within the community to such less familiar sources of support, exacerbated by a lack of experience on the part of some professionals.

D.   The *Marchioness* riverboat disaster

LINDA GOLDSMITH and JANET HADDINGTON

On 20 August 1989, the Thames riverboat the MV *Marchioness* set sail in the early hours of the morning. The boat was filled with party-goers who were celebrating the 26th birthday of Antonio Vasconcellos. Half an hour after she set sail, the *Marchioness* was struck by the Thames dredger, the *Bowbelle*. The *Marchioness* sank immediately. Fifty-one people died, including Antonio and his brother, while 83 people survived. A sense of shocked disbelief spread across London and large numbers of people converged on the site in order to comprehend and accept that the disaster had occurred.

Twenty-three bodies were found trapped on board the *Marchioness* when it was raised the following day. Over the next 14 days, 28 more bodies were recovered from the water. Twenty-four bodies were visually identified in the two days following the disaster but, after that, because of deterioration, visual identification was first of all discouraged and subsequently denied. As a result, 27 bodies were identified only by personal possessions and clothing, dental and fingerprint records. They were never seen by relatives and loved ones, in some cases, despite much pleading to be allowed to do so.

The coordinators of the psychosocial response to the sinking of the *Marchioness* were aware that the mental health and stability of those individuals whose grief remained unresolved would be at risk. An effort was made, therefore, to learn the lessons of the past in planning the response. One unique feature was that the Disaster Response Unit, staffed by local authority social workers and bereavement counsellors from the voluntary sector, was set up inside the designated police station. This meant that counsellors had access to all the available information as the police themselves acquired it, and avoided the pitfall, experienced in many disasters, of accurate information being difficult to find and rumours being perpetuated.

A crucial factor was the issue of whether or not relatives should be 'allowed' to see their loved one after their body had been in the water for two or more days, and deterioration had set in to the extent that they could no longer be visually identified. Social workers and counsellors had no doubts on this issue, believing that relatives should if they wanted to, and would benefit from the opportunity to see their loved ones in death. There was deep concern that people should be properly prepared for what might face them and that they should be appropriately supported throughout and after the viewing if that was their choice. The resources and the expertise to ensure that this happened was available, the coroner was persuaded that such a process would be positively beneficial, and yet achieving it was far from straightforward and sometimes obstructed by senior police and coroners' officers. This was especially true as time wore on and the bodies were being retrieved in a more and more deteriorated condition.

There was also a commitment from the social workers managing the psychosocial response to ensuring that the photographs of the bodies of those who had died were held for relatives to view for an indefinite period of time. It was believed that relatives might need to look at the photographs a long while after the event, and that this would be likely to help with the resolution of grief. This proved to be the case. Ultimately, the bodies of 42 victims were viewed by relatives, either directly or through photographs, leaving nine bodies which have still not been viewed either way. Of those nine, several people have expressed an interest to see the photographs when they are 'ready'.

The need to view the bodies is entwined with the overall need for as much detailed information as possible about how, why, when and where a loved one died. It is also enmeshed with a belief that 'seeing is believing', together with the desire to say goodbye. It is not unusual for relatives, at some stage, to want to receive every known detail of their loved one's death. Part of this process is to help people understand and assess how much suffering occurred up to, and at the time of, the actual death. Part of it is to begin the process of acceptance. Most survivors of the *Marchioness* described near-death experiences, having been submerged in the water for minutes while the massive length of the dredger passed over them. They were, therefore, forced to breath water and many gave themselves up for dead. Many people were particularly afraid to drown, believing that it would be an extremely painful death. Survivors, however, described feelings of peace and tranquillity when their lungs filled with water. Hearing survivors describe such experiences was of enormous value to the bereaved relatives who had expressed a desperate need to know such details.

In the UK a great deal of information, which is new to relatives, becomes available at the time of the personal inquests. Personal inquests often happen some months after the actual event and the transcript of the inquests and the photographs of the body become important reference points in the resolution of grief.

The actual viewing of the body seems, for most people, an immediate need, while others feel they have neither the emotional strength nor the desire for immediate viewing. However, when the expressed desire to see the body has been actively discouraged or refused, it is not uncommon for long-lasting anger to emerge which is easily displaced and difficult to resolve. Over a period of time, there is a great deal of evidence to suggest that the vast majority of people bereaved as a result of a traumatic event demonstrate a need to hear the truth in all its detail and to have the unadulterated facts made clear.

In the case of the *Marchioness*, most of the people who died were young people. The majority of the bereaved were, therefore, parents, sisters and brothers. Many families and friends were not aware, or not sure, that their loved one had been on board. Many bodies were missing and some remained so for two weeks. The age of those who died meant that many had been geographically mobile and living away from home, so that their families were not necessarily familiar with their lifestyles or social networks. Consequently, feeding into what one might describe as 'normal denial' were factors which overloaded the potential to prolong non-acceptance. These factors included excessive shock. The initial absence of bodies and subsequent identification difficulties, together with the fact that there was no guest list, added to the confusion. Geographical distance also prevented a number of bereaved relatives from immediately visiting the scene.

The parents and, in particular, the mothers who viewed the photographs of their dead children, stated, without exception, that it had helped them accept that the death had occurred. Also, without exception, they experienced extreme pangs of grief at the sight of the photographs which was, inevitably, very painful for the counsellor to observe.

Case W

Mrs W was told that her daughter's body, which had been recovered from the water four days after the accident, was badly deteriorated through swelling and heat. She, however, said that she believed that new-born babies are "often wrinkled and ugly . . . but, when it is your own, it is beautiful". When she saw the photographs she recognised her daughter immediately: "There is no mistaking her and she is still beautiful. How can a man tell me, her mother, that my child is no longer beautiful?"

Mrs W had been told by well-meaning people that she should remember her daughter as she was when she was alive and that there was a danger, if she viewed the photographs, that they would be her longest lasting memory. She refutes this, saying that she continues, in her thoughts, to see her child "flitting around doing normal things".

The funeral director had refused her request to see her daughter's body when it was released for burial. When her request continued to be refused she finally asked if she could just touch her daughter's hair. This, too, was refused on the grounds that it was falling out, so she settled, with reluctance, for a cut-off lock. This mother had felt and expressed a need to see, touch and say goodbye to her child. She was also haunted by fears of how disfigured her daughter's body must be. Her fears were immediately resolved as soon as she saw the pictures – reality being far less frightening than imagination. Mrs W asked to return to see the photographs a second time, in order to say goodbye. She says that the two hours enabled her, with the help of the counsellor, to fit together the pieces of the jigsaw which left her with a more complete picture of what had happened on the night her daughter died.

Case X

Mrs X and her family made a special long-distance journey several months after her daughter's death in order to view the photographs of her body. She was aware from the pathologist's report at the inquest that her daughter, after death, had been struck by a boat propeller. The counsellor had already viewed the photographs and could, therefore, prepare the family and offer to be present at their viewing.

Mrs X was the first to take the photographs. In silence she covered with one hand her daughter's nakedness and then with the other began to stroke her eyebrow. After several silent moments she passed the photographs to other family members and then began to cry quietly. Once the photographs had been passed back to her, she asked if she could be alone with them, but asked the counsellor to stay in the room. During this time, she held the photographs to her breast, cried with head bowed, and spoke inaudibly. After some 20 minutes she placed the photographs on the table, closed the folder and ran her fingers round the edge. She dried her eyes and said in a normal voice: "I'm glad I have seen her. That is my baby and I know now that she is dead."

Case Z

Mrs Z lost her daughter in the disaster. She was telephoned in the early hours of the morning by the parents of her daughter's boyfriend who had been rescued but was unable to locate his girlfriend. In a state of panic and confusion, Mrs Z drove to the River Police point nearest her home and pleaded with them to rescue her daughter. She returned home to collect a photograph which she gave to the police in the vain hope that it would help. She later found herself in her local church but was unable to gain comfort and returned home to await the dreaded news.

When her daughter's body was recovered she was discouraged from viewing it. She has since avoided discussion that would give details of her last moments and death. She decided initially not to proceed with a personal inquest which would have given details of the death and, to date, she has also chosen not to view the photographs.

This mother's use of denial has taken the form of avoiding the truth in order to postpone the pain of reality. She manipulates events to enable her to control her own version of reality. Her constant search for someone to blame, and her intense displaced anger, has so far protected her, but she presents as a person who is overwhelmingly fearful of losing control. It is likely that, unless she is enabled to experience the pain she feels, her grief may never reach the successful resolution which will allow her to move forward.

It is the job of the professionals involved to help bereaved individuals to the successful resolution of grief. In the case of Mrs Z, excessive denial may have been avoided if she had been encouraged to see her daughter's body.

Conclusions

Experience gained from the sinking of the *Marchioness* and other disasters demonstrates the importance of viewing the body of a deceased loved one and of having access to photographs immediately or at any future date. The manner in which some people bereaved as a result of the sinking of the *Marchioness* have been denied access to the bodies of their relatives has led to long-lasting anger and protracted grief.

The police need to understand that identification is not the sole, nor the most important, reason why relatives need to see the bodies of their loved one. Counsellors involved in responding to disasters should, as a matter of principle, enable bereaved people to reach an informed decision about whether or not they should view their relative's body and/or the photographs. The counsellor should be available before, during and after the viewing. The counsellor's role, at this stage, is to prepare the person, to be supportive and to offer information and clarification. It is not the time, nor the place, to enter into in-depth counselling. The environment in which a body is viewed should be conducive to and enhance dignity and privacy.

The role of the counsellor in supporting people while viewing bodies and photographs in such traumatic circumstances is extremely harrowing, but it is also important and potentially very rewarding. Counsellors involved in such work need to be given appropriate professional support throughout the process and beyond.

E.   The Kegworth air disaster

MARION GIBSON

At 8.26 p.m. on 8 January 1989, Flight BD 092, a British Midland Boeing 737-400 flying from London Heathrow to Belfast crash-landed on the M1 motorway in central England. Passengers had noticed a fire in one of the engines of this recently acquired plane. The aircraft flew low over the village of Kegworth, failed to reach the runway of East Midlands Airport by a short distance and crash-landed on an embankment of the motorway. On impact the fuselage of the aircraft broke up into three main sections.

There were 127 passengers and crew on board. Thirty-nine died at the scene of the crash and the 88 survivors were taken to the three main hospitals in the area. The final death toll from this disaster was 47.

Due to the location of the crash many organisations and agencies were involved across county boundaries; 70% of those on board came from Northern Ireland or had relatives living there. This incident challenged all the organisations involved, including social services, to collaborate across geographical and administrative boundaries.

Social workers from the Leicestershire Emergency Team worked at the airport hotel as relatives arrived to identify the dead. The fact that few relatives lived near the scene of the crash gave the social workers in the three main hospitals involved, Derby Royal Infirmary, Queen's Medical Centre, Nottingham and Leicester Royal Infirmary, some hours to plan their response to the multiple practical and emotional needs with which the relatives presented. Staff were involved in the initial response to the many telephone calls to the hospitals seeking information. British Midland staff were an integral part of all the support planned and delivered. Two social workers from Northern Ireland later joined these staff to act as a link between England and the support networks in Northern Ireland.

The relatives of those from Northern Ireland were supported by airport personnel at Belfast International Airport who were soon joined by clergy, social workers and representatives of voluntary organisations. As the media broke the news and pictures of the crash appeared on television screens, more relatives rushed to the airport. This scene of anguish was mirrored at Heathrow where relatives had bade farewell to the passengers as the flight had departed for Belfast.

The relatives from Northern Ireland were flown to England the following day. The bereaved were supported by social workers and local clergy as they took part in identification procedures and the recovery of the personal belongings of the deceased. Arrangements were made for the bereaved and some of the injured to visit the site of the crash. Floral tributes to those killed allowed the bereaved to say the unsaid farewells by writing messages on the cards. The relatives of the injured were accommodated near the hospitals.

As those who had been injured in the crash recovered physically, they had to come to terms with the fact that they had lived and others had died. Some examples of survivor guilt resulted from these experiences. There were a number of cases where the injured were also bereaved. It was noted that these bereaved were excluded from the visits to the crash site, participation in the identification process and funeral rituals. British Midland facilitated the photographic recording of the funeral of a deceased relative in one such case. These photographs and video were later used by the surviving relative to aid the grieving process. The injured may be somewhat cosseted in hospital with all the activity of acute care surrounding them, so their emotional reactions may be delayed until they are discharged and face the outside world again. This phenomenon was recorded by Kennedy & Johnston (1975). This is an important point to consider when planning for the aftercare of such patients.

In the hospitals the use of different types of wards was seen as a significant feature by some of the survivors. In one hospital, a large Nightingale-type ward was set aside for all the patients. This provided an opportunity for peer support among patients of both sexes and all ages. The relatives also got support from each other. Later some were to recall that they needed more "private space" for individual reactions. One patient did not feel that he could show his true feelings of distress in case he annoyed the other patients and "let the side down". Hence, after a traumatic event, it may be helpful for survivors to be in hospital together but there is also a need for private space to be provided. Hospital chaplains also played a significant role in helping patients, relatives and staff.

A Disaster Relief Fund was established and managed by the English local councils. A group of survivors and some of those who had been bereaved later formed the Air Safety Action Group (ASAG). They have campaigned vigorously for the air safety measures which were identified in the investigation report and coroner's recommendations.

A network of social workers was established in Northern Ireland to support those affected on their return from England. The on-going support of those affected continued for as long as they chose to use it. Many re-accessed the network at the time of the anniversary or when media attention focused on the crash again. Some of the survivors still struggle with their physical residue of the crash, but more significantly, many still carry the burden of the emotional scars.

The lessons learned by social workers who responded to this disaster were multiple but the most significant points were:

(a) the need for cross-administrative and organisational cooperation;
(b) the need for a strategy for closer collaboration with voluntary workers, statutory social work staff and health-based staff;
(c) the need for practical help and information in the initial stages before emotional and psychological needs could be addressed;
(d) the need for local knowledge to be available to staff responding to the needs of people involved in a transport disaster which occurred away from their normal support networks;

(e)   the support networks, including counselling, psychological and psychiatric services must be accessible and acceptable to those affected. These services may have to be provided when those affected return to their home area.

As a result of the experience gained by responding to this disaster, social work practice has developed. In Northern Ireland a network structure of social work teams has been developed to ensure that protocols exist to provide for the aftercare of those affected by major incidents.

F.   The King's Cross fire: second phase intervention

RACHEL ROSSER

The event

The King's Cross fire occurred at the end of the evening rush-hour on 18 November 1987. This station is the most complex in the UK. Five underground lines intersect at different depths below the surface. Above them, trains supply the whole of northeast England and Scotland. Some 40 000 people pass through the station in the two hours of the evening rush-hour.

Thirty-one people died in the fire, one of whom was never identified. One other died of 70% burns and lung damage three days later. Seven people survived with severe burns affecting especially the face and hands.

The fire was considered by many to have been preventable, a crucial point for the feelings of the bereaved, the survivors and their families. The smell of smoke had been reported to the ticket office several times over the previous two hours. No action was taken. Eventually, a passenger pressed the emergency stop button of one of the escalators, thus generating an obvious crisis and resulting in a call to the fire brigade. The nearest brigade had just been called out to a relatively minor incident. The neighbouring brigade set off immediately but its progress was impeded by crowds of London Christmas shoppers and visitors to the street illuminations which had just been switched on.

The phase 1 response: life-saving

Within two minutes of the brigade reaching the station, a flashover occurred, effectively eliminating the ticket hall, and preventing exit from the station. This flashover caused most of the deaths. The most senior fire officer present rushed into the blaze without breathing apparatus and died. The remaining members of the team carried on against great obstacles.

Below ground, transport staff and police, unaware of the catastrophe higher up, evacuated people from the station onto the escalators and into the blaze. Above ground, maps of the station had been covered by advertisements or locked into the destroyed ticket office. None were available at lower levels. The wooden escalators were antiquated. Their sprinklers were never switched on. Below the stairs were piles of oil-covered rags and other highly inflammable rubbish. The official enquiry (Fennell, 1988) concluded that the fire was almost certainly caused by a match, used by a smoker lighting up on the way out of the station, falling between the steps.

Some of the victims were left alone after 'rescue' because gates between passages had been locked. Others were laid in the smoke-filled street waiting for ambulances.

When the ambulances arrived, triage did not occur. Thus the remains of the dead were transported to University College Hospital, while the living and near moribund waited. Some onlookers rushed in to help; of these, one died and another sought emotional support from a survivor but declined professional psychological help. The hospital received no warning of the disaster until after the casualties had arrived. A temporary mortuary was created. Staff, students and visiting nurses worked through the night; the senior nursing officer was called back just after leaving the hospital and worked for 36 hours to ensure all junior nurses had received her personal support. Management briefed the media, cleared the emergency ward, and ensured that beds were available for survivors. Leaders of most of the religious denominations in the vicinity attended immediately and were greatly appreciated for their discretion, courage and comfort; religious leaders who arrived later the next day were barely acknowledged.

The acute stage of the physical management and the long drawn-out process of plastic surgery has been described elsewhere (Brough *et al*, 1991). So has the psychological work with the six people who survived in the plastic surgery wards of University College Hospital (UCH) (Sturgeon *et al*, 1991).

The number of those affected by this disaster was vast. The police reported 20 000 telephone enquiries in 48 hours. Those affected included those who had been at the station, those on crowded trains which had been routed through the station without stopping, while people on the platform tried to break windows and climb on board. Some people on the station platforms had jumped onto the rails, hoping to walk through the tunnel to the next station (where one young man was found in flames).

The phase 2 response: restoration of meaning

Following emergency physical intervention, the second phase of psychosocial help commenced.

Three members of the Academic Department of Psychiatry had previous experience of working with those affected by disasters (Kinston & Rosser, 1974). These three visited the wards where the victims were being treated, and the official mortuary outside the hospital where the dead had been transferred. They spoke both to those injured and those caring for them. An existing fund was, with permission, diverted to payment of the salary for three months of a disaster coordinator who was appointed on the following day. All subsequent funding came from research bodies.

On 20 November, a meeting was held of volunteers, all experienced psychotherapists, and many fluent in more than one language. Forty people gave their names, adding those of colleagues who could not be present. Contact was established with local social services and a local Helpline.

An experienced psychiatric nursing officer offered individual help and group support to nursing staff. The Health District Counselling Service was available to all staff. With the agreement of the medical school, medical students were offered therapeutic interviews.

More than 2000 people in distress were recognised, mainly through the Helpline. A steering committee was established with representatives from social services, voluntary organisations, a psychiatrist and a clinical psychologist. Apart from telephone counselling, it fell to the social services to focus on acute grief and to guide the bereaved relatives through the identification of the dead and the stressful coroners' inquest. In the absence of a definable community traumatised by the fire, a network was created by means of a newsletter.

Psychological screening

After the crisis of the first Christmas, it became clear that the demand for psychosocial help was increasing and swamping the capacity of available staff. An important decision was made to screen all people contacting our services by means of questionnaires: the General Health Questionnaire (Goldberg & Hillier, 1979) and the Impact of Event Scale (Horowitz *et al*, 1979). It must be emphasised that the prime reason for this was to identify and prioritise those who were most distressed and suicidal. Later the responses were valuable in our research, and in making comparisons with other disasters.

We decided to offer an initial individual contact of eight sessions, which could be renewed or reduced by the patient. Therapists used the models to which they were accustomed, bearing in mind that trauma work would generally precede grief work, since traumatic experiences can block the working through of grief. Supervisions took the form of group sharing and support. Senior therapists participated more as sharers than healers, and all took individual responsibility for treating patients and, when necessary, providing detailed Court reports. Two of the senior team members provided evidence to Mr Justice Fennell and this was noted in the Report of the Committee of Enquiry which he chaired (Fennell, 1988).

Therapeutic trials

We felt a responsibility to document our experiences so as to contribute to the international knowledge base about the most successful ways of helping survivors and witnesses of disasters. Furthermore, in the absence of public funding for our services, continued provision was dependent on research grants.

We experimented with many trial designs. Eventually, given the pressure to save severely mentally tortured people, we chose the simplest design – that is, a waiting list control group. Clients were allocated to the programme in order of severity. They were paired; one received immediate treatment, the paired partner receiving an appointment for eight weeks later. In practice, this was not rigorously sustained because of particular emergencies where pairing was neither feasible nor ethical, and because of the low show-up rate of those placed on the waiting list. We terminated this trial after 30 cases, concluding:

(a)   people do not improve between the disaster and initial contact with the clinical service;

(b)   once placed on a waiting list with a definite date for the first session, they begin to recover;

(c)   immediate therapy is preferable to delayed therapy in so far as people on the waiting list organised their lives prior to therapy and experienced some disruption of relationships in therapy, exposed by the Index of Health Related Quality of Life (Harmony scale) (IHQL; Rosser *et al*, 1993) and the Symptom Check-List SCL–90 (paranoid ideation and interpersonal hostility scales (Derogatis, 1977).

Thereafter we conducted a second trial. Clients received either just one day of individual assessment and debriefing, or the addition to this of eight sessions of therapy. It appeared that these additional sessions were neither more therapeutic, nor detrimental, but they were an extra cost to the service and the client.

Other disasters

Through media and legal work and oral presentations to many audiences, we received referrals from the *Marchioness* riverboat disaster (Thompson *et al*, 1994), the Clapham rail disaster, the Lockerbie relatives' group (Thompson *et al*, 1994), and other smaller group and individual catastrophes. These were included in therapeutic trials and the service (now called the Stress Clinic) became established within the Camden and Islington Community Services Trust.

National work

A UK researchers' group was convened at the Middlesex Hospital (UCL Hospitals). The response from academics and professionals working with victims was immense, peaking at the time of the Gulf War, when a meeting was led by senior medical representatives from the three armed services. Great interest was also expressed by the private medical sector. Our only concern was that a few individuals with minimal experience drew on these corporate discussions to sell their services at high fees in situations where extensive experience and on-going support to therapists was needed (see chapter 21).

International work

A European group was convened by Professor Wolfram Schüffel (Marburg, Germany), following his attendance at a King's Cross 12-hour presentation and his group's intervention in a neighbouring mining disaster. Because this involved Turkish immigrant workers (already vulnerable), a Turkish expert (Professor Gunsel-Kopta-Igel) agreed to participate.

This group, our local UCL-Middlesex group and others received visits from US and Australian experts. International psychosomatic, psychiatric and psychological societies became concerned. Eventually the International Society for the Study of Traumatic Stress was founded, with a research satellite group.

G.   The Hungerford massacre

ELIZABETH CAPEWELL

Metaphorically the massacre at Hungerford on 19 August 1987 represents our worst fears: the unknown 'stranger' from within rising up without warning for no particular reason and wreaking havoc.

Perhaps the most striking feature of the tragedy is that many details of the impact on individuals and community remain hidden and are difficult to uncover. Unlike other disasters, there is a lack of research and professional writing about the shootings. Nor were survivor/bereaved self-help groups formed. Those who try to uncover the stories are struck by the silence or anger that meets them. The Dunblane shootings of March 1996 have however refocused attention on Hungerford and a few bereaved people have joined those from Dunblane in campaigning for stricter gun laws.

The perpetrator

Michael Ryan, aged 27, was reported to be a loner, a man without friends and social skills who had never held down a job for long and who had difficulty in making close relationships. His elderly father, a strict disciplinarian, had died in 1984 and this had affected Ryan badly. His mother, a popular person in the town, was said to have spoilt him, and colluded with the world of fantasy (including an imaginary fiancée) that he had spun around him. From an early age he had been fascinated by guns and soon learnt that these gave him the power he lacked in himself, as did the fantasy games he later loved. He was described as well dressed and courteous, with no previous criminal record or mental health problems, and there were never any objections to him holding firearms licences.

The shootings

The massacre began at around noon in the Savernake Forest, Marlborough, close to where Ryan was born. It continued for an hour around the house in Hungerford where he grew up and finally ended at 6.52 p.m. with Ryan shooting and killing himself in the secondary school he had attended. In all he killed 16 people and his pet dogs, physically injured 15 others, and threatened, missed and mentally scarred many more. He set fire to four houses and in an hour fired not less than 119 shots – 84 from a Kalashnikov, 34 from a pistol and one from an M1 carbine. The dead included his mother, a police officer and five near-neighbours. He targeted adults, telling children to go indoors, and aimed only at the legs of the two teenagers he did injure.

The impact

In understanding the impact, it is helpful to be aware of some key features about the time, place, sequence of events, response of emergency services, and people involved. In disasters it is the details that influence perceptions and reactions of people but which are not always appreciated by those looking back with hindsight, with full information and without the fear and tension of those present at the time. These key factors include:

(a) The whole event was made up of a string of incidents lasting eight hours covering a distance of about seven miles, but mostly concentrated in an area of approximately half a mile square.

(b) This is a well populated area in which key community facilities are located.

(c) Hungerford is a quiet, traditional rural town of 5000 people.

(d) 19 August was market day and a hot sunny day in the school holidays. Many people were in the town visiting or shopping. Many children were out playing in the streets, on the common, or at the swimming pool and many were separated from their parents. Some residents were away on holiday, and so missed out on the 'experience' and/or community mourning. One family did not know their house was burnt down until they were on the ferry home from France ten days later.

(e) It happened during working hours so many people did not know what their families were experiencing, could not phone and were prevented from getting home until late in the evening.

(f) The community and visitors to the town were under siege for many hours not knowing what was happening or how long it would last. Many were alone or had to keep children safe. Added to the fear of uncertainty was the noise of helicopters, the smell and sound of gunfire, the sight of dead and injured bodies, and the scale and nature of the police action.

(g) Beliefs that rapid help from emergency services can be relied upon when in trouble were seriously challenged.

(h) There had been little preparation for a major incident of this kind. Existing County plans were geared to civil defence needs and the evacuation or rehousing of a community.

(i) The intrusive behaviour of the press during and since the incident has added to the distress of many people.

Unfortunately, the full impact on the survivors, bereaved and community can only be surmised because no official research has ever been conducted. Only anecdotal evidence can be gained from reports of work done by various professionals, and personal experiences. More recently some journalists have been able to unearth further evidence, especially when interviews are 'off the record'. Psychological assessments were mainly undertaken for the purposes of distributing the Memorial Fund money. It is known that people are still being seen by mental health personnel, while many are still getting by without formal interventions, still troubled by their experiences. Those of us who were involved continue to come across Hungerford stories in the most unexpected places as time goes by.

In the aftermath of the shootings, the streets were quiet, and children were kept indoors. "It was as if the Pied Piper had been through the town and taken all the children", reported one health visitor. The uncertainty continued until all the facts were known about who was dead and injured. The pulling together commonly found after disaster was evident in the assertions that this was a special community who would come through the horror. Although early offers of practical help and good wishes from around the world were received gratefully, the assertion that outsiders were not needed to deal with the emotional trauma was strong.

As people began to emerge from the safety of their homes, stories were exchanged, exaggerated or diminished in the telling. In the absence of concrete facts, rumours developed as well as stories. Children asked questions: "If daddy is in heaven, is Michael Ryan – and will they be friends?". People exhibited startle responses and other reactions to loud noises, the smell of blood, police cars and helicopters. One man was hyper-alert when anyone walked past his office window (as Ryan had done) for a year after. "Why us?", "Why them, not me?" and "If only . . ." were repeated throughout the community. Many had nightmares and slept badly, while others refused to return to their homes.

People worried about each other and, in particular, about the impact on their children, while denying their own reactions. Some felt guilty at having survived while others felt that they had not done enough to save the dead and help the injured. Differences in the community arose when offers of help were rejected and when attitudes and feelings polarised. Many people, especially the young, found fund-raising an appropriate response when other forms of helping seemed closed to them.

The community mourning lasted until a memorial service in October led by the Archbishop of Canterbury. Inclusion/exclusion issues emerged over invitations and seating at functions and the distribution of funds, and about who should receive psychological support. Those receiving normal social or health services were concerned that the disaster was taking away key staff and resources. There was an unspoken hierarchy of need. Many felt they did not deserve help or that others were in greater need. The stiff upper lip approach was praised. "We must forget" became the official view in later years.

Suppressed, disenfranchised grief has been, or may yet be, triggered by other traumatic events. Those not able to name their grief and seek help, even though services were available, included:

(a) Those protected by well-meaning relatives, friends or community figures, or by some volunteers and professionals who did not make appropriate referrals.
(b) Close relatives of the bereaved who had given up homes and jobs to live closer to them. Some sought help three years afterwards but still felt they did not deserve it as they "weren't the ones affected".
(c) Bereaved people who were also survivors and witnesses in their own right.

(d) A large proportion of the community whose symptoms and needs were overshadowed by the seemingly greater needs of the survivors and bereaved.

(e) Many rescue personnel and carers did not feel they should use resources for the community, or were told by managers and colleagues that they should not be affected. Some thought or were told that to be affected was a sign of weakness or incompetence.

(f) Children and young people caught in the myth that the school and community were so caring that no one would need extra help. The phrase "we have a wonderful pastoral care system" is reported following crisis in schools around the world. Many teachers and other adults were also caught in this way so that they dared not admit their own needs publicly or tell others about disturbing behaviour they observed in the children.

(g) People who lived outside Hungerford but who were involved in various ways. Even the most directly affected felt excluded in the aftermath as Hungerford 'owned' the disaster and the community mourning.

(h) Equally, those who lived in Hungerford but were out of the town at work or on holiday were given little permission to be affected. Their reactions to their fear for their families were not always recognised by friends and colleagues.

Different experiences, reactions and feelings caused problems. Some who had missed the events or mourning felt excluded and dismissed the feelings of others. The difference in energy of those who were involved and those who were not was marked – as if some had been exposed to a whole new dimension of understanding about life and death. This also manifested in different perceptions of time. By October, those on the outside felt it was a long time past, while those on the inside felt as if it had happened only yesterday. A distortion was still present some seven years later.

Anecdotal evidence exists about family functioning. For example, health visitors reported tensions. Husbands were accused of not understanding what their wives and children had been through and some did not want their wives to go out. A few responded by leaving their families, to enjoy themselves while they could as death could come so easily. Many women and the elderly lost confidence and were both afraid to go out and be in their own homes alone. Attempts to start confidence-building groups were thwarted by managers who feared they would cause family break-ups.

Trauma and grief has been exposed by other events. A small community tragedy in nearby Newbury in 1990 showed one family reacting strongly; they were related to two of the Hungerford dead. In 1992, volunteers from Hungerford rescued a large group of Croatian refugees, whose trauma stirred up in them issues which had lain dormant since the 1987 shootings. Some children are experiencing problems as they reach adolescence. One boy has hidden the truth about his father's death since people at school would not believe that he had been shot. He also had to endure a talk at school by a police officer about the shootings. Those who attend schools outside Hungerford have experienced a particular isolation. Children thought to be too young to be affected have experienced strong reactions to the trauma and its consequences.

The impact of dealing with the incident and its aftermath on rescue and recovery professionals has been immense and largely hidden. There have been suicides, family break-ups, loss of jobs and income, and poor health including depression, anxiety and nervous breakdown.

The response

The police provided essential detective work, and their work gave information important to an understanding of events. They also interviewed and prepared people for the inquest. Social Services set up a Family Help Unit and were authorised to lead the inter-agency response. Great efforts were made to contact all in need of help through distributing leaflets, personal contacts with follow-ups for the most directly affected, and media appeals for people to come forward if help was needed. Social workers and volunteer befrienders were assigned to help people through the funerals, inquest and public memorials, while the rest of the community could telephone or call at the Unit (Lane & Stacey, 1988).

The Hungerford Schools and Youth and Community Service combined to support staff and parents and to plan for the childrens' return to school after the summer holidays. The Youth and Community Officer was already involved in supporting staff who were in the school when Ryan entered, and was asked by local head teachers to prepare staff for the start of term and to help with requests for help from parents. Teams of experienced youth counsellors were coordinated and briefed to be ready to deal with what then was an unknown need. Sessions were run for parents and other education personnel. This response is described in detail elsewhere (Capewell, 1993).

The main incident response continued well into 1988 and extra support was available for the first anniversary. Help continued for some people but within the framework of regular services. The social services office set up in Hungerford after the shootings finally closed in 1994.

H. The Piper Alpha oil platform disaster

DAVID ALEXANDER

The Piper Alpha oil platform was designed to tap dry gas, wet gas and oil from a field in the North Sea, 120 miles off the coast of Aberdeen. The all-male crew numbered 226, most of whom were used to working in harsh and uncompromising conditions.

The disaster began at about 10 p.m. on 6 July 1988. At that time there was an initial explosion that served to trigger other explosions and fires, which ultimately led to the almost complete destruction of the installation above sea-level. Initial control of the burning wells was not achieved until 9 July and they were only finally brought under complete control on 4 September.

Because the communication system had been destroyed, confusion reigned and no instructions were given to abandon the platform. Many men sought refuge and awaited further instruction in the accommodation modules which were subsequently engulfed in flames and dense toxic fumes. Others sought escape by jumping into the sea (often from considerable heights) or by clambering down ropes, despite the fact that areas of the sea were also ablaze with oil and gas. Some inflatable life rafts were launched but they did not inflate properly. Fortunately, however, the sea was relatively calm, and those who had escaped from the fire and toxic fumes were eventually picked up by rescue craft.

Of the 226 men originally on board Piper Alpha, 164 (72%) were killed, and one man subsequently died in Aberdeen Royal Infirmary. Two men in a rescue craft also lost their lives while trying to rescue others. All survivors were taken first to Aberdeen Royal Infirmary where 21 were admitted for in-patient care. The majority of men had suffered burns, particularly to the head, face and hands. When they had recovered sufficiently the men were discharged to hospitals nearer their own homes.

Responses to the disaster

As survivors were brought in by helicopter to the accident and emergency department, a social work management team was set up to coordinate help for the survivors, the bereaved and the families of men who were still missing. A 24-hour Helpline was established to provide information and support for anybody affected by the disaster. Links were quickly made with other local authorities to provide information about individuals from their areas. Coordination between the Social Work Department and the medical, psychiatric and voluntary agencies was also quickly initiated. The owners of the oil platform, Occidental Petroleum, readily made available financial and other resources, and they also organised a series of meetings involving representatives of lay and professional agencies involved in the disaster.

Initial response

It was agreed that all victims' families should be visited by a representative of the employer as soon as possible after they had been contacted by the police (who had a statutory duty to inform them of the death of their family member). It was also agreed that all families should have one 'uninvited' visit by the social work team, with offers of further help if required. When possible, and where appropriate, debriefing was offered to specific groups. Efforts were made to identify survivors or bereaved persons who might be particularly at risk of adverse reactions or who might constitute 'hidden victims'. (These included some of the crew of Piper Alpha who would, but for chance, have been on the platform.) A memorial service to which all survivors, bereaved and others involved were invited took place the following week.

The psychiatric team

It was agreed that a small team of five senior and experienced clinicians from the psychiatric service should provide a continuous presence and involvement throughout the different stages of the aftermath of the disaster. Initially they were located in a room in the accident and emergency department of the main hospital. It was believed that a positive, preventative approach should be pursued rather than simply react to emergency requests for help. This was done, for example, by identifying individuals at particular risk and by being actively involved when various plans (such as those for the retrieval of human remains from the wreckage) were being discussed. Deliberately, the team adopted a positive view, emphasising the resilience of individuals when faced with adversity. This was done to counteract the rather pessimistic reiteration of gloomy statistics by the media.

In the accident and emergency department the team saw most of the survivors. Usually this was only on an informal basis, but every opportunity was taken to alleviate any anxieties about subsequent psychiatric help lest this be required at a later stage. Survivors and their families were forewarned of the kind of reactions they might experience later. Also, the author met, at their request, with a number of the nursing staff who had found the experience distressing. In some cases, however, the distress was not exclusively related to the disaster itself; rather, the intensity of the occasion had exacerbated pre-existing personal problems, a few of which involved staff relationships.

The more badly burned survivors were moved to the regional burns unit in Aberdeen Royal Infirmary. There they initially showed signs of euphoria and relief at having survived. However, after a few days most became irritable, tearful and anxious. Two became clinically depressed, and 'survivor guilt' soon emerged when it became evident there would be no more men rescued. The men suffered badly from uncertainties, becoming easily upset by unexpected changes in their routine or in their plans, but it was noticeable how quickly the victims emerged as a mutually supportive and cohesive group, at least while they remained in hospital together. One unfortunate consequence of this was that one survivor, who was alone in an orthopaedic ward, missed out on the support from the many visiting professionals and on the team spirit which developed in the burns unit. The two men who remained on their own for some time after the others had been discharged required additional support. It is important to note that the group cohesiveness that was created on the ward meant that discharge from hospital loomed as a threatening prospect associated with worries about how they would be received by family and friends on their return home.

The rescuers

The author visited the firefighting ship, the MSV *Tharos*, which was actively involved in combating the fires on Piper Alpha. Deliberately, he was not introduced as a 'counsellor' as it was anticipated that this would not be well-received by the men on board at that time. He was introduced as an expert on stress who had "come out to see how things were going". In this capacity he was able to have many informal meetings with the rescuers and firefighters without this giving rise to any suspicion or resistance. They were reassured by him that their reactions were 'normal' and appropriate to these tragic circumstances, and that they had done and were doing a 'good job'. The message which his presence gave, namely, that those on shore cared about their welfare and appreciated what they were doing, was well received by the men on the *Tharos*, whose work had been as emotionally unpleasant as it had been physically dangerous.

The police

At two sites local police officers were involved with the bodies from Piper Alpha. Forty-eight police officers (41 men and 7 women) were based at the temporary mortuary set up near Aberdeen Airport. Another 23 officers (22 men and 1 woman) were based on the island of Flotta in the Orkney archipelago, where Occidental Petroleum had an oil terminal. This was chosen as the site at which the raised accommodation modules would be searched by the police officers. After the initial rescue operation, 105 bodies were still missing; underwater surveys by remote operating vehicles indicated that many were entombed in the larger accommodation module of the platform. After a major feat of marine engineering this module (and its smaller counterpart) was raised from the sea bed and taken to the island of Flotta where it was searched by the police officers. In view of the unpleasant nature of the task, volunteer officers were selected principally on the basis of their having had some previous experience of dealing with death (although only one officer had been involved in a major catastrophe before).

Other selection criteria were used – older officers were preferred, as were those with a good sense of humour. All individuals on site were given an intensive induction at which particular attention was paid to physical safety, hygiene, security and to personal reactions (physical and psychological). The officers were informed that support was available from the author on an informal basis.

At three months and five years after the body retrieval exercise had been completed, all of these officers were followed up by the author using a number of measures frequently used in the aftermath of trauma. None of the officers showed major or persistent adverse reactions attributable to the body-handling exercise. This follow-up study was facilitated and enhanced by the fact that these officers had also been involved in an occupational health survey conducted by the author and his colleagues prior to the Piper Alpha disaster and, therefore, pre-disaster baseline data were available. In addition, there was a matched control group of police officers who had not been involved in the Piper Alpha disaster.

The results of the follow-up study indicated that there were a number of factors that combated the development of adverse post-traumatic reactions. These factors included the pre-operation induction (a form of 'stress inoculation'), a high degree of professionalism during the operation, a strong *esprit de corps*, and sensitive organisational and managerial practices.

Lessons learned

Immediately after the disaster there was an enormous and sympathetic response, both locally and nationally, and offers of help came from many parts of the country and abroad. It was clear, however, that this response had to be carefully organised such that new needs were quickly identified, offers of help were appropriately targeted and clear lines of communication were established among all those involved. The organisation also needed to be able to make the best use of outside 'experts' in a way which did not create antagonism among the local helpers. It was agreed that their knowledge and expertise should be used 'behind the scenes' to promote the response of the local community. Care was taken to ensure that it did not inhibit or supplant local agencies.

The problem of continuity of care became evident. Many of those who had become involved in the early stages of intervention found that they were unable to sustain this commitment (for perfectly legitimate reasons). However, unfortunately, it was often in the later phases of the disaster that many problems became intensified and new ones emerged. This was particularly evident at certain signal events, such as the retrieval of bodies, the demolition of the remains of the oil platform, the distribution of the Disaster Fund, and the inevitably protracted legal proceedings.

Managers have to be alert to the needs and difficulties of their staff. It was important to identify those rescuers and helpers who themselves required to be relieved of their duties, because rarely would any of them indicate that they had had enough. Those charged with organising a response to disaster must also acknowledge that some individuals who wish to be involved in the disaster response have had very little practical experience and have only limited skills. While their willingness to contribute is unquestionably well intended, it may, on occasions, do more harm than good.

For some of the survivors the disaster became too convenient an explanation for a variety of problems they encountered subsequently, including alcohol and drug misuse, marital disharmony and even criminal behaviour. In some cases there is no doubt that the Piper Alpha disaster exacerbated pre-existing problems or gave a sharp focus to them, but it certainly was not the case that the disaster caused all the problems that were subsequently reported. Hence, one of the challenges of counselling, and of more formal methods of psychiatric help, is to enable individuals and their families to develop a realistic perspective on the disaster and its sequelae and to avoid such false attributions.

Some of the helpers seemed, on the other hand, to develop an unrealistic view of the victims. Those who survive disasters are not saints – they have all the strengths and weaknesses of ordinary mortals. It is also too easy to create dependency among such victims and to become overprotective. One of the primary aims of any intervention is to help individuals to retrieve their sense of self-determination and self-control over their own lives. 'Rescue fantasies' abound after major incidents of this kind, and it is important that all helpers maintain a balanced and realistic perspective of their own contribution and of the role of the disaster in their lives. It was noticeable how some individuals found it almost impossible to disengage from their disaster work when it was appropriate to do so.

While the impact of a disaster is potentially overwhelming, and we should not expect disaster victims to 'get back to normal', we should not, on the other hand, assume that they will remain emotional cripples thereafter. The majority of people can come to terms with what has happened to them. Fortunately, even from great tragedy can come some good.

Positive outcomes after the Piper Alpha disaster included: the recognition by some individuals that they were able to cope with major problems; the reaffirmation of important relationships (some families became much closer) and the development of new ones; and the achievement of new solutions to difficult problems – both personal and technological.

More detailed accounts of this accident and its aftermath are available in the following publications: Alexander & Wells (1991); Alexander (1991, 1993*a,b,c*).

I.   Psychological consequences of road traffic accidents

MARTIN NEWMAN

Road traffic accidents, or motor vehicle accidents as they are termed in the US, are common. They may affect individuals of all ages. However, the psychological and psychiatric sequelae of road traffic accidents (RTAs) have been little studied until relatively recently. It is an important subject because of their common occurrence and because the psychological sequelae of RTAs are often severe, yet unrecognised, even in medico-legal work (Frank, 1993). The psychological consequences may affect not only those severely injured in an accident, but also those who only suffer minor injury or who are not injured at all (Mayou *et al*, 1993). It is to be anticipated that claims for compensation for psychological injury will become more frequent.

Feinstein & Dolan (1991) carried out a prospective study of 48 subjects, aged between 15 and 60 years, who had suffered an accidental fracture of the femur, tibia or fibula without loss of limb, who had required admission to an orthopaedic ward for surgical correction of the fracture, and who were discharged within six weeks. After the initial assessment within 4–7 days of admission, they were re-assessed at six weeks and at six months. In this study, the commonest causes of accidental injury were motorcycle accidents (29.2%), pedestrian injuries (20.8%) and sports injuries (14.6%). Assessment of psychiatric morbidity included the General Health Questionnaire (Goldberg & Hillier, 1979), the Clinical Interview Schedule (Goldberg *et al*, 1970), the Impact of Event Scale (Horowitz *et al*, 1979), the Standardized Assessment of Personality (Mann *et al*, 1981), and a self-report symptom checklist for symptoms of PTSD derived from DSM–III–R (American Psychiatric Association, 1987) criteria. Patients were also asked demographic information and to indicate whether they had been active or passive participants in the traumatic event, to assess their responsibility for it ('fully responsible', 'partially responsible', or 'not at all responsible') and to rate the stressfulness of the event. The findings were that approximately two-thirds of patients, within a week of injury, reported sufficient symptoms to be labelled as psychiatric 'cases' (although not necessarily full PTSD). Without intervention the natural history of these sequelae was towards improvement over time, with less than a quarter remaining as 'cases' by six months. The authors reported that two variables were the most powerful predictors of PTSD at six months – scores above the median for both the initial Impact of Event Scale and weekly alcohol consumption. The initial score on the Impact of Event Scale was the single most important predictor of psychiatric morbidity in general, and PTSD in particular, at six weeks and six months. Feinstein & Dolan (1991) suggested that levels of distress after the accident, possibly due to failure in having cognitively mastered a stressful situation, predict poor prognosis. This study also raised doubt about the appropriateness of the stressor criteria for PTSD as defined in DSM–III–R, which assumed the magnitude of severity of the trauma was of primary aetiological importance in the development of PTSD. Doubts regarding the stressor criteria were also raised by others (Breslau & Davis, 1987; March, 1993) and the definition was subsequently changed in DSM–IV (American Psychiatric Association, 1994).

Brom *et al* (1993), in Israel, reported that an average of 10% of RTA victims suffered from post-traumatic stress disorders. They found that, although counselling was appreciated by victims, it was not proven to be effective in preventing disorders.

Mayou *et al* (1993), in Oxford, carried out a prospective follow-up study of 188 consecutive road accident victims aged 18–70, with multiple injuries or whiplash neck injury, and who had not been unconscious for more than 15 minutes. They found that, at the first assessment after the accident, 18% of subjects suffered from an acute stress syndrome with mood disturbance and horrific memories of the accident. This was significantly associated with neuroticism and being conscious after the accident. These subjects had a poor psychological outcome at one year; 10% of patients had mood disorders, twice that expected in the general population. PTSD (according to DSM–III–R criteria) occurred during follow-up in 10% of patients, and phobic travel anxiety as a driver or passenger was more common and frequently disabling. Emotional disorder was associated with having pre-accident psychological or social problems and, in patients with multiple injuries, continuing medical complications. Post-traumatic syndromes were not associated with a neurotic predisposition but were strongly associated with horrific memories of the accident. They did not occur in any subject who had been unconscious and were amnesic for the accident. Mental state at three months was highly predictive of mental state at one year. The authors noted that the prospect of compensation did not predict psychiatric disorder.

Kuch (1993) suggested that accident phobias and post-traumatic stress disorders after RTAs may be more common in patients with chronic pain. Dalal & Harrison (1993) suggested that somatoform pain disorder may be an important psychiatric consequence of RTAs, and recommended that further research be carried out.

Thompson *et al* (1993) suggested that psychiatric morbidity after RTAs is also important in children, who may present with such symptoms as nightmares of the accident, separation anxiety, fear of the dark, sleep disturbance, reluctance to cross roads or travel by car, and a preoccupation with road safety. They recommended that those involved in the psychological treatment of the adult survivors of RTAs should be aware of the possible significance of any behavioural disturbance in children in the survivors' families, and that it may sometimes be appropriate to refer affected parents and their children to children's mental health services.

O'Brien (1993) suggested that becoming unconscious after a major trauma, with amnesia for what happened, may protect against the development of PTSD.

Bryant & Harvey (1995) suggested that there was an association between avoidant coping response and post-traumatic stress, and that it may therefore be helpful to elucidate what is adaptive avoidance behaviour after a trauma and what is maladaptive avoidance behaviour. This may then allow studies to determine whether a reduction in certain avoidance behaviours in the initial post-accident period reduces longer-term morbidity.

Blanchard *et al* (1995*a*) reviewed the studies on RTAs. They noted that most studies have used clinical interviews, rather than structured interviews of known reliability and validity. Also, the samples studied have been from a variety of sources, and the time between the accident and the assessments have varied considerably between studies. Thus, the importance of the variation in the results obtained between studies is uncertain. Blanchard *et al* (1995*a*, 1996), working in the US, carried out a study of 158 victims of recent motor vehicle accidents (MVAs) and 93 non-accident controls. They defined an MVA victim as someone aged 17 or over who had been in a recent MVA for which they had sought medical attention. They were assessed from 1–4 months after the accident. The MVA personnel came from a variety of sources – some from other medical practitioners who had been asked to refer any MVA victims they saw (not just those having problems), and some recruited by local media coverage and advertising. Entry criteria for the controls were that they had not been in any MVA for the previous year, and that they matched the age and gender distribution of the MVA victims. Some were friends of the MVA victim, others were from staff of referral sources and some were recruited by advertising. Blanchard *et al* acknowledge that there may be some referral bias in their study. Various clinical instruments were used. PTSD was diagnosed on the basis of DSM–III–R criteria. 'Subsyndromal PTSD' was defined as a group who met symptomatic criteria for criterion B (re-experiencing) and either criterion C (avoidance and numbing) or criterion D (hyperarousal) but not both. Other terms such as partial PTSD and subclinical PTSD have been used by others (Feinstein & Dolan, 1991; Weiss *et al*, 1992; Green *et al*, 1993) to describe morbidity which does not satisfy all the DSM criteria. Blanchard *et al* (1995*a*, 1996) found that 39% of their sample of recent MVA victims met the criteria for PTSD. This was higher than for comparable groups reported by Mayou *et al* (1993) or Malt (1988). Blanchard *et al* postulate that this may have been due to referral bias, or to their use of a more sensitive instrument (CAPS: the Clinician-Administered PTSD Scale; Blake *et al*, 1990; Blake, 1994; Weathers & Litz, 1994) than the Present State Examination (used by Mayou *et al*, 1993) or clinical interview (used by Malt, 1988). Blanchard *et al* (1995*a*) identified three subgroups of MVA victims: those with full PTSD (39.2%); those who met criteria for a subsyndromal form of PTSD (28.5%); and those with relatively few symptoms (32.3%). Among accident victims, age showed no significant effect. Significantly more female MVA victims met the criteria for full PTSD. Ethnic minorities (defined as black, Hispanic or Asian) were more likely than whites to meet the criteria for PTSD, although further research regarding this finding is needed (Blanchard *et al*, 1996).

Blanchard *et al* (1995*a*) looked at the effect of applying DSM–IV criteria to their study, and found that the incidence of full PTSD fell to 34.8% and the incidence of subsyndromal PTSD rose to 33.5%. Blanchard *et al* (1995*c*) found that changing the scoring rules used for the Clinician-Administered

PTSD Scale (CAPS) could result in significant effects on the incidence and severity of diagnosed PTSD. Thus, care is needed when interpreting results from different studies where differing scoring rules may be used.

Blanchard *et al* (1996) reported that the presence of a prior major depressive illness, fear of dying in the road traffic accident, the extent of physical injury, and having sought advice from a lawyer regarding the accident, were modest predictors of PTSD. The subject of compensation is discussed below.

Platt & Husband (1987) and Goldberg & Gara (1990) had noted a large degree of mood disturbance in MVA victims. Blanchard *et al* (1995*a*) also found that 53% of their PTSD subgroup met the criteria for current major depression. They found that those MVA victims who develop PTSD were significantly more likely to have a history of major depression than were those who had lesser responses to the trauma. There was a similar, but weaker, relationship between panic disorder and PTSD. Those MVA victims who developed PTSD were more likely to have a history of panic disorder (11.3%) than the other MVA victims (3.1%). There were no differences among the subgroups of MVA victims on current or lifetime alcohol or drug problems, eating disorders, somatoform disorders, or personality disorders. Over half of the controls had themselves been in a previous serious MVA. A risk factor for developing PTSD or subsyndromal PTSD from the current accident was having previously suffered from PTSD. Thus, prior trauma and PTSD apparently sensitise the individual, leaving him or her more vulnerable when a new trauma occurs.

Physical injury

It has been argued that those injured as a result of a trauma are more likely to develop PTSD than those who are not injured (Helzer *et al*, 1987; Kilpatrick *et al*, 1989; Pitman *et al*, 1989). Blanchard *et al* (1995*b*), in a preliminary report on 98 MVA victims, found that there was a significant but low-level correlation between extent of injury and development of PTSD. They used the Abbreviated Injury Scale (AIS-85; American Association of Automotive Medicine, 1985) which asks for ratings of the worst injury to each of seven body areas (head, face, neck, thorax, abdomen and pelvic contents, spine, extremities and external) using a 0–6 scale, where 1 represents a minor injury and 6 represents maximum injury which may well not be survivable. The seven ratings are then summed.

The study found that fear of death or perceived life threat also significantly predicted development of PTSD in MVA victims. This prediction was independent of the extent of physical injury. However, overall prediction combining these two variables was modest. They concluded that, for some MVA victims, it appears that it is the perceptions that result from the accident, rather than the seriousness of the injuries received, that are important in the development of PTSD.

Compensation

The effects of being involved in legal redress for psychological and physical injury is uncertain (Culpan & Taylor, 1973; Bryant & Harvey, 1995). Glaser *et al* (1981) did not find any significant differences between those involved in litigation and those who were not, in adult survivors of the Buffalo Creek disaster. Studies in children are lacking (Yule, 1994). Burstein (1986) pointed out that there was little research in this area, and that documenting the effects of monetary compensation, if any, would be difficult in acute PTSD. Mayou *et al* (1993) did not find that psychiatric disorder in those who had experienced RTAs was affected by the prospect of compensation. However, the legal processes and the delays involved may cause great distress (Tarsh & Royston, 1985).

Blanchard *et al* (1996) noted that there was a significant correlation between the development of PTSD and whether a MVA victim had contacted a lawyer or not and the time when he/she was assessed. However, they point out that this could be because those seriously injured and sufficiently distressed to meet the criteria for a diagnosis of PTSD are more likely to seek legal advice and seek compensation. Alternatively, it is possible that those who wish to initiate legal redress may be inclined to portray themselves as suffering from symptoms which lead to a diagnosis of PTSD being made.

Caution is needed when making legal reports in personal injury litigation. Neal (1994) pointed out that the DSM multiaxial classification may be a useful framework for presenting a diagnosis of PTSD, but over-rigid adherence to the diagnostic criteria, at the expense of clinical judgement and experience, should be avoided. Neal (1994) agrees with Sparr & Boehnlein (1990) that:

> "a diagnosis of PTSD by an expert witness based on personalized and vague descriptions is to be deplored, but too much preoccupation with precise diagnostic categories does not serve legal needs. A diagnosis may be met when not all the criteria are met, and vice versa. The DSM represents guidelines which should be subject to clinical judgement, and adherence to the diagnostic criteria is not mandatory, but advisory."

Summary

There is significant psychiatric and psychosocial morbidity associated with RTAs. Such accidents are common, yet the psychological consequences may frequently go unrecognised. Those who are suffering from PTSD may have impaired performance at work or at school, in their homes, and in their relationships. Early identification of those at greatest risk of long-term psychological problems, such as those who do not lose consciousness and have initial horrifying memories of the accident, or who suffer from a vulnerable personality, may be helpful (Mayou *et al*, 1993; Blanchard *et al*, 1996).

References

Alexander, D. A. (1991) Psychiatric intervention after the Piper Alpha disaster. *Journal of the Royal Society of Medicine*, **84**, 8–11.

—— (1993*a*) Stress among police body handlers – a long-term follow-up. *British Journal of Psychiatry*, **163**, 806–808.

—— (1993*b*) The Piper Alpha oil rig disaster. In *International Handbook of Traumatic Stress Syndromes* (eds J. P. Wilson & B. Raphael), pp. 461–470. New York: Plenum Press.

—— (1993*c*) Burn victims after a major disaster: reactions of patients and their care-givers. *Burns*, **19**, 105–109.

—— & Wells, A. (1991) Reactions of police officers to body-handling after a major disaster: a before-and-after comparison. *British Journal of Psychiatry*, **159**, 547–555.

American Association of Automotive Medicine (1985) *The Abbreviated Injury Score (Revised)*. Des Plaines, IL.

American Psychiatric Association (1987) *Diagnostic and Statistical Manual of Mental Disorders* (3rd edn, revised) (DSM–III–R). Washington, DC: APA.

—— (1994) *Diagnostic and Statistical Manual of Mental Disorders* (4th edn) (DSM–IV). Washington, DC: APA.

Blake, D. D. (1994) Rationale and development of the Clinician-Administered PTSD Scale. *PTSD Research Quarterly*, **5**, 1–2.

——, Weathers, F., Nagy, L., *et al* (1990) *Clinician-Administered PTSD Scale (CAPS)*. Boston: National Center for Post-Traumatic Stress Disorder, Behavioural Science Division.

Blanchard, E. B., Hickling, E. J., Taylor, A. E., *et al* (1995*a*) Psychiatric morbidity associated with motor vehicle accidents. *Journal of Nervous and Mental Disease*, **183**, 495–504.

——, ——, Mitnick, N., *et al* (1995*b*) The impact of severity of physical injury and perception of life threat in the development of post-traumatic stress disorder in motor vehicle accident victims. *Behaviour Research and Therapy*, **33**, 529–534.

——, ——, Taylor, A. E., *et al* (1995*c*) Effects of varying scoring rules of the Clinician-Administered PTSD Scale (CAPS) for the diagnosis of post-traumatic stress disorder in motor vehicle accident victims. *Behaviour Research and Therapy*, **33**, 471–475.

——, ——, ——, *et al* (1996) Who develops PTSD from motor vehicle accidents? *Behaviour Research and Therapy*, **34**, 1–10.

Breslau, N. & Davis, G. C. (1987) Post-traumatic stress disorder: the stressor criterion. *Journal of Nervous and Mental Disease*, **175**, 255–264.

Brom, D., Kleber, R. J. & Hofman, M. C. (1993) Victims of traffic accidents: incidence and prevention of post-traumatic stress disorders. *Journal of Clinical Psychology*, **49**, 131–140.

Brooks, D. N. & McKinlay, W. W. (1992) Mental health consequences of the Lockerbie Disaster. *Journal of Traumatic Stress*, **5**, 527–543.

Brough, M. D., & 26 co-authors (1991). The King's Cross Fire: the physical injuries. *Burns*, **17**, 7–9.

Bryant, R. A. & Harvey, A. G. (1995) Avoidant coping style and post-traumatic stress following motor vehicle accidents. *Behaviour Research and Therapy*, **33**, 631–635.

Burstein, A. (1986) Can monetary compensation influence the course of a disorder? *American Journal of Psychiatry*, **143**, 112.

Capewell, E. (1993) Responding to the needs of young people after Hungerford. In *Working With Disaster – Social and Welfare Interventions During and After Tragedy* (ed. T. Newburn). London: Longman.

Coyle, B. (1994) *The Families of the Pan Am 103 Disaster: Self-Help Groups*. Unpublished PhD thesis, University of Syracuse.

Culpan, R. & Taylor, C. (1973) Psychiatric disorders following road traffic and industrial injuries. *Australian and New Zealand Journal of Psychiatry*, **101**, 452–459.

Dalal, B. & Harrison, G. (1993) Psychiatric consequences of road traffic accidents – consider somatoform pain disorder. *British Medical Journal*, **307**, 1282.

Derogatis, L. R. (1977) *SCL–90: Administration, Scoring and Procedures. Manual 1*. Baltimore: Clinical Psychometrics Research.

Feinstein, A. & Dolan, R. (1991) Predictors of post-traumatic stress disorder following physical trauma: an examination of the stressor criterion. *Psychological Medicine*, **21**, 85–91.

Fennell, J. D. E. (1988) *Official Enquiry into the King's Cross Fire*. London: Her Majesty's Stationery Office.

Frank, A. (1993) Psychiatric consequences of road traffic accidents – often disabling and unrecognised. *British Medical Journal*, **307**, 1283.

Glaser, G. G., Green, B. L. & Winget, C. (1981) *Prolonged Psychosocial Effects of Disaster: A Study of Buffalo Creek.* New York: Academic Press.

Goldberg, D. P. & Hillier, V. F. (1979) A scaled version of the General Health Questionnaire. *Psychological Medicine,* **9,** 139–145.

——, Cooper, B., Eastwood, M. R., *et al* (1970) A standardized psychiatric interview for use in community surveys. *British Journal of Preventative and Social Medicine,* **24,** 18–23.

Goldberg, L. & Gara, M. A. (1990) A typology of psychiatric reactions to motor vehicle accident. *Psychopathology,* **23,** 15–20.

Green, M. M., McFarlane, A. C., Hunter, C. E., *et al* (1993) Undiagnosed post-traumatic stress disorder following motor vehicle accidents. *Medical Journal of Australia,* **159,** 529–534.

Helzer, J. E., Robins, L. N. & McEvoy, L. (1987) Post-traumatic stress disorder in the general population. *Findings of the Epidemiologic Catchment Area Survey,* **317,** 1630–1634.

Hodgkinson, P. E. & Stewart, M. (1991) *Coping with Catastrophe: A Handbook of Disaster Management.* London: Routledge.

Horowitz, M. J., Wilner, N. & Alvarez, W. (1979) Impact of Event Scale: a measure of subjective stress. *Psychosomatic Medicine,* **41,** 209–218.

Joseph, S. A., Brewin, C. R., Yule, W., *et al* (1991) Causal attributions and psychiatric symptomatology in survivors of the Herald of Free Enterprise disaster. *British Journal of Psychiatry,* **159,** 542–546.

——, Williams, R., Yule, W., *et al* (1992) Factor analysis of the Impact of Event Scale with survivors of two disasters at sea. *Personality and Individual Differences,* **13,** 693–697.

——, Hodgkinson, P., Yule, W., *et al* (1993*a*) Guilt and distress thirty months after the capsize of the Herald of Free Enterprise. *Personality and Individual Differences,* **14,** 271–273.

——, Yule, W., Williams, R., *et al* (1993*b*) The Herald of Free Enterprise disaster: Measuring post-traumatic symptoms thirty months on. *British Journal of Clinical Psychology,* **32,** 327–331.

——, Dalgleish, T., Thrasher, S., *et al* (1994) Crisis support and emotional reactions following trauma. *Crisis Intervention,* **1,** 203–208.

——, Yule, W. & Williams, R. (1995) Emotional processing in survivors of the Jupiter cruise ship disaster. *Behaviour Research and Therapy,* **33,** 187–192.

Kennedy, T. & Johnston, G. W. (1975) Civilian bomb injuries. Surgery of Violence. *British Medical Journal,* **1,** 382–383.

Kilpatrick, D. G., Saunders, B. E., Amick-McMullan, A., *et al* (1989) Victim and crime factors associated with the development of crime-related post-traumatic stress disorder. *Behaviour Research and Therapy,* **20,** 199–214.

Kinston, W. J. & Rosser, R. M. (1974) Disasters: effects on mental and physical state. *Journal of Psychosomatic Research,* **18,** 437–455.

Kuch, K. (1993) Psychiatric consequences of road traffic accidents – phobias linked to chronic pain. *British Medical Journal,* **307,** 1283.

Lane, S. & Stacey, T. (1988) *The Hungerford Family Help Unit.* London: National Institute of Social Work.

Livingston, H. M., Livingston, M., Brooks, D. N., *et al* (1992) Elderly survivors of the Lockerbie Air Disaster. *International Journal of Geriatric Psychiatry,* **7,** 725–729.

McIntosh, N. (1989) *Lockerbie: A Local Authority Response to Disaster.* Dumfries and Galloway Regional Council.

Malt, U. (1988) The long-term psychiatric consequences of accidental injury: a longitudinal study of 107 adults. *British Journal of Psychiatry,* **153,** 810–818.

Mann, A. H., Jenkins, R., Cutting, J. C., *et al* (1981) The development and use of a standardized assessment of abnormal personality. *Psychological Medicine,* **11,** 839–847.

March, J. S. (1993) What constitutes a stressor? The "Criterion A" issue. In *Post-Traumatic Stress Disorder: DSM–IV and Beyond* (eds J. R. T. Davidson & E. B. Foa), pp. 37–54. Washington, DC: APP.

Mayou, R., Bryant, B. & Duthie, R. (1993) Psychiatric consequences of road traffic accidents. *British Medical Journal,* **307,** 647–651.

Mitchell, M. (1993*a*) The eye of the storm: The police organisation of the recovery operation after the Lockerbie Disaster. In *Working With Disaster* (ed. T. Newburn). London: Longmans.

—— (1993*b*) The role of the general practitioner in the aftermath of disaster. In *Working with Disaster* (ed. T. Newburn). London: Longmans.

—— (1994) Help-seeking following traumatic exposure. Northern Ireland British Psychological Society Conference, Letterkenny, April 1994.

——, McLay, D., Boddy, J., *et al* (1991) The police response to the Lockerbie disaster. *Disaster Management*, **3**, 198–205.

Neal, L. A. (1994) The pitfalls of making a categorical diagnosis of post traumatic stress disorder in personal injury litigation. *Medicine, Science and the Law*, **34**, 117–122.

Newman, T. (1993) Social welfare after tragedy: what have we learnt? In *Working With Disaster* (ed. T. Newburn). London: Longmans.

O'Brien, M. (1993) Psychiatric consequences of road traffic accidents – loss of memory is protective. *British Medical Journal*, **307**, 1283.

Pennebaker, J. W. (1988) Confiding traumatic experiences and health. In *Handbook of Stress, Cognition and Health* (eds S. Fisher & J. Reason). London: Wiley.

Pitman, R. K., Altman, B. & Macklin, M. L. (1989) Prevalence of post-traumatic stress disorder in wounded Vietnam veterans. *American Journal of Psychiatry*, **146**, 667–669.

Platt, J. J. & Husband, S. D. (1987) Post-traumatic stress disorder and the motor vehicle accident victim. *American Journal of Forensic Psychology*, **5**, 39–42.

Raphael, B. (1986) *When Disaster Strikes*. London: Hutchison Education.

Rosser, R., Allison, R., Butler, C., *et al* (1993) The Index of Health Related Quality of Life (IHQL): a new tool for audit and cost per Qualy analysis. In *Quality of Life Assessment: Key Issues in the 1990s* (eds S. R. Walker & R. M. Rosser), pp. 179–184 & Appendix 4, pp. 455–463. London: Kluwer Academic Publishers.

Sparr, L. F. & Boehnlein, J. K. (1990) PTSD in tort actions: forensic minefield. *Bulletin of the American Academy of Psychiatric Law*, **12**, 443–467.

Stiff, J. B. (1989) *Lockerbie Air Disaster: Incident Report*. The Firemaster's Report on the Role of Dumfries and Galloway Fire Brigade at the Lockerbie Air Disaster, 21st December 1988.

Stroebe, M. S., Stroebe, W. & Hausson, R. (eds) (1993) *Handbook of Bereavement: Theory, Research and Intervention*. Cambridge: Cambridge University Press.

Sturgeon, D., Rosser, R. & Schoenberg, P. (1991) The King's Cross fire: the psychological injuries. *Burns*, **17**, 10–13.

Tarsh, M. J. & Royston, C. (1985) A follow-up study of accident neurosis. *British Journal of Psychiatry*, **146**, 18–25.

Thompson, A., McArdle, P. & Dunne, F. (1993) Psychiatric consequences of road traffic accidents – children may be seriously affected. *British Medical Journal*, **307**, 1282–1283.

Thompson, J., Chung, M. C. & Rosser, R. (1994) The Marchioness disaster: preliminary report on psychological effects. *British Journal of Clinical Psychology*, **33**, 75–77.

Thrasher, S., Dalgleish, T. & Yule, W. (1994) Information processing in post-traumatic stress disorder. *Behaviour Research and Therapy*, **32**, 247–254.

Tsui, E. P. (1990) The "Jupiter" sinking disaster: effects on teenagers school performance. Unpublished MSc dissertation, University of London, Institute of Psychiatry.

Weathers, F. W. & Litz, B. T. (1994) Psychometric properties of the Clinician-Administered PTSD Scale, CAPS-1. *PTSD Research Quarterly*, **5**, 2–6.

Weighill, V. E. (1983) 'Compensation neurosis': a review of the literature. *Journal of Psychosomatic Medicine*, **27**, 97–104.

Weiss, D. S., Marmar, C. R., Schlenger, W. E., *et al* (1992) Prevalence of lifetime and partial post-traumatic stress disorder in Vietnam theater veterans. *Journal of Traumatic Stress*, **5**, 365–376.

Williams, R., Hodgkinson, P. E., Joseph, S., *et al* (1995) Attitudes to emotion, social support and distress 30 months after the capsize of a passenger ferry disaster. *Crisis Intervention*, **1**, 209–214.

Yule, W. (1992) Post traumatic stress disorder in child survivors of shipping disasters: the sinking of the "Jupiter". *Psychotherapy and Psychosomatics*, **57**, 200–205.

—— (1994) Post-traumatic stress disorders. In *Child and Adolescent Psychiatry: Modern Approaches* (3rd edn) (eds M. Rutter, E. Taylor & L. Hersov), pp. 392–406. Oxford: Blackwell Scientific Publications.

—— & Udwin, O. (1991) Screening child survivors for post-traumatic stress disorders: experiences from the "Jupiter" sinking. *British Journal of Clinical Psychology*, **30**, 131–138.

—— & Gold, A. (1993) *Wise before the Event: Coping with Crises in Schools*. London: Calouste Gulbenkian Foundation.

—— & —— (1994) Wise before the event: planning with schools to help child survivors of catastrophes. In *Trauma and Crisis Management* (ed. G. Forrest), pp. 26–34. London: ACPP.

——, Udwin, O. & Murdoch, K. (1990) The "Jupiter" sinking: effects on children's fears, depression and anxiety. *Journal of Child Psychology and Psychiatry*, **31**, 1051–1061.

9 The effect of conflict on combatants

MARTIN DEAHL

War is, regrettably, one of man's oldest pastimes, and since the earliest recorded accounts of warfare the psychological effects of combat upon combatants have been recognised. Ancient historians observed fear provoking sudden blindness among soldiers at the battle of Marathon, and symptoms typical of traumatic stress in soldiers are described in Homer's epic poems. Shakespeare appeared aware of combat stress symptoms which are well described in Henry IV. In modern times the first detailed descriptions of what today we would recognise as combat stress disorders came from the American Civil War, which was the first conflict to subject large numbers of men to sustained heavy bombardment.

The psychopathology of combat veterans should be of more than passing interest to civilians. Although this chapter focuses on only a few of the more major recent conflicts, the sheer scale of warfare must not be underestimated. Since the end of the Second World War there have been more than 150 wars, 90% of which have taken place in the developing world. Although Britain may seem at peace, British servicemen have lost their lives on active service somewhere in the world in virtually every year since 1945. Of approximately 26 conflicts taking place at the present time, 21 are taking place in developing countries (who spend more than £100 billion between them on defence) and the remaining five are in the former Soviet Union and former Yugoslavia. The collective suffering of combatants and civilians currently living is beyond comprehension. From a purely pragmatic perspective, large numbers of servicemen leave the military and re-enter civilian life, bringing with them their combat experience and its psychological aftermath. Civilian psychiatrists are often called upon to treat ex-servicemen and their families, the secondary victims, in the course of their work. Many veterans are reluctant to discuss their military experiences with 'outsiders', especially mental health professionals, who they feel cannot possibly understand the experience of combat. It is important, therefore, that psychiatrists have some understanding of the nature and prevalence of mental disorder in ex-servicemen.

War has always been a fertile ground for studying the effects of traumatic stress, and much of our current understanding of the psychiatric consequences of psychological trauma derive from observations of combat veterans. No other setting exposes such large numbers of clearly identifiable individuals to stresses that are unequivocally extreme and outside normal experience. Indeed, the effects of traumatic stress were originally thought to be confined to the military, and it has only recently been recognised that civilian populations involved in disasters and personal tragedy such as rape and accident may suffer similar disorders.

Concepts of traumatic stress have evolved and been inextricably linked with the history of warfare, and each new conflict spawns new research, often relearning the forgotten lessons of previous wars (Andreassen, 1980). Prior to the mid 19th century, symptoms which today we would recognise as stress-related were termed 'nostalgia' and attributed to homesickness. During the American Civil War symptoms resembling those of post-traumatic stress disorder (PTSD) were described (Mitchell *et al*, 1864). Observers were at a loss to explain these, relying instead on the diagnosis of neurasthenia, a term introduced by Beard to indicate a state of mental and physical exhaustion. During this time Da Costa (1871) described the "irritable heart syndrome" illustrating the confusion that surrounded the aetiology of these disorders. By the beginning of the First World War the same clinical picture had been renamed 'shell-shock', a term introduced by Mott (1919) to describe a disorder believed to be caused by 'microstructural' alterations in the central nervous system as a result of blast injury or carbon monoxide toxicity. The concept of shell-shock barely survived the Great War, as it became apparent that the condition occurred in servicemen not exposed to shelling and that many of the symptoms improved when soldiers were removed from immediate danger. From a study of 589 shell-shock cases, Southward (1919) concluded that the majority of cases could be attributed to the "psychoneuroses" – hysteria, neurasthenia or psychasthenia. One of the major themes of military psychiatry during this period was to distinguish 'war neurosis' from other causes of mental disorder including organic states and major mental illness. Following the Second World War, DSM–I (American Psychiatric Association, 1952) described the "gross stress reaction", considered at the time a short-lived disorder that was completely reversible, far removed from present-day concepts of PTSD. Omitted altogether from DSM–II (American Psychiatric Association, 1968), the present term PTSD appeared for the first time in DSM–III (American Psychiatric Association, 1980) and owed much to the studies and observations of Vietnam war veterans. DSM–III criteria recognised that PTSD was not unique to warfare and that any form of extreme stress could produce the same disorder. The operational definition of PTSD was a landmark in traumatic stress research, allowing systematic epidemiological studies to be undertaken for the first time.

We have, perhaps, accepted combat uncritically as a model for the effects of catastrophe and disaster in civilian life (Deahl *et al*, 1994*a*). There is a body of evidence to suggest that there are differences between soldiers and civilians exposed to violence. Combat veterans are more likely than civilians to develop the full PTSD syndrome and are also more likely than their civilian counterparts to experience associated symptoms of survivor guilt and emotional numbing (North *et al*, 1994). The stresses associated with combat are unique, and any attempt to draw parallels between combat and civilian experience should be treated cautiously. Soldiers themselves are not typical or representative of the general population and, unlike the victims of disaster, are trained and prepared for war. They face combat in cohesive groups. Unlike much of the psychological trauma encountered in civilian life such as rape, accident and disaster, soldiers in combat face multiple, interacting and often prolonged traumatic events. These include the stresses associated with mobilisation – being uprooted from one's normal role and environment and losing the support of family and confiding relationships (Deahl, 1992). Further stress arises from the uncertainty about the duration and nature of combat facing an individual soldier, a perceived sense of helplessness and an inability to exercise control over his own fate.

Combat exposure itself, and events surrounding it (including fatigue, a hostile and uncomfortable environment, lack of privacy and personal space, threat to personal safety, witnessing of atrocities and body handling) all contribute to exacerbate stress. Medical personnel in particular witness the gruesome consequences of war, and evidence suggests that they are a group particularly likely to develop stress-related disorders (Baker, 1989). Servicemen also face considerable stresses associated with demobilisation and re-integration into normal family and working life. War veterans often find great difficulty in identifying a single distressing event, and more often describe multiple prolonged traumatic experiences set against a background of continuing chronic stress.

Historically, military psychiatry has made important contributions to civilian practice. The treatment of Second World War British army veterans made a major contribution to the development of post-war British psychiatry. The "Northfield experiments" in which psychiatrists such as Bion, Jones and Main successfully treated many traumatised servicemen were milestones in British psychiatry. They not only played an important role in the development of the post-war group psychoanalytical movement, refining concepts of group dynamics and developing new treatments such as the therapeutic community, but also created a sense of therapeutic optimism which was to form an important factor in the development of the community care movement.

The First and Second World Wars

During the two world wars, 12% of all British Army casualties (6% of total battle casualties) were psychiatric. "Neuroses" accounted for 37 out of every 1000 casualties evacuated from the front. The US Great War expeditionary force made efforts to exclude individuals prone to psychiatric disorder but, despite this, "functional nervous disease" accounted for 9.5 per 1000 admissions to US military hospitals. A total of 35 846 US veterans were considered to be suffering from mental disorder as a result of their wartime experience. During the First World War official attitudes to 'shell-shock' were ambivalent and it was often a matter of luck whether a soldier was deemed ill and deserving of treatment, or treated as a coward and deserter and punished. Although it is well known that 3500 death sentences were passed, of which approximately 282 were executed prior to 1917, many more soldiers were deemed ill. Sixty thousand psychiatric cases were ultimately in receipt of war pensions; 29 000 of these were still receiving pensions in 1938 (Brend, 1938).

The Second World War also produced large numbers of psychiatric casualties. This was despite more stringent recruit selection (2% of all British recruits were rejected on psychiatric grounds) (Belas, 1973) and a government policy urging regimental medical officers to give "strong reassurance" when servicemen reported sick with palpitations or other anxiety-related symptoms. More than 920 000 Allied servicemen were admitted to psychiatric hospitals, of which 258 000 were diagnosed as suffering from "war neurosis". Mental disorder accounted for 31% of medical discharges from the British Army. Prior to the end of the battle of Normandy in August 1944, 20% of all the British 2nd Army's casualties were psychiatric. After 44 days fighting in Italy, the US 2nd Armoured Division reported 54% of its casualties were psychiatric (Belas, 1973).

Research during the Second World War began to focus on personal vulnerability and the extent to which individuals were predisposed to stress reactions. In a study of 346 cases of war neurosis, Hadfield (1942) considered 82% were predisposed and that "constitutional and acquired predisposition" played a significant role in the genesis of such disorders. Sargent & Slater (1940), in a study of war neurosis following the Dunkirk evacuation, agreed that while constitutional factors were important, "men of reasonably sound personality" could also develop neurotic disorders. The importance of premorbid factors in the genesis of PTSD has been a matter of debate ever since.

Since the Second World War a number of studies have demonstrated increased rates of mental illness among service veterans, which in some cases persist for many years (e.g. Archibald & Tuddenham, 1965). In the 1987 US study of veterans (SOV–III; Department of Veterans Affairs, 1989), the overall prevalence of mental health problems in Second World War veterans was 4.8%. Veterans who saw combat were 36% more likely to experience subsequent mental health problems, more likely to be retired or disabled, and more than twice as likely to receive disability pensions and use Veterans Administration (VA) health services than non-combat veterans. In a study of 75 Second World War veterans attending VA hospitals, using structured clinical interviews, 55% received a diagnosis of PTSD (Rosenheck & Fontana, 1994). Among these, 89% experienced the onset of symptoms during the war, the remaining 11% experiencing a delayed onset of symptoms. Considerable comorbidity was noted in the sample: 19% were diagnosed as suffering from anxiety disorders and 41% from affective disorders. Only 5% had alcohol misuse problems and there was no recorded drug misuse.

Battleshock: the acute combat stress reaction

Battleshock, or the acute combat stress reaction (CSR) is an acute situational reaction of anxiety, distancing (numbing, fainting), restlessness, psychomotor retardation, stuttering, withdrawal, nausea, vomiting and disorientation, frequently associated with paranoid ideation and guilt about functioning, accompanied by increased sympathetic nervous system activity (Solomon, 1993).

The experience of recent warfare indicates that approximately a third of all casualties in a conventional war are psychiatric with even higher rates in mass casualty situations. This figure is likely to be considerably inflated in unconventional conflict including urban, guerrilla warfare, or with the use of nuclear, chemical or biological weapons. The additional fear of the invisible and unknown combines with the discomfort and degrading effects on physical performance associated with the use of individual protective equipment (IPE).

Although fear is universal in combat, and indeed may enhance performance, overwhelming fear seriously undermines combat efficiency and may jeopardise the success of an operation and the safety of others. Of a group of 4500 US airmen, all admitted to feeling frightened with accompanying symptoms of somatic anxiety. The majority felt this improved their efficiency, and less than a third felt it impaired it. Only 1% were so disabled that they were unable to fly (Bond, 1952). Anxiety and fear were closely related to perceived danger, and there was a high correlation between the number of aircraft lost during a mission and the number of subsequent psychiatric casualties. Among ground forces, fear during combat is almost universal. Of a group of 277 wounded American combat veterans, 65% reported that they had experienced fear sufficient to interfere seriously with their performance on at least one occasion. Twenty-three per cent said this had happened many times (Stouffer *et al*, 1949). Surveys of numerous battles have shown that many soldiers become 'paralysed' with fear. Only a minority (15–25%) of infantry riflemen actually shoot at available targets, even when they are under intensive attack and about to be overrun, choosing instead to stand their ground without fighting or defending themselves until they are killed (Marshall, 1947). Time takes its toll on the performance of any soldier who remains fully 'combat efficient' for only a limited period (between 10 and 30 days); beyond this all combatants eventually succumb to the effects of stress and the incidence of battleshock dramatically increases (Swank & Marchand, 1946).

Preventing and minimising the effects of battleshock are issues of major importance to the armed forces. Although fear can never be eliminated from the battlefield, steps can be taken to minimise the incidence and impact of battleshock. Numerous studies have demonstrated the vulnerability of soldiers with a significant past psychiatric history and, to a lesser extent, a significant family history of mental illness. Greater efforts could be made to exclude these individuals during recruit selection. The importance of motivation, discipline and training cannot be overemphasised, and raises serious concerns about the effectiveness of 'conscript' servicemen in combat.

Morale has long been recognised by commanders as crucial to combat efficiency and a positive effort to maintain and promote morale pays considerable dividends in minimising combat stress. Although the ingredients of morale are difficult to quantify, observations of returning Spanish Civil War veterans illuminate some of the more important factors: these included belief in war aims (77%), good leadership (49%), effective military training (45%), information on the military situation (38%), *esprit de corps* (28%), hatred of the enemy (21%), and distraction and keeping busy (17%) (Dollard, 1944). During the battle of Guadalcanal in the Second World War, the only factors that predictably boosted morale were the dissemination of accurate, up-to-date information and the 'mail call'.

Does battleshock predispose to PTSD and other long-term psychological sequelae? Solomon & Shavlev (1994) have suggested the occurrence and severity of battleshock is predictive of subsequent PTSD. Of 3553 Israeli soldiers who experienced battleshock, 56% suffered PTSD two years later, compared with only 18% of 235 soldiers who did not suffer a CSR. Of soldiers experiencing a CSR of sufficient severity to prevent them returning to duty, 74% experienced symptoms of PTSD one year later, compared with only 38% of soldiers who experienced a CSR but were returned to duty (Solomon, 1993). Many Israelis have seen service in several wars and evidence suggests that the effects of combat stress are cumulative: soldiers who had experienced battleshock were 57% more likely to experience a further CSR in the next war, 67% if they participated in two wars, and 83% if they participated in three wars.

If there is a clear association between battleshock and subsequent PTSD, can any measures be taken to reduce the incidence of long-term psychiatric sequelae? Battleshock is treated in the field using a system of psychological debriefing according to the principles of proximity (near the point of combat), immediacy (as soon as symptoms become apparent), and expectancy (of a full recovery and rapid return to duty) (PIE). These principles are not new and have been developed from the work of Salmon (1919) and Marshall (1944). Solomon & Benbenishty (1986) reported that only 20% of battleshock casualties treated according to these principles showed evidence of PTSD one year later, compared with 71% of soldiers treated in other ways. However, in a comparison study of debriefing versus no debriefing among a group of body-handlers during the Gulf war, Deahl *et al* (1994*b*) failed to find any effect of debriefing on PTSD symptomatology nine months later, although recipients appeared to value the experience at the time. Further work is clearly needed to demonstrate the efficacy of treatment (Bisson & Deahl, 1994).

The treatment of battleshock raises important ethical questions for military psychiatrists. It is claimed that as many as 90% of battleshock cases can, with appropriate treatment, be returned to normal duties within seven days, a potentially important source of reinforcement to the military. Nevertheless, if the long-term mental health of servicemen is seriously jeopardised by further combat exposure, the medical role of the psychiatrist is called into question. Indeed, it has been argued that the treatment of battleshock is a logistical rather than a medical activity, designed to return servicemen to combat. As such it should be not conducted in field hospitals but in separate facilities (the battleshock recovery unit or BRU) that do not enjoy the protection of the Geneva convention. Further research is needed to clarify these issues, which are of considerable importance for military psychiatrists.

The Korean War

The Korean war was a highly controversial war of containment that claimed more than 55 000 lives. It has been said that "Korean combat veterans, more than Vietnam combat veterans are the forgotten warriors of today" (Rosenheck & Fontana, 1994). Compared with the Second World War, Korean combat veterans were more likely to belong to hispanic or black ethnic minority groups and come from poorer socioeconomic backgrounds. As well as differences between the background of combatants and non-combatants, the nature of combat in Korea itself was also different from the Second World War. The Korean combat veterans were more likely to witness or participate in atrocities or abusive violence. In the US survey of veterans, Korean combat veterans showed significantly poorer social adjustment (e.g. unemployment, divorce, etc.) than their peers who did not participate in combat (Department of Veterans Affairs, 1989). Combatants were 2.5 times more likely to have mental health problems. Only 54 Korean ex-servicemen were studied in the VA survey (Rosenheck & Fontana, 1994), and of these, two-thirds were suffering from PTSD, 37% from affective disorder and 15% from anxiety disorders. Compared with the Second World War, Korean veterans were significantly more likely to have alcohol misuse problems, be divorced and be socially isolated. They were least likely to use the VA health services or receive disability pensions, compared with veterans of either the Second World War or Vietnam.

The Vietnam War

Between 1964 and 1975, 3.14 million US servicemen and women served in Vietnam. Approximately 58 000 died and 300 000 were wounded in what was a highly controversial war which enjoyed at best ambivalent public support. Combat itself was unconventional and many soldiers found themselves fighting a guerrilla army for which they were untrained and ill-prepared. Following the trend of the Korean war, 20% of combatants witnessed atrocities or abusive violence. Vietnam spawned a massive literature from which the concept of PTSD subsequently emerged. Importantly, it ultimately lead to widespread public recognition of the psychological suffering of veterans.

Only a small number of the studies based on Vietnam veterans can be reviewed. Of all US Vietnam veterans, 15.2% (450 000) currently suffer from PTSD (Kulka *et al*, 1990). An additional 11.1% of male and 7.8% of female veterans suffer from 'partial' PTSD. In total, therefore, 830 000 Americans currently suffer at least some symptoms of traumatic stress related to their experience in Vietnam.

The National Vietnam Veterans Readjustment Study (NVVRS; Kulka *et al*, 1988) demonstrated that nearly a third (30.6%) of male theatre veterans (> 960 000) and more than a quarter of female veterans (26.9%) have met full diagnostic criteria for PTSD at some point since returning from Vietnam. There is a strong relationship between PTSD and problems with almost every area of social adjustment, including occupational instability, chronic ill-health and family difficulties (Kulka *et al*, 1988). Studies of Vietnam veterans have identified specific aspects of combat that are most likely to predict post-war psychiatric disorder. These include the duration and intensity of combat exposure, being wounded in battle (disabled veterans are among the highest PTSD risk group), witnessing atrocities and 'grotesque' death. No differences have been found in rates of affective disorder, anxiety states or substance misuse between combat and non-combat veterans; participation in combat was the sole risk factor for PTSD. Interestingly, personal vulnerability factors include a past history of physical or sexual abuse, suggesting that diverse stressors occurring many years apart may cumulatively interact to produce PTSD.

The Second World War, Korea and Vietnam compared

The 1987 US study of veterans demonstrated roughly similar rates of mental illness among veterans of the three conflicts (Department of Veterans Affairs, 1989). Although there were no specific data on PTSD in this study, health status and social adjustment tended to follow trends in the general population for each age group.

The 1988 VA survey studied a help-seeking group of 1900 veterans (Rosenheck & Fontana, 1994). Apart from an increase in abusive violence in Korean and more so in Vietnam veterans, the prevalence of other forms of psychopathology were equivalent between veterans of all three conflicts. PTSD symptoms were similar in all groups and tended to diminish with time. The severity of PTSD was roughly proportional to war zone stress experienced in combat. Vietnam veterans were more likely to use mental health services compared with their Second World War counterparts. In addition they had increased rates of deliberate self-harm and divorce, and tended to be more socially isolated and vocationally unstable. They were also more likely to be involved in antisocial activities. The figures for Korean veterans fell mid-way between the Second World War and Vietnam samples. The study was unable to show whether the data between the three groups reflected differences in the nature of war or whether it simply reflected an age effect and differences in social behaviour between generations.

The Falklands conflict

In the conflict over the Falkland Islands, 237 British servicemen were killed and 777 wounded. The war was brief, the force was professional, motivated and commanded widespread public support. As a result of these factors, few psychiatric casualties were anticipated. Indeed, early observations suggesting PTSD rates as low as 2% (7% of all wounded) seemed to confirm this (Price, 1984).

By 1986, however, numerous press reports had suggested that significant numbers of Falklands veterans were suffering from PTSD and accused the ministry of defence (MoD) of complacency. Jones & Lovett (1987) published a series of case reports and concluded that "the comfortable conclusion that the Falklands war had remarkably few psychiatric casualties is not tenable". O'Brien & Hughes (1991) studied a group of 64 Falklands veterans five years after the conflict, and showed that 22% had the full syndrome of PTSD and 50% had at least some symptoms of PTSD. It is clear that significant numbers of Falklands veterans have suffered long-term psychological disabilities. They now claim, with justification, that in 1982, when Britain sent the task force to the South Atlantic, the extensive American literature on the psychological aftermath of the Vietnam war was already available. In this light the MoD should have been forewarned and prepared for the inevitable psychological casualties and arranged appropriate treatment and aftercare where necessary. The sole Royal Navy psychiatrist despatched to the South Atlantic never set foot on land, and there were no Army psychiatrists included in the task force. Numerous claims for compensation in the civil courts can be expected.

The Gulf War (Operation Desert Storm)

The Gulf War involved 697 000 US troops and 40 000 British servicemen, alongside many other coalition forces. Significant psychiatric casualties following the Gulf conflict would be surprising given that the war was brief, the coalition forces were highly motivated and enjoyed popular public support, the enemy was clearly defined, and the objectives, were, by and large, clear. Nevertheless, some servicemen underwent potentially traumatising experiences and most lived with the threat of chemical and biological warfare. The prevalence of PTSD in a group of 4500 US Gulf veterans was 9%, with an additional 34% reporting significant psychological distress in the months immediately following their return (Rosenheck, 1993). One year later, 19% of veterans complained of moderate or severe family adjustment problems (Figley, 1991) and 40% reported marital discord. Ford *et al* (1993) observed that marital discord was one of the best measures of adjustment. Substance misuse was associated with PTSD symptomatology, and family dysfunction in general was associated with chronicity of PTSD. Soldiers involved in body-handling during the conflict appear to be a particularly high-risk group. Deahl *et al* (1994*b*) found that half of 72 members of the British Army war graves registration team suffered from PTSD symptomatology nine months after the conflict. Like the US studies, substance misuse and relationship difficulties were also noted. Only a minority of these soldiers (18%) sought help. Similarly high rates of morbidity have also been found in US studies of servicemen involved in body-handling and grave registration duties (e.g. McCarroll *et al*, 1993, 1995).

Since it may take time for the development of post-traumatic stress disorders to develop, continued follow-up studies of Gulf War veterans are required (e.g. Southwick *et al*, 1993, 1995).

Following the Gulf war, 43 000 US and more than 400 British Gulf veterans have reported a variety of ailments in what has come to be known as Gulf War syndrome. Symptoms are diverse and apparently unrelated, including myalgias, poor concentration, memory impairment, chronic fatigue, respiratory, cardiac and gastrointestinal complaints and malignancy. In some cases it is claimed that the families of returning servicemen have also been affected. Gulf veterans were exposed to numerous potentially toxic hazards (multiple immunisations, prophylactic medication against the effects of nerve agents, pesticides, dust containing depleted uranium, and fumes from burning oil-wells). Whether a specific syndrome related to Gulf war service exists remains highly controversial and is currently denied by the British MoD. Further investigation of these cases is urgently required, and although some cases are likely to be entirely unrelated to Gulf war service, some may indeed be related to exposure to toxic hazards. Many of the reported symptoms are, however, reminiscent of the neurasthenic symptoms first described in soldiers during the American Civil War. Gulf War syndrome may well include some cases related to combat stress and perhaps will be seen as another failure to learn the lessons of history.

Prisoners of War (POWs)

POWs have been extensively studied and represent a particularly high-risk group for subsequent psychiatric disorder. In a 40-year follow-up study of former Far East POWs, 29% had PTSD (Goldstein *et al*, 1987). A 40-year longitudinal study in the US (Page, 1992) has shown Second World War POWs have suffered 4–5 times higher rates of in-patient psychiatric admissions compared with a group of matched controls. Rates were highest for former Far East POWs who received, in general, particularly harsh and inhumane treatment in captivity. As time went by, early post-release anxiety symptoms diminished and were overtaken by an increase in depressive symptoms. Compared with controls, former POWs had between three and five times the incidence of affective disorder both at 20 and 40-year follow-up. Lifetime PTSD rates are as high as 70%, with current rates at 40 years between 20–40%. POWs who lost more than 35% of their body weight in captivity had the poorest psychiatric outcome.

Despite their persisting symptoms, many former POWs have made an extremely good social adjustment and have gone on to have successful family and working lives. It has been suggested that some POWs use their ordeal as a framework to move towards greater psychological health.

Conclusions

What is perhaps most remarkable about combat experience is the fact that not more servicemen suffer long-term psychological and psychiatric sequelae. It is clear that a variety of factors, including personality, physical fitness, unit morale and motivation, all mitigate against the traumatising effects of combat. Nevertheless, the resilience of so many servicemen is remarkable, and perhaps future research should ask not why combatants break down, but what makes so many resilient in the face of adversity?

As the nature of war changes so the effects of combat on veterans can itself be expected to change in the future. With the increasing international commitment to the United Nations and other peace-keeping operations, servicemen are becoming increasingly removed from their traditional role, potentially placing them under even greater stress. A 'good' war, from the psychiatric point of view, is short, has a well-defined enemy, clear objectives and expectations of the servicemen involved. It also commands the widespread support of public opinion as well as from within the military itself (O'Brien, 1994). Peace-keeping operations are often the antithesis of this, with soldiers going to disparate regions of the world with ambivalent public support, unclear objectives and an ill-defined and often changing enemy. The additional burden of witnessing atrocities, but being powerless to intervene, places a further considerable stress on soldiers who are often ill-prepared and not properly trained for these duties.

PTSD is a disabling and potentially lifelong disorder. Half of former servicemen who develop symptoms of PTSD will have the disorder years later (Green, 1994). The psychological and psychiatric sequelae of service life can be as disabling as any physical handicap, yet because of the stigma of mental illness and the avoidance phenomena associated with PTSD, many ex-servicemen suffer in silence and fail to seek help or discuss their symptoms. To help overcome this reticence, services must be pro-active and include the possibility of outreach facilities.

Any psychiatric assessment of former servicemen with combat experience should include careful questioning for the symptoms of PTSD, which may easily go undetected and result in inappropriate and ineffective treatment. The likelihood of developing PTSD is closely related to the degree of combat exposure. In any suspected case, therefore, the assessment should include a detailed history of combat exposure including duration, intensity, being wounded, perception of personal threat, witnessing deaths and atrocities, body-handling, physical deprivation, perceived responsibility for the death or injury of others, and survivor guilt: all factors associated with an increased risk of PTSD in combat veterans. The presentation of PTSD in former servicemen may be protean and includes a wide range of psychiatric morbidity. Comorbidity frequently exists, and substance misuse, anxiety states and affective disorders as well as changes in personality and various somatic complaints may all mask the underlying symptoms of PTSD. Dissociative states and automatism have also been described as presenting features of traumatic stress, in some cases leading to criminal acts (Bisson, 1993). PTSD results in serious problems readjusting to normal life and may result in marital, family, and more generalised relationship difficulties, occupational instability and a variety of other social problems, such as antisocial and criminal behaviour. Despite the current awareness of PTSD, a recent US study of elderly former POWs showed that 25% had current PTSD that had gone unnoticed in previous psychiatric assessments (Schnurr, 1994). Failure to involve families in a comprehensive 'problem-orientated' treatment plan may further exacerbate the symptoms of PTSD and increase the likelihood of chronicity. The symptoms of PTSD are not static and run a fluctuating course and therefore require longitudinal assessment and regular review.

Unlike other countries, in particular the US and Israel, who have produced most of the current literature on combat stress and PTSD, the British armed forces have been accused of failing to conduct adequate research into combat stress and its sequelae, despite being in an apparently ideal situation to do so. On the battlefield the chaos and unpredictability of war makes research difficult under any circumstances. The military imperative during combat subordinates all other activity (including medicine) to the operational task in hand and winning the battle. In recent years the size of the UK defence medical services, including the psychiatric services, has reduced dramatically. In the absence of an organisation similar to the Department of Veterans Affairs in the US, which provides healthcare to former servicemen, the UK simply does not have the resources available to conduct large-scale research, or indeed provide even comprehensive medical care for service veterans. This is particularly worrying in the light of a recent survey of London homeless vagrants, 25% of whom were service veterans (Randell & Brown, 1994).

The psychopathology and changes in personality and behaviour that may result from war experience may seriously hamper a serviceman's attempts to reintegrate into his family, and into society as a whole. Families themselves become secondary victims if a serviceman fails to seek help. This in turn further exacerbates and reinforces the symptoms of PTSD, establishing a vicious circle of suffering and despair. Without help, former servicemen remain chronically disabled, denied treatment, pension rights and financial compensation to which many are entitled. Combat veterans develop PTSD as a direct result of serving their country. It is the duty of psychiatrists as citizens to serve them, by promoting awareness, diagnosing and effectively treating their disorder.

References

American Psychiatric Association (1952) *Diagnostic and Statistical Manual.* Washington, DC: APA.
—— (1968) *Diagnostic and Statistical Manual* (2nd edn) (DSM–II). Washington, DC: APA.

—— (1980) *Diagnostic and Statistical Manual of Mental Disorders* (3rd edn) (DSM–III). Washington, DC: APA.

Andreassen, N. (1980) Post traumatic stress disorder. In *Comprehensive Textbook of Psychiatry III* vol. 2 (eds H. I. Kaplan, A. M. Freedman & B. T. Sadock). Baltimore: Williams and Wilkins.

Archibald, H. C. & Tuddenham, R. D. (1965) Persistent stress reactions after combat: a 20 year follow up. *Archives of General Psychiatry*, **12**, 475–481.

Baker, R. R. (1989) The military nurse experience in Vietnam: stress and impact. *Journal of Clinical Psychology*, **45**, 736–744.

Belas, R. J. (1973) Combat psychiatry and preventative aspects of mental health. *Journal of the Royal Army Medical Corps*, **119**, 3.

Bisson, J. I. (1993) Automatism and post traumatic stress disorder. *British Journal of Psychiatry*, **163**, 830–832.

—— & Deahl, M. P. (1994) Does psychological debriefing work? *British Journal of Psychiatry*, **165**, 717–720.

Bond, D. D. (1952) *The Love and Fear of Flying*. New York: International Universities Press.

Brend, W. A. (1938) *Traumatic Mental Disorders in Courts of Law*. London: William Heinemann.

Da Costa, J. M. (1871) On irritable heart: a clinical study of a form of functional cardiac disorder following natural disaster. *American Journal of Psychiatry*, **153**, 470–475

Deahl, M. P. (1992) Doctors at war: psychiatry in the Gulf. *Psychiatric Bulletin of the Royal College of Psychiatrists*, **16**, 220–222.

——, Earnshaw, N. M. & Jones, N. (1994*a*) Psychiatry and war: learning lessons from the former Yugoslavia. *British Journal of Psychiatry*, **164**, 441–442.

——, Gillham, A. B., Thomas, J., *et al* (1994*b*) Psychological sequelae following the Gulf war. Factors associated with subsequent morbidity and the effectiveness of psychological debriefing. *British Journal of Psychiatry*, **164**, 60–65.

Department of Veterans Affairs (1989) *1987 Survey of Veterans*. Washington, DC: Department of Veterans Affairs.

Dollard, J. (1944) Fear in Battle. The Infantry Journal (n.p. Washington D.C.).

Figley, C. R. (1991) Gulf war veteran families: struggles on the home front. In *Operation Desert Storm Clinician Packet* (ed. A. Bollinger). Palo Alto, CA: National Centre for PTSD.

Ford, J. D., Shaw, D., Sennhauser, S., *et al* (1993) Psychosocial debriefing after Operation Desert Storm. Marital and family assessment and intervention. *Journal of Social Issues*, **49**, 73–102.

Goldstein, G., Van Kamman, W., Shelley, C., *et al* (1987) Survivors of imprisonment in the Pacific theatre during World War Two. *American Journal of Psychiatry*, **144**, 1210–1213.

Green, B. L. (1994) Long-term consequences of disasters. Paper presented at the NATO conference on Stress, Coping and Disaster in Bonas, France.

Hadfield, J. A. (1942) War neurosis: year in a neuropathic hospital. *Bulletin of War Medicine*, **3**, 31–37.

Jones, G. & Lovett, J. (1987) Delayed psychiatric sequelae among Falklands war veterans. *Journal of the Royal College of General Practitioners*, **37**, 34–35.

Kulka, R. A., Schlenger, W. E., Fairbank, J. A., *et al* (1988) *Contractual Report of Findings from the National Vietnam Veterans Readjustment Study*. Research Triangle Park, North Carolina: Research Triangle Institute.

——, Fairbank, J. A., Hough, R. L., *et al* (1990) *Trauma and the Vietnam Operation: Findings from the National Vietnam Veterans Readjustment Study*. New York: Brunner/Mazel.

McCarroll, J. E., Ursano, R. J. & Fullerton, C. S. (1993) Symptoms of post traumatic stress disorder following recovery of war dead. *American Journal of Psychiatry*, **150**, 1875–1877.

——, —— & —— (1995) Symptoms of PTSD following recovery of war dead: 13–15 month follow-up. *American Journal of Psychiatry*, **152**, 939–941.

Marshall, S. L. A. (1944) *Island Victory*. New York: Penguin Books.

—— (1947) *Men under Fire: the Problem of Battle Command in Future War*. New York: William Morrow & Co.

Mitchell, S. W., Morehouse, C. R. & Keen, W. S. (1864) *Gunshot Wounds and Other Injuries of Nerves*. Philadelphia: Lippincott.

Mott, F. W. (1919) *War Neuroses and Shellshock*. Oxford: Oxford Medical Publications.

North, C. S., Smith, E. M. & Spitznagel, E. L. (1994) Post traumatic stress disorder in victims of a mass shooting. *American Journal of Psychiatry*, **151**, 82–88.

O'Brien, L. S. (1994) What will be the psychiatric consequences of the war in Bosnia? *British Journal of Psychiatry*, **164**, 443–447.

—— & Hughes, S. J. (1991) Symptoms of post traumatic stress disorder in Falklands veterans five years after the conflict. *British Journal of Psychiatry*, **159**, 135–141.

Page, W. F. (1992) *The Health of Former Prisoners of War*. Washington, DC: National Academy Press.

Price, H. H. (1984) The Falklands: rate of British combat casualties compared to recent American wars. *Journal of the Royal Army Medical Corps*, **130**, 109–113.

Randell, G. & Brown, S. (1994) *Falling Out: a Research Study of Homeless Ex-servicemen*. London: Crisis.

Rosenheck, R. (1993) Returning Persian Gulf troops: first year findings. *NCP Clinical Newsletter*, **3**, 18–19.

—— & Fontana, A. (1994) Long term sequelae of combat on World War II, Korea and Vietnam: a comparative study. In *Individual and Community Responses to Trauma and Disaster* (eds R. J. Ursano, B. G. McCaughey & C. S. Fullerton), pp. 330–359. Cambridge: Cambridge University Press.

Salmon, T. W. (1919) The war neuroses and their lesson. *New York State Journal of Medicine*, **59**, 933–944.

Sargent, W. & Slater, E. (1940) Acute war neuroses. *Lancet*, **2**, 1–2.

Schnurr, P. P. (1944) The long term course of PTSD. *Clinical Quarterly*, **4**, 15–16.

Solomon, Z. (1993) *Combat Stress Reaction: The Enduring Toll of War*. New York: Plenum Press.

—— & Benbenishty, R. (1986) The role of proximity, immediacy and expectancy in frontline treatment of combat stress amongst Israelis in the Lebanon war. *American Journal of Psychiatry*, **143**, 613–617.

—— & Shalev, A. Y. (1994) Helping victims of military trauma. In *Traumatic Stress from Theory to Practice* (eds J. R. Freedy & S. E. Hobfoll). New York: Plenum Press.

Southward, E. E. (1919) *Shellshock*. Boston: W.M. Leonard.

Southwick, S. M., Morgan, A., Nagy, L. M., *et al* (1993) Trauma-related symptoms in veterans of Operation Desert Storm: a preliminary report. *American Journal of Psychiatry*, **150**, 1524–1528.

——, ——, Darnell, A., *et al* (1995) Trauma-related symptoms in veterans of Operation Desert Storm: a 2-year follow-up. *American Journal of Psychiatry*, **152**, 1150–1155.

Stouffer, S. A., Lumsdaine, R., Williams, M., *et al* (1949) *The American Soldier: Combat and its Aftermath*. Princeton: Princeton University Press.

Swank, R. L. & Marchand, W. E. (1946) Combat neurosis. Development of combat exhaustion. *Archives of Neurology and Psychiatry*, **55**, 236.

10 The effect of conflict on civilian populations

A. The impact of war and atrocity on civilian populations

DEREK SUMMERFIELD

An epidemiology of conflict

There have been an estimated 160 wars and armed conflicts in the developing world since 1945, with 22 million deaths and three times as many injured (Zwi & Ugalde, 1989). Torture is routine in over 90 countries. In the First World War 5% of all casualties were civilians, 50% in the Second World War, over 80% in the US war in Vietnam, and in present conflicts over 90% (UNICEF, 1986). At present the United Nations High Commission for Refugees counts 18 million refugees who have fled across an international border, a six-fold increase on 1970, but as many again are internally displaced and often no less destitute. This totals one person in 125 of the entire world population; 80% of all war refugees are in developing countries, many among the poorest on earth.

A core element of modern political violence is the creation of states of terror to penetrate the entire fabric of social relations, as well as subjective mental life, as a means of social control. No distinctions are drawn between combatants and civilians and the valued institutions and ways of life of a whole population are routinely targeted. Sexual violation is another endemic feature (Swiss & Giller, 1993). So-called 'low intensity' war, frequently played out on a terrain of subsistence economies, has high-intensity consequences for its victims.

Worldwide, violations of medical neutrality are a consistent feature of conflict. For example, in Nicaragua 300 000 people (15% of the rural population) were left without any healthcare (Garfield & Williams, 1989). In El Salvador surgeons were assassinated in mid-operation by death squads who suspected that they were prepared to treat wounded activists, and in the Philippines 102 health workers were subjected to extrajudicial killing or arbitrary detention by the army or government agents in 1987–1989 (Summerfield, 1992). Hospitals in Croatia and Bosnia have been repeatedly fired upon by Serb forces and patients and staff killed.

Another key dimension of armed conflict is the crushing of the social and cultural institutions which connect a particular people to their history, identity and values. Middle East Watch *et al* (1993) documents that the Iraqi government campaign against their Kurdish population in the 1980s amounted to genocide within the meaning of the Genocide Convention of 1951. This included the use of poison gas – a mixture of mustard and nerve gas – dropped by aircraft.

Specific effects

Relatively little has been documented of the overwhelming majority of survivors who must endure in or near a war-devastated social setting. War, drawing in male combatants and disrupting agriculture and other forms of economic life, brings harsh pressures to bear upon women. In parts of Central America, 50% of households are headed by a woman and these are much more likely to be poor. In some areas of the militarised countryside in Guatemala, up to 80% of children are reported to have some degree of malnutrition. In Africa war and famine formed a malignant combination during the 1980s.

Mortality rates during the acute phase of displacement by war are up to 60 times expected rates. Sixty per cent of refugees in Africa get no assistance, but even those who reach official refugee camps may not escape daily physical hardship or violence. Despite the presence of aid agencies, there have been mass outbreaks of vitamin deficiency diseases – pellagra, scurvy and beri-beri – and thousands of children can die in a measles epidemic in a single camp in a year.

In Brazil people have come to express their physical and emotional responses to violent oppression and poverty through the metaphor of mental disorder ('nervos' or nerves). It is safer to be 'ill' than to name the political factors which make their lives so distressing. Presentations in a somatic idiom are central to the subjective experience and communication of the distress wrought by war and its upheavals. Most common are variously described headaches, non-specific bodily pains, chest or abdominal discomfort, dizziness, weakness and fatiguability. This does not mean that these subjects do not have psychological insights, but that somatic complaints often reflect what they view as the elements of illness relevant to a medical setting (Lin *et al*, 1985). Some researchers see somatic complaints as stress-driven physiological responses; others emphasise that they are the only available expressions of the collective distress of powerless and persecuted people denied a social validation of their suffering and humanity (Farias, 1991). In Nicaragua, terrorised rural peasants often expressed themselves in a mixed somatopsychological idiom: for example, "there is a sadness in my body" and "my blood is frightened".

The standard literature has described war refugees in terms of vulnerability to depression, anxiety, marital and intergenerational tension, antisocial behaviour (including violence against women), alcohol misuse and paranoid psychosis. Those at extra risk are: households headed by an unprotected woman, often widowed; those without a community or marginalised in an alien culture; those at serious socio-economic disadvantage or in frank poverty; those with poor physical health or disability. This group includes those mutilated by landmines.

The emotional well-being of children remains reasonably intact for as long as their parents, or other significant figures, can absorb the continuing pressures of the situation (see chapter 10C). Once parents can no longer cope, day-to-day care breaks down, child well-being deteriorates rapidly and infant mortality rates rise (Richman, 1993). Orphaned or otherwise unprotected children face significant extra risks.

The elderly are also at risk, as described in chapter 12, although they have been little studied. The upheavals of war expose their relative physical frailty, diminished capacity for work and vulnerability to loss of social status. In a rare study of older adults displaced by war and famine in Ethiopia, over half of those over 60 years of age had to be left behind by their families, mostly to die (Godfrey & Kalache, 1989).

Recent trauma literature is mostly based on the tiny minority of survivors, particularly from Indo-China and Latin America, who reach North America or western Europe. Subjects presented clinically and there is a lack of non-helpseeking comparison groups. Western diagnostic classifications are problematic when applied to diverse non-Western survivor populations. The view of trauma as an individual-centred event bound to soma or psyche is in line with the tradition in this century for both Western biomedicine and psychoanalysis to regard the singular human being as the basic unit of study. At source is the Western scientific approach to knowledge, positivist and empiricist: facts are unearthed rather than constructed.

However, a checklist of mental state features cannot provide a rigorous distinction between subjective distress and objective disorder. Much of the distress experienced and communicated by victims of extreme trauma is normal, even adaptive, and will be coloured by active interpretations and choices. Signs and symptoms can be identified in different social settings, but may have differing meanings. This is what Kleinman (1987) called a category fallacy. Thus, to one man, recurrent violent nightmares might be an irrelevance, revealed only through direct questioning; to another it might indicate a need to visit a medical clinic; to a third it might represent a helpful message from ancestors.

PTSD prevalences of 14–50% have been found in various studies of survivor populations in both Third World and Western settings, generally with concurrent higher prevalence of major depression (50–70%). However, sufferers often have good social and work function. A community sample of war-displaced rural peasants in Nicaragua, all survivors of atrocities, demonstrated many PTSD features, yet subjects themselves were not attending to these symptoms. They were fearful, grieving and wearied but not psychiatric casualties; they were active and effective in maintaining their social world as best they could in the face of poverty and the continuing threat of further attacks. In this context, PTSD "symptoms" such as hypervigilance could be lifesaving (Summerfield & Toser, 1991). Three-quarters of injured ex-soldiers in the same country with diagnosable PTSD were basically well-adjusted and functioning unremarkably (Hume & Summerfield, 1994). Thus, a diagnosis of PTSD is poorly predictive of capacity to function, nor a reliable indicator of a need for psychological treatment.

Long-term effects

Eitinger & Strom (1973) studied Norwegian survivors of Nazi concentration camps through to the early 1970s. They found that subjects, matched with a control group, maintained higher than expected mortality and morbidity rates over three decades. They had significantly more tuberculosis, neurosis, alcohol and drug misuse, and also less successful work lives, more time on sick leave, and more and longer hospital admissions. Elsewhere there has been considerable attention given to the possibility of transgenerational transmission of effects to the children and grandchildren of Jewish Holocaust survivors. In a review of the literature, Solkoff (1992) noted that psychoanalytically oriented studies tended to support this conclusion, but that community-based research did not bear it out. There are little or no empirical data on long-term effects in developing world settings.

Trauma as collective experience

Western debate about experiences like torture or rape has focused on the psychological effects of what is seen as an extreme violation of individual integrity and identity. This is in line with the Western view of the individual as the basic – and autonomous – unit of society, and that our psychological nature is closer to our essence than are our social or religious ones. But non-Western peoples have different notions of the self in relation to others, and the maintenance of harmonious relations within a family and community is generally given more significance than an individual's own thoughts, emotions and aspirations. The cultural emphasis is on dependency and interdependency rather than the autonomy and individuation on which many Western ideas about mental injury are predicated. When conflict routinely involves the terrorisation or destruction of whole communities, even survivors of individual acts of brutality are likely to register their wounds as social rather than psychological.

Suffering is at the centre of the social order and in this sense is 'normal'. Violent conflict is part of social experience and memory (Davis, 1992). We should not assume that the stresses of war are necessarily discontinuous with those arising from other sources of social destabilisation. Development benefiting only an economic and military elite, unbridled exploitation of natural resources, chaotic urbanisation and the plight of impoverished, landless peasants is linked to the withering away of many traditional self-sufficient ways of life. Victimised social groups may find what has happened incomprehensible and their traditional recipes for handling crisis useless. Meaninglessness leaves people feeling helpless and uncertain what to do. When important structures are targeted – community organisations, trade unions, health and educational institutions, religious leadership – the social fabric may no longer be able to perform its customary role, so that socially managed mourning and adaptation is difficult. Such effects may be planned as psychological warfare, creating a situation where it is impossible to mourn and honour properly the murdered and disappeared, reinforcing isolation and mistrust.

Diverse ideologies and identities govern the repertoire of explanations, beliefs and ceremonies available to particular peoples. For example, in Cambodia the word for torture derives from the Buddhist term for karma, an individual's thoughts and actions (often bad) in a prior existence which affect life in the present. Survivors may feel responsible for their suffering (Mollica & Caspi-Yavin, 1992). In Mozambique guerrillas and government forces sought to heighten the impact of their military efforts by incorporating traditional sources of ritual power – ancestors' spirits and myths of male invincibility, including ceremonies conferring 'vaccination' against bullets. The rural peasantry did the same thing to bolster their capacity to resist, so that a war driven by old South Africa's destabilisation policies has been imbued by local understandings and world views, becoming in part a "war of the spirits" (Wilson, 1992). Spiritual revitalisation and other cultural shifts may outlast such wars, with as yet unknown effects upon the social order.

Refugeedom in a country with a distinctly different culture brings other variables to bear. For example, torture has been endemic in Turkey and is well enough understood, but not all ill-treatment there is considered torture by everyone. Kurdish men are routinely assaulted during interrogation in police stations, including beatings on the soles of the feet (*falaka*). Such treatment is part of the victimisation of this persecuted ethnic group, but also of their capacity to endure and resist. When some finally seek refuge in the West, they can find their experiences reconstructed *in toto* as torture. With this comes Western ideas of hapless victimhood, and of exquisite and enduring individual mental injury, to which they would not have subscribed back home. The impact of this on their attitude to themselves, on their capacity to feel whole and effective, has not yet been studied.

Fifty years ago, at Auschwitz, those incarcerated as communists rather than as Jews could draw on their political ideals to better withstand what was happening to them (Bettelheim, 1960). The most telling recent evidence of this kind has emerged from a secret military prison, Tazmamart, in Morocco. For 18 years, 59 men were held incommunicado and in almost complete darkness in small single cells which they never left. They were exposed to extremes of temperature, poor food, little water and no medical care. They were split between two separated wings of equal size. In one wing, where prisoners had structured their time with joint activities from their cells, including recitations from memory from the Koran, 24 survived. However, in the second wing, where this did not happen and there was always chaotic argument and tension, only four survived (Van Ginneken & Rijnders, 1993). The capacity to draw on social or religious ideals, and on cooperative effort and solidarity, can bolster psychological and physical defences in even the most extreme situation. My clinical practice in London with survivors of torture bears this out regularly: former activists seem less likely than others to continue to be painfully plagued by the question "Why me?".

It is simplistic to see those exposed to political violence only as helpless victims, unable to act on their environment. Violent crises constitute positive challenges for some, even if they expect to suffer. Children, too, are active citizens with values and causes. For example, in Gaza, strong identification with the aspirations of Palestinian nationhood seemed to offer psychological protection to children facing high levels of violence from the Israeli army. The more they were exposed to political hardship the more they deployed active and courageous coping modes (Punamaki & Suleiman, 1990). This did not mean they did not also suffer from fear, grief, nightmares and bedwetting.

The attitudes and responses of people in adversity may change as circumstances change: some are sustained by pride in sacrifice; some are later sufficiently disappointed by post-war events to abandon the sense of having suffered in a good cause and to fear it was in vain. Public acknowledgement of the cost of struggle towards an egalitarian society or in war assists those who have suffered. US Vietnam war veterans returned to find that their nation, and even their families, had disowned their own guilt, blaming them. Feelings of shame, guilt, betrayal and a sense of wasted sacrifice continued their trauma. In contrast, British Falklands war veterans came home to national acclaim for an honourable job well done (Summerfield & Hume, 1993).

Some implications for interventions

Analysis of human agency in the context of violence, terror and social upheaval is complex, and psychological insights in one setting will not necessarily carry over to another. From one culture to another, local traditions and points of view give rise to psychological knowledge and the paradigms guiding the interpretation and collection of psychological material; there is more than one true description of the world. The taxonomies of Cambodian traditional healers, for example, range across the physical, supernatural and moral realms, and are at odds with the linear causal thought of Western practitioners. The dominance of Western psychological concepts and practices, accompanying the global diffusion of Western culture, risks perpetuating the colonial status of the Third World mind (Berry *et al*, 1992). Even the 'new' cross-cultural psychiatry, which recognises the ethnocentricity of Western categories of mental disorder and seeks to understand people from non-Western cultures in their own terms, must grapple with the core conundra: are there shared features which unite all mankind? How can one culture be made truly intelligible to another? (Skultans, 1991).

It would be unfortunate if the experiences of non-Western survivors and the silence of those left speechless by what they have witnessed were transmuted only into the words of Western professionals, and suffering routinely reframed as psychological distress or disorder. Professional compassion, allied to psychological models which can construe an inappropriate sick role, may confirm their humiliation.

Socially constructed meanings and attributions are central to the way individuals register, elaborate and communicate traumatic events, and what they do about them. Psychological trauma is not like physical trauma; people do not passively register the impact as, for example, a leg registers a bullet, but engage in a social and problem-solving way. It is important that health workers do not see trauma only as a static isolatable entity lodged within the psychology of a victimised individual. Research must try to delineate the relative contribution of pre- and post-flight traumas to the overall burdens that a particular set of refugees are carrying, and to outcomes.

The millions who remain in or near the war-torn areas of their country are the overwhelming majority. We have only sketchy knowledge of baseline prevalence of mental disorders in developing world societies, let alone during turmoil. We need to know more about traditional coping patterns mobilised at a time of crisis in a particular society, and what ensues when these too are engulfed by the conflict on the ground. The narratives of survivors can give a graphic illustration of their experiences, and also insight into the psychological processes brought to bear on them (Ager, 1993). A body of indigenous writings about these questions does exist, but is rarely translated into Western languages or published in major journals (Baker, 1992). The central question is perhaps not so much how or why individuals become psychosocial casualties, but how or why the vast majority do not, the study of survivors rather than victims. This knowledge, which could better inform interventions for war-affected peoples and prevent some negative psychological consequences, is not yet being reflected in programme and policy initiatives (McCallin, 1996).

The victims of Nazi Germany have been the only population studied concerning the long-term consequences of war, atrocity and social upheaval. Tracing outcomes over time is not simple, since variables extend beyond individual subjects. Those who emerged alive in 1945 mostly sought to rebuild their social and work lives and put their traumas behind them. Most did not seek, nor were offered, psychological help, and post-war societies did not see them as carrying a permanent psychological wound. But public definitions of what constitutes health are not static. Today's trauma victims are commonly held to have a kind of life sentence and to merit psychological treatment to moderate the damage. Socially held beliefs about trauma outcomes will influence individual victims, shaping what they feel has been done to them, whether or how they seek help and their expectations of recovery. Research into long-term effects must take account of the way these social constructions of trauma change over time, and from one setting to another.

From the human rights perspective, moral outrage pushes us to recognise victims, but it would be an affront to the uncounted millions who reassemble their lives afterwards to assume that they are intrinsically damaged human beings who cannot but hand this on to their children. The question of transgenerational effects in survivor populations remains open. Closer working alliances between the mental health field and other disciplines – anthropologists, sociologists, historians and political economists – would afford the best chance of a more richly textured understanding of the range of human responses to extreme violence and their determinants.

Mental health is not generally a thing apart, and therapeutic interventions do not necessarily have to be 'psychological'. War-affected peoples make determined efforts to preserve what they can of their culture and way of life, since these embody what it means to be human and civilised. Collective recovery over time will be fundamentally linked to the bolstering or rebuilding of social and economic networks and ways of life; herein lie the sources of resilience for adults and children alike. Interventions should be directed to the damaged social fabric, guided by the expressed priorities of the communities in each case. These will include health and education services.

Human rights and social justice: the role of advocacy

Some victims of political violence seek psychological help but all of them want justice. History has shown that social reform is the best medicine: can health professionals go beyond the 'binding of wounds' to promote the wider rights of victimised and persecuted groups? It is an ethical imperative that a human rights framework informs the way those in the trauma field address their patients, colleagues and the wider public. There are too few studies that 'bridge' individual psychological responses and the sociopolitical dynamics of marginalisation and persecution.

If prevention is to be as important as cure, there must be as much rigour in the analysis of the causes of massive trauma as of its effects. Much political violence is rooted in gross social inequities. Most victims are the poor and those who speak for them, or members of persecuted ethnic minorities with few advocates in the West. The Western political and economic order tacitly insists that issues of social justice and human rights should not seriously influence the alliances they make in the developing world. Regimes serving Western geopolitical interests provoke mere routine denunciations when they murder or torture their citizens. The most sophisticated technology passing from rich to poor nations is in arms sales, weaponry which is wielded by entrenched elites against the deprived masses of their own societies. Average expenditure per capita on arms in the developing world is US$98, compared with US$12 on health (Siward, 1989).

Relatively empowered and unpersecuted professionals are in a position to publicise the human costs of these philosophies. Local human rights organisations need to be helped to publish their findings; the solidarity of colleagues abroad offers activists some protection against elimination by the state. The testimonies they collect can provide for a more complete counting of the human costs of exposure to extreme violence.

Allied to this is the vital question of official reparation for human rights crimes. Victims may more easily become survivors if some part of the legacy of the past can be addressed, preferably in an official form, such as a war crimes tribunal or financial compensation. After the Second World War Germany apologised to its victims (and has continued to do so) and made financial restitution. It is possible that Japan, which has yet to do this or to give an open account in history books read by its own children, has left its victims with greater tasks in personal adjustment and acceptance. Investigation of past human rights offences is an essential feature of democratic civilian government.

B.   Civil violence

GERARD LOUGHREY

Civil violence, such as that within Northern Ireland, has essentially taken two forms: firstly, rioting and general civil disorder with marked social displacement, then episodes of lethal shooting and bombing incidents set against a background of chronic community tension. The first phase occurred principally in the late 1960s and early 1970s and was similar to, and virtually coincident with, civil disorder in the US, featuring 'race riots' and also other social upheavals. The second phase, lasting more than 20 years, is similar to the urban crime experience in some US cities, and has also coincided with sporadic incidents in England.

Civil violence features many of the stresses encountered elsewhere, but where conflict engulfs an entire population, violence and trauma are not only experienced directly, but also vicariously through social contacts, the media and so on, in such a way as to broaden the range of vulnerable people. This psychological process is, of course, the principal goal of terrorism.

The study of the effects of civil violence allows comparison of the effects of various kinds of stress, such as the influence of social changes and the impact of civil violence on mental health services. Some of the most interesting insights are sociological and the concept of PTSD has been useful, enabling analysis of hospital referral patterns and community studies.

Studies of hospital referral rates are bedevilled by the impact of civil violence on mental health service provision. However, in Northern Ireland these have been largely maintained. Two separate studies (Fraser, 1971; Lyons, 1971) concluded that the impact was slight. Lyons (1971) found no increase in referral of mental health problems to specialist mental health services, nor to general practitioners. Fraser (1971) found no difference in referral patterns between areas which were severely affected by civil violence and those less severely affected. These findings have been mirrored elsewhere. Fishbain *et al* (1991) studied the impact on the local psychiatric emergency service of a riot in a black area of Miami in 1980, over a 12-week cycle before and after a three-day outbreak of violence which led to 16 deaths, 40 admissions to hospital and 35 major surgical procedures. They found no evidence that the riot had a significant effect.

Nasr *et al* (1983) studied the impact of an outbreak of civil violence in the Lebanon in the mid 1970s, and found a decrease both in referrals to clinics and admissions to hospital. However, in the aftermath there did seem to be a rebound increase in referrals. After a week of rioting in Kuala Lumpur in 1969, Tan & Simons (1973) found an increase in referrals over the next six months, but no increased demand on beds. Admissions actually fell in Baltimore after four days of rioting in 1968 (Klee & Gorwitz, 1970), and Mira (1939), the Chief Inspector to the Spanish Republican Army, reported that there was no increase in the need for beds during the Spanish Civil War.

The conclusion from these data is that, perhaps surprisingly, civil conflict has little immediate impact on mental health services, with perhaps some rebound increase in the aftermath, either because services are disrupted or because reactions may be delayed. It is important when looking at reports of the impact on services to pay attention to the time period studied.

Demand on conventional mental health services is a crude measure, as most traumatised people choose not to go to them and because the effect on those who are already suffering mental health problems is disproportional. A reluctance by the more severely ill disaster victims to use services has been reported both in Europe (Weisaeth, 1989) and the US (Schwarz & Kowalski, 1992). In the latter study, which followed up adult victims of a school shooting over an 18-month period, non-participation in treatment was associated with avoidance-type symptoms and generally increased levels of psychological distress at the initial assessment. This led the authors to invoke the concept of 'malignant memories' which are re-awakened by entry into treatment, and avoided by non-compliance. This concept was acknowledged as perhaps speculative, requiring replication.

As for the already ill, Mira (1939) commented:

> "I had the impression that many depressed and other mentally ill people were better when confronted with the actual demands and situations that arose during the war than when they were concerned only with their conflicts."

The anecdotal account by Ierodiakonou (1970) of 14 patients in long-term therapy at the time of the outbreak of the Cyprus civil war was that four felt more insecure and fearful, whereas ten felt more calm, actually reporting increased self-confidence with a compensatory optimism, hoping that war would change them for the better. The conclusion from this would be that a proportion of those who are already mentally ill will improve, at least superficially, when they can contribute their symptoms to an external cause. One should also bear in mind the effects of the social environment on neurotic symptoms.

The use of psychotropic drugs has been studied by King *et al* (1982), who analysed drug prescribing in Northern Ireland from 1966 until 1980. Although drug use was high, increasing during the years of greatest civil violence, there was no clear evidence that the trend towards an increase in rates of prescribing was any different from that in other European countries.

The immediate impact of conflict has been mainly on surgical services, although attempts have been made to estimate the early prevalence of psychological morbidity. Findings vary widely, from "emotional shock" in 24 of 160 victims of the Old Bailey bomb explosion (Caro & Irving, 1973), to "psychological disturbance" in 50% of the patients of Hadden *et al* (1978) in a Northern Ireland sample of bomb victims. Masking of psychological symptoms in the aftermath may lead to an underestimation of prevalence. Kennedy & Johnston (1975) speak graphically of the "bilateral amputee [who remains] calm, co-operative and stoical in the protective hospital environment, only to break down on discharge from hospital". Curran *et al*

(1990) found evidence of a latency period before presentation by the more severely injured victims of a large bomb in Enniskillen, Northern Ireland.

In the Lebanon, Hourani *et al* (1986) carried out a study of almost 6000 civilians, of whom just over half had been displaced, during an outbreak of violence in 1982. They used a rather crude measure of mental health, a symptom checklist; the most frequently endorsed items were those reflecting irritability and sleep disturbance. They found a relatively low level of mental health problems, in that only 8% reported at least one or more items of unusual or inappropriate behaviour. There were significantly higher levels where the war trauma had been associated with loss of physical health, loss of income and loss of home. In their analysis of those displaced, it was postulated that those who had suddenly acquired refugee status were disproportionately at risk, compared with those groups who had been repeatedly displaced, who may have been habituated to the stress, or those who had been acutely displaced, but were perhaps still buoyed by the increased social integration in the aftermath of the violence.

Within Northern Ireland, Cairns & Wilson (1985) have been engaged for a number of years in a detailed analysis of the interactions between the incidence of violence and perception of violence and levels of psychological morbidity. In their first study, they compared two towns, 'Hitown', with a high level of political violence, and 'Lotown', with a low level. In addition to higher levels of civil violence, Hitown also had various other socio-economic disadvantages. The General Health Questionnaire (GHQ) caseness in Hitown was 32%, as opposed to 21% in Lotown: a statistically significant difference. A three-way analysis of covariance for actual town, the respondent's sex and his/her perception of town violence showed that in Hitown, but not in Lotown, a perception of violence was associated with an elevated GHQ score. Even then, 85% of the respondents in Hitown perceived the level of violence as "at worst only a little", indicating that denial of violence is a significant factor.

Breslau, Davis and colleagues (Breslau *et al*, 1991; Breslau & Davis, 1992) reported on the prevalence of post-traumatic stress disorder in an urban population of young adults in Detroit. They found that, of the sample of 1007 young adults, 394 (39.1%) had been exposed to traumatic events of a type or a severity that the authors judged fitted the stressor criterion of PTSD. The most frequent stresses were a sudden injury or serious accident, physical assault, seeing someone seriously hurt or killed, or the news of sudden death or injury of a close relative or friend, and threat to one's life. All these were reported by more than 2.5% of the population. Rape was reported by 16, or 1.6% of the population. The rates of PTSD after these incidents were broadly similar, with the exception of the rate of PTSD after rape, at 80%. For the rest, the rate of PTSD after exposure to traumatic stress was nearly 24%. The stresses enumerated are similar to those experienced in a civil violence scenario, and the incidence of PTSD is similar to figures found by Loughrey *et al* (1988) in a retrospective study of PTSD and civil violence in Northern Ireland. This study found that PTSD occurred in 116 (23.2%) of 499 victims.

They also found that exposure to stress was not random, in that male sex, absence of a college education, a history of three or more early conduct problems and a family history of psychiatric illness, were all associated with an increased risk of exposure. The risk factors for PTSD after exposure to trauma included female sex, a history of neuroticism, early separation, pre-existing anxiety or depression, and a family history of anxiety or antisocial behaviour. These findings would be broadly consistent with clinical experience in Northern Ireland, in that exposure to civil violence does vary greatly according to different populations and geographical areas. Whereas overwhelming stress is generally held to be of overriding significance, most of the stresses encountered in civil violence are such as to allow the impact of vulnerability factors, such as pre-existing symptomatology, background problems, social support or enforced relocation, to be identified. This study also identified high rates of other illnesses, notably anxiety and affective disorders.

The authors found that, among the study group, the median duration of PTSD was one year. Chronic PTSD, lasting more than one year, was associated with higher levels of comorbidity, and with various self-reported medical conditions. They commented that war trauma is associated with moral complexities. Civil violence also has complex meaning; political background, the breakdown of social order, and the effects of terrorisation transcend single events individually experienced.

The literature on drug treatment of PTSD suggests that the outcome of PTSD after war stress is much worse than after other more acute events. Davidson *et al* (1990) found no effect of amitriptyline on PTSD in 46 war veterans with a chronic illness. Elsewhere, the response to treatment with tricyclic antidepressants or monoamine oxidase inhibitors (MAOIs) has been reported to be good (see chapter 19).

There has been a long-recognised association between PTSD and suicide and suicidal behaviour. In Northern Ireland, Lyons (1972) reported a decreased rate of suicide in the early years of the civil violence. Curran *et al* (1988) noted an increased rate of suicide in recent years, postulating that other factors, notably the availability of firearms, may play a part.

Durkheim (1951) studied suicide in Europe at a time of civil violence and social upheaval. There was a reduction in the rates of suicide in those countries affected by civil violence. Whereas Lyons opted for the intra-psychic explanation of civil violence affording the opportunity to externalise aggressive impulses which would otherwise be turned on the self, Durkheim looked to social factors and stated:

> "These facts are therefore susceptible of only one interpretation; namely, that great social disturbances and great popular wars rouse collective sentiments, stimulate partisan spirit and patriotism, political and national faith, alike, and concentrating activity on a single end, at least temporarily cause a stronger integration of society. The salutary influence which we have just shown to exist is not due to the crisis, but to the struggles that it occasions. As they force men to close ranks and confront the common danger, the individual thinks less of himself and more of the common cause."

This powerful description was virtually recapitulated by a study of American riots in the 1960s (Greenley *et al*, 1975). Sears & MacConaghy (1969), studying riots in Watts, Los Angeles, noted that while 15% of the population were actually involved directly, a further 30% were involved vicariously, reported to be close spectators and sympathetic to the rioters. In a review paper, Fogelson (1970) noted that, during the American 1960s riots, the "outpouring of fellow feeling, of mutual respect and common concern . . . camaraderie . . . carnival spirit . . . exhilaration so intense as to border on jubilation . . . a sense of pride, purpose and accomplishment . . . their common predicament revealed in the rioting, blacks looked again at one another and saw only brother".

The literature on the psychiatric effects of civil violence is therefore consistent, despite the differences in the nature of the civil violence, the population studied, and the historical and political context of the violence. Taken as a whole, there seems to be only limited impact on mental health services and, while, to a degree, this may be attributed to the reluctance of trauma victims to identify themselves as psychiatric cases and to seek help, reports from community studies indicate that other factors play a part.

While it seems reasonable to conclude that a minority of people with severe psychological trauma are profoundly affected, are subject to chronic PTSD and may indeed be difficult to identify or treat, for the majority of the population certain factors, such as increased social cohesion, attribution factors, denial and habituation, militate against very severe psychiatric outcomes. Even when the standard measure of outcome severity, namely PTSD, is identified, the course of this condition may not be malignant, as extrapolation from the large body of work on war veterans might suggest. Where there is severe physical injury or social displacement one may look for comparisons with combat trauma. However, clinical experience suggests that research on victims of violent crime, which points to the significant importance of vulnerability factors, may be more relevant.

Further research on the psychiatric effects of civil conflict is likely to continue to rely on the opportunistic use of ongoing epidemiological studies where civil violence happens to break out, plus retrospective studies with their various flaws. It is essential to attempt to identify other areas of study, such as those of disaster or crime victims, which allow useful comparisons. Interpretation of findings is likely to pay increasing heed to the complexity of the trauma and the need to be aware of, and if possible to quantify, the non-random nature of civil violence-related trauma.

C.   Children and conflict

ANULA NIKAPOTA

Terrorism, war and oppressive political regimes have effects on children which depend on the type of conflict, the level of disruption and the context. Parents may be victims or aggressors, children victims themselves, combatants or participants. Impact may be assessed during conflict or after there has been some form of resolution or cessation of hostilities. Children may be within their community, displaced or refugees.

It is difficult to study the impact of organised violence during hostilities as, particularly in protracted civil war situations, access to groups such as child combatants may be impossible and there are also methodological limitations of current instruments (Richman, 1993).

This section focuses on organised violence. Interactions between actual experiences, individual characteristics such as gender, age, development and temperament, which influence the capacity to cope, family and social support, social, political and economic context, the material and ideological structure of society require exploration in relation to child populations.

Children in civil war experience killing as attack, mutilation, seeing the killing of family or friends, kidnapping or conscription, whereas those under an oppressive political regime experience killing and detention, as well as discrimination organised by civil authorities. A report by UNICEF (1989) also emphasised common features such as the widespread impact on children of malnutrition, physical morbidity or disablement, disruption of social and community life and multiple deprivations irrespective of ideology or type of conflict.

The focus is not on diagnosis or symptoms specifically, but on the meaning and effects of conflict in relation to the child. In this it resembles accepted multiaxial approaches to the classification of child psychiatric disorders.

Emotional and behavioural responses to conflict-related experience

Children do experience PTSD reactions (Yule, 1994). Some recent studies have focused on children's reactions to attack, for example by SCUD missiles during the Gulf war (Schwarzwald *et al*, 1993), or exposure to an episode of terrorist activity (Frazer, 1974). Others have looked at children's reactions and experiences in war settings or soon after cessation of hostilities in diverse sites, confirming features of PTSD in children, the severity of symptoms relating usually to the degree of trauma experienced. Children may be exposed repeatedly to conflict-related traumas (Punamaki, 1983; Arroyo & Eth, 1985; Chimienti *et al*, 1989; Richman *et al*, 1989) and predominant symptomatology may vary accordingly. Grief and depressive features may predominate in children coping with significant losses, such as family, home, mutilation or rape (Kaffman & Elizur, 1984), and there may be more somatisation in some cultural settings (Abu-Hein *et al*, 1993).

Studies have been undertaken on the variety and numbers of traumas that wars inflict on children, including the death (which may be witnessed) of family or friends, torture, rape, exposure to bombardment, shelling, terrorist activity, coping with witnessing parental fears, separation from or loss of family, displacement and refugee status, extreme poverty, and participation as combatants. Feelings of hopelessness and uncertainty about survival persist, and exposure to such traumas may result in significant psychological impairment. The development of culture-specific trauma profiles may allow the impact of trauma to be better understood (Macksoud *et al*, 1993).

The persistence of PTSD symptomatology may indicate children at long-term risk, yet the diagnosis does not indicate the extent to which children have understood their situation, nor the degree of associated functional impairment (Richman, 1993). Symptoms such as fearfulness or hyper-vigilance may sometimes be appropriate for monitoring threat and hence for survival (Richman, 1993; Pynoos, 1993).

Increased attachment behaviour towards parents or siblings and separation anxiety may be part of a child's reaction to trauma. Children who had experienced terrorist attack refused to leave their mothers to attend pre-school, fearing that mother or teacher would run away and leave them at risk. This is a survival strategy when risk continues, but a maladaptive response when the threat is over.

Case example
A 10-year-old girl was at school, as was her 12-year-old brother, when their home was destroyed by bombing during military action and her parents killed. The children moved to live with an aunt in an area subject to terrorist attack. One year later this girl, who was exhibiting a number of PTSD features, was still refusing to attend school. She would leave the house only with her brother.

High-risk groups can be identified in relation to the degree of psychiatric morbidity or in terms of specific situations. Any child exposed to war-related trauma is at risk, and factors relevant to children are the same as those described earlier in this chapter.

Some factors are of particular relevance to children. Displacement, with loss of family links, is a high-risk bereavement. The needs of orphaned or unaccompanied children for maintenance of links with existing family and familiar community should be remembered immediately and in the longer term (Ressler *et al*, 1988). Children are often exposed to threat and abuse due to lack of care.

Torture and mutilation

Anecdotal information from interviews with children and young people, as well as comment from other sources (Macksoud *et al*, 1993; Richman, 1993), suggests that children who have experienced torture and mutilation may be among those displaying severe distress, anger, hostility and high rates of somatisation. Studies of refugee children, as in, for example, one recent Swedish study on children from Chile (Hjern *et al*, 1991), and another study in Hong Kong studying Vietnamese children (Tsoi *et al*, 1986), describe the significantly higher prevalence of PTSD-type symptoms in persecuted refugee children.

The child combatant

Age and gender contribute to risk, conscription as combatants being more likely for boys. Child combatants may show violent, aggressive behaviour patterns, and guilt and depression when active involvement ceases. Variables that affect their later function (Richman, 1993) may depend more on the ideology and morality of their group and on their experiences rather than the age at which they were conscripted. Children inducted into fighting and trained to commit atrocities by initial brutalisation may be at higher risk of later dysfunction than those who voluntarily joined guerrilla armies. While not systematically brutalised to the same extent, these children nevertheless have few experiences to help them adapt to normal life and peacetime activities (Centre on War and the Child, 1987, 1989).

Factors contributory to coping and adjustment

These are no different to those identified in general for acute and chronic stresses (Garmezy & Rutter, 1985; Pynoos, 1993; Garmezy & Marsten, 1994). Developmental competency, temperament, self-esteem, quality of previous experiences, prior psychopathology, attachments, as well as support from family and social structures such as school, are all relevant.

Young children are particularly vulnerable to the impact of poor physical health and malnutrition, which make an impact on psychosocial and cognitive development. This is relevant to the assessment of resilience and adjustment. Evidence on the probable impact is already available, for example, in a recent study in Kenya. The importance of health and nutrition to the psychosocial well-being of children in developing countries has been reviewed (Minde & Nikapota, 1993). Lack of education is associated with poverty and is created by conflict. Large-scale destruction of schools and massacre of teachers may occur in civil war. Closure of schools is used as one means of controlling terrorist or rebel activity. Family distress or coping is consistently found to affect significantly the response of younger children to conflict (Frazer, 1974; Chimienti & Abu-Nasr, 1992–93). Parental depression in Lebanon correlated with war experiences, and maternal depression was the best predictor of child morbidity (Bryce *et al*, 1989). The previous quality of family relationships is relevant (Kinzie, 1993).

The erosion of traditional values has been noted in many conflict situations. Parents find they have lost their authority over their children, who disobey and may even threaten their parents with reprisal. Parents are dismayed and disempowered at the role reversal and flouting of traditional authority (Arafat, 1990; Reynolds, 1990).

Studies have attempted to delineate the impact on children and adolescents growing up in societies where conflict results in chronic adversity. Available evidence indicates that young people directly involved in active opposition, or those detained and persecuted, are most at risk of continuing risk-taking, antisocial and aggressive behaviour, especially if they were exposed to other adverse experiences and deprivation (Arafat, 1990; Straker, 1992). Older children and those developmentally more competent are more aware of the reasons for their situation and better able to appreciate the threat and the implication that one's own side is good, the other bad. This leads to difficulties in accepting and adjusting to traditional norms and values, especially where violence was initially socially sanctioned and approved. Adjustment will be a new experience, not a welcome return to normality.

Research

Research that focuses on defined symptomatology is easier than that which looks at changes in attitude, culture and coping styles. This wider field is relevant to children.

> "I don't think I have a future" said a 14-year-old girl who had been abused within a child labour situation in Sri Lanka.

> "I don't worry about the future. There will not be many of us alive by the year 2000, everyone is armed around here" was the view expressed by a conduct-disordered 14-year-old girl living in a deprived inner city area of London.

D. Concepts, causes and magnitude of population displacement

WILLIAM PARRY-JONES

For centuries, populations have been uprooted forcibly and displaced for a wide variety of reasons. During the 20th century, large-scale involuntary migration has been precipitated by: war and political turmoil; persecution or the threat of persecution, related to nationalistic, ethnic, religious or racial tensions; natural disasters, including earthquakes, floods, cyclones and famines; and by planned development projects, such as dam or road-building, which produce major changes in land usage and availability. Populations affected by the first three of these causes are customarily referred to as refugees. Their displacement may be internal, in that they remain within national borders, or external, involving international flow. Populations displaced by development projects (oustees, or development refugees) do not usually cross international boundaries and this criterion has been used to distinguish refugees from other displaced groups and migrants. Generally, external refugees have attracted the greatest attention from international organisations, and much less institutional support is available for internally displaced people of all categories (Cernea, 1990). While the plight of all displaced people warrants the attention of mental health professionals, this chapter is primarily concerned with external refugees.

The internationally accepted definition of refugee status was embodied in the 1951 United Nations Convention Relating to the Status of Refugees and its 1967 Protocol. In this context, a refugee is defined as "a person who is outside his or her former home country owing to a well-founded fear of persecution for reasons of race, religion, nationality, membership of a particular social group or political opinion, and who is unable or unwilling to avail himself or herself of the protection of that country, or to return there for reasons of fear of persecution" (United Nations High Commissioner for Refugees, 1993a). Further, the Convention established the principle of non-refoulement, whereby "no person may be returned against his or her will to a territory where he or she may be exposed to persecution". The 1967 Protocol made the Convention universal and, by June 1993, 111 states had signed both, and seven had signed one or the other (United Nations High Commissioner for Refugees, 1993a). In addition, there have been extensions of refugee definitions to cover the care of other groups of people, particularly those internally displaced and in need of international protection, such as the Kurds in northern Iraq and large numbers of people in Bosnia-Herzegovina. Current definitions can be seen, increasingly, as a compromise between the provision of humanitarian regimes for forced migrants and the restrictions imposed on immigration by member states (Hathaway, 1991).

Although precise numbers will never be obtained, estimates indicate that, globally, there are 18.2 million refugees, with a much higher number of internally displaced people (approximately 24 million) (United Nations High Commissioner for Refugees, 1993a). Only a small proportion of the refugee population is resident in Western countries, the majority living in developing nations in Asia and Africa, often under impoverished conditions because of the prevailing economic situation (Clinton-Davis & Fassil, 1992). In most cases, half of the displaced populations are children and adolescents, many of whom are orphaned or abandoned and, consequently, have special care and protection needs (Ressler *et al*, 1988). In addition to greatly increased refugee flows, the number of people seeking asylum has been rising rapidly, heightening governmental restrictive reactions. In total, approximately 3.7 million applications for asylum were recorded from 1983 to 1992 (United Nations High Commissioner for Refugees, 1993a).

Process of displacement

Displacement does not occur in isolation from other psychological and physical stressors but, to clarify the components involved, it is useful to distinguish the process, phases and psychological concomitants of displacement, from secondary, compounding factors. A number of distinct phases are identifiable and their sequence forms a useful framework for planned intervention. Following war, violence, social or economic upheaval in the home country, there may be a period of internal exile. The provision of services for people displaced in this way, in countries with repressive regimes, is particularly limited and often there is restricted access for international humanitarian organisations. This is followed by flight, often hazardous in itself. The next phase is entry into the country of first asylum, possibly with an insecure period of stay in one or more transit or long-term refugee camps, before either returning home, settling in that country or moving on. Finally, for a proportion of refugees, there is entry to a third country of resettlement. At a later stage there may be repatriation to the homeland, with all the inherent problems of re-integration. It is estimated that 2.4 million refugees were able to return home in 1992 (United Nations High Commissioner for Refugees, 1993a).

Forcible displacement carries with it a series of psychological concomitants. Inevitably there is loss of home, possessions and livelihood, breakdown of community structure and security, and there can be isolation from persons of similar cultural and religious background. Personal, social and economic status is diminished and movement from one country to another, prior to resettlement, can lead to emotional and adjustment difficulties, exacerbated by the frequently unwelcoming reception by host populations. Resettlement may be followed by a phase of continuing stress and adjustment problems associated with cultural, educational and employment difficulties and the possibility of intergenerational conflict, due to differences in the rate of acculturation. The psychological impact of displacement may be compounded by a wide range of other stressors, including the effects of political oppression, economic hardship, family separation, death of relatives or friends, exposure to violence, warfare, physical injury, rape, torture, or involvement in combat. The cumulative effect of such experiences is probably a critical factor in increasing the risk of psychological distress and mental disorder. At all stages of displacement, therefore, refugees have to develop new coping strategies to reduce stress and to enable adaptation to changing circumstances, including those imposed by relief programmes and therapeutic intervention (Knudsen, 1991).

Mental health of displaced people

Consideration of symptomatic responses to forced migration and of the mental health of refugees and other displaced populations raises the controversial issue of differentiation between normal, predictable psychological distress and mental disorder. Although migration and refugee experiences are frequently associated with psychological suffering and altered behaviour, they do not lead necessarily to mental disorder. In this context, a range of individual, family, social, cultural and environmental factors are likely to influence vulnerability (Ager, 1993). Consideration of mental health issues, therefore, requires awareness of the risks of medicalising essentially normal responses, and the need for rigorous application of customary diagnostic criteria of mental disorder.

Clinical and research studies

Despite the magnitude of population displacement, relatively little is known about the pattern of morbidity and the natural history of psychological disorders in refugees. The scientific literature is patchy and, until recently, most findings were derived from medically-orientated studies of the small proportion of refugees living in Western resettlement countries, the emphasis being on psychiatric problems arising after arrival (Liebkind, 1993). It has been difficult, therefore, to generalise such findings to refugees in other phases of displacement and in other societies. Furthermore, there has been a tendency for reliance on an ethnocentric interpretation of disorder, based upon Western medical theories of traumatisation, adjustment problems and psychiatric treatments. While this tendency is beginning to be corrected, there is a lack of research using explanatory models and culture-relevant illness typologies, derived from within-the-culture studies (Eisenbruch & Handelman, 1989).

Ager (1993) comprehensively reviewed recent literature on refugee mental health, summarising the findings in relation to the phases of refugee experience. There is evidence that the psychiatric consequences of forced migration differ according to the degree of control held by the migrants over the process of displacement. In this context, for example, it has been found that refugees carry an increased risk of psychotic disorder, compared with other groups of displaced people. Rates of psychiatric disorder appear to be related to the severity of war experiences, and the duration of stay within the country of resettlement does not appear to reduce vulnerability to psychiatric problems. Many studies have suggested that a diagnosis of PTSD is the most appropriate for the constellation of symptoms shown by war-traumatised refugees, and that these symptoms can persist over time, although usually becoming less intense (Mollica *et al*, 1987; League of the Red Cross and Crescent Society, 1988; Sack *et al*, 1993). Although the concept of PTSD may be pertinent and individual refugees may have had discrete stressful experiences compatible with the current definition of the stressor criterion, of greater importance is recognition of the cumulative effects of continuing psychological traumatisation and duress associated with displacement (Muecke, 1992). In addition, it is possible to take the view that the diagnostic criteria of PTSD reflect an ethnocentric view of health, and that for refugees a preferable term might be cultural bereavement (Eisenbruch, 1991). Cross-cultural studies, however, do indicate similar post-traumatic symptoms (Carlson & Rosser-Hogan, 1994). Depression emerges consistently as the most common symptom, even when it coexists with manifestations of other disorders (Kroll *et al*, 1989). In one of several long-term follow-up studies of post-World War II refugees, Eitinger & Strom (1973) found that depression and paranoid reactions occurred more frequently in refugees in Norway than in indigenous Norwegian patients. Physical complaints feature prominently, especially in refugees from cultures such as that of southeast Asia, where emotional expression is discouraged and experience of psychological treatments is minimal or non-existent.

There is growing evidence of the impact of displacement on children and young people. It is recognised that the type and severity of distress reactions and behavioural problems are related closely to age, developmental stage and parental and family support, and also that the maturation of refugee children can be severely disrupted by their experiences, especially if exposed to long-term duress (Ahearn & Athey, 1991; Ahmad, 1992). The current view is that children benefit from remaining with their parents, whatever the nature of the potentially traumatising experience (Ressler *et al*, 1988). The special needs of unaccompanied children, who have been orphaned or abandoned, are considerable, and under most circumstances, especially with younger children, family reunification is a priority. In this context, the United Nations High Commissioner for Refugees (UNHCR) has identified the family as the basic planning unit for the provision of assistance.

Particular stresses arise as a result of long-term displacement, possibly for years or decades, especially if there is internment in intentionally inhospitable transit or refugee camps (De Girolamo *et al*, 1989). This becomes a period of passive waiting, characterised by dependency, loss of self-esteem, apathy, a sense of anonymity and helplessness, feelings of being unwanted, exposure to neglect, abuse and exploitation, overcrowding, lack of privacy and segregation from the host population.

Identification and diagnosis of mental disorder in refugees

Effective mass-scale screening of displaced populations, to identify those with severe, persistent symptoms, presents major difficulties. Generally it relies on information derived from a network of sources, including healthcare and social welfare services, schools and camp officials. More systematic techniques have relied on PTSD-related questionnaires, supplemented, to a varying extent, by a battery of standardised and purpose-designed measures. Less structured methods have been used, especially with children exposed to warfare. These have included essays, interviews, story-telling and artwork and provide an effective way of acquiring a better understanding of how children cope with adversity (Dodge & Raundalen, 1987). Conventional Western diagnostic assessment techniques, based on clinical history-taking and mental state examination, need to be modified to take into account cultural differences in understanding mental illness and its treatment, and resistance to external intervention and to expectations of self-disclosure or emotional expression (Beiser & Fleming, 1986).

Principles and objectives of intervention

Systematic, culturally-sensitive interventions

During the last few years, the first attempts have been made to identify the psychosocial and mental health needs of refugee populations, exemplified by studies concerning displaced people in former Yugoslavia (World Health Organization, 1992; Pharos Foundation for Refugee Health Care, 1993). A variety of services and models for intervention are beginning to be established for the general and specific case of refugees, especially of vulnerable groups such as children (Macksoud, 1993; United Nations High Commissioner for Refugees, 1993b). These require a variety of community-based interventions to stabilise the background, and a spectrum of preventive and remedial strategies, including crisis intervention, counselling, psychotherapy and psychiatric treatment. In the absence of a single therapeutic framework, a pragmatic, eclectic approach has to be taken to promote improvement in levels of functioning, well-being and social integration. As far as possible, services should be "realistic, concrete, economical, flexible, unstigmatizing, culturally sensitive and non-medicalized" (United Nations High Commissioner for Refugees, 1993b).

There are likely to be difficulties penetrating the protective 'trauma membrane', in order to undertake any form of intervention. While resistance to treatment is a frequently recognised phenomenon following psychological traumatisation, avoidance behaviour and denial of the need for assistance in refugees may be closely related to a natural wish for privacy, cultural beliefs about disorder, and a sense of shame and stigma at being identified publicly as needing assistance, particularly following rape. This highlights the need for adherence to the strictest ethical standards, with respect for the autonomy and personal rights of refugees. Exploratory and diagnostic interviews must be slow-paced, with due regard for reluctance in expressing feelings or sexual issues, and with appropriate respect for cultural values and natural coping styles (Mattson, 1993). Although discussion and working through trauma experiences is widely used as a therapeutic strategy, exploration of the 'trauma story' may not be appropriate in all circumstances, especially after a lengthy time interval or in victims of torture or sexual violence. Instead, there is need for emphasis on more direct, pragmatic techniques concerned with symptom reduction, self-sufficiency, self-empowerment and enhanced coping with current adjustment problems. Bilingual or bicultural workers, recruited preferably from refugee communities, can play a key part in complementing the role of professional therapists, not simply as interpreters but as trusted intermediaries (Cunningham & Silove, 1993). All refugee workers need an understanding of the relevance of traumatic stress in refugee mental health, and familiarity with different methods for working with trauma survivors. The work is stressful, demanding and sometimes dangerous, and managers need to be alert to the possibility of burnout and exhaustion.

Psychological and social support in refugee camps

The tasks facing mental health professionals working in transit or long-stay camps in countries of first asylum are rendered more difficult by the continuing insecurity of the population, often under arduous living conditions, and the tendency towards passivity and dependency. Local mental health services may be inaccessible to refugees. An attempt needs to be made to introduce and maintain screening procedures to identify those disabled by symptoms and to establish priorities for intervention. Unaccompanied children are at special risk of neglect, abuse, exploitation, unwanted physical displacement, and inadequate efforts to provide resettlement or reunification with their families (Ressler *et al*, 1988; Williamson & Moser, 1988). The training, supervision and support of care providers, teachers and other relief workers are essential pre-requisites.

Services in countries of resettlement

Countries vary widely in their management of the resettlement needs of refugees being integrated into local communities (Cunningham & Silove, 1993). It is usually during this phase of displacement that mental and behavioural disorders are first recognised and treatment is initiated. The wider tasks concern the facilitation of long-term integration into new societies and include the organisation of housing, material needs, education and employment and the resolution of intergenerational conflict. The achievement of a new ethnic and cultural identity, however, is likely to be difficult and, for adults, there may be limited opportunity for socio-economic self-sufficiency and for active contribution to the culture and economy of the host country. In this context, interaction between refugees and the host populations can generate problems, and there may be resentment or frank hostility towards incomers once the initial humanitarian response has faded. These effects may be compounded by the separate problem of factionalism within refugee communities.

Role of international agencies and non-governmental organisations

During the last decade, worldwide growth in large-scale displacement and the plight of refugees has thrown into sharp relief the need for concerted action by United Nations agencies, national and international governmental bodies, and a wide range of non-governmental organisations (NGOs) and foundations, capable of mobilising and delivering medical, psychosocial and humanitarian aid promptly. The principal organisations include the International Committee of the Red Cross, the United Nations High Commissioner for Refugees, UNICEF, the International Social Service, the World Health Organization, the International Organization for Migration, and OXFAM.

Conclusions

Development of specialised mental health programmes

The number of displaced people is increasing relentlessly and the massive refugee flows following turmoil in the Balkans, the former Soviet Union, the Middle East, parts of the Asian subcontinent and Rwanda illustrate the continuing difficulty for governments and international humanitarian agencies in coping adequately, promptly and comprehensively with large-scale population displacement. In addition to the provision of international protection and humanitarian assistance, there is urgent need to develop models for delivering a sequence of coordinated services capable of meeting the mental health needs of refugees at all the different stages of displacement.

Training

Throughout the phases of displacement, contact with a range of professional personnel and relief workers offers multiple opportunities for psychological support and preventive measures. It follows that major emphasis should be placed on staff training to understand normal responses to trauma and to identify and meet the special needs of refugees. In addition to social welfare and healthcare personnel, with responsibility for therapeutic intervention, it is necessary to include lay workers engaged in organised protection and assistance, drawn from the refugee services and communities. In all training programmes, an essential feature is the dissemination of information about cross-cultural psychology and religious differences.

Programme evaluation and research

In addition to the need for systematic evaluation of all forms of intervention, substantial research programmes are required to guide the multiple mental health interventions being funded by humanitarian organisations, mainly in the developing world. Much more needs to be known, for example, about the impact of economic deprivation and social upheaval in the pre-flight phase, and the relevance of risk factors, such as previous coping strategies, premorbid psychiatric disorder and abnormal psychosocial factors, in the generation of post-trauma mental disorders. Longitudinal studies are necessary to clarify the natural history of disorders arising as a result of displacement and to identify predictors of severe impairment and chronicity. Finally, the development of culture-relevant approaches to screening and intervention is an overriding necessity.

References

Abu-Hein, F., Thabet, A. A. & El-Sarraj, E. (1993) Trauma and violence in Gaza. *British Medical Journal*, **306**, 1030–1031.

Ager, A. (1993) *Mental Health Issues in Refugee Populations: A Review.* Boston: Harvard Centre for the Study of Culture and Medicine.

Ahearn, F. L. & Athey, J. L. (eds) (1991) *Refugee Children: Theory, Research and Services.* Baltimore: Johns Hopkins University.

Ahmad, A. (1992) Symptoms of posttraumatic stress disorder among displaced Kurdish children in Iraq: victims of a man-made disaster after the Gulf war. *Nordic Journal of Psychiatry*, **46**, 315–319.

Arafat, C. (1990) *Childhood. Impressions of the Intifada: Psychological Barriers to Peace.* Jerusalem: Imut Publications.

Arroyo, W. & Eth, S. (1985) Children traumatised by Central American warfare. In *Post-Traumatic Stress Disorder in Children* (eds S. Eth & R. Pynoos), pp. 103–120. Washington, DC: APP.

Baker, R. (1992) Psychosocial consequences for tortured refugees seeking asylum and refugee status in Europe. In *Torture and its Consequences* (ed. M. Basoglu), pp. 83–106. Cambridge: Cambridge University Press.

Beiser, M. & Fleming, J. A. E. (1986) Measuring psychiatric disorder among Southeast Asian refugees. *Psychological Medicine*, **16**, 627–639.

Berry, J., Poortinga, Y., Segall, M., *et al* (1992) Psychology and the developing world. In *Cross-Cultural Psychology, Research and Applications*, pp. 378–391. New York: Cambridge University Press.

Bettelheim, B. (1960) *The Informed Heart.* New York: Free Press.

Breslau, N. & Davis, G. C. (1992) Post traumatic stress disorder in an urban population of young adults: risk factors for chronicity. *American Journal of Psychiatry*, **149**, 671–675.

——, ——, Andreski, P., *et al* (1991) Traumatic events and post traumatic stress disorder in an urban population of young adults. *Archives of General Psychiatry*, **48**, 216–222.

Bryce, J.-W., Walker, N., Ghorayeb, F., *et al* (1989) Life experiences, response styles and mental health among mothers and children in Beirut, Lebanon. Special Issue: Political Violence and Health in the Third World. *Social Science and Medicine*, **28**, 685–695.

Cairns, E. & Wilson, R. (1985) Psychiatric aspects of violence in Northern Ireland. *Stress Medicine*, **1**, 193–201.

Carlson, E. B. & Rosser-Hogan, R (1994) Cross-cultural response to trauma: a study of traumatic experiences and posttraumatic symptoms in Cambodian refugees. *Journal of Traumatic Stress*, **7**, 43–58.

Caro, D. & Irving, M. (1973) The Old Bailey Bomb Explosion. *Lancet*, **i**, 1433–1435.

Centre on War and the Child (1987) *Uganda: Land of the Child Soldier.* Eureka Springs: Centre on War and the Child.

—— (1989) *Youth under Fire: Military Conscription in El Salvador.* Eureka Springs: Centre on War and the Child.

Cernea, M. M. (1990) Internal refugee flows and development-induced population displacement. *Journal of Refugee Studies*, **3**, 320–339.

Chimienti, G. & Abu-Nasr, J. (1992–93) Children's reactions to war-related stress: II. The influence of gender, age, and the mother's reaction. *International Journal of Mental Health* **21**, 72–86.

——, —— & Khalifeh, I. (1989) Children's reactions to war-related stress: affective symptoms and behaviour problems. *Social Psychiatry and Psychiatric Epidemiology*, **24**, 282–287.

Clinton-Davis, L. & Fassil, Y. (1992) Health and social problems of refugees. *Social Science and Medicine*, **35**, 507–513.

Cunningham, M. & Silove, D. (1993) Principles of treatment and service development for torture and trauma survivors. In *International Handbook of Traumatic Stress Syndromes* (eds J. P. Wilson & B. Raphael), pp. 751–762. New York: Plenum Press.

Curran, P. S., Finlay, R. J. & McGarry, P. J. (1988) Trends in suicide. Northern Ireland 1960–1986. *Irish Journal Psychological Medicine*, **5**, 98–102.

——, Bell, P., Murray, A., *et al* (1990) Psychological consequences of the Enniskillen Bombing. *British Journal of Psychiatry*, **156**, 479–482.

Davidson, J., Kudler, H., Smyth, R., *et al* (1990) Treatment of post traumatic stress disorder with amitriptyline and placebo. *Archives of General Psychiatry*, **47**, 259–266.

Davis, J. (1992) The anthropology of suffering. *Journal of Refugee Studies*, **5**, 149–161.

de Girolamo, G., Diekstra, R. & Williams, C. (1989) *Report of a Visit to Border Encampments on the Kampuchea–Thailand Border*. Geneva: WHO.

Dodge, C. P. & Raundalen, M. (1987) *War, Violence and Children in Uganda*. Oslo: Norwegian University Press.

Durkheim, E. (1951) *Suicide* (transl. J. A. Spaulding & G. Simpson). Glencoe, IL: Free Press.

Eisenbruch, M. (1991) From post-traumatic stress disorder to cultural bereavement: diagnosis of Southeast Asian refugees. *Social Science and Medicine*, **33**, 673–680.

—— & Handelman, L. (1989) Development of an explanatory model of illness schedule for Cambodian refugee patients. *Journal of Refugee Studies*, **2**, 243–256.

Eitinger, L. & Strom, A. (1973) *Mortality and Morbidity after Excessive Stress: A Follow-up Investigation of Norwegian Concentration Camp Survivors*. New York: Humanities Press.

Farias, P. (1991) Emotional distress and its socio-political correlates in Salvadoran refugees: analysis of a clinical sample. *Culture, Medicine and Psychiatry*, **15**, 167–192.

Fishbain, D. A., Aldrich, T. E., Goldberg, M., *et al* (1991) Impact of a human-made disaster on the utilization pattern of a psychiatric emergency service. *Journal of Nervous and Mental Disease*, **179**, 162–166.

Fogelson, R. M. (1970) Violence and grievances: reflections on the 1960s riots. *Journal of Social Issues*, **26**, 141–163.

Fraser, R. M. (1971) The cost of commotion: an analysis of the psychiatric sequelae of the 1969 Belfast riots. *British Journal of Psychiatry*, **118**, 257–264.

Frazer, M. (1974) *Children in Conflict*. Harmondsworth: Penguin.

Garfield, R. & Williams, G. (1989) *Health and Revolution. The Nicaraguan Experience*. Oxford: Oxfam.

Garmezy, N. & Rutter, M. (1985) Acute reactions to stress. In *Child and Adolescent Psychiatry: Modern Approaches* (2nd edn) (eds M. Rutter, E. Taylor & L. Hersov), pp. 152–176. Oxford: Blackwell.

—— & Marsten, A. (1994) Chronic adversity. In *Child and Adolescent Psychiatry: Modern Approaches* (2nd edn) (eds M. Rutter, E. Taylor & L. Hersov), pp. 191–208. Oxford: Blackwell.

Godfrey, N. & Kalache, A. (1989) Health needs of older adults displaced to Sudan by war and famine: questioning current targeting practices in health relief. *Social Science and Medicine*, **28**, 707–713.

Greenley, J. R., Gillespie, D. P. & Lindenthal, J. J. (1975) A race riot's effects on psychological symptoms. *Archives of General Psychiatry*, **32**, 1189–1195.

Hadden, W. A., Rutherford, W. H. & Merrett, J. D. (1978) The injuries of terrorist bombing: a study of 1532 consecutive victims. *British Journal of Surgery*, **65**, 525–531.

Hathaway, J. C. (1991) *The Law of Refugee Status*. London: Butterworths.

Hjern, A., Angel, B. & Hojer, B. (1991) Refugee children from Chile. *Child Abuse and Neglect*, **15**, 245–248.

Hourani, L. L., Armenian, H., Zurayk, H., *et al* (1986) A population-based survey of loss and psychological distress during war. *Social Science and Medicine*, **23**, 269–275.

Hume, F. & Summerfield, D. (1994) After the war in Nicaragua: a psychosocial study of war wounded ex-combatants. *Medicine and War*, **10**, 4–25.

Ierodiakonou, C. S. (1970) The effect of a threat of war on neurotic patients in psychotherapy. *American Journal of Psychotherapy*, **24**, 643–651.

Kaffman, M. & Elizur, E. (1984) Children's bereavement reactions following death of the father. Family therapy in the Kibbutz. *International Journal of Family Therapy*, **6**, 259–283.

Kennedy, T. & Johnston, G. W. (1975) Civilian bomb injuries. In *Surgery of Violence* (ed. Martin Ware). London: British Medical Association Publications.

King, D. J., Griffiths, K., Reilly, P. M., *et al* (1982) Psychotropic drug use in Northern Ireland, 1966–1980: prescribing trends, inter- and intra-regional comparisons and relationship to demographic and socio-economic variables. *Psychological Medicine*, **12**, 819–833.

Kinzie, J. D. (1993) Post traumatic effects and their treatment in Southeast Asian refugees. In *International Handbook of Traumatic Stress Syndromes* (eds J. P. Wilson & B. Raphael), pp. 311–319. New York: Plenum Press.

Klee, G. D. & Gorwitz, K. (1970) Effects of the Baltimore riots on psychiatric hospital admissions. *Mental Hygiene*, **54**, 447–449.

Kleinman, A. (1987) Anthropology and psychiatry: the role of culture in cross-cultural research on illness. *British Journal of Psychiatry*, **151**, 447–454.

Knudsen, J. C. (1991) Therapeutic strategies and strategies for refugee coping. *Journal of Refugee Studies*, **4**, 21–38.

Kroll, J., Habenicht, M., MacKenzie, T., *et al* (1989) Depression and posttraumatic stress disorders in Southeast Asian refugees. *American Journal of Psychiatry*, **146**, 1592–1597.

League of the Red Cross and Crescent Society (1988) *Refugees: The Trauma of Exile*. Geneva: League of the Red Cross and Crescent Society.

Liebkind, K. (1993) Self-reported ethnic identity, depression and anxiety among young Vietnamese refugees and their parents. *Journal of Refugee Studies*, **6**, 25–39.

Lin, E., Carter, W. & Kleinman, A. (1985) An exploration of somatization among Asian refugees and immigrants in primary care. *American Journal of Public Health*, **75**, 1080–1084.

Loughrey, G. C., Bell, P., Kee, M., *et al* (1988) Post traumatic stress disorder and civil violence in Northern Ireland. *British Journal of Psychiatry*, **153**, 554–560.

Lyons, H. A. (1971) Psychiatric sequelae of the Belfast riots. *British Journal of Psychiatry*, **118**, 265–273.

—— (1972) Depressive illness and aggression in Belfast. *British Medical Journal*, **i**, 342–345.

McCallin, M. (1996) The impact of current and traumatic stressors on the psychological well-being of refugee communities. In *The Psychological Well-Being of Refugee Children. Research, Practice and Policy Issues* (ed. M. McCallin). Geneva: International Catholic Child Bureau.

Macksoud, M. (1993) *Helping Children Cope with the Stresses of War*. New York: UNICEF.

——, Dyregrov, A. & Raundalen, M. (1993) Traumatic war experiences. In *International Handbook of Traumatic Stress Syndromes* (eds J. P. Wilson & B. Raphael), pp. 625–633. New York: Plenum Press.

Mattson, S. (1993) Mental health of Southeast Asian women: an overview. *Health Care for Women International*, **14**, 155–165.

Middle East Watch and Physicians for Human Rights (1993) *The Anfal Campaign in Iraqi Kurdistan. The Destruction of Koreme*. New York: Human Rights Watch.

Minde, K. & Nikapota, A. D. (1993) Child psychiatry and the developing world: recent developments. *Transcultural Psychiatric Research Review*, **30**, 315–346.

Mira, E. (1939) Psychiatric experience in the Spanish war. *British Medical Journal*, **i**, 1217–1220.

Mollica, R. & Caspi-Yavin, Y. (1992) Overview: the assessment and diagnosis of torture events and symptoms. In *Torture and its Consequences* (ed. M. Basoglu), pp. 253–274. Cambridge: Cambridge University Press.

——, Wyshak, G. & Lavelle, J. (1987) The psychosocial impact of war trauma and torture on Southeast Asian refugees. *American Journal of Psychiatry*, **144**, 1567–1572.

Muecke, M. A. (1992) New paradigms for refugee health problems. *Social Science and Medicine*, **35**, 515–523.

Nasr, S., Racy, J. & Flaherty, J. A. (1983) Psychiatric effects of the civil war in Lebanon. *Psychiatric Journal of the University of Ottawa*, **8**, 208–212.

Pharos Foundation for Refugee Health Care (1993) *Care and Rehabilitation of Victims of Rape, Torture and Other Severe Traumas of War in the Republics of Ex-Yugoslavia*. Utrecht: Pharos Foundation.

Punamaki, R. L. (1983) Psychological reactions of Palestinian and Israeli children to war and violence. In *Children and War* (eds S. Kahnert, D. Pitt & I. Taipale), pp. 103–120. Siunto Baths, Finland: GIPRI, IPB, Peace Union of Finland.

—— & Suleiman, R. (1990) Predictors and effectiveness of coping with political violence among Palestinian children. *British Journal of Social Psychology*, **29**, 67–77.

Pynoos, R. S. (1993) Traumatic stress and developmental psychopathology in children and adolescents. *American Psychiatric Press Review of Psychiatry*, **12**, 205–238.

Ressler, E. M., Boothby, N. & Steinbock, D. J. (1988) *Unaccompanied Children. Care and Protection in Wars, Natural Disasters, and Refugee Movements*. New York: Oxford University Press.

Reynolds, P. (1990) Children of tribulation: the need to heal and the means to heal war trauma. *Africa*, **60**, 1–38.

Richman, N. (1993) Annotation: Children in situations of political violence. *Journal of Child Psychology and Psychiatry*, **34**, 1286–1302.

——, Ratilal, A. & Aly, A. (1989) *The Psychological Effects of War on Mozambiquan Children*. Maputo: Ministry of Education.

Sack, W. H., Clarke, G., Him, C., *et al* (1993) A 6-year follow-up study of Cambodian refugee adolescents traumatized as children. *Journal of the American Academy of Child and Adolescent Psychiatry*, **32**, 431–437.

Schwarz, E. D. & Kowalski, J. M. (1992) *Journal of Nervous and Mental Disease*, **180**, 767–772.

Schwarzwald, J., Weisenberg, M., Waysman, M., *et al* (1993) Stress reaction of school-age children to the bombardment by SCUD missiles. *Journal of Abnormal Psychology*, **102**, 404–410.

Sears, D. O. & MacConaghy, J. B. (1969) Participation in Los Angeles Riots. *Social Problems*, **17**, 3–20.

Siward, R. (1989) *World Military and Social Expenditures*. Washington, DC: World Priorities.

Skultans, V. (1991) Anthropology and psychiatry: the uneasy alliance. *Transcultural Psychiatric Research Review*, **28**, 5–24.

Solkoff, N. (1992) The Holocaust: survivors and their children. In *Torture and its Consequences* (ed. M. Basoglu), pp. 136–148. Cambridge: Cambridge University Press.

Straker, G. (1992) *Faces in the Revolution*. Ohio: Ohio University Press.

Summerfield, D. (1992) Philippines: Health, human rights and "low-intensity" war. *Lancet*, **339**, 173.

—— & Toser, L. (1991) 'Low intensity' war and mental trauma in Nicaragua: a study in a rural community. *Medicine and War*, **7**, 84–99.

—— & Hume, F. (1993) War and post-traumatic stress disorder: the question of social context. *Journal of Nervous and Mental Disease*, **181**, 522.

Swiss, S. & Giller, J. (1993) Rape as a crime of war: a medical perspective. *Journal of American Medical Association*, **270**, 612–615.

Tun, E. S. & Simons, R. C. (1973) Psychiatric sequelae to a civil disturbance. *British Journal of Psychiatry*, **122**, 57–63.

Tsoi, M.-M., Yu, G.-K. & Lieh-Mak, F. (1986) Vietnamese refugee children in camps in Hong Kong. *Social Science and Medicine*, **23**, 1147–1150.

UNICEF (1986) *Children in Situations of Armed Conflict*. New York: UNICEF.

—— (1989) *Children on the Front Line. The Impact of Apartheid, Destabilisation and Warfare on the Children of Southern Africa*. Geneva: UNICEF.

United Nations High Commissioner for Refugees (1993*a*) *The State of the World's Refugees. The Challenge of Protection*. Harmondsworth: Penguin Books.

—— (1993*b*) *Guidelines on the Evaluation and Care of Victims of Trauma and Violence*. Geneva: UNHCR.

Van Ginneken, E. & Rijnders, R. (1993) *Tazmanart: Fort-Militaire Secret du Maroc. Consequences d'un Internement du 18 Annees*. Amersfoort: Johannes Weir Foundation for Health and Human Rights.

Weisaeth, L. (1989) Importance of high response rates in traumatic stress research. *Acta Psychiatrica Scandinavica*, **80** (suppl. 353), 131–137.

Williamson, J. & Moser, A. (1988) *Unaccompanied Children in Emergencies. A Field Guide for their Care and Protection*. Geneva: International Social Service.

Wilson, K. (1992) Cults of violence and counter-violence in Mozambique. *Journal of Southern African Studies*, **18**, 527–582.

World Health Organization (1992) *United Nations Programme of Humanitarian Assistance in Yugoslavia: WHO Mission on the Mental Health Needs of Refugees, Displaced Persons and Others affected by the Conflict*. Geneva: WHO.

Yule, W. (1994) Post traumatic stress disorders. In *Child and Adolescent Psychiatry: Modern Approaches* (eds M. Rutter, E. Taylor & L. Hersov) (3rd edn), pp. 392–406. Oxford: Blackwell.

Zwi, A. & Ugalde, A. (1989) Towards an epidemiology of political violence in the Third World. *Social Science and Medicine*, **28**, 633–642.

11 Psychological responses to interpersonal violence

A.   Adults

GILLIAN MEZEY

There is a marked reluctance to accept the accidental nature of violent crime. The notion of the legitimate or deserving victim versus the innocent victim and victim precipitation (Wolfgang, 1958; Amir, 1967) is intrinsically linked to concepts of blame and responsibility, thereby affecting the way the victim is treated by society and the criminal justice system. The 'Just World Hypothesis' (Lerner & Miller, 1978) assumes that people get what they deserve and deserve what they get. Thus, the morally reprobate are seen as more deserving of victimisation and blamed more than the respectable or 'innocent' victim. In a similar way, criticism and blame is frequently extended to certain categories of rape victims, such as women who dress 'provocatively', act without caution in accepting a lift home, who drink excessively, or who are 'promiscuous' (Adler, 1987). Similarly, victims of domestic violence are often represented as enjoying and actively seeking out punishment (Scott, 1974). Given such widespread accusations of irresponsibility and criticism and neglect, it is perhaps not surprising that self-blame and feelings of guilt are such prominent concerns among many victims of crime.

The experience of crime is a commonplace event, particularly in Western urban society, and carries with it negative social connotations as well as adverse health and financial consequences which are largely unrecognised. The British Crime Survey (Mayhew *et al*, 1993) found that, of an estimated 2.64 million incidents, some 20% were domestic assaults involving partners, ex-partners and other relatives or household members. Domestic violence formed the largest category of assault for women, 19% of the violent incidents were street assaults (affecting men more than women), and a third of all violent incidents against Afro-Caribbeans and Asians were felt to be racially motivated.

Criminal violence, sexual and physical assault represent, for the individual victim, a personal disaster and their response can be expected to parallel that described in victims of 'natural' and war-related traumas. The impact of personal violence on the victim is no less devastating because she experiences terror and helplessness alone, rather than as part of a community. Criminal victimisation is no less significant because the media does not consider it newsworthy, and it is certainly no less traumatic for the victim by virtue of being man-made, rather than perceived as an arbitrary act of God. Indeed, it has been argued that victims of deliberate human malevolence may fare worse than victims where no immediate human scapegoat is identifiable and the victim's relationship with his fellow man is not so directly challenged.

Crime and post-traumatic stress disorder

The effects of criminal violence are variable and diffuse. The majority of victims of violence are not referred to health practitioners or psychiatrists, and even if they are referred they may not associate the violence with their current problems; they may not, for a variety of reasons, choose to disclose the experience to the doctor who, in turn, rarely makes any specific direct enquiry about victimisation experiences (Jacobson *et al*, 1987; Saunders *et al*, 1989). It can sometimes be difficult to distinguish the primary harm (i.e. that caused directly by the trauma of the assault), from the secondary damage, which results from the victim's sense of isolation, blame and rejection, compounded by negative responses from society or within the criminal justice process. The response following victimisation is also influenced by the victim's belief system, attributions and core assumptions and the extent to which these are challenged and undermined by the experience (Abramson *et al*, 1978; Janoff Bulman, 1988).

Maguire & Corbett (1987) have claimed that one in four victims of crime (excluding victims of serious sexual assault) are in need of some form of psychological support. Shapland *et al* (1985) found that 26% of victims of wounding reported extra worry, fear, or loss of confidence, 11% reported depression, stress or sleep problems, and 5% were 'very upset'. Wykes & Whittington (1994) described a range of victim responses following assaults on hospital staff in the workplace, including fears and phobias, guilt and self-blame, anger and hatred.

Post-traumatic stress disorder has been identified as a response among families of homicide victims (Rynearson, 1984; Rynearson & McCreery, 1993), and indeed the trauma of killing may result in PTSD in a proportion of perpetrators (Thomas *et al*, 1994).

Criminal victimisation appears to be more pathogenic than other forms of traumatic experience in terms of its propensity to precipitate lifetime and current PTSD. Victims of personal assault appear to have more severe reactions than victims of accidents, even when the degree of injury is controlled for (Helzer *et al*, 1987; Janoff-Bulman, 1988; Shepherd *et al*, 1990; Breslau *et al*, 1991).

The following factors predispose to crime-related PTSD: experiencing a sexual assault, being female, belonging to an ethnic minority, being younger, having a family history of anxiety or instability, early experiences of separation in childhood, a history of anxiety and previous trauma (Breslau *et al*, 1991; Norris, 1992). Higher rates of PTSD are associated with exposure to violent crimes compared with other 'non-deliberate' environmental hazards (Helzer *et al*, 1987; Janoff-Bulman, 1988; Breslau *et al*, 1991). Within experiences of personal crime, physical injury, threat to life and serious sexual assault predict a worse prognosis, resulting in high rates of PTSD: indirect victimisation (e.g. burglary) appears to produce lower rates (Kilpatrick *et al*, 1987; Koss, 1988; Breslau *et al*, 1991; Resnick *et al*, 1993).

The effects of crime tend to be worse and qualitatively different if the victim knows the offender well than if the perpetrator is an unknown stranger (Mawby & Gill, 1987). Rape victims experience greater difficulties re-establishing intimate relationships following acquaintance rape than stranger rape: this may relate to the victim's greater tendency to blame herself and her lack of judgement when the perpetrator is someone she previously liked and trusted. An attack by a stranger does not so directly challenge the victim's pre-existing assumptions about vulnerability, predictability and trust-worthiness.

Long-term studies of the effects of serious physical and particularly sexual assault suggest that the effects can last for months or years (Burt & Katz, 1985; Kilpatrick *et al*, 1985*a;* Shapland *et al*, 1985). Recovery can be predicted by the initial psychological reaction (the higher the initial level of distress, the greater the likelihood of a severe and persistent reaction (Feinstein & Dolan, 1991)), as well as by the continuing presence of demonstrable distress after three months (Kilpatrick *et al*, 1985*a*).

Crime victims also appear to be less healthy on measures of general physical health than non-victims (Koss, 1988). Women who had experienced a physical or sexual assault had significantly higher rates of medical consultation than victims of burglary, and for rape victims this effect persisted for two years after the rape attack.

There are conflicting opinions on the extent to which the 'severity' of the crime predicts the victim's response. It is difficult to judge 'severity' retrospectively, or to define which crimes are more frightening for the victim, or entail a greater level of threat. The observer's judgement about level of severity and risk involved may not match up to the victim's perception of her ordeal or her cognitive appraisal of the event, her response and its likely consequences. While some authors have found worse effects following completed versus attempted criminal assault (Kilpatrick *et al*, 1987), this has not been replicated in other studies (Mezey & Taylor, 1987; Resnick *et al*, 1993). Attempted assaults or 'near misses' leave room in the victim's mind for ambiguity regarding the assailant's intentions and the likely danger facing them. Resnick *et al* (1993) found that 35% of victims of attempted molestation versus 18% where molestation was completed thought they were likely to be killed or seriously injured. The victim may also react differently depending on whether she attributes her narrow escape to events within her control or merely to serendipity.

Although there is evidence that the elderly are less likely to be victims of criminal assault than their younger counterparts, the elderly are generally more fearful of crime. They tend to go out less and are less likely to expose themselves to situations where they feel vulnerable (Hough & Mayhew, 1985). Older victims tend to experience fewer psychological and emotional effects subsequently, but express greater concerns about the practical and financial consequences of crime (Mawby & Gill, 1987; Breslau *et al*, 1991). Thus, it appears that the fear arising from the anticipation of crime may be worse than the reality, in the elderly population.

Racially and sexually motivated violence

The diagnostic formulation of PTSD derives primarily from observations of survivors of relatively circumscribed traumatic events. This model is less relevant to prolonged and repeated trauma such as domestic violence, sexual abuse, sexual and racial discrimination or torture, which give rise to more complex, diffuse and long-term disturbance than simple PTSD.

Racial and sexual victimisation and family violence cannot be conceptualised as a set of discrete, unrelated episodes, but represent a constantly evolving social process which is diffuse, contextually bound and profoundly dislocating for its victims (Bowling, 1993). Such experiences are more likely to give rise to a chronic stress reaction than a time-limited traumatic stress response. The devastating impact of racially motivated assaults has been highlighted by Cooper & Pomeiye (1988) who assessed 30 cases in north London. The victims' lives had been blighted, they were prisoners in their own homes, frequently being forced to move, and experiencing marked disruption to their children's education and social life.

Victims of sexual harassment report an array of psychological, emotional and interpersonal problems over and above the negative employment and financial repercussions (Charney & Russell, 1994; Mezey, 1994). Victims of sexual harassment in the workplace find themselves unable to complete daily tasks or function due to perpetual fear and anxiety. Continuing harassment may impair the victim's ability to trust, which interferes with her relationships with others, undermines her confidence and self-esteem and makes her perceive herself as vulnerable and defenceless. If the situation does not resolve, she is at risk of developing mental illness, including generalised and phobic anxiety, depression and PTSD (Mezey & Rubenstein, 1992).

Rape and sexual assault

The emotional, cognitive and behavioural response to rape and sexual assault was first described in the 1970s as rape trauma syndrome (Burgess & Holmstrom, 1974). Following the inclusion of PTSD in the psychiatric classification system, sexual assault was conceptualised as a stressor that could potentially meet the DSM–III–R criteria for PTSD. Thus the response to sexual assault has come to be conceptualised as a generic stress response, in common with responses to a wide range of violent and traumatic events.

Rape victims are more likely to develop PTSD than victims of any other form of crime; this relationship holds true even when elements of risk and dangerousness are controlled for (Kilpatrick *et al*, 1987). In the days to weeks following sexual assault, more than 90% of victims have symptoms of PTSD (Steketee & Foa, 1977). Levels of distress rapidly decline, so that within 4–6 weeks the majority of rape victims are no longer significantly different from a comparison group of non-victims. However, re-experiencing and avoidance phenomena, including intrusive images, numbing of responsiveness, and reduced involvement in other people and former interests including sexual activity, have been noted to persist for up to three years following the rape (Kilpatrick *et al*, 1979; Atkeson *et al*, 1982; Becker & Skinner, 1983).

Kilpatrick *et al* (1987) found that 75% of 391 adult women they surveyed in the community had been victimised by crime. Of all crime victims, 27.8% subsequently developed PTSD. Lifetime prevalence and current prevalence of PTSD was highest for victims of completed rape; victims of attempted sexual molestation were less likely to develop PTSD. Symptoms of PTSD, once developed, were very tenacious in a proportion of survivors; 16.5% of rape victims still had PTSD on average 17 years after the assault. Among victims of sexual assault, three elements make a significant individual contribution to the development of PTSD: perception of life-threat, actual injury, and being the victim of a completed as opposed to an attempted rape (Kilpatrick *et al*, 1989).

In addition to PTSD, rape victims also go on to experience high rates of generalised and phobic anxiety (Kilpatrick *et al*, 1985a), depression (Atkeson *et al*, 1982; Kilpatrick *et al*, 1985a), suicidal attempts (Kilpatrick *et al*, 1985b), drug misuse (Frank & Anderson, 1987), lowered self-esteem (Murphy *et al*, 1988) and social adjustment (Resick *et al*, 1981) and physical complaints (Koss, 1988).

The reactions of men following sexual assault, although relatively under-researched, appears to parallel the responses of female rape victims, resulting in long-term sexual dysfunction, feelings of vulnerability, rage and anger (Mezey & King, 1989).

Adult survivors of child sexual abuse

A wide range of symptoms have been reported by adult survivors of child sexual abuse, including higher rates of depression, guilt, chronic tension, sexual dysfunction, impaired 'interrelatedness' and lower self-esteem than the general population (Runtz & Briere, 1986; Russell, 1986; Briere, 1989; Mullen *et al*, 1993, 1994). PTSD has also been described as a consequence of childhood sexual abuse (Lindberg & Distad, 1985), although the nature of the traumatic stressor with adult survivors may have become lost in the passage of time, resulting in a prevailing clinical picture of a personality disturbance, rather than a discrete, circumscribed stress response.

The cycle of violence

The victim to victimiser cycle is not a predetermined inevitability but represents an interplay and interaction of multiple factors, both internal and external. Physical abuse of children is a risk factor for later aggressive behaviour (Dodge *et al*, 1990). Child sexual abuse is associated with increased rates of adult convictions for violent and property offences, but not specifically for sexual offending (Widom, 1989). The re-enactment of early experiences of abuse may represent a form of repetition compulsion, replaying and re-experiencing the original trauma, with the victim in the role of the perpetrator (Van der Kolk, 1989). The repetition of early traumatic experiences may represent a defence against overwhelming feelings of vulnerability and helplessness, or a form of identification with the aggressor. Oliver (1993) reviewed 60 studies on intergenerational transmission of child abuse, which suggested that a third of child victims grow up to continue a pattern of "seriously inept, neglectful or abusive" rearing as parents, while a third do not. The remaining third are vulnerable to becoming abusive parents through the mediating effects of social stress.

The experience of early victimisation is associated with a later vulnerability to physical and sexual abuse (Fromuth, 1986; Russell, 1986). When adult victimisation is superimposed on a background of childhood deprivation or abuse, this is likely to result in a more severe and prolonged reaction, representing a compounded reaction to the present trauma with earlier unresolved grief and conflict.

Victims of domestic violence

The growing body of research on the subject of domestic violence has recently begun to shift deeply entrenched societal and institutional attitudes which tend to blame and stigmatise the victim. Domestic violence is increasingly understood within a feminist and political context of unequal power relations between men and women, as well as women's unequal access to and experiences within certain vocational, educational and judicial institutions (Dobash & Dobash, 1979; Edwards, 1985; Hoff, 1990). Domestic violence has been defined as "an act carried out with the intention, or perceived intention of physically injuring another person" (Straus *et al*, 1980). Most definitions include psychological abuse and sexual assault, as well as threatened and actual physical violence (Frieze, 1983; Bowker, 1983; Rath *et al*, 1989). The violence is repetitive and tends to escalate both in frequency and severity. Certain factors appear to increase the risk of violence occurring or may cause it to escalate, such as alcohol use by the perpetrator, or pregnancy (Bowker, 1983; McFarlane, 1989; Bohn, 1990).

A characteristic pattern of psychological, emotional and behavioural responses, described as battered woman syndrome, has been identified in a substantial number of women who experience domestic violence (Hilberman & Munson, 1977; Walker, 1979; Dobash & Dobash, 1979; Hilberman, 1980; Pagelow, 1981; Gelles & Cornell, 1985; Bergman *et al*, 1987; Gelles & Harrop, 1989; Bergman & Brismar, 1991). Women seeking refuge from domestic violence show higher rates of anxiety and fear, depression, physical complaints and PTSD (Jaffe *et al*, 1986; Gianakos & Wagner, 1987; West *et al*, 1990; Dutton & Goodman, 1994; Scott-Gliba *et al*, 1995).

With repeated violence, the battered woman tends to become gradually incapacitated, her coping strategies are progressively undermined, rendered ineffective and eventually extinguished, until she retreats into "a state of passivity, paralysis and an inability to act" (Hilberman & Munson, 1977). This terminal state is reminiscent of learned helplessness in the face of uncontrollable and inescapable threat (Seligman, 1975; Walker, 1979). Learned helplessness in women who are battered is predicted by the following factors (Walker, 1985):

(a) battering in the home as a child;
(b) history of sexual abuse or molestation;
(c) traditionality;
(d) health problems;
(e) pathological jealousy;
(f) sexual assault (in addition to the physical violence);
(g) threats to kill;
(h) psychological torture (as defined by Amnesty International this includes: isolation, induced debility, monopolising of perceptions, verbal degradation, hypnosis, drugs, threats to kill, occasional indulgences).

Gelles (1976) also noted that a history of past childhood abuse meant that a woman was more likely to remain in a battering relationship.

Disclosure to legal or health professionals is rare. Of 60 victims of domestic violence seen in a general medical clinic, the history of violence was known to the referring clinician in only four cases (Hilberman & Munson, 1977). Stark *et al* (1979) found that a history of domestic violence was identified in only 1 in 25 battered women attending a hospital emergency clinic.

Paradoxically strong emotional bonds between the battered woman and her abuser may develop, making it difficult for her to leave her partner or to behave in a way that he would regard as disloyal (Dutton & Painter, 1981). The apparent acquiescence of the woman to her partner's demands and her acceptance of his brutality is reminiscent of the relationship between hostage and torturer (Symonds, 1975; Ochberg, 1978; Dutton & Painter, 1981). Traumatic bonding is facilitated by the unequal power relationship between abused and abuser, the victim's internalisation of blame, lack of access to safe havens in the community, inadequate protection afforded by the criminal justice system, and a lack of financial resources. Battering destroys the woman's sense of self-esteem and efficacy, the qualities she needs in order to believe that survival without her partner is viable.

The formation of strong emotional bonds under conditions of inter-mittent torture and maltreatment have been well described among captors and their hostages (Bettelheim, 1960; Ochberg, 1978; Keenan, 1992), between abused children and their parents (Kempe & Kempe, 1978) and among followers of extremist religious cults (Halperin, 1983; Lifton, 1987). Symonds (1975) described similar regressed and dependent behaviour in victims of crime as traumatic psychological infantilism: an automatic response to their sense of fear and threat to their lives. The victim of prolonged and repeated violence and abuse may adopt the belief system of the abuser, tending to internalise feelings of aggression in the form of guilt and self-blame, a dynamic which has been incorporated into the new psychiatric category proposed, 'disorders of extreme stress not otherwise specified' (Herman, 1992). Traumatic bonding and identification with the batterer's judgements and value system should be understood not as a mark of affection and respect, but an indication of the victim's terror and constant vigilance.

In some tragic cases, the end result is that the woman resorts to violence herself and may end up killing her partner. Homicide tends to be the last resort for a woman who, after years of violence, degradation and abuse and without the means to escape or protect herself, kills in order to avoid being killed (Browne, 1987).

B.   Children

TONY KAPLAN

Children and adolescents are exposed to violence in different ways. This discussion is limited to those forms of violence that children on the British mainland more commonly experience. For clarity, violence directed against the child (intrafamilial abuse, bullying) will be distinguished from violence the child witnesses, either in the family or on television. In reality these categories often overlap, and violence for the multiply-exposed child is usually only one aspect of a harsh life which may include deprivation, disruption and loss, all of which will have a marked impact on the emotional life of the child, his/her behaviour and attitudes and on the relationships he/she will seek out or form.

Witnessing violence

The plight of the witness to violence may in some ways be worse than that of the victim. Victims may be more egocentrically preoccupied with pain and physical injury, internal sensations (which may operate as distracters) providing some protection against PTSD in the short term but predisposing the victim to dissociative symptoms and to traumatic amnesia (Pynoos & Eth, 1985). The uninjured witness, however, will perceive events from the points of view of victim, assailant, others present, as well as from their perspective of helpless onlooker, and later imagine him/herself as, or identify with, any of these roles. The witness has less powerful distracters than the victim, and hence PTSD may be more intense and more immediate, and post-traumatic guilt and shame at not having intervened effectively more keenly felt. Children may be especially vulnerable to feelings of guilt. If the victim is a parent, child witnesses older than 4–5 years may be so preoccupied with the welfare of their loved one and with the urgent need for intervention that they may disregard threats to their own safety, and this tendency may persist and generalise.

Effects of inter-parental violence on the child

It has been estimated that more than 3 million children in the US, where 1 in 14 marriages deteriorate into chronic violence, are at risk of witnessing the serious assault of one parent by the other. As much as 70% of domestic violence is witnessed by a child in that home, and 70% of women seeking sanctuary in women's refuges bring children with them (Jaffe *et al*, 1990). In the UK, 40–50 families each year will be devastated by the death of one parent at the hands of the other (Harris-Hendriks *et al*, 1993); nearly one in three of the children having seen or heard the killing.

The effects on a child of living in a violent family have been studied in community samples (Jenkins & Smith, 1990), in clinic samples (Pynoos & Eth, 1986; Harris-Hendriks *et al*, 1993), in samples of children with their mothers in women's refuges (Jaffe *et al*, 1990), and in the retrospective accounts of adults who grew up in violent surroundings (Straus *et al*, 1980). Wolfe *et al* (1985) found that boys from violent homes differed significantly from their peers in social and academic competence; they were more aggressive, overactive, communicated less effectively, and were more prone to depression, obsessive–compulsive behaviour and delinquency. Jaffe *et al* (1990) reported research which found higher rates of school non-attendance and poor academic performance, contributed to by noticeably impaired concentration, more oppositional behaviour and a tendency to respond to frustrations in relationships with violent retaliation or with overpassivity.

Younger children are, on the whole, more severely affected. Because young children are more dependent on their mothers, threats to their mother's safety and threats to their own safety are inextricably tied. Many of the symptoms seen in young children of abused mothers (such as irritability, regressive behaviour and sleep problems) (Alesi & Hearn, 1984), may be attributable to a combination of insecure attachment (with separation anxiety) and PTSD. This pattern of behaviour, meant to elicit care, is unfortunately more likely, in their stressed mothers with their low self-esteem and inadequate social support, to elicit rejection. This exacerbates the insecure attachment, ensures the persistence of symptoms of post-traumatic stress, and confirms the sense that they are to blame for the troubles between their parents. Since most rows between couples are ostensibly over childcare issues and because younger children, through immature cognitive and emotional development, are more egocentric, their conclusion (that they must be the cause of their mother's victimisation) is not surprising.

Boys are especially vulnerable for a number of reasons. Their attachment to their mothers may be in conflict with their gender identity formation. Goldner *et al* (1990) described how both boys and girls tend to be primarily attached to their mothers in infancy, but boys, to develop a male gender identity, have to become different from their mother. Genetically and through early socialisation, boys become more aggressive than girls. Young boys who witness violence are more likely to deal with their overwhelming fear and powerlessness by assuming the role of assailant in their play (identification with the aggressor) or by repeatedly playing through the traumatic event to desensitise themselves or to find a more satisfactory resolution (mastery through repetition). With PTSD, from which many children exposed to violence suffer, there is a general irritability, which may be seen as aggressiveness, for which they are punished by mother and teacher, and rejected by peers. Whether they identify with their father's violence *per se*, their acting out is often interpreted as such by their victimised mother, since their aggression may serve as a traumatic reminder to a mother with PTSD, and they may be branded as like their father ('bad genes') and suffer further rejection.

Girls, especially early on, show more anxiety, dependency and withdrawal. Interestingly, when asked to rate their own symptoms, boys acknowledged fear, sadness, and other 'internalising symptoms' to the same degree as girls (Wolfe *et al*, 1985; Jenkins & Smith, 1991). Girls, through their identification with their mothers, are, in adolescence and adult life, prone to depression, victimisation and psychosexual problems.

Both boys and girls may suppress any angry feelings (indeed, they may inhibit all strong feelings) that they may harbour towards their fathers for their violence and towards their mothers for not finding ways to avoid confrontation and, in many cases, for not protecting them from abuse. (There is a significant overlap between spouse abuse and child abuse (Straus *et al*, 1980).) From about the age of five, children exposed to violence become intensely preoccupied with fantasies of rescuing the victim (their mothers in this case); the younger ones will tend to imagine the intervention of a powerful or resourceful adult, while the older ones will torment themselves with what they might have done, if only they had been bigger/stronger/braver/more quick-witted. With these fantasies come fears of retaliation or repetition (Pynoos & Eth, 1985). Since it is the child's impotent rage that provokes these fantasies, inhibiting the angry feeling may feel like the best self-protection from their father's retaliation and from their mother's rejection. These children may seem distant and emotionally constricted, excessively well-behaved and solicitous of adults; they disguise their anxiety, sense of hurt and lack of trust.

It is not inevitable that boys from violent homes will go on to become violent themselves; in fact, this will occur in about 30% of cases (Jaffe *et al*, 1990). Most men who assault their wives witnessed their father assaulting their mother. Sons of the *most* violent parents have a rate of spouse abuse 1000 times greater than the sons of non-violent parents (Straus *et al*, 1980). Women in violent relationships will commonly have seen their mother beaten by a partner. The most obvious explanation for this comes from social learning theory. Children learn to behave like the adults around them – they assume from what they see that violence is a powerful, effective and acceptable way to resolve disagreements or to discharge feelings. Attachment theory helps to explain the prediction, born out by research (Goldner *et al*, 1990), that predisposed men will most commonly lash out against their partners when the partner threatens to leave, withdraws affection or loyalty, or at least gives indication of diminished dependency on the man. These men are likely to have expectations ("internal working models"; Bowlby, 1980) of insecure attachments generated in and confirmed since infancy. Goldner *et al* (1990) explained that dependency feelings in these men provoke gender identity conflict, which is resolved by identification with their violent fathers from whom they derive their sense of maleness.

There may be many direct and indirect stresses and changes which may influence the development of symptoms and personality. Jaffe *et al* (1990) pointed out that children may react not only to the violence between their parents, but also to the disruption to their lives (for example, having to move out of their homes, away from their schools, friends, and familiar social networks to go with their mothers into women's refuges, or into local authority care). They face accruing financial hardship if the mother leaves the father (if he is the breadwinner), and complex organisational and relationship problems around contact with estranged fathers. Much depends on the mother's capacity to care for them, which is mediated by her mental and physical health. Other factors that coexist in violent families and which may influence the development of behavioural problems include the increased rate of violence from parent to child (an estimated overlap of 30–40% according to Straus *et al*, 1980), a relative lack of parental supervision and control of the children (Patterson, 1982) and the greater likelihood of parental disagreement related to differing childrearing styles and attitudes (Block *et al*, 1981).

Jaffe's group found that women in shelters scored very highly on measures of physical and emotional distress, which was predicted largely on the amount of violence they had endured and on the social disruption and disadvantage that had resulted as measured by 'negative life-events'. The children's levels of behavioural and social relationship problems were related mostly to the degree of violence to which they had been exposed, their mother's adjustment (how well she was coping) and to the deprivation and disadvantage they were suffering as a consequence. As predicted by Rutter (1979), the factors were potentiating rather than merely additive.

Jenkins & Smith (1991) found that the factor that most influenced the development of problems in the children living in disharmonious families was the amount of *overt* conflict between the parents. They were also able to demonstrate that as parental conflict increased, the care the child received diminished and the amount of aggression *towards* the child increased. The more this was the case, the greater the likelihood and degree of behavioural problems on the part of the child. This effect was exaggerated if there were also major discrepancies in childrearing attitudes and practices between the parents.

Both sets of researchers also point out that, although the at-risk children show more distress and behavioural problems than the general population of children from low-intensity conflict homes, it is by no means invariable that all children from violent homes will have problems. In the group studied by Jaffe *et al* (1990), only a third of boys and a fifth of girls in shelters had problems in the clinical range. There are aspects of personality as well as qualities of relationship and circumstances in the child's life which ameliorate the distress a child may feel. Jenkins & Smith (1990) gave an informative account as to how these factors operate. Children with a good relationship with at least one parent, whether from homes with high conflict or low conflict, had fewer problems. The authors regard this as a relative absence of vulnerability. However, other factors, regarded as truly protective against stress, ameliorated symptoms more in children from high conflict than from low conflict households. Conferring true protection were a trusting relationship with an adult outside of the immediate family (commonly a grandparent, but potentially also teachers or counsellors), school success and other achievements which brought acclaim and popularity, and a good relationship with a sibling. In other studies, resilience against stress develops from greater cognitive abilities (higher intelligence and problem-solving skills), secure attachment from infancy, and previous exposure to stresses with which the child could cope adequately. It is likely that these factors also apply to children living with violence in their homes.

Others have studied the effects on children of one parent killing the other (Black & Kaplan, 1988; Harris-Hendriks *et al*, 1993). In such cases, the children effectively lose both parents suddenly and simultaneously. They are, in most cases, dislocated from home, school and familiar and significant adults and friends, and are exposed to conflict by proxy in their extended families and to multiple placements. Children who had witnessed the killing were much more likely to have post-traumatic symptoms. As in other studies, girls tended to have more neurotic symptoms, while boys were more behaviourally disturbed. Not surprisingly, attachment problems were common.

Violence from outside the family

Homicide

Pynoos & Eth (1985) and Malmquist (1986) have described the post-traumatic effects on children who were witness to their parent's violent death by homicide by an assailant from outside the family. Fantasies of revenge are not contaminated by conflicts of loyalty and may be more florid as a result. In some cases, the child witness's impotent rage may be displaced onto the surviving parent, relatives or friends, for not intervening. Because, in the main, these events will be less explicable to the child than violence which is the culmination of a parental dispute, and the threat which their parents were unable to resist and protect them from came from outside their family, the illusion of the inviolability of home and family is shattered, and fundamental trust in adults and in the future is profoundly affected. Since the arrest and conviction rate of non-domestic homicide is lower, many of these children will not be able to achieve 'psychological closure', without which symptoms will be maintained at a higher level of intensity than would otherwise have been the case.

Rape

In Pynoos & Eth (1985) and Pynoos & Nader (1988), there are descriptions of PTSD in a group of children who had witnessed the sexual assaults of their mothers. Girls were more affected, especially with regard to their fear of repetition and insecurity about their future relationships. They found that all the children they saw repressed the sexual aspects of the attack and focused on the violence. Because the sexual content was also the most difficult for the adults to talk about, especially to the children, cognitive and perceptual distortions for the child remained uncorrected. The sexual elements came through in the repetitive games of the younger children and in heightened masturbatory activity. Older boys were particularly affected by guilt at not having intervened effectively and by identification with the aggressor at times of sexual arousal, with a strong fear of loss of impulse control. Constriction of affect was common. Family relationships and gender attitudes were compromised. Rape places a great strain on the mother's relationship with her partner, and up to 50% of relationships will break down. This increases the adversity for the child. Furthermore, because the mother, with whom the child is usually left, will almost invariably be suffering from a degree of PTSD, the child will find it harder to recover (McFarlane, 1987).

Random violence

It is no longer unusual for a child from an inner-city area to witness extreme violence in their neighbourhood. This applies especially where there is poverty, big differentials between rich and poor, discrimination, and access to dangerous weapons. In the US, drug-related and gang violence is endemic in certain areas, and the effect of this on children in these areas is currently receiving a great deal of professional and political attention.

In a study into the aftermath of a sniper attack on a children's school playground, Pynoos *et al* (1987) found that 40% of children were suffering from moderate or severe PTSD. Children who were in the playground at the time of the shooting were significantly more affected than their peers who were in the school building, who in turn were more affected than children who were on their way home or at home. Vulnerability factors, as predictors of PTSD, applied only to less exposed children. In a follow-up study one year later (Nader *et al*, 1990), children who had been severely affected at the time were still highly symptomatic. Having been a close friend of a child who had been killed in the attack, 'survivor guilt', and concern at the time for a sibling added to the prediction, and contributed to the emergence of depressive symptomatology.

Violence by proxy: the effect of seeing violence on television

Viewing graphic portrayals of violence on television and video is no longer uncommon, even for young children. A UK community survey (Gunter & McAleer, 1990) found that 25% of 4–6-year-olds regularly watched television after the 9pm watershed on a Saturday night, and 5% were still watching at midnight. Barlow & Hill (1985) reported that almost 10% of 7–8-year-olds had seen an '18' rated video, as had 25% of 11–12-year-olds.

The issue of causation is complex and research results are confusing. Laboratory studies have been most influential in highlighting individual causative mechanisms, but attributions of causality are generally lineal. Field studies have been better at showing up interactions between causal and contributory social and personality factors, and longitudinal studies have been focused on these effects over time. Naturally, with greater complexity of design, outcome is less categorical and even contradictory.

Psychologists explain the increased aggressivity observed in laboratory studies as mediated by arousal, imitation, desensitisation and disinhibition (Gunter & McAleer, 1990). The arousal theory posits that the more exciting the programme is to the viewer, the more the viewer becomes emotionally engaged, and hence the more likely the viewer is to be affected. The effect may be non-specific, but is exaggerated in amplifying aggressive behaviour if the programme contained violence. This is the obverse of the desensitisation theory which predicts that heavy viewing of violence without real-life consequences will cause children to stop, or intervene to stop, fighting less often. There is evidence for this in controlled studies, and inferentially from a longitudinal study in Canada in which the rate of behavioural problems in young children increased much more rapidly after watching a prescribed diet of television in a town which had not had access to television before the study commenced. There is also evidence that the more realistic the violence is, the less easy it is for the viewer to detach, so that studies that used cartoon violence as the test stimulus have limited validity. Josephson (1987) described the interaction between imitation and disinhibition. The social learning theory of imitated violence is perhaps the better known and summed up by Bandura's (1973) assertion that violent acts by heroic characters portrayed as justified, successful and unpunished counteract the inhibition of violent behaviour which is based on fear and guilt. Berkowitz & Rogers (1986), in their revised model of disinhibition (originally based on a laboratory experiment in which volunteers were more likely to 'get even' with an 'aggressor' by administering what they thought were genuine electrical shocks after watching violent videos), proposed a dual process of 'priming' and 'elicitation', connected non-specifically by cognition of aggression (meaning). Josephson (1987) demonstrated this latter theory in a well-designed study and was able to show that Feshbach & Singer's assertion (1971) that viewing violence had a 'cathartic' effect was limited and applied only to boys who were not predisposed to aggression. Boys assessed as aggressive before watching television violence were more aggressive after, were more easily and non-specifically provoked, and their aggression was not exclusively directed against 'justifiable' targets, as was the case with the non-aggressive boys. This was in keeping with a field study that found that delinquent boys' aggression was much more exaggerated after violent videos than their non-delinquent peers (Gunter & McAleer, 1990).

Although not all longitudinal studies have shown a link between television violence and aggressivity, most have, including the most recent (and cross-national) study (Weigman *et al*, 1992). The relationship, however, is not a simple one. For example, children who are aggressive *choose* to watch more violent programmes, and come from homes in which there is less parental supervision, with parents who have the same viewing preferences, with punitive disciplinary styles and, in some cases, more domestic violence or conflict. Children of lesser intelligence are more predictably affected by violence on television. In putting together the available data, and by including trauma theory which hitherto has not been done, the chain of causation is likely to be as follows. Vulnerable or behaviourally disturbed children, especially those children from disharmonious homes, sensitised to violence by exposure to real-life violence, growing up in families and peer-groups in which violence is approved of, and especially those of lower intelligence, will choose to watch more violent television, both as a way of coping with trauma through mastery by proxy and because they become progressively more desensitised and 'need' greater levels of stimulation to achieve the same effect. They are allowed to watch more because it is consonant with what their parents watch and/or because they are under-supervised.

What it amounts to is that the least well-looked-after, most aggressive children are made more aggressive by what they see and have the least good chance of reversing this. Other children either get scared because they are still able to identify with the victim, or are fundamentally secure in their families and assume that everything will turn out all right in the end. Paradoxically, it may be most difficult to recognise that what they are seeing is having a disturbing effect upon them in those children who are more prone to aggression. Indeed, they may appear to be enjoying themselves, with laughter and cynicism, distancing themselves from their fears. Their parents may be the parents least likely to notice and understand the detrimental effect on their children, and to offer limit-setting, reassurance, support, and a corrective prosocial perspective.

Children as victims of violence: stranger attacks, physical and sexual abuse, and bullying

Perhaps surprisingly, other than in the growing literature on sexual abuse, there are few traumatic stress formulations or analyses in relation to children as direct victims of interpersonal violence. Although in two of the most influential studies of PTSD in children (Terr, 1979, 1983; Pynoos *et al*, 1987) they were as victims of crime, the research emphasis has been on children in wars and disasters, and as witnesses of violence. Of course, all victims are also witnesses but, as has been pointed out before, victims tend to have a more narrowly-focused, more egocentric perspective.

In the case of children under sniper fire in a school playground (Pynoos *et al*, 1987) and in the case of a bus-load of children kidnapped and entombed in the dark for more than 24 hours (Terr, 1979, 1983), children were both victims and witnesses. However, as victims they were non-specific targets and, as such, attribution of causality and with it preoccupations of recurrence would be different from an attack that had more specific personal meaning and hence greater predictability, as is the case with intrafamilial abuse and bullying.

Reviewing post-traumatic reactions to childhood physical and sexual abuse, Green (1993) pointed out that, unlike extrafamilial traumatic situations, where parents buffer stress and provide protection and support, in intrafamilial abuse one of the parents is the 'instrument' of trauma and the other parent is demonstrably unable or unwilling to protect the child. Abused children are usually subjected to distorted relationships and complex psychosocial adversity. Furthermore, traumatic stress is predictably, although erratically, recurrent and enduring. Repeated traumata, once patterned, are accommodated to (Summit, 1983) and there may be symptom differentiation with the greater likelihood of dissociative symptoms, compared with the reaction to single traumatic events (Terr, 1991). This is certainly the case with sexual abuse.

For physical abuse there have been no studies to date which have adequately differentiated the effects of witnessing violence (without also being a victim) from the effects of the abuse in its own right. There is, of course, a high degree of overlap (Jaffe *et al*, 1990), both in terms of incidence and developmental psychopathology. Numerous studies have described the anxiety and fearful hypervigilance of the physically abused child (Kempe & Kempe, 1978; George & Main, 1979; Green, 1985). 'Hyper-aggression' in physically abused children has been noted in toddlers (George & Main, 1979) and older children (Livingston, 1987), and adolescents convicted of crimes involving violence were much more likely to have been abused compared with non-violent delinquents (Lewis *et al*, 1979). Unfortunately, there is significant continuity into adult life and parenting of the next generation. Other than the studies already referred to, Egeland *et al* (1987), in a controlled study, found that 70% of mothers who had experienced physical abuse in their own childhood were abusive or neglectful towards their children.

Physically abused children are also prone to depression, with self-destructive or frankly suicidal behaviour (Allen & Tarnowski, 1989). This derives from their accommodation to their abuser's view of them as bad, blameworthy and undeserving of love or protection (Green, 1978) but may also function as a distance-regulator in circumstances of motivational conflict (that is, to act out rage towards the parent while simultaneously eliciting their care and concern). The protectiveness they elicit in professionals will, in many cases, facilitate the disclosure of abuse for the first time.

PTSD in sexually abused children was reviewed by Goodwin (1985), who speculated that PTSD may be more severe and long-lasting than in victims of rape because the sexual assaults were repeated over time. In general, the psychological repercussions of child sexual abuse increase the longer the abuse persists (Browne & Finkelhor, 1986), and is much more common in children abused by their father, especially when compared with children abused by older children (McLeer *et al*, 1988). Nearly half the sexually abused children in a clinic-referred sample had PTSD, with a further 40% having symptoms of post-traumatic stress insufficient to qualify for a DSM–III–R diagnosis of PTSD (McLeer *et al*, 1992). Intrusive thoughts are particularly common (Allen *et al*, 1991), especially in those children that develop stable and global attributions of causality of the abuse in terms of perpetrators ("all adults are capable of abusing children") and themselves as victims ("I remain liable to be abused in the future") (Wolfe *et al*, 1989). The latter attributional style also predicts impaired social competence and depression.

Depression is common in sexually abused children with PTSD (McLeer *et al*, 1992) and in adult survivors (Finkelhor, 1986), with a high incidence of suicidal behaviour and self-mutilation, often coexisting with bulimia and borderline personality disorder (Herman *et al*, 1989). Anorexia nervosa may occur, in part functioning to help the adolescent to delay the challenges of sexual development. Dissociation symptoms may be particularly common after penetrative sexual abuse (Pynoos, 1993), and abuse (physical and sexual) is the factor common to most people with multiple personality disorder (Braun & Sachs, 1985). Hysterical symptoms are also described.

Green (1993) proposed a continuum of defensive reactions from hypervigilance through phobic avoidance to hysterical conversion and dissociation.

> "In PTSD, the avoidant and dissociative defences buttressed by a constricted affect fail to prevent a breakthrough of intrusive recollections of the traumatic event accompanied by autonomic arousal." (Green, 1993)

PTSD may well persist into adult life and may be activated in its acute form by traumatic reminders (Lindberg & Distad, 1985; Pynoos, 1993). Alternatively, defensive adaptation may become entrenched, with the development of personality disorder.

Bullying in schools has until recently been underrated as a source of intense stress to victims. The subject is comprehensively examined in Tattum & Lane's *Bullying in Schools* (1988), in Olweus (1994), and in companion articles by Lowenstein (1978*a,b*), describing the characteristics of the bully and the bullied. School phobia in some of the bullied children may represent a social syndrome of PTSD and may need to be treated accordingly.

Conclusion

Interpersonal violence cannot be wished away and will inevitably be part of the lives of some unfortunate children. However, our growing understanding of the causes of violence and the mechanisms and mediators of its effects will help us to develop more effective primary and secondary preventive treatment programmes, to gradually reduce the morbidity that arises from violence and attenuate the cycle of violence for the generations to come.

References

Abramson, L. Y., Seligman, M. E. P. & Teasdale, A. D. (1978) Learned helplessness in humans: critique and reformulation. *Journal of Abnormal Psychology*, **87**, 47–49.

Adler, Z. (1987) *Rape on Trial*. London: Routledge and Keegan.

Alesi, J. S. & Hearn, K. (1984) Group treatment for battered women. In *Battered Women and their Families* (ed. A. R. Roberts), pp. 49–61. New York: Springer.

Allen, D. M. & Tarnowski, K. J. (1989) Depressive characteristics of physically abused children. *Journal of Abnormal Child Psychology*, **17**, 1–11.

Amir, M. (1967) Victim precipitation in rape. *Criminology and Police Science*, **59**, 493–502.

Atkeson, B. M., Calhoun, K. S., Resick, P. A., *et al* (1982) Victims of rape: repeated assessment of depressive symptoms. *Journal of Consulting and Clinical Psychology*, **50**, 96–102.

Bandura, A. (1973) *Aggression: A Social Learning Analysis*. Englewood Cliffs, NJ: Prentice-Hall.

Barlow, G. & Hill, A. (1985) *Video Violence and Children*. Hodder and Stoughton.

Becker, J. V. & Skinner, L. J. (1983) Assessment and treatment of regulated sexual dysfunctions. *Clinical Psychologist*, **3**, 102–105.

Bergman, B. & Brismar, B. (1991) A 5 year follow-up study of 117 battered women. *American Journal of Public Health*, **81**, 1468–1488.

——, Larsson, G., Brismar, B., *et al* (1987) Psychiatric morbidity and personality characteristics of battered women. *Acta Psychiatrica Scandinavica*, **76**, 678–683.

Berkowitz, L. & Rogers, K. H. (1986) A priming effect analysis of media influences. In *Perspectives on Media Effects* (eds J. Bryant & D. Zillman), pp. 57–81. Hillsdale, NJ: Erlbaum.

Bettelheim, B. (1960) *The Informed Heart*. Harmondsworth: Penguin Books.

Black, D. & Kaplan, T. (1988) Father kills mother: Issues and problems encountered by a child psychiatric team. *British Journal of Psychiatry*, **153**, 624–630.

Block, J. H., Block, J. & Morrison, A. (1981) Parental agreement – disagreement on child-rearing orientations and gender-related personality correlates in children. *Child Development*, **52**, 965–974.

Bohn, D. K. (1990) Domestic violence and pregnancy: implications for practice. *Journal of Nurse-Midwifery*, **35**, 86–98.

Bowker, D. K. (1983) *Beating Wife Beating*. Lexington, MA: Lexington Books.

Bowlby, J. (1980) *Attachment and Loss, vol. 3*. London: Hogarth.

Bowling, B. (1993) Racial harassment and the process of the victimisation. *British Journal of Criminology*, **33**, 231–250.

Braun, B. G. & Sachs, R. G. (1985) The development of multiple personality disorder: predisposing, precipitating and perpetuating factors. In *Childhood Antecedents of Multiple Personality* (ed. P. Kluft), pp. 38–64. Washington, DC: APP.

Breslau, N., Davis, G. C., Andreski, P., *et al* (1991) Traumatic events and post traumatic stress disorder in an urban population of young adults. *Archives of General Psychiatry*, **48**, 216–222.

Briere, J. (1989) *Therapy for Adults Molested as Children*. New York: Springer.

Browne, A. (1987) *When Battered Women Kill*. New York: Free Press.

—— & Finkelhor, D. (1986) Initial and long-term effects: a review of the research. In *A Sourcebook on Child Sexual Abuse* (ed. D. Finkelhor), pp. 143–179. Beverley Hills, CA: Sage.

Burgess, A. W. & Holmstrom, L. L. (1974) Rape trauma syndrome. *American Journal of Psychiatry*, **131**, 981–986.

Burt, M. R. & Katz, B. L. (1985) Rape, robbery and burglary: responses to actual and feared criminal victimisation with special focus on women and the elderly. *Victimology*, **10**, 325–358.

Charney, D. A. & Russell, R. C. (1994) An overview of sexual harassment. *American Journal of Psychiatry*, **151**, 10–17.

Cooper, J. & Pomeiye, J. (1988) Racial attacks and racial harassment: lesson from a local project. In *Victims of Crime: a New Deal* (eds M. Maguire & J. J. Pointing), pp. 83–89. Milton Keynes: Open University Press.

Dobash, R. P. & Dobash, R. E. (1979) *Violence Against Wives. A Case Against the Patriarchy*. New York: Free Press.

Dodge, K. A., Bates, J. E. & Pettit, G. S. (1990) Mechanisms in the cycle of violence. *Science*, **250**, 1678–1683.

Dutton, D. & Painter, S. L. (1981) Traumatic bonding: the development of emotional attachments in battered women and other relationships of intermittent abuse. *Victimology: An International Journal*, **61**, 139–155.

Dutton, M. A. & Goodman, L. A. (1994) Post traumatic stress disorder among battered women: analysis of legal implications. *Behavioural Sciences and the Law*, **12**, 215–234.

Edwards, S. M. (1985) A socio-legal evaluation of gender ideologies in domestic violence assault and spousal homicides. *Victimology: An International Journal*, **1**, 186–205.

Egeland, B., Jacobvitz, D. & Papetola, K. (1987) Intergenerational continuity of parental abuse. In *Biosocial Aspects of Child Abuse* (eds J. Lancaster & R. Gelles), pp. 255–276. San Francisco: Jossey-Bass.

Feinstein, A. & Dolan, R. (1991) Predictors of post traumatic stress disorder following physical trauma: an examination of the stressor criterion. *Psychological Medicine*, **21**, 85–91.

Feshbach, S. & Singer, R. D. (1971) Television and aggression. San Francisco: Jossey-Bass.

Finkelhor, D. (1986) *A Sourcebook on Child Sexual Abuse*. Beverley Hills, CA: Sage.

Frank, E. & Anderson, B. P. (1987) Psychiatric disorders in rape victims: past history and current symptomatology. *Comprehensive Psychiatry*, **28**, 77–82.

Frieze, I. H. (1983) Investigating the causes and consequences of marital rape. *Signs*, **8**, 532–553.

Fromuth, M. E. (1986) The relationship of child sexual abuse with altered psychological and sexual adjustment. *Child Abuse and Neglect*, **10**, 5–15.

Gelles, R. J. (1976) Abused wives, why do they stay? *Journal of Marriage and the Family*, 659–668.

—— & Cornell, C. P. (1985) *Intimate Violence in Families*. Beverly Hills, CA: Sage.

—— & Harrop, J. W. (1989) Violence, battering and psychological distress in women. *Journal of Interpersonal Violence*, **4**, 400–440.

George, C. & Main, M. (1979) Social interactions in young abused children: approach, avoidance and aggression. *Child Development*, **50**, 306–319.

Gianakos, I. & Wagner, E. E. (1987) Relations between hand test variables and the psychological characteristics and behaviours of battered women. *Journal of Personality Assessment*, **51**, 220–227.

Goldner, V., Penn, P., Sheinberg, M., *et al* (1990) Love and violence: gender paradoxes in volatile attachments. *Family Process*, **29**, 343–364.

Goodwin, J. (1985) Post-traumatic symptoms in incest victims. In *Post-traumatic Stress Disorder in Children* (eds S. Eth & R. Pynoos), pp. 157–168. Washington, DC: APP.

Green, A. (1978) Self-destructive behaviour in battered children. *American Journal of Psychiatry*, **135**, 579–586.

—— (1985) Children traumatised by physical abuse. In *Post-traumatic Stress Disorder in Children* (eds S. Eth & R. Pynoos), pp. 135–154. Washington, DC: APP.

—— (1993) Childhood sexual and physical abuse. In *The International Handbook of Traumatic Stress Syndromes* (eds J. P. Wilson & B. Raphael), pp. 577–592. New York: Plenum.

Gunter, B. & McAleer, J. (1990) *Children and Television: The Eye of the Monster?* London: Routledge.

Halperin, D. A. (1983) *Group Processes in Cult Affiliation and Recruitment. Psychodynamic Perspectives on Religion, Sect and Cult.* Boston: John Wright.

Harris-Hendriks, J., Black, D. & Kaplan, T. (1993) *When Father Kills Mother: Guiding Children through Trauma and Grief.* London: Routledge.

Helzer, J., Robins, L. & McEvoy, L. (1987) Post traumatic stress disorder in the general population: findings of the Epidemiologic Catchment Area Survey. *New England Journal of Medicine*, **317**, 1630–1634.

Herman, J. L. (ed.) (1992) *Trauma and Recovery. From Domestic Abuse to Political Terror.* London: Harper-Collins.

——, Perry, J. C. & van der Kolk, B. (1989) Childhood trauma in borderline personality disorder. *American Journal of Psychiatry*, **146**, 490–495.

Hilberman, E. (1980) Overview: The wife-beater's wife reconsidered. *American Journal of Psychiatry*, **137**, 1336–1347.

—— & Munson, K (1977) Sixty battered women. *Victimology: An International Journal*, **2**, 460–470.

Hoff, L. A. (1990) *Battered Women as Survivors.* London: Routledge.

Hough, M. & Mayhew, P. (1985) *Taking Account of Crime: Key Finds from the 1984 British Crime Survey Home Office Research Study.* London. HMSO.

Jacobson, A., Koehler, J. E. & Jones-Brown, C. (1987) The failure of routine assessment to detect histories of assault experienced by psychiatric patients. *Hospital and Community Psychiatry*, **38**, 387–389.

Jaffe, P., Wolfe, D. A., Wilson, S., *et al* (1986) Emotional and physical heath problems of battered women. *Canadian Journal of Psychiatry*, **31**, 625–629.

——, —— & —— (1990) *Children of Battered Women.* Newbury Park: Sage.

Janoff-Bulman, R. (1988) Victims of violence. In *Handbook of Stress, Cognition and Health* (eds S. Fisher & J. Reason), pp. 101–113. Chichester: John Wiley.

Jenkins, J. M. & Smith, M. A. (1990) Factors protecting children living in disharmonious homes: maternal reports. *Journal of the American Academy of Child and Adolescent Psychiatry*, **29**, 60–69.

—— & —— (1991) Marital disharmony and children's behaviour problems: aspects of a poor marriage that affect children adversely. *Journal of Child Psychology and Psychiatry*, **32**, 793–810.

Josephson, W. (1987) Television violence and children's aggression: testing the priming, social script and disinhibition predictions. *Journal of Personality and Social Psychology*, **53**, 882–890.

Keenan, B (1992) *An Evil Cradling.* London: Vintage.

Kempe, R. S. & Kempe, C. H. (1978) *Child Abuse.* London: Fontana.

Kilpatrick, D. G., Veronen, L. J. & Resick, P. A. (1979) The aftermath of rape: recent empirical findings. *Journal of Orthopsychiatry*, **149**, 658–669.

——, —— & Best, C. L. (1985a) Factors predicting psychological distress among rape victims. In *Trauma and its Wake* (ed. C. E. Figley). New York: Brunner.

——, Best, C. L, Veronen, L. J., *et al* (1985b) Mental health correlates of criminal victimisation: a random community survey. *Journal of Consulting and Clinical Psychology*, **53**, 866–873.

——, Saunders, B. E., Veronen, L. J., *et al* (1987) Criminal victimisation: lifetime prevalence, reporting to the police and psychological impact. *Crime and Delinquency*, **33**, 479–489.

——, ——, Amick-McMullen, A., *et al* (1989) Victim and the crime factors associated with the development of crime-related post traumatic stress disorder. *Behaviour Therapy*, **20**, 199–214.

Koss, M. P. (1988) Criminal victimisation among women; impacted on health status and medical services usage. Paper presented at the American Psychological Association, Atlanta, GA.

Lerner, M. J. & Miller, D. T. (1978) Just world research and attribution process; looking back and ahead. *Psychiatry Bulletin*, **85**, 1030–1051.

Lewis, D., Sharok, S., Pincus, J., *et al* (1979) Violent juvenile delinquents: psychiatric, neurological, psychological and abuse factors. *Journal of the American Academy of Child Psychiatry*, **18**, 307–319.

Lifton, R. J. (1987) *Cults: Religious Totalism and Civil Liberties. The Future of Importality and Other Essays for a Nuclear Age*. New York: Basic Books.

Lindberg, F. & Distad, L. (1985) Post-traumatic stress disorder in women who experienced childhood incest. *Child Abuse and Neglect*, **9**, 329–334.

Livingston, R. (1987) Sexually and physically abused children. *Journal of the American Academy of Child Psychiatry*, **26**, 413–415.

Lowenstein, L. F. (1978*a*) The bullied and non-bullied child. *Bulletin of the British Psychological Society*, **31**, 316–318.

—— (1978*b*) Who is the bully? *Bulletin of the British Psychological Society*, **31**, 147–149.

McFarlane, A. C. (1987) Post-traumatic phenomena in a longitudinal study of children following a natural disaster. *Journal of the American Academy of Child and Adolescent Psychiatry*, **26**, 764–769.

—— (1989) Battering during pregnancy: tip of an iceberg revealed. *Women and Health*, **15**, 69–84.

McLeer, S. V., Deblinger, E., Atkins, M. S., *et al* (1988) Post-traumatic stress disorder in sexually abused children. *Journal of the American Academy of Child and Adolescent Psychiatry*, **27**, 650–654.

——, ——, Henry, D., *et al* (1992) Sexually abused children at high risk of post-traumatic stress disorder. *Journal of the American Academy of Child and Adolescent Psychiatry*, **31**, 875–879.

Maguire, M. & Corbett, C. (1987) *The Effects of Crime and the Work of Victims Support Schemes*. Aldershot: Gower.

Malmquist, C. (1986) Children who witness parental murder: post-traumatic aspects. *Journal of the American Academy of Child and Adolescent Psychiatry*, **25**, 320–325.

Mawby, R. I. & Gill, M. L. (1987) *Crime Victims Needs, Services and the Voluntary Sector*. London: Tavistock.

Mayhew, P., Aye Maung, N. & Mirrlees-Black, C. (1993) *The 1992 British Crime Survey*. London: HMSO.

Mezey, G. C. (1994) Sexual victimisation in the work place. In *Violence and Health Care Professionals* (ed. T. Wykes), pp. 89–102. London: Chapman & Hall.

—— & Taylor, P. (1987) Psychological reactions of women who have been raped. *British Journal of Psychiatry*, **17**, 249–253.

—— & King, M. (1989) The effects of sexual assault on men – a survey of 22 subjects. *Psychological Medicine*, **19**, 205–209.

—— & Rubenstein, M. (1992) Medico-legal aspects of sexual harassment. *Journal of Forensic Psychiatry*, **3**, 221–233.

Mullen, P. E., Martin, J. C., Anderson, S. E., *et al* (1993) Childhood sexual abuse and mental health in adult life. *British Journal of Psychiatry*, **163**, 721–732.

——, ——, ——, *et al* (1994) The effects of child sexual abuse on social, interpersonal and sexual function in adult life. *British Journal of Psychiatry*, **165**, 35–47.

Murphy, S. M., Amick McMullan, A., Kilpatrick, D. G., *et al* (1988) Rape victims self-esteem: a longitudinal analysis. *Journal of Interpersonal Violence*, **3**, 355–370.

Nader, K., Pynoos, R. S., Fairbanks, L., *et al* (1990) Post traumatic stress disorder reactions one year after a sniper attack at their school. *American Journal of Psychiatry*, **147**, 1526–1530.

Norris, F. H. (1992) Epidemiology of trauma: frequency and impact of different potentially traumatic events on different demographic groups. *Journal of Consulting and Clinical Psychology*, **60**, 409–418.

Ochberg, F. (1978) The victim of terrorism, psychiatric considerations. *Terrorism: an International Journal*, **1**, 147–167.

Oliver, H. E. (1993) Intergenerational transmission of child abuse: rates and research implications. *American Journal of Psychiatry*, **150**, 1315–1324.

Olweus, D. (1994) Bullying in schools: basic facts and effects of a school based intervention programme. *Journal of Child Psychology and Psychiatry*, **35**, 1171–1190.

Pagelow, M. D. (1981) *Women-Battering: Victims and their Experiences*. Beverley Hills, CA: Sage.

Patterson, G. R. (1982) *Coercive Family Process*. Eugene, OR: Castalia.

Pynoos, R. (1993) Traumatic stress and developmental psychopathology in children and adolescents. *American Psychiatric Press Review of Psychiatry*, **12**, 205–238.

—— & Eth, S. (1985) Children traumatized by witnessing acts of personal violence: homicide, rape or suicidal behaviour. In *Post-traumatic Stress Disorder in Children* (eds S. Eth & R. Pynoos), pp. 19–43. Washington, DC: APP.

—— & —— (1986) Witness to violence: the child interview. *Journal of the American Academy of Child Psychiatry*, **25**, 306–319.

—— & Nader, K. (1988) Children who witness the sexual assaults of their mothers. *Journal of the American Academy of Child and Adolescent Psychiatry*, **27**, 567–572.

——, Frederick, C., Nader, K., *et al* (1987). Life threat and post-traumatic stress in school age children. *Archives of General Psychiatry*, **44**, 1057–1063.

Rath, G. D., Jarratt, L. G. & Leonardson, G. (1989) Rates of domestic violence against adult women by men partners. *Journal of American Board Family Practice*, **2**, 227–233.

Resick, P. A., Calhoun, K. S., Atkeson, B. H., *et al* (1981) Social adjustment in sexual assault victims. *Journal of Consulting and Clinical Psychology*, **49**, 705–712.

Resnick, H., Kilpatrick, D. G., Dansky, B. S., *et al* (1993) Prevalence of civilian trauma and post traumatic stress disorder in a representative national sample of women. *Journal of Consulting and Clinical Psychology*, **61**, 984–991.

Runtz, M. & Briere, J (1986) Adolescent 'acting-out' and childhood history of sexual abuse. *Journal of Interpersonal Violence*, **1**, 326–334.

Russell, D. E. H. (1986) *The Secret Trauma: Incest in the Lives of Girls and Women*. New York: Basic Books.

Rutter, M. (1979) Protective factors in children: responses to stress and disadvantage. In *Prevention of Psychopathology: Vol. 3. Promoting Social Competence and Coping in Children* (eds M. W. Kent & J. E. Rolf), pp. 49–74. Hanover, NH: University Press of New England.

Rynearson, E. K. (1984) Bereavement after homicide: a descriptive study. *American Journal of Psychiatry*, **141**, 1452–1454.

—— & McCreery, J. M (1993) Bereavement after homicide: a synergism of trauma and loss. *American Journal of Psychiatry*, **150**, 258–261.

Saunders, B. E., Kilpatrick, D. G., Resnick, H. S., *et al* (1989) Brief screening for lifetime history of criminal victimisation about mental health intake. *Journal of Interpersonal Violence*, **4**, 267–277.

Scott (1974) Battered wives. *British Journal of Psychiatry*, **125**, 433–441.

Scott-Gliba, E., Minne, C. & Mezey, G. C. (1995) The psychological, behavioural and emotional impact of surviving an abusive relationship. *Journal of Forensic Psychiatry*, **6**, 343–358.

Seligman, M. E. (1975) *Helplessness: on Depression, Development and Death*. San Francisco: Freeman.

Shapland, J., Willmore, J. & Duff, P. (1985) *Victims in the Criminal Justice System*. Aldershot: Gower.

Shepherd, J., Qureshi, R. & Preston, M. (1990) Psychological distress after assaults and accidents. *British Medical Journal*, **301**, 849–850.

Stark, E., Flitcraft, A. & Frazier, W. (1979). Medicine and patriarchal violence: The social construction of a private event. *International Journal of Health Services*, **9**, 461–493.

Steketee, G. & Foa, E. (1977) Rape victims: post traumatic stress responses and their treatment. *Journal of Anxiety Disorders*, **1**, 69–86.

Straus, M., Gelles, R. & Steinmetz, S. (1980) *Behind Closed Doors: Violence in the American Family*. New York: Anchor Press/Doubleday.

Summit, R. (1983) The child sexual abuse accommodation syndrome. *Child Abuse and Neglect*, **7**, 177–182.

Symonds, M. (1975) Victims of violence: psychological effects and after effects. *American Journal of Psychoanalysis*, **35**, 19–26.

Tattum, D. P. & Lane, D. A. (1988) *Bullying in Schools*. Trentham Books.

Terr, L. (1979) Children of Chowchilla. *Psychoanalytic Study of the Child*, **34**, 547–623.

—— (1983) Chowchilla revisited: the effects of psychic trauma four years after a school bus kidnapping. *American Journal of Psychiatry*, **140**, 1543–1550.

—— (1991) Childhood traumas – an outline and overview. *American Journal of Psychiatry*, **148**, 10–20.

Thomas, C., Adshead, G. & Mezey, G. (1994) Traumatic responses to child murder. *Journal of Forensic Psychiatry*, 5, 168–176.

van der Kolk, B. A. (1989) The compulsion to re-enact the trauma: re-enactment, re-victimisation and masochism. *Psychiatric Clinics of North America*, 12, 389–411.

Walker, L. E. A. (1979) *The Battered Woman*. New York: Harper and Row.

—— (1985) Psychological impact of the criminalization of domestic violence on victims. *Victimology: An International Journal*, 10, 281–300.

Weigman, O., Kuttschreuter, M. & Baarde, B. (1992) A longitudinal study of the effects of TV viewing on aggressive and prosocial behaviour. *British Journal of Social Psychology*, 31, 147–164.

West, C. G., Fernandez, A., Hillard, J. R., *et al* (1990) Psychiatric disorders of abused women at a shelter. *Psychiatric Quarterly*, 61, 295–301.

Widom, C. S. (1989) Child abuse, neglect and adult behaviour: research design and findings on criminality, violence and child abuse. *American Journal of Orthopsychiatry*, 59, 355–367.

Wolfe, D. A., Jaffe, P., Wilson, S. K., *et al* (1985) Children of battered women: the relation of child behaviour to family violence and maternal stress. *Journal of Consulting and Clinical Psychology*, 53, 657–665.

Wolfe, V. V., Gentile, C. & Wolfe, D. (1989) The impact of sexual abuse on children: a post traumatic stress disorder formulation. *Behaviour Therapy*, 20, 215–228.

Wolfgang, M. E. (1958) *Patterns in Criminal Homicide*. Philadelphia, PA: University of Pennsylvania Press.

Wykes, T. & Whittington, R. (1994) Reactions to assault. In *Violence and Health Care Professionals* (ed. T. Wykes), pp. 105–126. London: Chapman & Hall.

12 Post-traumatic stress disorder in the elderly

INGE HYMAN

"We have a responsibility to the elderly to ensure that their ability to enjoy as normal a life as possible, to the full, is maintained throughout the whole life span." (Woods & Britton, 1988)

If we accept this as an obvious and humane attitude, it then seems extraordinary that when we examine the most recent literature on post-traumatic stress disorder in the elderly we find there is some research on its prevalence, but very little on its treatment.

Two main types of circumstance could lead to PTSD in the elderly. Firstly, PTSD may be chronic after someone has experienced severe trauma perhaps decades earlier, as in some Holocaust or war survivors, or the survivors of a major natural catastrophe. In such instances PTSD may still be present, or the survivor may be apparently symptom-free for years until PTSD is reactivated by vicissitudes of ageing. Secondly, PTSD may occur after a recent catastrophic event, ranging from such experiences as unexpected bereavements to rape, mugging or natural disasters. In such cases its presence may be overshadowed or obscured by either physical illnesses or damage, depression, or other major diagnosable psychiatric disorders. Although there is an almost folkloric acceptance that recent events are immediately forgotten by the elderly and, therefore, acute recent trauma would not affect the elderly as much as younger victims, there is no evidence that this is the case. Even in the severely demented we cannot be sure that such a trauma has not affected them emotionally, even if cognitively they are unable to describe or verbally articulate what has happened.

Chronic or reactivated PTSD in the elderly

There have been a number of studies in the last two decades designed to ascertain the long-term effects of their experiences on Holocaust survivors and on war veterans. Davidson (1981) emphasised most importantly that generalisations tended to be made and applied to Holocaust survivors as if they were a homogeneous group. In particular, general conclusions were often drawn from observations of biased samples, i.e. from particular groups of survivors who were already receiving or presenting themselves for

199

psychiatric help. Many writers, including Marcus & Rosenberg (1989), agree that a proportion of Holocaust survivors who do seek professional help may have been more severely affected by their traumatic experiences.

However, conclusions drawn from work with clinical groups cannot be assumed to apply to other Holocaust survivors who have not sought such help. Harel *et al* (1993) reviewed the gerontological and Holocaust survivor literature, and found from their own subsequent research data with non-clinical elderly subjects that "the availability of social support and of communication with members of one's primary group and friends are indeed important contributors towards higher levels of psychological well-being", and that in this respect these groups did not significantly differ from other populations of older persons.

However, when Kuch & Cox (1992) investigated the incidence of PTSD in 124 Holocaust survivors who were judged to be free from bipolar affective disorder, obsessive–compulsive disorder and organic brain disorder, a different picture emerged. Their psychiatric assessments made for West German compensation boards (and not for psychiatric treatment purposes) were re-examined for explicit descriptions of current PTSD symptoms according to the DSM–III–R diagnostic criteria; 46% of the total sample met the criteria. The tattooed Auschwitz survivors were three times more likely to meet diagnostic criteria than those survivors who had not been in camps. Most survivors had not received adequate psychiatric care.

Others, who appear to have had well-adjusted personal and professional lives, may endure symptoms of PTSD in the absence of any other psychiatric disorder. The most frequently reported symptoms are sleep disorders, recurrent nightmares and intense distress over reminders, and for some survivors these have remained a chronic and considerable problem over 45 years (Rosen *et al*, 1991; Kuch & Cox, 1992).

In contrast to instances of symptoms of PTSD being chronically present, Christenson *et al* (1981) described the reactivation of traumatic conflicts after many symptom-free years. They stated that losses associated with invo-lutional age, including parental loss, children leaving home, pending or actual retirement, and increasing medical disabilities, all serve as stressors that may reactivate latent PTSD. Similarly, Danieli (1982) stated that (the survivors') "physical frailty and psychological vulnerability may stimulate memories of traumatic experiences which occurred in camps, in ghettos, or in hiding".

Furthermore, it is not just psychiatric illnesses which must be assessed with early trauma in mind. It has been shown by Zilberfein & Eskin (1992) that physical illness, and in particular hospitalisation, can "trigger intense reactions for Holocaust survivors" and crisis intervention is necessary. Baider *et al* (1992) investigated whether surviving stressful life-threatening situations (LTSs) had an influence on coping with new LTSs. They found that cancer patients who were Holocaust survivors had a much higher level of psycho-logical distress on an appropriate Scale than their controls without such experience. Another study by Solomon & Prager (1992) investigated the notion that "prior experience with extreme stress has an inoculating effect that leads to greater resilience in dealing with other forms of stress". On the contrary, Holocaust experience was found to render the elderly more vulnerable rather than less. Their findings are of particular significance as they were working with a non-clinical group. It thus becomes extremely important when faced with elderly survivors of either the Holocaust, or wars, or atrocities, or even natural catastrophes such as earthquakes or volcanic eruptions, for the therapist "to identify patients whose past traumatic conflicts may contribute to their present illness" (Christenson *et al*, 1981). The presenting psychiatric picture could be obscuring the reactivation of PTSD in the individual.

A number of studies have concentrated on the presence of PTSD in veterans of the Second World War, Vietnam, and other conflicts round the world. Many of these are flawed for the purposes of this review chapter by not differentiating between ages of the subjects. For example, age range can be reported as between 34–60 years compared with another group aged 20–80 years (Hryvniak & Rosse, 1989). Hennessy & Oei (1991) used subjects whose ages ranged from 42 to 70 years. Another study (Wolfe *et al*, 1992) of female Vietnam veterans used subjects ranging from 37–72 years. In contrast, a Dutch study by Hovens *et al* (1992) assessed 147 male Dutch Second World War Resistance veterans of similar age and found that 56% were currently suffering from PTSD; of the remaining 44% who did not meet the criteria for current PTSD, only 4% had no symptoms at all. All these studies used the DSM–III criteria for PTSD. A similar study of 108 Second World War veterans in Australia by Kidson *et al* (1993) gave a picture of active PTSD in 45% of veterans attending a psychiatric clinic 45 years after the war. The authors also found that "the presence of both an anxiety and a depressive disorder was substantially and significantly more common in the veterans who had PTSD". Sutker *et al* (1993) reported that 70% of Second World War prisoners of war fulfilled criteria for a current diagnosis, and 78% for a life-time diagnosis, of PTSD 40 years on.

In an excellent review article, Orner (1992) discussed studies of European war veterans up to the date of his paper. They "reveal how little reliable and valid knowledge we have about this large population found in all parts of our continent". He stated that he had been unable to find a single controlled study of treatment outcomes carried out with European war veterans. He continued: "This scarcity of information remains a severely limiting factor for clinicians seeking guidance on how to plan and prioritise their therapeutic endeavours." He quoted Op den Velde's (1988) reports of disillusionment, alienation and resentment among war veterans, and suggested that these should be registered as "serious complaints rooted in factual failure to meet [veterans'] needs". Op den Velde (1988) also questioned whether apparently successful post-war adaptation can be achieved without any symptoms at all being chronically present. De Loos (1990) categorised the long-term psychosomatic sequelae of chronic PTSD in war veterans and advocated great caution in using drugs for such conditions, in case they reinforced somatisation of emotional problems and possibly made them less amenable to other appropriate psychological forms of therapy. This paper also warned that the therapists in this very complex medical and psychological area may well need specific peer support to avoid 'burn-out'.

Acute PTSD in the elderly

Very little research seems to have been done on the effect on elderly people of recent traumatic events. On the whole, if studies in this area do include a number of elderly people in the age range of subjects examined, they do so without differentiating them from the group. This could be, of course, because the elderly do not differ from younger individuals in their response to recent trauma. For example, Mayou *et al* (1993) studied 188 consecutive road-accident victims aged 18–70. The elderly were not apparently distinguishable from others in this group. However, in another study by Goenjian *et al* (1994), the elderly were compared with younger adults 18 months after the 1988 Armenian earthquake. The elderly scored higher on arousal symptoms and lower on intrusive symptoms. Once again, sleep difficulties were a major problem in the elderly after trauma. There was also a positive correlation between loss of family members and severity of PTSD. Livingston *et al* (1992) reported that after the Lockerbie disaster the elderly had a similar response to the younger survivors as assessed on the DSM–III–R criteria for PTSD. However, it is interesting and important to note that there was a "high incidence of co-existing major depression, unlike the younger population".

As far as rape, mugging, burglary and so on are concerned, there seems to be very little studied with particular reference to the elderly. Whether this is because it is accepted that the elderly will react in the same way as younger adults, or whether it is due to neglect of the reality of the psychological difficulties of the elderly after such events, is hard to know. Tyra (1993) has examined the effect of rape on older women, and although the symptoms after such an event are given the term "rape trauma syndrome", "a diagnosis made by nurses", it is clearly very much like PTSD. 'Nursing actions' are described which are clearly therapies for the acute and more chronic stages of the reaction. In Illinois a study by Durks & Hayes (1986) described a programme designed in part to train elderly volunteers to help other elderly victims of crime.

Treatment

Although psychodynamic, behavioural and cognitive therapies have been used with sufferers of PTSD, very little has, to date, been reported on using these techniques with the elderly. More research is needed.

Auerhahn *et al* (1993) reported on psychotherapy with Holocaust survivors and gave clinical examples, but basically their approach did not recognise PTSD as such. At present, it would seem that there are no journal reports of active research in the use of behavioural or cognitive therapy specifically with the elderly suffering from chronic, reactivated or acute PTSD. Krell (1990) suggested that at the end of the Second World War "there was a conspicuous absence of response by the psychiatric profession to the challenge of rehabilitating Holocaust survivors", and that textbooks largely ignored this group. However, in the last 20 years in his practice Krell has seen "a steady stream of Holocaust survivors and their children". An increasing number of elderly Holocaust or war survivors are presenting themselves perhaps for the first time, at old-age psychiatric clinics in this country (personal communications from consultants in old-age psychiatry: Nori Graham, Royal Free Hospital; Martin Blanchard, Queen Mary's Hampstead; Gill Livingston, Whittington Hospital; Bob Woods, Department of Psychology, University College, London).

It is, therefore, important to recognise firstly, that if an elderly person admitted into hospital for a medical reason (other than that resulting from an immediate acute trauma) shows unusually stressed or anxious behaviour out of proportion to the medical procedure, it would be advisable to take a more detailed history of earlier life events; and secondly, if there is evidence in the history of a psychiatric patient that he or she has been involved in an early severe trauma, even where a good social adjustment seems to have been made thereafter, the possibility of PTSD being present should be taken into account. This could well be an important factor in diagnosis (particularly where an atypical pattern is presented) and, therefore, also in determining treatment. The majority of the elderly are neither cognitively impaired nor dementing (only 18% over the age of 80, and 25% over 90 show forms of dementia). Thus research into the best possible treatment for the traumatised elderly, including cognitive therapy, is fundamentally worthwhile.

References

Auerhahn, N. C., Laub, D. & Peskin, H. (1993) Psychotherapy with Holocaust survivors. *Psychotherapy*, **30**, 434–442.

Baider, L., Peretz, T. & De Nour, A. (1992) Effect of the Holocaust on coping with cancer. *Social Science and Medicine*, **34**, 11–15.

Christenson, R. M., Walker, J. I., Ross, D. R., *et al* (1981) Reactivation of traumatic conflicts. *American Journal of Psychiatry*, **138**, 984–985.

Danieli, Y. (1982) Families of survivors of the Nazi Holocaust: some short-term and long-term effects. In *Stress and Anxiety* (eds C. D. Spielberger, I. G. Sarason & N. A. Milgram). Washington, DC: Hemisphere Publishing.

Davidson, S. (1981) Clinical and psychotherapeutic experience with survivors and their families. *The Family Physician*, **10**, 313–321.

De Loos, W. S. (1990) Psychosomatic manifestations of chronic post-traumatic stress disorder. In *Post-traumatic Stress Disorder: Etiology, Phenomenology and Treatment* (eds M. E. Wolf & A. D. Mosnaim). Washington, DC: APP.

Durks, M. J. & Hayes, R. L. (1986) Peer counselling for elderly victims of crime and violence. *Journal for Specialists in Group Work*, **11**, 107–113.

Goenjian, A. K., Najarian, L. M., Pynoos, R. S., *et al* (1994) Posttraumatic stress disorder in elderly and younger adults after the 1988 earthquake in Armenia. *American Journal of Psychiatry*, **151**, 895–901.

Harel, Z., Kahana, B. & Kahana, E. (1993) Social resources and the mental health of ageing Nazi Holocaust survivors and immigrants. In *International Handbook of Traumatic Stress Syndromes* (eds J. P. Wilson & B. Raphael), pp. 241–252. New York: Plenum Press.

Hennessy, B. & Oei, T. P. (1991) The relationship between severity of combat exposure and army status on post-traumatic stress disorder among Australian Vietnam war veterans. *Behaviour Change*, **8**, 136–144.

Hovens, J. E., Falger, P. R., Op den Veld, W., *et al* (1992) Occurrence of current PTSD among Dutch World War II resistance veterans according to the SCID. *Journal of Anxiety Disorders*, **6**, 147–157.

Hryvniak, M. R. & Rosse, R. B. (1989) Concurrent psychiatric illness in inpatients with post-traumatic stress disorder. *Military Medicine*, **154**, 399–401.

Kidson, M. A., Douglas, J. C. & Holwill, B. J. (1993) Post-traumatic stress disorder in Australian World War II veterans attending a psychiatric outpatient clinic. *Medical Journal of Australia*, **158**, 563–566.

Krell, R. (1990) Holocaust survivors: a clinical perspective. *Psychiatric Journal of the University of Ottawa*, 15, 10–21.

Kuch, K. & Cox, B. J. (1992) Symptoms of PTSD in 124 survivors of the Holocaust. *American Journal of Psychiatry*, **149**, 337–340.

Livingston, H. M., Livingston, M. G., Brooks, D. N., *et al* (1992) Elderly survivors of the Lockerbie air disaster. *International Journal of Geriatric Psychiatry*, **7**, 725–727.

Marcus, P. & Rosenberg, A. (eds) (1989) *Healing their Wounds: Psychotherapy with Holocaust Survivors and their Families*. New York: Praeger.

Mayou, R., Bryant, B. & Duthie, R. (1993) The psychiatric consequences of road traffic accidents. *British Medical Journal*, **307**, 647–651.

Op den Velde, W. (1988) Specific psychiatric disorders. In *Stress, Medical and Legal Analysis of Late Effects of World War II Suffering in the Netherlands* (eds J. F. P. Hers & J. Terpstra). Alphen aan den Rijn: Samson Sijthoff.

Orner, R. J. (1992) Post-traumatic stress disorders and European war veterans. *British Journal of Clinical Psychology*, **31**, 387–403.

Rosen, J., Reynolds, C. F., Yeager, A. L., *et al* (1991) Sleep disturbances in survivors of the Nazi Holocaust. *American Journal of Psychiatry*, **148**, 62–66.

Solomon, Z. & Prager, E. (1992) Elderly Holocaust survivors during the Persian Gulf War: a study of psychological distress. *American Journal of Psychiatry*, **149**, 1707–1710.

Sutker, P. B., Allain, A. N. & Winstead, D. K. (1993) Psychopathology and psychiatric diagnoses of World War II Pacific Theater prisoner of war survivors and combat veterans. *American Journal of Psychiatry*, **150**, 240–245.

Tyra, P. A. (1993) Older women: victims of rape. *Journal of Gerontological Nursing*, **19**, 7–12.

Wolfe, J., Brown, P. & Bucsela, M. L. (1992) Symptom responses of female Vietnam veterans to Operation Desert Storm. *American Journal of Psychiatry*, **149**, 676–679.

Woods, R. T. & Britton, P. G. (1988) *Clinical Psychology with the Elderly*. London: Chapman & Hall.

Zilberfein, F. & Eskin, V. (1992) Helping Holocaust survivors with the impact of illness and hospitalisation. *Social Work in Health Care*, **18**, 59–70.

13 Torture

STUART W. TURNER and RONAN MCIVOR

Torture is the intentional use of severe pain or suffering to gain information, confession, punishment, intimidation, coercion, or for any reason based on discrimination. Under the United Nations definition, this attack is always carried out by or with the approval of a public official (United Nations, 1984). It therefore forms part of the systematic process of state control of dissident beliefs and the repression of individuals, groups and communities. So, it is not only the survivor of torture who suffers. This systematic and repressive violence stands to affect all people who share ethnicity, religion or political ideology with the immediate victim. Indeed, it is the intention of the state that this should be the case.

Seen in this way, torture can be identified as part of a broader spectrum of activities, perhaps best described under the phrase 'organised state violence', a process well illustrated by Ignacio Martin-Baro, Vice-Rector of the University of Central America and one of the Jesuits tragically murdered in El Salvador in 1989 because of his human rights work. In his account of the developing conflict in his country between 1980 and 1983, he described how one out of every 200 Salvadorans was a direct victim of the open civil conflict; many were killed by the so-called "death squads", operating with state support and impunity. From 1984 onwards, he reported that there was a shift to a more sophisticated (and politically more acceptable) covert psychological warfare. Brutal actions were carried out on a few individuals in such a way that the wider population was terrorised. For this to be successful, the perpetrators had to make sure that the population was well informed about the violence taking place and was maintained in a state of fear by a sequence of unpredictable actions involving acts of intimidation alternating with conditional protection (Martin-Baro, 1988).

So systematic harassment, detention, interrogation and searches, which do not fall within a narrow definition of torture, clearly share similar repressive intentions and must be understood in similar psychological and political terms. Jacobo Timerman, in his autobiographical writing (Kolff & Doan, 1985), gave a different insight into the importance of considering meaning rather than form of violence in this context of violent intimidation and repression. Fear induced in this way may lead to profound long-term psychological changes regardless of the degree of objective life risk or even of the actual experience of physical violence.

"Nothing can compare to those family groups that were tortured often together, sometimes separately, but in view of one another or in different cells, while one was aware of the other being tortured. The entire affective world, constructed over the years with utmost difficulty, collapses with a kick in the father's genitals, a smack on the mother's face, an obscene insult to the sister or the sexual violation of a daughter. Suddenly an entire culture based on familial love, devotion, the capacity for mutual sacrifice collapses. Nothing is possible in such a universe, and that is precisely what the torturers know." (Timerman, in Kolff & Doan,1985)

It seems that an essential function of torture is its ability to shatter relationships, in fact to destroy trust between individuals and within communities. Information extracted under torture becomes a weapon of repression. Even when the individual has been able to resist the pressure to inform, he or she still has the battle to convince friends and family that this is the case. They may hesitate to trust the released survivor because of assumptions about his or her behaviour under torture; similarly, the likelihood that anyone released will deny passing information makes it all the more difficult to be believed even when this is the case. In much the same way, Cambodian women who were known to have been detained sometimes faced stigmatisation by their communities because it was assumed they had been sexually violated. A denial had no meaning; it was not believed. The mere fact of detention was sufficient to break trust within family and community.

Torture is part of a larger process – organised state violence – and both narrow and broad perspectives must be understood within a framework of deliberate and complex traumatisation intended to disrupt an individual's model of the world and self and to lead to complex trauma reactions.

The trauma, of course, may not end in the country of persecution. Refugees are people who have a "well-founded fear of persecution for reasons of race, religion, nationality, membership of a particular social group or political opinion" (United Nations, 1951). Many will have experienced torture, but all to some degree will have been made aware of the broader aspects of organised state violence.

Although the British media tend to portray refugees and asylum-seekers arriving in "floods, influxes, waves, torrents, streams" (Doveling & Hoffman, 1989), this is a stereotypic, false representation. In any comparison (e.g. with the number of refugees in the world as a whole or the number arriving in other European countries), the number of asylum-seekers to the UK is tiny (Nettleton & Simcock, 1987) and the proportion gaining refugee status smaller still.

Given that the asylum-seeker has often already sustained severe trauma, through no fault of his or her own, and has often been left with psychological injuries, a caring and just response might involve official procedures which are not just neutral but are positively designed to facilitate recovery. It would require an understanding of the overwhelming pressures acting to make some people risk everything in flight. This process would inevitably need to include work on the re-establishment of trust relationships, between individuals and between individual and state. Sadly, this does not appear to be the case (e.g. Rudge, 1989).

Individual psychological reactions

Given the complexity of the assault, the notion that either post-traumatic stress disorder or a single torture syndrome can explain the complexity of the reaction has been challenged; instead it has been proposed that at least four common themes can be identified in the psychological sequelae of torture (see Turner & Gorst-Unsworth, 1990, 1993, for more detailed accounts and reference lists). These themes are: (a) incomplete emotional processing (akin to PTSD); (b) depressive reaction; (c) somatic symptoms; and (d) the existential dilemma. This approach also highlights the abnormality of the experience rather than the individual, and by pointing to a series of dimensional (quantitative) reactions rather than a categorical (qualitative) disorder, it relies on theories of normal rather than abnormal functioning.

Implicit in this approach is a recognition both that individuals react differently to state violence, as they do to many other psychological stressors, and that the persecutory experiences may continue. Torture is an activity with particularly complex psychological and physical sequelae. The survivor has not merely been an accidental victim of a natural disaster; he has received the focused attention of an adversary often determined to cause the maximum possible psychological change. This perversion of an intimate relationship (Ritterman, 1987; Schlapobersky & Bamber, 1988) for socio-political reasons may involve a deliberate intention to disrupt the normal healing process in order to maximise the psychological scars.

Given that one of the main covert purposes of torture is the destruction of trust as a basis for interpersonal and intercommunity relationships, an individual psychology is an insufficient explanation of these events. Both individual and social understandings and approaches must complement each other in achieving a resolution of this pain.

For refugees in particular, the possibility of social reconstruction within a changing country (for example, Chile or the countries of the former Yugoslavia) may have been abandoned with the decision to seek exile. The refugee may have had to face multiple traumas in his or her search for sanctuary. These may add to the experience of alienation and may significantly limit the opportunity for successful return and resettlement to the country of origin, even if the political climate there changes. A refugee may have had to accept not only enforced exile, but also separation from family and dependants, prolonged periods of uncertainty and fear, further detention and official interrogation. Moreover, the processes of isolation and cultural bereavement are enhanced with the fear that the refugee community may well contain people acting as informants to the country of origin.

Incomplete emotional processing

The trauma of organised repressive violence causes for many a characteristic reaction best understood in terms of a (hypothesised) normal function, emotional processing, which has been overwhelmed by the scale of the damage. Similar reactions follow disasters and other extreme traumatic events.

It is suggested that each of us carries a set of predictions about our own social and physical environment (internal models of the world or cognitive schemata). It is this facility which allows us to plan in advance ways of dealing with difficulties. Each daily event is compared with this set of predictions, and when discrepancies are identified the internal psychological model can be adjusted accordingly (or alternatively, that aspect of reality can be ignored or distorted to make a fit). This internal adjustment has been termed cognitive processing. Some discrepancies also have emotional consequences. Passing or failing an examination, gaining or losing a job, for example, all require more than a factual cognitive change; they also involve important emotional reactions.

Emotional processing is a parallel process by which the emotional reactions are worked through (Horowitz, 1976; Rachman, 1980).

Using conventional categorical diagnoses, PTSD (DSM–III–R; American Psychiatric Association, 1987) has been shown to be a common sequel of torture (e.g. Ramsay *et al*, 1993). In this case-note survey of 100 refugees and asylum-seekers in the UK, 31% met strict research criteria for PTSD and 54% received a clinical diagnosis of PTSD. However, these data did not support the suggestion of a discontinuity between the two conditions of 'well' or 'disordered'. Instead the evidence indicated a wide range of degrees of difficulty. Moreover, it was also found that different patterns of traumatic stress reaction could be identified. Straightforward violence appeared to be more closely associated with subsequent intrusive behaviours (unpleasant thoughts, dreams or flashbacks); the more intimate and humiliating attack of sexual torture on men and women appeared to lead to a strongly defensive avoidance state (Ramsay *et al*, 1993). PTSD, not formally validated with groups of torture survivors in DSM–III–R or DSM–IV (American Psychiatric Association, 1994), is likely to be an oversimplification in theory and application.

Depressive reactions to loss

Associated with the experience of organised state violence are many consequential loss events, a class of life events recognised as capable of leading to a major depressive reaction (Brown & Harris, 1978). In torture survivors, losses may include bereavement, personal injury (loss of function), loss of home and loss of employment. Leaving the country of oppression may only serve to increase the problem, with separation from family, community, culture and language. The reception of asylum-seekers is obviously of critical importance. Attempts to reduce the impact of these further traumas following arrival in the country of asylum are seldom made.

In an American series of 52 southeast Asian refugees (Mollica *et al*, 1987), major depression was the most common diagnosis in the whole sample, being diagnosed in 37 subjects. Moreover, the relationship with loss was demonstrated. Those Cambodian widows who had experienced at least two of the three traumas of rape, loss of spouse or loss of children had the highest levels of depressive symptoms. They perceived themselves as socially isolated and living in a hostile social world.

Ramsay *et al* (1993) found that 42% of their sample of refugees and asylum-seekers met DSM–III–R criteria for major depressive disorder, and 55% had received a clinical diagnosis of depression. Again, the evidence suggests a dimensional response with a range of severities. In another interview study of refugees and asylum-seekers in the UK, Van Velsen *et al* (1996) found major depression in 35%; measures of trauma exposure, loss of health and social impact in the UK all showed statistically significant relationships with major depression. This report therefore provides some evidence that factors involved in the manner of reception have an impact on depressive symptoms.

Somatic symptoms

It is hardly surprising that following physical torture applied to the individual as a means of achieving psychological change, there should be complex meanings assigned to physical symptoms (Turner & Gorst-Unsworth, 1990, 1993). Nowhere is it more important to move away from a Cartesian mind–body dualism and accept an interactional psychosomatic model (Turner & Hough, 1993).

The existential dilemma

Torture is a "catastrophic existential event" (Bendfeldt-Zachrisson, 1985). Those who survive have to come to terms with a world in which such acts of barbaric cruelty are not just nebulous possibilities, but are stark personal realities. Even survival may bring its own guilt, whether by virtue of the enforced confessions, the information painfully extracted, the actions needed to survive, or the more magical notion that one death might have led to another being saved. Life in such a condition has a powerful capacity to change developmental direction, and is best described in personal autobiography.

> "Writing and publishing *If This is a Man* (1960) and *The Truce* (1965) marked a decisive turn in my life not only as a writer. For several years afterward, I had the feeling that I had performed a task, indeed the only task clearly defined for me. At Auschwitz, and on the long road returning home, I had seen and experienced things that imperiously demanded to be told. And I had told them, I had testified." (Levi, 1987)

One of the common themes of these testimonies is the shift from a more comfortable position of greater or lesser denial into a more radical reaction – the "decisive turn" of Primo Levi. Survivors must to some extent come to reconcile the 'new self' with the 'new reality' of the external world. This may lead to active opposition to a system, as well as to repression under the burden of violence and threat. There is the potential for personal growth, but commonly the reactions seem to be more mixed and problematic.

Just as interpersonal relationships are changed, so the relationship between a person and larger entities such as the qualities of love and goodness, religious faith or even a political ideology may be damaged by torture or other organised state violence. Similarly, the man or woman who was 'betrayed' by a close friend or relative may never again have quite the same confidence in anyone. They may also find that their personal world philosophy is irreparably dented by their experience.

Often of equal significance, the trust of an asylum-seeker in his chosen safe country may be misplaced. One man asked why it was that he had been detained in his own country for a matter of days but was held in the UK in prison-like circumstances for three months. Implicit in the concept of trust is the notion of hope. Those who hope for little may have their trust in others less damaged by such experiences than those with higher expectations.

In an attempt to unravel this issue, data on some of these attitudes and feelings have been collected as part of a pilot interview survey (Gorst-Unsworth *et al*, 1993). Survivors of torture and other forms of organised violence (n = 31) frequently reported feeling that the experience had changed them, that they felt different and misunderstood by others who had not shared their experiences. More seriously, many reported that they felt misunderstood even by those friends, doctors or lawyers trying to help. This sense of alienation, of being apart from others, is probably common to many victims of trauma and may be an important reason behind the development of self-help groups, such as rape counselling or survivor groups following natural disasters. Another factor likely to be important among survivors of torture in producing alienation from health professionals is the latter's possible role in torture (Van Velsen *et al*, 1996).

Those who had been expecting torture or who had prepared themselves for torture reported feeling less alienated after the event. Perhaps it had been less of a challenge to their prior beliefs or schemata about the world in which they lived. Guilt was reported by the majority, and was associated chiefly with separation from other family members (Gorst-Unsworth *et al*, 1993). Nearly half were separated from all family members including dependants. For many this separation will continue for long periods, the fear and uncertainties so produced being a major cause of continuing distress. Worse than this, the mere fact that the asylum-seeker had escaped would make it more likely to draw the attention of the authorities to his or her family and friends left behind.

Treatment

There is, as yet, no consensus concerning the most effective way of treating survivors of torture (McIvor & Turner, 1995). Common elements of therapy have not yet been satisfactorily defined, and controlled research into the available options is in its infancy. Nevertheless, recurrent themes do occur, in terms of the therapist, the setting and the treatment process itself, which allow us to draw some tentative conclusions regarding principles that are of importance in the therapeutic process.

The therapist

The trauma story may have a profound and disturbing impact on the therapist. Some may feel powerless and hopeless in the face of such an overwhelming experience. Countertransference reactions may be potentially antitherapeutic, and may lead to intense emotional reactions ranging from denial to over-identification or fear of failure (Comas-Diaz & Padillo, 1990; Fischman, 1991). In contrast with many other therapeutic situations, the therapist should be prepared to adopt openly a commitment to supporting human rights issues, while at the same time remaining objective (Agger & Jensen, 1990; Turner, 1992). This commitment may need to be made explicit for some survivors to be able to trust their therapist. For therapists working in the country of repression, this often places them at considerable personal risk (Cienfuegos & Monelli, 1983).

It is important that the therapist should have some understanding of the cultural background of the client. This includes not only some knowledge of the social and political context of their country, but also the unique meaning of the torture, and the symbolic significance of the symptoms. In some communities, there may be more or less reluctance or inability to differentiate between psychological, physical or supernatural causes of symptoms. There may also be varying tendencies towards somatisation, often a more acceptable way of seeking help. Physical or pharmacological methods, rather than psychotherapy, may be the expected treatment in some cultures, but in others there may be a rejection of 'medical' approaches and a greater reliance on psychotherapeutic approaches. Whichever treatment is adopted, it must be consistent with the cultural expectations of the survivor.

The setting

Ideally, therapy should take place in a setting which provides a sense of safety and encourages trust. The past 20 years have seen the development of centres dedicated to the treatment of torture survivors (Chester, 1990; van Willigen, 1992). The first of these was the International Rehabilitation and Research Centre for Torture Victims (RCT) in Copenhagen, which grew out of the combined work of Amnesty International and the Danish Medical Group in 1974. Most centres provide a multidisciplinary approach to assessment and treatment, dealing not only with psychological and physical problems, but also with social and occupational difficulties. Mollica (1988) provided an eloquent description of the development and methods of the Indochinese Psychiatric Clinic (IPC), which evolved in the early 1980s in a primary care setting in Boston. Some workers have found that a specialist centre may not be the most appropriate response, particularly in developing countries (Bracken *et al*, 1992). There, community-based services may be more acceptable, involving the participation of local health workers who possess a more complete understanding of the social and political context in which the trauma occurred.

Careful explanation and reassurance at each stage of therapy are important non-specific elements of care. These encourage openness and reduce fear. Anything resembling interrogation should be avoided, and particular care should be taken when uncontrolled reminders of torture occur as part of the assessment procedure. This applies particularly to physical investigations, such as a venepuncture or electrocardiograph, but may also be experienced in the enclosed space of the therapy session.

Treatment is greatly complicated in the bicultural setting. Where the survivor is unable to speak the language of their adopted country, the interpreter or bicultural worker become essential components in the process of assessment and treatment (McIvor, 1994). They should be used not merely as translators, but as cultural bridges between the therapist and client, allowing a clearer understanding of both verbal and non-verbal communication and evaluating the cultural significance of what is being said (Kinzie, 1985). It goes without saying that a particular interpreter should be acceptable to the client in terms of political and ethnic beliefs.

There is scope to develop new models of service delivery in which skills developed and available within mainstream health services in host countries are made available for the benefit of new refugee communities. Working with individuals, in a broad outline, there are three levels at which this cultural and linguistic bridging function can operate.

(a)   At the lowest level is the translator. Here literal and mechanical conversion of words from one language to another takes place. The broader cultural issues are largely ignored and the translator takes a passive role in the three-way relationship between patient/user, therapist and bridge worker. This is an inadequate approach.

(b)   At the next level is the interpreter/advocate. This is still a bridging role between patient/user and therapist but more active, and with the training and ability to recognise that cultural interpretation and advocacy is also important.

(c)   At the highest level is the bicultural worker (e.g. Mollica *et al*, 1990). Still a bridge, the bicultural worker accesses education, supervision and validation from the developed service and applies these to the benefit of the local refugee community. He or she will be a member of the community and will be selected on the basis of pre-existing skills. Typically, refugee communities include many people with high levels of ability, including some whose qualifications are not recognised by local regulatory authorities. In a new job role, recruitment can take place on the basis of skills rather than recog- nised qualifications. The bicultural worker, through employment in a mainstream service, is empowered to operate in an effective way. He or she would also be able to provide a culturally appropriate model of treatment.

The therapy

Emphasis in therapy varies from one centre and one therapist to another, but common themes emerge which appear to contain the main ingredients for improvement. Many of the treatments used today originate from established models of cognitive–behavioural or psychodynamic psychology. The retelling of the trauma story appears to be, as Mollica (1988) pointed out, the centrepiece of therapy, for it is the working-through of the traumatic process that permits the development of a new story – a story that is no longer about shame, humiliation or guilt. This process of catharsis is as important in other therapies as it is in psychodynamic therapy and should be clearly distinguished from fixation to the trauma, characterised by pathological repetition of the story without movement.

Testimony (Agger & Jensen, 1990) was a method first used in South America (Cienfuegos & Monelli, 1983) as a mechanism of political opposition, whereby a written record, or testimony, was produced which could then be used as evidence that torture had taken place. Gradually, its therapeutic benefits became apparent and it now provides a general basis for psychotherapy with survivors of torture and other forms of state organised violence. Its central tenet is again the retelling of the trauma story, but through the process of tape-recording, writing and editing, the patient is left with a permanent record or testimony which can be used for personal purposes or which can be widely distributed. The purpose of this cathartic experience is to help the patient to "integrate the traumatic experience into their lives by identifying its significance in the context of political and social events as well as the context of their personal history" (Cienfuegos & Monelli, 1983). Thus the patient becomes an active participant in therapy, the therapist acting as a witness, to clarify and encourage.

This method has been modified for use in host countries. As testimony proceeds, psychological reactions such as aggression are addressed and symptoms are reframed. For example, the guilt or humiliation felt after divulging information against comrades or family members can be reframed as understandable and inevitable in the face of pain and powerlessness.

This theme of cognitive restructuring is a common element in many forms of therapy, be they individual, group or family-based, although its effectiveness is not yet clear. Denial, self-blame, humiliation, poor self-esteem and existential questions are discussed, and through cognitive reappraisal or reframing, cognitive schemata and belief systems can be appropriately reassigned, providing meaning to experience.

Experiences of organised violence appear commonly to have profound and probably long-term effects on attitudes and priorities. Political and religious outlooks may change. Experiences of this type often force the survivor to confront very basic human assumptions. It is no longer possible to assume that the world is a comfortable place or to reconcile new understandings with previous beliefs. A process of radicalisation may follow, leaving the individual either more oppressed or more determined to fight for change. In both cases, trust will have been one of the first casualties.

Conclusions

Torture and organised state violence therefore stand to have dramatic effects on individuals and communities. In this chapter, the concept of PTSD has been criticised: (a) it is hard to see the survivor of torture as *disordered* – perhaps 'injured' is a better description where relevant; (b) the evidence suggests a dimensional rather than categorical reaction; and (c) the pattern of symptoms within the PTSD syndrome description appears to vary according to trauma type (sexual torture appears different from other forms of torture). Torture is a complex trauma with a correspondingly complex series of reactions not encompassed within PTSD. Moreover, it occurs within a social and political context, affecting interpersonal and intercommunity functioning as well as intrapersonal development.

A multidimensional approach has been advocated. Perhaps the effect torture has on attitudes and beliefs is of particular importance in relation to personal development. Those survivors who come from countries where torture and state violence are widespread have higher expectations and levels of preparation for torture. They are less affected by the experience itself, but only by virtue of longer-term adaptation to these unacceptable pressures. On the other hand, its impact on individuals has been well recorded. Primo Levi described a decisive turn which affected the whole of his subsequent life. Torture appears to be a radicalising force, pushing some into retreat, exile or submission, and others into active opposition – sometimes armed conflict. It leaves few unaffected. Transgenerational effects in families of Holocaust survivors also illustrate the power of horrifying traumatic events to change and shape the developmental path. Finally, in therapy, the importance of tackling belief systems through some sort of cognitive or meaning-based approach is apparent. Testimony that encourages a reframing of the primary experience is an obvious example, but many others exist. Torture challenges fundamental beliefs and attitudes to self and world; often this continues to have an impact through the rest of a person's life.

Given these patterns of reaction, the way in which survivors are received in exile becomes especially important. It is easy for the traumatisation to continue. In host countries, access to reasonable levels of support with basic needs being met is of paramount importance. If trust is to be recovered, there must be a positive approach to asylum-seekers. Nowhere is it more important to ensure that justice is done, and seen to be done, than in work with victims of major trauma and, perhaps especially, in the case of torture.

References

Agger, I. & Jensen, S. (1990) Testimony as ritual and evidence in psychotherapy for political refugees. *Journal of Traumatic Stress*, **3**, 115–130.

American Psychiatric Association (1987) *Diagnostic and Statistical Manual of Mental Disorders* (3rd edn, revised) (DSM–III–R). Washington, DC: APA.

—— (1994) *Diagnostic and Statistical Manual of Mental Disorders* (4th edn, revised) (DSM–IV). Washington, DC: APA.

Bendfeldt-Zachrisson, F. (1985) State (political) torture: some general, psychological, and particular aspects. *International Journal of Health Services*, **15**, 339–349.

Bracken, P. J., Giller, J. E. & Kabaganda, S. (1992) Helping victims of violence in Uganda. *Medicine and War*, **8**, 155–163.

Brown, G. W. & Harris, T. (1978) *Social Origins of Depression*. London: Tavistock.

Chester, B. (1990) Because mercy has a human heart: centers for victims of torture. In *Psychology and Torture* (ed. P. Suedfeld), pp. 165–184. New York: Hemisphere Publishing Corporation.

Cienfuegos, A. J. & Monelli, C. (1983) The testimony of political repression as a therapeutic instrument. *American Journal of Orthopsychiatry*, **53**, 43–51.

Comas-Diaz, L. & Padillo, A. M. (1990) Countertransference in working with victims of political repression. *American Journal of Orthopsychiatry*, **60**, 125–134.

Dovelong, B. & Hoffman, K. H. (1989) Proposals to project accurate, positive images: the view of the German Red Cross. In *Refugees – the Trauma of Exile* (ed. D. Miserez), pp. 307–310. Dordrecht: Martinus Nijhoff.

Fischman, Y. (1991) Interacting with trauma clinicians' responses to treating psychological after-effects of political repression. *American Journal of Orthopsychiatry*, **61**, 179–185.

Gorst-Unsworth, C., van Velsen, C. & Turner, S. W. (1993) Prospective pilot study of survivors of torture and organised violence – examining the existential dilemma. *Journal of Nervous and Mental Disease*, **181**, 263–264.

Horowitz, M. J. (1976) *Stress Response Syndromes*. New York: Jason Aronson.

Kinzie, J. D. (1985) Cultural aspects of psychiatric treatment with Indochinese refugees. *American Journal of Social Psychiatry*, **1**, 47–53.

Kolff, C. A. & Doan, R. N. (1985) Victims of torture: two testimonies. In *The Breaking of Minds and Bodies* (eds E. Stover & F. O. Nightingale), pp. 45–57. New York: W. H. Freeman.

Levi, P. (1987) *If This is a Man* and *The Truce*. London: Penguin.

McIvor, R. (1994) Making the most of interpreters. *British Journal of Psychiatry*, **165**, 268.

—— & Turner, S. W. (1995) Assessment and treatment approaches for survivors of torture. *British Journal of Psychiatry*, **166**, 705–711.

Martin-Baro, I. (1988) From dirty war to psychological war: the case of El Salvador. In *Flight, Exile, and Return: Mental Health and the Refugee* (ed. A. Aron). San Francisco. Committee for Health Rights in Central America.

Mollica, R. F. (1988) The trauma story: the psychiatric care of refugee survivors of violence and torture. In *Post-traumatic Therapy and the Victim of Violence* (ed. F. M. Ochberg), pp. 295–314. New York: Brunner/Mazel.

——, Wyshak, G. & Lavelle, J. (1987) The psychosocial impact of war trauma and torture on southeast Asian refugees. *American Journal of Psychiatry*, **144**, 1567–1572.

——, ——, *et al* (1990) Assessing symptom change in southeast Asian refugee survivors of mass violence and torture. *American Journal of Psychiatry*, **147**, 83–88.

Nettleton, C. & Simcock, A. (1987) *Asylum Seekers in the United Kingdom: Essential Statistics*. London: British Refugee Council Research and Development Unit.

Rachman, S. (1980) Emotional processing. *Behaviour Research and Therapy*, **18**, 51–60.

Ramsay, R., Gorst-Unsworth, C. & Turner, S. W. (1993) Psychological morbidity in survivors of organised state violence including torture: a retrospective series. *British Journal of Psychiatry*, **162**, 55–59.

Ritterman, M. (1987) Torture, the counter therapy of the state. *Networker*, Jan/Feb, 43–47.

Rudge, P. (1989) Reflections on the status of refugees and asylum seekers in Europe. In *Refugees – the Trauma of Exile* (ed. D. Miserez), pp. 62–70. Dordrecht: Martinus Nijhoff.

Schlapobersky, J. & Bamber, H. (1988) Rehabilitation and therapy with the victims of torture and organised violence. Paper presented to the American Association for the Advancement of Science Annual Meeting.

Turner, S. (1992) Therapeutic approaches with survivors of torture. In *Intercultural Therapy: Themes, Interpretations and Practice* (eds J. Kareem & R. Littlewood), pp. 163–174. Oxford: Blackwell Scientific.

—— & Gorst-Unsworth, C. (1990) Psychological sequelae of torture – a descriptive model. *British Journal of Psychiatry*, **157**, 475–480.

—— & —— (1993) Psychological sequelae of torture. In *The International Handbook of Traumatic Stress Syndromes* (eds J. Wilson & B. Raphael), pp. 703–713. New York: Plenum Press.

—— & Hough, A. (1993) Hyperventilation as a reaction to torture. In *The International Handbook of Traumatic Stress Syndromes* (eds J. Wilson & B. Raphael), pp. 725–732. New York: Plenum Press.

Van Velsen, C., Gorst-Unsworth, C & Turner, S. W. (1996) Survivors of torture and organised state violence: demography and diagnosis. *Journal of Traumatic Stress*, **9**, 181–193.

van Willigen, L. (1992) Organization of care and rehabilitation services for victims of torture and other forms of organized violence: a review of current issues. In *Torture and its Consequences: Current Treatment Approaches* (ed. M. Basoglu), pp. 277–298. Cambridge: Cambridge University Press.

United Nations (1951) *Convention Relating to the Status of Refugees*. New York: United Nations.

—— (1984) *Convention Against Torture and Other Cruel, Inhuman or Degrading Treatment or Punishment*. New York: United Nations.

Part III. Diagnosis, intervention and treatment

14 Diagnosis and treatment

A. Diagnosis

MARTIN NEWMAN and DEBORAH LEE

Here, we consider the assessment and diagnosis of psychological morbidity after a traumatic event. We include reference to some of the aids to assessment which are available. We also discuss prognosis.

Making a diagnosis of PTSD

Post-traumatic stress disorder is a psychiatric diagnosis requiring the framework of a psychiatric history. Assessment specifically for legal purposes is described in chapter 24. There are, of course, other professional assessments which may be independent or complementary and which require different types of information.

In order to make a diagnosis the following information should be sought.

(1) Presenting complaint(s) and their duration.
(2) History of presenting complaints (further details and relevant questioning, including what help has already been received, if any, and whether anything else has been noticed to be of benefit or made the problem(s) worse).
(3) Details of the traumatic event. This should include:
    (a) details of what actually happened (the facts)
    (b) what the person's thoughts and feelings were at the time (thoughts and emotions)
    (c) what decisions they made and how they came to make them – including what happened
    (d) what the subjective experiences were, and the significance of this within the individual's inner world. (Also, it is important that the clinician gains a clear understanding of the client's perception/ representation of the traumatic event and how they fit it into their framework of their self, their world and others.)
    (e) a clear understanding of how this event challenges pre-existing beliefs, attitudes and thoughts about the traumatic event, the self and others should be sought. This process will give the clinician

vital insight into the thinking patterns of the client and in particular will allow for identification of dysfunctional or distorted thinking processes which may be hindering the emotional processing of the event.

(4)   Family history (details of important and close relatives, and any history of physical or psychiatric illness in the family).

(5)   Personal history (pregnancy, birth, neonatal period, early development and milestones, temperament, close and intimate relationships).

(6)   School (progress, dates of changing or leaving school, relationships with peers and staff, attainments).

(7)   Work (jobs held, reason for any changes, plans for the future).

(8)   Previous medical history (operations, illnesses).

(9)   Previous psychiatric history (any problems or any help recommended or received).

(10) Menstrual history (in females).

(11) Social history (alcohol, smoking, use of illicit drugs, religion, friendships, hobbies and interests).

(12) Forensic history (any criminal records or behaviour).

(13) Medication (prescribed or self-prescribed).

(14) Allergies (if any).

(15) An accurate assessment of premorbid personality. In particular, attention needs to be paid to how the individual dealt with stress and with problems – their preferred coping style. By questioning around social history, a picture of main personality traits should emerge, i.e. shy, introverted, anxious, a worrier, extrovert, easy going, indecisive, a ruminator, prone to feelings of guilt, overdeveloped sense of responsibility, etc. Also any previous traumatic events and/or traumatic bereavements should be identified.

(16) Information from other informants.

(17) Mental state examination.

(18) Physical examination.

(19) Investigations as appropriate.

(20) Any ongoing/forthcoming criminal trials or litigation which may prolong/intensify symptomatology.

A problem in the diagnosis of PTSD is its high level of comorbidity with other disorders, which frequently overlap and mask the underlying PTSD. Other disorders which may coexist with PTSD include depression, generalised anxiety disorder, phobic anxiety, panic disorder, obsessive–compulsive disorder, eating disorders, alcohol and drug addiction (the latter two may develop in the context of extreme avoidance behaviour).

It is important to distinguish the symptoms of PTSD from those of the following:

(a)   *Adjustment disorder:* where the stressor may be a single event or there may be multiple stressors. The stressor may be of any severity and there is a wide range of possible symptoms. Hill (1994) provides a useful review of adjustment disorders.

(b) *Acute stress disorder.* The symptom pattern must occur within four weeks of the traumatic event and have resolved within that four-week period. If symptoms continue after the four-week period and follow the pattern of PTSD, then the diagnosis must change.

(c) *Obsessive–compulsive disorder.* Here, the intrusive phenomena are experienced as inappropriate and have no relation to a traumatic event.

(d) *Malingering:* whereby the client fakes illness in order to gain financially from litigation, be eligible for benefits, or have mitigating circumstances in a forensic context.

(e) The 'flashbacks' in PTSD, if present, need to be distinguished from hallucinations and delusions typical of schizophrenia and other psychotic disorders.

The diagnostic criteria of ICD–10 (World Health Organization, 1992) and DSM–IV (American Psychiatric Association, 1994) provide guidance. When used, multiaxial systems of classification make it possible to record several different facets of a condition (Cantwell & Rutter, 1994).

As a diagnostic category, PTSD has clear construct validity (Malloy *et al*, 1983). However, there are legal and ethical issues involved in assessing and interpreting the DSM criteria (Neal, 1994). Clinical judgement and experience are essential, rather than simply making a diagnosis on the presence of symptoms in accordance with the diagnostic criteria. A mild post-traumatic stress disorder may be less psychologically debilitating than a severe post-traumatic stress reaction where the individual fails to meet the DSM–IV diagnostic criteria by, say, one symptom in the avoidance criterion but experiences several distressing symptoms of intrusion (when only one is needed to fulfil that criterion).

DSM–IV contains the statement that it "reflects a consensus about the classification and diagnosis of mental disorders derived at the time of its initial publication . . . the text and criteria sets included in DSM–IV will require reconsideration in light of evolving new information". DSM–IV states that "in most situations, the clinical diagnosis of a DSM–IV mental disorder is not sufficient to establish the existence for legal purposes of a 'mental disorder', 'mental disability', 'mental disease' or 'mental defect'". It recommends that, in order to determine whether an individual meets a specified legal standard, further information (such as details of any functional impairments, abilities and disabilities) is required.

PTSD ranges from mild to severe, acute to chronic; the severity is an arbitrary clinical judgement. It is important to consider whether there may be any possible physical cause for the symptoms and signs, as organic illness may present with psychological sequelae, or coexist with psychiatric illness.

A difficulty may arise when the professional carrying out the assessment does not speak the same language as the person being examined. Difficulties in communication may lead to inaccuracies in assessment and effective treatment (Deahl *et al*, 1994). An untrained interpreter may make errors in communication, such as omission, addition, condensation, substitution, and role exchange (Vasquez & Janvier, 1991). However, the use of properly trained interpreters, who have a knowledge of the political and cultural background of the patient or survivor, and who are socially, ethically and politically acceptable to that person, may provide insight into the cultural significance of what is being said and contribute significantly to the assessment (McIvor, 1994). Questionnaires may need to be carefully translated (e.g. Kuterovac *et al*, 1994), and their suitability for the population under study re-evaluated. Thus, care is needed in making a diagnosis. The complexity of each individual's response needs to be considered. It should be noted that carrying out an assessment may, by itself, have a therapeutic effect.

The patient or client may present with a clear history of having experienced a traumatic event, and the subsequent development of some symptoms which suggest a diagnosis of PTSD and/or other psychiatric illness which may be present. However, in some cases, the patient may not initially present with a clear history of having experienced a traumatic event, as in the following example.

Case example

A 35-year-old man presented with an addiction to gambling. His family reported that he had also been drinking excessively, and driving increasingly recklessly. His marital relationship had deteriorated. Initially, he gave a brief history of former military service but details of his military career were not volunteered nor elicited. It was not until some time later, when initial interventions had not been helpful, that more detailed questioning revealed that, during his military service, the man had served in a war and experienced a missile attack. This attack had resulted in numerous deaths and casualties, and he had been lucky to survive. A careful review of his symptoms showed that, in addition to the problems listed already, he suffered from recurrent and intrusive distressing recollections of the incident (he found that these recollections were temporarily relieved if he was concentrating on gambling), recurrent distressing nightmares, a desire to avoid thinking or talking about what had happened, a wish to avoid activities associated with the incident (hence, he had left military service), feelings of detachment from others, including members of his family, associated with poor concentration, outbursts of anger, and difficulty in sleeping. Careful consideration of the possibility of other psychiatric conditions, including depression, was made. A diagnosis of PTSD was made, and he received appropriate psychotherapeutic interventions, with benefit. There was an improvement in his marital relationship, he ceased to gamble or drink alcohol excessively, and his interpersonal relationships improved. His nightmares diminished.

Research

Green (1994) reviewed the psychosocial research into the psychological effects of trauma, including the epidemiology in the general adult population, diagnoses associated with exposure to trauma and PTSD, the course and longevity of PTSD, the symptomatology, and risk factors for the diagnosis. At present, there are still many unanswered questions about PTSD. For example, there is still inadequate knowledge about the natural history of PTSD, so it is difficult to assess the effectiveness of specific treatments (McFarlane, 1987). The adverse effects of treatment may often go unreported, and there is still little knowledge about the attitude of PTSD sufferers to treatment. McFarlane (1987) makes a number of recommendations for further research studies. Those relevant to the initial assessment include recording the impact of the traumatic event on other family members, describing any treatment that they have received, and carefully noting the age of the patient at the time of the trauma. The different phenomenological components of PTSD should be separately assessed, using well-accepted measures. Each study should have independent assessors.

Lindy *et al* (1981) pointed out that traumatised people may be reluctant to engage in treatment with a person who is perceived to be distant from the traumatic experience. Also, Lindy found that the level of clinical experience of the therapist was an important predictor of success. Therefore, reports should describe the therapists' knowledge of the trauma, their level of training and their experience.

Use of assessment questionnaires

Assessment questionnaires may be useful for both clinical and research purposes. Unstructured interviews tend to be too selective and omit important information. It is often more helpful to use semistructured interviews, questionnaires and research instruments. Mann & Murray (1986) and Berger (1994) have described the principles which underlie the use of instruments for the measurement of psychiatric disorder. The choice of appropriate instruments is essential.

Assessment in adults

The use of questionnaires and semistructured interview techniques is widely accepted with adult sufferers of PTSD. Typically, self-rating questionnaires are used to establish baseline measures before treatment and as outcome measures after treatment. Furthermore, such questionnaires have been extensively used for research purposes.

Although there are numerous questionnaires available to measure psychological distress, typically a core batch have been frequently used by researchers and clinicians alike. These include the following:

(1) The Impact of Event Scale (Horowitz *et al*, 1979). This is a 15-item, self-rating questionnaire with two subscales: intrusion and avoidance. It was specifically designed to measure the effects of traumatic events and gives a subjective estimate of the frequency of intrusive recall of the traumatic event and any attempts to avoid such recall, and thus a measure of psychological disturbance when compared with normative data. It does not include questions about physiological reactivity and cannot be used to make a diagnosis. Also, the Impact of Event Scale (IES) is best used with discrete traumatic incidents. It is not effective

or meaningful to use it with people who have suffered multiple traumas. This is possibly the most widely used questionnaire in either research or clinical work. In civilian groups in peacetime, a score of 20 or more is often taken as indicating cause for concern. Others (McFarlane, 1988; Bryant & Harvey, 1995) have used a score of 30 or above to indicate significant post-traumatic stress.

(2)   The General Health Questionnaire (GHQ-28; Goldberg & Hillier, 1979). This is a 28-item self-report questionnaire with four subscales: somatic, anxiety and insomnia, social dysfunction, and severe depression. It gives a probability measure that the person on interview will be found to be a psychiatric case.

(3)   The Symptom Checklist (SCL–90; Derogatis, 1977). A 90-item self-report questionnaire with nine subscales of somatisation, obsessive–compulsive, interpersonal sensitivity, depression, anxiety, anger–hostility, phobic anxiety, paranoid ideation and psychoticism. Comparisons can be made with normal and psychiatric populations.

This package of questionnaires has been frequently used in research and to demonstrate clinically relevant change in intervention studies. Thompson *et al* (1995) demonstrated significant reductions in symptomatology using the IES, GHQ–28 and the SCL–90 (the IES reduced by 42%, the GHQ by 62% and the SCL–90 by 38%) as pre- and post-treatment measures in an open trial. In this study, 23 subjects with PTSD were given a debriefing session followed by eight sessions of exposure and cognitive restructuring therapy, termed CEASE.

Turner *et al*(1995) looked at the psychological reactions of 50 survivors of the 1987 King's Cross Underground fire (see also chapter 8F). They used the IES, GHQ–28, Eysenck Personality Questionnaire (EPQ; Eysenck & Eysenck, 1976) and a King's Cross Events Schedule (Thompson & Turner, personal communication). The survivors were interviewed between 1 and 12 months after the event. Two-thirds (66%) of the sample were found to have significant levels of psychological distress (as measured by the GHQ–28). Mean IES scores were well above the cut-off point. Also, personality and degree of exposure to trauma were related to subsequent reaction.

Other than self-rating questionnaires, which are useful measures of psychological distress following trauma, there exist specific instruments designed to aid diagnosis of PTSD. As stated earlier, semistructured interview schedules and structured interview checklists offer higher validity and allow for an in-depth assessment of the symptomatology. One of the most comprehensive and widely used structured interviews is the Clinician Administered Post-traumatic Stress Scale (CAPS; Blake *et al*, 1990). This has been used both for research purposes and in clinical settings. It consists of 17 items based on the diagnostic criteria for PTSD (DSM–III–R). Each item is divided into frequency and severity of distress associated with the symptom. An overall rating of severity can be obtained, although interpretation of this score is somewhat arbitrary. It does, however, provide a comprehensive assessment of PTSD symptomatology and can be used as a diagnostic instrument. (NB. At the time of print, the revised CAPS based on DSM–IV was not yet available.)

Assessment in children

The assessment of children poses additional problems (Harris-Hendriks & Newman, 1995). The principles underlying assessment of psychiatric disorder in children have been described (Cox, 1994). Age and developmental factors need to be considered. It needs to be decided who is to provide standardised information – parent, carer, teacher or relative. This may be especially important as when, for example, one parent has killed the other (Harris-Hendriks *et al*, 1993).

Pynoos & Eth (1986) recommended a child interview structure. The child begins by drawing a picture, or telling a story about a picture of his or her choice. The child's experiences of the traumatic event are then explored (including the physical, sensory and affective experiences and fantasies, with re-enactment of events). This is followed by closure, during which there is a review of concerns; mourning is supported, the contents of the interview are reviewed, the child is invited to return for another interview, and goodbyes are said.

It needs to be remembered that a child's concept of death will depend on age as well as on other factors. Speece & Brent (1984) described how young children may regard death as temporary and reversible, believe that dead people still have some feelings or bodily functions, that death may be avoidable in some way, or that some people will not die. Gradually, a child learns that death is irreversible, final, irrevocable and permanent, that the body ceases to function, and that death is universal – all living things die. Lansdown & Benjamin (1985) questioned 105 children aged between 5–9 years on their concept of death. They found that approximately 60% of the 5-year-olds had a complete or almost complete concept of death. Almost all had a fully developed concept of death by the age of 8–9 years.

Pynoos (1992) proposed that, in children, factors which may be relevant in assessing resistance and vulnerability to trauma include: current developmental competencies and challenges; temperament; prior psychopathology; a child's ability to make cognitive discriminations and to tolerate the internal changes and reactivity to reminders; and the strength and importance of attachments, with an increased vulnerability if there is a threat to a parent or family member. He noted that adolescents who were worried about a younger sibling have reported greater post-traumatic distress and more somatic complaints than their peers (Dohrenwend *et al*, 1981). It has been found that separating children from their parents during rescue or post-disaster clear-up can measurably increase their post-disaster morbidity (McFarlane, 1987). The response of the parent or adult care-giver and pre-existing personality, temperament or psychopathology are also relevant. Hence, a comprehensive assessment should include information on all these factors. It is also important to remember that special care is needed when examining young children, as they may be suggestible (Ceci & Bruck, 1993).

Assessment questionnaires for children

Yule & Williams (1990, 1992) have suggested that early studies of children failed to identify the extent of their difficulties after exposure to traumatic events because a number of them had used screening instruments which did not pick up PTSD symptomatology or because they relied upon parent and/or teacher reports, which have been found to underestimate the level of children's disturbance (Udwin, 1993). The appropriate use of such recording methods may provide useful information, both for an individual case and for research purposes, although they are still in the process of development and refinement. For those who have experienced a bereavement, it is important to obtain some measure of their grief (Raphael, 1995).

Questionnaires or research instruments that have been used with children include the following:

(1) The Impact of Event Scale (Horowitz *et al*, 1979) as discussed earlier. This was not originally intended to be used with children, but has been used with those aged 8 and over (Yule & Williams, 1990; Yule & Udwin, 1991; Yule, 1992). Yule & Udwin (1991) administered the IES to 24 girls aged 14–15 years, ten days after the sinking of the cruise ship *Jupiter*. They also completed the Children's Manifest Anxiety Scale (Reynolds & Richmond, 1978), which has been widely used in studies of children from 8–16 years of age, and the Birleson Depression Inventory (Birleson, 1981; Birleson *et al*, 1987), an 18-item scale developed as a clinical instrument to be completed by children and adolescents. Yule & Udwin showed that this combination of tests predicted psychopathology at five months, and also correlated with later help-seeking. They concluded that this selection of tests appeared useful for screening adolescents after a disaster, so as to identify those most at risk of difficulties. Kuterovac *et al* (1994), in a study of displaced and non-displaced children in Croatia, have also found the IES to be useful for children over 10 years of age.

(2) The Child Post Traumatic Stress Reaction Index (CPTSRI; Pynoos *et al*, 1987*a*; Frederick & Pynoos, 1988). This was originally devised by Pynoos *et al* (1987*a*) and revised by Pynoos & Nader (1988). It is a 20-item questionnaire developed to assess the severity of PTSD in children. Nader *et al* (1993) stated that the following are guidelines – a total score of 12–24 indicates a mild level of PTSD reaction, 25–39 a moderate level, 40–59 a severe level, and above 60 a very severe reaction. Yule *et al* (1992) found that CPTSRI total scores related very highly to IES, to Manifest Anxiety, and to Birleson Depression scores, and to clinical judgement of severity of PTSD. The revised form of the CPTSRI has been used after large-scale disasters such as the Armenian earthquake (Pynoos *et al*, 1993) and war (Nader *et al*, 1993). The index is completed by a trained adult who interviews the child. In the Armenian study (Pynoos *et al*, 1993), scores on the CPTSRI were very good predictors of a clinical diagnosis of PTSD using DSM criteria.

(3) The Saigh Children's Post-traumatic Stress Disorder Inventory (Saigh, 1989). This was constructed on the basis of DSM–III PTSD diagnostic

criteria, in a study of Lebanese children. It has good psychometric properties (Yule, 1994).

(4)   There are a number of instruments which have been used to measure grief. One is the Hogan Sibling Inventory of Bereavement, which consists of 109 items (Hogan, 1990). Another that has been used (for example, by Nader *et al*, 1990, 1993) is a brief (9-item) children's grief inventory (Pynoos *et al*, 1987*b*). This asks questions about dreams of the deceased person, thoughts of seeing the dead person, crying about the dead person, disbelief, thoughts of the deceased, changes in play or activities that remind the child of the deceased, anger with thoughts about the deceased, a desire to be more like the deceased, and whether time passing and new friends have helped the child to feel better.

(5)   The Orvaschel Questionnaire (Orvaschel, 1990; McLeer *et al*, 1992) and the KIDDIE–SADS (Puig-Antich & Chambers, 1978) may be useful. The K–SADS – Present Episode (K–SADS–P) is a semistructured diagnostic interview designed to record information about a child or adolescent's functioning and symptoms for the current episode of psychiatric disorder. It is modified from the Schedule for Affective Disorders and Schizophrenia (Spitzer *et al*, 1978) that has been employed with children between the ages of 6 and 17 years by Puig-Antich and colleagues (Orvaschel *et al*, 1982; Chambers *et al*, 1985). It is a reliable instrument for measuring symptoms of depression and conduct disorder (Kolvin *et al*, 1991). The recommended procedure is for the parents to be interviewed, then the child – the child interview being guided by information from the parents. However, this is not essential. The examiner is required to make a clinical judgement of the presence or absence of the symptom under inquiry and, if present, its severity. A wide range of symptoms is covered and all have been found to be assessed with acceptable reliability, except for pathological guilt and impaired concentration (Chambers *et al*, 1985). The advantages of the K–SADS–P are that it provides a detailed clinical picture, achieves a clinical diagnosis, allows exploration of responses and clarification of ambiguous answers. It allows for a Global Assessment Rating: a rating is obtained for two time points – when most severe during the episode (e.g. over the past six months) and during the week prior to interview. In order to assess interrater reliability, it is necessary for interviews to be videotaped, and a proportion assessed by an experienced, independent, rater.

Assessment of children under four years of age

When younger children are being assessed, it is still unclear which questionnaires, if any, should be used. One study (Scheeringa *et al*, 1995) found that when more behaviourally anchored and developmentally sensitive criteria were applied to 12 new cases of traumatised infants, nine of them were diagnosed with PTSD by three out of four raters, who had not been able to make the diagnosis using DSM–IV criteria. Scheeringa *et al* (1995) concluded that a post-traumatic syndrome does appear to exist in infants and children exposed to traumatic events, and that the sequelae can be severe if untreated. However, not every infant who is traumatised will develop PTSD. Further research is needed.

Further work is required to identify which instruments are the most helpful clinically and for research purposes, across the age range, and to establish the level of agreement between different methods of assessment. Certain types of trauma, such as the experience of children in a war situation, may require special consideration. It may be possible to develop instruments which measure levels of anger and aggression, and changes in assumptions about life, about personal vulnerability and mortality, and changes in interpersonal factors such as trust.

Screening

Sometimes a selection of questionnaires and tests can be administered to a population considered to be at risk (for example, children who are living in a war-zone). It may be appropriate to administer tests to preschool children, schoolchildren, adolescents, parents and teachers. When screening a large number of individuals, the methods should be simple, repeated to monitor change and progress and implemented as soon as possible after traumatic events. Screening identifies those at risk and may help in the targeting of limited resources. Screening provides a documentary record, raises awareness of the psychological needs of the population under study, of the possible effects of the trauma on the population, and assists in the evaluation of intervention. Records may also be useful in any legal proceedings, such as claims for compensation. Those involved in the gathering of information (which may include teachers and volunteers, as well as healthcare professionals) should be offered training and support. Questionnaires have been devised for use in recent conflicts, such as in Bosnia (e.g. Stuvland, 1992).

Prognosis

McFarlane (1987) rightly pointed out that PTSD is a relatively unknown concept. In particular, little is known about its natural course or indeed its spontaneous remission in some cases. The lack of longitudinal studies make it difficult to be confident about the long-term effectiveness of treatments and the risk of recurrence. However, as a general rule, without treatment it can take two to three years to regain normal functioning. After three years, the chances of a spontaneous recovery are greatly reduced. Also, it is not uncommon for traumatised individuals to be involved in lengthy litigation, perhaps for years, making it difficult for sufferers to put the event behind them and begin to rebuild their lives. However, there is no evidence that survivors who are involved in compensation claims exaggerate their symptoms. Glaser *et al* (1981) interviewed survivors and found no significant difference in the level of reported symptoms between those involved in litigation and those who were not. Similar studies with child survivors involved in litigation are needed (Yule, 1994).

Recent data from research involving survivors of a disaster, who were studied over a nine-year period, showed that there was a clear increase in the general level of morbidity after a traumatic event. The most striking increase was in the occurrence and persistence of psychiatric problems. The increased likelihood of suffering from a major psychiatric disorder was eight times higher than average and persisted over the nine-year period of study (Holen, 1990).

On a human level we know that people do not forget traumatic experiences and they are often etched clearly in their minds for life. Thus the goal of any therapeutic intervention is not to help them forget what happened, but to help facilitate emotional processing and integration of the event, in a way that allows return to normal functioning as soon as possible.

Summary

The assessment of any person who has undergone a traumatic experience needs to be done with care and sensitivity. It should be remembered that there may be coexisting psychiatric and/or physical conditions, and psychosocial issues. A thorough and complete assessment provides a sound basis for diagnosis and therapeutic intervention and for extending our knowledge about post-traumatic stress disorders. As a result of further studies, it may be possible to determine the processes that lead to differences, and predictors of long-term outcome. These may include non-specific factors, such as IQ, personality, temperament, self-esteem, self-reflection, etc.; specific factors, such as aspects within the therapy, premorbid fears and event factors; and mediating factors, such as attachments.

B.   Interventions and treatments

WILLIAM PARRY-JONES

This section seeks to review the rationale and selection of intervention strategies in relation to the concept of psychological traumatisation (when viewed in its widest sense), the range of possible reactions, the stages following potentially traumatising events, and the professional personnel involved.

Ambiguities in the concept of psychological traumatisation

Stress, grief and trauma

The fact that the terms stress, grief and trauma can all be applied to the impact of stressor events may obscure the therapeutic focus, making definitional clarification necessary. While grief connotes bereavement phenomena, following death and other loss experiences, stress and trauma are less easily distinguished and may be used to refer to both the cause and effect of distress. If the ambiguous term *trauma* is to be retained, its distinctive features and meaning should be defined. Etymologically, trauma means a bodily wound from external violence. When used psychologically, it is possible to conceptualise a state of emotional and cognitive wounding, in which the individual's coping capacity is overwhelmed for a period exceeding the aftermath of a stressful event; psychological and physiological responses are disorganised, and the ability to continue normal life is impaired. Experienced events are best referred to as stressors, which can be single or multiple incidents, brief or prolonged, and of low or high magnitude. It is evident that intense, single incidents of relatively short duration generate different responses than multiple, prolonged, repeated experiences. The more diffuse nature of prolonged-duress stress disorders may render treatment more difficult.

Normal distress and mental disorder

The possibility of construing some, if not all, post-trauma reactions as normal, predictable responses to extreme stress, challenges the justification of intervention, as discussed below by Richman (chapter 25). In the eagerness to respond to trauma survivors and to acquire new intervention techniques, the complex issue of causation can be allocated less than the requisite attention. This is not surprising since, despite the plethora of explanatory theories, there is no single, satisfactory view of causation, with a corresponding therapeutic rationale, and the current state of the art signals the need to adopt a discriminating approach to new theoretical formulations.

Recent research provides encouraging empirical support for a cognitive processing model for post-trauma stress and its treatment (Creamer, 1993), but a holistic approach to individual treatment and the necessity for comprehensive services suggest that familiarity with other models is essential.

The time of onset, form, severity and duration of reactions varies widely, ranging from minimal and normal distress reactions to prolonged, incapacitating, treatment-resistant PTSD. This range of reactions necessitates an equally diverse spectrum of crisis, supportive and therapeutic interventions, delivered by personnel from various professional backgrounds, employed by different agencies and services. Some interventions are interdisciplinary; others require highly specialised experience and training. When viewed as a whole, comprehensive post-trauma services require substantial collaboration and coordination to maintain cohesion and minimise uncertainty and conflict about roles and responsibilities (see chapter 26).

Screening and diagnosis

Screening

This aims to identify groups of people at high risk for developing adverse reactions and should be undertaken as soon as possible after potential traumatisation. Ideally, all intervention decisions should be based on the findings of prior screening. This is not an easy task, especially when large numbers are involved, since there are no well-established protocols. Screening procedures should be concerned, at least, with identifying factors likely to increase susceptibility to psychological traumatisation, signs of early post-trauma reactions, and of serious or potentially serious disorders. Three groups of factors influence variations in response.

(a) Characteristics of the stressor. Certain experiences carry greater risks of traumatisation, and the degree and duration of exposure form major components of risk screening.

(b) Characteristics of the person: developmental stage, cognitive style, coping resources, previous experience of loss or trauma and pre-existing medical and psychiatric problems.

(c) Characteristics of the recovery environment: the extent of support provided by family, peer group and community, and the social and societal context of personal distress.

Diagnosis

The diversity of individual post-trauma reactions and the frequent occurrence of comorbidity necessitate detailed clinical interviews in addition to questionnaire-based methods of assessment. Despite the prominence accorded to PTSD in the professional literature, not all medium or long-term adverse reactions meet its diagnostic criteria, and consideration of other diagnoses is essential. Adjustment reactions, including complicated grief reactions, and a range of anxiety symptoms commonly occur. Major depression can arise, especially if secondary adversities accumulate as a result of the trauma. There may be exacerbations of pre-existing vulnerabilities and disorders, and such features may either lower the threshold for the development of PTSD or aggravate its course.

Stages and strategies of intervention

Rationale for intervention

It is widely accepted that early intervention, characterised by risk anticipation, reduces the adverse psychological effects of potentially traumatic experiences. Scope may exist for removing stressors, or reducing their potency, strengthening ameliorative factors and mobilising natural coping skills. Scientific support for prevention remains limited. The psychological and psychiatric treatment of those suffering from PTSD or other specified post-trauma mental disorders follows well-established lines, but there are few outcome evaluation studies.

Although they vary in timing, intensity and complexity, the interventions outlined in this section form essential components of a comprehensive programme. While there is no single theoretical or practical framework, it is possible to identify common features, including the examination, confrontation and mastery of stressful experiences, emotions and thoughts; the ventilation of impressions, reactions and feelings; the clarification of dysfunctional meanings; the discouragement of avoidance; normalisation and preparation for dealing with future stress. Acknowledgement of this degree of commonality facilitates the assembly of intervention programmes from multiple information sources.

Differentiation and selection of intervention models

Descriptive titles of psychological interventions, especially counselling, tend to be used loosely and even interchangeably, although objectives, methods and requisite skills vary considerably. Clear definition and differentiation facilitates selection of the appropriate intervention style, thereby increasing the practitioner's confidence. Associated confusion can arise also because titles such as counsellor, therapist or disaster worker tend to predetermine expectations of specialist roles, and for this reason a neutral term, such as interventionist, might be preferable.

Since there is likely to be a constellation of symptoms or levels of traumatisation in PTSD and other long-term reactions, a multidimensional treatment protocol may be appropriate, using behavioural, psychodynamic and pharmacological techniques (Southwick & Yehuda, 1993). The interventions selected should match individual psychological and social needs, developmental stage, the pattern and duration of presenting features, the post-trauma stage, as well as the interventionist's experience and expertise. There should be detailed advance planning and delineation of the roles of interventionists, and objectives should be well-defined and realistic.

Crisis intervention

In the first 24 hours after traumatic events, survival takes precedence and it is usually appropriate to postpone psychological intervention until medical attention, food, transport and shelter have been provided, yet prompt involvement facilitates the interventionist's role (Alexander, 1990). Psychological first-aid (see chapter 15) aims to help people to get their bearings, reducing the duration and progress of distress and preventing onset of disorder, reducing further disturbance by secondary stressors, facilitating grief-work, promoting confidence in natural coping efforts, and identifying those at risk for adverse reactions.

Empirical data are lacking at present (Robinson & Mitchell, 1993), but the aims of individual or group psychological debriefing comprise: ventilation of impressions, reactions and feelings; promotion of clear understanding of events and reactions; decreased individual or group tension; normalisation through sharing experiences; increasing group support, solidarity and cohesiveness; education about typical post-traumatic reactions; and identification of sources of further assistance and those likely to benefit from follow-up counselling (Hodgkinson & Stewart, 1991).

Longer-term interventions

Counselling

This term creates ambiguous expectations about objectives and it should be distinguished clearly from psychotherapy, emphasising the different, non-specialist, but exacting skills required, including the provision of opportunities for trauma survivors to share experiences. Counselling facilitates emotional expression, understanding, problem-solving and normalisation. Those likely to need more specialised psychological or psychiatric assessment and treatment can be identified.

Psychotherapy

There are extensive reports of the use and contribution of psychotherapy, but outcome evaluation tends to be anecdotal. Horowitz (1976) provided the central conceptual model for dynamic approaches. Generally, cognitive–behavioural treatment, employing cognitive restructuring, fear extinction and skills training, have been subjected to the most rigorous empirical studies (Foy, 1992). In most cases, psychotherapy is indicated for longer-term or chronic reactions. There is a view well established in Western psychiatry that the guided reappraisal of the traumatic experience, using imagery and memories, can be beneficial, in addition to the exploration of such features as revenge fantasies, guilt, self-blame, grief and worries about the future.

With some multiply-traumatised individuals, especially war-exposed refugees, clinical experience suggests that evoked verbalisation of the trauma narrative may be less appropriate than direct efforts at symptom reduction and enhanced coping with daily living. Psychotherapy is the prerogative of trained medical and non-medical psychotherapists and always requires supervision.

Other assessments and treatments by mental health teams

Indications for psychiatric assessment and treatment include evidence suggesting specific mental disorder or suicide risk: requests for reassurance by trauma survivors that they are not mentally ill and situations where counselling or other therapeutic interventions have proved ineffective, leaving mental functioning impaired. There is a growing body of evidence about the adjunctive use of psychopharmacological treatment, but there have been few controlled studies (Friedman, 1993; see chapter 19).

Interventions across the age range

Recognition of developmental variation of symptoms and the family orientation is essential, yet continuity of treatment concepts and methods across age-groups should be maintained (Saylor, 1993; and see chapter 12). In addition to the separate interviewing of children and adolescents, detailed evaluation of parental reactions, marital and family adjustment and coping strategies is essential. Special problems arise when families have been separated and re-unification is delayed or impossible. The school may provide an optimum setting for intervention (Yule & Gold, 1993; see chapter 20C). The role of medication should be considered, particularly in the treatment of anxiety and depressive disorders in the context of predominantly psychotherapeutic approaches.

Welfare of counsellors and therapists

This commences with careful recruitment and selection of personnel, their regular training, supervision and support, and the use of stress-mitigation activities, based, for example, on role clarification and rehearsal. Signs of secondary trauma need to be understood clearly by the managers of disaster programmes and stress clinics (Parry-Jones, 1992; and see chapter 21).

Transcultural aspects

The transcultural generalisation of Western paradigms of traumatisation, mental disorder and treatment requires caution, as discussed by Richman (chapter 25) and in chapter 10.

Community-level intervention and future directions

Comprehensive mental health programmes for trauma survivors should incorporate a range of community-based strategies, including crisis hotlines, educational, school or church-based programmes, and other techniques designed to mobilise social networks and stabilise the social background (Department of Health, 1991; Parry-Jones, 1992). These require detailed advance preparation and efficient inter-agency liaison (see chapter 26).

References

Alexander, D. A. (1990) Psychological intervention for victims and helpers after disasters. *British Journal of General Practice*, **40**, 345–348.

American Psychiatric Association (1994) *Diagnostic and Statistical Manual of Mental Disorders* (4th edn) (DSM–IV). Washington, DC: APA.

Berger, M. (1994) Psychological tests and assessment. In *Child and Adolescent Psychiatry: Modern Approaches* (3rd edn) (eds M. Rutter, E. Taylor & L. Hersov), pp. 94–109. Oxford: Blackwell Scientific.

Birleson, P. (1981) The validity of depressive disorder in childhood and the development of a self-rating scale: a research report. *Journal of Child Psychology and Psychiatry*, **22**, 73–78.

——, Hudson, I., Buchanan, D., *et al* (1987) Clinical evaluation of a self-rating scale for depressive disorder in childhood (Depression Self-Rating Scale). *Journal of Child Psychology and Psychiatry*, **28**, 43–60.

Blake, D., Weathers, F., Nagy, L., *et al* (1990) *Clinician-Administered PTSD Scale (CAPS)*. Boston, MASS: Behavioral Science Division, Boston National Center for Post-traumatic Stress Disorder.

Bryant, R. A. & Harvey, A. G. (1995) Avoidant coping style and post-traumatic stress following motor vehicle accidents. *Behaviour Research and Therapy*, **33**, 631–635.

Cantwell, D. P & Rutter, M. (1994) Classification: conceptual issues and substantive findings. In *Child and Adolescent Psychiatry: Modern Approaches* (3rd edn) (eds M. Rutter, E. Taylor & L. Hersov), pp. 3–21. Oxford: Blackwell Scientific.

Ceci, S. J. & Bruck, M. (1993) Suggestibility of the child witness: a historical review and synthesis. *Psychological Bulletin*, **113**, 403–469.

Chambers, W. J., Puig-Antich, J., Hirsch, M., *et al* (1985) The assessment of affective disorders in children and adolescents by semi-structured interview. *Archives of General Psychiatry*, **42**, 696–702.

Cox, A. D. (1994) Diagnostic appraisal. In *Child and Adolescent Psychiatry: Modern Approaches* (3rd edn) (eds M. Rutter, E. Taylor & L. Hersov), pp. 22–33. Oxford: Blackwell Scientific.

Creamer, M. (1993) Recent developments in post-traumatic stress disorders. *Behaviour Change*, **10**, 219–227.

Deahl, M., Earnshaw, N. M. & Jones, N. (1994) Psychiatry and war – learning lessons from the former Yugoslavia. *British Journal of Psychiatry*, **164**, 441–442.

Department of Health (1991) *Disasters: Planning for a Caring Response*. London: HMSO.

Derogatis, L. R. (1977) *Symptom Checklist–90–R: Administration, Scoring and Procedure Manual 1*. Baltimore: Clinical Psychometrics Research.

Dohrenwend, B. P., Dohrenwend, B. S., Warheit, G. J., *et al* (1981) Stress in the community: a report to the President's Commission on the accident at Three Mile Island. *Annals of the New York Academy of Sciences*, **365**, 159–174.

Eysenck, H. J. & Eysenck, S. B. (1976) *Manual of the Eysenck Personality Inventory*. San Diego: Educational and Industrial Testing Service.

Foy, D. W. (ed.) (1992) *Treating PTSD. Cognitive–Behavioural Strategies*. New York: Guilford Press.

Frederick, C. J. & Pynoos, R. (1988) *The Child Post-traumatic Stress Disorder (PTSD) Reaction Index*. Los Angeles: University of California.

Friedman, M. J. (1993) Psychobiological and pharmacological approaches to treatment. In *International Handbook of Traumatic Stress Syndromes* (eds J. P. Wilson & B. Raphael), pp. 785–794. New York: Plenum Press.

Glaser, G. G., Green, B. L. & Winget, C. (1981) *Prolonged Psychosocial Effects of Disaster: A Study of Buffalo Creek*. New York: Academic Press.

Goldberg, D. P. & Hillier, V. F. (1979) A scaled version of the General Health Questionnaire. *Psychological Medicine*, **9**, 139–145.

Green, B. L. (1994) Psychosocial research in traumatic stress: an update. *Journal of Traumatic Stress*, **7**, 341–362.

Harris-Hendriks, J. & Newman, M. (1995) Psychological trauma in children and adolescents. *Advances in Psychiatric Treatment*, **1**, 170–175.

——, Black, D. & Kaplan, T. (1993) *When Father Kills Mother: Guiding Children Through Trauma and Grief.* London: Routledge.

Hill, P. (1994) Adjustment disorders. In *Child and Adolescent Psychiatry: Modern Approaches* (3rd edn) (eds M. Rutter, E. Taylor & L. Hersov), pp. 375–391. Oxford: Blackwell Scientific.

Hodgkinson, P. E. & Stewart, M. (1991) *Coping with Catastrophe.* London: Routledge.

Hogan, N. S. (1990) Hogan Sibling Inventory of Bereavement. In *Handbook of Family Measurement Techniques* (eds J. Touliatos, B. Perlmutter & M. Straus), p. 524. Newbury Park, CA: Sage.

Holen, A. (1990) *A Long-Term Outcome Study of Survivors from a Disaster: the Alexander L. Kielland Disaster in Perspective.* Oslo: University of Oslo.

Horowitz, M. J. (1976) *Stress Response Syndromes.* New York: Jason Aronson.

——, Wilner, N. & Alvarez, W. (1979) Impact of Event Scale: a measure of subjective stress. *Psychosomatic Medicine*, **41**, 209–218.

Kolvin, I., Barrett, M. L., Bhate, S. R., *et al* (1991) The Newcastle Child Depression Project. Diagnosis and classification of depression. *British Journal of Psychiatry*, **159** (suppl. 11), 9–21.

Kuterovac, G., Dyregrov, A. & Stuvland, R. (1994) Children in war: a silent majority under stress. *British Journal of Medical Psychology*, **67**, 363–375.

Lansdown, R. & Benjamin, G. (1985) The development of the concept of death in children aged 5–9 years. *Child: Care, Health and Development*, **11**, 13–20.

Lindy, J. D., Grace, M. C. & Green, B. L. (1981) Survivors: outreach to a reluctant population. *American Journal of Orthopsychiatry*, **51**, 468–478.

McFarlane, A. (1987) Post-traumatic phenomena in a longitudinal study of children following a natural disaster. *Journal of the American Academy of Child and Adolescent Psychiatry*, **26**, 764–769.

—— (1988) The longitudinal course of post-traumatic morbidity: the range of outcomes and their predictors. *Journal of Nervous and Mental Disease*, **176**, 30–39.

McIvor, R. J. (1994) Making the most of interpreters (letter). *British Journal of Psychiatry*, **165**, 268.

McLeer, S. V., Deblinger, E., Henry, D., *et al* (1992) Sexually abused children at high risk for post-traumatic stress disorder. *Journal of the American Academy of Child and Adolescent Psychiatry*, **31**, 875–879.

Malloy, P., Fairbank, J. & Keane, J. (1983) Validation of a multimethod assessment of PTSD in Vietnam veterans. *Journal of Consulting and Clinical Psychology*, **51**, 48–94.

Mann, A. & Murray, R. (1986) Measurement in psychiatry. In *Essentials of Postgraduate Psychiatry* (2nd edn) (eds P. Hill, R. Murray & A. Thorley), pp. 55–77. London: Grune & Stratton.

Nader, K., Pynoos, R., Fairbanks, L., *et al* (1990) Children's PTSD reactions one year after a sniper attack at their school. *American Journal of Psychiatry*, **147**, 1526–1530.

——, ——, ——, *et al* (1993) A preliminary study of PTSD and grief among the children of Kuwait following the Gulf crisis. *British Journal of Clinical Psychology*, **32**, 407–416.

Neal, L. A. (1994) The pitfalls of making a categorical diagnosis of post traumatic stress disorder in personal injury litigation. *Medicine, Science and the Law*, **34**, 117–122.

Orvaschel, H. (1990) Early onset psychiatric disorder in high risk children and increased familial mortality. *Journal of the American Academy of Child and Adolescent Psychiatry*, **29**, 184–188.

——, Puig-Antich, J., Chambers, W., *et al* (1982) Retrospective assessment of prepubertal major depression with the Kiddie–SADS–E. *Journal of the American Academy of Child Psychiatry*, **21**, 392–397.

Parry-Jones, W. Ll. (1992) Disaster management and experiences from the United Kingdom. In *Critical Incident Stress Management across the Lifespan* (ed. J. Westerink), pp. 18–28. Turramurra, NSW: Australian Critical Incident Stress Association.

Puig-Antich, J. & Chambers, W. J. (1978) *K–SADS (The Schedule for Affective Disorders and Schizophrenia for School Aged Children).* Unpublished - obtain through New York State Psychiatric Institute, 722 West 168 Street, New York 10032, US.

Pynoos, R. S. (1992) Grief and trauma in children and adolescents. *Bereavement Care*, **11**, 2–10.

—— & Eth, S. (1986) Witness to violence: the child interview. *Journal of the American Academy of Child Psychiatry*, **25**, 306–319.

—— & Nader, K. (1988) Children who witness the sexual assaults of their mothers. *Journal of the American Academy of Child and Adolescent Psychiatry*, **27**, 567–572.

——, Arroyo, W., Steinberg, A., *et al* (1987*a*) Life threat and post traumatic stress in school-age children. *Archives of General Psychiatry*, **44**, 1057–1063.

——, Nader, K., Frederick, C., *et al* (1987*b*) Grief reactions in school-age children following a sniper attack at school. *Israel Journal of Psychiatry and Related Sciences*, **24**, 53–63.

——, Goenjian, A., Tashjian, M., *et al* (1993) Post-traumatic stress reactions in children after the 1988 Armenian Earthquake. *British Journal of Psychiatry*, **163**, 239–247.

Raphael, B. (1995) The measure of grief. In *Grief and Bereavement: Proceedings from the Fourth International Conference on Grief and Bereavement in Contemporary Society, Stockholm 1994*. Stockholm: Swedish National Association for Mental Health.

Reynolds, C. R. & Richmond, B. D. (1978) What I think and feel: a revised measure of children's manifest anxiety. *Journal of Abnormal Child Psychology*, **6**, 271–280.

Robinson, R. C. & Mitchell, J. T. (1993) Evaluation of psychological debriefings. *Journal of Traumatic Stress*, **6**, 367–382.

Saigh, P. A. (1989) The development and validation of the Children's Postttraumatic Stress Disorder Inventory. *International Journal of Special Education*, **4**, 75–84.

Saylor, C. F. (ed.) (1993) *Children and Disasters*. New York: Plenum Press.

Scheeringa, M. S., Zeanah, C. H., Drell, M. J., *et al* (1995) Two approaches to the diagnosis of post-traumatic stress disorder in infancy and early childhood. *Journal of the American Academy of Child and Adolescent Psychiatry*, **34**, 191–200.

Southwick, S. M. & Yehuda, R. (1993) The interaction between pharmacotherapy and psychotherapy in the treatment of post-traumatic stress disorder. *American Journal of Psychotherapy*, **47**, 404–410.

Speece, M. W. & Brent, S. B. (1984) Children's understanding of death: a review of three components of a death concept. *Child Development*, **55**, 1671–1686.

Spitzer, R. L., Endicott, J. & Robins, E. (1978) Research Diagnostic Criteria: rationale and reliability. *Archives of General Psychiatry*, **35**, 773–782.

Stuvland, R. (1992) *43-item War Trauma Questionnaire*. Zagreb: UNICEF.

Thompson, J. A. & Turner, S. W. (1987) *The King's Cross Event Schedule* (available from the Traumatic Stress Clinic, 73 Charlotte Street, London W1P 1LB).

——, Charlton, P. F. C., Kerry, R., *et al* (1995) An open trial of exposure therapy based on deconditioning for post-traumatic stress disorder. *British Journal of Clinical Psychology*, **34**, 407–416.

Turner, S. W., Thompson, J. A. & Rosser, R. M. (1995) The King's Cross Fire: psychological reactions. *Journal of Traumatic Stress*, **8**, 419–427.

Udwin, O. (1993) Children's reactions to traumatic events. *Journal of Child Psychology and Psychiatry*, **34**, 115–127.

Vasquez, C. & Janvier, R. A. (1991) The problem with interpreters: communicating with Spanish-speaking patients. *Hospital and Community Psychiatry*, **42**, 163–165.

World Health Organization (1992) *The ICD–10 Classification of Mental and Behavioural Disorders*. Geneva: WHO.

Yule, W. (1992) Post-traumatic stress disorder in child survivors of shipping disasters: the sinking of the "Jupiter". *Journal of Psychotherapy and Psychosomatics*, **57**, 200–205.

—— (1994) Posttraumatic stress disorders. In *Child and Adolescent Psychiatry: Modern Approaches* (3rd edn) (eds M. Rutter, E. Taylor & L. Hersov). Oxford: Blackwell Scientific Publications.

—— & Williams, R. (1990) Post-traumatic stress reactions in children. *Journal of Traumatic Stress*, **3**, 279–295.

—— & Udwin, O. (1991) Screening child survivors for post-traumatic stress disorders: experiences from the 'Jupiter' sinking. *British Journal of Clinical Psychology*, **30**, 131–138.

—— & Williams, R. (1992) The management of trauma following disasters. In *Child and Adolescent Therapy – a Handbook* (eds D. A. Lane & A. Miller), pp. 157–176. Milton Keynes: Open University Press.

—— & Gold, A. (1993) Wise before the event: planning with schools to help child survivors of catastrophes. In *Trauma and Crisis Management* (Occasional Paper No. 8) (ed. G. Forrest), pp. 26–34. London: Association for Child Psychology and Psychiatry.

——, Bolton, D. & Udwin, O. (1992) Objective and subjective predictors of PTSD in adolescents. Paper presented at World Conference of International Society for Traumatic Stress Studies, 'Trauma and Tragedy', Amsterdam, June 1992.

15 Debriefing and crisis intervention

WALTER BUSUTTIL and ANGELA BUSUTTIL

Crisis intervention and *debriefing* are related techniques. They can be employed in the prevention of the stress response syndrome (SRS). SRS may be viewed as beginning with an initial 'fluid' post-traumatic stress reaction (PTSR) which can progress to the 'fixed' post-traumatic stress disorder (PTSD) (Horowitz, 1976).

This chapter will describe the development of debriefing as a form of crisis intervention and refer to published research investigating the technique in the prevention of post-traumatic psychological sequelae. Postulated therapeutic components of debriefing will be presented with reference to aetiological models of the SRS.

Crisis intervention

Crisis intervention principles have been used in military settings since the middle of the First World War for dealing with acute combat psychiatric casualties (Glass, 1975; Kormos, 1978; Price, 1984; Copp & McAndrew, 1990). Four treatment principles have been used (Salmon, 1919; Artiss, 1963; Levav *et al*, 1979).

> *Proximity*: treatment is delivered close to the battle front and the soldier's social network.
> *Immediacy*: immediate treatment when stress symptoms compromise fitness for duty.
> *Expectancy*: soldiers are made aware that return to active combat is expected.
> *Brevity*: management lasts for a maximum of ten days.

The principles are summarised as PIEB. If they fail, transfer to a rear hospital is indicated. Empirical studies demonstrate that the benefits of PIEB include a decreased incidence of PTSD at follow-up, and the increased ability of soldiers to return to active duty (Levav *et al*, 1979; Solomon & Benbenishty, 1986).

Classical crisis intervention principles are similar to PIEB. Initial screening identifies those in need of psychiatric assessment or hospitalisation. Where this is not indicated, supportive procedures commence within the victim's social setting. Intervention is not designed to address all problems, but aims to restore pre-crisis levels of emotional and functional equilibrium. Techniques include: promoting an understanding that the crisis and psychological responses are linked; ventilation of feelings; exploration of alternative coping styles; mobilising social support; promoting resolution of the crisis; and planning for any future difficulties (Aguilera, 1990).

Debriefing

Samuel Marshall, a military historian, described a technique similar to debriefing (Shalev, 1994). His Second World War, Korean and Vietnam war diaries document benefits to the psychosocial functioning of small combat units when groups of soldiers were encouraged to talk in detail in a structured format about their traumatic combat experiences soon after exposure. Marshall was interested in group communication and social cohesiveness of small combat units under fire. His technique was devised as a means for gathering factual data for this research (Shalev, 1994).

Debriefing after subjection to traumatic stress was developed separately by Mitchell (1983) and Dyregrov (1989), and more informally by Raphael (1986). The need for a preventative psychological programme was identified after observing that some emergency workers showed psychological distress after exposure to traumatic incidents involving direct and indirect personal physical or psychological threat (Mitchell, 1983; Dyregrov, 1989; Parkes, 1991).

Mitchell called his technique 'critical incident stress debriefing' (CISD), while Dyregrov referred to 'psychological debriefing' (PD). These similar techniques have been conceptualised as part of a "supportive crisis intervention format" (Mitchell, 1983).

Debriefing aims to diminish the impact of catastrophic events by promoting support and encouraging processing of traumatic experiences in a group setting. It facilitates the piecing together of traumatic information while personal experiences are normalised and participants are helped to look to the future. It attempts to accelerate recovery before harmful stress reactions have a chance to damage the performance, careers, health and families of victims (Mitchell, 1983, 1988; Dyregrov, 1989).

A group meeting of those exposed to a common traumatic event is conducted by a credible facilitator. Talking about factual experiences, associated feelings and reactions after exposure to a traumatic incident is promoted in a positive, supportive manner to foster the understanding and assimilation of events.

Mitchell (1983) described four types of CISD. Each may be used at different periods during and in the aftermath of traumatic exposure.

I.   The *on-scene* or *near scene debriefing* is brief and conducted by a mental health professional familiar with the operational task. The role incorporates the detection of early signs of PTSR, offering encouragement and support and advising commanding officers when individuals or groups need work routine changes or rest breaks.

II.   The *initial defusing* is performed within a few hours of the incident, usually organised and led by the section commander but perhaps occurring spontaneously within the emergency team. Feelings and reactions relating to the incident are discussed.

III.   *Formal CISD* is similar to the PD technique described by Dyregrov (1989) and is usually led by a mental health practitioner or a trained manager. The leader must be credible to all participants and knowledge of SRS and operational procedures are essential. This type of debriefing is recommended 24 to 48 hours post-incident. Mitchell (1983) reasoned that emergency workers 'train' themselves to suppress psychological reactions during and for a brief period after an incident, and that during this period they were too aroused to deal with an in-depth discussion of the events. It has been argued that formal CISD and PD should be mandatory for all involved in a traumatic incident (Mitchell, 1983; Dyregrov, 1989).

Mitchell & Dyregrov (1993) recently jointly detailed a seven-phase debriefing protocol. They advised that all individuals involved in an incident should participate and suggested that the debriefing process should take 2.5–3 hours. A team of four debriefers including a mental health professional lead the debriefing. The first phase described is the introduction. Ground rules are set, confidentiality is stressed, and it is explained that while group members are encouraged to participate, no-one is compelled to talk. It is emphasised that debriefing is not intended to be "psychotherapy", but a discussion with educational and psychological components.

The second phase addresses the facts of the incident with individuals presenting the event from their own perspective. In the third phase, participants describe their thoughts about the event. According to Mitchell & Dyregrov this enables participants to move from describing the facts of the event to developing a more personal perspective. The fourth phase encourages participants to openly discuss emotions experienced in relation to the event. Free and open discussion of the most difficult aspects of the event is encouraged.

In the fifth phase the symptoms of stress occurring in relation to the trauma are addressed. Cognitive, physical, emotional and behavioural reactions are discussed. This phase includes review of the symptoms experienced at the scene of the event, those occurring immediately after and those still present at the time of debriefing. Education about stress reactions and the symptoms experienced by the participants takes place in the sixth phase. The purpose of this is to 'normalise' the bewildering range of symptoms that commonly occur and which might otherwise become a further source of stress as the individual struggles to make sense of them. Instruction in adaptive coping techniques may be given. This phase may be adapted in accordance with the specific needs of the group.

The last phase, the 're-entry phase', allows participants to raise questions, address issues in more depth or raise new issues. Previous descriptions of debriefing have indicated that this phase can include future planning and advice on where to obtain further help if needed (Mitchell, 1983; Dyregrov, 1989).

A firm theoretical rationale for psychological debriefing has never been presented. However, a number of therapeutic elements appear to be included:

(a) group support factors: including a reassuring and supportive environment, a credible group leader and the reassurance of the explanatory introduction and "ground rules";

(b) cognitive factors: Detailed disclosure of expectations, facts, thoughts, emotional reactions and sensory impressions;

(c) coping factors: education about SRS, normalisation and anticipatory guidance, future planning and "re-entry phases".

IV. The *follow-up CISD* takes place several weeks after the incident and is not always required. Its main function is to resolve issues arising as a result of the original incident. Mitchell (1983) asserted that this is perhaps the hardest to conduct and that it is closely associated with therapy.

Innovations and debriefing

Bergmann & Queen (1986) developed an educational package aimed at helping emergency personnel gain insight into the nature of traumatic experiences. Techniques included: helping individuals to anticipate a list of potentially traumatic events; teaching them what the symptoms and causes of SRS are; offering options for dealing with the trauma; and teaching basic peer support skills. Other workers have made similar suggestions (Raphael, 1986; Mitchell, 1988; 1989). The setting-up of a network of trained CISD teams which could be called in to supervise CISDs has also been suggested (Mitchell, 1988, 1989; Mitchell & Dyregrov, 1993). This concept has a forerunner, the so-called Special Psychiatric Rapid Intervention Teams (SPRINT). SPRINT was used by the US Navy following a shipping disaster in the 1970s. It aims to deliver immediate crisis intervention by means of reassurance and support (Taylor, 1991). A Royal Air Force SPRINT team was used after the release of British hostages from Lebanon in 1991 and with British Gulf Conflict prisoners of war (POWs). After crisis intervention, debriefing of victims and close family members was conducted (Turnbull, 1992; Psychiatric Division of the Royal Air Force Medical Service, 1993).

Technical debriefings and psychological debriefings may be merged (Turnbull, 1992; Psychiatric Division of the Royal Air Force Medical Service, 1993) in situations where operational contingencies dictate that victims must immediately divulge what they have witnessed as part of a legal process (after rape, for example), or to prevent similar accidents or disasters. A debriefer can 'sit in' during such debriefings, offering psychological support to the victim and advice to the technical debriefers, at the same time noting areas of emotional upset which can be used later in therapeutic individual or group debriefings. It should be noted that there are suggestions that the debriefing of the debriefers (or secondary debriefing) may be beneficial (Talbot *et al*, 1992).

Research evidence

There is little empirical evidence demonstrating the efficacy of debriefing and crisis intervention in the prevention of PTSD. Recent reviews have highlighted this (Bisson & Deahl, 1994; Raphael *et al*, 1995).

Until empirical evidence exists demonstrating the efficacy of the technique it is difficult to support calls that it should be mandatory after traumatic events. However, it would similarly be unwise to dismiss the evidence that debriefing or some elements within the debriefing format may be beneficial for some.

Emergency workers welcome the opportunity to talk, but they appear most verbal immediately after traumatic exposure (Jones, 1985). An expressed inability to talk about experiences in the immediate aftermath of traumatic exposure has been demonstrated to predict poor psychological outcome (Fowlie & Aveline, 1985) and PTSD at long-term follow-up (O'Brian & Hughes, 1991).

A prospective study which included 172 emergency service personnel who participated in 31 separate debriefings assessed the value of debriefing positively. Unfortunately, only subjective evaluations were used (Robinson & Mitchell, 1993).

In a before-and-after comparison study, the effects of induction training, stress inoculation, daily debriefing led by trained senior police officers, and supportive liaison by psychiatrists, were assessed over time in a controlled group of 54 police officer body-handlers of the Piper Alpha oil rig disaster (Alexander & Wells, 1991; Alexander, 1993; and see Chapter 8H). Officers completed their duties satisfactorily, emerged relatively unscathed, and most gained from the experience. At three-month follow-up, no increase in psychiatric morbidity was detected. Assessment using the Impact of Event Scale (IES; Horowitz *et al*, 1979) demonstrated that post-traumatic stress (PTS) symptoms were present but did not amount to PTSD. No significant differences were detected between experienced and inexperienced officers. Coping strategies measured using a specially devised questionnaire revealed that humour, talking to colleagues (including debriefing), and thinking about positive operational aspects were helpful. Avoiding issues was the most unhelpful strategy. Good morale, organisation and team spirit were thought to promote healing. Reassessment of 35 of the original group three years later revealed a significant decline in psychiatric morbidity including PTS symptoms as compared with the three-month assessments. A general shift towards a positive appraisal of the operation was detected (Alexander, 1993).

Comparisons with groups of officers who had not received debriefing, induction training, stress inoculation or their relative combinations were not made in this study. It has been demonstrated that induction training, by preparing emergency workers for what to expect in disaster situations, was superior to stress inoculation alone (previous disaster work experience), and that both were effective in reducing PTS symptoms after comparisons with cohorts of emergency workers for whom no preventative provisions were made (Paton, 1992, 1994).

A recent study incorporating a control group failed to demonstrate the efficacy of debriefing which was delivered in addition to induction training. This study was conducted with 62 Gulf Conflict British military body-handlers (Deahl *et al*, 1994). Sixty-nine per cent of participants attended a single debriefing session on completion of their duties. After nine months, 50% were found to have evidence of PTSD. Neither prior induction training nor debriefing appeared to have made any difference to subsequent morbidity at nine months. At face value the results of this study suggest that the prevention measures did not work. However, debriefing was conducted on a single occasion and only after return to the UK in most cases. Only 20% reported they found it useful. Moreover, debriefing was led by two professionals drawn from a pool of chaplains, a psychologist, psychiatrists and social workers who were (presumably) not personally known to the soldiers and who were 'removed' from the traumatic incidents. This raises issues of credibility and is in contrast to the debriefers involved in the Piper Alpha study where these issues appear not to apply.

It can also be postulated that the "one-off end of trauma debriefing session" did not facilitate the working-through of all the traumatic material, and regular debriefing sessions might have promoted this, along with ongoing peer support as was the case in the Piper Alpha study. Further controlled studies are required to clarify these issues.

Important questions emerge from these studies. What are the relative contributions to outcome of induction training, stress inoculation through previous experience, and debriefing? Further empirical research is required.

Debriefing and aetiological models of PTSD

Horowitz's information processing (aetiological) model can be seen as the most influential model from which others such as the psychosocial (Green *et al*, 1985) and cognitive appraisal models (Janoff-Bulman, 1985) have developed. The central assumption made by Horowitz (1975, 1976, 1979) is the *completion tendency*. In explaining this, a rationale pertaining to normal cognitive operations was put forward.

(a) Active memory storage has an intrinsic tendency towards repeated representation of its contents.
(b) This tendency continues indefinitely until storage of the particular contents in active memory is terminated.

(c)   Termination of contents in active memory occurs when cognitive processing has been completed: in effect, active memory contents follow an automatic 'completion tendency'.

SRS, characterised by the oscillation of intrusive and avoidance phenomena, emerges if the completion tendency is not achieved by the processing of traumatic information. Progression to PTSD results from non-completion of the tendency. Information processing requires the modification and accommodation of cognitive schemata before the completion tendency can be achieved (Horowitz, 1975, 1976).

Thus the duration of psychological disturbance is limited by information processing mechanisms which may become arrested. Several studies have confirmed that the spontaneous resolution of PTSR becomes less likely as time from traumatisation elapses (Taylor & Frazer, 1982; Duckworth, 1986; McFarlane, 1988*a,b*; Rothbaum & Foa, 1993; McCarroll *et al*, 1993). Processing appears more likely to become blocked as time goes on.

Pre-trauma personality characteristics can affect the course of SRS in positive or negative directions: promoting spontaneous resolution of the initial fluid PTSR, or precipitating a fixed PTSD. Progression to the disorder is more likely with increasing degrees of exposure and if maladaptive coping behaviours are adopted (Horowitz, 1976).

Several studies confirm the exposure dose–response relationship with the formation of PTSD (Shore *et al*, 1986; Helzer *et al*, 1987; Goldberg *et al*, 1990; Buydens-Branchey *et al*, 1990). Other studies fail to confirm these findings and emphasise predisposing personality traits (McFarlane, 1989).

Studies suggest that coping style and control expectancies are important in the spontaneous recovery from PTSR. A predominant problem focused coping style rather than emotion focused coping style (Lazarus, 1981) and internal rather than external locus of control (Rotter, 1966) promote recovery from PTSR (Noy, 1987; Mikulincer & Solomon, 1988; Solomon *et al*, 1989). These findings are in keeping with Horowitz's assertions.

Is debriefing likely to facilitate the completion tendency? This question has not been fully explored but it may be relevant to consider what the therapeutic components of debriefing might be in this context.

Group factors

Traumatic exposure often compromises social networks, precipitating isolation, confusion and helplessness (Shalev & Munitz, 1988). Group debriefing counteracts this by promoting a safe understanding environment, allowing reconstruction of social networks and the mobilisation of other helping agencies if required. These factors are in keeping with the psychosocial model of PTSD which states that a socially supportive recovery environment protects against the development of SRS (Green *et al*, 1985).

Cognitive factors

Detailed disclosure of the experience on four dimensions is promoted during debriefing: the expectations and facts, thoughts, emotional reactions and sensory impressions. Identification of expectations and facts addresses what the individual expected might happen and what in fact happened. Disclosure in a supportive group format allows individuals to share common ground to piece factual evidence together. A clear factual picture allows resolution of doubts about individual and general performance.

Similarly, the disclosure of individual thoughts, feelings and actions allows reassurance that others may have similar experiences. Uniformity of response can help promote understanding of what is expected and 'normal'. Disclosure of sensory impressions (smell, taste, touch, etc.) is important, and individuals should be warned that strong sensory inputs gained during traumatic incidents may serve to act as triggers for later intrusive phenomena.

Cognitive reorganisation is therefore facilitated on four dimensions (expectations and facts, thoughts, emotional reactions and sensory impressions). Resultant schemata can accommodate the traumatic incident seen from the individual's perspective and also from the perspective of others involved. These assertions are in keeping with theoretical perspectives concerning appraisal processes, which act in order to accommodate and incorporate the new traumatic information (Lazurus, 1981; Horowitz, 1976).

Shalev (1994) considered an assertion made by Greenberg & van der Kolk (1987) as being relevant to the therapeutic mechanisms of debriefing. They postulated that traumatic memories are stored as iconic recollections rather than verbal ones, and that their persistence precludes further processing of the traumatic experience until the symbolic function of language allows it to proceed. Thus, talking about traumatic experiences may serve to enhance information processing.

Debriefing also allows individuals to conjure a vivid imaginal picture of what has happened by ensuring that all pieces of the 'jigsaw' are disclosed in detail. From a cognitive–behavioural perspective it might be that debriefing generates a detailed image of the traumatic event, fully exposing the individual to all the components of the 'fear structure' (Lang, 1979) and thus facilitating the habituation of arousal.

Coping style factors

The debriefing stages involving normalisation, anticipatory guidance and coping, future planning, and disengagement, sanction the understanding that post-trauma emotions and feelings are usual. Adaptive coping strategies are promoted, as is the appreciation of the 'meaning' of what has happened. These phases also allow further mobilisation of social support networks and buffers (Figley, 1985; Flannery, 1990; see also chapter 20).

Debriefing may not suit everyone, and there is a risk that those who use coping mechanisms such as denial may be damaged through re-traumatisation (Shalev, 1994). Resiliency studies have demonstrated, however, that outcome in terms of psychosocial function is improved if traumatic situations are confronted and not denied, avoided or repressed (Kobasa, 1979; Elder & Clipp, 1989); disclosure of traumatic experiences can serve to decrease longer-term psychological morbidity (Jones, 1985; Fowlie & Aveline, 1985; O'Brian & Hughes, 1991).

Further research might demonstrate that those who do not benefit from debriefing tend to use these defence mechanisms as part of their normal coping repertoire to a greater extent. Indeed, such individuals would probably tend to avoid attendance and active participation in debriefing (if available). Research into the coping repertoires of individuals in relation to objective measures of the benefits of debriefing is required. Bearing in mind the studies cited earlier concerning the relationship between problem-focused coping style, internal locus of control and the recovery from PTSR, it could be postulated that where these strategies are utilised, benefit from debriefing is more likely than where emotion-focused strategies and external locus of control are in evidence (Noy, 1987; Mikulincer & Solomon, 1988; Solomon *et al*, 1989).

One study has suggested that supportive networks can in themselves shift locus of control towards internality (Novaco *et al*, 1983). Perhaps this is one of the therapeutic mechanisms of debriefing.

Children and the elderly

Detailed descriptions of intervention with these groups identified as having special requirements is beyond the scope of this chapter, but some general points can be made.

Follow-up studies of traumatised children demonstrate that, contrary to popular belief, they do not spontaneously 'outgrow' their trauma (Terr, 1983). PTSD can interfere with natural developmental processes in children (Pynoos & Nader, 1993). Debriefing techniques have been modified for use in children, often incorporating drawing to facilitate communication (Pynoos & Eth, 1986). Developmental factors must be taken into account as these modulate the child's appreciation of the trauma, threat appraisal, adopted coping strategies, and therefore symptom presentation. Unique features of SRS include that children may not recall the trauma as a single event but as a series of traumatic incidents within one event. Re-experiencing phenomena often include 'intervention fantasies' – things children wish they had been able to do in the situation (Pynoos & Nader, 1993).

Little is known about the psychological response of the elderly to trauma. In a comparison study, presence of PTSD with comorbid depression was reported more commonly in this group than in younger survivors of the Lockerbie disaster (Livingston *et al*, 1992). Anecdotal reports concerning a survivor group set up in the aftermath of the Bradford fire suggest that survivor guilt and guilt feelings for not going back to rescue others were commoner issues compared with the younger survivor groups, and that expression of emotions was more difficult (Hodgkinson & Stewart, 1991; see chapter 12).

Conclusions

Debriefing may be useful as a form of crisis intervention after major trauma, but it should be seen as only one part of a crisis intervention approach. While anecdotal reports attest to its usefulness, there is a need for controlled studies to evaluate claims that it can prevent or ameliorate symptoms of post-traumatic stress. In this chapter, attempts have been made to identify therapeutic elements with reference to aetiological models. As yet the research literature allows only speculation about what the beneficial components of the technique might be. Further research should also assess its efficacy in different classes of victims in the context of different types of trauma. Whether 'ongoing trauma' requires 'ongoing debriefing' to achieve benefit is another research question yet to be addressed (Busuttil & Busuttil, 1995).

References

Aguilera, D. C. (1990) *Crisis Intervention, Theory and Methodology* (6th edn). St Louis: C. V. Mosby.

Alexander, D. A. (1993) Stress among police body handlers. A long-term follow-up. *British Journal of Psychiatry*, **163**, 806–808.

——— & Wells, A. (1991) Reactions of police officers to body handling after a major disaster. A before and after comparison. *British Journal of Psychiatry*, **159**, 547–555.

Artiss, K. (1963) Human behaviour under stress from combat and social psychiatry. *Military Medicine*, **128**, 1011–1019.

Bergmann, L. H. & Queen, T. R. (1986) Critical incident stress: Part 1. *Fire Command*, April, 52–56.

Bisson, J. I. & Deahl, M. P. (1994) Psychological debriefing and the prevention of post-traumatic stress. *British Journal of Psychiatry*, **165**, 717–720.

Busuttil, A. M. C. & Busuttil, W. (1995) Psychological debriefing. *British Journal of Psychiatry*, **166**, 676–677.

Buydens-Branchey, L., Noumair, D. & Branchey, M. (1990) Duration and intensity of combat exposure and post-traumatic stress disorder in Vietnam veterans. *Journal of Nervous and Mental Disorders*, **178**, 582–587.

Copp, T. & McAndrew, B. (1990) *Battle Exhaustion. Soldiers and Psychiatrists in the Canadian Army, 1939–1945*. Montreal & Kingston: McGill–Queen's University Press.

Deahl, M. P., Gillham, A. B., Thomas, J., *et al* (1994) Psychological sequelae following the Gulf War. Factors associated with subsequent morbidity and the effectiveness of psychological debriefing. *British Journal of Psychiatry*, **165**, 60–65.

Duckworth, D. H. (1986) Psychological problems arising from disaster work. *Stress Medicine*, **2**, 315–323.

Dyregrov, A. (1989) Caring for helpers in disaster situations: psychological debriefing. *Disaster Management*, **2**, 25–30.

Elder, G. H. & Clipp, E. C. (1989) Combat experience and emotional health: impairment and resilience in later life. *Journal of Personality*, **57**, 311–341.

Figley, C. R. (1985) From victim to survivor: social responsibility in the wake of catastrophe. In *Trauma and its Wake, The Study and Treatment of Post-Traumatic Stress Disorder*, vol. 1 (ed. C. R. Figley), pp. 398–451. New York: Brunner Mazel.

Flannery, R. B. (1990) Social support and psychological trauma: a methodological review. *Journal of Traumatic Stress*, **3**, 593–611.

Fowlie, D. G. & Aveline, M. O. (1985) The emotional consequences of ejection, rescue and rehabilitation in Royal Air Force aircrew. *British Journal of Psychiatry*, **146**, 609–613.

Glass, A. J. (1975) Mental health programs in the armed forces. In *American Handbook of Psychiatry*, vol. 6 (ed. S. Arieti), pp. 800–809. New York: Basic Books.

Goldberg, J., True, W. R., Eisen, S. A., *et al* (1990) A twin study of the effects of the Vietnam war on post-traumatic stress disorder. *Journal of the American Medical Association*, **263**, 1227–1232.

Green, B. L., Wilson, J. P. & Lindy, J. D. (1985) Conceptualizing post-traumatic stress disorder: a psychosocial framework. In *Trauma and Its Wake: The Study and Treatment of Post Traumatic Stress Disorder*, vol. 1 (ed. C. R. Figley), pp. 53–69. New York: Brunner Mazel.

Greenberg, M. S. & van der Kolk, B. A. (1987) Retrieval and integration of traumatic memories with the "painting cure." In *Psychological Trauma* (ed. B. A. van der Kolk), pp. 191–216. Washington, DC: APP.

Helzer, J. E., Robins, L. N. & McEvoy, L. (1987) Post-traumatic stress disorder in the general population. Findings of the epidemiological catchment area survey. *New England Journal of Medicine*, **317**, 1630–1634.

Hodgkinson, P. E. & Stewart, M. (1991) *Coping with Catastrophe: A Handbook of Disaster Management*. London: Routledge.

Horowitz, M. J. (1975) Intrusive and repetitive thoughts after experimental stress. *Archives of General Psychiatry*, **32**, 1457–1463.

—— (1976) *Stress Response Syndromes*. New York: Jason Aronson.

—— (1979) Psychological response to serious life events. In *Human Stress and Cognition* (eds V. Hamilton & D. M. Warburton), pp. 235–263. New York: Wiley.

——, Wilner, N. & Alvarez, W. (1979) Impact of event scale: a measure of subjective stress. *Psychosomatic Medicine*, **41**, 209–218.

Janoff-Bulman, R. (1985) The aftermath of victimisation: rebuilding shattered assumptions. In *Trauma and its Wake: The Study and Treatment of Post Traumatic Stress Disorder*, vol. 1 (ed. C. R. Figley), pp. 15–35. New York: Brunner Mazel.

Jones, D. J. (1985) Secondary disaster victims: the emotional effects of recovering and identifying human remains. *American Journal of Psychiatry*, **142**, 303–307.

Kobasa, S. C. (1979) Stressful life events, personality, and health: an inquiry into hardiness. *Journal of Personality and Social Psychology*, **37**, 1–11.

Kormos, H. R. (1978) The nature of combat stress. In *Stress Disorders Among Vietnam Veterans: Theory Research and Treatment* (ed. C. R. Figley), pp. 3–22. New York: Brunner Mazel.

Lang, P. J. (1979) A bio-informational theory of emotional imagery. *Psychophysiology*, **16**, 495–512.

Lazarus, R. (1981) The stress and coping paradigm. In *Models for Clinical Psychopathology* (eds C. Eisdorfer, D. Cohen, A. Kleinman, *et al*), pp. 177–214. New York: Spectrum.

Levav, I., Greenfield, H. & Baruch, E. (1979) Psychiatric combat reactions during the Yom Kippur war. *American Journal of Psychiatry*, **136**, 637–641.

Livingston, H. M., Livingston, M. G., Brooks, D. N., *et al* (1992) Elderly survivors of the Lockerbie air disaster. *International Journal of Geriatric Psychiatry*, **7**, 725–729.

McCarroll, J. E., Ursano, R. J. & Fullerton, C. S. (1993) Symptoms of post-traumatic stress disorder following recovery of war dead. *American Journal of Psychiatry*, **150**, 1875–1877.

McFarlane, A. C. (1988a) The longitudinal course of post traumatic morbidity: the range of outcomes and their predictors. *Journal of Nervous and Mental Disease*, **176**, 30–39.

—— (1988b) The phenomenology of post-traumatic stress disorders following a natural disaster. *Journal of Nervous and Mental Disease*, **176**, 22–29.

—— (1989) The aetiology of post-traumatic morbidity: predisposing, precipitating and perpetuating factors. *British Journal of Psychiatry*, **154**, 221–228.

Mikulincer, M. & Solomon, Z. (1988) Attributional style and combat-related post-traumatic stress disorder. *Journal of Abnormal Psychology*, **97**, 308–313.

Mitchell, J. T. (1983) When disaster strikes. The critical incident stress debriefing process. *Journal of Emergency Medical Services*, **8**, 36–39.

—— (1988) The history and status and future of critical incident stress debriefings. *Journal of Emergency Medical Services*, November, 47–52.

—— (1989) Development and functions of a critical incident stress debriefing team. *Journal of Emergency Medical Services*, December, 43–46.

—— & Dyregrov, A. (1993) Traumatic stress in disaster workers and emergency personnel. Prevention and intervention. In *International Handbook of Traumatic Stress Syndromes* (eds J. P. Wilson & B. Raphael), pp. 905–914. New York: Plenum Press.

Novaco, R., Cook, T. M. & Sarason, I. G. (1983) Military recruit training. An arena for stress-coping skills. In *Stress Reduction and Prevention* (eds D. Mietchenbaum & M. E. Jaremko), pp. 377–417. New York: Plenum Press.

Noy, S. (1987) Stress and personality as factors in the causation and prognosis of combat reactions during the 1973 Arab–Israeli war. In *Contemporary Studies in Combat Psychiatry* (ed. G. L. Belenky), pp. 21–29. Westport, CT: Greenwood Press.

O'Brian, L. S. & Hughes, S. J. (1991) Symptoms of post-traumatic stress disorder in Falklands veterans five years after the conflict. *British Journal of Psychiatry,* **159,** 135–141.

Parkes, C. M. (1991) Planning for the aftermath. *Journal of the Royal Society of Medicine,* **84,** 22–25.

Paton, D. (1992) Disaster research: the Scottish dimension. *The Psychologist: Bulletin of the British Psychological Society,* **5,** 535–538.

—— (1994) Disaster relief work: an assessment of training effectiveness. *Journal of Traumatic Stress,* **7,** 275–288.

Price, H. H. (1984) The Falklands: rate of British psychiatric combat casualties compared to recent American wars. *Journal of the Royal Army Medical Corps,* **130,** 109–113.

Psychiatric Division of the Royal Air Force Medical Service (1993) The management of hostages after release. *Psychiatric Bulletin of the Royal College of Psychiatrists,* **17,** 35–37.

Pynoos, R. S. & Eth, S. (1986) Witness to violence: the child interview. *Journal of the American Academy of Child Psychiatry,* **25,** 306–319.

—— & Nader, K. (1993) Issues in the treatment of post-traumatic stress in children and adolescents. In *International Handbook of Traumatic Stress Syndromes* (eds J. P. Wilson & B. Raphael), pp. 535–549. New York: Plenum Press.

Raphael, B. (1986) *When Disaster Strikes.* London: Hutchinson.

——, Meldrum, L. & McFarlane, A. C. (1995) Does debriefing after psychological trauma work? *British Medical Journal,* **310,** 1497–1480.

Robinson, R. C. & Mitchell, J. T. (1993) Evaluation of psychological debriefings. *Journal of Traumatic Stress,* **6,** 367–382.

Rothbaum, B. O. & Foa, E. B. (1993) Subtypes of post traumatic stress disorder. In *Post-traumatic Stress Disorder: DSM–IV and Beyond* (eds J. R. T. Davidson & E. B. Foa), pp. 23–35. Washington, DC: APP.

Rotter, J. B. (1966) Generalized expectancies for internal versus external control of reinforcement. *Psychological Monographs: General and Applied,* **80** (609), 1–28.

Salmon, T. W. (1919) The war neuroses and their lessons. *New York Journal of Medicine,* **109,** 993–994.

Shalev, A. (1994) Debriefing following traumatic exposure. In *Individual and Community Responses to Trauma and Disaster: The Structure of Human Chaos* (eds R. J. Ursano, B. G. McCaughey & C. S. Fullerton), pp. 201–219. Cambridge: Cambridge University Press.

—— & Munitz, H. (1988) Psychiatric care of acute stress reactions to military threat. In *Groups and Organisations in War, Disaster and Trauma* (2nd edn) (eds R. J. Ursano, C. S. Fullerton, M. S. Dixon, *et al*), pp. 107–119. Bethesda, Maryland: USUHS.

Shore, J. H., Vollmer, W. M. & Tatum, E. (1986) Psychiatric reactions to disaster. The Mount St Helens experience. *American Journal of Psychiatry,* **143,** 590–595.

Solomon, Z. & Benbenishty, R. (1986) The role of proximity, immediacy and expectancy in frontline treatment of combat stress reaction among Israelis in the Lebanon war. *American Journal of Psychiatry,* **143,** 613–617.

——, Mikulincer, M. & Benbenishty, R. (1989) Locus of control and combat-related post-traumatic stress disorder: the intervening role of battle intensity, threat appraisal and coping. *British Journal of Clinical Psychology,* **28,** 131–144.

Talbot, A., Manton, M. & Dunn, P. J. (1992) Debriefing the debriefers: an intervention strategy to assist psychologists after a crisis. *Journal of Traumatic Stress,* **5,** 45–62.

Taylor, A. J. W. (1991) Individual and group behaviour in extreme situations. In *Handbook of Military Psychology* (eds R. Gal & D. Mangelsdorff), pp. 491–505. Chichester: John Wiley.

—— & Frazer, A. G. (1982) The stress of post-disaster body handling and victim identification work. *Journal of Human Stress,* **8,** 4–12.

Terr, L. C. (1983) Chowchilla revisited: the effects of psychic trauma four years after a school-bus kidnapping. *American Journal of Psychiatry,* **140,** 1543–1550.

Turnbull, G. (1992) Debriefing British POWs after the Gulf war and released hostages from Lebanon. *WISMIC Newsletter,* **4,** 4–6.

16 Bereavement counselling

BILL YOUNG and DORA BLACK

Humans experience many kinds of bereavement – the loss of a relationship, a limb, a home, a job, even a hope for the future. Each and every bereavement entails, to a greater or lesser extent, a period of mourning during which the mental suffering of grief has to be endured and expressed and a psychological and social adjustment has to be made to life without the lost object (Bowlby, 1980; Parkes & Weiss, 1983).

Of all human afflictions, mourning highlights both our psychological isolation from, and our social connectedness with, those around us. It is a psychobiological process occurring within a specific social and cultural milieu which not only colours the meaning of the loss for the individual but shapes their response to it. Since recorded history, different societies have developed their own ways of coming to terms with death and of accommodating and helping those who are left in its wake (see Enright, 1983). In recent times there has been an increasing awareness among different professional groups of the psychological needs and vulnerabilities of those afflicted by bereavement (Parkes, 1972; Osterweis *et al*, 1984). In addition, the sociopolitical processes of humanisation and secularisation have resulted in shifting attention away from preparing the deceased for their journey into the afterlife, towards helping the bereft on their journey through this one. Modern funerals increasingly reflect this trend (Walter, 1994). One result of these public and professional trends has been the development of a wide range of psychological interventions which are collectively referred to as bereavement counselling.

After outlining the rationale and theoretical underpinnings of bereavement counselling as a specific form of psychological intervention, we will consider the different aims, principles, methods and techniques as well as their application in different circumstances. A final section summarises empirical support for the effectiveness of bereavement counselling.

Theoretical foundations of bereavement counselling

While grief is a natural human response to loss, it is also a painful and potentially isolating state of mind in which the individual may become temporarily or permanently stuck. In the past, many cultures developed their own rituals to help the bereaved adjust to their new circumstances. Many cultures also appropriated their own 'ritual specialists' to preside over such matters (Rosenblatt *et al*, 1976). These individuals were often invested with apparent magical powers or religious authority.

In contrast, many Western societies have witnessed a decline in the status of established religion and this, along with the dissolution of extended family and community networks, has meant that those structures which would have supported the bereaved in times past are now often unavailable or inadequate. Sometimes these structures may actually be experienced by the bereaved as a source of additional stress (Stylianos & Vachon, 1993). This has highlighted the unmet needs of the bereaved, and mobilised new structures within society to deal with them. One 'solution' has been for society to delegate mental health professionals as the 'ritual specialists' for those who become stuck in their bereavement.

Much of our current thinking can be traced back to Freud (1957) and his concept of mourning as a mental activity in which the necessary struggle and pain of grief have to be 'worked through' if it is to be satisfactorily completed. Engel (1961) likened unresolved grief to a psychological wound which, like an open bodily wound, fails to heal properly with the formation of a mental scar. An early study of human grief also described mourning within a medical model using psychiatric phenomenology (Lindemann, 1944). Bowlby (1963) and Parkes (1972) considered mourning as a phased recovery with characteristic stages. These earlier accounts resulted in the development of notions of 'normal' and 'pathological' bereavement and interventions which aimed to ameliorate abnormal mental states.

Partly as a reaction to these prevailing medical views of mourning, bereavement counselling gained momentum from the sweeping popularity of Carl Rogers' humanistic and essentially pragmatic approach to counselling those in distress (Rogers, 1967). His client-centred methods emphasised the healing potential within a relationship based on acceptance, empathy and positive regard of the client's unique experience.

Models of intervention have increasingly incorporated a developmental perspective which highlights the ongoing interaction between the individual and the surrounding environment. Mourning is conceptualised as a process consisting of various adaptive tasks which have to be negotiated over time. Fewer assumptions are made about the precise way the tasks are managed, and grief resolution is considered satisfactory when all tasks have been accomplished. By adopting a developmental formulation of the mourning process, it is possible to link the timing and goals of counselling with the specific tasks of mourning. This is well exemplified by Worden (1991) who described a model of intervention that involves helping the bereaved to complete four basic tasks of mourning:

  (a) accepting the reality of the loss;
  (b) working through the pain of grief;
  (c) adjusting to an environment in which the deceased is missing;
  (d) relocating the deceased and moving on with life.

Other writers have emphasised bereavement as a shared human phenomenon, and mourning as a process which is fundamentally embedded in a social context. Systemic theorists (e.g. Walsh & McGoldrick, 1991; Kissane & Bloch, 1994; Shapiro, 1994) have described how an individual's efforts to cope with loss are influenced by intergenerational processes, shared family beliefs, family life-cycle tasks, and family structure and functioning, which may also create the conditions for maladaptation. Likewise, those adopting an anthropological or sociocultural framework (Rosenblatt *et al*, 1976; Irish *et al*, 1993) demonstrate the wide variety of beliefs and rituals across cultures and societies for dealing with death and bereavement, and how much the individual mourner needs these to give meaning to their experience and to help them find a new role within their community.

Finally, several theorists have emphasised the potential for positive outcomes after bereavement, for instance in terms of increased existential awareness and personal growth (Yalom & Lieberman, 1991). There is certainly anecdotal evidence that adults who coped successfully with a significant childhood bereavement can feel better able to deal with subsequent losses and may even show accelerated development resulting from being orphaned (Eisenstadt *et al*, 1989).

General aims of bereavement counselling

The important question of whether or not counselling is really appropriate or necessary for the majority of the bereaved can be approached by considering three potentially different aims of bereavement counselling. While in practice these aims often overlap, each implies a different level of intervention and sophistication of counselling methods.

(a) Humanitarian: providing human comfort and support

The lack of meaningful rituals and social structures supporting the bereaved (noted earlier) has resulted in the growth of many voluntary agencies and self-help groups which serve a humanitarian prerogative to offer counsel to the bereaved, if only to help relieve their burden of suffering. While there is no firm evidence that counselling 'speeds up' the mourning process itself, many can testify that their grief is ameliorated by sharing it with another.

(b) Preventive: facilitating mourning and readjustment

Counselling as a preventive intervention can be viewed as having two main aims: firstly, to promote the onset and progression of normal mourning; and secondly, to help individuals stop grieving and get on with their lives. A preventive approach usually implies targeting groups considered to be at particularly high risk of either short or long-term morbidity as a result of bereavement. This risk may be attributable to the onset of pathological grief. However, it is worth noting that the many psychosocial readjustments required after bereavement may act as non-specific triggers for other psychiatric disorders, particularly for those who are genetically or psychologically predisposed (Jacobs & Kim, 1990). A preventive approach would also justify counselling prior to an anticipated bereavement, and several studies have demonstrated the value of anticipatory work with adults (Cameron & Parkes, 1983; Stedeford, 1984) and children (Adams-Greenly & Moynihan, 1983; Siegel *et al*, 1990). Indeed, this is a practice which has been widely disseminated by the Hospice movement.

(c) Therapeutic: ameliorating pathological grief

Ever since Freud's original distinction between mourning and melancholia (Freud, 1957), workers have attempted to delineate the atypical variants of grief through descriptive categories, such as absent, delayed and chronic grief (Raphael, 1984). While there is a general consensus that pathological grief is a clinically valid and useful concept (Jacobs, 1993), only moderate agreement seems to exist among 'experts' on how to define the boundaries around, and subtypes within, this condition (Middleton *et al*, 1994). It is also worth noting that classification systems have tended to avoid describing pathological grief as a diagnostic entity. In DSM–IV, only uncomplicated bereavement is mentioned and given a V coding under additional conditions (American Psychiatric Association, 1994).

Nevertheless, some workers (e.g. Worden, 1991; Stroebe *et al*, 1993) make a distinction between grief counselling (i.e. directed towards resolving normal grief) and grief therapy (directed towards those individuals whose grief has taken a pathological course or who have developed a psychological problem related to their bereavement). In these latter cases, bereavement counselling often involves more sophisticated and instrumental techniques and a higher level of training and competence in the practitioner.

Practical aspects of bereavement counselling

Assessment for counselling

Given that only a proportion of bereaved people will not require additional support, there is a need to make an early assessment of several broad areas which help establish a risk profile and may help distinguish those who might benefit from preventive intervention. These areas include:

(1) Circumstances of the death (e.g. sudden, traumatic).
(2) Relationship with deceased (e.g. dependent or ambivalent).
(3) Associated losses (e.g. change of home, work, school).
(4) Extent of social support (e.g. support perceived as unhelpful).
(5) Coping ability of bereaved (e.g. previous psychological problem).
(6) Family variables (e.g. family functioning, economic).

Different studies have identified different risk factors for specific groups, such as children (Black, 1978), widowers (Young *et al*, 1963) and parents (Black, 1994). Furthermore, there is a recognition that certain factors may protect individuals and even counteract the effects of risk factors (see Parkes & Weiss, 1983, for an account of an Index of Bereavement Risk.)

Common features of bereavement counselling

(1)   Main aim is to facilitate 'normal' grief.
(2)   Initiated soon after the bereavement.
(3)   Usually conducted one-to-one, but group and family formats are used.
(4)   Structured sessions with explicitly agreed objectives.
(5)   Time-limited and often relatively brief.
(6)   May be undertaken by trained non-professionals.
(7)   Eclectic approach – draws on a wide range of techniques.
(8)   Often conducted in non-clinical settings, e.g. client's home.
(9)   May be insufficient if client gets stuck or shows clear evidence of psychiatric disorder.

Common issues dealt with during counselling

(1) *Establishing a therapeutic alliance*

There is universal agreement that bereavement counsellors must be both willing and able to work with any painful feelings which the bereaved person may bring. This requires the counsellor to be self-aware and to have dealt satisfactorily with their own previous losses, particularly recent bereavements. However, this non-intrusive readiness is usually communicated to the client through basic human qualities such as acceptance, empathy and positive regard, rather than any specialised techniques. This is particularly crucial if the client is still in the post-bereavement crisis of shock, confusion and denial. A therapeutic alliance also involves explicit agreement about the therapeutic contract which determines the structure, duration and goals of the counselling. Given that bereavement counselling is a relatively brief intervention, the counsellor has to discourage dependency, offering themselves as an additional support and facilitating the client's use of other family and social supports.

(2) *Providing practical support*

Alongside the emotional turmoil of grief, bereavement often brings many other changes and associated losses in its wake. Consider the circumstances of a widow and her dependent children who lose their main income, resulting in a change of home, school and community. A counsellor who is familiar with statutory provisions and other community resources is often in the best position to direct the bereaved towards these sources of support, and may, in certain situations, act as their advocate in obtaining entitlements. In the crisis of bereavement, many people feel the need to keep busy but at the same time feel less able to make decisions. The counsellor is often involved in helping the client to solve practical problems, while discouraging them from making major life decisions until the crisis period is over.

(3) *Realising the loss*

Most workers agree that the counsellor has to help the client "give sorrow words", that is, articulate the full range of their experiences of, and feelings about, the loss. Encouraging the client to "tell their own story" about the loss often brings relief from ventilation of the underlying feelings. It also provides an opportunity, perhaps their first, to explain themselves to another person and to begin to organise their experience in a more coherent and manageable way. In many cases, a major loss awakens the pain of earlier losses which may also need to be identified and worked through.

(4) *Resolving the lost relationship*

More specific skills are often required to explore painful and potentially overwhelming feelings, such as anger, blame, shame and guilt, which may be related to the nature of the death. Likewise, the counsellor may have to carefully challenge pathological defences such as prolonged denial and idealisation, or identify maladaptive coping strategies such as excessive drinking and avoidance of reminders. At the same time, the counsellor has to be aware of and respect the natural time course of each client's grief reaction and not to jeopardise their day-to-day functioning. Exploring the many meanings of the client's attachment to the deceased – in the past as well as currently – allows them to develop a more realistic and stable 'internal' connection with the deceased. As the client emotionally relocates this relationship, the counsellor can help them to reinvest in life's new opportunities and relationships.

(5) *Achieving a satisfactory termination*

The ending of counselling may bring to the surface the full impact of the client's loss, highlighting the intensity of the relationship that often develops between counsellor and client. Termination provides an opportunity to review where the client has reached in their own grief process, to begin to plan for the future, and to anticipate grief-related stresses such as anniversary reactions (Renvoize & Jain, 1986). The counsellor may help the client to develop their own informal support systems and can identify sources of additional help, including further counselling or therapy, if need be.

Specific techniques used in bereavement counselling

The practice of bereavement counselling is primarily conducted using the basic techniques common to most counselling approaches. These include clarification, reflecting back and summarising, all of which are non-directive and help create a safe space for the client to explore and resolve the issues discussed above. However, bereavement counselling has also 'borrowed' from various schools of therapy – psychoanalytical, humanistic, behavioural, cognitive, and the creative arts therapies – resulting in many practitioners adopting an eclectic approach. The following examples include directive techniques which are often employed when dealing with more complicated or protracted grief reactions. Several practical handbooks are available which describe these and other techniques in work with both adults (Worden, 1991; Lendrum & Syme, 1992) and children (Dyregrov, 1990).

(1) Using photographs, possessions and other symbols of the deceased to promote both registration of the loss and the formation of an internal relationship.

(2) Writing or drawing, which can tap emotions that may be difficult to verbalise. These methods may also be used as symbolic communication with the deceased allowing "unfinished business" to be dealt with.

(3) Using relaxation techniques and guided imagery. These may be useful in dealing with the physical symptoms of anxiety and panic which may accompany grief. They may also help to restore a sense of control to counteract feelings of helplessness.

(4) Creating rituals, which may be private or shared, and which can be a way of remembering or commemorating the dead person. They may also help to mark a change or transition, particularly for those who are 'stuck'.

(5) Role playing or rehearsing for new situations.

(6) Cognitive restructuring, which involves confronting and testing out distorted beliefs that may be uncovered by grief and may be maintaining a pathological response (Kavanagh, 1990).

(7) Bibliotherapy or the use of written material to facilitate mourning. This may be in the form of educational aids (e.g. Ward *et al*, 1993), biographical accounts (e.g. Fabian, 1988) or fictional stories. Such methods have been found particularly useful with children (Ayalon, 1987).

Bereavement counselling in specific circumstances

Helping bereaved children

Childhood bereavement, particularly of a parent, is a psychological crisis and merits attention from mental health professionals for two important reasons.

Firstly, a number of controlled studies based on population samples have confirmed that bereaved children have a significantly increased risk of developing psychiatric disorders and may suffer considerable psychological and social difficulties throughout childhood (Black, 1978; Berlinsky & Biller, 1982; Kaffman & Elizur, 1983; Van Eerdewegh *et al*, 1985; Kranzler *et al*, 1990) and later in adult life (Brown & Harris, 1978; Breier *et al*, 1988; Finkelstein, 1988). Furthermore, other types of bereavement, such as siblings, close friends and teachers, also carry the potential for significant and enduring effects (Dyregrov, 1988).

Secondly, major bereavement is not an uncommon event in the lives of children. The most recent UK census figures suggest that about 170 000 children, nearly 1.5%, are currently dependent on widowed lone parents, of whom about a third are fathers. These figures are considerably higher in developing countries or in those afflicted by natural disasters and wars, whose orphaned refugee children are increasingly being rehabilitated within developed nations. With children, it may be beneficial to facilitate and possibly accelerate normal grief as this will not only protect a mourning child from the noxious effects of grief, but may also reduce the time period during which they are exposed to all the other stresses children face (Black & Young, 1995).

If one considers the tasks of mourning outlined earlier, it soon becomes clear that each task presents additional risks for children:

(1) Adjusting to the reality of the loss is complicated by children's incomplete concepts related to dying and death, which often give rise to false beliefs and unrealistic fears. This lack of understanding is further compounded by the lack of accurate, age-appropriate information given by adults – often with a spurious rationale of 'protecting' them from the truth.

(2) Likewise, children have a more limited capacity to experience and tolerate painful affects. Their sadness often occurs in brief bursts, perhaps while playing, and often goes unrecognised by others.

(3) Due to their dependency, children are reliant on others to care for them and to help them adjust to their new circumstances. Children adjusting to the physical absence of a dead parent may have to manage the emotional absence of a surviving parent consumed in their own grief.

(4) Psychological autonomy develops throughout childhood, and young children particularly are not so able to separate their own identity from those close to them. This complicates the task of finding a new identity, because their hopes and aspirations for the future are still tied up with the deceased.

Many forms of bereavement counselling employed with adults have been adapted for children, with generally positive results. Examples include individual counselling (Furman, 1974), group counselling (Zambelli & Derosa, 1992; Smith & Pennells, 1993; Lohnes & Kalter, 1994) and family counselling (Black & Urbanowicz, 1985, 1987; Shapiro, 1994). There have also been a number of approaches described which are specific to children (Dyregrov, 1990).

Pathological and complicated grief

Several studies have demonstrated that specialised forms of bereavement counselling may be effective in ameliorating pathological grief. One example of this, often referred to as 'guided mourning', involves repeated confrontation with aspects of the loss within sessions and as homework assignments. This 'floods' the client with previously avoided memories and feelings which diminish in intensity over time. Using this method, several controlled intervention studies in adults (Mawson *et al*, 1981; Sireling *et al*, 1988) have reported significant and sustained improvement in pathological grievers. Other types of intervention have also been used successfully in pathological grief, including family therapy (Rosenthal, 1980), cognitive–behavioural methods (Kavanagh, 1990), and non-verbal approaches using art, music, dance and drama (Schut *et al*, 1994).

In contrast to treating pathological grief *per se*, a wide range of psychiatric disorders may occur in association with bereavement (Jacobs & Kim, 1990). These include major depressive disorder, post-traumatic stress disorder, panic disorder and substance misuse. It is often the presence of psychiatric comorbidity that limits the effectiveness of bereavement counselling alone and which necessitates more specialised therapeutic, including pharmacological, interventions (Jacobs & Kim, 1990).

Finally, grief complicated by psychological trauma carries a high risk of maladjustment and responds poorly to bereavement counselling alone. In these circumstances, many advocate dealing with the trauma before attempting to resolve grief (see chapters 4 and 15).

Counselling the bereaved of different cultures

Despite the ubiquity of bereavement, the status of a bereaved person and the expression of grief seems to vary widely across cultures. Indeed, a vigorous debate is opening up among workers in the field of bereavement research about the validity of many of our hypotheses about how individuals cope with loss. Those such as Wortman & Silver (1989) cite a lack of empirical support for many "commonly-held myths", while others (see Stroebe *et al*, 1995) assert that untested and untestable assumptions are not represented by the current state of knowledge or research efforts. Hence there is probably much to be gained from studying how different cultures deal with death and bereavement (Parkes *et al*, 1996).

However, it is increasingly recognised that those from ethnic minorities may be at increased risk for a variety of reasons (Neuberger, 1987; Irish *et al*, 1993). They may have become dislocated from their parent culture where help would normally be available. Their concepts and patterns of grief and psychiatric disorder may be unfamiliar to professionals, resulting in their either avoiding involvement through fear or ignorance, or delivering inappropriate forms of intervention. While there is much clinical and research work to suggest that those from ethnic minorities can benefit from counselling, there are often problems in providing accessible and appropriate services for them, particularly if they do not speak the host culture's language (Lago & Thompson, 1989).

Efficacy of bereavement counselling

Despite the substantial corpus of clinical literature describing successful bereavement interventions, few of these have been systematically evaluated. Parkes (1980), in an earlier review, cited only five well-conducted studies: Raphael's (1977) case-control study of widows showed that professional counselling improved the outcome of "high-risk" cases; Gerber's controlled study (Gerber *et al*, 1975) showed that a brief intervention (50% telephone contact only) resulted in lower health service utilisation in the following year; Vachon's comparative study (Vachon *et al*, 1980) suggested that self-help groups could provide valuable support, particularly in those showing most distress; Parkes's own study of St Christopher's Hospice in London showed that help from a volunteer service reduced the risk of a poor outcome in the high-risk group. In contrast to the above, one study (Polak *et al*, 1975) yielded negative results, although the supported group had suffered far greater economic losses than the control group, which may have undermined any treatment benefit. More recently, Relf (cited by Parkes, 1994) used a risk assessment strategy to obtain a high-risk group of bereaved relatives of hospice patients before random assignment into two groups: an index group receiving bereavement counselling from trained volunteers and a control group. At 20 months follow-up, she found that the index cases had made less use of healthcare services and were less anxious than controls. Apart from the clinical significance of these findings, they also carry resource implications, particularly in the current climate of NHS reforms in the UK. The general conclusion from these controlled studies is that the bereaved, particularly those considered at higher risk, can indeed benefit from a variety of early interventions, including support from skilled volunteers.

More recently, a number of studies are beginning to compare different forms of intervention. For example, Schut *et al* (1994) described how a brief group intervention combining cognitive–behavioural techniques and art therapy resulted in a better outcome for bereaved in patients than an equally intensive but conventional therapy format. They attributed the increased benefits to two factors: the structure provided, which reduced uncertainty and anxiety, and the non-verbal facilitation of 'blocked' emotions.

Despite much recent progress in intervention research, there is still a need for studies that systematically address and rectify the methodological problems which have flawed earlier attempts to evaluate bereavement counselling. These include:

(1) Conceptual and definitional issues. As noted earlier, the concepts of mourning, both typical and complicated, need to be operationally defined and reliably described (Middleton *et al*, 1994). Likewise, the content of counselling interventions needs more accurate description in terms of aims, structure (i.e. timing, duration and place) and methods.

(2) Study design. Many studies have been flawed by retrospective strategies, small numbers of cases, lack of an appropriate control group, poor

descriptions of important variables such as the sociodemographic, family and clinical characteristics of the sample, and inadequate length of follow-up. Furthermore, many studies have used a referred or clinical sample, which may limit generalisation of findings to the majority of bereaved in the normal population.

(3)   Instruments and measures. Few satisfactory measures of grief and post-bereavement adjustment exist (Stroebe *et al*, 1993). Furthermore, as for psychotherapy generally, measures of the process and outcome of bereavement counselling have to be refined. This includes non-specific aspects of the counselling relationship, which may in itself account for much of the benefit.

Services for the bereaved

Through his seminal account of adult grief, Parkes (1972) established a firm scientific basis for the organisation and delivery of support to the bereaved. He noted that many professionals do not receive any formal training in bereavement counselling, and that trained volunteers with a year or more experience in bereavement work may exceed the expertise of these professionals. The value of trained volunteers is borne out by organisations like Cruse – Bereavement Care who provided counselling support for nearly 20 000 people in the year 1993/4. Many other organisations, often charitable, are being set up locally to address the needs of the bereaved, and there has been a growth of self-help groups.

At the same time, there are several reasonable arguments for involving mental health specialists in the development of services for the bereaved and in the training and supervision of those who might counsel them. Firstly, there is now a substantial body of research showing that the bereaved are at a higher risk of developing a wide variety of physical and psychological disorders (Osterweis *et al*, 1984; Stroebe & Stroebe, 1987). Indeed, there is an increased mortality associated with major bereavement. These individuals may be more effectively identified and treated by mental health professionals.

Secondly, there is a wider appreciation of the needs of particular groups who may require more specialised attention and help, such as children, refugees, those with a learning disability, and pregnant women (Woodward *et al*, 1985). One group who are at substantially higher risk are those who suffer traumatic bereavement (see chapter 4).

Services for the bereaved need to include wider preventive aims. A preventive approach means taking a more collaborative and proactive stance at all levels (individual, family, community and sociopolitical) in order to improve the quality of people's lives. Because bereavement is and should be handled largely by families and informal social networks, public education about children's reactions to bereavement, and how they differ from adult's reactions, should be encouraged so that people are better prepared for the death of someone close to them and to respond sensitively to others in similar situations. In the case of children, schools, youth facilities and media coverage provide the most appropriate contexts for education about death and bereavement. The Royal College of Psychiatrists has recently produced an educational leaflet on bereavement for the public.

Conclusions

The needs of those bereaved through death, as well as other major losses, should be a major concern for all mental health professionals, whether in the role of therapist, service-provider or policy-maker. The total cost of these unmet needs in terms of human suffering, chronic health problems and economic losses is incalculable.

There is now good evidence that many bereaved people can be helped considerably by a time-limited intervention from a suitably trained counsellor, preferably in consultation with a professional. This applies even more to those identified as high-risk and to particular groups such as children, parents and the learning disabled.

However, more needs to be done and this will involve mental health professionals working collaboratively with policy-makers, other professional groups and voluntary groups in order to create services which are comprehensive, coherent and appropriate to the specific needs of different groups. In this respect, more research is required, particularly on the differential benefits of different forms of bereavement counselling, particularly in non-clinical settings, and their application to certain groups, particularly children, ethnic minorities and those suffering from traumatic psychopathology.

References

Adams-Greenly, M. & Moynihan, R. T. (1983) Helping the children of fatally ill parents. *American Journal of Orthopsychiatry*, **53**, 219–229.

American Psychiatric Association (1994) *Diagnostic and Statistical Manual of Mental Disorders* (4th edn) (DSM–IV). Washington, DC: APA.

Ayalon, O. (1987) *Rescue! Helping Children Cope with Stress*. Haifa: Nord Publications.

Berlinsky, E. B. & Biller, H. B. (1982) *Parental Death and Psychological Development*. Toronto: Lexington.

Black, D. (1978) Annotation. The bereaved child. *Journal of Child Psychology and Psychiatry*, **19**, 287–292.

—— (1994) Bereavement. In *Care Of The Dying Child* (ed. A. Goldman), pp. 145–163. Oxford: Oxford University Press.

—— & Urbanowicz, M. A. (1985) Bereaved children – family intervention. In *Recent Research in Developmental Psychopathology* (ed. J. E. Stevenson), pp. 179–187. Oxford: Pergamon.

—— & —— (1987) Family intervention with bereaved children. *Journal of Child Psychology and Psychiatry*, **28**, 467–476.

—— & Young, B. (1995) Bereaved children: risk and preventive intervention. In *Handbook of Studies on Preventive Psychiatry* (eds B. Raphael & G. P. Burrows), pp. 225–244. Amsterdam: Elsevier.

Bowlby, J. (1963) Pathological mourning and childhood mourning. *Journal of the American Psychoanalytic Association*, **11**, 500–541.

—— (1980) *Attachment and Loss: Vol. III. Loss: Sadness and Depression*. London: Hogarth.

Breier, A., Kelsoe, J., Kirwin, P., *et al* (1988) Early parental loss and development of adult psychopathology. *Archives of General Psychiatry*, **45**, 987–993.

Brown, G. W. & Harris, T. (1978) *Social Origins of Depression.* London: Tavistock.

Cameron, J. & Parkes, C. M. (1983) Terminal care: evaluation of effects on surviving families of care before and after bereavement. *Postgraduate Medical Journal,* **59,** 73–78.

Dyregrov, A. (1988) The loss of a child: the sibling's perspective. In *Motherhood and Mental Illness 2* (eds R. Kumar & I. F. Brockington), pp. 270–280. London: I. F. Wright.

—— (1990) *Grief in Children: A Handbook for Adults.* London: Jessica Kingsley.

Eisenstadt, M., Haynal, A., Rentchnick, P., *et al* (1989) *Parental Loss and Achievement.* Connecticut: International Universities Press.

Engel, G. L. (1961) Is grief a disease? A challenge for medical research. *Psychosomatic Medicine,* **23,** 18–22.

Enright, D. J. (1983) *The Oxford Book of Death.* Oxford: Oxford University Press.

Fabian, A. (1988) *The Daniel Diary.* London: Grafton.

Finkelstein, A. (1988) The long-term effects of early parent death: a review. *Journal of Clinical Psychology,* **44,** 3–9.

Freud, S. (1957) Mourning and melancholia. In *Standard Edition of the Complete Psychological Works of Sigmund Freud.* (ed. J. Strachey), Vol. 14, 243–258. London: Hogarth Press

Furman, E. (1974) *A Child's Parent Dies: Studies in Childhood Bereavement.* New Haven, CT: Yale University Press.

Gerber, I., Weiner, A., Battin, D., *et al* (1975) Brief therapy to the aged bereaved. In *Bereavement: Its Psychological Aspects* (eds B. Schoenberg & I. Gerber), pp. 310–313. New York: Columbia University Press.

Irish, D. P., Lundquist, K. F. & Nelsen, V. J. (1993) *Ethnic Variations in Dying, Death and Grief: Diversity in Universality.* Bristol, PA: Taylor & Francis.

Jacobs, S. (1993) *Pathologic Grief.* Washington, DC: APA.

—— & Kim, K. (1990) Psychiatric complications of bereavement. *Psychiatric Annals,* **20,** 314–317.

Kaffman, M. & Elizur, E. (1983) Bereavement responses of kibbutz and non-kibbutz children following the death of father. *Journal of Child Psychology and Psychiatry,* **24,** 435–442.

Kavanagh, D. G. (1990) Towards a cognitive–behavioural intervention for adult grief reactions. *British Journal of Psychiatry,* **157,** 373–383.

Kissane, D. & Bloch, S. (1994) Family grief. *British Journal of Psychiatry,* **164,** 728–740.

Kranzler, E. M., Schaffer, D., Wasserman, G., *et al* (1990) Early childhood bereavement. *Journal of the American Academy of Child and Adolescent Psychiatry,* **29,** 513–520.

Lago, C. & Thompson, J. (1989) *Counselling and Race (Handbook of Counselling in Britain).* London: Routledge.

Lendrum, S. & Syme, G. (1992) *Gift of Tears: A Practical Approach to Loss and Bereavement Counselling.* London: Routledge.

Lindemann, E. (1944) Symptomatology and management of acute grief. *American Journal of Psychotherapy,* **101,** 141–148.

Lohnes, K. L. & Kalter, N. (1994) Preventive intervention groups for parentally bereaved children. *American Journal of Orthopsychiatry,* **64,** 594–603.

Mawson, D., Marks, I. M., Ramm, L., *et al* (1981) Guided mourning for morbid grief: a controlled study. *British Journal of Psychiatry,* **138,** 185–193.

Middleton, W., Moylan, A., Raphael, B., *et al* (1994) An international perspective on bereavement-related concepts. *Australian and New Zealand Journal of Psychiatry,* **27,** 457–463.

Neuberger, J. (1987) *Caring for People of Different Faiths.* London: Austen Cornish.

Osterweis, M., Solomon, F. & Green, M. (1984) *Bereavement: Reactions, Consequences and Care.* Washington, DC: National Academic Press.

Parkes, C. M. (1972) *Bereavement: Studies of Grief in Adult Life.* London: Tavistock.

—— (1980) Bereavement counselling: does it work? *British Medical Journal,* **281,** 3–10.

—— (1994) Report on the Fourth International Conference on Grief and Bereavement in Contemporary Society. *Bereavement Care,* **13,** 32–33.

—— & Weiss, R. S. (1983) *Recovery from Bereavement.* New York: Basic Books.

——, Laungani, P. & Young, B. (1996) *Death and Bereavement Across Cultures.* London: Routledge.

Polak, P. R., Egan, D., Lee, J. H., *et al* (1975) Prevention in mental health: a controlled study. *American Journal of Psychiatry,* **132,** 146–149.

Raphael, B. (1977) Preventive intervention with the recently bereaved. *Archives of General Psychiatry,* **34,** 1450–1454.

—— (1984) *The Anatomy of Bereavement.* London: Hutchinson.

Renvoize, E. B. & Jain, J. (1986) Anniversary reactions. *British Journal of Psychiatry*, **148**, 322–324.

Rogers, C. R. (1967) *On Becoming a Person*. London: Constable.

Rosenblatt, P. C., Walsh, R. P. & Jackson, D. A. (1976) *Grief and Mourning in Cross-Cultural Perspective*. New Haven, CT: Human Relations Area Files Press.

Rosenthal, P. A. (1980) Short-term family therapy and pathological grief resolution with children and adolescents. *Family Process*, **19**, 151–159.

Schut, H., de Keijser, J. & van den Bout, J. (1994) Short-term inpatient grief therapy in groups. Paper presented at the Fourth International Conference on Grief and Bereavement in Contemporary Society, Stockholm, Sweden.

Shapiro, E. R. (1994) *Grief as a Family Process*. New York: Guilford.

Siegel, K., Mesagno, F. P. & Christ, G. (1990) A prevention programme for bereaved children. *American Journal of Orthopsychiatry*, **60**, 168–175.

Sireling, L., Cohen, D. & Marks, I. (1988) Guided mourning for morbid grief: a replication. *Behaviour Therapy*, **29**, 121–132.

Smith, S. & Pennells, M. (1993) Bereaved children and adolescents. In *Group Work with Children and Adolescents* (ed. K. N. Dwivedi), pp. 195–208. London: Jessica Kingsley.

Stedeford, A. (1984) *Facing Death: Patients, Families and Professionals*. London: Heinemann.

Stroebe, M. S., Stroebe, W. & Hansson, R. O. (1993) *Handbook of Bereavement: Theory, Research and Intervention*. New York: Cambridge.

——, van den Bout, J. & Schut, H. (1995) Myths and misconceptions about bereavement: the opening of a debate. *Omega*, **29**, 187.

Stroebe, W. & Stroebe, M. (1987) *Bereavement and Health*. New York: Cambridge University Press.

Stylianos, S. K. & Vachon, M. L. S. (1993) The role of social support in bereavement. In *Handbook of Bereavement: Theory, Research and Intervention* (M. S. Stroebe, W. Stroebe & R. O. Hansson), pp. 397–410. New York: Cambridge University Press

Vachon, M. L. S., Sheldon, A. R., Lancee, W. J., *et al* (1980) A controlled study of self-help intervention for widows. *American Journal of Psychiatry*, **137**, 1380–1384.

Van Eerdewegh, M., Clayton, P. & Van Eerdewegh, P. (1985) The bereaved child: variables influencing early psychopathology. *British Journal of Psychiatry*, **147**, 188–194.

Walsh, F. & McGoldrick, M. (1991) Loss and the family: a systemic perspective. In *Living Beyond Loss: Death in the Family* (eds F. Walsh & M. McGoldrick), pp. 1–29. New York: W. W. Norton

Walter, T. (1994) *The Revival of Death*. London: Routledge.

Ward, B. (1993) *Good Grief: Exploring Feelings, Loss and Death with Over-Elevens and Adults*. London: Jessica Kingsley.

Woodward, S., Pope, A., Robson, W.J., *et al* (1985) Bereavement counselling after sudden infant death. *British Medical Journal*, **290**, 363–365.

Worden, W. (1991) *Grief Counselling and Grief Therapy*. London: Routledge.

Wortman, C. & Silver, R. (1989) The myths of coping with loss. *Journal of Consulting and Clinical Psychology*, **57**, 349–357.

Yalom, I. D. & Lieberman, M. A. (1991) Bereavement and heightened existential awareness. *Psychiatry*, **54**, 334–345.

Young, M., Benjamin, B. & Wallis, C. (1963) Mortality of widowers. *Lancet*, **2**, 454–456.

Zambelli, G. & Derosa, A. (1992) Bereavement support groups for school age children: theory, intervention, and case examples. *American Journal of Orthopsychiatry*, **62**, 484–493.

17 Treatment of adults

A. Behavioural and cognitive approaches

DAVID RICHARDS and KARINA LOVELL

Behavioural and cognitive approaches to psychotherapy have developed rapidly during the last 30 years and have been increasingly applied to PTSD within the last 15 years. Many different techniques are subsumed under the term 'cognitive–behavioural' but all behavioural and cognitive methods emphasise (Hackman, 1993):

(a) the empirical validation of treatment
(b) a treatment focus on the 'here and now'
(c) the use of explicit, agreed and operationally defined treatment strategies
(d) the specification of treatment goals (usually chosen by the patient) to bring about desired changes in their life
(e) the use of collaborative therapeutic strategies between patient and therapist.

PTSD is clearly a good candidate for behavioural approaches. Any disorder which stems from exposure to a traumatic event lends itself very well to behavioural conceptualisations of conditioned fear (e.g. Keane *et al*, 1985). More recently the development of cognitive therapy has given possible insights into the way in which dysfunctional thinking patterns may contribute to the onset and maintenance of the disorder (Parrott & Howes, 1991). Both approaches have been reported in the literature on PTSD treatment, although exposure-based techniques have been cited more frequently than cognitive ones. Much of the literature is case-study or case series material, but there are eight reported studies randomly assigning patients to alternative treatment cells and/or including a placebo control group (Table 17.1).

Behavioural and cognitive therapists have generally taken one of three directions when attempting to treat PTSD. These are:

(a) exposure or related techniques
(b) cognitive therapy
(c) anxiety management training (stress inoculation training).

TABLE 17.1
Randomised studies of cognitive and behavioural treatments of PTSD

Study	Treatments	Patients	Average % improvement	Relative improvements
Peniston (1986)	Biofeedback assisted desensitisation, no treatment	Vietnam veterans	PTSD not measured Muscle tension 79% improved	Desensitisation > no treatment
Keane *et al* (1989)	Implosion (flooding), wait-list	Vietnam veterans	21–50%	Implosion > wait-list
Cooper & Clum (1989)	Imaginal flooding, 'standard' control treatment	Vietnam veterans	21–43%	Imaginal flooding > standard treatment
Brom *et al* (1989)	Systematic desensitisation, hypnotherapy, psychodynamic psychotherapy	Bereavement, criminal assault, accidents	29–41%	All treatments produced similar improvement
Boudewyns & Hyer (1990)	Direct therapeutic exposure, counselling	Vietnam veterans	20%	Exposure > counselling
Foa *et al* (1991)	Prolonged exposure (PE), stress inoculation training (SIT), supportive counselling (SC), wait-list	Rape survivors	35–71%	SIT > PE at post-treatment, PE > SIT at follow-up
Resick & Schnicke (1992)	Cognitive processing therapy, wait-list	Sexual assault survivors	40–60%	Cognitive processing therapy > wait-list
Richards *et al* (1994)	Real-life exposure, imaginal exposure – in cross-over design	Accident, disaster, crime survivors	63–83%	Combined real life + imaginal exposure highly effective. Order of treatments unimportant

Exposure

Exposure has been shown to be the treatment of choice for many anxiety disorders such as specific phobias, social phobias and agoraphobia, obsessive–compulsive disorder and panic disorder (Marks, 1987). Research has refined the process of exposure so that best practice now involves the prolonged (one continuous hour or more) confrontation with feared objects and situations, repeated at least daily by the patient, until habituation of anxiety (i.e. a reduction in the fear associated with the stimuli) has occurred. A modified hierarchy is employed, but the emphasis is on patients choosing exposure exercises which cause arousal levels to rise before dropping with time as habituation occurs. Recent research has shown that self-exposure, where patients essentially conduct their own treatment with minimal guidance from therapists, is as effective as long courses of treatment involving much therapist–patient contact (Al-Kubaisy *et al*, 1992).

Exposure has been used to treat PTSD in rape victims (Wolff, 1977; Foa *et al*, 1991), Vietnam veterans (Cooper & Clum, 1989; Keane *et al*, 1989; Boudewyns & Hyer, 1990), accident victims (McCaffrey & Fairbank, 1985; Muse, 1986), assault survivors (Richards & Rose, 1991) and disaster victims (Richards *et al*, 1994). Earlier studies report systematic desensitisation, whereas in later reports, direct therapeutic exposure to trauma stimuli is used. The most common form of exposure is imaginal exposure to trauma memories (Keane *et al*, 1989; Vaughan & Tarrier, 1992). A combination of real-life and imaginal exposure has been used in two studies by Foa *et al* (1991) and Richards *et al* (1994).

Imaginal exposure

This technique involves patients reliving their trauma in imagination using their vivid visual memories as the feared stimuli. Patients imagine their traumatic memories, relating them aloud to the therapist in the first person and present tense. Details of the event are relayed to the therapist as if the patient were actually back in the traumatic situation. Patients are encouraged to give rich detail about environmental stimuli during the trauma, their behaviour in response to events, and the meaning this had for them at the time.

Normally patients run through the complete sequence of their traumatic memory. Over time, however, more detail emerges, connections between events are made and patients become less fearful imagining some elements of the memory than others. This often enables patients to make a hierarchical list out of the elements of their traumatic memories, and it is then possible to work through this list by imagining less distressing elements first.

Quite often a very traumatic memory will quickly break down into critical elements, where certain key memories are much more feared than others. When exposure to these memories is undertaken a procedure called "rewind and hold" can be used. Patients concentrate on these aspects of the memory, freeze-frame the images and hold them while repeatedly describing in detail all they can possibly remember about this part of their trauma. This enables exposure to these very relevant stimuli to be prolonged so that habituation can occur.

Exposure sessions typically last for 1–1.5 hours. The sessions are taped and the patient is instructed to repeat the imaginal exposure at home using the tape as a guide. This should be done daily for at least one hour. Further studies are recommended (Bisson & Jones, 1995).

Real-life exposure

When treating PTSD using real-life exposure it is important to tailor the exercises to the specific avoidances that are handicapping the individual patient. These are often not the same situations as the trauma. Many trauma-tised patients avoid a wide range of situations. For example, rape survivors may fear being alone at home, shipwreck survivors often avoid other forms of public transport, and crime victims may avoid many objectively safe situations, suffering from an exaggerated fear of attack.

Live exposure, therefore, involves patients re-entering situations that they have been avoiding, remaining in the feared situation until anxiety begins to reduce – usually at least one hour – and repeating this exercise daily. Patients work through a graded list of feared situations and objects until their fear reduces. Often, the final avoidance to be tackled will be more closely related to the trauma, for example, going on a ship for a shipwreck victim. However, the difference between appropriate avoidance of objectively dangerous situations (not appropriate for treatment) and phobic avoidance (suitable for treatment) must always be weighed up carefully with each individual patient. As Wolff (1977) noted while referring to the treatment of a crime victim, the goal of real-life exposure is:

> "not to feel relaxed while walking through high crime districts . . . rather to alter specific behaviours which were preventing her from living her life in the manner of her choosing."

Cognitive therapy

The last two decades have witnessed a vast increase in our knowledge of the effectiveness and applicability of cognitive therapy. The term 'cognitive therapy' refers to Beckian-style therapy described by Beck (1993) as:

> ". . . the application of the cognitive model of a particular disorder with the use of a variety of techniques designed to modify the dysfunctional beliefs and faulty information processing characteristic of each disorder."

Cognitive therapy is based on the premise that an individual's emotional disturbance is maintained as a result of negative thinking. For example, Beck's model of depression proposes that dysfunctional assumptions are laid down as cognitive schemata during early experience, lying dormant until they are activated by a critical incident. The meshing of dysfunctional assumptions and the incident leads to "negative automatic thoughts". These thoughts are distorted, negative, dysfunctional and unhelpful. They maintain an individual's emotional disturbance by interacting with the mood state, creating a "vicious circle" of depression.

Cognitive therapy aims to educate the client to identify and monitor their 'surface' negative thoughts and underlying assumptions, to identify the logical errors contained in these thoughts, underlying beliefs and assumptions, and to try to find more realistic and helpful alternatives to their current way of thinking. It is a structured, directive, collaborative, problem-orientated and time-limited intervention. Furthermore, it draws upon Socratic questioning methods and guided self-discovery, thus enabling the client to view their negative thoughts and beliefs as hypotheses to be validated (called 'reality testing') in a systematic and scientific way.

A whole range of techniques, beyond the scope of this chapter but detailed in Hawton *et al* (1989) and Williams (1986), are available to the therapist and patient to achieve this cognitive change.

Cognitive therapy has been found to be more effective than antidepressants in the treatment of depression (Elkin *et al*, 1989). A meta-analysis (Dobson, 1989) found cognitive therapy to be superior to behaviour therapy, pharmacotherapy and other psychotherapies in treating depression. It has been found to be effective in many other disorders, for example panic disorder (Clark *et al*, 1991), eating disorders (Fairburn *et al*, 1991), and generalised anxiety disorders (Butler *et al*, 1991). The application of cognitive therapy has now widened to many other disorders (Robins & Hayes, 1993).

A number of cognitive and information processing models of PTSD have been described in the literature (e.g. Krietler & Krietler, 1988; Chemtob *et al*, 1988; Foa *et al*, 1989; Resick & Schnicke, 1992; Janoff-Bulman, 1992). While these models may differ in detail, all suggest that distorted assumptions and beliefs about the traumatic event, self and world occur in individuals with PTSD. It is proposed that fear structures (Chemtob *et al*, 1988; Foa *et al*, 1989), shattered assumptions (Janoff-Bulman, 1992) and negative conflicting schemata (Resick & Schnicke, 1992) resulting from a traumatic experience can be modified by cognitive interventions. Appraisal and modification of these distorted beliefs and assumptions will result in the amelioration of PTSD symptomatology. These models suggest the following slightly different foci for therapy.

Resick & Schnicke (1992) developed an intervention called 'cognitive processing therapy' (CPT) for the treatment of survivors of rape and sexual assault. Although CPT is similar to Beckian cognitive therapy, it differs most significantly in that it holds that PTSD occurs when an experience is deemed so traumatic that it is completely at odds with the individual's previously held schemata. Efforts by the traumatised individual to absorb the event result in the formation of distorted cognitive systems. Therapy aims to elicit and challenge maladaptive beliefs and thoughts, focusing particularly on five themes developed from McCann *et al* (1988): safety, power, intimacy, esteem and trust.

Janoff-Bulman (1985, 1992) argued that following a traumatic incident assumptions about ourselves and the world are shattered. She highlighted three basic assumptions shared by most people which are particularly affected: (a) the belief in personal invulnerability; (b) the perception of the world as meaningful and comprehensive; and (c) the way we view ourselves in a positive light. She argued that treatment of PTSD should focus on cognitive interventions that rebuild and reevaluate these shattered assumptions.

Although many writers, for example Parrott & Howes (1991), Jehu (1988) and Rothbaum & Foa (1992), advocate the use of cognitive therapy with PTSD (either alone or as an adjunct to other forms of therapy), there is a paucity of studies investigating its effectiveness with these patients (Solomon *et al*, 1992). However, Resick & Schnicke's (1992) controlled study found that CPT did reduce PTSD in women following sexual assault. Cognitive therapy has in fact been used most commonly as part of anxiety management packages, such as stress inoculation training with rape survivors (Foa *et al*, 1991).

Anxiety management training

One alternative approach to the treatment of anxiety taken by many therapists is to teach patients more effective ways of coping with their anxiety. In this model, anxiety is recognised as a normal part of the human condition which results not only from environmental stimuli but also from a breakdown or insufficiency in the coping mechanisms used by the individual. A range of techniques is available, often used in combination with each other, to help people to manage their anxiety. These techniques include:

(a) Education on the nature of anxiety, its components (physical, behavioural and cognitive) and the normality of such reactions after traumatic events.

(b) Muscle relaxation training, usually based on Jacobson's progressive techniques (Jacobson, 1938) and sometimes biofeedback assisted (e.g. Peniston, 1986).

(c) Controlled breathing – slow, shallow, diaphragmatic breathing – to reduce hyperventilation and control severe panic (e.g. Clark *et al*, 1985).

(d) Thought-stopping, a technique to interrupt the intrusive mental thoughts and images typical of PTSD.

(e) Cognitive restructuring as described above.

(f) Guided self-dialogue, where patients learn to use a personal mental script to manage their anxiety and 'talk' themselves through difficult situations, controlling the more distorted thoughts common in these situations.

(g) Problem-solving, in which apparently overwhelming difficulties are analysed and broken down into their component parts, alternative solutions generated, and the solution most likely to be successful selected and applied in order to deal with the problem in a structured fashion.

(h)   Role-play practice of difficult situations, including role play of social skills such as assertiveness and often including elements of exposure.

Such combined treatment programmes have been shown to be effective in general anxiety disorder (GAD) (Blowers *et al*, 1987) and have been most commonly applied in PTSD research to rape victims (Veronen & Kilpatrick, 1983).

The particular variant of anxiety management training developed in PTSD research is based on Meichenbaum's work on stress inoculation training (SIT; Meichenbaum, 1985). This was used extensively by Kilpatrick *et al* (1982) in the treatment of rape victims. Typically SIT has three phases.

(1)   The conceptualisation phase, where patient and therapist assess the way in which the patient is dealing with anxiety-provoking situations. Self-monitoring, using diaries, is a feature of this phase.

(2)   The skill acquisition phase, where patients are taught the anxiety management techniques appropriate to their problems. In SIT the focus is on teaching patients how to cope with the way in which they think about their trauma, as well as managing anxiety-provoking situations in real life.

(3)   The rehearsal and application phase, where patients practice the techniques they have been taught in real-life situations between treatment sessions with the therapist.

In clinical practice, exposure and cognitive restructuring are often included in an anxiety management package. However, although PTSD researchers have usually omitted one or more of these techniques in order to identify the other active SIT components, the programme still remains a batch of techniques best seen as alternatives, and which must be carefully tailored to the individual patient's needs.

Case vignettes

Case example 1 (exposure)

Adele had been involved in an armed robbery three years ago while working in a branch of a building society. During the raid she was directly threatened by the raider and hid below a desk, fearing for her life. She initially had few symptoms, but over the next three years developed severe anxiety symptoms when reminded of the raid. Triggers for her intrusive thoughts and images included people talking about crime, TV and radio programmes, her husband continuing to work at a bank, and a training programme produced by the building society which aimed to prepare staff to cope better with robberies. She avoided these triggers for fear of the intrusions bringing on a panic. Her sleep was also disturbed and her concentration was at 70% of her normal level.

Treatment: Adele was treated with a combination of imaginal and real-life exposure. Initially she was asked to write out in her own words the events of the robbery. Homework was to read this through daily and write it out again every second day. She self-rated her anxiety as a maximum 8 out of 8 during the first write-through, but this had reduced to 40% of maximum by the end of several repeats.

She then had two sessions of therapist-assisted imaginal exposure, audiotaped to facilitate homework practice. The first session, an overall 'run through' of the robbery, was repeated twice in the session and produced anxiety ratings of 8 and 7 respectively. Homework reduced this to 3 during the next seven days. The second session was a 'rewind and hold' on two particularly distressing scenes. Anxiety was rated at 5, reducing to 1 after only two homework repeats.

The final session reviewed her progress during which she arranged to do some real-life exposure to discussing robberies with colleagues and her husband. She also arranged to watch the training video of robberies and to join a 'raid support team' of staff who attend branches to support staff immediately after a robbery. Follow-up by telephone has confirmed that she has remained symptom free for one year.

Case example 2 (cognitive therapy)

John was a 42-year-old married man with two children aged 8 and 11. He was employed as a guard collecting money for a security firm. He arrived home one afternoon and was jumped on by three men and a woman while entering his front door. They tied him up and held a knife to his throat, threatening to kill him if he failed to obey their instructions. He was held hostage at home for the next 14 hours and then instructed to go to work as normal and deliver a van-load of money to his captors. When his wife and children arrived home they were also tied up and threatened until two hours prior to going to work, when they were taken away in a car. He was informed that if the money was not delivered his family would be killed. John went to work as normal and told a colleague who called the police. As the police had been informed, the van left the depot three hours later than usual. John was convinced that his family had been killed and that the assailants would be watching him. However, when John finally arrived at the rendezvous point the assailants had not arrived and in fact his family had been freed a number of hours earlier.

Treatment: The initial stages of therapy involved identifying unhelpful thoughts and mapping out the central themes of thought distortion. The thoughts and beliefs contained in these themes (e.g. guilt, anger, anxiety, lowered self-esteem, etc.) were challenged using a variety of methods to elicit more rational and realistic alternatives. For example, John felt particularly guilty because he believed himself to be responsible for the trauma. He described a stream of negative automatic thoughts (strength of beliefs in brackets), such as "I am totally responsible for the trauma" (100%); "I should have been able to stop the assailants taking my family away" (100%).

Using cognitive therapy techniques John was able to examine the evidence for and against these cognitions and to replace them with rational responses such as: "I am not at all responsible for the incident, the responsibility lies entirely with the assailants"; "I had a gun to my head and if I had tried to stop them taking my wife and children I or my family could have been seriously injured". He then rated his belief in these alternative cognitions as 100% and the original dysfunctional thoughts as 0%.

Following ten sessions of cognitive therapy John had made a 75% improvement and continued to improve further during follow-up.

Case example 3 (package of techniques)

Jean was a 30-year-old single unemployed woman, who between the ages of 9 and 15 was repeatedly sexually abused, raped and beaten by her father and also on occasions by her uncle. This abuse occurred in her room at night 2–3 times weekly. In total she suffered approximately 750 separate incidents of rape, buggery, sexual abuse and violent assault. At age 14 she became pregnant as a result of the abuse and was sent away for a termination.

Fifteen years after the abuse she continued to experience symptoms consistent with post-traumatic stress disorder. Flashbacks occurred 2–3 times weekly, during which she was frequently incontinent. Intrusive thoughts and images of the abuse were present for 80% of the day. Her sleep was disturbed by nightmares and frequent wakening. She avoided any cues that reminded her of the abuse (e.g. striped pyjamas, certain male characteristics, reading or seeing anything where sexual or physical abuse was portrayed). She was consumed with guilt that the abuse was her fault. She also felt extreme anger towards her mother as she believed that her mother knew about the abuse (because of the blood-stained sheets and nightwear) but never acknowledged or tried to stop it.

Her life was severely impacted. She was unable to work or socialise with other people due to her fears. She had many sexual difficulties, could not look at or touch her own body and could not maintain sexual relationships. She could not touch her own son. She had a major depressive illness, clear suicidal plans and had made three serious attempts to take her own life. She drank between 40–60 units of alcohol weekly to reduce the intrusive thoughts and images of the abuse and to enable her to sleep.

Treatment: Treatment involved using most of the behavioural, cognitive and anxiety management interventions described previously and is summarised in Table 17.2. Treatment lasted for 30 sessions, much longer than the average duration of most behavioural and cognitive treatments of PTSD, thus reflecting the complexity of this case.

Evidence for the efficacy of behavioural and cognitive treatments

Of the eight randomised and/or controlled studies shown in Table 17.1, two have used systematic desensitisation, three direct imaginal exposure,

TABLE 17.2
Complex cognitive–behavioural treatment programme of sexual abuse survivor

Session	Target problem area	Intervention	Outcome
1–4	Reduce frequency and intensity of suicidal thoughts and plans	Suicide prevention plan	Suicidal thoughts and plans reduced by 70%
5–7	Reduce alcohol and manage increase in intrusive thoughts	Distraction to cope with thoughts and anxiety management	Alcohol reduced to 3–6 units weekly
8–14	Identify and modify negative thoughts and beliefs	Cognitive restructuring	Reduced guilt and depression. Self-esteem improved
15–22	Intrusive thoughts and images, flashbacks, nightmares and sleep disturbance	Imaginal exposure	Intrusive thoughts and images reduced by 85%
22–23	Inability to hug young son	Real-life exposure	Able to show affection
24–28	Fear of cues associated with abuse	Real-life exposure	Avoidances resolved
29–30	Termination of therapy. Ensure maintenance of treatment gains	Relapse prevention. Structured follow-up arranged	Treatment gains maintained

two imaginal and real-life exposure, one anxiety management training and one cognitive therapy. Exposure, anxiety management training and cognitive therapy all improve PTSD by between 20–80%.

As techniques have improved, so have the results. It is clear that a combination of imaginal and real-life exposure is currently the most efficacious technique, although cognitive therapy shows great promise. Unfortunately, the only controlled study to compare behavioural and psychodynamic therapies directly (Brom *et al*, 1989) used systematic desensitisation as the behavioural treatment. Although this study showed no superiority of behavioural therapy, systematic desensitisation is the least effective of the exposure-based therapies and so little can be deduced from this comparison.

Studies are urgently required, therefore, which pitch exposure against cognitive, drug and brief psychodynamic interventions before definitive statements can be made about the treatment of choice for PTSD. Currently, two UK studies (one at the Maudsley Hospital, London under the direction of Professor Isaac Marks and the other at the Withington Hospital, Manchester under the direction of Professor Nick Tarrier) are comparing cognitive and behavioural treatments in controlled designs. The results are awaited with interest.

B.   Psychodynamic psychotherapy

CLEO VAN VELSEN

Previously I have attempted to sketch an outline of the complex nature of the interaction between a trauma and an individual's internal world (deriving from nature and environment) in the context of an external world (chapter 6B).

With respect to longer-term psychoanalytically informed psychotherapy for those suffering from PTSD, the task of the psychotherapist is to assist a survivor to manage their experience, which is, as Garland (1991) says, about "getting on with it rather than getting over it". Patients often ask to return to "how I was" and this is probably unrealistic as there has been major internal upheaval. Hopefully, however, people should be able to get on with their lives.

The basic principles of treatment associated with psychoanalytical psychotherapy are: the development of a working alliance, catharsis, the process of rebuilding trust, and understanding of the elements of the complex traumatic event in a way that acknowledges, but contains, overwhelming anxiety. Use is made of the transference, which is the patient's emotional attitude to his or her therapist, affected as it is by the nature of the patient's internal world with its particular object relationships.

Such work will involve the analysis of defence mechanisms. There are a number of different manoeuvres adopted by people faced with severe external threat, but I shall discuss those commonly associated with PTSD.

(1)   *Denial* or disavowal, where the reality of a traumatic perception is not recognised, for example, a patient who refuses to recognise the impact of being involved in a major accident at work although colleagues have noticed the effect on his work.

(2)   *Dissociation*, where perceptual consciousness is reduced, allowing the individual to 'cut off' from the trauma: as reflected in amnesic symptoms and possibly in 'flashbacks' (Putnam, 1990; Spiegel, 1990). It is this mechanism that has been postulated in the development of multiple personality disorder, although the validity of such a diagnosis is doubtful (Fahy, 1988).

(3)   *Splitting* consists of keeping the good and bad aspects of oneself, and others, totally separate, thus avoiding uncomfortable states of ambivalence associated with idealisation and denigration. Everyone has aggressive and destructive aspects of themselves which early on in life are dealt with by splitting, and 'good enough' development enables the integration, toleration and moderation of these split-off aspects. Individuals who have been victimised, perhaps particularly at the hands of others, can suffer a breakdown of their whole view of themselves and others. An example is a woman who, after being raped, perceives

all men as "bad". The situation can become stuck, with little development in thought or affect possible.

(4) *Projection* and projective identification is a process whereby unacceptable feelings are unconsciously located in others. Garland (1991) concentrated on this mechanism, stating that the survivor makes "a desperate and unconscious attempt to rid himself of intolerable states of terror and helplessness" in order to let the object or other (for example helper) know about the condition of his internal world so that something can be done about it. Thus projective identification may be a method of "communicating and evacuating intense anxiety". Affects such as rage and vengefulness may be unconsciously split off and projected by a victim, meaning that he or she is unable to 'know', 'think' or process them.

(5) *Identification* with the aggressor is based on the reaction to an external threat. There may be appropriation of the aggression itself, physical or moral emulation of the aggressor, or adoption of particular symbols of power associated with the aggressor (Catherall, 1991). An example is the identification with Nazi guards by the 'promoted prisoners' in concentration camps (Bettelheim, 1960).

All these defensive strategies contribute to a state in which the person is both cognitively and emotionally 'trapped' in the trauma. This relates to repetition compulsion and such a situation predisposes to action rather than thought. For example, the constant telling of a traumatic event often has the flavour of an action rather than a process of remembering, thinking and working through. The use of thought as action is developed in Bion's (1967) theory of thinking.

Manoeuvres such as these interact with a variety of affects, namely helplessness, loss, guilt, rage and shame, which may become organised as depression, vengefulness and aggression, both conscious and unconscious. Lindy (1993) has described the "special configuration" of a traumatic event which includes "the multiplicity of stressors which are active in and around the period of trauma such as fright, loss, threat of bodily harm or exposure to grotesqueness" plus "multiple inter-acting affect states" and "expectable compensatory fantasies . . . such as omnipotence or murderous aggression".

Individual psychotherapy

Lindy (1986, 1993) also described a focal psychoanalytic psychotherapy which pays particular attention to the modifications of technique required to work with survivors, and the basic principles of treatment are illustrated by referring to this model.

Lindy highlighted a common finding, namely the difficulty of engaging people in treatment, often associated with negative transference reactions, especially if the therapist is experienced as silent and distant. His treatment consists of three phases. In opening the therapist will need to express empathy, explain PTSD and specifically link present symptoms to the traumatic experience. Only in the middle phase will there be more emphasis on the transference/countertransference matrix to help give in-depth understanding to the special configuration. He emphasises the importance of using the transference to interpret the traumatic event, and counsels against incautiously introducing added affect into an already intense here-and-now situation in the therapy. The interaction between the therapist and the patient will often reflect transference phenomena from the trauma itself, rather than from the early past. The termination phase allows integration of the pretraumatic and current selves, as well as providing an opportunity to work through issues of mourning and loss highlighted by the forthcoming separation from the therapist.

It is important to note here that patients who require psychodynamic psychotherapy may need psychiatric support, partly due to common comorbidity with other psychiatric disorders such as substance misuse or depression.

The transference/countertransference matrix is basic to the technique of psychoanalytical psychotherapy and this may be very uncomfortable for both therapist and patient. Use of the transference and countertransference is vital to obtaining information about the patient's state of mind, but 'acting out' in either may be harmful. Repetition compulsion is fundamental to PTSD, and the strength of the compulsion to re-enact the trauma in the therapeutic space cannot be overemphasised (Adshead & Van Velsen, 1996). This can be avoided by careful attention to boundaries as well as by supervision and case discussion. 'Getting better' means having to face destruction and loss, which in object relation terms means having to achieve the 'depressive position' (Krystal, 1988; Garland, 1991).

The only controlled study of psychodynamic psychotherapy is by Brom *et al* (1989) who compared patients receiving psychodynamic therapy, systematic desensitisation and hypnotherapy with a waiting-list control group. All treatment groups had significantly improved symptom scores in comparison with the control group, with psychotherapy having more impact on avoidance symptoms (associated with chronicity) than the other two treatments, which achieved greater reduction in symptoms of intrusion. Solomon *et al* (1992) concluded in their review that psychodynamic therapy is promising but that more empirical data are required. This is particularly so in regard to long-term psychotherapy.

Group psychotherapy

Yalom (1975) discussed curative factors in group therapy which are relevant in patients suffering from PTSD. Groups are of particular use for people who have suffered the same trauma, such as those used extensively, and usefully, in the treatment of Vietnam veterans and rape and incest survivors (Dye & Roth, 1991; Marmar, 1991; Koller *et al*, 1992).

Overall there seems little agreement as to how groups should be constructed, for example whether they should be time-limited, open or closed, and therapist-led or not. Efficacy studies are lacking.

Family therapy

The impact of major trauma on an individual is not in a vacuum but in a social context, often a family. Difficulties can be experienced by the families of trauma survivors and traumatic stress symptoms exacerbated in an individual because of family dynamics. Conversely, there can be a positive effect on PTSD symptoms with improvement in family functioning (Figley, 1978, 1985; Silver & Iacono, 1986; Masters *et al*, 1988). Figley (1988) has thus developed a five-phase treatment of PTSD in families with the aim of enabling a family member to return to pre-traumatic functioning within a family system. Again, outcome studies are required.

Conclusion

The range of traumatic and individual variation, both in personality and experience, imply a variety of treatments. Psychodynamic understanding and psychodynamic psychotherapies (individual, group, brief and long-term) have an important place in the therapeutic repertoire. Understanding of PTSD and its treatment is now much richer, but more research of all kinds is required to underpin clinical descriptions and hunches. Outcome studies are lacking at present; their establishment is essential.

C. Eye movement desensitisation

MARTIN NEWMAN

A relatively new treatment for post-traumatic stress disorder is that of eye movement desensitisation (Shapiro, 1989*b*, 1995, Wolpe & Abrams, 1991; Spector & Huthwaite, 1993; Walsh, 1993). Shapiro tried the technique on approximately 70 clients and volunteers, and then made a systematic study of 22 rape/molestation and Vietnam veterans (Shapiro, 1989*a*). The results of this study indicated that a single session of the eye movement desensitisation procedure was sufficient to desensitise completely the traumatic memories of the subjects and to alter their cognitive self-assessments. The treatment is reported to be both rapid and successful. Shapiro reported that, following the instructions, 60–70% of PTSD-related traumatic memories could be expected to be relieved, although specialised training is necessary to achieve the highest success rates. Improvements were reported to be maintained at one-year follow-up. Full instructions regarding the technique are given by Shapiro (1989*b*). Spector & Huthwaite (1993) reported the technique to be useful in a case report concerning a 41-year-old woman who had been involved in a road traffic accident. Further research on this technique is needed.

References

Adshead, G. & Van Velsen, C. (1996) Psychotherapeutic work with victims of trauma. In *Forensic Psychotherapy; Crime, Psychodynamics and the Offender Patient* (eds C. Cordess & M. Cox), pp. 355–370. London: Jessica Kingsley.

Al-Kubaisy, T., Marks, I. M., Logsdale, S., *et al* (1992) The role of exposure homework in phobic reduction: a controlled study. *Behaviour Therapy*, **22**, 599–622.

Beck, A. T. (1993) Cognitive therapy, past, present and future. *Journal of Consulting and Clinical Psychology*, **61**, 194–198.

Bettelheim, B. (1960) *The Informed Heart.* London: Penguin.

Bion, W. (1967) *Second Thoughts.* Reprinted (1993). London: Karnac.

Bisson, J. I. & Jones, N. (1995) Taped imaginal exposure as a treatment for post-traumatic stress reactions. *Journal of the Royal Army Medical Corps*, **141**, 20–25.

Blowers, C. M., Cobb, J. P. & Matthews, A. M. (1987) Treatment of generalised anxiety disorders: a comparative study. *Behaviour Research and Therapy*, **25**, 493–502.

Boudewyns, P. A. & Hyer, L. (1990) Physiological response to combat memories and preliminary treatment outcome in Vietnam veteran PTSD patients treated with direct therapeutic exposure. *Behaviour Therapy*, **21**, 63–87.

Brom, D., Kleber, R. J. & Defares, P. B. (1989) Brief psychotherapy for posttraumatic stress disorders. *Journal of Consulting and Clinical Psychology*, **57**, 607–612.

Butler, G., Fennell, M., Robson, P., *et al* (1991) Comparison of behaviour therapy and cognitive therapy in the treatment of generalised anxiety disorder. *Journal of Consulting and Clinical Psychology*, **59**, 167–175.

Catherall, D. R. (1991) Aggression and projective identification in the treatment of victims. *Psychotherapy*, **28**, 145–149.

Chemtob, C., Roitblat, H. L., Hamada, R. S., *et al* (1988) A cognitive action theory of post-traumatic stress disorder. *Journal of Anxiety Disorders*, **2**, 253–275.

Clark, D. M., Salkovskis, P. M. & Chalkley, A. J. (1985) Respiratory control as a treatment for panic attacks. *Journal of Behaviour Therapy and Experimental Psychiatry*, **16**, 23–30.
——, ——, Hackmann, A., *et al* (1991) Long-term outcome of cognitive therapy for panic disorder. Paper presented to the meeting of the Association for Advancement of Behaviour Therapy, New York, November.
Cooper, N. A. & Clum, G. A. (1989) Imaginal flooding as a supplementary treatment for PTSD in combat veterans: a controlled study. *Behaviour Therapy*, **20**, 381–391.
Dobson, K. (1989) A meta-analysis of the efficacy of cognitive therapy for depression. *Journal of Consulting and Clinical Psychology*, **57**, 414–419.
Dye, E. & Roth, S. (1991) Psychotherapy with Vietnam veterans and rape and incest survivors. *Psychotherapy*, **28**, 103–120.
Elkin, I., Shea, M. T., Watkins, J. T., *et al* (1989) NIMH treatment of depression collaborative research program. General effectiveness of treatments. *Archives of General Psychiatry*, **46**, 971–982.
Fahy, T. (1988) The diagnosis of multiple personality disorder: a critical review. *British Journal of Psychiatry*, **153**, 597–606.
Fairburn, C. G., Jones, R., Peveler, R.C., *et al* (1991) Three psychological treatments for bulimia nervosa. *Archives of General Psychiatry*, **48**, 463–469.
Figley, C. R. (ed.) (1978) Psychosocial adjustment among Vietnam veterans: In *An Overview of the Research in Stress Disorders Among Vietnam Veterans: Theory, Research and Treatment*, pp. 57–90. New York: Brunner/Mazel.
Figley, C. R. (1985) The family as victim: mental health implications. *Psychiatry*, **6**, 283–291.
Figley, C. R. (1988) A five-phase treatment of post traumatic stress disorder in families. *Journal of Traumatic Stress*, **1**, 127–141.
Foa, E. B., Steketee, G. & Rothbaum, B. O. (1989) Behavioural/cognitive conceptualisations of post-traumatic stress disorder. *Behaviour Therapy*, **20**, 155–176.
——, Rothbaum, B. O., Riggs, D. S., *et al* (1991) Treatment of posttraumatic stress disorder in rape victims: a comparison between cognitive–behavioural procedures and counselling. *Journal of Consulting and Clinical Psychology*, **59**, 715–723.
Garland, C. (1991) External disasters and the internal world: an approach to psychotherapeutic understanding of survivors. In *Textbook of Psychotherapy in Psychiatric Practice* (ed. J. Holmes), pp. 507–532. London: Churchill Livingstone
Hackman, A. (1993) Behavioural and cognitive psychotherapies: past history, current applications and future registration issues. *Behavioural and Cognitive Psychotherapy*, **21** (suppl. 1), 1–75.
Hawton, K., Salkovskis, P. M., Kirk, J., *et al* (1989) *Cognitive Behaviour Therapy for Psychiatric Problems: A Practical Guide*. New York: Oxford University Press.
Jacobson, E. (1938) *Progressive Relaxation*. Chicago: University of Chicago Press.
Janoff-Bulman, R. (1985) Aftermath of victimization: rebuilding shattered assumptions. In *Trauma and its Wake* (ed. C. R. Figley), pp. 15–35. New York: Brunner/Mazel.
—— (1992) *Shattered Assumptions*. New York: Free Press.
Jehu, D. (1988) *Beyond Sexual Abuse: Therapy with Women who were Childhood Victims*. Chichester: John Wiley.
Keane, T. M., Zimmerling, R. T. & Caddell, J. M. (1985) A behavioural formulation of post-traumatic stress disorder in Vietnam veterans. *The Behaviour Therapist*, **8**, 9–12.
——, Fairbank, J. A., Caddel, J. M., *et al* (1989) Implosive (flooding) therapy reduces symptoms of PTSD in Vietnam combat veterans. *Behaviour Therapy*, **20**, 245–260.
Kilpatrick, D. G., Veronen, L. J. & Resick, P. A. (1982) Psychological sequelae to rape: assessment and treatment strategies. In *Behavioural Medicine: Assessment and Treatment Strategies* (eds D. M. Dolays & R. L. Meredith), pp. 473–497. New York: Plenum Press.
Koller, P., Marmer, C. & Kanas, N. (1992) Psychodynamic group treatment of PTSD in Vietnam veterans. *International Journal of Group Psychotherapy*, **42**, 225–245.
Krietler, S. & Krietler, J. (1988) Trauma and anxiety: the cognitive approach. *Journal of Traumatic Stress*, **1**, 35–56.
Krystal, H. (1988) *Integration of Self Healing: Affect, Trauma and Alexithymia*. Hillsdale, NJ: Analytic Press.
Lindy, J. D. (1986) An outline for the psychoanalytic psychotherapy of post traumatic stress disorder. In *Trauma and its Wake: Traumatic Stress Theory, Research and Intervention*, vol. 2 (ed. C. R. Figley), pp. 195–212. New York: Brunner/Mazel.
—— (1993) Focal psychoanalytic psychotherapy of post traumatic stress disorder. In *International Handbook of Traumatic Stress Syndromes* (eds J. P. Wilson & B. Raphael), pp. 803–809. New York: Plenum.

McCaffrey, R. J. & Fairbank, J. A. (1985) Behavioural assessment and treatment of accident-related PTSD: two case studies. *Behaviour Therapy*, **16**, 406–416.

McCann, I. L., Sakheim, D. K. & Abrahamson, D. J. (1988) Trauma and victimization: a model of psychological adaption. *The Counselling Psychologist*, **16**, 531–594.

Marks, I. M. (1987) *Fears, Phobias and Rituals*. Oxford: Oxford University Press.

Marmar, C. (1991) Brief dynamic psychotherapy of PTSD. *Psychiatric Annals*, **21**, 405–414.

Masters, R., Friedman, L. N. & Getzel, G. (1988) Helping families of homicide victims: multidimensional approach. *Journal of Traumatic Stress*, **1**, 109–125.

Meichenbaum, D. (1985) *Stress Inoculation Training*. New York: Pergamon.

Muse, M. (1986) Stress related post-traumatic chronic pain syndrome: behavioural treatment approach. *Pain*, **25**, 389–394.

Parrott, C. A. & Howes, J. L. (1991) The application of cognitive therapy to posttraumatic stress disorder. In *The Challenge of Cognitive Therapy: Applications to Nontraditional Populations* (eds T. Vallis & J. Howes), pp. 85–109. New York: Plenum Press.

Peniston, E. G. (1986) EMG biofeedback assisted desensitization treatment for Vietnam combat veterans post-traumatic stress disorder. *Clinical Biofeedback and Health*, **9**, 35–41.

Putnam, F. W. (1990) Disturbances of "self" in victims of childhood sexual abuse. In *Incest Related Syndromes of Adult Psychopathology* (ed. R. Kluft), pp. 113–131. Washington, DC: APP.

Resick, P. A. & Schnicke, M. K. (1992) Cognitive processing therapy for sexual assault victims. *Journal of Consulting and Clinical Psychology*, **60**, 748–756.

Richards, D. A. & Rose, J. S. (1991) Exposure therapy for post-traumatic stress disorder: four case studies. *British Journal of Psychiatry*, **158**, 836–840.

——, Lovell, K. & Marks, I. M. (1994) Post-traumatic stress disorder: evaluation of a behavioural treatment program. *Journal of Traumatic Stress*, **7**, 669–680.

Robins, C. J. & Hayes, A. M. (1993) An appraisal of cognitive therapy. *Journal of Consulting and Clinical Psychology*, **6**, 205–214.

Rothbaum, B. O. & Foa, E. B. (1992) Cognitive behavioural treatment of posttraumatic stress disorder. In *Posttraumatic Stress Disorder: A Behavioural Approach to Assessment and Treatment* (ed. P. Saigh), pp. 85–110. New York: Macmillan.

Shapiro, F. (1989a) Efficacy of the eye movement desensitization procedure in the treatment of traumatic memories. *Journal of Traumatic Stress*, **2**, 199–223.

—— (1989b) Eye movement desensitization: a new treatment for post-traumatic stress disorder. *Journal of Behavioural Therapy and Experimental Psychiatry*, **20**, 211–217.

—— (1995) *Eye Movement Desensitisation and Reprocessing*. New York: Guilford.

Silver, S. M. & Iacono, C. (1986) Symptom groups and family patterns of Vietnam veterans with post-traumatic stress disorders. In *Trauma and its Wake*, vol. 2 (ed. C. R. Figley), pp. 232–263. New York: Brunner Mazel.

Solomon, S. D., Gerrity, E. T. & Muff, A. M. (1992) Efficacy of treatments for post-traumatic stress disorder. *Journal of the American Medical Association*, **268**, 633–638.

Spector, J. & Huthwaite, M. (1993) Eye-movement desensitisation to overcome post-traumatic stress disorder. *British Journal of Psychiatry*, **163**, 106–108.

Spiegel, D. (1990) Trauma, dissociation and hypnosis. In *Incest Related Syndromes of Adult Psychopathology* (ed. R. Kluft), pp. 247–261. Washington, DC: APP.

Vaughan, K. & Tarrier, N. (1992) The use of image habituation training with post-traumatic stress disorders. *British Journal of Psychiatry*, **161**, 658–664.

Veronen, L. J. & Kilpatrick, D. G. (1983) Stress management for rape victims. In *Stress Reduction and Prevention* (eds D. Meichenbaum & M. E. Jaremko), pp. 341–373. New York: Plenum Press.

Walsh, J. A. (1993) Eye-movement desensitisation to overcome post-traumatic stress disorder (letter). *British Journal of Psychiatry*, **163**, 697.

Williams, J. M. G. (1986) *The Psychological Treatment of Depression: A Guide to the Theory and Practice of Cognitive–Behaviour Therapy*. London: Croom-Helm.

Wolff, R. (1977) Systematic desensitization and negative practice to alter the after-effects of a rape attempt. *Journal of Behaviour Therapy and Experimental Psychiatry*, **8**, 423–425.

Wolpe, J. & Abrams, J. (1991) Post-traumatic stress disorder overcome by eye movement desensitization: a case report. *Journal of Behaviour Therapy and Experimental Psychiatry*, **22**, 39–43.

Yalom, I. D. (1975) *The Theory and Practice of Group Psychotherapy*. New York: Basic Books.

18 Children and adolescents

A. Treatment of children and families

DORA BLACK

It is to be expected that if a child who has experienced an acute traumatic event has been well debriefed at the right time, and if bereaved, has had some brief bereavement counselling, the incidence of later psychiatric disorders directly attributable to the trauma or to the bereavement will be substantially reduced (Black & Urbanowicz, 1985, 1987, Robinson & Mitchell, 1993). Nevertheless, the practitioner is likely to see some children for the first time long after the time when debriefing might have prevented the onset of PTSD, and similarly with bereavement, past the time when a coun selling intervention might have prevented the onset of school refusal, depression, academic failure or other problems known to be associated with bereavement. Children presenting at these later stages may be suffering from any of a wide range of psychological and psychiatric disorders, and it is beyond the scope of this book to give a complete description of these and their treatments. The reader is referred to a textbook of child psychiatry for fuller details (e.g. Black & Cottrell, 1993; Rutter *et al*, 1994). In this section we will discuss treatments for traumatised children that help them to deal with aspects of the trauma or traumatic bereavement which continue to be present for some time after the trauma, or which begin within a few months of it. These might include specific phobias related to the trauma, compulsive repetitive traumatic play, troublesome dreams and nightmares, flashbacks, anxiety and depression.

Treatment approaches

The child, unlike many adults, must always be considered within the context of the family with whom he lives and the school where he spends half his waking hours. Many of his problems arising from the trauma may be maintained or even enhanced by the reactions of members of his family. Even when it is considered that the child should receive individual treatment, some sort of support and guidance for his parents, and possibly his siblings and teachers, may be necessary.

Case example

Two brothers aged 7 and 5 survived a fire, started by one of them playing with matches, which killed their baby sister. Their mother, devastated by grief and guilt, dealt with her feelings by shunning the children who had to be cared for by their maternal grandmother. At her home also lived her son aged 13, (the uncle of the children) who never let them forget it was their 'fault' that the baby died and that their mother would not care for them. Helping the children to recognise that at their age it is not possible to anticipate the results of one's actions, and that they should have been better supervised, would involve: helping the mother to cope with her guilt and grief in more mature ways than by rejecting the children; helping the grandmother to find ways to deal with the adolescent anxieties of her younger son and with her own grief at losing a grandchild; and working with the family as a whole, perhaps using family therapy techniques to deal with the issues thrown up by this tragedy and to help them mourn. At the same time the specific post-traumatic symptoms of the older child, nightmares and traumatic repetitive play (fire-setting), needed to be addressed.

In what follows, various specific therapies are described and the reader is referred to studies which establish their efficacy, where available. In practice, it is common and sensible to combine two or more therapies, so that in the above case, the family were offered a contract of six family therapy sessions by the consultant child psychiatrist, the mother received brief individual counselling from the psychiatric social worker, the psychologist saw the older boy individually and with his grandmother for behaviour modification to deal with his repetitive play, and dream rehearsal techniques were used to change the traumatic nature of his dreams within the family therapy sessions. The technique chosen for the fire-setting was highly effective but would not have worked unless other related issues were being dealt with in the family therapy sessions. Similarly, dealing with his guilt in these sessions might not have resulted in his relinquishing his compulsive play without the specific behavioural techniques being used as well.

Behaviour modification

These treatments are based on learning theory and fall into four main groups.

(1) *Pavlovian (classical) conditioning*

This assumes that an individual becomes conditioned to react to frightening stimuli in certain chance ways. This is probably the mechanism for the excessive startle reaction shown by children (and adults) with post-traumatic stress reaction. The sound of a car back-firing may produce excessive startle in a child who was subject to shelling in a war zone or who witnessed his mother being shot. Treatment may include graduated exposure to noises which increasingly approximate to the actual original stimulus using relaxation techniques simultaneously (*systematic desensitisation*), or the child is exposed to the stimulus in full intensity, while using relaxation, holding, etc. (*flooding*). Both these techniques are helpful in extinguishing fears and phobias but should be used by practitioners who are trained and experienced, and the parents' and child's consent should be obtained before using them (see Gelfand & Hartmann, 1984, for studies of efficacy of all behavioural approaches).

Case example
Norman, a 4-year-old boy, developed a fear of going in boats after spending many hours in cold water in the dark when the *Herald of Free Enterprise* car ferry overturned and sank off the coast of Belgium in 1987. He had been on the boat with his parents, and his father received injuries when he had tried to clamber out to find help. Among other treatments (which included marital therapy to address the problems between the parents arising from the father's injuries which led to his being unable to work), Norman received systematic desensitisation. The psychologist started by showing him pictures of small boats and then encouraging him to play with toy boats in a bath; they then graduated to drawing boats, watching larger boats on videos; to sailing boats on a pond, to rowing on the lake and eventually to taking a trip to Zeebrugge on another ferry. At the same time she taught him how to relax his muscles while imagining pleasant scenes involving water (such as fountains playing) and she included the parents on all the trips, desensitising them at the same time. The family were able to take a ferry to France the following year.

(2) *Operant conditioning*

Behaviour is shaped by being reinforced differentially. Maladaptive behaviour develops because a child is rewarded for those behaviours while other (more desirable) behaviours are extinguished because they are not rewarded. Behaviour modification therapy utilises rewards (and rarely, punishments) differentially to reinforce desired behaviour. Children who have developed behaviours following trauma which have been encouraged (reinforced) by parents at the time, such as coming into the parental bed at night when they are troubled by fears or bad dreams, can be helped to relinquish such behaviours when they have continued after the need for them has faded, by the use of a rewards chart (*shaping behaviour*). The child is given a star on a calendar chart if he first goes back to his bed after a cuddle, then if he stays in bed for ten minutes, and eventually by stages, if he manages to stay in his room all night. The intervening stages must be worked out carefully so that the child receives sufficient reward to overcome his fears, and not so large a reward that maintaining interest is defeated. Stars are cheap so can be given frequently, but are of little reward in themselves unless backed up by a larger one. Five stars might earn him a trip to the cinema, or a favourite video or a small packet of sweets.

Some undesired behaviours, especially ones of an obsessional or repetitive kind, can be extinguished by the use of *satiation* or *massed practice*. The behaviour is practised by the child to destruction. For example, the child with traumatic repetitive fire-setting was taught to make a safe fire (one in the open air, with an adult in attendance, away from trees and with water on hand to extinguish it). He was then encouraged to light fires (and extinguish them) one after the other, for over two hours. He got very fed up and did not continue this behaviour. *Response prevention* is another effective way of extinguishing obsessional symptoms and thoughts. The parent is taught to intervene to prevent the child carrying out the full compulsive ritual (Bolton *et al*, 1983). This is useful for children who compulsively repeat parts of a traumatic experience.

Case example

A 9-year-old girl, who saw all her family killed in a civil war in Africa, came to this country to live with an aunt who could not understand why the girl insisted on eating *under* the table rather than with the others. She had in fact escaped the slaughter of her family by hiding under the table, and resorted to this in a compulsive way when she felt under stress. Mealtimes were stressful as she recalled the loss of her family most at that time. The child was given specific bereavement counselling which enabled her to grieve for her dead parents, but did not alter this particular behaviour. Her aunt was taught to prevent her going under the table by holding her tight and talking gently to her about her sad feelings and about her love for the child and her wish to give her a home. After this had been repeated at every meal for a week, the girl sat at the table and began to join the family meals.

(3) *Cognitive therapy*

Cognitive therapy is based on the concepts of *cognitive deficiency* (an absence of the accurate information processing that enables an individual to understand and retain an accurate perception of an experience) and *cognitive distortion* (a tendency to misconstrue perceptions, usually to the individual's detriment). The former is particularly likely with children because of their limited knowledge and experience, and much helpful work with children can be done by helping them to understand their perceptions and process them more accurately (Kendall, 1991). The recent research on how information about traumatic events is processed (Siegel, 1995) is relevant to these approaches.

Therapies designed to help with cognitive distortions have been particularly successful with depressed adults, usually in conjunction with other treatments such as antidepressant medication. There have as yet been few trials of cognitive therapy with depressed children, but in principle the same techniques should be as successful (see above).

Case example

A 4-year-old boy lived with his maternal aunt following the death of his mother at his father's hands, which it was believed he had witnessed. His aunt was distraught that Jimmy followed her everywhere complaining that everything smelled of "poo" (faeces). He wouldn't eat his food because of the smell of "poo", and he smelled it on his hands and his toys. This appeared to be an olfactory hallucination, which is a form of cognitive distortion. Knowing that his mother had been strangled, the therapist talked to the boy about how his mummy and daddy had had a big fight, and daddy had hurt mummy so much that she was very frightened. When people are frightened they sometimes do a "poo" in their pants. Mummy had poohed in her pants because she was frightened. Maybe daddy didn't mean to hurt mummy so much, but he hurt her body so much it didn't work any more and so she died. Four-year-old children, having not long achieved continence, understand very well how fear can cause loss of bowel control. Having made sense of his experience for him he was able to process the olfactory perception and could move on to grieving for his dead mother. He no longer complained of the smell.

(4) *Social skills training*

This involves the use of role play, teaching children and adolescents how to manage anxiety in social situations. These techniques are derived from social learning theory and may be helpful in the adolescents under consideration who withdraw from social contact and then find it difficult, after processing the traumatic events, to find their way back into their peer group (Herbert, 1981).

Pharmacotherapy

Medication has a small but useful part to play with children and adolescents. It can often be used to relieve specific symptoms to enable one of the psychological therapies to be more effective (see chapter 19 for details).

Family therapy

Family therapy, a group treatment in which the family is regarded as a unit for treatment purposes, can be applied in two main situations with traumatised children. If the family shared the trauma, working with them as a group enhances their understanding of each individual's idiosyncratic experience of the trauma, and enables the parents to help the children to resolve some of their distress. If the child was the traumatised person and the others did not share the experience, family therapy can help the child to convey his or her experiences to the others, and enable the therapist to help the family to help the traumatised individual. Family therapy may also be useful when the individual traumatised is one of the parents, and the children are suffering because of parental psychopathology. The various theoretical bases for family therapy are described by Dare, and the techniques are fully covered in Dare (1985). Many of the techniques described above can be used in the setting of family meetings.

Case example
Two young children survived a car crash in which their mother, who was driving, was killed. The children were trapped in the car, suspended upside-down but conscious, while flames engulfed the car. They had moderate burns which kept them in hospital for several weeks. They were first referred two months after the accident. They were now living with their father who had been divorced from their mother. Family therapy was felt to be indicated in order to help the father to understand the children's ordeal and to help him manage them, as he had not lived with them for over a year. In the sessions the older child, who had nightmares in which she recalled a screaming red monster coming to get her, repetitively drew pictures of cars in flames. It was known from those who had rescued the children that the mother's death screams were extremely disturbing. The screaming red monster nightmare was thought to be the child's abnormal processing of these various traumatic experiences. Because of their young ages (5 and 3 years) they had a very

imperfect conceptualisation of death (Lansdown & Benjamin, 1985). It was helpful to the father to have this demonstrated by the therapist and then, with help, to talk to the children about mother's death within the family belief system but in a mentally healthy way. He explained that the fire had burned mummy a lot and so her body stopped working. Her spirit had gone to heaven, but her body was buried in the ground as it didn't work any more, and the doctors had not been able to make it better as they had made the children better. So there was nowhere on earth for mummy's spirit to live because spirits had to have a body to live on earth. Mummy didn't hurt any more but she could not be with them. God was looking after her spirit. By father establishing his authority and helpfulness with the children, and demonstrating that he too cared about mummy (the children had witnessed their quarrels in the past), it was easier for the children to accept their father's care. The work of grieving for the dead mother could then be done as a family group.

Group therapy

Children who have shared in the same traumatic experiences but were then parted are often helped by being able to meet together for sessions to share their memories and their subsequent experiences. Yule (1989) described how group meetings were helpful to the children involved in the *Herald of Free Enterprise* ferry capsize, who had in some cases felt unable to burden their parents with their own worries as the parents had been traumatised, and the children sensed that they could not cope with the children's problems too. His work with two schools whose pupils were on board the *Jupiter* showed the effectiveness of early intervention. The *Jupiter* was a boat that was holed and sank within ten minutes after leaving port and before any lifeboat drill had occurred (see chapter 8A). There had been little loss of life, but both schools were offered group therapy: one refused and the other accepted. There were marked differences in outcome in the treated group, early intervention bringing about a lessening of fear, intrusion and avoidance phenomena (Yule & Udwin, 1991).

B. Psychodynamic psychotherapy

RICKY EMANUEL and ANNETTE MENDELSOHN

Freud (1926) described the essence of a traumatic situation as the experience of helplessness. A traumatic experience evokes feelings which cannot be processed and thus overwhelms the person. In order to recover from trauma, some processing of the experience has to take place. Psychodynamic psychotherapy with traumatised children attempts to help them assimilate, digest and process experiences that have hitherto proved impossible to manage.

Attaining control or regaining control is a vital step in overcoming a sense of traumatising helplessness. A common way people achieve a sense of power or control is to try to pass on the trauma they have suffered passively, by triumphantly inflicting it, actively, onto someone else. This mechanism perpetuates the cycle of abuse and can be thought of as turning trauma into triumph.

In trying to help traumatised children, it is important to know what factors can foster the development of real resilience and inner strength to face adversity, rather than the more antidevelopmental method of compulsively repeating an experience which was suffered by doing it to someone else. An everyday example encountered in school playgrounds would be of a bully who torments and hurts younger children to make them feel unsafe and vulnerable, when the bully himself maybe at the receiving end of mal-treatment by older siblings or a parent. It is also reflected in the fact that the majority of child abusers have been abused as children themselves.

In a study on resilience, Fonagy *et al* (1994), rather surprisingly, isolated one factor termed 'reflective self-function' that serves as a protection against adversity. This essentially means the capacity to make sense of one's own, and by extension others', emotional experiences.

This function arises out of the child's relationship with its care-giver. Before the baby can make sense of its own experience it has to have repeated experiences of its care giver trying to understand it. This requires the parent to be able to tune in and be responsive a good deal of the time to the baby's communications, and then to be able to think about what is being communi-cated and respond accordingly.

Many psychoanalytical writers, including Winnicott (1985), Bion (1962), Stern (1985) and Fonagy *et al* (1994), see this process as providing the foundation for establishment of the mental equipment necessary for the baby to be able to reflect and think about itself and others. The receptive parent's mind is described by Bion (1962) as a container for the baby's communications. The process of thinking or reflecting upon these communications by the parent, which informs his or her response to the baby, is termed containment.

Child psychotherapy

The setting for psychotherapy

The psychotherapist's primary task in working with traumatised children is to help them make sense of their emotional experience and thus develop their reflective self-function. The therapist is primarily interested in the 'inner world' of the child – that is, the personalised way the child views and experiences life.

The first task in treatment is to establish a setting in which the child can communicate his or her innermost feelings and anxieties. The provision always of the same room, the same time, and so on, facilitates observations and offers a certain predictability and consistency to the child. A further very important ingredient of the total setting is the therapist's receptive frame of mind, open to whatever the child wishes to communicate and whichever way the child wishes to do this. Depending on the age of the child, the therapist provides a range of toys, drawing and modelling equipment to facilitate emotional expression. The child's behaviour is observed in close and continuous detail and an attempt is made to understand what is being communicated both verbally and non-verbally. The therapist also pays close attention to what the child makes him or her feel, as the therapist's mind is used by the child as a container for unbearable feelings, images and emotions. In the same way as we described how a mother has to make sense of her baby's communications before the baby can think for itself (reflective self-function), so the therapist has to think about what is being communicated and *where appropriate*, hand this back in a more understandable and bearable way to the child, by putting these communications into words.

Therapy with traumatised children

Since trauma overwhelms or shatters the mental equipment necessary for thinking, the traumatic experience is usually still raw and undigested where it may have been encapsulated, even after many years. The child first has to learn to label or give names to the elements of his emotional experience. Only then is thought possible about *why* something has happened. You first have to be able to talk about *what* has happened. The naming process can only take place within the context of a relationship with a receptive person. Over time the child begins to identify with the functions performed by the therapist.

The post-traumatic stress debriefing interview is primarily a naming process, and although naming what was previously unnameable and unthinkable is an essential part of containment, it is only the beginning of the process of recovery.

In psychotherapy it is the meaning of that experience that also needs to be worked through. In order to recover fully, Hopkins (1986) writes that we have to help people "not only accept the reality of the traumatic events and the feeling which they engendered but to become able to grieve about the damage done to them and to express appropriate anger about this".

Case vignettes

Case example 1 – bearing the unbearable

Sally was 5 years old when her estranged father, in a jealous rage about her mother having a boyfriend, murdered her mother with a machete while Sally was in the room next door. Sally heard her mother's pleas for help but could not get to the telephone. After the murder her father had blood and bits of her mother's flesh on his clothing, as he took Sally to her relatives before giving himself up to the police.

Sally was cut off and remote in the sessions. She used whatever means she could to distract herself from thinking or using her imagination. Her whole mind seemed to be in a state of traumatised constriction.

In one session, she began using the red and brown paints to make an enormous mess, spilling them over some paper and all over the tiles above the sink. As was usually the case, she denied any feelings or memories associated with this scene, but the therapist's mind was filled with vivid images of the slaughter. This became acute, as Sally squeezed the red and brown paint-covered paper into an oval shape and flattened it on the table so that it looked exactly like an uncooked piece of meat. The therapist's mind was full of horror as he imagined the mother's flesh Sally saw on her father's clothes, images which stayed with the therapist for many hours afterwards. It was easy to understand why a small child would find it virtually impossible to entertain them, and would have no choice but to project them wholesale into someone else's mind, where they could begin to be processed. It was not appropriate to name this experience for Sally, as she was not strong enough emotionally to tolerate any real contact with the full impact of her horror at this stage. It was important that she could communicate it to someone else.

Case example 2 – symbolising experience and naming in play

Three months later Sally was becoming able to 'open up her mind' on some occasions during the sessions, but would rapidly 'close it' again. One of the main difficulties for a child is when trauma in the external world coincides with pre-existing fantasies in the internal world. External and internal reality become confused and responsibility for the trauma becomes difficult to allocate, creating anxiety.

Sally drew a picture of the sun and sky, with some grass and flowers reaching towards the sun. She drew a series of N's in brown, like birds flying towards the sun. She painted a face on the sun and put some glitter onto it. She then painted prominent red lips on the sun and added "nail polish" onto the sun's arms. The therapist commented on the nail polish Sally too was wearing that day like a grown-up lady. Sally said the "sun-girl" was hated by the girls because she was loved by all the "boy-flowers". The big brown N's in the sky started to attack the sun to deface her beauty. The therapist interpreted the N's as No's. Sally said "Yes, they are saying No, No, No we don't want you here".

In the next picture, the No's dirty and spoil the sun-girl by covering her face in red and brown paint. The boy-flowers are helpless to stop it. The sun-girl had to leave and Sally painted in two big brown suitcases. The boy-flowers are sad because they loved the sun-girl, and they bend their heads and lose their colours. The therapist commented on the jealous attacks by the No's on the sun-girl, because she was all glittery and loved by all the boy-flowers. He commented also on the sadness and helplessness of the flowers.

The naming that was taking place was kept at the level of the drawing as it did not seem appropriate to link the feelings to Sally's own feelings directly. She was jealous of her mother who by all accounts was a glamorous young woman and who often went out 'raving' and to parties leaving Sally with a baby-sitter. Sally often wore her mother's make-up and nail varnish and since her death had taken to wearing her clothes.

She often spoke about her wish to be a grown-up lady and not a child. Her rivalry with her mother would have been a normal developmental stage. In her fantasies, a jealous part of her may have wished to spoil her mother's beauty and send her packing, which was matched in external reality when her mother was murdered and defaced (literally) by her jealous father. Sally thus felt she had some inexplicable responsibility for the murder. This could not be dealt with by reassurance alone and had to be expressed and worked through in psychotherapy.

Some months after this painting Sally told the therapist that her mother's killing was "half her fault". The therapist could then begin to work directly on helping Sally differentiate internal and external reality, and clarify that what happened in the external world when her mother was killed was different to what happened in Sally's mind.

Case example 3 – reworking the effects of early trauma in adolescence

At the age of four, Caroline was seriously disfigured as a result of a fire which started when she was alone at home. During the ensuing hospitalisation and for a while subsequently, Caroline was seen by a child psychotherapist and some working-through of the trauma had been achieved.

However, at the age of 12 when Caroline started secondary school in another district, in unfamiliar surroundings and with an unfamiliar peer group, she began to get depressed and withdrawn and was having angry outbursts at home.

Caroline was eager to talk and reveal her preoccupations. The therapist was rapidly flooded with vivid descriptions of the various members of her peer group and her struggle to form relationships. She said she hated school and she hated her class. The only thing she ever looked forward to was going into hospital, to the children's ward she was familiar with, to have her recurrent operations.

During her sessions there seemed to be very little space for thinking with her as the time was filled with excessive detail. The content and flow of the sessions was to be under her direction and control, without time to think.

After several sessions in a similar vein, Caroline one day disclosed, with some trepidation, her preoccupation with organising time. She explained that getting herself through the day involved a series of elaborately planned rituals which began every morning at the crack of dawn. There were various clocks and watches in her bedroom all set to signal the end of one ritual and the start of another. Everything had to be planned and set out in advance so that she could go from one activity to another without having to think about them. Nothing was allowed to disturb her plans.

What Caroline could not prevent was the onset of adolescence. Her world no longer felt certain, predictable or manageable. What had been shelved in latency to allow for adjustment and development was now returning to consciousness, triggered by physiological and psychological changes which seemed to be forcing her to confront once more the full impact of her injuries and how this was going to affect her body image and perception of herself and of others. Angry outbursts also seemed linked to the trauma, the rage she felt at the damage done to her, and the effect this may have on her future life. The attraction to hospital, in spite of painful medical procedures, also became understandable since this rescued her from the arduous task of growing up too quickly, offering respite from having to face a world populated by budding adolescents whose preoccupations about their intact bodies she could hardly bear.

Significant associations between past trauma and present developmental task delineated the direction of psychotherapy, which may never be complete. This reinforces the need to look at trauma from a developmental perspective and underlines the necessity of providing victims with a way to reflect on the continuing emotional impact of trauma on their lives.

These examples, in order of increased complexity, demonstrate some constituents of psychotherapeutic work with traumatised children. The task starts with the need to receive and contain the emotional experience followed by a naming process at one remove, through the medium of painting or play. Putting experiences into words is described as the need for repeated working through of traumatic experiences at different developmental stages.

Research

As far as we are aware there have been no systematic evaluation studies of the outcome of psychodynamic psychotherapy with traumatised children. There have been other studies with different patient groups whose findings may be relevant. Heinicke & Ramsey-Klee (1986) reported a study of psychotherapy with children with emotionally-based learning problems. Children with intensive four-times-weekly therapy improved more than the once-weekly sample. Moran *et al* (1991) reported a study of psychoanalytical treatment with children suffering from poorly controlled brittle diabetes. Two equivalent groups of 12 diabetic children were compared. The treatment group received 3–4 times weekly psychotherapy in addition to medical treatment for an average of 15 weeks. This group showed considerable improvements in diabetic control maintained at one-year follow-up compared with the control group who were offered medical treatment only.

Lush *et al* (1991) compared 35 children in psychotherapy who were fostered or adopted with 13 similar children for whom psychotherapy had been recommended but did not commence. There were indications that psychotherapy benefited these deprived children over several external and internal measures compared with the untreated group. A larger-scale retrospective study by Fonagy & Target (1994) at the Anna Freud Centre looked at extensive documentation of 270 cases of child psychoanalytical therapy. The majority of patients received intensive treatment (4–5 times per week). Half the group had disruptive disorders (DSM–III–R diagnosis) and half had emotional disorders. There were significant improvements in both groups with the number of diagnosable cases decreasing from 100% at the beginning of treatment to 33% at termination. A large-scale long-term prospective study is now in progress, and a large-scale evaluation study of shorter term psychotherapy with sexually abused girls is in progress at the Tavistock Clinic, London.

Summary and conclusion

We have tried to show how a psychodynamic approach to traumatised children provides them with the opportunity to assimilate hitherto unbearable, unthinkable experiences given that the essence of trauma as a feeling of helplessness (Freud, 1926) can overwhelm the capacity to process the emotional experience.

Psychodynamic child psychotherapy requires a consistent structure and setting. The therapist needs to be receptive to the whole range of the child's communications, deep-seated anxieties and feelings, and through a process of naming and description, enables the child to begin to make sense of emotional experiences. This fosters the development of 'reflective self-function' (Fonagy *et al*, 1994). Case vignettes highlight the need to took at trauma from a developmental perspective.

There is a serious problem in the lack of adequately trained practitioners, like child and adolescent psychotherapists, to carry out this kind of work. Provision is patchy throughout the UK. Funding for child psychotherapy training is still lacking in most regions.

We would stress that it is essential that anyone undertaking this kind of work without proper training would require close supervision from a suitably qualified person.

References

Bion, W. R. (1962) *Learning from Experience.* London: Heinemann; reprinted by Maresfield Reprints.

Black, D. & Urbanowicz, M. A. (1985) Bereaved children – family intervention. In *Recent Research in Developmental Psychopathology* (ed. J. E. Stevenson), pp. 179–187. Oxford: Pergamon.

—— & —— (1987) Family intervention with bereaved children. *Journal of Child Psychology and Psychiatry*, **28**, 467–476.

—— & Cottrell, D. (eds) (1993) *Seminars in Child and Adolescent Psychiatry*. London: Gaskell.

Bolton, D., Collins, S. & Steinberg, D. (1983) The treatment of obsessive–compulsive disorder in adolescence: a report of fifteen cases. *British Journal of Psychiatry*, **142**, 456–464.

Dare, C. (1985) Family therapy. In *Child and Adolescent Psychiatry: Modern Approaches* (2nd edn) (eds M. Rutter & L. Hersov), pp. 809–825. Oxford: Blackwell.

Fonagy, P. & Target, M. (1994) The efficacy of psychoanalysis for children with disruptive disorders. *Journal of the American Academy of Child Psychiatry*, **33**, 45–55.

——, Steele, M., Steele, H., *et al* (1994) The theory and practice of resilience. *Journal of Child Psychology and Psychiatry*, **35**, 231.

Freud, S. (1926) *Inhibitions, Symptoms and Anxiety*. Standard Edition 20, 1959. London: Hogarth Press.

Gelfand, D. M. & Hartmann, D. P. (1984) *Child Behaviour Analysis and Therapy* (2nd edn). Oxford: Pergamon.

Heinicke, C. M. & Ramsey-Klee, D. M. (1986) Outcome of child psychotherapy as a function of frequency of sessions. *Journal of the American Academy of Child Psychiatry*, **25**, 247–253.

Herbert, M. (1981) *Behavioural Treatment of Problem Children – A Practice Manual*. London: Academic Press.

Hopkins, J. (1986) Solving the mystery of monsters: steps towards the recovery from trauma. *Journal of Child Psychotherapy*, **12**, 61.

Kendall, P. C. (1991) *Child and Adolescent Therapy: Cognitive–Behavioral Procedures*. New York: Guilford.

Lansdown, R. & Benjamin, G. (1985) The development of the concept of death in children aged 5–9 years. *Child Care, Health and Development*, **11**, 13–20.

Lush, D., Boston, M. & Grainger, E. (1991) Evaluation of psychoanalytic psychotherapy with children: therapist's assessments and predictions. *Psychoanalytic Psychotherapy*, **5**, 191–234.

Moran, G. S., Fonagy, P., Kurtz, A., *et al* (1991) A controlled study of the psychoanalytic treatment of brittle diabetes. *Journal of the American Academy of Child Psychiatry*, **30**, 241–257.

Robinson, R. C. & Mitchell, J. T. (1993) Evaluation of psychological debriefings. *Journal of Traumatic Stress*, **6**, 367–382.

Rutter, M., Taylor, E. & Hersov, L. (eds) (1994) *Child and Adolescent Psychiatry: Modern Approaches* (3rd edn). Oxford: Blackwell.

Siegel, D. J. (1995) Memory, trauma and psychotherapy: a cognitive science view. *Journal of Psychotherapy Practice and Research*, **4**, 93–122.

Stern, D. (1985) *The Interpersonal World of the Infant*. London: Basic Books.

Winnicott, D. (1985) *The Maturational Process and the Facilitating Environment*. London: Hogarth Press and Institute of Psychoanalysis.

Yule, W. (1989) The effects of disasters on children. *Newsletter of the Association of Child Psychology and Psychiatry*, **11**, 3–6.

—— & Udwin, O. (1991) Screening child survivors for post-traumatic stress disorders – experiences from the *Jupiter* sinking. *British Journal of Clinical Psychology*, **30**, 131–138.

19 Psychopharmacology

MARTIN NEWMAN

The main treatments for PTSD are psychological, as described elsewhere in this book. However, an increasing understanding of the physiological and neurophysiological changes that occur in PTSD has led to the hope that certain medications may be helpful in their treatment.

However, most of the investigations into the physiological changes that occur in PTSD have been in male Vietnam combat veterans suffering from chronic PTSD. It is not clear how applicable these findings are to PTSD due to other causes, and in other people. It is not clear to what extent the findings apply to children.

In addition, while many drugs have been reported to be helpful in the treatment of PTSD, there are very few satisfactory studies (Davidson *et al*, 1990). Most of the reports are case reports or uncontrolled studies, often carried out in male combat veterans suffering from chronic PTSD. Since the natural course of PTSD over time is still unclear, it is difficult to evaluate the effects of treatment accurately in some studies. It is still unclear for how long, and at what doses, medication should be prescribed in the treatment of PTSD. Methods of assessing the severity of PTSD and the response to treatment vary. It is unclear how drug treatments should be combined with psychological treatments, if at all. Hence, in reading this chapter, it is important to bear in mind that pharmacotherapy for PTSD is not, at the present, the main approach to treatment.

Physiological changes in PTSD

As already mentioned, most of the studies have been on male Vietnam combat veterans. There appears to be overactivity of the autonomic nervous system in these patients (van der Kolk, 1987; Friedman, 1993). The locus coeruleus may also be involved. It has been suggested that lasting neurobiological and behavioural changes are produced by repeated traumatisation, as in child abuse, or by one trauma followed by intrusive re-experiences ('kindling') (van der Kolk, 1987). Changes of sleep architecture in PTSD have also been found by some (Schlosberg & Benjamin, 1978; Lavie *et al*, 1979; Friedman, 1988; Ross *et al*, 1989*a,b*; Lipper *et al*, 1989).

These findings have led to the study of drugs that affect the autonomic nervous system, reducing physiological arousal or reducing anxiety, or which may have effects on any disturbances in sleep patterns.

Comorbidity

Some studies have identified a significant level of coexisting psychiatric illness in certain PTSD sufferers. For example, depression, substance misuse and personality disorder may coexist with PTSD (Sierles *et al*, 1983; Davidson *et al*, 1985; Kauffman *et al*, 1987; Friedman, 1993). These studies were small, and the patients were not randomly selected. Further studies are required to determine the frequency of other psychiatric disorders in PTSD sufferers, and to determine what factors may influence their occurrence – for example, the type of trauma experienced, the characteristics of the patient and his family, the characteristics of the disorder experienced, and the length of time since the trauma.

Goals for drug treatments in PTSD

These have been summarised (Davidson, 1992) as reducing avoidant symptoms and intermittently intrusive symptoms, reduction of symptoms of persistent hyperarousal, relief of depression and anhedonia, improvement of impulse regulation, and control of acute dissociative and psychotic features. Davidson pointed out that treatment goals may differ from one time to another in the same patient, according to the symptoms that are prominent at the time. The aim is to bring troublesome symptoms under greater control, thereby assisting the patient to deal with psychological factors.

Uses of medication

Yule (1994) pointed out that the distinction between acute and chronic subtypes of PTSD is arbitrary. Acute PTSD is defined in DSM–IV (American Psychiatric Association, 1994) when the duration of symptoms is less than three months. Chronic PTSD is defined when symptoms have lasted three months or more. Most studies have been on patients with chronic PTSD as determined by DSM–III (American Psychiatric Association, 1980) or DSM–III–R (American Psychiatric Association, 1987) criteria.

Tricyclic antidepressants

Marshall (1975) reported that imipramine appeared to reduce night terrors in patients with PTSD. Burstein (1984) administered imipramine (50–350 mg/day) to ten patients with PTSD of recent onset, and noted improvement in forced recollections, sleep and dream disturbance, and flashbacks. Falcon *et al* (1985), in a retrospective, uncontrolled study, reported tricyclic antidepressants to be helpful. Bleich *et al* (1986) retrospectively studied 25 patients with PTSD, and noted that antidepressants had had good or moderate results in 67% of cases. Amitriptyline alone was given to 14 patients, and gave good or moderate improvement in four and eight cases respectively (85%) after it had been prescribed for a period of six months. This finding might suggest that, for pharmacotherapy to achieve its fullest effect in PTSD, it is necessary to exceed the usual period for response to treatment seen in most anxiety or depressive disorders (Davidson *et al*, 1990).

Frank *et al* (1988) carried out a double-blind, randomised 8-week clinical trial in 34 male Vietnam veterans with PTSD. They gave placebo, imipramine or phenelzine to each patient. The dose of imipramine was initially 50 mg/day, and it was adjusted up to 300 mg/day to achieve blood levels in a therapeutic range. The starting dose of phenelzine was 15 mg/day and was adjusted up to 75 mg/day to achieve more than 90% MAO inhibition. They found that symptoms of PTSD, but not depression, improved significantly after treatment with imipramine or phenelzine, compared with placebo.

Davidson *et al* (1990) compared amitriptyline with placebo in 46 veterans with chronic PTSD. They found that, in a group completing eight weeks of treatment, amitriptyline was superior to placebo on certain assessment scales. Drug–placebo differences were greater in the presence of comorbidity in general, although recovery rates were uniformly low in the presence of major depression, panic disorder, and alcoholism. At the end of treatment, 64% of the amitriptyline and 72% of the placebo samples still met diagnostic criteria for PTSD.

A more recent study (Kosten *et al*, 1991) was an 8-week randomised trial of 60 male combat veterans suffering from PTSD. Both imipramine and phenelzine were found to reduce PTSD symptoms significantly as assessed by the Horowitz Impact of Event Scale (Horowitz *et al*, 1979), with a 44% improvement with phenelzine and a 25% improvement with imipramine. Initial mild to moderate depressive symptoms did not significantly improve.

Reist *et al* (1989) found no significant difference between desipramine (at doses up to 200 mg/day) and placebo in a four-week crossover trial. It has been suggested (Kudler *et al*, 1989; Frank *et al*, 1990; Davidson, 1992) that this may be because of the design of the study, small study size, the failure to evaluate comorbidity, insufficient doses of antidepressant, and the fact that the trial lasted only four weeks.

Davidson *et al* (1993) attempted to identify predictors of response to pharmacotherapy in PTSD in their 8-week placebo-controlled, double-blind study of 62 combat veterans with PTSD. Amitriptyline was prescribed; 46 patients completed eight weeks of treatment. They found that drug response was related to lower baseline levels of depression, neuroticism, combat intensity, and one intrusion and four avoidance symptoms of PTSD. A number of individual symptoms were associated with a poor response to treatment, including impaired concentration/memory, somatic anxiety, psychic anxiety, and feelings of guilt.

Chen (1991) reported the use of clomipramine to treat seven Vietnam veterans who were in-patients with PTSD, and found that it was of benefit in six of the seven in reducing the severity of intrusive symptoms.

Monoamine oxidase inhibitors (MAOIs)

Hogben & Cornfield (1981) reported five cases of PTSD who, when prescribed phenelzine (45–75 mg/day), experienced reduction in traumatic dreams, startle reactions and violent outbursts. Phenelzine has also been reported to be helpful by others (Levenson *et al*, 1982; Walker, 1982).

Davidson *et al* (1987) described the results of a pilot study of phenelzine in 11 veterans of the Second World War or Vietnam. Ten patients completed four weeks of treatment, at which point two were removed from the study because of poor response or deterioration, while another was removed because of side-effects. The daily dose of phenelzine was 45 mg/day in all but one of the patients. After four weeks treatment, 70% of the group were rated as showing clinical global improvement, whilst 80% rated themselves as having improved. After six weeks treatment, the figures were 85% and 100% respectively. Side-effects of the medication were common. The authors point out the limitations of this study and recommend a double-blind placebo-controlled assessment of phenelzine.

Frank *et al* (1988), in the 8-week trial mentioned earlier, found phenelzine to be somewhat more effective than imipramine. However, Shestatzky *et al* (1988) carried out a study of 13 patients meeting DSM–III criteria for PTSD who participated in a random-assignment, double-blind crossover trial comparing phenelzine (45–75 mg/day) and placebo. Ten patients completed at least four weeks of each treatment phase. Clinical response to phenelzine did not differ from placebo, and overall improvement at the end of the study could not be attributed to the active drug.

Kosten *et al* (1991) reported treating 60 male combat veterans with PTSD in an 8-week, randomised trial comparing phenelzine, imipramine and placebo. As mentioned earlier, they found that both phenelzine and imipramine were of benefit.

Fluoxetine

Early reports suggest that fluoxetine, a serotonin reuptake inhibitor, may be helpful in PTSD (Shay, 1992; Davidson, 1992). Shay (1992) reported an uncontrolled study in which 28 depressed male Vietnam combat veterans were prescribed fluoxetine, after other antidepressants had not been helpful. Four discontinued the drug. The remaining 24 received fluoxetine for 12 months or more. Shay reported a reduction in explosive outbursts and elevation of mood in the majority of the veterans. A frequent side-effect was insomnia. Davidson *et al* (1991) gave fluoxetine to five non-veteran patients with PTSD. The maximum doses ranged from 20–80 mg/day, and treatment was continued for between 8 and 32 weeks. Fluoxetine was associated with marked improvement of both intrusive and avoidant symptoms. They also noted that fluoxetine facilitated trauma-focused psychotherapy in two adult victims of childhood sexual trauma. Further research is needed to ascertain the value of fluoxetine, and other serotonin reuptake inhibitors, in the treatment of PTSD (March, 1992; Friedman, 1993; van der Kolk & Fisler, 1993).

Anxiolytics

PTSD patients exhibit symptoms associated with anxiety disorders, such as anxiety, fear, autonomic hyperarousal, irritability and insomnia. In addition to antidepressants, which have an anxiolytic effect, sympatholytic drugs (such as propranolol and the alpha-2 adrenergic agonist, clonidine, which reduces sympathetic activity through inhibition of the locus coeruleus) and benzo-diazepines (such as diazepam and alprazolam) have been used in the treatment of PTSD. Buspirone has also been reported to be useful.

Famularo *et al* (1988), in one of the few studies of the treatment of children, reported 11 cases of acute PTSD in children (mean age 8.5 years), each of whom had been physically or sexually abused. Propranolol, at a starting dose of 0.8 mg/kg/day, was gradually increased over a two-week period until a top dosage of approximately 2.5 mg/kg/day was reached. Scores for PTSD symptomatology decreased during treatment with propranolol. The authors stated that they considered it likely that at least some of the improvement may have been caused by a placebo effect associated with the belief that the medication would be helpful rather than by an actual pharmacological effect.

In another study (Kolb *et al*, 1984), propranolol was given to 12 Vietnam combat veterans with chronic PTSD, and clonidine was given to nine such veterans. The dose of propranolol was gradually raised until the patients were taking from 120–160 mg propranolol daily. The dose of clonidine given was 0.2–0.4 mg daily. They were followed up for a six-month period; 11 of the 12 men on propranolol reported a positive change in self-assessment. When asked about specific symptoms, 11 of 12 reported reduced explosive-ness, 11 had fewer nightmares and dreams, 9 had improved sleep, 10 had fewer intrusive thoughts of combat, 7 had a lessened startle reaction, and 6 had lessened hyperalertness. Eight of the 12 reported evidence of improve-ment on psychosocial adaptation. Side-effects included depression, fatigue, forgetfulness, sexual impairment, bradycardia, hypotension, and mental confusion at higher dosage.

In the patients prescribed clonidine, eight of the nine patients assessed themselves more able to control their emotions. Eight of the nine reported decreased explosiveness, seven reported fewer dreams and nightmares, six had better sleep, and four each reported lessened startle, less intrusive thinking, and reduced hyperalertness. All had symptomatic improvement, and four returned to work. The authors noted that six of the nine patients prescribed clonidine had accompanying chronic physical disorders.

Clonidine in combination with a tricyclic antidepressant has been reported to be useful by Kinzie & Leung (1989), who described the addition of clonidine to imipramine in the treatment of PTSD in a prospective pilot study of 12 Cambodian patients. The authors reported that the combination of imipramine and clonidine was well tolerated, and recommended further studies of this combination as a possible treatment for severely depressed and traumatised patients.

Van der Kolk (1987) observed that clonidine attenuated PTSD-driven self-mutilatory behaviour when given on an as-required basis. Further studies of clonidine in the treatment of PTSD are required.

With regard to benzodiazepines, there are reports that clonazepam and alprazolam may be of benefit (Davidson, 1992). Braun *et al* (1990) reported a random assignment, double-blind crossover trial comparing alprazolam and placebo in PTSD. Ten patients fulfilling DSM–III criteria for PTSD completed five weeks of treatment on each agent. Improvement in anxiety symptoms was significantly greater during alprazolam treatment, but modest in extent. Symptoms specific to PTSD were not significantly altered.

However, benzodiazepines have a high risk of addiction and dependency, and this may be especially important in PTSD, where patients already have a high risk of alcohol and drug misuse and dependency (Branchey *et al*, 1984). There is also a risk that benzodiazepines will release impulsive or antisocial behaviour (Davidson, 1992). It may be that benzodiazepines may be helpful in PTSD for carefully selected patients (Friedman, 1993), but care is needed in their use.

Buspirone has been reported to be useful (Silver *et al*, 1990; Wells *et al*, 1991; LaPorta & Ware, 1992), but these case reports need to be substantiated by further research.

Carbamazepine and lithium

Lipper *et al* (1986) studied the use of carbamazepine in ten Vietnam combat veterans with PTSD, in a five-week open clinical trial. They found that it reduced intrusive symptoms such as traumatic nightmares, flashbacks, and intrusive recollections. Wolf *et al* (1988) found that carbamazepine reduced impulsivity, irritability and violent behaviour in ten war veterans with PTSD.

There are no published systematic double-blind trials of lithium in PTSD. However, there are uncontrolled clinical reports that lithium is of benefit in PTSD, even for patients without a personal or family history of bipolar affective disorder or cyclothymia (van der Kolk, 1983; Kitchner & Greenstein, 1985). Van der Kolk (1987) reported that 14 out of 27 patients treated with lithium exhibited diminished sympathetic arousal, a decreased tendency to react to stress as if it were a recurrence of their original trauma, and reduced alcohol intake.

Valproate

Valproate is another drug which, like lithium and carbamazepine, has been shown to interfere with limbic kindling. Fesler (1991) reported an open clinical trial conducted in 16 Vietnam veterans with combat-related PTSD. Ten out of the 16 patients were reported as showing significant improvement, especially in hyperarousal/hyperreactivity symptoms. The use of valproate and carbamazepine in the treatment of panic and PTSD, withdrawal states and behavioural dyscontrol syndromes is reviewed by Keck *et al* (1992).

Naltrexone

Naltrexone is an oral opiate antagonist. Bills & Kreisler (1993) postulated that flashbacks may represent a form of self-injurious behaviour and that painful stimuli, leading to increased release of endorphins, might explain repetitive behaviour through a positive reinforcement mechanism. They report using naltrexone on two patients and found that, at a dose of 50 mg/day, both patients experienced a decrease in the number of flashbacks. However, the authors themselves pointed out that further controlled studies would be needed to assess the value of such treatment.

Neuroleptics

Friedman (1989) stated that neuroleptics can be useful in the treatment of PTSD, but that they are not part of routine treatment. Dillard *et al* (1993) reported a case involving a 44-year-old combat veteran who experienced severe flashbacks of the time that he spent in Vietnam, whose symptoms improved while he was taking thioridazine. However, there are no published controlled clinical trials of the effects of neuroleptic drugs on PTSD patients. Some argue that they do have a role in the treatment of refractory PTSD marked by paranoid behaviour, fragmented ego boundaries, self-destructive behaviour, and frequent flashback episodes with frank auditory and visual hallucinations of traumatic episodes (Friedman, 1981, 1991; Walker, 1982; Atri & Gilliam, 1989), while Meuser & Butler (1987) suggested that PTSD patients with auditory hallucinations constitute a distinct subgroup for whom neuroleptics are specifically indicated. Davidson (1992) pointed out that psychotic symptoms may be dissociative experiences in PTSD patients, and be better managed by other techniques.

Recommendations for use

Most of the studies to date suggest that successful drug treatments for PTSD generally result in a decrease in DSM–III intrusive recollection and arousal symptoms. Avoidant symptoms, grief, problems with intimacy and moral pain do not appear to respond to medication (Friedman, 1993). Medication may have a role when the intensity of symptoms (e.g. anxiety, depression, sleep disturbance, autonomic arousal) is so great that adaptive coping is prevented. Reduction of these symptoms may prevent additional traumatisation and facilitate other therapeutic work (van der Kolk, 1987). McFarlane (1989) argued that the successful treatment of PTSD is difficult unless any associated psychiatric disorder is also treated, and this view was supported by Friedman (1993).

Davidson (1992) suggested that, when deciding whether to use drugs in the treatment of PTSD, it is necessary to exclude the effects of any head injury, and to identify any alcohol or drug misuse. He suggested that a reasonable first-choice drug treatment for PTSD is a tricyclic antidepressant. He recommended that treatment should continue for at least eight weeks, and improvement looked for within specific areas. Davidson stated that fluoxetine or another selective serotonin reuptake inhibitor may be another reasonable early-choice treatment. He suggested that propranolol, clonazepam, lithium or carbamezepine may be second-line drug treatments, while non-response to one or more of these agents might then lead to the use of phenelzine or clonidine. Occasionally, the use of two or more psychotropic drugs may be indicated. The duration of drug treatment is unclear, but it may need to be continued long-term.

Future research directions

Many of the reports into possible drug treatments are unsatisfactory, for a number of reasons (McFarlane, 1989; Davidson *et al*, 1990). At present, the number of published research findings with regard to drug therapies of PTSD is relatively small. Almost all quantitative research is on male combat veterans. There is a lack of standardised protocols. Many reports are uncontrolled studies or case reports. In order to establish the role of pharmacotherapy in PTSD, carefully designed, double-blind controlled studies are required, with larger clinical samples. More work needs to be done with patients who have experienced other types of trauma. The use of drugs to treat PTSD in children requires further careful research. There needs to be better attention to dosage, and the results of treatment need to be assessed with well-validated observer rating scales (Kudler *et al*, 1989). Studies need to be controlled and double-blind, with attention paid to placebo effects. There is a need to consider the possibility that PTSD patients may have coexisting psychiatric illnesses, such as depression. The beneficial effects of drugs, and the long-term outcomes, need to be carefully recorded.

McFarlane (1989), in his review of treatment studies of PTSD, pointed out that there is little knowledge of the natural history of PTSD against which to measure the effectiveness of specific treatment interventions. He also pointed out that there has been little discussion of sufferers' attitudes to treatment or of their acceptance of different forms of treatment. McFarlane recommended that, in future studies of PTSD, there should be a careful description of selection bias, past and concurrent treatments received by the patient, the time between exposure to the trauma and the start of treatment, the impact of the traumatic event on other family members, and the age of the patient, and the different phenomenological components of PTSD should be separately assessed. McFarlane also recommended case-control design, and careful documentation of negative effects of treatment. Davidson (1992) pointed out that it remains unclear how important PTSD subtypes are in relation to response to drug treatments, and the optimum length of treatment and relapse rates over time are uncertain. The effect of comorbidity on selection and effectiveness of treatment also needs further investigation, as does the question of whether earlier intervention leads to a more favourable prognosis. Further studies are needed to find out more about predictors of response to pharmacotherapy, as this is both clinically and economically important (Davidson *et al*, 1993).

Conclusions

At present, drug treatments alone do not provide complete relief of the suffering in PTSD, and the main use of drug treatments would seem to be in support of psychological treatments (McFarlane, 1989; Friedman, 1993). Further research is required to compare drug and psychological treatments of PTSD, and to identify the mechanisms by which drugs may be helpful. In addition, further studies of the effects of trauma on neurophysiological functioning may provide a basis for more rational pharmacotherapy for PTSD (Friedman, 1988).

References

American Psychiatric Association (1980) *Diagnostic and Statistical Manual of Mental Disorders* (3rd edn) (DSM–III). Washington, DC: APA.
—— (1987) *Diagnostic and Statistical Manual of Mental Disorders* (3rd edn, revised) (DSM–III–R). Washington, DC: APA.
Atri, P. B. & Gilliam, J. H. (1989) Comments on posttraumatic stress disorder. *American Journal of Psychiatry*, **146**, 128.
Bills, L. J. & Kreisler, K. (1993) Treatments of flashbacks with naltrexone (letter). *American Journal of Psychiatry*, **150**, 1430.
Bleich, A., Siegel, B., Garb, R., *et al* (1986) Post-traumatic stress disorder following combat exposure: clinical features and psychopharmacological treatment. *British Journal of Psychiatry*, **149**, 365–369.
Branchey, L., Davis, W. & Lieber, C. S. (1984) Alcoholism in Vietnam and Korea veterans: a long-term follow-up. *Alcoholism: Clinical and Experimental Research*, **8**, 572–575.
Braun, P., Greenberg, D., Dasberg, H., *et al* (1990) Core symptoms of posttraumatic stress disorder unimproved by alprazolam treatment. *Journal of Clinical Psychiatry*, **51**, 236–238.
Burstein, A. (1984) Treatment of post-traumatic stress disorder with imipramine. *Psychosomatics*, **25**, 681–687.
Chen, C.-J. (1991) The obsessive quality and clomipramine treatment in PTSD (letter). *American Journal of Psychiatry*, **148**, 1087–1088.
Davidson, J. (1992) Drug therapy of post-traumatic stress disorder. *British Journal of Psychiatry*, **160**, 309–314.
——, Swartz, M., Storck, M., *et al* (1985) A diagnostic and family study of posttraumatic stress disorder. *American Journal of Psychiatry*, **142**, 90–93.
——, Walker, J. I. & Kilts, C. (1987) A pilot study of phenelzine in the treatment of post-traumatic stress disorder. *British Journal of Psychiatry*, **150**, 252–255.
——, Kudler, H., Smith, R., *et al* (1990) Treatment of posttraumatic stress disorder with amitriptyline and placebo. *Archives of General Psychiatry*, **47**, 259–266.
——, Roth, S. & Newman, E. (1991) Fluoxetine in post-traumatic stress disorder. *Journal of Traumatic Stress*, **4**, 419–423.
——, Kudler, H. S., Saunders, W. B., *et al* (1993) Predicting response to amitriptyline in posttraumatic stress disorder. *American Journal of Psychiatry*, **150**, 1024–1029.

Dillard, M. L., Bendfeldt, F. & Jernigan, P. (1993) Use of thioridazine in post-traumatic stress disorder. *Southern Medical Journal*, **86**, 1276–1278.

Falcon, S., Ryan, C., Chamberlain, K., *et al* (1985) Tricyclics: possible treatment for posttraumatic stress disorder. *Journal of Clinical Psychiatry*, **46**, 385–389.

Famularo, R., Kinscherff, R. & Fenton, T. (1988) Propranolol treatment for childhood posttraumatic stress disorder, acute type. *American Journal of Diseases of Children*, **142**, 1244–1247.

Fesler, F. A. (1991) Valproate in combat-related posttraumatic stress disorder. *Journal of Clinical Psychiatry*, **52**, 361–364.

Frank, J. B., Kosten, T. R., Giller, E. L., *et al* (1988) A randomized clinical trial of phenelzine and imipramine for posttraumatic stress disorder. *American Journal of Psychiatry*, **145**, 1289–1291.

——, Kosten, T. R. & Giller, E. L. (1990) Antidepressants in the treatment of PTSD (letter). *American Journal of Psychiatry*, **147**, 260.

Friedman, M. J. (1981) Post-Vietnam syndrome: recognition and management. *Psychosomatics*, **22**, 931–943.

—— (1988) Toward rational pharmacotherapy for posttraumatic stress disorder: an interim report. *American Journal of Psychiatry*, **145**, 281–285.

—— (1989) Comments on posttraumatic stress disorder (reply). *American Journal of Psychiatry*, **146**, 129.

—— (1991) Biological approaches to the diagnosis and treatment of post-traumatic stress disorder. *Journal of Traumatic Stress*, **4**, 67–91.

—— (1993) Psychobiological and pharmacological approaches to treatment. In *International Handbook of Traumatic Stress Syndromes* (eds J. P. Wilson & B. Raphael), pp. 785–794. New York: Plenum Press.

Hogben, G. L. & Cornfield, R. B. (1981) Treatment of traumatic war neurosis with phenelzine. *Archives of General Psychiatry*, **38**, 440–445.

Horowitz, M., Wilner, N. & Alvarez, W. (1979) Impact of Event Scale: a measure of subjective stress. *Psychosomatic Medicine*, **41**, 209–218.

Kauffman, C. D., Reist, C., Djenderedjian, A., *et al* (1987) Biological markers of affective disorders and posttraumatic stress disorder: a pilot study with desipramine. *Journal of Clinical Psychiatry*, **48**, 366–367.

Keck, P. E. Jr, McElroy, S. L. & Friedman, L. M. (1992) Valproate and carbamazepine in the treatment of posttraumatic stress disorders, withdrawal states, and behavioural dyscontrol syndromes. *Journal of Clinical Psychopharmacology*, **12** (suppl. 1), 36S–41S.

Kinzie, J. D. & Leung, P. (1989) Clonidine in Cambodian patients with posttraumatic stress disorder. *Journal of Nervous and Mental Disease*, **177**, 546–550.

Kitchner, I. & Greenstein, R. (1985) Low dose lithium carbonate in the treatment of post traumatic stress disorder: brief communication. *Military Medicine*, **150**, 378–381.

Kolb, L. C., Burris, B. C. & Griffiths, S. (1984) Propranolol and clonidine in treatment of the chronic post-traumatic stress disorders of war. In *Post-Traumatic Stress Disorder: Psychological and Biological Sequelae* (ed. B. A. van der Kolk), pp. 97–105. Washington, DC: APA.

Kosten, T. R., Frank, J. B., Dan, E., *et al* (1991) Pharmacotherapy for posttraumatic stress disorder using phenelzine or imipramine. *Journal of Nervous and Mental Disease*, **179**, 366–370.

Kudler, H. S., Davidson, J. R., Stein, R., *et al* (1989) Measuring results of treatment of PTSD. *American Journal of Psychiatry*, **146**, 1645–1646.

LaPorta, L. D. & Ware, M. R. (1992) Buspirone in the treatment of posttraumatic stress disorder. *Journal of Clinical Psychopharmacology*, **12**, 133–134.

Lavie, P., Hefez, A., Halperin, G., *et al* (1979) Long-term effects of traumatic war-related events on sleep. *American Journal of Psychiatry*, **136**, 175–178.

Levenson, H., Lanman, R. & Rankin, M. (1982) Traumatic war neurosis and phenelzine (letter). *Archives of General Psychiatry*, **39**, 1345.

Lipper, S., Davidson, J. R. T., Grady, T. A., *et al* (1986) Preliminary study of carbamazepine in post-traumatic stress disorders in Vietnam veterans. *Psychosomatics*, **27**, 849–854.

——, Edinger, J. D. & Stein, R. M. (1989) Sleep disturbance and PTSD. *American Journal of Psychiatry*, **146**, 1644–1645.

McFarlane, A. C. (1989) The treatment of post-traumatic stress disorder. *British Journal of Medical Psychology*, **62**, 81–90.

March, J. S. (1992) Fluoxetine and fluvoxamine in PTSD (letter). *American Journal of Psychiatry*, **149**, 413.

Marshall, J. R. (1975) The treatment of night terrors associated with the posttraumatic syndrome. *American Journal of Psychiatry*, **132**, 293–295.

Meuser, K. T. & Butler, R. W. (1987) Auditory hallucinations in combat-related chronic posttraumatic stress disorder. *American Journal of Psychiatry*, **144**, 299–302.

Reist, C., Kauffman, C. D., Haier, R. J., *et al* (1989) A controlled trial of desipramine in 18 men with posttraumatic stress disorder. *American Journal of Psychiatry*, **146**, 513–516.

Ross, R. J., Ball, W. A., Sullivan, K. A., *et al* (1989*a*) Sleep disturbance as the halimark of posttraumatic stress disorder. *American Journal of Psychiatry*, **146**, 697–707.

——, ——, ——, *et al* (1989*b*) Sleep disturbance and PTSD: reply. *American Journal of Psychiatry*, **146**, 1645.

Schlosberg, A. & Benjamin, M. (1978) Sleep patterns in three acute combat fatigue cases. *Journal of Clinical Psychiatry*, **39**, 546–549.

Shay, J. (1992) Fluoxetine reduces explosiveness and elevates mood of Vietnam combat vets with PTSD. *Journal of Traumatic Stress*, **5**, 97–101.

Shestatzky, M., Greenberg, D. & Lerer, B. (1988) A controlled trial of phenelzine in posttraumatic stress disorder. *Psychiatry Research*, **24**, 149–155.

Sierles, F. S., Chen, J.-J., McFarland, R. E., *et al* (1983) Post-traumatic stress disorder and concurrent psychiatric illness. *American Journal of Psychiatry*, **140**, 1177–1179.

Silver, J. M., Sandberg, D. P. & Hales, R. E. (1990) New approaches in the pharmacotherapy of posttraumatic stress disorder. *Journal of Clinical Psychiatry*, **51** (suppl.), 33–38.

Van der Kolk, B. A. (1983) Psychopharmacological issues in posttraumatic stress disorder. *Hospital and Community Psychiatry*, **34**, 683–691.

—— (1987) The drug treatment of post-traumatic stress disorder. *Journal of Affective Disorders*, **13**, 203–213.

—— & Fisler, R. E. (1993) The biologic basis of posttraumatic stress. *Primary Care*, **20**, 414–432.

Walker, J. L. (1982) Chemotherapy of traumatic war stress. *Military Medicine*, **147**, 1029–1033.

Wells, B. G., Chu, C. C., Johnson, R., *et al* (1991) Buspirone in the treatment of posttraumatic stress disorder. *Pharmacotherapy*, **11**, 340–343.

Wolf, M. E., Alavi, A. & Mosnaim, A. D. (1988) Posttraumatic stress disorder in Vietnam veterans – clinical and EEG findings: possible therapeutic effects of carbamazepine. *Biological Psychiatry*, **23**, 642–644.

Yule, W. (1994) Posttraumatic stress disorders. In *Child and Adolescent Psychiatry: Modern Approaches* (3rd edn) (eds M. Rutter, E. Taylor & L. Hersov), pp. 392–406. Oxford: Blackwell Scientific.

20 Service provision

A. The role of the police

THOMAS DICKIE

The statutory duty of the police is to guard, patrol and watch so as to prevent the commission of offences, preserve order and protect life and property. In the context of a major incident this role requires enlargement as follows:

(a) the notification of emergency services;
(b) coordination and facilitation of the efforts of essential services;
(c) to perform police functions;
(d) to contribute, wherever necessary, to the function of any of the essential services.

(The task is not to take over the work of colleagues in the fire and ambulance services, but to provide assistance, for example as stretcher-bearers or in the movement of equipment.)

The task of the first officer is as follows:

(a) (S)he must not get involved in rescue work.
(b) (S)he must assess the situation, correctly identify what has happened and ensure that the necessary people are told about it.
(c) (S)he must commence a log. Since it often happens in times of stress and confusion that we lose all perception of time, the log should have a time section and action sheet so as to allow an accurate record and assistance in the assessment of performance in subsequent debriefing.

The following specific information is required from the first officer.

(a) The exact location must be known. If it is an urban area, streets and roads must be identified and in a rural area the grid reference, nearest landmark and identifiable features should be pinpointed.
(b) The type of incident should be defined, e.g. a serious fire, gas explosion or a bomb attack.
(c) The police need to know hazards and potential hazards, for example, an emergency response to the release of toxic fumes requires knowledge of wind direction.

(d)   Specific information about access to the disaster site, particularly with reference to approach routes for emergency vehicles.

(e)   The police need an estimate of the number of casualties, the extent of their injuries, and liaison with ambulance services and health authorities so as to estimate response requirements and the possibility of activating hospitals to a major incident alert status.

(f)   Which emergency services are present and what others are required.

Good communication is essential; a police service must create a forward control point serviced by a senior police incident officer with specific tasks such as the role of coordination between the resources. Liaison between services and agencies should not be initiated only with the onset of disaster; as indicated in chapter 26, pre-planned liaison is essential.

The police incident officer must establish an incident control post at which will be found representatives of all services and agencies. A rendezvous point must also be established and manned sufficiently for accurate tabulation of the arrival of resources, without delay. People arriving at a major incident look to such a point for direction as to their duties and functions, and it is imperative that this rendezvous is easily found in a suitable location to accommodate large numbers of people from the emergency services, from the medical profession and from voluntary organisations.

Security is another primary concern both for the proper conduct of police and other emergency activities and for protection of the scene, particularly if a crime has been committed. Normally two cordons of police officers achieve this; an inner cordon where only rescue resources are present and an outer cordon to keep public and unauthorised persons at bay. The rendezvous point should touch the outer cordon and the incident control post, with emergency services working between the inner and outer cordons.

Setting up this system may cause chaos to the motoring public, and traffic control is an important task which the incident officer often will delegate via the senior traffic officer present.

Major incidents create crowd problems, and no matter how often personnel dealing with an incident go to the media requesting the public to stay away, they continue to come. For example, the disaster at Lockerbie encroached onto the A74 road and many accidents occurred on the stretch of this road adjacent to the incident scene, caused by members of the motoring public who were either stopping or travelling slowly past. Accidents were caused by vehicles shunting into each other. An essential police task is to make sure that the public are going to be safe, are not going to interfere with rescue attempts, and are not able to interfere with evidence.

If required, police will assess the setting-up of a casualty clearing station and, along with colleagues in the ambulance service, will move casualties to this temporary place of refuge for further treatment, stabilisation and transportation to casualty-receiving hospitals.

The protection of property continues to be a police duty, not just because of its ownership but because of a need to secure information for evidential purposes.

Temporary mortuary facilities may be required, and there is a moral responsibility to look after the deceased and to ensure that their dignity is maintained. The temporary mortuary should not be a garden shed or town hall, and an important planning task of police divisions is, in advance of need, to identify suitable premises for use in an emergency. What is required is a level standing unit with good ventilation and drainage, a supply of power and water, with office facilities. The number of deceased persons involved in the incident will affect the decision as to whether a body-holding area is required prior to transfer to an existing mortuary, or whether the creation of a full-scale temporary mortuary is required. Team work should take place in liaison with environmental health officers.

With regard to the media, it is important that the public be aware of what is happening at the incident and police will appoint officers whose responsibility it is to provide regular briefing on changing situations and the role of essential services. The police must not underestimate the speed with which media can arrive at a scene and the technology available to them. A media unit complete with satellite facilities arrived at Lockerbie within 2.5 hours of the incident becoming known, and where incidents such as this one are of worldwide interest, media briefing is a round-the-clock task. At Lockerbie, 500–600 media people were in attendance, requiring the services of some 11 police officers and civilian personnel.

The Chief Constable, or a nominated senior officer, is responsible for the initiation of the alert, site coordination, public safety, casualty evacuation, the establishment of a casualty bureau, and most importantly, has a duty to guard and collect any evidence required to satisfy the judicial system.

In a multi-casualty incident the casualty bureau is likely to receive a large number of enquiries, which would disrupt control rooms of receiving hospitals to such an extent that they would be prevented from continuing their normal daily routines. Therefore, the bureau should issue several specified telephone numbers. The public may telephone via the local exchange which at the same time must also cope with enquiries from press, other agencies, emergency services, hospitals and mortuaries as well as normal traffic. At the height of the Hillsborough disaster in Sheffield, the local exchange tried to cope with 10 000 calls an hour, which indicates the enormity of the problem.

The casualty bureau has several functions, including the establishment of a missing-persons enquiry unit and an information unit, which gather information from mortuaries, hospitals and reception centres. A collation unit tries to link the two together and to pass this information to a message unit which will work with other authorities to identify those involved in the disaster. A liaison unit will dedicate an individual police officer to the task of linking with the family of a deceased person, ensuring continuity and allowing the bereaved family to have a point of contact.

Thus there are a number of problems related to the establishment of a casualty bureau, mainly the number of telephone lines available and the potential call rate. There is need for national standardisation of police procedures for smoother handling of manual and computerised recording procedures; this requires further evaluation and systematisation. A British

Telecom system called "the Advanced Link Line Network" can now separate and divert calls throughout the country and move them around to take the load off local exchanges, and it is anticipated that many separate police forces may become involved in one major incident. Each has access to the police national computer, and new software packages are in the process of development.

In summary, communication and the systematisation of good practice in the emergency services is essential to the establishment of a coordinated response to major tragedies in which the police force has a central role.

Adapted, with permission, from Dickie, T. I. (1991) The role of the police at major incidents. *Journal of the Royal Society of Health*, **8**, 152–155.

B.   Social work in disasters

MARION GIBSON

The expectations of the role of social services in the aftermath of disasters has changed significantly over the last decade. Prior to this time, they were expected to respond to the needs of the community in a reactive way; their ability to do so, and the nature of their response, was dependent on local resources. The relationship which existed between social services, the police and other emergency services was also a significant factor. Where major incident plans existed, the role for social services was usually practical, associated with the setting-up of rescue centres, supplying 'welfare' to the more vulnerable groups in the community. A review of the literature on the aftermath of disasters, prior to the last decade, reveals little reference to the need for on-going social and psychological support.

In the last decade there have been two main influences on the type of response which is now expected. First is the development of research and clinical studies described elsewhere in this book. The second influence is a change in the role of social services. More professional training has produced a greater understanding of the underlying psychological basis for the work. Statutory responsibilities increased, but strategies for early intervention to support those at risk were viewed more positively by the community and policy-makers. Early intervention was seen to minimise the need for more intensive services or later intervention. The core of the social work task now is assessment of need, the mobilisation of resources to ameliorate harm, and support for people in stressful situations.

Adaptation of practice to meet the needs of a community experiencing the aftermath of a disaster is well demonstrated by the response of Bradford Social Services to the fire in their local football stadium in 1985. They adopted a proactive approach to those who were bereaved or sustained injuries. The setting-up of a helpline and the use of a newsletter were features of this response, providing a service which was accessible to a large number of people. This was to become a model used by other social services. Core elements of the Bradford model were adapted and refined to match the particular needs presented by subsequent disasters.

Lessons learned from this and subsequent disasters were to inform the growing body of knowledge. Information was disseminated by personal contact, journal articles or by conferences. During the 1980s there were a number of significant disasters and the role of voluntary organisations and social services became more integrated. One valid criticism of this evolutionary process was that many social services staff, faced with the need to respond, asked colleagues with previous experience "What did you do?". There was little systematic evaluation of the outcome of the services provided.

A typology of disasters as described in chapter 7 and by Gibson (1996) who includes the dimension of Man-made or natural in her typology can be used by managers of social services response teams to identify specific elements that will dictate the nature of the services required, and as an indicator of the elements that will cause psychological distress to those affected. The task requires a flexible approach, as it will vary not only by the type of disaster, but also by the time at which the intervention takes place.

Pre-crisis

This is significant when providing support. People need to talk about relationships prior to the disaster and about preceding events and alternative outcomes (the 'if only' syndrome).

Crisis stage

The need for rescue and damage limitation is paramount. Social services may have little involvement, but by joint training they can influence some of the procedures and attitudes of emergency services. The way people are treated by emergency personnel can be the beginning of their psychological recovery. Methods of rescue that preserve the dignity of those being rescued or the handling of bodies can have a significant influence on those involved.

Immediate post-crisis stage

There is a feeling of chaos when little information is available on how many have been injured or killed. Social workers can provide a valuable service by dealing with the immediate practical issues and supporting vulnerable people who are in severe shock.

Following a terrorist assassination in a betting shop in the Ormeau Road area of Belfast in 1992, when five men died and eight were severely injured, distressed people ran to the nearby City Hospital where casualties were being taken. Social workers, senior nursing staff and chaplains were involved in managing these people in a designated area away from the accident and emergency department. Family groups were identified and a social worker was allocated to each group. Through the anxious hours which followed, family members were supported by social workers who were also available to relatives when they were taken to the mortuary to identify the dead. People in shock are numb and feel depersonalised, helpless and overwhelmed. The response provided must be proactive and structured in a way which does not add to these feelings. People in shock do not always hear what is being said, they have difficulty in concentrating, and they may become hyperactive with associated aggression. The opposite reaction of catatonic apathy has also been observed. Social workers need to listen, since the information gained may aid the identification process for the police.

This stage can be called the *T stage* (Gibson, 1996):

Talk – staff must keep talking with the relatives even where there is little information.

Tears – need to be accepted and comforted.

Touch – may be more appropriate than words.

Tissues – need to be readily available.

Telephones – coins must be available, as does assistance with directories.

Toilets – practical details are important.

Tea – food and tea provide comfort.

Transport – may be needed to homes, hospitals or the mortuary.

Tablets – provision needs to be made for people on regular medication.

Time – helpers need to make time to listen and to reassure people of ongoing support in the future.

Short-term post-crisis stage

The numbness of shock gives way to the pain of realisation. The event is not a nightmare which is going to disappear. This can happen as a body is identified, belongings are returned, when media attention centres on distressed families, or when an injured person leaves the supportive environment of the hospital. Social services need to be accessible, if required, at this stage.

On 23 September 1992 at 9 p.m. a terrorist bomb devastated the forensic laboratory in South Belfast. No-one was killed and there were relatively few casualties, but 1002 homes were damaged and the area was plunged into darkness as the electricity failed. Churches, schools and health centres were also damaged. The team of social workers responded immediately, but the home-helps were the first on the scene to help the elderly and disabled. They left their own devastated homes to run to the aid of their clients. Neighbours used car headlights to illuminate the way out for people through falling ceilings and shattered glass. Terrified children were showered with glass in their beds. There were a number of cases of lacerated feet as people ran over broken glass in their homes or gardens.

The social services set up a rescue centre, but the majority of the homeless were accommodated by relatives. Many feared leaving their homes because of the possibility of looting. On the night of the incident there was chaos, and people reacted to their trauma either by high levels of activity promoted by anger, or by inactivity as a result of the overwhelming feelings of helplessness. Social workers involved noticed a phenomenon which had been observed at other bomb incidents. Following the initial shock and the associated noise of alarms ringing, masonry and glass falling, some hours later people wandered around silently and aimlessly with a "zombie-like" appearance. The realisation came with the dawn when the full extent of damage was visible. On one occasion police and fire brigade officers had difficulty in communicating with an elderly lady who was sitting in her devastated home cradling a broken ornament in her hands. Her distress was centred on a china donkey bearing the inscription "Present from

Blackpool". This had been bought on a honeymoon trip. The husband had died some years ago but the lady was focusing her distress on a single object which represented her lost memories and the sense of insecurity which she now felt in her home. She could not deal with the reality of all the damage. This meant that she could not accept the practical help that was needed to clear up the damage and secure her home. The social work role was to deal with both the emotional trauma, represented by the china donkey, and to provide practical help.

Long-term post-crisis stage

Northern Ireland has not had a major disaster in terms of numbers killed or injured. However, when one considers the police statistics associated with acts of terrorism – 3112 killed and 36 236 people injured in the 25 years of the "troubles" up to the end of 1993 – it could be described as an ongoing disaster. The model for social services has been targeted crisis response with follow-up provided through our integrated health and social services network. The recommendations of the Disasters Working Party (chapter 26) have been incorporated into service provision, and a network of crisis support teams is being established.

The number of bereaved and injured people resulting from a particular incident can be recorded statistically, but the category of 'others traumatised' is incalculable. Service provision must be specific and targeted to the identified groups but extensive enough to be accessible and acceptable to 'others traumatised' who may need help. In the category of others traumatised, we must include helpers (see chapter 21).

Social services are uniquely placed to provide a coordinating role in the provision of psychosocial support in the aftermath of disasters. This includes networking with emergency services, voluntary groups and health professionals. At a time of disaster need is experienced by people who would not normally be users of their service, and social workers need additional training in the effects of disaster, which can also have a positive effect on non-disaster practice. The elements necessary in providing a response following a major incident can be used to support those who are experiencing personal disaster in their lives. Lessons learned by the team in the South and East Belfast Health and Social Services Trust have been developed to provide a staff care service based on needs identified by staff involved in traumatic events. The service is provided to a number of statutory, voluntary or private organisations including the ambulance service.

The provision of support must be such that its accessibility continues. People may wish to access help long after the event when their initial stress reactions have been reactivated.

The 'long-term post-crisis stage' had taken on a new meaning in our work in Northern Ireland since the declaration of a ceasefire by the two main paramilitary groups in the autumn of 1994. Organisations providing support had an increase in self-referrals from victims who felt that they needed to discuss their feelings. They were experiencing:

(a) Feelings of confusion at the futility of the terrorist attacks: "The ceasefire came too late for my son." For some they feel their loss contributed to the ceasefire: "At least they did not die in vain if their death advanced the peace process."

(b) Fear that their needs will be forgotten as society is urged to forget the past and look to the future. This may be necessary, but to deny the past is to forget their loved ones.

(c) Anger – some feelings of anger have remained suppressed. The suggestion that prisoners imprisoned for terrorist crimes may have an early release angers some families who feel that they continue to serve a life sentence of bereavement and shattered hopes through the result of disabled bodies or scarred minds.

(d) The need for new coping strategies. Many people who were traumatised coped by using the collective community reaction of 'business as usual': "we must keep going". Now they can express anger and they have time to reflect on what might have been "if only . . .".

These reactions were valid in a changing situation with new challenges arising. Long-term care now needs to provide an open door for those experiencing such reactions. They need to tell their stories in the confidence that they will be listened to with empathy and understanding.

With the breakdown of the IRA ceasefire with the massive bomb in the Canary Wharf area of London on 9 February 1996, reactions from those who had suffered were again thrown into turmoil. The uncertainty of the future and the fragility of the peace process adds to the emotional distress of many.

Conclusion

Disasters can have a positive as well as a negative outcome for organisations, the people and the communities affected. The current role of social services in disasters is a result of lessons learned. Austin (1967) ends his book on the Aberfan disaster of 1966 with these words: "Dedicated to the hope that the lessons will not only be appreciated but applied". Past experience must be researched and current practice evaluated to enable future practice to be developed.

C.   The school in disasters

WILLIAM YULE and ANNE GOLD

Most of us do not like to contemplate that we might be caught up in a disaster. Many of us hesitate before drawing up a will in the superstitious belief that it may hasten our end. We may resent the waste of time involved in regular fire-drills at our place of work. All in all, we are not too good at planning for the unexpected and schools are no different.

And yet, accidents and tragedies are part of everyday experience in schools across the country. True, few schools get caught up in terrible disasters such as the collapse of buildings with pupils inside, or fatal fires, but many schools do have to cope with a stream of smaller events which have major significance for those involved.

Some small-scale disasters hit the national headlines: the children swept off the rocks in Cornwall; children who fell over a cliff in Switzerland during a skiing holiday; the teenagers who drowned in the canoeing tragedy in Dorset. How many other dreadful accidents occur during school journeys? Fortunately, most pass smoothly and are important growth points for the children involved. Children travelling to or from school may be involved in fatal road traffic accidents. Teachers or pupils may die in front of children in school premises. Intruders may assault or kill teachers or pupils in school. How can schools prepare to deal with such eventualities?

It is our belief that they can by considering coolly what sort of accidents may happen to their particular school. Teachers, particularly those with pastoral care responsibilities, can learn how such accidents can produce stress reactions and other psychopathology in children (and staff). They can learn to spot the signs of such stress and distress so that children who are not coping can get effective help. They can learn to talk to children so that the burden can be shared in a sympathetic and trusted setting. They can adjust the demands of the teaching timetable so that children can maintain as near as possible a regular routine while they are coming to terms with any trauma. They can develop recording systems in order to keep an eye on vulnerable children. Above all, they can develop a contingency plan so that when news of a tragedy breaks, they are better able to respond.

In our book for schools, *Wise Before the Event: Coping with Crises in Schools* (Yule & Gold, 1993), we illustrate for schools how disasters can affect children of different ages. By describing some real-life cases in which we were involved, we bring it home to teachers that these are not rare or isolated events, but that it is important that they understand PTSD and other reactions such as depression, anxiety, acquired fears and bereavement reactions. Teachers need to be able to monitor children's reactions carefully over many months after a disaster. They also need to monitor their educational progress. Problems in concentration and learning may be the most obvious manifestations, but what should a teacher do when a child is obviously miserable or looking as if they need to talk? Many teachers, and parents for that matter, have the unrewarding experience of offering to listen to a child only to have their offer rebuffed. Many are concerned that if they encourage the child to talk about horrendous things they have experienced, this may do some harm. When should they talk and when should they let well alone? There are no easy guidelines but these are issues that teachers need to discuss and take advice on. What most mental health professionals agree on is that survivors do need to talk, but in a helpful way.

Who is most likely to be affected?

Sometimes it is immediately obvious when young people are affected by some of the symptoms of PTSD. Others, however, take longer to surface. It is important, therefore, to know who is most likely to be affected, so that teachers can keep an eye on those who are most likely to need help. Here we list pointers to identifying the most vulnerable (Yule, 1992).

(a) People whose lives were at greatest risk are most likely to suffer emotional consequences.
(b) Those who witness death and carnage.
(c) Children who come from less stable family relationships.
(d) Children who are less able intellectually.
(e) There is a higher proportion of problems among girls than among boys.

Schools cannot do anything about most of these risk factors, but if a disaster does strike, the factors can be used to identify children who should be especially carefully monitored.

What should schools do?

What can a school do to plan ahead to minimise the impact of any critical incident? We strongly recommend that schools should develop a *contingency plan* to see them through emergencies as well as reflect on the implications for their curriculum. Thus, it is far easier for staff and pupils to think through the issues of coping with death, if death has already been discussed more normally as part of the everyday curriculum in a variety of lessons.

Here, we can only give an outline of the tasks that schools must undertake as a crisis develops. We discuss them roughly in the order in which decisions have to be made, but obviously they have implications for prior preparation. We recommend that headteachers should be clear about which tasks should be delegated to which staff members, particularly in relation to taking children away on school journeys.

Immediate tasks

On learning that a crisis has occurred, the first task is to obtain accurate information and to relay that to senior management within the school. There needs to be an easy way to get information out as well as in to the school, and the use of a portable telephone may help. Someone needs to deal with enquiries, both from anxious parents and from press and other outsiders. This can be quite stressful. Whoever is on telephone duty will need to keep good records, but will also need some support on leaving the shift.

Parents will need to be informed as soon as possible. Staff should be told what is happening, and in turn they should tell the pupils in as straight-forward a way as possible. As far as possible, the school's normal routine should be followed.

Even in the first few hours, some thought should be given to whether children should attend the funerals of any pupils or staff killed in a disaster, since some religions have burial rites that demand burial within 24 hours where feasible. This is an example of where prior discussion as part of the normal curriculum can prepare one to deal with what can be a very delicate matter.

Short-term action

Once it is confirmed that the school is facing a major crisis, staff and pupils may feel shocked, numbed, and also feel a great pressure to talk. The headteacher and staff will face a number of decisions that will be informed by understanding these reactions and needs.

If a disaster happens outside school, the first thing that is needed is to ensure the physical safety of all the children and then to inform the parents. Children should be reunited with their families as soon as practicable.

This is the time to refer to the list of contacts in the contingency plan. The time spent developing the links will now ensure that the outside contacts are reliable and fit the way the school would like to work. As soon as practicable, arrangements should be made for formal help within the school – whether from specially chosen teaching staff or from outside mental health professionals. All staff, both teaching and support staff, will need an opportunity to share their emotional reactions to the crisis and support should be organised, as far as possible, from within the school itself.

The job of the psychologists, psychiatrists, social workers or volunteers should be to support the efforts of the staff, not to replace them. The head-teacher has legal responsibility for what happens to the pupils in school and for deciding who has access to the children in school. The Head needs to be aware that many unknown people will offer help, which is why it is a good idea to identify potential helping agencies earlier rather than having to risk accepting help from people of unknown background and experience.

Pupils will have a need to talk about what happened one minute, and shy away from it the next. Not all children are ready to discuss things at the same time. Pupils who were not present at an incident will also need an opportunity to talk about their own reactions. They need help in deciding what to say to children who were directly involved.

A debriefing meeting

Many people recommend that there should be a formal meeting to 'debrief' all those involved. Such a meeting serves a number of important purposes:

(a)   to clarify what happened;
(b)   to share reactions;
(c)   to learn that such reactions are not abnormal;
(d)   to mobilise resources.

During a major trauma, people are often numbed. They feel as if things are not really happening to them. For a few days afterwards, they are often in a state of shock. Thereafter, as upset as they may be, it is important that someone helps them to make a little sense of what did actually happen. Debriefing is a way of sharing not only what happened, but of sharing the often frightening emotional reactions to the events. By holding a debriefing meeting in the school, preferably led by an experienced person from outside, the school is giving the pupils and staff permission to share their reactions and educating them in how best to cope in the following period. A separate debriefing meeting may be necessary for directly affected staff.

The normal ground rules, clarified in the Children Act 1989 (England and Wales), apply. Schools cannot take unilateral decisions without the permission of parents and of the older pupils themselves. Schools will need to decide on whether and how to commemorate what happened and will want to involve pupils in this. They need to continue to keep the families of all children informed on what is happening, as well as to continue monitoring the progress of pupils.

Medium-term action

As the school begins to settle back into its usual routines after a few days, staff and pupils realise more clearly what has happened to them. The initial period of numbed feelings may move on to a period of more public expressions of distress. While wanting to maintain as normal a routine as possible, some alterations will be inevitable. Decisions about continuing monitoring of pupils, referring on for specialist help, and about attendance at funerals or memorial services have to be taken.

Staff must think carefully about what arrangements to make to help children get back into a school routine after a period of absence. Decisions will be made about missed schoolwork and about preparing other children for the absentees' re-entry to the school. If the children's concentration remains impaired, then alternative teaching methods may have to be considered.

Some staff may need to have individual help in their own right to come to terms with the effects of the trauma. Others may benefit from some sessions with an outside helper. In relation to their support of affected children, staff may benefit from advice and support from child mental health professionals.

Where the school chooses to have an outside consultant (such as a psychologist, social worker, counsellor or psychiatrist) to advise staff on how to help the children, a few ground-rules concerning sharing of information and confidentiality need to be developed and made explicit to avoid misunderstandings.

Longer-term planning

Many people report that their lives are completely changed by a major disaster. After a brush with death, we all re-examine our values and priorities. Not everything that happens is negative, and schools, too, can learn to be better places as a result of experiencing a major crisis.

Schools should remember that the effects of a major incident can reverberate for years. Arrangements should be made to keep an eye on vulnerable staff and pupils, and to ensure that new staff are informed about the trauma and its possible effects. Anniversaries inevitably come round and so thought needs to be given as to how to mark them. Many disasters will be complicated by legal actions, and these may prolong the time before the crisis can be put behind everyone. As time goes on, so the trauma is reinterpreted and when similar incidents receive publicity, so the earlier survivors may need to talk again.

Implications for the curriculum

Schools should not have to deal with such enormously difficult issues as death and bereavement for the first time following a crisis. These issues can be embedded into the curriculum of a school, whatever the age of the children, so that the school and the young people in it are used to talking about such subjects, and they are not shrouded in mystery and taboo. As with sex education, parents and governors can be involved in the planning, so that there is a shared development of the teaching about these issues and an agreed way of acknowledging them that does not separate the children from their parents.

Issues such as life, death, bereavement and other rites of passage should be explored through well-chosen literature, poetry, religious education, drama, history, humanities, sociology, and so on. Primary schools often include them in projects about the self, health, or families. Some teachers find it uncomfortable to explore ideas that they are not completely at ease with themselves. Increasingly, schools include staff development sessions for dealing with difficult feelings. These sessions may include specialist consultants working with small groups of teachers to address uncomfortable feelings and to develop strategies for dealing with them in themselves as well as in the young people they work with.

Most schools will be aware of the diversity of backgrounds from which their pupils come. They need an understanding of different cultural and religious attitudes to disability, disasters, death, bereavement, mourning and funerals. Such awareness of diverse views and expectations is all part of creating a supportive ethos within the school.

Implications for child mental health services

The model we are proposing here starts from the premise that the headteacher has the responsibility for what happens within the school. However, they have to work within the framework of the law and especially the Children Act, and so require parental and pupil permission to involve other professionals in the care of the children. This sounds a bit pompous, but it is necessary to understand where responsibility lies in this modern age when aggressive outreach within community settings is all the rage. However well-intentioned, mental health staff have no right to enter schools to provide services unless they are invited in.

In an ideal world, schools and clinic or other mental health staff will already know each other and have developed mutual respect and trust. Part of our advice on setting up a contingency plan is for schools to identify potential local agencies and to get to know them. There can be no substitute for personal contact prior to an emergency happening.

It is important for mental health professionals to think through the implications of 'normal' people suddenly being acutely distressed. These are not psychiatric patients who have learned over months or years how to be a patient and seek help; rather, these are people for whom any suggestion that they are "psychiatric cases" can add to their distress. The manner in which help is offered and the personnel introduced to the children and their families is crucial.

As always when one is invited into any system in a consultative role, one has to be clear who is the client. Given that schools call in help and the teachers want practical advice on how to help the children within the classrooms, it is vital that the ground rules of what information is to be shared, with whom, and how, should be known to teachers, mental health workers and children alike. Clearly, some children will take the opportunity of individual sessions to discuss material that is very personal and should remain confidential, but teachers will still expect, rightly, to be treated as partners in helping the children and not just as passive conduits of information.

There is increasing evidence that early intervention after a disaster can help to reduce the psychopathology, but there are no studies of how best to support schools. This is a task that should be addressed over the next few years as more disasters inevitably strike at children in school settings.

D.   The role of volunteers

DORA BLACK

In Britain, as in many Western countries, there is a well-developed network of voluntary agencies which had their origins in the philanthropic movement of the Victorian era. To some extent the need for them was lessened by the development of state-funded social services, but specific voluntary charitable agencies have tended to spring up to meet perceived gaps in the statutory provision of social services. As those needs have been adopted as legitimate ones for government agencies to meet, so the charitable drive in those who 'have' has been directed to new ventures for the 'have-nots'.

This section can describe only a few of the many charitable agencies which provide counselling and support to victims of trauma and their families. New ones arise almost daily to meet the needs of survivors of specific disasters. Here I will describe four main charities relevant to the theme of this book: Cruse, the national charity for bereavement care; Victim Support; The Medical Foundation for the Care of Victims of Torture; and SAMM (Support after Murder and Manslaughter). As has been described elsewhere in this book under specific disasters (chapter 8), a new development has been the coming together of statutory and voluntary agencies to form a Disaster Response Unit (see chapter 8D) to provide counselling and support services at the site of a disaster. This is discussed in more detail in chapter 26.

Cruse Bereavement Care

Cruse Bereavement Care was named by its founder, Margaret Torrie, after the widow's *cruse* of oil which was a symbol in biblical times of neighbourly care of the bereaved. It is a charity largely funded by donations, with contributions from the Department of Health and local authorities, which started in 1959 to support widows and help them with the practical and emotional problems that faced them upon the death of their husband. Concurrently with the development of branches all over the UK, Cruse expanded its services gradually to meet the needs of all bereaved people. It now has 192 branches providing social support groups, bereavement counselling to adults, children and families by selected and trained volunteers, and provides its counsellors with training, ongoing professional supervision and consultation. Initial training is a ten-session course involving lectures and discussion groups. This is followed by skills training combined with supervision of individual counselling for 20 hours, followed by accreditation and group supervision for a further 60 hours of counselling, and consultation with the supervisor at regular intervals thereafter. There are specialist courses and supervision for those working with children and families.

An evaluation of the training of counsellors at the Aberdeen branch of Cruse in 1988 found that the counsellors had a sound grasp of the bereavement process and had a unified view on helpful counsellor qualities, of which empathy was the most highly rated. They were able to recognise when clients needed to be referred for psychiatric help and when to use publications, but they had relatively little interest in theory despite the fact that it had been taught. The author concluded that bereavement counselling might be considered a suitable test for the future of psychotherapy in the National Health Service (Le Poivedin, 1988). Cruse has recently begun to develop specialised training for its volunteers in debriefing techniques and working with survivors of disasters and their families. It played a major role in the teams set up to help with the psychosocial consequences of the Zeebrugge Ferry disaster and the Hungerford Massacre (see chapter 8) among others, and initiated and convened the Disasters Working Party (see chapter 26). It provides a telephone helpline and a number of relevant publications of help to professionals and the public. It publishes a journal, *Bereavement Care*, three times a year with original and other papers of interest to bereavement counsellors, as well as a newsletter for the bereaved ten times a year.

Following the publication of controlled studies of the effectiveness of counselling in reducing post-bereavement morbidity (see chapter 16), bereavement counselling services became much more widely available from statutory and voluntary agencies. The National Association of Bereavement Services was formed in 1988 to collate and disseminate information about bereavement services. It publishes a national directory of these services, a newsletter, and guidelines on setting up a bereavement service as well as holding seminars and workshops.

Cruse Bereavement Care, 126 Sheen Road, Richmond, Surrey TW9 1UR. Tel. 0181 940 4818, fax 0181 940 7638, helpline 0181 332 7227.
National Association of Bereavement Services, 20 Norton Folgate, London E1 6DB. Tel. & fax 0171 247 0617.

Victim Support

In 1974 the first Victim Support scheme was started in Bristol by people who perceived a gap in the provision of services for victims of crime. The National Association was founded in 1979, with Helen Reeves, OBE, as current Director. Victim Support now has over 370 offices in England, Wales and Northern Ireland. Scotland has its own separate organisation. It offers volunteer support for victims of crime, and training to police and magistrates. Volunteers are checked by the police and then trained in 6–10 sessions on the emotional impact of crime, police and court procedures, compensation and insurance, and listening and counselling techniques. After experience in working with victims of minor crimes there is further intensive training for more serious aspects of crime such as racial harassment, violent crime, helping families of murder victims and helping women who have been raped.

The police give information about the services provided by Victim Support to victims of crime who are invited to contact the local branch for a counsellor. The service given is short-term and essentially practical, and may include accompanying clients to court to support them when giving evidence. Specific publications of interest include a survey of domestic violence, a project on families of murder victims, and one on road deaths.

Victim Support, Cranmer House, 39 Brixton Road, London SW9 6DZ. Tel. 0171 735 9166, fax 0171 582 5712.

Medical Foundation for the Care of Victims of Torture

This is a London-based charity founded in 1986 to continue the work carried out for more than a decade by professionals volunteering their services, under the auspices of the British section of Amnesty International. They offer comprehensive services to victims of torture who have sought refuge in Britain, which include: help in preparing reports to establish refugee status; medical and psychiatric treatment, including psychotherapy, family therapy and medication; careers counselling; social work help; and work with the families of torture victims (Turner, 1989). Although unpaid, all the clinical work is done by professionally qualified doctors, nurses, psychologists, physiotherapists and psychotherapists. They are funded mainly by donations. There has as yet been no evaluation of the work of the Foundation.

Medical Foundation for the Care of Victims of Torture, 95–98 Grafton Road, London NW5 3EJ. Tel. 0171 284 4321, fax 0171 284 4265.

SAMM – Support after Murder and Manslaughter

This is the new name of the charity formerly known as Parents of Murdered Children, which was founded by June Patient and Ann Robinson in 1984 originally as a self-help group within The Compassionate Friends, an international organisation of bereaved parents. Since 1990 it has been a separate charity. They aim to offer understanding and support to families and friends who have been bereaved as a result of murder or manslaughter by enabling them to meet others who have been through similar experiences. They hold informal meetings in various parts of the UK. The only paid staff are administrative and are funded with the help of other charities including Victim Support who also accommodate them. The organisation acts as a resource for journalists and others, bringing to the public information about the effect of murder and manslaughter on the relatives and friends of the victim. They also publish a quarterly newsletter. There has as yet been no evaluation of their work and there is no training or supervision for the befrienders, although they have recourse to the director for advice.

SAMM, Cranmer House, 39 Brixton Road, London SW9 6DZ. Tel. 0171 735 3838, fax 0171 735 3900.

E. The role of employers

DAVID RICHARDS

With crime at record levels, many retail, security and financial services companies face an almost daily assault on their workplaces and employees. Increasingly this has led employers to recognise the personal and financial impact of crime on their businesses. The late 1980s and 1990s have seen many such companies develop counselling services to support employees caught up in traumatic events in the workplace.

In 1993 the Health and Safety Executive, in consultation with the banks and building societies, produced guidelines on good practice for preventing violence to employees and managing the impact of crimes such as armed robberies (Health and Safety Executive, 1993). The main points of this guidance are:

(a) a risk management process, including security procedures;
(b) an education and training programme;
(c) a post-robbery support system;
(d) a predefined public relations policy.

The guidance emphasises the collaborative nature of post-traumatic stress management before, during and after an incident. There is particular emphasis on counselling, critical incident stress debriefing (CISD) and pre-trauma training.

The actual provision of such services may be by 'internal' salaried company employees or 'external' consultancies. Either way, the challenge is to integrate the various elements into a service which is intelligible, consistent and needs-led. An example of such a service was the internal post-raid counselling service at the Leeds Permanent Building Society (now merged with the Halifax Building Society), detailed below and in more detail in Richards (1994).

(1) *Pre-trauma training*

The Leeds Permanent Building Society put all its branch-based and regional support staff through a training programme called 'Coping With Robberies'. This was based on Meichenbaum's work on stress inoculation training (Meichenbaum, 1985), analogous to biological immunisation. It followed the premise that pre-exposure to modified examples of an actual traumatic incident, together with instruction on coping with the incident and its aftermath, protected employees from the worst effects of the future trauma.

The training took the form of four short video films seen one at a time by employees for four consecutive months in the branch environment where they worked. The video films exposed employees to a number of likely robbery scenarios, with the emphasis on both practical security and psychological coping skills. In addition, simple exercises were contained within a personal 'workbook' retained by each employee after the training has finished.

Effective coping strategies, social support in a crisis and self-efficacy are the three factors (other than the severity of the traumatic event) that many authors regard as crucial to post-trauma recovery (Joseph *et al*, 1993). The workbook exercises, therefore, backed up the coping messages contained in the films and focused primarily on: (a) enhancing self-control of anxiety during a robbery; (b) the effective use of social support post-raid; and (c) managing post-traumatic stress symptoms.

(2) *Immediate post-incident support*

Immediately after a traumatic incident such as a robbery, information was available to all those involved on what to do next. Simple procedural checklists and information on post-trauma symptoms were contained in an emergency 'raid pack', the emphasis being on taking the active thinking out of what to do next by making the procedures automatic, thereby reducing confusion.

A senior manager would attend the incident as soon as possible afterwards with the aim of helping to 'defuse' the emotional aftermath. They did this by adopting an empathic stance, concentrating on the human needs of victims and delivering support which may be merely as simple as making the tea and ferrying employees home.

Within the raid pack were contact cards for the Leeds' system of 'professional counsellors'. Within the next 2–3 days a critical incident stress debriefing was carried out with *all* staff at the branch, whether they were directly involved in the incident or not. This was facilitated in a group by one of the two full-time, professionally qualified counsellors employed by the Leeds and used the standard CISD procedures detailed in chapter 15. The branch would be resourced by supernumerary staff while this was carried out.

(3) *Long-term support*

During the debriefing, assessments of group and individual mental health would be carried out. In addition, a system of psychological health screening was started using self-report symptom checklists such as the Impact of Event Scale (Horowitz *et al*, 1979). These were repeated at one week, and at 1, 3, 6 and 12 month intervals. Furthermore, a follow-up visit was made by one of the full-time counsellors one month after the debriefing, with particular attention paid to employees who were directly involved or highly distressed by the incident.

This psychological screening and follow-up system would allow the counsellors to pick up potential cases of PTSD and intervene early using the effective cognitive or behavioural interventions described in chapter 17B. Where other conditions such as depression were identified, rapid referral to GPs or local psychiatric services could be made.

Summary

As employers increasingly recognise the human resource benefits of actively intervening to support staff before, during and after traumatic incidents, more and more systems such as the one detailed here at the Leeds are being implemented. The Leeds' service was recognised as a model for others (Reynolds, 1994) because of its "sophisticated and professional approach". It included all the elements of trauma support currently recognised as best practice – pre-trauma training, management defusing, debriefing, peer support and professional therapy. Wykes (1994) provides a valuable overview of employers' responsibilities in healthcare settings.

The service was not cheap, but the benefits, including increased morale, team rebuilding, a more confident workforce and a healthier workforce, were thought to outweigh the costs. It is the integration of all the diverse elements of a trauma support programme, so that care is delivered to those who need it, when they need it and where they need it, which is one of the greatest challenges facing responsible employers into the next century.

References

Austin, T. (1967) *The Story of a Disaster*. London: Hutchinson.
Gibson, M. (1996) *Order from Chaos* (2nd edn). Birmingham: Venture Press.
Health and Safety Executive (1993) *Prevention of Violence to Staff in Banks and Building Societies*. Suffolk: HSE Books.
Horowitz, M., Wilner, N. & Alvarez, W. (1979) Impact of event scale: a measure of subjective stress. *Psychosomatic Medicine*, **41**, 209–218.
Joseph, S., Yule, W. & Williams, R. (1993) Post-traumatic stress: attributional aspects. *Journal of Traumatic Stress*, **6**, 501–515.
Le Poivedin, D. (1988) An evaluation of the training of bereavement counsellors. *Bereavement Care*, **7**, 14–17.
Meichenbaum, D. (1985) *Stress Inoculation Training*. New York: Pergamon Press.
Reynolds, P. (1994) *Violence and Crime at Work: A Guide for Organisational Action*. New York: McGraw-Hill.
Richards, D. A. (1994) Traumatic stress at work: a public health model. *British Journal of Guidance and Counselling*, **22**, 51–64.
Turner, S. (1989) Working with survivors. *Psychiatric Bulletin*, **13**, 173–176.
Wykes, T. (ed.) (1994) *Violence and Health Care Professionals*. London: Chapman & Hall.
Yule, W. (1992) Resilience and vulnerability in child survivors of disasters. In *Vulnerability and Resilience: A Festschrift for Ann and Alan Clarke* (eds B. Tizard & V. Varma), pp. 82–98. London: Jessica Kingsley.
—— & Gold, A. (1993) *Wise Before the Event: Coping with Crises in School*. London: Calouste Gulbenkian Foundation.

21 Effects of disasters on helpers

RACHEL ROSSER

"We will stay with the people of the camp until the danger is over. We will remain with them – to live or die with them." Pauline Cutting, OBE (1988)

PTSD can affect anyone. Rescue workers, health professionals and bystanders are vulnerable to the full spectrum of post-disaster syndromes including PTSD with comorbidity such as affective disorders. These occur as a result of direct exposure or indirect transmission, including:

(a) prolonged and over-intense exposure and threat to life (however courageous);
(b) emergency service working, where cumulative exposure to traumatic experiences, particularly when rescue fails, may lead to PTSD;
(c) direct exposure of helpers to the mental disturbance of victims;
(d) revisiting of past traumas, both direct and indirect, by the therapist.

There is a pressing need for systematic research on the impact on the helper of such work.

Phenomenology

The phenomenology of the PTSD spectrum is gradually emerging but is still poorly defined. Hence it is not established whether the symptom complex of victims and helpers differs systematically. Often there is difference in exposure: sudden and predominantly passive in survivors with a sense of helplessness; drawn-out action for helpers. Helpers at the scene range from chronically exposed professionals (senior fire officers, police, armed forces officers, etc.) to novices and volunteers. These include bystanders and victims who have just escaped themselves and return to try to rescue others.

Responses and the concept of countertransference

People who help victims of a disaster, whether at the scene or later, develop feelings about those they aid (the counterdisaster syndrome) which range from total denial or 'black humour' through panic and impotence to subtle responses which may obstruct or be of use in the healing process.

The term 'countertransference' is used by psychodynamic therapists to describe their feelings about their patients. It is being discussed as a concept which may be applicable to a wide range of emergency helpers. Recent literature classifies countertransference reactions (CTR) (Wilson *et al*, 1994; Lindy & Wilson, 1994), but it does not convey the unique intensity of these painful experiences and the burden on helpers' families and friends. Type 1 CTR comprises withdrawal of empathy or repression of feelings, the equivalent of high avoidance in victims. 'Compassion fatigue' is a comparable concept used by the media of themselves and of their audiences. Type 2 CTR comprises empathic enmeshment or disequilibrium, the equivalent of the experience of highly intrusive imagery and arousal in victims (Horowitz, 1976; Weisaeth, 1989; Wilson *et al*, 1994). Roles may be exchanged. The media may cease to be dispassionate recorders and assist the frail, perhaps feeling that detached reporting is not acceptable today (John Simpson reporting from Rwanda, *The Times*, 16 July 1994).

Case example 1 – CTR1: neglect

A skilled and empathic psychiatric trainee assessed and took into therapy a schoolteacher who was working full-time and also taking care of her 7-year-old child as a single parent. After the King's Cross fire the victim began to drink considerable amounts of alcohol. She did not attend the fourth session. The therapist did not make further contact despite supervisory advice.

Case example 2 – CTR2: interminable problem

An Afro-Caribbean woman lost a child in the King's Cross fire. She developed pathological grief. Her therapist re-negotiated the initially brief treatment and eventually it continued for several years.

Models

Predisposing factors in the survivors (McFarlane, 1989) are likely to be equally applicable to helpers. A quantitative model of the importance of traumatic vulnerability and risk factors has yet to be derived. It is difficult to extrapolate from observations of survivors to helpers without adequate empirical data.

In the absence of facts, models take the form of lists, or more obscure representations such as decision trees, helices ('the hermeneutic spiral') (McCann & Colletti, 1994) or mandala representations (Lindy & Wilson, 1994). More comprehensive models are required of the interaction between the intensity and duration of exposure to a traumatic event, and vulnerability and risk factors in the victim or helper.

Recently there has been interest in the concept of 'borderline personality disorders' as perhaps attributable to early chronic or recurrent trauma and the PTSD syndrome. Whether borderline states constitute a vulnerability factor is not known.

Diagnosis of general reactions

The phenomenological descriptions of PTSD are only crude summaries of the symptoms that helpers may develop. They may identify intensely with the victims and the bereaved and obsessionally review their own performance at the time. As for the victims, the *content* of their thoughts and feelings is their principal preoccupation, and formal mental phenomena are difficult to elicit because of their seeming irrelevance.

Some helpers fit neatly into the diagnostic categories of major affective disorder or PTSD, but more obscure phenomena may be missed, such as depersonalisation, *déjà vu* (easily confused with flashbacks), *jamais vu*, pseudo-dementia and unusual hallucinations, especially visual phenomena and motor perceptions (such as a sense of falling through the air while treating survivors of air disasters). As recognised in the earlier literature on psychogenic psychosis, and on the impact of life events in precipitating or bringing forward a psychotic illness, psychotic phenomena may emerge (Murphy & Brown, 1980)

The psychophysiology of these phenomena is complex. Temporal lobe symptoms may be the result of hyperventilation, the particular content being attributable to the specific disaster experience. More precise physiological and biochemical data, particularly concerned with the transmitters in the limbic system, feature elsewhere in this volume (chapter 6A). Knowledge of the biological aspect is crucial to the choice of treatment. In future it may provide much needed objective indicators to aid in diagnosis and for medico-legal purposes.

Helpers also develop pathological grief about victims who died despite their rescue attempts. Meeting relatives of victims may aggravate the experience but can provide a means of resolution. Survivor guilt (Lifton, 1967) may occur if some rescuers survived and others died.

Examples of rescuers and high-risk occupations

Different professions face different problems. Firemen, ambulance staff and the armed forces are at high risk, blaming themselves for being emotionally vulnerable, yet knowing they chose this type of work despite the pressures that fall on their families. Transport workers, recruited through financial necessity, are increasingly at risk. The armed forces are slowly changing in attitudes and their families now tend to obtain confidential psychological and practical support. However, recent data suggest that training, early debriefing and counselling have minimal preventive effect on survivors of active combat (Deahl *et al*, 1994). Also, PTSD may present in unusual ways, for example, dissociative phenomena and pseudo-epileptic fits in soldiers.

Fire service

Objective data on cardiac arrhythmias, carbon monoxide and cyanide blood levels in fire officers are available (Douglas *et al*, 1988). A raised incidence of ventricular ectopic beats has been observed in staff in busy fire-stations.

Case example 3
The most senior fire officer fighting the King's Cross fire in London 1987, after a fire-ball explosion in the ticket hall, perceiving a crisis, rushed in without pausing to put on his ventilation mask. He died immediately. His colleagues, who respected him as a friend and leader, worked through their shock and grief by staging an impressive march past the site of the fire to his funeral and by supporting his young family.

Police service

When well-trained police undertake the gruesome task of body-handling, traumatic symptoms are typically short-lived (Thompson & Solomon, 1991; Alexander, 1993).

Case example 4
A transport policeman at the King's Cross fire survived with severe burns. He worked on rescuing victims throughout the fire, and attributed his survival to the mental images of his children, one just six weeks old. Severely burned, he developed a hypomanic illness followed by depression and later lost his sense of vocation. He gave testimony to many newspapers and television programmes. After six years he took part in a programme about delayed reactions in heroes. Other survivors similarly described the disruptive effect on family lives (Sheridan & Kenning, 1993).

Armed services

Armed service personnel may not be viewed as "helpers", yet they are servants of their country.

Case example 5
A family man in his 30s was involved in Operation Desert Storm during the Gulf War. He was unprepared for hand-to-hand fighting which was purposely concealed by the media. He also experienced instant commands, some of which he misunderstood to instruct him to kill. On returning from the Gulf he developed florid PTSD and received treatment in an army hostel. During this time he coped with his anxiety by misusing alcohol. At the end of a year he resigned his army position.

Transport workers

Transport workers are at risk. The difficulties of railway drivers 'responsible' for 'person under the train' deaths have been investigated in detail with international comparisons. Again, short-term distress is normal but usually resolves over the following six months (Tranogh & Farmer, 1992; O'Donell & Farmer, 1992; Malt *et al*, 1993; Theorell *et al*, 1994; Williams *et al*, 1994).

Hospital services

At the site of accidents, bystanders may confuse rescuers; professionals do not follow standard procedures. Triage may not occur immediately. Thus the dead may be sent to makeshift mortuaries while suffering survivors lie in corridors, trenches or pavements terrified of what may happen to them. Hospitals may not be alerted until after the first injured arrive. Such problems arose in the King's Cross fire (see chapter 8F).

These events cause even more distress to staff in accident and emergency departments. Ironically it may be junior staff and non-professionals who receive maximum exposure and minimal support.

Senior staff

At the other extreme, little is known of the coping mechanisms of senior managers, consultant medical staff and nurses but there can be no more vivid description of the combination of technical expertise, courage and coping through good personal relationships than that of Pauline Cutting (1988).

The stress on politicians is rarely regarded as a cause for public concern, yet they are expected to take a public supportive role. Little consideration has been given to the effect on the direction of national politics after incidents such as the IRA bombing at the Conservative Conference at Brighton. Several more recent individual and group disasters internationally have involved heads of state, royalty and other public figures.

> "Weep
> If you can,
> Weep,
> But do not complain.
> The way chose you –
> And you must be thankful."
> (Dag Hammarskjold (1974), Secretary General of the United Nations.
> Shot down over Africa, posthumous publication.)

At a lower managerial level, the confusion of officials after the Armenian earthquake was thoroughly documented (Goenjin, 1993).

Role of therapists and supervisors

It is now clear that previously healthy people who become disaster victims may respond positively to brief structured interventions without the necessity of interpretative techniques relating to earlier experiences (Thompson *et al*, 1994). Junior therapists should engage in time-limited but renewable contracts with individual patients which minimise the pressure on both members of the 'dyad', backed up by a senior clinician also able to take rapid referrals for people needing medication. Similar back-up is needed in prolonged dynamically-based therapy. Case-loads must be limited and supervised and resource implications cannot be ignored. It is now usual for victims to form self-help groups which may call in a variety of experts including psychiatrists or psychologists. The emphasis for the bereaved is on the achievement of lives curtailed. One problem is that their family doctor may not be kept informed (Rosser, 1994).

Religious leaders

These are needed at the site to offer the last rites or similar types of relief. Later they may offer further support, sometimes under the guise of 'confession'. This counselling role has put stress on priests, rabbis and imams who have experienced a 'secularisation' of their most consecrated roles.

The media as helpers

The world wants to know what has happened; families and friends of the victims need information and helplines and the media provide this, yet the presence of journalists and television interviewers may be experienced as intrusive. The appointment of a media spokesperson minimises rumour.

The media employee may become a victim. John McCarthy spent just three weeks reporting in Beirut before being kidnapped and held hostage for several years (McCarthy & Morrell, 1994). Would-be rescuer of John McCarthy and others, Terry Waite, special ambassador to the Archbishop of Canterbury, was himself abducted and held hostage (Waite, 1994).

The wounded healer

Jung (1983) wrote about the necessity of "being wounded" prior to treating patients who have experienced particular traumata. Without this experience, the therapist had a "traumatic scotoma" and could not identify the patient's central problem. The Freudian equivalent is "the creative illness". Not every expert agrees on this (Ellenberger, 1970). However, many accept that an experience of exceptional trauma successfully managed may provide "inoculation", enhancing their capacity to help other victims while empathising with them. The concept of the wounded healer is elaborated metaphorically at the end of this chapter.

Case example 6
It is not clear whether therapists are easier or more difficult to treat and the answer may not be the same for all. A gifted woman therapist in her mid-30s was referred from an accident and emergency department because of her extreme distress after a minor neck injury in a crash in a car driven by her boyfriend. It emerged that after an appalling childhood she had obtained an education and postgraduate training, created a home and a private practice and taught in a police school. Several serious traumatic events had happened

to her (some derived from her own vulnerabilities). She sought help and waited several months over the summer vacation. During therapy, it emerged that she had suppressed memories of a more serious accident in her teenage years. She renegotiated her initial 8-week psychotherapy contract to 16 weeks. Seen later, she reported that she was relaxed and happy.

Multigeneration effects

The cycle of trauma has attracted recent attention (e.g. the autobiographical *Wild Swans* (Chang, 1993), and the semi-fictional work of Amy Tan (1991)). This should be distinguished from the cycle of deprivation (Rutter & Madge, 1976). Essentially it is the transmitted consequence of woundedness through the generations.

Two examples below illustrate the similarity of descriptive accounts 70 years apart.

Case example 7: Lockerbie
"A low rumble like thunder came first, then the whole sky lit up, the noise was deafening. I was absolutely petrified. Everything started falling down. Lumps of plane, bits of seat belts, bits of bodies. There were bits of burning bodies all over the forecourt. Ruth ran inside and hid under a shelf. For six months she was depressed and on tranquillisers. It was impossible to take in what had happened. It was impossible to believe I might have died." (Sheridan & Kenning, 1993)

We now understand better the full effects of such a disaster on child development through prospective follow-ups. The description is comparable with the example below where a chain of consequences is clear.

Case example 8
The Low Moor explosion of 1916 (near Bradford, Yorkshire) was described by the author's grandmother, May, in unpublished memoirs and thoroughly documented by Blackwell (1986). "Miss Ada Gumshall on Daisy Hill heard a rumbling noise like thunder and she looked just in time to see the gas holder at Low Moor rise into the air and disintegrate into fragments. Mr Hird heard the explosion in his garden at Kitson Hill Road and looking towards Low Moor he saw a huge swirling sphere rushing up into the sky. The sphere suddenly turned from grey to red before rushing sky-high as a mass of smoke. Flying debris had hit and fractured the gasometer."
May adds the individual perspective of her child, the present author's mother, born into a vulnerable family and acutely traumatised at a young age. "Madge, aged 2, looking over Gran's shoulder saw fragments of men's bodies being thrown up into the air. Eventually we got Madge home. But the effect on Madge was rather alarming. She just lay for many hours suffering from shock for rather a long time. The effect of this experience was very obvious. The doctor suggested that she be allowed to take up piano lessons so that by the use of her fingers she would find an outlet for her nervous trouble. This proved a good thing for her; Madge seemed to recover over the next four years (passing her first piano exam at six), although she seemed terrified of candles or fire. Her brother Harry, born a month after the fire was well-adjusted but terrified by any noise."

The explosion site was a tourist attraction, there being many thousands of visitors during the following week. Local newspapers gave this major disaster a high profile (Blackwell, 1986).

Madge married a pacifist and they were conscripted in 1939 to work in ammunition factory areas. One day at noon, a high-flying Messerschmitt wrote a smoke-trail question mark in the air over Coventry. That night the bombing of the provinces began, and the opening-up of the life and mind-saving communal air-raid shelters. In the following two years they lost two homes and all their possessions in air raids. Madge turned her back on the privilege of teaching her subject (history) in private sixth forms to become head of a nursery and primary school in an exceptionally deprived area. They had a daughter (the present author). Brought up in the black-out, perhaps she too became unconsciously a wounded healer.

Generational transmission may be one mechanism which produces the wounded healer. A daughter of holocaust survivors developed a depressive illness with obsessional features after the birth of her first child. Centres specialising in holocaust survivors are familiar with the breakdown of survivors' children when they reach important points in their own life-cycle.

Burnout

Burnout is a lay term which is acquiring specific meaning (Schaufeli *et al*, 1993). There are a number of rating scales, the best known being the Maslach Inventory (Maslach & Jackson, 1986). Typically, burnout starts with poor performance at work and lack of professional or recreational interest. Tedium (an extreme form of boredom) follows: life has lost its meaning. Thereafter a number of symptoms of psychiatric illness may emerge, with prominent irritability, anxiety and agitation, and then proneness to the whole range of somatic symptoms. Burnout is a severe condition difficult to reverse, but experienced employers and supportive partners may help. Nonetheless, it can break central relationships, and change or even destroy careers. If the dominant emotions are sadness, loss and grief the individual may be accessible to help. Anger, despair and depersonalisation are more difficult to work through. The worst scenario is the presence of undetected physical illness (prevalent in association with any stress) (Bennet, 1970; Brown *et al*, 1973; Murphy & Brown, 1980) with symptoms attributed exclusively to psychopathology.

Burnout classically occurs in people who are idealistic and conscientious about their work. This devotion to duty renders them more difficult to help, being work-centred to the exclusion of other values. As yet, the literature on burnout in disaster helpers is minimal, but the 'coal face' experience is substantial. There is a considerable literature relating to AIDS workers (Bennett *et al*, 1994) and to critical care nurses, one example of a serious attempt at quantitative modelling (Stechmiller & Yuarandi, 1993).

Various preventative and therapeutic strategies are available (Kelly, 1994).

Prevention

Primary

Primary prevention (i.e. intervention with at-risk staff prior to a traumatic event) may be attained in several ways.

(a)   *Staff selection.* A sensitive and non-intrusive interview is necessary, but it must be probing. This may exclude those who are themselves irreparably damaged by exposure to trauma, but not those who may become creative wounded healers.
(b)   *Staff education.* Work on staff attitudes should start before the first experience of active service. The principal lessons are:
   (1)   Grieving and trauma reactions are normal.
   (2)   Staff should be told that it is usually a responsible act to accept advice after a disaster or an isolated traumatic event and to seek this if it is not immediately offered. Following a mass disaster, full debriefing should be provided. However, individual staff may opt out of this and longer-term individual help be made available.
   (3)   A stand-by counselling service should be available to all affected employees and their families.
   (4)   Confidentiality is absolute but employees should feel free to consult their GPs, helplines, or other experts in public or private services, as they prefer.

Secondary (treatment)

Despite precautions, some helpers will develop PTSD with related symptoms. Prompt intervention sometimes prevents chronicity; family involvement may be appropriate.

Tertiary (preventing relapse)

Staff who have treatment may need special surveillance or transfer to less exposed jobs to minimise the risk of relapse.

Therapists

Case-loads should be limited and mixed (i.e. including some patients with different problems). Supervisors of therapists should advise about the importance of rest, recreation, hobbies, pleasurable interests and ordinary physical exercise as a protection and enhancement of therapeutic capacity. Supervisors must provide adequate time.

A short but renewable contract should take the pressure off both patient and therapist, and permit a more relaxed approach to transference and countertransference issues as these intervene in a therapeutic relationship.

Both concentrated formal supervisions and informal sharing are important. Supervisors should avoid criticism of juniors and be actively encouraging.

Group issues

Rescue workers and counsellors are vulnerable to interprofessional or interpersonal rivalry. The danger of a leadership vacuum or of overt hostility and leadership competition has to be recognised. Zealous but naïve volunteers may aggravate the situation. Furthermore, counselling for victims or staff has been commercialised. There is a fear that with high fees coming in, private companies with inexperienced counsellors may offer too prolonged and intensive interventions, some of which may be actively harmful. This problem will be difficult to prevent since, in the UK, therapists have failed to agree on any form of professional register of psychotherapists.

Court cases

Court appearances are considered in the final section of this book. However, any helper may have to give evidence with respect to compensation or a survivor's claim of disaster exposure as a mitigating circumstance in a subsequent crime. Cross-examination will question any lack of objective evidence and issues of malingering may arise. It is common for expert witnesses to be required to give evidence at public inquiries.

> **Case example 9**
> A young man accused of a sexual offence against a 15-year-old boy gave a detailed account of a deprived childhood and his decision to take part in first-aid work (ostensibly a transgenerational effect). He described his work immediately after the King's Cross disaster where he claimed to have been the first person, himself an ambulance driver, to open the ambulance filled with the dead and the dying. He responded accurately to questions of every detail of the disaster and its timing. In the light of expert evidence, his prison sentence was reduced to two years by the judge and was suspended at appeal to probation. He was not required to have compulsory treatment and exercised his entitlement to drop out of therapy while remaining on probation. The case was widely publicised through national newspapers.
> Eventually he recovered from the overt symptoms which had been attributed to PTSD and became employed by a highly respected company. Years later, after the probation order had ceased, he re-offended and produced a somewhat histrionic account of his bravura and experiences at the fire which were inconsistent with his former descriptions.

New work on objective indicators of simulated PTSD is urgently needed (Orr & Pitman, 1993). The pitfalls for expert witnesses have been described (Neal, 1994).

Disaster planning

This is detailed in other chapters. Many of the stresses on helpers can be avoided if there is a disaster plan, usually led by social services and a team of psychologists, psychiatrists, paramedics and voluntary organisations. Pre-defined leadership is essential. A standing interprofessional committee with social, health and voluntary organisations is important, minimising the effects of disaster and allocating those in immediate crisis to appropriate professionals.

Motivation of helpers: why do we do it?

Altruism is a major factor, but motivations are complex. We can sublimate the effort into a higher cause. For example, the Phoenix Appeal arose from the King's Cross ashes. At the press conference the media were briefed by plastic surgeons, accident and emergency consultants, anaesthetists, psychiatrists and survivors of the fire. The result was the first professorial unit of plastic surgery in the UK based at University College, London.

Perhaps the next generation will understand better from those who have recorded their experiences.

Summary

The characteristics of traumatic reactions which are general to any helper were considered briefly, then experiences more characteristic of helpers in specific roles were discussed. These include people involved in the physical act of rescue as professionals or as volunteers, such as fire officers, ambulance staff, police and those involved in the immediate aftermath, including religious leaders, those involved in identifying the dead, accident and emergency staff, cleaners and mortuary attendants. Those with particular occupational hazards, especially transport workers, are also considered.

Therapists' experiences and the timing of their interventions are explored. Role confusions, reversals and misunderstandings are described in relation to all helpers, victims, expert witnesses and professionals in senior positions. This leads into two new notions of the 'wounded healer' and the multigenerational transmission of trauma.

Group interactions are crucial, including inadvertent inter- and intra-professional misunderstandings.

> "Onlookers can't look in
> Nor mind look out
> I huddle, insensible
> As blank air
> And fear the vertigo of the night
> Seeing myself
> Dropped
> God knows where
> From such a height."
> (Brian Keenan, 1992, hostage in Beirut for over four years)

Acknowledgements

Rosalind Rabin for editorial assistance; Greyfriars Hall and Nuffield College, Oxford for receiving me as Research Fellow with the support of UCL while preparing this chapter; ESRC, the Mental Health Foundation and NETRA for funding.

References

Alexander, D. A. (1993) Stress among police body handlers: a long term follow-up. *British Journal of Psychiatry*, **163**, 806–808.

Bennet, G. (1970) Bristol Floods 1968. Controlled survey of effects on health of local community disaster. *British Medical Journal*, **III**, 454–458.

Bennett, H. L., Kelaher, M. & Ross, M. (1994) Quality of life in health care professionals: burnout and its associated factors in HIV/AIDS related cases. *Psychology and Health*, **9**, 273–284.

Blackwell, R. (1986) *The Low Moor Explosion August 21st, 1916. A Mystery Explained?* Coventry Polytechnic.

Brown, G. W., Sklair, F., Harris, T. O., *et al* (1973) Life events and psychiatric disorders. Part 1: some methodological issues. *Psychological Medicine*, **3**, 74–87.

Chang, J. (1993) *Wild Swans*. London: Harper Collins.

Cutting, P. (1988) *The Children of the Siege*. London: Pan Books/William Heinemann.

Deahl, M. P., Gillham, A. B., Thomas, J., *et al* (1994) Psychological sequelae following the Gulf War: factors associated with subsequent morbidity and the effectiveness of psychological debriefing. *British Journal of Psychiatry*, **165**, 60–65.

Douglas, R. B., Blanks, R., Crowther, A., *et al* (1988) A study of stress in West Midlands firemen using ambulatory electrocardiograms. *Work and Stress*, **2**, 309–318.

Ellenberger, H. F. (1970) *The Discovery of the Unconscious: The History and Evolution of Dynamic Psychiatry*. New York: Basic Books.

Freud, S. (1991) *Analysis Terminable and Interminable* (ed. J. Sandler). New Haven: Yale University Press.

Goenjin, A. (1993) A mental health programme in Armenia after the 1988 earthquake. Implementation and clinical observations. *British Journal of Psychiatry*, **163**, 230–239.

Hammarskjold, D. (1974) *Markings*. London: Faber & Faber.

Horowitz, M. (1976) *Stress Response Syndrome*. New York: Jason Aronson.

Jung, C. G. (1983) *Memories, Dreams, Reflections* (ed. A. Jaffe). London: Fontana.

Keenan, B. (1992) *An Evil Cradling*. London: Hutchinson.

Kelly, D. (1995) Burnout and alcohol problems. In *Health Risks to the Health Care Professional* (ed. P. Litchfield), pp. 63–75. London: Royal College of Physicians.

Lifton, R. J. (1967) *Death in Life. Survivors of Hiroshima*. New York: Random House.

Lindy, J. P. & Wilson, J. P. (1994) Empathic strain and countertransference roles: case illustrations. In *Counter Transference and the Treatment of PTSD* (eds J. P. Wilson & J. D. Lindy), pp. 62–82. New York: Guilford.

McCann, I. L. & Colletti, J. (1994) In *Counter Transference and the Treatment of PTSD* (eds J. P. Wilson & J. D. Lindy), pp. 87–121. New York: Guilford.

McCarthy, J. & Morrell, J. (1994) *Some Other Rainbow*. London: Corgi Books.

McFarlane, A. (1989) The aetiology of post traumatic morbidity: predisposing, precipitating and perpetuating factors. *British Journal of Psychiatry*, **154**, 221–228.

Malt, V., Karleghen, S., Holt, H., *et al* (1993) The effect of major railway accidents on the psychological health of train drivers: 1. Acute psychological responses to accidents. *Journal of Psychosomatic Research*, **17**, 793–805.

Maslach, C. & Jackson, S. E. (1986) *The Maslach Burn-Out Inventory. Manual* (2nd edn). Palo Alto, CA: Consulting Psychologists Press.

Murphy, E. & Brown, G. W. (1980) Life events, psychiatric disturbance and physical illness. *British Journal of Psychiatry*, **136**, 326–338.

Neal, L. A. (1994) The pitfalls of making categoric diagnosis of post-traumatic stress disorder in personal injury litigation. *Medicine, Science and the Law*, **34**, 117–122.

O'Donnell, I. & Farmer, R. T. (1992) Suicidal acts on metro systems: an international perspective. *Acta Psychiatrica Scandinavica*, **86**, 60–63.

Orr, S. P. & Pitman, R. K. (1993) Psycho-physiological assessment of attempts to simulate post-traumatic stress disorder. *British Journal of Psychiatry*, **33**, 127–129.

Raphael, B. (1986) *When Disaster Strikes. How Individuals and Communities Cope with Catastrophe.* New York: Basic Books.

Rosser, R. M. (1994) Post-traumatic stress disorder. *The Practitioner*, **238**, 393–397.

Rutter, M. & Madge, N. (1976) *Cycles of Disadvantage – A Review of Research.* London: Heinemann.

Schaufeli, W. B., Maslach, C. & Marek, T. (1993) *Professional Burn-Out: Recent Developments in Theory and Research.* Washington, DC: Taylor & Francis.

Sheridan, G. & Kenning, T. (1993) *Survivors.* Basingstoke: Pan Books.

Stechmiller, J. K. & Yuarandi, H. N. (1993) Predictors of burnout in critical care nurses. *Heart and Lung*, **22**, 534–541.

Tan, A. (1991) *The Kitchen God's Wife.* New York: Harper-Collins.

Theorell, I. T., Leymann, H., Jodko, M., *et al* (1994) "Person under train" incidents from the subway drivers' point of view. A prospective 1-year follow-up study: the design and medical and psychiatric data. *Social Science and Medicine*, **38**, 471–475.

Thompson, J. & Solomon, M. (1991) Body recovery teams at disaster: trauma and challenge? *Anxiety Research*, **4**, 235–244.

——, Cheung, M. C. & Rosser, R. (1994) The Marchioness Disaster. Preliminary report on psychological effects. *British Journal of Clinical Psychology*, **33**, 75–77.

Tranogh, T. & Farmer, R. T. (1992) Effects on train drivers. *Social Science and Medicine*, **38**, 459–469.

Waite, T. (1994) *Taken on Trust.* London: Hodder & Stoughton.

Weisaeth, L. (1989) A study of behavioural responses to an industrial disaster. *Acta Psychiatrica Scandinavica*, suppl. **355**, 25–37.

Williams, C., Miller, J., Watson, G., *et al* (1994) A strategy for trauma debriefing after railway suicides. *Social Science and Medicine*, **38**, 483–487.

Wilson, J. P., Lindy, J. D. & Raphael, B. (1994) Empathic strain and therapist defense: Type 1 and 2 CTRs. In *Counter Transference and the Treatment of PTSD* (eds J. P. Wilson & J. D. Lindy), pp. 31–61. New York: Guilford.

Part IV. Legal aspects: victims as witnesses and claimants

22 Civil law and psychiatric injury

MICHAEL NAPIER and KAY WHEAT

Claiming damages for psychiatric injury presents special problems not associated with claiming damages for physical injury. Quite understandably, non-lawyers may be somewhat mystified by this. In order to try to explain this, it is necessary to look at the causes of action that are open to the litigant in such cases. Generally, English civil law recognises two areas in which damages may be awarded: when the defendant is in breach of contract, and when the defendant has no contract with the plaintiff but owes her a tortious duty. Although in this chapter we propose to concentrate on the area of tortious liability (i.e. non-contractual civil liability), it may be helpful to mention the position under the law of contract. Claims for damages for psychiatric injury in breach of contract cases are possible, although they will be rare as the type of damages claimed will have to relate to the terms of the contract, either express or implied. An example of the way a contractual cause of action may arise would be a contract in which a solicitor is engaged to obtain a protective court order by a woman subjected to domestic violence. If the solicitor, in breach of contract, fails to take the appropriate steps towards obtaining such an order, and the woman is attacked or threatened and thereby suffers psychiatric injury, then, as one of the very purposes of the contract was to protect her from such injury, the solicitor will be liable in damages to her for the injury caused.

Although the law of contract will at times imply terms into a contract, generally it can be said that most of the terms will be specifically agreed by the parties concerned. However, the essence of the law of tort is that there is no such *agreement* as to liability. The law imposes liability when appropriate to do so. The main area of tort in which these issues arise is in the tort of negligence. The definition of negligence revolves around the concept of 'duty of care'. The defendant must have a duty of care towards the plaintiff, so, for example, the user of the highway owes such a duty to other road users. The further requirements of the tort of negligence are that the defendant has breached the duty of care by failing to meet the required standard, and that the damage has been *caused* by the breach complained of. Deciding who is owed a duty of care by whom has created a huge body of case law, largely since 1932 when the ubiquitous case of *Donoghue v. Stevenson* [1932] AC 562 was decided. The House of Lords held that a manufacturer of a defective article could be liable in the tort of negligence to someone

341

other than the person with whom he has a contractual relationship. Every law student knows the facts of the case (a consumer of ginger beer discovered a snail in the bottle), and every law student should know the legal principle formulated in that case by Lord Atkin, at p. 580:

> "You must take reasonable care to avoid acts or omissions which you can reasonably foresee would be likely to injure your neighbour. Who, then in law is my neighbour? The answer seems to be – persons who are so closely and directly affected by my act that I ought reasonably to have them in contemplation as being so affected when I am directing my mind to the acts or omissions which are called in question."

In other words, a duty is owed to a foreseeable person or class of persons who may suffer if the defendant is careless, including legal minors who may sue via their guardians.

This 'neighbour principle' formulated by Lord Atkin is still the starting point when considering negligence claims, but through subsequent case law the application of the principle has developed in a number of ways. The notion of 'proximity' is one such development. For example, physical proximity between the plaintiff and the allegedly negligent acts of the defendant can determine whether they are neighbours for the purpose of Lord Atkin's principle.[1] The social or economic relationship between the parties can also determine whether they are legally proximate so as to justify implying a duty of care into the relationship. We will look at this aspect in more detail as it is an essential part of the framework to be established if a successful claim for psychiatric injury can be made in negligence.

The notion of 'foreseeability' is crucial in establishing negligence, although it must be said that it is a necessary but not a sufficient condition. It relates to the foreseeability of the plaintiff himself and also to the type of harm suffered by that plaintiff, although the distinction between the two aspects can become blurred. The plaintiff him or herself must be foreseeable by the defendant, i.e. their presence at the time and place that the injury occurs. For example, in *Haley v. London Electricity Board* [1965] AC 778, the plaintiff, who was blind, fell into a hole which was surrounded by adequate warnings for sighted people. The Court of Appeal decided that the plaintiff was 'unforeseeable'; the House of Lords overturned their decision by stating that it *was* foreseeable that blind people would be in the vicinity. We will look at the particular application of this in relation to psychiatric injury.

The type of injury suffered should also be foreseeable. As Lord Bridge said in the case of *Caparo Industries plc v. Dickman* [1990] 1 All ER 568 (at 574), "One of the most important distinctions always to be observed lies in the law's essentially different approach to the different kinds of damage which one party may have suffered in consequence of the acts or omissions of another". So, in the case of *Bourhill v. Young* [1943] AC 92, the woman who suffered psychiatric injury as a result of being within the sound of a road accident and subsequently saw blood on the road, and who had no special relationship to the participants in the collision, was unsuccessful in her claim. It was not foreseeable that someone in her position (her presence, of course was foreseeable) would suffer *this kind* of damage.

To return for a moment to the facts of *Donoghue v. Stevenson*, it must be stressed that the woman concerned did not *just* discover a snail in her ginger beer: she was also made ill by it. In other words she suffered physical injury. Psychiatric injury poses particular problems in negligence because it is not *physical* injury. It can easily be understood that if the harm suffered by the plaintiff is caused by physical impact, generally the laws of physics restrict the area of damage caused. (It should be noted that physical damage caused by contamination can be huge; at the time when the requirement as to physical damage was imposed, however, the potential for destruction through radiation and chemical contaminants was perhaps not readily appreciated.) Generally, however, limiting damage to physical damage has had the required restrictive effect. On the other hand, in certain areas, often for not very logical reasons, the courts have allowed claims for non-physical damage,[2] and one of these areas is psychiatric injury. We will presently consider the requirement that a plaintiff suffers a 'recognised psychiatric injury'; emotional distress (described somewhat insensitively in the cases as 'ordinary' grief) will not do.

Is the reason for generally limiting claims to those of physical damage based just on lack of foreseeability? As we have said, foreseeability is not a sufficient condition to establish a duty of care. The other consideration is one of policy, which really means public policy. There are many judgements that seek to analyse the role of policy in the establishment of a duty of care, and, indeed, in the law of tort generally, and we do not see this as the appropriate place to examine them in detail. Suffice to say that there is disagreement as to the exact role of policy and whether it is different to the issue of whether there is a duty of care or not, or whether that is precisely what the duty of care issue is about.[3] However, in the area of psychiatric injury policy has played a large and, we submit, depressing role and is much to blame for the present state of the law. A distinguished American judge once said that the law should avoid burdening defendants with "liability in an indeterminate amount for an indeterminate time to an indeterminate class".[4] Opening the floodgates to admit unacceptably large numbers of claims is not permitted, with its anticipated results of soaring insurance premiums, huge delay in settlement of claims and overwhelming pressure on the civil justice system. As we shall see, the devices used by the courts to restrict the class of plaintiff who can pursue a claim for psychiatric injury have been constructed to keep the floodgates closed. The fact that there may be little in the way of a flood behind those gates has been suggested by certain judges,[5] but in the latest House of Lords case, not accepted.[6]

The other elements of negligence are that the duty has been breached, i.e. that the defendant has not behaved in accordance with the appropriate standard of care. This standard will vary according to the position of the defendant, although as a general statement it can be said that it is an objective standard (i.e. the reasonably competent motorist, the reasonably competent brain surgeon, etc).[7] Finally, the breach of the duty must be causatively linked with the damage that the plaintiff has suffered. The tort of negligence looks at factual and legal causation. The latter is another limiting device and asks the question whether the damage caused was too remote, which is decided by whether it was foreseeable. Factual causation is a question of eliminating other causes of the injury.

It is illustrative of the above factors in the development of the tort of negligence, that, firstly, the expression still commonly used to describe a claim for psychiatric injury in negligence is 'nervous shock', and secondly, that some of the early cases involved women who either miscarried or gave birth to dead or damaged children as a result of their experiences. The word 'shock' indicates sudden impact upon the senses, and 'nervous' refers to the nervous system. In other words, implicit in the expression is the physical closeness of the act or event concerned and the subsequent psychiatric illness. Secondly, the cases involving childbirth show some 'physical' evidence of the shock sustained.

It is hoped that this brief, and inevitably simplified, history of the law's manipulation of certain concepts will set the scene for the following consideration of the essential elements of bringing a claim when the plaintiff suffers psychiatric injury as a result of another's carelessness. We use the word 'carelessness' advisedly, as to use the term 'negligence' implies that the legal requirements of negligence have been satisfied.

First of all it can be said that if the plaintiff suffers psychiatric injury as a result of physical injury, or because of the traumatic effect of being involved in the incident which gave rise to the physical injury, then the claim for psychiatric injury will generally not be contentious. The real difficulties arise when there is no associated physical injury. The requirements in such a case are that the plaintiff must either have witnessed an event which had a sudden impact upon her senses, or she must have witnessed the immediate aftermath of that event, and that either she was frightened for her own safety or for a specified other who is sufficiently proximate to her, either through emotional ties or through another proximate relationship. Finally, she must have suffered a recognisable psychiatric injury. Children and other dependants of those injured or killed may also claim for bereavement, loss of the services of a care-giver, and dislocation, all of which compound and prolong the effects of trauma. We will now examine these requirements in more detail.

The causative event

The event must be such as to be distressing to someone of normal fortitude. This requirement has developed out of the foreseeability principle, i.e. it would not be foreseeable that an unremarkable event would cause psychiatric injury.[8] However, the case of Page v. Smith ([1995] 2WLR 644) has established that this is only the case when the victim is not a direct participant in the event but merely witnesses it. In addition to this, the event itself or its immediate aftermath must have been experienced through the unaided senses of the person who has suffered psychiatric injury. This was established in the House of Lords case of *McLoughlin v. O'Brian*.[9] In that case, Mrs McLoughlin was informed that her husband and three children were involved in a road accident and arrived at the hospital where they were being treated some two hours or so after the accident. One of the children had died and she was told of this. However, this did not entitle her to claim damages for her subsequent psychiatric injury. She did, however, recover damages for the injury on the basis that it was caused by the sight of the remaining children and her husband who were still covered in blood and dirt and in states of distress. This was held to constitute part of the 'immediate aftermath' of the event itself, which she witnessed at the hospital through her unaided senses. It is illustrative of the unsatisfactory nature of the present law that it was, presumably, pure chance that she saw her family before they had been cleaned up and sedated, and that if she had seen them in the latter state, she would have had no claim.

In *Alcock v. Chief Constable of South Yorkshire Police*,[10] the case concerning the Hillsborough Football Stadium disaster, it was held that a man who identified a body eight hours or so after it had been crushed to death was not participating in the immediate aftermath. What follows from all this, of course, is the fact that people who suffer psychiatric injury as a result of being told of the death/injury of a loved one will not succeed in negligence (but would succeed if it was a deliberate lie[11]), and since the Alcock decision, those who witness the event via live television will not succeed in negligence either.

Fear for oneself

The test here is whether it is reasonable to fear for one's own safety, given the nature of the event and the physical closeness of the injured party to the event itself. This was considered in *McFarlane v. EE Caledonia*,[12] where it was found that a plaintiff could not reasonably have been in fear for his own safety when he was on a support vessel which was some 550 m away from the Piper Alpha oil rig which exploded in the North Sea in 1988. This case will be considered further in connection with whether a 'mere bystander' can ever recover damages.

Fear for others

The law will only allow damages for psychiatric injury which is a result of witnessing an event which damages or threatens to damage another person, if the injured party and the threatened/injured person are in a sufficiently 'proximate' relationship with one another. This does not necessarily have to be an intimate relationship. It has long been acknowledged that someone who goes to the rescue of another is entitled to claim damages for both physical and psychiatric injury which he may suffer as a result of his involvement.[13] Similarly, someone who is negligently put in a position of threatening the safety of others, may be compensatable. An example is the case of *Dooley v. Cammell Laird & Co Ltd*,[14] where the psychiatrically injured plaintiff had believed that his non-negligent actions had caused injury to his fellow workers.

As far as emotional relationships are concerned, the question of whether there should be a required degree of kinship was considered in *Alcock*. Although the only classes of relationship to have been recognised so far have been those of spouse/spouse and parent/child, the House of Lords said in Alcock that there should be no legally fixed relationships, but each case should be considered on its merits. There could, for example, be a successful claim in the case of cohabitees, siblings, and grandparents/grandchildren. In fact, if the evidence of the strong emotional attachment was cogent enough, then there is no relationship which is excluded.

Again, in *Alcock*, the position of the 'mere bystander' was considered. This is someone who witnesses a traumatic event, but does not stand in a relationship of proximity with someone who has been injured. It was said in *Alcock* that if the event was horrific enough then it may be possible that a mere bystander could recover damages. However, this was again considered in the case of McFarlane, which dealt with the Piper Alpha disaster, and the Court of Appeal took a more harsh view: "In my judgment both as a matter of principle and policy the court should not extend the duty to those who are mere bystanders or witnesses of horrific events unless there is a sufficient degree of proximity, which requires both nearness in time and place and a close relationship of love and affection between plaintiff and victim".[15] This does not accurately sum up the law (for example, it does not acknowledge the other, non-intimate relationships) and the correct view should still be taken to be that of the House of Lords in *Alcock*, so that it can still be argued that if the event is sufficiently horrifying a claim may be possible.

Recognised psychiatric injury

Despite a few anomalous decisions,[16] it is now generally well-established that the compensation is not for mere 'shock', but for a recognised psychiatric injury. Having said that, it is worth pointing out that, as 'acute stress reaction' is specified as an identifiable psychiatric illness in both DSM–IV (American Psychiatric Association, 1994) and ICD–10 (World Health Organization, 1992) with its symptoms of daze, disorientation, agitation, sweating and breathlessness, then surely this is compensatable, even though it is probably only what we would colloquially think of as ordinary 'shock'.

Although many forms of psychiatric injury may result from trauma, it was not until the hearing in 1989 of ten test cases of survivors of the "Herald of Free Enterprise" disaster that the terms 'post-traumatic stress disorder' and 'pathological grief' were first legally recognised. The arbitration panel that heard the case also recognised that it is possible to suffer from more than one psychiatric illness. On the specific issue of the level of compensation, the panel also stated that it may be reasonable for survivors to refuse to undergo treatment for psychiatric illness and that account should be taken in individual cases of any vulnerability to future psychiatric illness.

Lawyers must, of course, take great care when obtaining and presenting evidence of psychiatric injury because the courts have been much less ready to accept the causative link between an accident causing non-physical injury, than one causing physical injury.

The level of compensation for psychiatric injury

The amount of compensation recoverable has to fit within the conventional awards handed down by the courts for physical injuries. The *Guidelines for the Assessment of General Damages in Personal Injury Cases* produced by the Judicial Studies Board in 1994 provide for four categories:

    (a)   severe psychiatric damage: £22 500 to £45 000;
    (b)   moderately severe psychiatric damage: £ 8500 to £20 000;
    (c)   moderate psychiatric damage: £2500 to £7500;
    (d)   minor psychiatric damage: £500 to £1500.

Psychiatric damage will, of course, encompass any recognised psychiatric illness, including PTSD.

The faults of the present system

As we have seen, claims for psychiatric injury in negligence present particular problems because of the special requirements of the tort of negligence. Such limiting devices do not necessarily operate in some other areas of tort, for example where harm is deliberately inflicted in assaults, deceit, or harassment. It is, however, outside the scope of this chapter to examine other areas, as by far the most common cause of action will arise out of negligence.

The law is not satisfactory in this area. It must be said that the aspect which probably leads to the most injustice is the requirement that the plaintiff experiences the event or its immediate aftermath with her own senses. In *McLoughlin* their Lordships were by no means unanimous about this, both Lord Bridge and Lord Scarman preferring tests based on foreseeability alone. Lord Bridge stated that he could see no reason for denying the claim of a mother who suffered injury on reading a newspaper report of a fire at a hotel where her children were staying. Similarly, in the case of *Wigg v. British Railways Board* [1986] 136 NLJ 446, the issue was decided on foreseeability alone. However, in *Alcock* their Lordships applied the 'immediate aftermath' test, and, as we have seen, refused to extend this to television broadcasts. At least in part, this was because the broadcasting authority's code of practice would prevent them from showing pictures of recognisable individuals. With respect, we submit that this is irrelevant: for example, the mother does not have to make a positive identification of her child in order to suffer injury.

The 'floodgates' argument has, of course, played a large part in encouraging judicial caution, but the judgment of Lord Edmund-Davies in *McLoughlin* deals neatly with this point: "My Lords, the experiences of a long life in the law have made me very familiar with this 'floodgates' argument. I do not, of course, suggest that it can invariably be dismissed as lacking cogency; on the contrary, it has to be weighed carefully, but I have often seen it disproved by later events . . . I remain unconvinced that the number and area of claims in 'shock' cases would be substantially increased or enlarged were the respondents here held liable".[17]

One of the matters which has affected judicial minds is the ease with which fraudulent claims may be constructed. However, this did not deter the judge in the case of *Hevican v. Ruane* [1991] 3 All ER 65, from giving a brave judgement in favour of the plaintiff who had suffered psychiatric injury after the death of his 14-year-old son in a road accident. The accident happened at 4 p.m.; the plaintiff was told about the accident very soon afterwards and was told by police at 5.50 p.m. that his son was dead. At 7 p.m. he identified his son's body in the mortuary. He suffered a reactive depression. Mantell J could not see the justification for what he referred to as 'arbitrary' limits on these sorts of claims. Regrettably, following *Alcock* which specifically disapproved the decision, the case was successfully appealed. However, it is instructive to look at the judgement where it considers the specific point about the possible faking of claims: "to sustain a claim based on nervous shock, no matter what the circumstances in which the shock was received, a plaintiff would be bound to submit himself or herself over a protracted period to the close scrutiny of psychiatrists well able to detect humbug".[18]

It can surely be argued that so-called physical pain is an elusive concept: can an orthopaedic consultant, for example, ever be certain that his patient does *not* experience the back pain of which he complains? It may even be arguable that physical pain is *easier* to fake than psychiatric distress; certainly there is no justification for putting them in entirely separate categories. In our submission it is a veiled insult to the profession of psychiatry to suggest that its practitioners are unscientific and easily duped.

In the case of *R. v. Chan Fook* [1993], *The Times*, 19 November, the court held that for the purposes of the criminal law, psychiatric injury was a form of bodily harm; a recognition of this by the civil law may be a welcome development.

Another possible development would be the introduction of legislation, something which was urged by the judges in several of these cases. For example, in the Australian territories of New South Wales and the Australian Capital Territory, legislation[19] allows for the recovery of damages for nervous shock regardless of whether the injury was foreseeable. Under these provisions: (a) a parent (broadly defined) or husband or wife of a person killed, injured or put in peril by the defendant's (wrongful) act, neglect or default may recover damages for nervous shock arising out of the accident regardless of whether it occurred within the sight or hearing of the person suffering the shock; (b) other members of the family (broadly defined) of the victim may recover damages for nervous shock if the accident occurred within the sight or hearing of that member of the family. Those who are not specifically covered by the legislation have to satisfy the ordinary common law requirements, which are more or less the same as in the UK.

Disasters and implications for psychiatrically injured victims

Apart from their proper search for compensation, the reasonable expectations of survivors and bereaved relatives following a disaster include the need for the legal response to provide an open investigation of the facts that will produce answers as to how the disaster occurred; how each deceased met his or her death; how to prevent it happening in future; and how blame and punishment should be apportioned.

However, under the law of England and Wales there is no clear and obvious method of simultaneously addressing all of these questions (which combine civil and criminal issues) in one form of hearing. Indeed, since the Manchester air crash in 1985, the nature and sequence of inquiries held in the aftermath of different disasters has been so varied that it has produced no discernible pattern that could be described as a systematic legal response at all. Furthermore, research by Dr James Thompson[20] at the Middlesex Hospital showed that the experience of confronting the problems that arise in the aftermath of a disaster can add to the trauma of the disaster itself. The complaint most commonly voiced by those involved in the study related to the post-disaster legal and official procedures.

Understandably, those involved in a disaster expect their legal advisers to explain at the outset with some certainty how the legal process can be expected to unfold and operate. However, the uncertain sequence of post-disaster procedures is such that today the legal adviser's predictions have to cover the full range of possibilities. These may include a public inquiry ordered by the Secretary of State, an internal (private) inquiry, specialised (private) Government investigations into aviation, maritime and rail accidents, a shortened form of inquest, a full inquest, a criminal investigation that may or may not lead to prosecution and, in the last resort, judicial review proceedings in the Divisional Court. This situation is hardly satisfactory and does little to ease the troubled minds of clients. Most of them expect that after a disaster a public inquiry will be set up, but this is a decision apparently taken at Cabinet Office level based upon unknown criteria.

To take but one example of the problems that can arise, it is instructive to record the events following the sinking of the passenger cruiser *Marchioness* by the dredger *Bowbelle* on the River Thames in August 1989. After the Government had refused to hold a public inquiry there followed two written reports by the Department of Transport, three unsuccessful criminal prosecutions, and a dispute between some bereaved relatives and HM Coroner over his refusal to hold a 'full' inquest, resulting in judicial review proceedings up to the level of the Court of Appeal which ordered that a new coroner should take over. After a second inquest which lasted four weeks, on 7 April 1995 the jury delivered a verdict of unlawful killing of the 51 people who died. The verdict was in spite of the direction by the coroner that a verdict of unlawful killing could not apply to anyone cleared by a court (referring to the earlier unsuccessful criminal prosecutions of the master of the dredger and its owners, South Coast Shipping). The opportunity for evidence to be presented as to the events of that night had a cathartic effect on the families of the dead and injured,[21] but it had taken nearly six years to achieve a public hearing of the events which had caused the tragedy.

If the risk of the aftermath of a disaster causing an increase to the trauma suffered by those involved is to be removed, then it is time that the working party set up by the Government as long ago as 1991 to look at methods of reforming the machinery of post-disaster inquiries actually produced its report, with proposals that should promote speed and certainty in the resolution of the above questions, for the benefit of both the victims and the public.

Endnotes

1. See, for example, *Home Office v. Dorset Yacht Co Ltd* [1970] AC 1004.
2. For example, economic loss caused by negligent misstatement: see *Hedley Byrne & Co Ltd v. Heller & Partners* [1964] AC 465.
3. See *Anns v. Merton London Borough Council* [1978] 1 AC 728 (the policy statement of Lord Wilberforce, particularly, which is now generally out of favour); *Caparo Industries plc v. Dickman* [1990] 2 AC 605 (the three point test of the relationships of the parties, the nature of the risk involved and the just and reasonableness of imposing a duty); and, in particular see the words of MacDonald J. in *Nova-Mink v. Trans Canada Airlines* [1951] 2 DLR 241, at 254, where he stressed the role of policy "however it may be obscured by the traditional formulae".
4. *Ultramares Corporation v. Touche* [1931] 174 NE 441, 444 per Cardozo C. J.
5. See, for example, the comments of Lord Edmund-Davies in *McLoughlin v. O'Brian* [1983] 1 AC 410 at 425.
6. *Alcock v. Chief Constable of South Yorkshire Police* [1992] 1 AC 310.
7. There are many cases on this point, see for example *Wells v. Cooper* [1958] 2 QB 265.
8. See, e.g. *Bourhill v. Young* [1943] AC 92.
9. [1983] AC 410.
10. [1992] 1 AC 310.
11. *Intentionally caused* psychiatric injury does not have to satisfy the special 'negligence' criteria; see *Wilkinson v. Downton* [1897] 2 QB 57.
12. [1994] 2 All ER 1.
13. *Chadwick v. British Railways Board* [1967] 1 WLR 912.
14. [1951] 1 Lloyd's Rep 271.
15. Per Stuart-Smith L.J., at 14e.
16. Such as *Whitmore v. Euroways Express Coaches Ltd* [1984] *The Times*, May 4.
17. At 425 D-G.
18. At 71.
19. Law Reform (Miscellaneous Provisions) Act 1944 (NSW), s 4 as amended, and Law Reform (Miscellaneous Provisions) Act 1955 (ACT) s 24.
20. BBC Radio 4 broadcast, "Shockwaves", 28 April 1991.
21. See, for example, *The Guardian*, 8 April 1995, p. 7.

References

American Psychiatric Association (1994) *Diagnostic and Statistical Manual of Mental Disorders* (4th edn) (DSM–IV). Washington, DC: APA.

Judicial Studies Board (1994) *Guidelines for the Assessment of General Damages in Personal Injury Cases*. Blackstone Press.

World Health Organization (1992) *The ICD–10 Classification of Mental and Behavioural Disorders: Clinical Descriptions and Diagnostic Guidelines*. Geneva: WHO.

23 Post-traumatic stress reactions and the criminal law

GWEN ADSHEAD and GILLIAN MEZEY

This chapter will focus on the association between post-traumatic stress reactions and criminal, violent or antisocial behaviours, and how this relates to the criminal justice process. The principal focus of this chapter will be on the violence following trauma in adulthood, rather than on aggression and violence manifested in survivors of childhood trauma.

There are few reports of criminal behaviour in survivors of trauma and the significance of any violent or antisocial behaviour may be overlooked. Clearly the majority of offenders do not describe any significant antecedent history of trauma, nor is criminal behaviour an automatic sequela to a traumatic event. Even if the two events are temporally associated, this does not necessarily demonstrate any causal connection (i.e. their association may be apparent rather than real).

Criminal behaviour arises as a result of a complex interplay between the traumatic event and factors such as personality, coping strategies, lifestyle and substance misuse (Shaw *et al*, 1987). However, there are some specific features of mental disorder that are associated with violence (see Monahan, 1992, for review). Symptoms of paranoia or suspiciousness are related to violence, as are anger and irritability (Kennedy, 1992). Increased arousal and impulsivity may make violence more likely, as may substance misuse, by reducing inhibitions and impairing judgement. All these symptoms may occur in post-traumatic stress disorder.

Crime and war trauma

One must be cautious about extrapolating findings from war veterans to a non-combat population of survivors: premorbid factors, as well as the violent, 'manmade' nature of the stressor in combat veterans, may produce a differential response.

However, an increase in violent and non-violent crimes and antisocial behaviours has been noted in a proportion of combat veterans (Lifton, 1973; Boman, 1987; Wilson, 1988; Resnick *et al*, 1989; Bremner *et al*, 1993; Chemtob *et al*, 1994). A quarter of those who saw heavy combat in Vietnam were charged with a criminal offence on their return (Marciniak, 1986), and a third of the US federal prison population are veterans (Jordan *et al*, 1986). Among veterans seeking help, uncontrollable and impulsive aggression is a prominent concern (Blum *et al*, 1984; Silver & Iacono, 1984). Veterans who have combat-related PTSD score higher ratings of anger than veterans without PTSD: a difference that cannot be explained by concurrent psychiatric diagnosis or by increased impulsivity in the PTSD group (Chemtob *et al*, 1994). Yager *et al* (1984) suggested that wartime participation in abusive violence was associated with a 14% increase in arrests, even after controlling for pre-service antisocial behaviours. An increase in domestic violence and marital breakdown has been recorded after trauma (Carroll *et al*, 1985; Gibbs, 1989); 38% of Vietnam veterans were divorced within six months of their return home (Jordan *et al*, 1986). Studies of Second World War veterans have also found increased irritability and aggression in this population, and all veterans appear to have an increased risk of dying a violent death (Segal *et al*, 1976; Boman, 1987).

Post-traumatic psychiatric illness and antisocial behaviour

Re-experiencing phenomena and crime

Intrusive images may be reactivated by conditions similar to those experienced at the time of the original trauma, associated with heightened physiological arousal and anxiety. The survivor feels "as if" they are reliving and re-experiencing the original trauma, and thus may react in a violent or disturbed way (Wilson & Ziegelbaum, 1983, 1986) – so-called 'traumatic re-enactments' (van der Kolk, 1989). Conscious awareness may be impaired during traumatic re-enactments, so that the subject may be either wholly or partially unaware of their actions at the time.

Cognitive–perceptual deficits and crime

There is some empirical evidence that physically abused children are prone to aggressive behaviour (Dodge *et al*, 1990; Otnow-Lewis, 1992). This effect is an indirect one, mediated by the effect of abuse on social information processing styles. Adult survivors of trauma may, like abused children, perceive objectively neutral stimuli as threatening and respond in an aggressive or defensive way.

Anger is common in survivors of trauma (Novaco & Robinson, 1984; Boulanger, 1986; Riggs *et al*, 1992) and this may intensify with the passage of time (Green *et al*, 1990). Angry people with high impulsivity and poor control may behave in an aggressive or violent way.

Individuals with PTSD tend to show cognitive rigidity and polarised thinking, and may turn to anger as a means of problem resolution (Alford *et al*, 1988). Poor memory, reduced concentration and increased sensitivity to perceptual stimuli can lead to increased risk-taking behaviour and impaired judgement (Zeitlin & McNally, 1991; Cassiday *et al*, 1992), which may bring the individual into contact with the law.

Social and interpersonal dysfunction and crime

Irritability, poor concentration and distractibility can lead to deterioration in work performance and sometimes loss of employment, with consequent financial worries. Loss of trust and general irritability can also result in alienation from others, causing loss of friends and marital disharmony (Lane & Hobfoll, 1992). The combination of loss of work, family and friends can exacerbate feelings of isolation, betrayal and generalised suspiciousness, lower self-esteem, and increase anxiety and resentment. These factors may independently make the individual more liable to act in a reckless, hostile or destructive way.

Alcohol and drug use

Post-traumatic stress disorder is commonly associated with increased use of drugs (legal and illegal) and alcohol (Jordan *et al,* 1986). The misuse of alcohol or illegal drugs, particularly in combination with high levels of arousal, suspiciousness, social withdrawal and alienation, may lead to violent or disturbed behaviour. Crime may also be committed in order to support drug or alcohol misuse or to combat financial hardship due to unemployment, as a pragmatic but maladaptive coping behaviour.

PTSD and the law

Since post-traumatic stress reactions can, in certain circumstances, give rise to antisocial or criminal behaviour, this knowledge may be used as the basis for a legal defence by lawyers, especially if the alternative is likely to be a long prison sentence. Controversy about the use and misuse of post-traumatic stress reactions as mitigation or as a defence has particularly arisen in the US, in relation to the large number of veterans who have been involved in violent crime (Jordan *et al,* 1986; Sparr & Atkinson, 1986).

The jurisprudential and philosophical basis for the role of psychological evidence in criminal trials will not be described in great detail. Suffice to say that most Anglo-Saxon jurisdictions recognise that mental illness may affect intention to carry out actions which are deemed criminal. Without intention (*mens rea*), there can be no crime (*actus rea*).

The effect of any mental illness on *mens rea* may be:

(a) to abolish it altogether, so that intention is said to be absent (e.g. sleepwalking, post-ictal states);
(b) to make it irrational or 'insane': e.g. not knowing that an act is wrong;
(c) to make it less blameworthy than it might otherwise be. This is an extension of a common social policy that those who are ill are not as responsible as others for their actions.

If it is accepted by the jury that a mental illness abolished *mens rea*, or made it 'insane', then the defendant may be acquitted of the charges. If it is thought that the defendant should be held to be less responsible for his actions because of the illness, then he will be found guilty of a lesser charge.

Mental illness following trauma, including PTSD, may also be used in mitigation after conviction; a successful outcome may result in acquittal, a lighter sentence, or a therapeutic as opposed to a punitive disposal.

In order to argue this, defence lawyers require expert evidence from psychiatrists, psychologists or other 'experts' in mental health. Expert witnesses may be required to give evidence on the nature of post-traumatic responses and their relationship with offending behaviour. They may also be required to comment on the effect of any mental illness present on the individual's capacity to form intent (although strictly speaking this is a matter for the jury). They may also be invited to comment on the availability of treatment and disposal, as well as the implications of their findings for the defendant's future dangerousness.

There are restrictions on the extent to which expert evidence may be allowed into court. Experts may only give evidence on matters of which the jury could not reasonably be expected to have knowledge (*R. v. Turner*)[1]. Judges are often reluctant to hear general expert evidence, rather than specific evidence about a case.

Psychiatric defences and PTSD

The principal psychiatric defences in English law are described below, in relation to PTSD and other post-traumatic states.

Insanity defences

The insanity defence (see Criminal Procedures: Insanity and Unfitness to Plead Act 1991) may be raised to any charge. If successful, this leads to a finding of legal insanity and acquittal. Where there is a mandatory sentence, judges will have to impose a hospital order, but less serious charges may receive community treatment orders, or guardianship equivalents. The test for the insanity defence is that the mental illness caused the defendant *either* not to know what he was doing, *or* not to know it was wrong (McNaughton rules; see West & Walk, 1977).

The symptoms of PTSD may form the basis for an insanity defence on both limbs of the McNaughton rules. A patient in a dissociative state might fulfil both criteria, and therefore a defendant who commits an offence while in a dissociative state may be deemed to be legally insane. (This argument has been further developed in relation to automatisms, and will be discussed further below.)

In the US, it has been argued that a defendant's experience of 'flashbacks' constitute dissociative states for the purposes of insanity defences (Sparr & Atkinson, 1986). This argument has principally been used for Vietnam veterans, but not without some reservations being expressed about the risk of false acquittals.

In principle, it should be possible for PTSD to provide a basis insanity defence in English courts. However, recent reforms to the i defence have meant a lack of opportunity to test this out. 'Temporary insanity' is a legal notion accepted in the US, but as yet untried in the UK. Arguments may be put forward that a crime was carried out while the individual was temporarily in a post-traumatic dissociative state (Bisson, 1993, describes just such a case, but does not give the outcome).

Diminished responsibility

Section 2 of the Homicide Act 1957 states that a charge of murder may be reduced to manslaughter if, at the time of the offence, the defendant suffered from an "abnormality of mind", and if that abnormality "substantially impaired [his] responsibility for the killing". Strictly speaking, experts should confine themselves to the first clause, and leave the second to the jury, but in practice, most experts are invited to comment on both. A successful defence results in a manslaughter conviction, which allows the judge a wider range of sentence options, from suspended sentence to life detention.

Psychiatrists have lacked consensus over the definition of and criteria for 'abnormality of mind' for the purposes of Section 2 of the Homicide Act 1957. The legal view is that an abnormality of mind is any state of mind the "reasonable man would find abnormal" (Parker L. J., in *R. v. Byrne*)[2]. In practice, most psychiatrists would see 'abnormality' as being equivalent to any mental state that met current internationally recognised diagnostic criteria (e.g. DSM–III–R (American Psychiatric Association, 1987) or ICD–10 (World Health Organization, 1992)).

Post-traumatic psychiatric illnesses could all qualify as 'abnormalities of mind' and, if accepted, should result in a conviction for manslaughter rather than murder. It remains to be seen if a traumatic stress response as a result of chronic victimisation (e.g. 'battered woman syndrome') will be the basis of future 'diminished responsibility' defences in English courts, but in principle, battered woman syndrome (Walker, 1979) could be reformulated as chronic PTSD.

Herman (1992) postulated the existence of a 'complex' post-traumatic stress disorder, DESNOS (disorders of extreme stress not otherwise specified), as a sequel to repeated and chronic interpersonal violence, including domestic violence and sexual abuse. However, until DESNOS is formally recognised as a mental illness by American or British classificatory systems, its usefulness as a psychiatric defence is likely to be limited.

Automatism defences

An automatism defence must show that, at the time of the offence, the defendant had no *mens rea* at all (i.e. his mental state was such that no intention was possible). A paradigm was of a sleepwalker, although the appropriateness of this has now been questioned: see *R. v. Burgess*.[3] If the defence is successful, the defendant is acquitted with no disposal conditions (unlike insanity).

Two separate automatism defences have developed in English law; 'sane' and 'insane' (*R. v. Kemp*)[4]. If the automatism is caused by a mental state which arises from an "external force" (e.g. a blow on the head; *R. v. Quick*)[5], then it is deemed to be a sane automatism, and if successful, results in complete acquittal. However, if the automatism arises from an internal cause (as determined by the court), then it is equivalent to "disease of the mind", and results in a finding of legal insanity.

Prior to the recent reforms which allowed for a range of disposal options, a finding of legal insanity previously resulted in automatic detention in a hospital, sometimes for prolonged and indeterminate periods of time. Not surprisingly, defendants were keen to plead to lesser charges rather than use the automatism defence (e.g. *R. v. Sullivan*)[6].

In practice, the range of mental disorders giving rise to 'sane' automatisms is becoming increasingly restricted. This is usually because most mental disorders are seen by the courts as an 'internal' rather than an 'external' cause. For example, sleepwalking and sleep disorders used to be the basis of sane automatism; however, sleepwalking is now said to be an 'insane' automatism (e.g. *R. v. Burgess*). Psychological states which are themselves the result of an 'external' cause might still qualify. The notion of a 'psychological blow' causing a sane automatism has not been accepted (in re Rabey; quoted in *R. v. T.*)[7]. However, PTSD, and especially dissociative states as a feature of PTSD, might now be the only psychological states to give rise to 'sane' automatism.

The case of *R. v. T.* bears this out. T. was charged with actual bodily harm. Her offence was that, in the course of an altercation with a stranger, she had injured the stranger with a knife. She claimed that, at the time of the offence, she was in an "automatic state", as a result of an acute post-traumatic stress reaction. Three days prior to the alleged offence, she had been raped by a stranger who had forced his way into her home. She had told no-one about the rape, but there was physical evidence to support her account. Psychiatric evidence was called to explain that T. was suffering from acute PTSD including dissociative episodes after having been raped. The judge allowed the defence of 'sane' automatism to be heard by the jury, based on PTSD, and accepted that PTSD was not a "disease of the mind". Although T. was convicted, the judge acknowledged her experience and she received a suspended sentence.

Other charges which require specific intent may be reduced to lesser charges if it can be shown that, at the time of the offence, the defendant was suffering from a psychiatric illness which might affect the capacity to form intent.

Dissociation and excuse: as clear as mud?

Given the difficulty of diagnosing dissociative states and determining their scope and duration, psychiatrists and lawyers should be cautious about offering evidence on this issue. Objective evidence which confirms the presence of a dissociative state is likely to be unavailable, although third-party accounts of the defendant's behaviour should be sought. Psychiatric experts may be asked to distinguish between a 'flashback' and a 'dissociative state', in terms of the effect on consciousness. They may have to comment on the effect of dissociative states on intent, and be prepared to defend this view under cross-examination.

With the acceptance of PTSD-induced dissociative states as the basis of a psychiatric defence comes the possibility of accepting dissociative states which are a feature of borderline personality disorder, and the spectre of multiple personality disorder, in the courtroom. Given the current confusion and controversy about the status of multiple personality disorder, psychiatrists will therefore want to think carefully about these issues before putting pen to court report. Malingering is considered to be a real risk in such cases. Blank (1985, cited in Sparr & Atkinson, 1986) suggested that the diagnosis of PTSD must be established before accepting that the criminal behaviour is the result of a flashback or dissociative state. The features which suggest a dissociative state episode include amnesia for all or part of the episode, lack of obvious motivation for the behaviour, sudden or unpremeditated behaviour, the presence of other symptoms of PTSD and the fortuitous or accidental choice of victim.

Provocation and self-defence

Strictly speaking, provocation and self-defence do not require psychiatric evidence, but are among a range of defences to murder which, if successful, result in a defendant being convicted of the lesser charge of manslaughter.

In a provocation case, the jury must ask themselves whether the 'reasonable man' (or woman) with the characteristics of the accused would have been provoked to react in such a way under the same circumstances. The accused's characteristics may be taken to represent physical character-istics (e.g. ethnicity, height, build, or psychological characteristics) providing they are of sufficient permanence and significance. In cases where women kill their battering partners, it has been suggested that having battered woman syndrome (Walker, 1979, 1984) could represent enduring psycho-logical 'characteristics' (*R. v. Camplin*)[8]. Psychiatric expert evidence may be admitted to inform the jury as to whether the defendant's response to previous trauma might be construed as 'enduring characteristics', and the jury would then be required to consider whether the reasonable 'battered woman' would have behaved as the defendant did. Psychiatrists or psycholo-gists may also be asked to testify on the nature of battering relationships and associated concepts: learned helplessness (Seligman, 1975), traumatic re-enactments (van der Kolk, 1989) and traumatic bonding (Dutton & Painter, 1991).

In relation to self-defence and murder, the jury must ask whether the 'reasonable man' would have perceived himself to be in imminent danger and whether the amount of force used was reasonable. This is an absolute defence to a charge of murder, and if successful, the defendant is acquitted and allowed to walk free from the court. In relation to battered women, the defence will seek to show that it would be 'reasonable' for a battered woman to perceive danger where another person might not. This is a developing area in law in England, and the responses of juries and judges is uncertain. However, it has been raised in some cases in the US.

Post-traumatic stress reactions and mitigation

It is possible for post-traumatic mental illnesses to stand as mitigation in the usual way. Evidence may be given by psychiatrists about post-traumatic stress reactions which may result in sentences being reduced on appeal (e.g. *R. v. Emery*[9]; *R. v. Parker*[10]). This is not always successful, for example, in those cases where the Appeal Court has not been convinced of the link between the offences and the post-traumatic stress (*R. v. Brown*[11]; *R. v. Slaughter*[12]).

Post-traumatic stress reactions and prosecution evidence

In the US expert evidence has been used to describe the psychological effects of rape and the rape victim's reactions, including submissive behaviour during the assault, delayed reporting and retraction of complaints, as well as commenting on whether the alleged victim's demeanour and behaviour are consistent with descriptions of rape trauma syndrome and PTSD (Raum, 1983; Frazier & Borgida, 1985; Tetreault, 1989; Block, 1990).

Evidence on the effects of sexual assault on victims is important, because this is arguably an area where both juries and judges may be unaware of specific relevant information. To date, the English judiciary has been reluctant to admit such evidence. One concern about such evidence within an adversarial system is that any victim is only an 'alleged' victim until the defendant is convicted. If evidence about rape trauma syndrome is admitted, then this might suggest to the jury that a rape has occurred; evidence could be highly prejudicial to the defence (Frazier & Borgida, 1985).

Effects on the crime victim can be influential when sentencing offenders (e.g. *R. v. W.*[13]), which may mean that the absence of any obvious traumatic stress response including PTSD could be used to justify a more lenient sentence being passed.

The psychiatrist as expert witness

The psychiatrist called to give expert witness in relation to post-traumatic stress has the same task as any expert in court. It is his/her job to educate the court and jury about the disorder in question, and to elucidate the psychological 'dynamics' of a patient's behaviour. Most juries and judges (and sometimes other psychiatrists) may need particular information about post-traumatic stress reactions and PTSD. The expert in the criminal court will have to review and emphasise the traumatic event, and demonstrate the connection between the experiences and the alleged offence.

Evidence about the defendant's pre-traumatic state is crucial for demonstrating the contrast with post-traumatic behaviour, and as much detailed information about this as possible should be obtained. The defendant's account alone should not be relied on, and interviews with independent informants can be very useful to support any arguments put forward. Diagnoses of PTSD should be made on the basis of detailed accounts of symptoms, and where possible with reference to DSM–IV (American Psychiatric Association, 1994) criteria, and using relevant standardised instruments. The relevance of PTSD to the whole personality should be discussed, plus the likely prognosis of the condition and recommendations for treatment.

As with all medico-legal work, it is the expert's task to decide if there is a psychiatric issue on which she can appropriately comment. A history of trauma may be unrelated to any subsequent crime, and many people do survive extraordinary trauma without acting criminally. Psychiatric expert witnesses have a responsibility to contribute what they can, but without either medicalising crime or criminalising mental disorder (see chapter 24).

Childhood trauma and later acting-out

Trauma in childhood can give rise to post-traumatic stress reactions, which may have a profound effect upon subsequent development. The most common form of childhood trauma is abuse by care-givers. In childhood itself, abuse may cause PTSD, anger and aggressive behaviours (McCleer *et al*, 1988; Otnow-Lewis, 1992). Abused children appear to have reduced empathy with the distress of others (Main & George, 1985).

The effects of childhood trauma may persist into adulthood. Retrospective studies of psychiatric in-patients and out-patients suggest that the prevalence of abuse histories is higher in these groups than the general population (Carmen *et al*, 1984). Trauma may have a specific pathological effect on the personality, causing it to change and become disordered (Wilson, 1988). Specifically, a history of abuse in childhood appears to be very common in those patients with a diagnosis of borderline personality disorder (BPD) (Herman *et al*, 1989). This is of relevance because of the association between some personality disorders (e.g. BPD) and aggressive outbursts (Gardner *et al*, 1991). Herman's (1992) concept of 'complex PTSD' has similarities with the symptoms of BPD and with the ICD–10 category of 'personality change after trauma'.

Histories of abuse in childhood have been found in a high proportion of child sex abusers (Araji & Finkelhor, 1986; Seghorn *et al*, 1987), wife batterers (Caesar, 1988) and aggressive and self-harming women (Adshead, 1994).

It is not suggested that all those who suffer abuse in childhood will become violent: the evidence for a 'cycle of violence' is inconclusive (Widom, 1989, 1991). Some children may be more resilient than others, by virtue of temperament or factors in the external environment (Rutter, 1985). Nevertheless, it appears that for a proportion of those abused in childhood, there is an increased risk of psychiatric illness in adulthood (Mullen *et al*, 1993) or violence (Coid, 1992; Dutton & Hart, 1992).

Conclusion: trauma and the wider stage

Crime is to some extent in the eyes of the beholder, as is the definition of what constitutes a traumatic event. It would be foolish to reduce all violence and criminal behaviour to a variant of post-traumatic response: violence may be rational, instrumental, politically inspired or provoked. One should hesitate to attribute wartime atrocities and group violence to a collective post-traumatic reaction, nor would such an exercise be particularly enlightening.

There is some evidence that in conditions where abuse is made legitimate, certain people who have been maltreated could re-experience their abuse either as victims or as abusers, depending on the power they are given (de Zulueta, 1993). The judgement of unacceptable behaviour as irrational raises important questions related to self-determination, personal responsibility, power and control. Clearly, there is concern about the interference of psychiatry in matters related to crime, justice, and inevitably social order. An understanding of the effects of trauma on individuals and communities and how this relates to violent behaviour needs to take into account how power is distributed within those communities. The use of a concept like PTSD may be too simplistic an explanation, and may not accurately reflect the realities of injustice and victimisation within a community.

Endnotes

1. *R. v. Turner* [1975] 60 Cr. App. R. 80 (C.A.).
2. *R. v. Byrne* [1960] 2 QB 398.
3. *R. v. Burgess* [1991] Court of Appeal, Criminal Division. *The Times*, 28 March.
4. *R. v. Kemp* [1957] 1QB 399.
5. *R. v. Quick* [1973] 3 All ER 347.
6. *R. v. Sullivan* [1983] 2 All ER 673.
7. *R. v. T.* [1990] Criminal Law Review 256.
8. *D.P.P. v. Camplin* [1978] 2 All ER 168.
9. *R. v. Emery* [1992] 14 Cr App R (S) 394.
10. *R. v. Parker* [1990] Ct. Of Appeal, Criminal Division, 1/2/90.
11. *R. v. Brown* [1989] Court of Appeal, *The Times*, 25 October.
12. *R. v. Slaughter* [1989] Court of Appeal. *The Times*, 25 October.
13. *R. v. W.* [1993] 14 Cr. App. R (S), Crim. LR 472.

References

Adshead, G. (1994) Damage: trauma and violence in a group of women referred to a forensic psychiatric service. *Behavioural Sciences and the Law*, 12, 235–249.

Alford, J., Mahone, C. & Fielstein, E. (1988) Cognitive and behavioural sequelae of combat: conceptualisations and implications for treatment. *Journal of Traumatic Stress*, 1, 489–501.

American Psychiatric Association (1987) *Diagnostic and Statistical Manual of Mental Disorders* (3rd edn, revised) (DSM–III–R). Washington, DC: APP.

—— (1994) *Diagnostic and Statistical Manual of Mental Disorders* (4th edn) (DSM–IV). Washington, DC: APP.

Araji, S. & Finkelhor, D. (1986) Abusers: a review of the research. In *A Source Book on Child Sexual Abuse* (ed. D. Finkelhor), pp. 89–118. Dewberry Park, CA: Sage.

Bisson, J. (1993) Automatism and post-traumatic stress disorder. *British Journal of Psychiatry*, **163**, 830–832.

Block, A. P.(1990) Rape trauma syndrome and scientific expert testimony. *Archives of Sexual Behaviour*, **19**, 309–323.

Blum, M. D., Kelley, E. M., Meyer, K., *et al* (1984) An assessment of the treatment needs of Vietnam-era veterans. *Hospital and Community Psychiatry*, **35**, 691–696.

Boman, B. (1987) Anti-social behaviour and the combat veteran: a review. *Medicine and Law*, **6**, 173–187.

Boulanger, G. (1986) Violence and Vietnam veterans. In *The Vietnam Veteran Redefined* (eds G. Boulanger & C. Kadushin), pp. 79–90. Hillsdale: Erlbaum.

Bremner, J. D., Southwick, S., Johnson, D., *et al* (1993) Child physical abuse and combat related PTSD in Vietnam veterans. *American Journal of Psychiatry*, **150**, 235–239.

Caesar, P. L. (1988) Exposure to violence in the families of origin among wife abusers and maritally non-violent men. *Violence and Victims*, **3**, 49–63.

Carmen, H., Rieker, P. & Mills, T. (1984) Victims of violence and psychiatric illness. *American Journal of Psychiatry*, **141**, 378–383.

Carroll, E. M., Reuger, D. B., Foy, D. W., *et al* (1985) Vietnam combat veterans with post traumatic stress disorder. *Analysis of Marital and Cohabiting Adjustment*, **94**, 329–337.

Cassiday, L., McNally, R. & Zeitlin, S. (1992) Cognitive processing of trauma cues in rape victims with PTSD. *Cognitive Research and Therapy*, **16**, 283–295.

Chemtob, C. M., Hamada, R. S., Roitblat, H. I., *et al* (1994) Anger, impulsivity and anger control in combat related post traumatic stress disorder. *Journal of Consulting and Clinical Psychology*, **62**, 827–832.

Coid, J. (1992) DSM–III diagnoses in criminal psychopaths: the way forward. *Criminal Behaviour and Mental Health*, **2**, 78–95.

de Zulueta, F. (1993) *The Traumatic Roots of Destructiveness. From Pain to Violence*. London: Whurr.

Dodge, K. A., Bates, J. E. & Pettit, G. S. (1990) Mechanisms in the cycle of violence. *Science*, **250**, 1678–1683.

Dutton, D. & Painter, S. (1991) Traumatic bonding: the development of emotional attachment in battered women and other relationships of intermittent abuse. *Victimology*, **6**, 139–155.

—— & Hart, S. (1992) Evidence for long-term specific effects of childhood abuse and neglect on criminal behaviour in men. *International Journal of Offender Treatment and Comparative Criminology*, **31**, 129–138.

Frazier, P. & Borgida, E. (1985) Rape trauma syndrome evidence in court. *American Psychologist*, **40**, 984–993.

Gardner, D. C., Leibenluft, E., O'Leary, K., *et al* (1991) Self-ratings of anger and hostility in borderline personality disorder. *Journal of Nervous and Mental Disease*, **179**, 157–161.

Gibbs, M. (1989) Factors in the victim that mediate between disaster and psychopathology. *Journal of Traumatic Stress*, **2**, 489–514.

Green, B. L., Grace, M. C., Lindy, J. D., *et al* (1990) Buffalo Creek survivors in the second decade: stability of stress symptoms. *American Journal of Orthopsychiatry*, **60**, 43–54.

Herman, J. (1992) Complex PTSD: a syndrome in survivors of prolonged and repeated trauma. *Journal of Traumatic Stress*, **5**, 377–391.

——, Perry, C. & Van der Kolk, B. (1989) Childhood trauma in borderline personality disorder. *American Journal of Psychiatry*, **146**, 490–495.

Jordan, H., Howe, G., Gelsomino, J., *et al* (1986) Post-traumatic stress disorder: a psychiatric defence. *Journal of the National Medical Association*, **78**, 119–126.

Kennedy, H. (1992) Anger and irritability. *British Journal of Psychiatry*, **161**, 145–153.

Lane, C. & Hobfoll, S. (1992) How loss affects anger and alienates potential supporters. *Journal of Consulting and Clinical Psychology*, **60**, 935–942.

Lifton, R. J. (1973) *Home from the War: Learning from Vietnam Veterans*. Boston: Beacon Press.

McCleer, S., Deblinger, E., Atkins, M. S., *et al* (1988) Post-traumatic stress disorder in sexually abused children. *Journal of the American Academy of Child and Adolescent Psychiatry*, **27**, 650–654.

Main, M. & George, C. (1985) Responses of abused and disadvantaged toddlers to distress in age mates: a study in a day care setting. *International Journal of Child Abuse and Neglect*, **8**, 203–217.

Marciniak, R. (1986) Implications for forensic psychiatry of PTSD: a review. *Military Medicine*, **151**, 434–437.

Monahan, J. (1992) Mental disorder and violent behaviour. *American Psychologist*, **47**, 511–521.

Mullen, P., Martin, J., Anderson, J., *et al* (1993) Child sexual abuse and mental health in adult life. *British Journal of Psychiatry*, **163**, 721–730.

Novaco, R. W. & Robinson, G. (1984) Anger and aggression among military personnel. In *Aggression in Children and Youths* (eds R. Kaplan, V. J. Konecni & R. W. Novaco), pp. 209–241. The Hague: Martinus Nijhoff.

Otnow-Lewis, D. (1992) From abuse to violence. *Journal of the American Academy of Child and Adolescent Psychiatry*, 31, 383–391.

Raum, B. A. (1983) Rape trauma syndrome as circumstantial evidence of rape. *Journal of Psychiatry and the Law*, Summer, 203–213.

Resnick, H. S., Foy, D. W., Donahoe, C. P., *et al* (1989) Antisocial behaviour and post traumatic stress disorder. *Journal of Clinical Psychology*, 45, 860–866.

Riggs, D. S., Dancu, C. V., Gershuny, B. S., *et al* (1992) Anger and PTSD in female crime victims. *Journal of Traumatic Stress*, 5, 613–625.

Rutter, M. (1985) Resilience in the face of adversity: protective factors and resistance to psychiatric disorder. *British Journal of Psychiatry*, 147, 598–611.

Segal, J., Hunter, E. J. & Segal, A. (1976) Universal consequences of capitivity: stress reactions among divergent populations of prisoners of war and their families. *International Journal of Social Science*, 28, 593–609.

Seghorn, T. K., Prentky, R. A. & Boucher, R. J. (1987) Childhood sexual abuse in the lives of sexually aggressive offenders. *Journal of the American Academy of Child and Adolescent Psychiatry*, 26, 262–267.

Seligman, M. (1975) *Helplessness: On Depression, Development and Death.* San Francisco: Freeman.

Shaw, D., Churchill, C., Noyes, R., *et al* (1987) Criminal behaviour and PTSD in Vietnam veterans. *Comprehensive Psychiatry*, 28, 403–411.

Silver, S. M. & Iacono, C. V. (1984). Factor analytic support for DSM–III's post traumatic stress disorder for Vietnam veterans. *Journal of Clinical Psychology*, 40, 5–14.

Sparr, L. & Atkinson, R. (1986) Post-traumatic stress disorder as an insanity defence: medico-legal quicksand. *American Journal of Psychiatry*, 143, 608–613.

Tetreault, P. A. (1989) Rape myth acceptance: a case for providing educational expert testimony in rape jury trials. *Behavioural Sciences and the Law*, 7, 243–257.

van der Kolk, B. (1989) The compulsion to repeat the trauma: re-enactment, re-victimisation and masochism. *Psychiatric Clinics of North America*, 12, 389–411.

Walker, L. E. A. (1979) *The Battered Woman.* New York: Harper & Row.

—— (1984) Battered women, psychology and public policy. *American Psychologist*, 39, 1178–1182.

West, D. J. & Walk, A. (1977) *Daniel McNaughton, His Trial and the Aftermath.* London: Gaskell.

Widom, C. (1989) Does violence beget violence? A critical examination of the literature. *Psychological Bulletin*, 106, 3–28.

—— (1991) Avoidance of criminality in abused and neglected children. *Psychiatry*, 54, 162–174.

Wilson, J. P. (1988) Understanding the Vietnam veteran. In *Post-Traumatic Therapy and Victims of Violence* (ed. F. Ochberg), pp. 227–253. New York: Brunner Mazel.

—— & Ziegelbaum, S. D. (1983) The Vietnam veteran on trial: the relationship of PTSD and criminal behaviour. *Behavioural Science and the Law*, 1, 115–130.

—— & —— (1986) PTSD and the disposition to criminal behaviour. In *Trauma and its Wake*, vol. II (ed. C. Figley). New York: Brunner Mazel.

World Health Organization (1992) *The ICD–10 Classification of Mental and Behavioural Disorders: Clinical Descriptions and Diagnostic Guidelines.* Geneva: WHO.

Yager, T., Laufer, R. & Gallops, M. A. (1984) Some problems associated with war experience in men of the Vietnam generation. *Archives of General Psychiatry*, 41, 327–333.

Zeitlin, S. & McNally, R. (1991) Implicit and explicit memory bias for threat in post-traumatic stress disorder. *Behaviour Research and Therapy*, 29, 451–457.

24 Psychiatric assessment of stress disorders for legal purposes

NIGEL EASTMAN

This chapter is concerned with the assessment of actual or potential litigants. Although focusing on adults, the principles and practice of psycho-legal assessment can equally be applied to children (Black *et al*, 1991).

Assessment of any medical condition for the courts must be carried out on the clear understanding that it represents the provision of medical information for an entirely non-medical (legal) purpose. Hence, although the method of clinical assessment is similar to an 'ordinary' assessment, it must be carried out in clear awareness of the issues of specific relevance to the court, and must also avoid presentation of information which is ultimately legally irrelevant or which does not assist understanding of the medical opinion expressed.

Medical or psychiatric concepts and legal concepts rarely directly cohere with each other and it is necessary for the clinician to have an understanding of the way in which they fail to do so. The specific relationship between (legal) 'nervous shock' and neurotic psychiatric injury is briefly dealt with below under 'Theoretical issues'.

Assessment should not be attempted without clear 'instructions' from the lawyers as to the legal issues to which psychiatric information may be relevant. The psychiatrist should clarify what the relevant psycho-legal interfaces are likely to be before seeing the client, and furthermore, should ensure that they have read at least some of the relevant papers before first interviewing the client. It is useful to have sight of all the client's medical records (from birth) at this early stage; this may avoid an otherwise unnecessary second appointment. It is also helpful to know from the outset whether there is a potentially useful informant who could conveniently be asked to attend with the client.

General principles

It is crucially important in any medico-legal interview to emphasise to the client at the outset the very unusual medical circumstances that pertain. In particular, the person seen is not a 'patient' of the doctor and, as a result, the ethical and clinical boundaries are entirely different from the usual doctor–patient relationship. (Where the clinician is assessing and treating someone clinically and carrying out a psycho-legal assessment, even greater ethical issues arise; see below.) Hence, the ordinary expectations of the boundaries of confidentiality do not apply, since the report will go to the client's lawyers and may, depending upon its contents, go to the other side and to the court. The clinician may be placed in the position of feeling unusually constrained in his or her contact with other practitioners who have treated the person; (s)he needs to obtain the client's specific permission not only to gain information about past treatment, but also to inform another clinician of any clinical findings, because the information was gained in a psycho-legal context.

Simulation and dissimulation are of unusual relevance where potential litigation is at stake. Hence, although clinicians are always properly cautious about the information they are given by their patients, particular caution must apply where there is a non-medical purpose behind the client's willingness to be assessed. Aside from ordinary sensible scepticism, specific approaches can be applied to estimate the likely reliability or validity of the assessment and conclusions. These include: limiting the use of closed questions in the early stages of an assessment of symptoms; noting negative answers to direct questions about possible valid symptomatology that might have been present; and observation of mental state changes concurrent with discussion of particular topics. This may be of particular use in the assessment of stress disorders if the client is confronted with thoughts which they would usually try to avoid. Also, any characteristic pattern of symptoms and/or of their waning may be of use in determining validity. Use of validated psychometric tests may be of further value in addressing faking, even though these may also be open to possible simulation. Validity is also, of course, assessed through addressing the totality of current and past available information (see below). Further advice on validation appears in Eastman (1995).

In conducting the clinical interview(s) it is always advisable to begin with the collection of background historical information before addressing psychological issues of direct relevance to litigation. It almost certainly assists reliability and validity to gain an initial clinical view of the person in isolation from the main purpose of the assessment.

For further general advice, both about the assessment of clients for legal purposes and about good practice in the preparation and provision of medico-legal reports, the reader is referred to Carson *et al* (1993).

Assessment of stress disorders

Assessment for a legal purpose relies upon 'ordinary' methods of psychiatric assessment. However, the specific legal purpose for which the information will be used, as well as adversarial testing of any opinions, determines that it is important to modify usual clinical practice. Hence, clinical information collection must often be more comprehensive and detailed than is usually necessary for ordinary therapeutic purposes and it is also necessary to emphasise particular areas which are of legal relevance, for example, concerning 'causation' (see below).

Theoretical issues

Legal 'nervous shock' is defined so as not to include the ordinary psychological suffering which is expected to accompany a stressful event (see chapter 22). The courts themselves specifically require there to be a recognised psychiatric condition in order to establish 'nervous shock'. Particularly in relation to neurotic conditions, there is always the potential for gradation into 'normality'. This problem may be particularly acute for clinical psychologists, whose constructs tend inherently to eschew notions of categorical disease and to emphasise continua and dimensional disorder. However, even psychiatrists, who do use the concept of categorical 'disease', may feel reduced to 'symptom counting', particularly with DSM–IV (American Psychiatric Association, 1994). A clear difference of diagnostic approach to PTSD is adopted by ICD–10 (World Health Organization, 1992) and DSM–IV, emphasising the problem of presenting psychiatric evidence; both the narrow 'checklist' approach (DSM–IV) and the looser 'clinical judgement' approach (ICD–10) are internationally accepted. A further issue of principle arises from the requirement of the courts that, for the symptoms complained of to amount to legal 'nervous shock', they must be predictable in the ordinary person by virtue of the extent of the trauma to which the person was subjected. This test of 'forseeability' implies that personal vulnerability to the development of PTSD must not amount to any element of the 'cause' of the disorder in order for an individual to be able to claim successfully. This goes against the generally accepted notion that the aetiology of disease is multifactorial and arises out of a mix of environmental and constitutional factors. Where psychiatric injury is secondary to some reasonably forseeable physical injury then the situation is different, since the 'eggshell personality principle' applies.[1] That is, the defendant must take the plaintiff as (s)he finds him or her, with whatever particular vulnerabilities (s)he may have; this is by analogy with the defendant who delivers a blow to the head of a plaintiff who proves to have had an 'eggshell skull'. It would seem clear that the legal principle of the 'eggshell personality' should also be allowed to operate in relation to solely 'nervous shock', such that defendants would have to take the plaintiff as they found him/her, vulnerable or not, causation being adjudged on the basis of 'material contribution'. The developmental thrust of this book emphasises the problem. In practice, the greater the severity of any trauma, particularly if it involved major physical trauma, the greater is likely to be the presumption that environment and not constitution determined the psychological injury. This perhaps properly reflects research that suggests that major disasters determine a very high frequency of PTSD pathology (Raphael, 1986).

The acceptance by the courts of PTSD as a diagnostic basis for determining the presence of legal 'nervous shock' has emphasised the importance of the diagnostic elements used therein. However, developing and changing professional and scientific perceptions of PTSD may well lay the basis for future medico-legal confusion, particularly in relation to category A of the DSM–IV symptom checklist. Any diagnostic approach which emphasises the subjective experience of the person (whatever the objective severity of the trauma) would raise a potential for conflict with the courts in relation to 'forseeability'. From a psychiatric viewpoint, such a diagnostic shift reflection in DSM–IV might make great sense, particularly given that the primary purpose behind diagnosis is treatment. Indeed, even from a primary nosological perspective, subjective symptomatology may seem a more valid disease basis, not only because the experience of the patient in terms of symptoms and signs makes an obviously sensible basis for diagnosis *per se*, but also because any assessment of trauma severity must clearly have a subjective element. However, psychiatric sense may not amount to legal sense.

Use of the alternative international classificatory system, ICD–10, raises different problems. The diagnostic 'definition' offered is so much looser than that of DSM–IV that medical subjectivity is enhanced. Although it may be thought that this offers an opportunity to avoid engaging in over-rigid and potentially unreal or unjust 'symptom counting', it increases the risk of substantial interrater unreliability between experts, except in 'obvious' diagnostic cases. Such a system also runs the risk of devaluing the diagnostic concept in the legal context through the spectacle of individual psychiatrists of different diagnostic persuasions and 'thresholds' repeatedly appearing for only plaintiffs or defendants. This raises the question of whether it should be for the courts to determine issues which, although apparently psychiatric, are intrinsically linked with issues of public policy. Perhaps psychiatry and psychology should be required to restrict themselves to 'symptomatological' aspects of diagnosis, separately from diagnostic criteria and thresholds *per se*.

The narrow legal view of the necessary 'proximity' of the psychologically traumatised plaintiff to the direct perception of the trauma (if not physically involved himself) further emphasises a difference between the perspective and purpose of clinicians and of the courts. Hence, an observer or 'bystander' may be traumatised in psychological reality but not in legal theory.

In summary, it seems clear that the tendency of the courts is, on public policy grounds, to take a much 'narrower' approach than many clinicians. Given that the professional purpose of clinicians is treatment, and that the purpose of the courts is just recompense, then this difference is perhaps not unsupportable. Whether it delivers justice, however, is open to question.

Practical aspects

The interview

The assessment interview follows that of any psychiatric assessment and what is well known will not be repeated. However, some aspects of particular importance in relation to assessment of stress-related disorders specifically for medico-legal purposes need to be emphasised.

The *background history* of a client is of some potential relevance to any medico-legal assessment, if only by virtue of giving some general understanding of the client and of his family and social context. It will also lay some foundations for a pre-trauma base-line of social and family functioning which will be of relevance to questions concerning the 'life impact' of the alleged trauma and of its psychological sequelae. The plaintiff's past social and family relationships, including aspects of his/her personality, are likely to be of direct relevance to possible symptoms in all of categories B, C and D of PTSD (see chapter 3). It may be important, in some circumstances, to lay stress on the person's psychosexual history, since that sometimes offers a somewhat objective measure of changed function. Clearly, any aspect of daily functioning which relates to specific avoidance (or other relevant) symptoms should be dealt with. The background history may also give clues to earlier life events which may have primed the person to be particularly vulnerable to the specific subsequent trauma which is the subject of litigation.

A plaintiff's pre- and post-trauma *drug and alcohol history* may be of direct relevance to assessment of any neurotic sequelae of trauma, where the person may have used substances as a means of controlling or countering specific symptoms, or may have turned more generally to substances. Specifically in the context of avoidance symptoms, substances may be used as 'tranquillisers', including as a means of controlling autonomic symptoms of arousal.

The *past medical and psychiatric history* will be of great importance in relation to questions of pre-existing conditions and of personality vulnerability. Although perhaps greater weight will be laid upon objective past evidence, such as past medical records, the detail of previous symptoms given by the client may be of great legal importance and may not be recorded adequately in past records, especially if present only in general practice records. It is not uncommon for traumatised litigants to give a history of earlier neurotic symptoms, including anxiety and perhaps depression. It is crucially important to determine whether they had any diagnosable condition already present at the time of the trauma, and if they did, whether the symptoms altered markedly either in quality or degree after the trauma. Faced with the sophisticated litigant, this is an area where 'faking' is possible, particularly where there is a large group action arising out of a disaster. This said, it is probably unusual for plaintiffs subjected to substantial trauma to exaggerate symptoms greatly and, in general, sophistication about the niceties of pre-existing conditions is not to be expected.

It is very important to take a detailed history of the *traumatic event* itself, even if there is an apparently adequate description of it in the papers. The person's own account may be invaluable, particularly if extracted by a clinician with an eye on the possible content of subsequent mental symptoms. The importance may be emphasised if re-experiencing symptoms emerge.

The *history of subsequent mental symptoms*, including a detailed description of their development and degree of resolution, will be important not only diagnostically, but also in relation to causation (should there be any possible confounding intervening life events) and to prognosis (of great importance in relation to the question of 'quantum'). The description of current symptoms will offer a basis for assessing the effect on the person's lifestyle and behaviour pattern.

It is important to record a clear history of the *life impact* of apparent mental symptoms. These must be clearly separated from sequelae of physical disability or from life events unrelated to the trauma. The information will be important in relation to quantum.

The *mental state examination* offers an aspect of objectivity to the interview assessment. Hence, evidence of hyperarousal in association with discussion of feared and 'avoided' thoughts and topics will tend to confirm the validity of claimed symptoms.

Taking of *a history from another informant* will also assist with verification, sometimes reversing minimisation by the client of the life impact of symptoms, particularly in relation to interpersonal relationships.

The examining psychiatrist must have access to relevant *documentation*, including medical records and legal papers (such as pleadings and statements from the litigant and others). It is crucially important that the medical records are complete and any gaps should be pursued with vigour. Records may contain details of pre-existing conditions or of specific vulnerabilities. The legal papers should be read for inconsistencies with the accounts given by those interviewed.

Tests

If standardised instruments (including self-report questionnaires) have been administered, these should be noted.

The report

The report should include much of the foregoing information, under appropriate headings. The sources of information, including the interview with the client, informants and other individuals, professionals or agencies should be listed. It should then address specifically the following areas.

Psychiatric status

Diagnosis is, in one sense, straightforward. However, clearly the courts may have difficulty understanding any diagnostic conclusion which describes (more than one) overlapping diagnostic categories, by comparison with the perceived greater diagnostic simplicity of medicine or surgery. Hence, it may assist the court if an explanation is given of the possibility of diagnostic overlap and of possible diagnostic hierarchies. The author should make clear which international classificatory system is adhered to and, once the diagnosis is made, the relevant diagnostic reference should be offered. If the client falls below the accepted threshold for a given diagnosis the reason should be made clear. If making the diagnosis involves at least one element of subjective judgement, either medical or general, then this should also be made clear. The advantages of using an accepted diagnostic classificatory system include improved inter-case consistency for the clinician and limitation of unnecessary inconsistency, or only apparent differences of view, between experts. If the person satisfies more than one diagnostic category then the relation between the categories should be explored in such a fashion that the court can understand that there is no inherent contradiction in what is being described.

A view should be given as to the level of confidence which the clinician has in the diagnosis (s)he has reached, and if there is evidence which points away from the preferred conclusion, this should be highlighted and reasons given for reaching the overall conclusion. Where appropriate, references from standard texts or seminal papers may be quoted in support of a particular view. Where different elements of an assessment point in different directions diagnostically (for example, interview material and standardised instruments), this should be commented upon.

If the client suffered from any *pre-existing condition* then this must be clearly identified and (if appropriate) contrasted in detail with the condition which supervened.

Other psychiatric information of possible relevance to specific legal issues should be described, including an estimate of *prognosis*. Prognosis will be very important medico-legally. Any view of prognosis should clearly include an estimate of the level of confidence placed in the conclusion. In many cases a better estimate will be possible after a trial of treatment, and this raises the issue of the difficult mix, in terms of purposes and timescale, of psychiatry and law. However, if a better estimate of prognosis is likely to be achieved after such a trial then this should be stated. Where known studies offer information likely to assist in estimating prognosis, they may properly be quoted. Hence reference to studies relevant to premorbid factors (for example, McFarlane, 1989) or the nature of the trauma (Green *et al*, 1985), or the detail of the trauma in terms of its suddenness, intensity and inherent dangerousness (Rachman, 1980) may assist.

Legal implications

Ideally the expert should be responding to specific questions posed by the instructing solicitor. In any event at least the following issues will be relevant.

Causation

Causation is often much more difficult to establish in relation to mental than physical disorders. A pre-existing condition identical to that complained of clearly rules out establishing causation. A supervening condition must be clearly distinguished from any pre-existing condition in order for any possibility of damage *per se* to be established, but again, clearly identified separate causation will have to be established also. If some earlier life event 'primed' the person to be susceptible to the alleged trauma, then the likely mechanism through which this occurred should be explained so that the court can, if necessary, attempt to disentangle the relative contributions of the different factors.

Establishing causation to the legal standard of 'the balance of probabilities' can be problematic in relation to mental illness. Sometimes the content of symptoms may assist. Hence, major re-experiencing symptoms may suggest a causal link by virtue of symptom content. Also, evidence of a temporal relationship between the trauma and the symptoms may assist, but there will have to be the clear absence of any possible confounding supervening causal factor(s). Where the person is thought to have been predisposed to respond symptomatically to the trauma, then the question will be asked "would (s)he have developed the disorder anyway?", that is, irrespective of the trauma which is the subject of litigation.

Establishing causation is particularly difficult where there was a demonstrable neurotic disorder, or even merely diathesis, existent prior to the trauma and where a more severe disorder supervened. Hence, a tendency towards generalised and unfocused anxiety symptoms in a person may both obscure some of the (category D) symptoms of PTSD and make it difficult to argue for a traumatic causation. Similarly, a prior tendency towards depressive symptoms or illness may obscure those PTSD symptoms which tend to overlap with depressive symptoms, even if it can be established that the person has had an episodic depressive illness in the past and that they were symptom-free prior to the trauma.

Generally, cases where there are few problems in establishing causation tend to be characterised by:

(a)   the lack of any prior neurotic (or other) psychiatric symptomatology;
(b)   the occurrence of a clearly identifiable and major (possibly life-threatening) trauma (possibly including substantial physical injury to the plaintiff);
(c)   the development of PTSD within a characteristic time-scale;
(d)   the presence of clear re-experiencing symptomatology which is directly linked by content with the traumatic event.

The absence of any one of these features will tend to weaken the case on causation, and the case will be increasingly weakened as more of these helpful features fall away.

Where there has been a previous 'priming' experience which was then 'kindled' by a subsequent trauma (which is litigated), the courts may, in some circumstances, determine that the defendants have to take the plaintiff as they find him/her. However, there may be problems in establishing that the plaintiff was, indeed, only 'primed' and not made frankly symptomatic by the earlier event.

Where there has been brain damage resulting from a trauma, it may be difficult, or impossible, to distinguish neuropsychiatric damage from neurotic damage; indeed, there may well be substantial overlap in individual cases. However, this will present few problems in relation to causation so long as all the psychiatric symptoms can, in some way or another, be linked to the traumatic event.

Finally, it is crucially important to make a clear distinction between psychological symptoms which amount to ordinary 'pain and suffering', or which have arisen as a direct result of physical injury, which are not separately dealt with legally, and a diagnosed (separate) psychiatric condition which arises as a result of both the psychological and physical experience of the trauma (and not the physical injuries which resulted therefrom).

Quantum

The quantum of damages is for the court to determine, although based at least partly on the medical evidence. The aim of the court is to put the successful plaintiff back, as near as possible, to the position they would have been in had the negligent trauma not occurred. Where lost earnings are demonstrated, whether or not resultant from psychiatric symptoms, these are relatively easily translated into damages. However, where loss of life itself, or loss of quality of life (including from psychiatric symptomatology), constitutes the damage, the conversion of 'damage' into 'damages' is inherently impossible. Hence the courts simply decide on a scale.

Expert evidence will assist both in relation to aspects of damages and a statement of prognosis. It is often wise to suggest that a trial of treatment be attempted prior to the final determination of damages, since this may greatly increase the validity of any estimated prognosis, assuming that the legal timetable of the case will allow this.

Estimation of prognosis may be assisted and validated in the court's eyes by quoting scientific papers which are directly relevant to issues of prognosis in the particular case assessed.

A specific problem arises where, for example in mass disasters, a surviving plaintiff has lost a close relative, so that there may be substantial difficulty in distinguishing 'personal' trauma symptoms from symptoms arising from grief and bereavement reactions which are not separately actionable in terms of damages. This is important in relation to quantum.

Combining medico-legal assessment and treatment

The ethical problems of combining assessment for a legal purpose with treatment have already been touched upon (see chapter 25). In purely scientific terms there may be great advantages in combining the two. The clinician who has had (hopefully) early and extensive contact with the patient will, in one sense, be best placed to offer an assessment to the court. However, ethics aside, 'closeness' to the person may not be the best guarantee of objectivity. A medico-legal assessee is more properly perceived as a 'client', indeed not even strictly a client of the clinician but of the solicitor, who then forms a contractual relationship directly with the clinician. From a psychological rather than legal viewpoint, the dynamics which may be set up between patient and clinician may not, for example in the context of an 'unhelpful' court report, assist the therapeutic process. Hence, both forensic and therapeutic purposes may be inhibited in terms of efficiency by conjoining assessment and therapy.

Clinician assessors will clearly take their own individual stance on this issue, but the foregoing description of some of the factors relevant to the decision may be of help in making the decision.

Criminal injuries compensation

In the UK since 1964, the State, via the Criminal Injuries Compensation Board, provides financial relief within the civil framework for the victims of violent crime. It is not necessary that there should be a criminal prosecution nor an identified perpetrator, and the effects of the crime may be indirect, for example bereavement or psychological illness such as the existence of PTSD.

Claims to the Board may be supported by medical evidence including that of psychiatrists. Minors may claim via their guardians or legal representatives and on their own behalf until three years after they have reached their majority. Clinical records should be retained accordingly.

Initially the principle was that claimants should be compensated as though they had sued their assailant via the civil court. Statutory legislation was passed in 1987 but has never been brought into force. Currently an attempt by central government is being made to simplify and narrow a tariff system such that compensation is assessed within defined bands by civil servants. Personal circumstances such as loss of earnings and pension rights will no longer be taken into account.

The argument is that this process will be speedy and clear-cut, but the financial disadvantage to victims may be substantial, since the proposed bands of compensation are likely to bear no relationship to, for example, a lifetime's expense for chronic disability. The current appeal and review system is in question. Victims of psychological trauma and their legal advisers should remain alert to this debate and to future legislative change.

Conclusion

Any court report represents use of the methods of one discipline (or disciplines) for the purposes of another. There is therefore the inherent potential for incongruence and 'mistranslation' from one to the other. Good court reporting starts from an acknowledgement of this and minimises the mistranslation which is actually experienced. Similarly, good legal use of court reports understands the essential incongruities and works within them. In summary, valid translation from the one discipline into the other is maximised by mutual, or bilateral, knowledge of the two disciplines and by detailed court reporting which lays bare not only the clinical data but the scientific method which lies behind it. Even more importantly, it lays bare the limitations of the method.

References

American Psychiatric Association (1994) *Diagnostic and Statistical Manual of Mental Disorders* (4th edn) (DSM–IV). Washington, DC: APA.
Black, D., Wolkind, S. & Harris-Hendriks, J. (1991) *Child Psychiatry and the Law* (2nd edn). London: Gaskell.

Carson, D., Eastman, N. L. G., Gudjonsson, G., *et al* (1993) Psychiatric reports for legal purposes in the United Kingdom. In *Forensic Psychiatry: Clinical, Legal and Ethical Issues* (eds J. Gunn & P. J. Taylor), pp. 826–856. Oxford: Butterworth-Heinemann.

Eastman, N. L. G. (1995) Assessing for psychiatric injury and 'nervous shock'. *Advances in Psychiatric Treatment*, 1, 154–160.

Green, B. L., Grace, M. C. & Gleser, G. C. (1985) Identifying survivors at risk: long term impairment following the Beverley Hill's supper club fire. *Journal of Consulting and Clinical Psychology*, 53, 672–678.

McFarlane, A. C. (1989) The aetiology of post traumatic mordibity: predisposing precipitating and perpetuating factors. *British Journal of Psychiatry*, 154, 221–228.

Rachman, S. (1980) Emotional processing. *Behaviour Research and Therapy*, 18, 51–60.

Raphael, B. (1986) *When Disaster Strikes*. London: Unwin Hyman.

World Health Organization (1992) *The ICD–10 Classification of Mental and Behavioural Disorders: Clinical Descriptions and Diagnostic Guidelines*. Geneva: WHO.

Endnote

1. *Malcolm v. Broadhurst* [1970] 3 ALL ER 508.

25 Ethical issues in disaster and other extreme situations

NAOMI RICHMAN

The topics of 'trauma' and 'post-traumatic stress disorder' are highly fashionable. As the numbers involved in helping victims of disasters or other traumatic events increase, so does the need to examine ethical aspects of research and of clinical interventions in this field, and to question whether our actions are truly in the best interests of those expected to benefit.

This chapter considers ethical issues related to working with people affected by disasters or other extreme situations. We always need to be aware of the ethical implications of our work, but when dealing with people in extreme situations we are obliged to give special thought to ethical issues. Firstly, such people are in particularly vulnerable situations, and therefore at risk of exploitation or further abuse. Secondly, there is often great media interest in the victims of these events and this raises issues about confidentiality and privacy. Thirdly, there is an issue as to whether we have an obligation to act as advocates in order to fulfil our clinical responsibilities properly.

Responsibility to behave ethically

As a framework for this chapter I have taken the definition of ethical responsibilities of those working in the field of psychiatry identified by Chodoff (1991): the need to behave ethically, to be accountable, to be competent, and to be involved in advocacy. These are discussed specifically in relation to disaster responses.

The basic ethical principle must be to promote the well-being of clients or research subjects and to ensure that the *benefits* of any intervention outweigh the *risks* of ill effects. Although it is possible to produce guidelines about the risks involved in particular procedures, idiosyncratic factors affect how risk is assessed by individuals, and what degree of risk is acceptable to them in a given situation. Thus a person prepared to accept the perils of hang-gliding may object to a much less dangerous procedure in a research project. It is more difficult for both researchers and subjects to assess the risk of participating in interviews about sensitive issues, and there is practically no research on this topic. Even those who have freely given their consent to do so may find themselves extremely upset afterwards and regret their participation, although the numbers so affected may be small.

It has been suggested that people who have been in traumatic situations are too psychologically vulnerable to be suitable subjects for non-therapeutic investigations, i.e. research where there is no possibility that they will benefit. Nicholson (1987) pointed out that it is often the already vulnerable who are involved in research, for example the chronically ill and the disadvantaged. However, it is just these groups who may benefit from good research, if it brings attention to their needs or identifies ways of helping them.

We must recognise that people often benefit from the opportunity to bear witness to their experiences, or to behave in an altruistic manner by contributing information that could help others (Graham, 1993).

It would seem reasonable to be particularly cautious when involving vulnerable children in non-therapeutic research (Nicholson, 1987; Munir & Earls, 1992; Graham, 1993).

Accountability

Professionals must be accountable both to their clients and to the wider scientific community. The principle of autonomy demands that people are fully informed about the nature of an intervention, understand the possible benefits and risks and, in the light of this information and understanding, have freely given their consent to participate.

The capacity to give informed consent will depend on many circumstances, including intelligence and maturity, and the nature of the intervention. Severe mental illness and impaired intellectual capacity can hinder this process. In general, children from around the age of 7–8 years have the capacity to understand the nature of risk and the issues involved in an intervention and are capable of assenting to their participation; most over the age of 14 years are competent to give consent (Graham, 1994). If at all possible, even children under 7 years of age should have the opportunity to express their wishes about participation in non-therapeutic research. Parents or guardians can overrule their child if it is considered vital for the child's well-being, and it is suggested that they should always be asked for their permission in any procedure involving more than minimal risk (Nicholson, 1987). Following injury or trauma there may be no parent or guardian available to give consent.

There is always a risk that people will give consent because they think this will bring some kind of benefit, or that refusal will have unfortunate consequences for them, but in catastrophes the vulnerable find it even more difficult to assert themselves or make their wishes known.

In some countries payment is given to those who participate in research trials, and this may be considered unethical practice (apart from payment of expenses or a small honorarium) and increases the likelihood of exploitation. It is especially questionable where parents receive payment on giving consent for their child to participate in an intervention. On the other hand it could be argued that unless people are adequately reimbursed for their cooperation, a different kind of bias ensues, in which the least well off are excluded and deprived of a possible source of assistance.

Autonomy also concerns the proper protection of privacy and confidentiality. It is unethical to release the name of a research subject without their consent, or any details that could lead to identification.

Competence

Various guidelines produced by official bodies have attempted to summarise clinical and research obligations, both for doctors in general and for psychiatrists in particular (see Bloch & Chodoff, 1991), because of the therapist's power to manipulate the patient or in other ways to abuse their position of trust (Karasu, 1991).

Different psychological treatments raise different issues. Behaviour therapy techniques have been accused of sometimes exerting undue control over subjects without obtaining properly informed consent; analytical techniques can foster dependency and prejudice a patient's independent decision-making (Karasu, 1991).

In order to be ethical a proposed intervention must be expected to produce some benefit, or some useful result, either currently for the participants or later for other beneficiaries should this be a clinical trial. This requires that practitioners are competent in their field and strive for excellence, maintaining "constant interpretation and creativity in light of patient needs" (O'Rourke *et al*, 1992). Practitioners must not adopt an inflexible theoretical framework which is applied wholesale to all patients, (especially important since the indications for particular kinds of treatment in psychiatry are far from well established), but must learn from their own and others' experience. Thus a psychotherapist must be aware of the indications for drug treatments, the 'biological' psychiatrist of the value of the different psychotherapies, and both must ensure that their patients benefit from the whole range of available treatments.

In this respect, misgivings have arisen about the exclusive emphasis on PTSD as the response to 'trauma' (American Psychiatric Association, 1987). The diagnosis of PTSD has provided one useful focus for research on the effects of overwhelming experiences, but is now being more and more widely applied, in line with the recent tendency to absorb ever more phenomena under the umbrella of psychiatry. The criteria for a diagnosis of PTSD do not allow assessment along a continuum of severity, so that it is difficult to decide when symptoms are serious enough to warrant a psychiatric diagnosis. Questionnaires based on the symptoms of PTSD provide measures of 'trauma', but usually lack any indication of functional impairment. The diagnosis should not be applied indiscriminately, so as to devalue it.

It is pertinent to recognise here the general difficulties in psychiatry of establishing diagnostic criteria and the concern that "ethical problems may . . . arise out of the application of disease theories to [those] who have no mental illness" (Munir & Earls, 1992). The problems of labelling people who have no psychiatric illness, but are extremely distressed following a severe adverse event, have been frequently reviewed (Fulford, 1991). While in no way denying the reality of the symptoms of PTSD, there are increasing criticisms about its application in practice (Lansen, 1992; Richman, 1993). The arbitrary structure of DSM–III–R with its strict criteria gives a spurious air of well-researched 'truth' (Kirk & Kutchins, 1993), but the designated symptoms provide only a partial view of the effects of severe events. There are a wide variety of overlapping influences that must be addressed, such as violence, displacement, bereavement and other losses, as well as the secondary consequences of the events, which often give rise to a train of adversity (Raphael, 1986).

> "What is needed is a system that recognises and understands the difficulties; . . . strategies, implemented within a mental health or sickness model, may be limited in focus and not necessarily address the broader psychosocial implications of events experienced . . ." (McCallin, 1992)

The presence of the symptoms of PTSD do not give clear indications for treatment, especially as it is not an exclusive diagnosis and many of the symptoms occur in other diagnostic categories (Lansen, 1992). In some cases rigidly applied regimes of treatment have been adopted, ranging from behavioural to more psychodynamic modes, that do not take into account the client's cultural background, social situation or current life difficulties.

Treatment must also take into account the reality that defences may fulfil a crucial role long after the time of acute crisis is over, perhaps because the daily level of tension remains high. Recounting the story of the traumatic experience, and exploring the emotions and feelings aroused by this, is frequently presented as the major focus of treatment. Such an approach can overlook the need for clients to create some structure and meaning out of their distressing circumstances, and their reluctance to discuss important details of their experiences. We know there can be long delays in revealing painful facts, for example in cases of sexual abuse or torture, even in people who have sought help. Straker *et al* (1987) concluded that South African youth involved in township confrontations were not helped by intensive explorations of their feelings, and that they benefited from help in maintaining their defences in the face of a chronically threatening situation.

The importance of the social context is of particular relevance when considering evacuation in time of disasters or conflict, which may serve more to satisfy the emotional needs of the helpers than the recipient. It is suggested that people in threatening situations are more likely to feel secure when they can stay with their relatives in a familiar place, and that removal to places of safety often causes extreme insecurity and anxiety about the fate of relatives (Raphael, 1986). Separation may be unexpectedly prolonged because it is impossible to return to the family or because the family is compelled to move on and contact is lost. Once removed from their homes, there must be a proper reception for evacuees to ensure adequate care and to prevent any form of exploitation (Ressler, 1993).

Advocacy and therapeutic neutrality

According to Chodoff (1991), "the . . . final responsibility of psychiatrists, no matter what their particular interests, is to serve as advocates for the emotionally disturbed and mentally ill". As well as being concerned with the rights of individual patients, advocacy would include promoting ethical codes of conduct in clinical work and research, informing others about the ethical issues involved, and encouraging adequate and equitable services. The lack of adequate therapeutic trials and of consensus about treatments can make this problematic.

Many would argue that advocacy and clinical commitment are incompatible and that it is essential for the clinician to remain impartial. But this ignores the importance of social and economic factors in recovery, and the reality that treatment inevitably entails value judgements. Even the decision of what constitutes a psychiatric disorder is not always value-free (Kirk & Kutchins, 1993).

People coping with overwhelming ordeals have to construct a framework for understanding the experiences, and come to terms with the existence of violence, evil and negligence. They demand that the guilty should be known and if possible punished. The existence of impunity in relation to the detained and disappeared in South America has seriously distressed the survivors and their families; 'therapeutic neutrality' in these cases, and in the case of torture, may be seen as condoning the acts of the perpetrators.

Even in so-called natural disasters there are frequently 'man-made' factors that affect the severity of impact, and turn a hazard into a disaster. As Maskrey (1989) pointed out, disasters, rather than being characteristic of hazards, are "a result of socioeconomic and political structures and processes". Thus vulnerable groups forced onto marginal land, living in poverty, with poor housing and few resources, are seriously affected by situations that do not affect those cushioned by greater affluence. Compare the large number of deaths in the Indian earthquake of 1993 with the few following the stronger earthquake in Los Angeles some months later. In other cases, negligence is suspected by the victims as an important factor in disaster, such as the Lockerbie air crash, capsizing of ships, the Aberfan tip slide, the Bhopal chemical disaster, and Chernobyl.

This raises the question as to whether it is possible to treat symptoms without taking into account the social context in which they occurred, whether they be disasters or political conflict. Psychological *assessment* of asylum-seekers, or in cases of insurance claims and litigation, does require an impartial evaluation of the degree of impairment and of its relation to the events experienced. Psychological *assistance* must consider why these events happened, and their long-term implications for the individual: economic, physical and emotional.

Research and scientific integrity

Here wider issues are discussed specifically in relation to disaster research. Subjects of research are protected by various charters such as the Declarations of Helsinki and the Nuremberg Code. The need to make specific recommendations about ethical behaviour is highlighted by recent developments in the US where it is recognised that pressure on academics and clinicians to produce large numbers of publications in order to advance their careers is inimical to scientific integrity and the protection of ethical standards. Efforts are now being made to "emphasise quality over quantity" in publications and to control the way in which research is published. Multiple authorship involving sleeping participants is discouraged, and grant applicants are requested to give only three relevant publications. There are moves to prevent publication of the same data under different guises, or of unfinished research prematurely so that the same data-sets are included in different analyses. Institutional Review Boards are charged with overseeing these processes (Munir & Earls, 1992).

It can be difficult to balance the need for research into the impact of threatening events, and the need to protect people from unwelcome intrusion. For this reason it is imperative for the researchers to show that their work is necessary and scientifically valid, and will be carried out in a responsible way. They also need to demonstrate that all the principles already described above are taken into account: the costs and benefits have been considered, the risks are acceptable, and the subjects have the opportunity to consider these and to give informed consent to participate in the research without coercion (Wing, 1991).

Support or treatment of some sort should be available to vulnerable participants. Research interviews must be linked with the possibility of offering support when people talk about distressing occurrences, and with adequate intervention if this is required. After the Armenian earthquake in 1988, measures of psychological morbidity were combined with a programme of first-aid for those who appeared to be most affected (Goenjian, 1993).

Unfortunately, 'disaster research' is often not linked with any form of support, nor are these basic ethical aspects considered. Such research should be reviewed by an ethical committee that is sufficiently familiar with the issues to be able to form an adequate opinion of whether the work meets ethical criteria.

In times of disaster or conflict it is more difficult to ensure that the rights of individuals are respected, and it is easier to slip through the net without adequate perusal by a scientific committee or an ethical committee.

Ethical committees

Research workers are increasingly required to submit their proposals to ethical committees for consideration. The committees are becoming more sophisticated in assessing ethical dilemmas, in considering risks and benefits, and in demanding clarification, for example to ensure that informed consent is properly obtained, before granting permission for the research to proceed (Wing, 1991). Nevertheless, there are still concerns about how the role of the committees can be strengthened.

It is somewhat contradictory that ethical committees do not always consider it their responsibility to assess the scientific worth of the proposals they receive, and yet it seems logical to suppose that research that is not scientifically sound cannot be ethical. The ethical committee must scrutinise the credentials of research applicants and ensure that their project has been adequately assessed, for example, by a grant-giving body that uses proper scientific evaluation. The composition of ethical committees varies, and they may not have anyone with expertise in psychology or mental health who can assess the validity of the proposed research. Where doubts exist, an appropriate person must be nominated by the committee to carry out this assessment.

A serious limitation is that, because ethical committees emerged in medical settings, related to drug and other treatment trials, they are not always available to other professions or in research that takes place outside clinical settings, such as schools or even some community health projects. Increasingly, professional bodies whose members conduct social research are devising their own ethical guidelines.

Media intervention

The role of the media in extreme situations is controversial. On the one hand there is a need to tell the public about events, so that help can be offered and the rights of individuals can be promoted (e.g. with kidnap victims). There is no doubt that the pictures of the Ethiopian famine in 1984 set off a worldwide wave of sympathy and brought in a large amount of money to help alleviate the misery. However, media information is often sensationalised and insensitive to the needs of the participants, seemingly responding to, or creating a voyeuristic interest in, suffering, rather than giving an informed view of the situation. Journalists may pressurise witnesses or experts to present the most dismal view, for example, that all those affected by a disaster will inevitably become psychiatric casualties, rather than looking for constructive responses. The way they are presented in the media can be very distressing and humiliating to affected communities. Aid organisations may attempt to present recipients as coping with their difficulties, but they find it is easier to raise money by presenting victims.

Caution should be exercised when exposing people to media interviews since it may not be possible to know in advance who might be adversely affected or feel exploited by the experience. The purpose of the interview should be clearly explained to them and they should have the opportunity to refuse cooperation. A familiar person should be available to provide support after the interview, and individual victims should not be subjected to repeated interviews about their experience.

In a recent bus accident affecting a group of pupils from one school, there were many images of weeping children and an interview with a distressed headmaster. Later the headteacher said that he thought the interviews were helpful, but the long-term effects of such interviews with strangers, and their utility, are questionable.

It could be argued that bearing witness about what they have endured is helpful to those people who willingly offer to participate. It helps them to feel that their suffering and the presence of injustice has been acknowledged. It may be encouraging to others to see how people withstand adversity. However, volunteers who talk about their personal lives on television sometimes regret this afterwards. One has to be aware of the dangers of publicity, especially for the psychologically vulnerable, who may receive media attention to the detriment of their understanding of, and dealing with, their current situation.

Conclusion

Those offering psychological support in devastating situations have to protect themselves from feeling overwhelmed by the experiences. They must deal with their own emotional responses, as well as with those of the people they are trying to help. One way of coping is to maintain a degree of distance from the victims, a necessary defence in order to be able to continue working in this field. But there is a risk of ignoring the existentialist and practical problems encountered by those affected, and concentrating on the phenomenology of their responses. In a sense the term 'victimology' raises the danger of reifying the experiences and turning the subjects into objects of study in a mechanistic way. The humanity of the sufferers must be affirmed by seeing them as partners and 'survivors', rather than as just 'victims' with symptoms.

It could be said that our area of expertise lies in treating the mentally ill and not in advocacy. However, the question remains of whether we are abrogating our responsibility if we know that justice and improved social conditions might be as important in recovery as 'treatment'? Should we be extending our own and other's awareness of ethical issues as an essential part of our therapeutic roles?

References

American Psychiatric Association (1987) *Diagnostic and Statistical Manual of Mental Disorders* (3rd edn, revised) (DSM–III–R). Washington, DC: APA.

Bloch, S. & Chodoff, P. (eds) (1991) *Psychiatric Ethics* (2nd edn). Oxford: Oxford University Press.

Chodoff, P. (1991) The responsibility of the psychiatrist to his society. In *Psychiatric Ethics* (2nd edn) (eds S. Bloch & P. Chodoff), pp. 449–460. Oxford: Oxford University Press.

Fulford, W. (1991) The concept of disease. In *Psychiatric Ethics* (2nd edn) (eds S. Bloch & P. Chodoff), pp. 77–100. Oxford: Oxford University Press.

Goenjian, A. (1993) A mental health programme in Armenia after the 1988 Earthquake. *British Journal of Psychiatry*, **163**, 230–239.

Graham, P. (1994) Children: problems in paediatrics. In *Principles of Health Care Ethics* (ed. R. Gillon), pp. 657–669. Chichester: Wiley.

Karasu, B. (1991) Ethical aspects of psychotherapy. In *Psychiatric Ethics* (2nd edn) (eds S. Bloch & P. Chodoff), pp. 135–166. Oxford: Oxford University Press.

Kirk, S. A. & Kutchins, H. (1993) *The Selling of DSM*. New York: Walter de Gruyton.

Lansen, J. (1992) A critical view of the concept: post-traumatic stress disorder. In *Health Situation of Refugees and Victims of Organised Violence* (ed. L. van Willigen), pp. 151–155. The Hague: Ministry of Welfare, Health and Cultural Affairs.

McCallin, M. (1992) Introduction. In *The Psychological Well-Being of Refugee Children* (ed. M. MacCallin), pp. xv. Geneva: International Catholic Child Bureau.

Maskrey, A. (1989) *Disaster Mitigation. A Community Based Approach*. Oxford: OXFAM.

Munir, K. & Earls, F. (1992) Ethical principles covering research in child and adolescent psychiatry. *Journal of the American Academy of Child and Adolescent Psychiatry*, **31**, 408–414.

Nicholson, R. H. (ed.) (1987) *Ethics and Medical Research in Children: Ethics, Law and Practice*. Oxford: Oxford University Press.

O'Rourke, K., Snider, B. W., Thomas, J. M., *et al* (1992) Knowing and practising ethics. *Journal of the American Academy of Child and Adolescent Psychiatry*, **31**, 393–397.

Raphael, B. (1986) *When Disaster Strikes*. London: Unwin Hyman.

Ressler, E. (1993) *Evacuation of Children from Conflict Areas*. Geneva: UNHCR/UNICEF.

Richman, N. (1993) Annotation: children in situations of political violence. *Journal of Child Psychology and Psychiatry*, **34**, 1286–1302.

Straker, G. & the Sanctuaries Counselling Team (1987) The continuous traumatic stress syndrome: the single therapeutic interview. *Psychology in Society*, **8**, 48–78.

Wing, J. (1991) Ethics and psychiatric research. In *Psychiatric Ethics* (2nd edn) (eds S. Bloch & P. Chodoff), pp. 415–434. Oxford: Oxford University Press.

26 Organising psychosocial responses to disasters

DORA BLACK and JEAN HARRIS-HENDRIKS

This chapter describes and discusses two reports: the 1991 report of a Disasters Working Party (Allen, 1991) funded by the Department of Health; and a subsequent project at the University of London Institute of Psychiatry (Adshead *et al*, 1993), also supported by the Department of Health, which surveyed the current provision of psychosocial care following the publication of the Disasters Working Party report and made further recommendations.

The Allen report

In 1989 a Disasters Working Party was set up, funded by the Department of Health following requests from Cruse Bereavement Care, a voluntary agency, and the Association of Local Authorities. The aim was to bring together a group of people able to consider the psychosocial needs of those involved in disasters. Under the chairmanship of Allen, membership was selected with advice from the above agencies, the Association of County Councils and Metropolitan Authorities, and the Convention of Scottish Local Authorities.

After the working party was set up, the Hillsborough stadium tragedy, the sinking of the *Marchioness* riverboat in the Thames, floods in Wales and the Gulf War "added to the growing number of occasions when there has been an unquestionable need to consider the provision of social and psychological support to those affected". Additionally, as work continued, the effects upon individuals of major and minor disasters were recognised, as described in reports from inquests, inquiries and court cases (Allen, 1991).

The working party accepted the police definition of a major incident (*Association of Chief Police Officers: Emergency Procedures Manual*):

"A major incident is any emergency that requires the implementation of special arrangements by one or all of the emergency services for:

(a) the rescue and transport of a large number of casualties
(b) the involvement either directly or indirectly of large numbers of people

(c)   the handling of a large number of enquiries likely to be generated
      both from the public and the news media, usually to the police
(d)   any incident that requires the large-scale combined resources of
      the three emergency services (police, ambulance and fire services)
(e)   the mobilisation and organisation of the emergency services and
      supporting organisations, e.g. local authority, to cater for the threat
      of death, serious injury or homelessness to a large number of
      people."

The working party comments that the rate of disasters within the UK has
increased significantly in the last decade. This is not in dispute in relation
to transport disasters, given that the volume of traffic and complexity and
density of our transport system has increased. Yet older members of farming,
seafaring, mining and manufacturing communities and members of the
armed forces and police may smile wryly at such an assertion, given that it
has long been their norm to live with events which today would fit all the
criteria for police-defined major incidents except those in category (c).
Modern technology facilitates rapid, extensive reporting.

The task began with an overview of current work, much of which, in
updated form, is described elsewhere in this book. This chapter concentrates
on the working party's published guidelines for an action plan, based
particularly on experiences of disasters within the UK in the last decade.
These in the main have been from man-made rather than natural causes
and have involved less than 1000 people. Further work must be done
regarding preparation for natural disasters, for those involving large numbers
of people, and for those with international or global dimensions. There is
also a need to extrapolate, from these small or medium-scale disasters,
principles for practice concerning domestic violence, kidnapping, homicide
or arson which affect smaller numbers of individuals on each occasion, yet
are overwhelming in their impact on those involved.

Given its brief, therefore, the working party accepted that social or
psychological support following a medium-scale disaster within the UK was
best managed by social services departments of the local authority, in
association with health authorities, the police and voluntary organisations.

Its terms of reference were to consider what lessons can be learned by
social service and social work departments and other local agencies from
experiences gained in recent major disasters in the UK, and in particular,
taking account of the resources likely to be available, to consider:

(a)   what steps should be taken to provide social and psychological
      support in the aftermath of such disasters
(b)   how best to achieve coordination among agencies in the arrange-
      ment of the necessary support
(c)   how lessons learnt from recent disasters might best be disseminated;
(d)   the setting-up of an information service.

It was not within the remit of the working party to consider the resource
implications of an effective, nationwide disaster service, nor the much larger

implications in terms of funding and manpower of setting up services to deal with catastrophic or international disasters.

The report

The guidelines provided are prefaced by an outline of responsibilities designed to help departments of social services, health authorities and education authorities to identify tasks to be accomplished in planning before disaster strikes, at the time of the impact of a disaster, and in the longer term. Throughout, advice is related to the establishment of protocols for psychological and social support, for the sharing of information and for communication with the media. The provision of medical and surgical treatment for the injured is outside the brief undertaken, except for appropriate discussion of the need of emergency workers for support, debriefing, rest, recovery and counselling. Emphasis is placed on joint and regular training with other agencies and the voluntary sector.

There are seven areas of work to be coordinated by the director of the lead agency – usually the Director of Social Services of the local authority These cover:

(a) immediate support
(b) administrative resources
(c) the coordination of voluntary and statutory organisations
(d) the provision of social and psychological services
(e) the provision, training and support of staff
(f) media relations
(g) formal public relations (including setting up memorial services and other civic events).

The second part of the report details the actions to be taken at different times before, at impact, and in the aftermath of the disaster, and has action pages to guide those entrusted with each area of work.

There is a brief section on planning civil events and memorial services, emphasising the need for coordination to obviate bereaved or distressed people having to attend multiple services, taking care to involve the people affected by the disaster in the planning of these events, and ensuring that they are ecumenical or humanist in nature where appropriate.

Since, until within the last decade, almost all disaster research focused either on adults or on children's responses to disaster as described by adult caretakers, the report contains an Appendix (Black) specifically on children's needs. She writes:

"Many of the needs of children following a disaster are identical to adults, but workers involved in helping should keep the following in mind:

(1) Protect children, especially young ones, as a priority from visual and auditory sensations which are distressing even to adults but which appear to have an even more profound and adverse effect on children.

(2)   Avoid separating children under five (and preferably all children) from familiar caretakers. The old adage 'women and children first' in a rescue was based on sound observation.

(3)   When a caretaker is incapacitated or unavailable, allocate a helper specifically for each child (or sibship) who has some understanding of the developmental limitations of that age group and who attempts to keep the child informed and to answer and anticipate questions.

(4)   All children involved in a disaster (which includes children who are not present but who are affected because of the injury or death of a family member, friend or teacher, or the destruction or severe damage of home or school) should be screened for signs of psychological problems immediately and at intervals over the next two or three months, and arrangements should be made for appropriate help, which should be family-based but include a separate evaluation of the child.

(5)   Group or individual psychological debriefing should be available within hours of the disaster.

(6)   Bereavement counselling, if there has been a significant bereavement, should be made available to all children and their families.

(7)   Group counselling for the children affected.

(8)   Help parents to help the children."

Main recommendations

Local authorities are seen as having the lead function in disaster planning and management (the resource implications are substantial). Their duty is to ensure effective social and psychological support services are freely available to those who need them as a result of the disaster, making full use of statutory, voluntary and private resources. These should be available for "a considerable period of time" with priority to the most vulnerable. Professional advice should be directed towards the achievement of long-term health goals for survivors.

All local authorities should require the preparation of social and psychological support plans as part of emergency planning procedures, and chief executives, besides ensuring that these requirements are met by their own staff, should liaise regularly with relevant heads of police, fire, ambulance, health and voluntary agencies. Directors of Social Services or Social Work should be responsible for devising protocols and delegating responsibility as indicated in the guidelines. They should be able to expect support from Chief or County Emergency Planning Officers.

Health authorities should ensure that their resources, particularly psychological and psychiatric services, are fully integrated with local authority social and psychological support plans. (Therefore, NHS business plans should take account of the resultant financial and manpower resource implications.) Similarly, health authorities should take part in joint planning, training exercises and rehearsals of disaster plans with social services and voluntary organisations. General practitioners are recognised as playing a critical role in diagnosing stress and seeking help for those suffering stress following disasters, and should be included in all emergency planning.

Health authorities should be responsible for ensuring psychological debriefing for all staff members involved in disaster work.

Voluntary organisations are expected to ensure that local authority social and psychological support plans recognise their role, to take part in joint planning and training, and, along with health authorities, to organise psychological debriefing for volunteers and staff members. (It is noted that the requirement to liaise rests with voluntary rather than statutory organisations.)

The police should review procedures with a view to recognising the rights of victims and families to receive information about the disaster and allowing relatives to view the bodies of those who have died. This may or may not be necessary for identification purposes, but it is often a prerequisite for the task of grieving. Police are required to supply necessary information to disaster support workers about individuals and families directly affected as soon as accurate information becomes available, but with due consideration of the possibility of criminal proceedings, security and confidentiality. This is a complex task requiring further consultation and discussion. The police are asked to consider involving social workers or other support workers in their first visits to families and should organise psychological debriefing for all staff members.

Central government departments are advised to clarify how their lead role in disasters will be exercised so as to avoid confusion, gaps or duplication of communication of responsibility "at a time when speed and certainty are a primary consideration". They are advised to include detailed guidelines on planning for social and psychological support in emergency plans, to review their policy of contributing to disaster funds on an apparently *ad hoc* basis, and to make public clear criteria for the release of resources for providing social and psychological care following a disaster. A central information service is recommended, as is the central monitoring and evaluation of the effectiveness of social and psychological support services and research into the efficacy of different types of intervention. Central government is asked to consider establishing a training and research organisation and to review and simplify the law on compensation and assessment of liability. A system for accreditation and training which ensures national consistency in service provision is a central responsibility.

The Press Council should be commissioned to produce an advice leaflet on how to respond to the press following a disaster. Press officers should plan together concerning the handling of relevant tasks. Media skills training for key members of the lead agency is advised, as is the proactive use of the media to promote understanding of the tasks of support workers and public awareness of mental health issues. Psychological debriefing, it is noted, may also be required for journalists, reporters, cameramen and photographers.

Relevant professional bodies should include information about the social and psychological effects of disasters and the teaching of skills related to crisis and bereavement counselling in basic and post-qualifying training for counsellors, health service professionals, teachers and social workers. Specialist courses should be available in these subjects.

Industry should be involved in emergency planning. This could include collaboration of industries where workers are at high risk of injury or accident, and those such as banks, building societies and transport facilities where there are risks of robbery, transport accidents or terrorism.

Finally, the *coroners and chairmen of disaster inquiries* should take part in coordinated discussions with support services so as to be fully briefed about issues which may cause distress to friends and relatives. Those involved in such inquiries may themselves be in need of psychological support.

Conclusions of the Allen report

Disasters create high levels of distress which may be alleviated by appropriate and timely intervention. Many authorities were not well prepared and, although this was recognised, it was difficult to afford priority to contingency planning or new resources, other services taking precedence. The report concludes: "We cannot however condone inaction. We believe that as a minimum, every authority's emergency planning procedures should include production of a social and a psychological support plan. There must be proper liaison and training to ensure that it would work in practice."

Department of Health report

Although the Allen report was the subject of nationwide multidisciplinary consultation at draft stages, little interest was shown by local authorities. In 1993 Adshead *et al* took the existing 14 regional health authorities as the framework of their inquiry. Their hypothesis was that Allen (1991), focusing on local authorities and district-based services, provided advice which was difficult to implement because subsequent restructuring of the National Health Service, and the impact of new legislation on local authorities and education services, had created gaps in the planning network which compounded continuing problems with resources.

The research team contacted 14 regional departments of public health; most enquiries were passed on to Regional Health Emergency Planning Officers. Detailed information about health emergency planning was sought and a sample of districts were also approached. Psychosocial care was studied specifically from a health perspective, as was the role of healthcare provision within the wider network, aiming to discover what provision existed at a regional level for the psychosocial care of disaster victims at all levels (see below), and whether regional emergency plans were kept under review. Was a lead agency identified and did plans specify the timing and duration of the psychosocial response?

Victims were defined as occurring at six levels:

(a)   survivors of the disaster
(b)   bereaved friends and relatives of primary victims
(c)   rescue and recovery personnel

(d) members of the public who converge on a disaster site or who altruistically offer help, who share grief and loss or who are in some way responsible

(e) people whose emotional equilibrium is such that, although not directly involved, they may be precipitated into states of distress or disturbance

(f) people who but for chance occurrences, would have been primary victims themselves or were indirectly or vicariously involved in the tragedy.

Finally, regions were asked whether any estimate had been made of the potential costs of an adequate psychosocial response.

Results

Provision was "mentioned" in most plans but this was general rather than specific; emergency plans emphasised hospital-based services with little psychosocial provision except for primary victims. Often it was assumed that this work could be carried out by hospital chaplains and social workers. Only three regions had adopted a code of practice ensuring comprehensive psychosocial responses, with the recommendation that district health authorities should identify clinical psychologists with responsibility for coordinating psychosocial responses to disasters. Many health regions were candid in saying that they did not know the level of district provision, nor were they aware of what clinical services were available in general for sufferers from post-traumatic stress. The Allen report recommendation that local authorities should be lead agencies in general had been accepted by health regions; plans were based around this premise but liaison was fragmentary. Psychosocial care in some cases was seen as purely a health responsibility, and in others as provided via a counselling service by the local authority.

Whichever agency was given the lead role, there seemed to be poor communication between health, social services and the voluntary sector. Furthermore, in many regions there was no mention of the timing and duration of response and little recognition of the long-term needs of those who develop chronic psychological disorders as a result of a disaster, nor of those who develop problems months or years after an event. No regional health authority had made any estimate of the possible cost implications of providing a psychosocial response.

Recommendations

(1) Local and accessible specialist units should be provided to meet the needs of victims of traumatic stress. (These could be based on the eight new health regions created in April 1994 by the Department of Health.)

(2) The tasks of these units would be:

(a) delivery of healthcare to victims of trauma, including victims of crime

(b)   developing strategies for the rapid expansion of the service in the event of a local or large-scale disaster

(c)   developing effective liaison with emergency and social services as well as the voluntary sector

(d)   developing links with similar provider units in neighbouring health regions to provide effective cross-boundary cover

(e)   negotiating funding for the provision of both day-to-day and emergency services

(f)   where possible to make links with academic departments and to facilitate research.

Report conclusions

There is a somewhat haphazard approach to victim services, with pockets of excellence and a complete absence of services in some areas. Victims have a range of needs but it is clear that some more complex or chronic needs are not addressed by major incident plans and require specialist assessment and treatment.

Users of a traumatic stress service need to be able to obtain help locally, since morbidity often makes travelling difficult for reasons related to anxiety or denial.

Proactive interventions are invaluable, and may play an important part in reducing later morbidity and subsequent demands on services.

They are in agreement in effect with the Allen report in saying that local agencies are better placed to initiate such interventions and to liaise. They regard disaster care as of equal importance to people not addressed in major incident plans, such as victims of crimes and accidents.

A national resource is required for research, audit, maintenance of a national database of resources, and international liaison, particularly within the European Union.

They recommend specific research projects:

(a)   epidemiological studies of PTSD and related disorders in the UK;

(b)   evaluation of early therapeutic interventions;

(c)   the effects of the legal process on morbidity;

(d)   efficacy of treatment for chronic disorder;

(e)   a developmental account of the effects of childhood trauma.

Comments

These reports contain effective overviews of recent UK disaster responses, a pioneering attempt to evaluate existing service provision, plus sensible and well thought-out guidelines for contingency planning by statutory and voluntary services. They give clear guidance to local authorities and central government on their roles. There is increasing need to audit and evaluate the provision of services, given that the changing framework of local government, local management of schools, and the establishment of fund-holding general practices and health service trusts has created a network of service provision substantially different from that which existed when the Disasters Working Party made its report. Adshead emphasised coordinated services at the regional level, yet the Department of Health changed and weakened the regional framework immediately after publication.

Plans for what may happen, constantly revised and kept up-to-date, are expensive both in themselves, in their prospective use of manpower, and because reorganisation of statutory services may make them obsolete. Much disaster planning continues to be *ad hoc* and in response to emergency. The value for money and measurable benefits from social and psychological support can only be established by extensive and thorough research at each disaster; a schema is provided by Raphael *et al* (1989). In practice, as each disaster is evaluated, the incentive to plan on economic and humanitarian grounds is likely to be reinforced.

In both reports, the specific needs of children caught up in disasters receive disproportionately little attention. Children make up at least a quarter of the population, and disasters in which they are involved bring in their wake specific problems such as the need to provide substitute parenting for bereaved survivors and the relative lack of training of counsellors concerning the developmental limitations of children's understanding and functioning. Few education authorities participated in discussion of the Allen report, although all were invited. In spite of the fact that some disasters primarily occur to schools (see Pynoos *et al*, 1987; Yule & Gold, 1993; Capewell, 1994), education authorities had done even less than health authorities to plan for and train teachers to deal with a disaster affecting their school.

References

Adshead, G., Canterbury, C. & Rose, S. (1993) *Current Provision and Recommendations for the Management of Psychosocial Morbidity following Disaster in England.* London: Institute of Psychiatry, University of London.

Allen, A. J. (1991) *The Disasters Working Party. Planning for a Caring Response.* London: HMSO.

Capewell, E. (1994) Responding to children in trauma: a systems approach for schools. *Bereavement Care*, **13**, 2–7.

Pynoos, R. S., Nader, K., Frederick, C., *et al* (1987) Grief reactions in school age children following a sniper attack at school. *Israel Journal of Psychiatry*, **24**, 53–63.

Raphael, B., Lundin, T. & Weisaeth, L. (1989) A research method for the study of psychological and psychiatric aspects of disaster. *Acta Psychiatrica Scandinavica*, **80**, suppl. 353.

Yule, W. & Gold, A. (1993) *Wise before the Event: Coping with Crises in Schools.* London: Calouste Gulbenkian Foundation.

27 Overview and comment

JEAN HARRIS-HENDRIKS, MARTIN NEWMAN, DORA BLACK and GILLIAN MEZEY

Our aim in this book has been to provide a comprehensive account of the many different aspects of post-traumatic stress disorder and to bring together the accumulating knowledge about reactions to traumatic experiences. The authors of the chapters come from a variety of professional backgrounds. Some contributions are written from a mental health point of view, some from a sociological point of view, and others from a general point of view. Some chapters are written specifically by or for psychiatrists (for example, chapter 24).

We have tried to include information across a wide spectrum. For example, we have devoted a large chapter to some of the disasters that have occurred in the UK, or which have affected UK personnel, over recent years, in order to gather together in an accessible form the UK experience.

Potentially traumatic experiences are common (Solomon *et al*, 1992) and inevitable, ranging from private events affecting only one or a few individuals to national or international events affecting many. Individuals vary in their responses, depending on many factors including their stage of development, their constitutional make-up, the resilience of their personality, their previous experiences, the nature of the event itself, and factors which precede and follow the event or sequence of events, including the social and political context in which it occurs.

It has been found that, following crises, disasters and war, girls report or acknowledge psychological distress more than boys (Burke *et al*, 1986; Green *et al*, 1991; Kuterovac *et al*, 1994). It remains unclear whether this represents a true difference, or is due to differences in reporting or acknowledging reactions (Kuterovac *et al*, 1994).

We have concentrated on exploring the effect of extremes of interpersonal and mass violence and disaster on the psychological functioning of people of all ages. We have not looked at the effects on children of physical and sexual abuse, as there are many texts which deal ably with this. Nor have we looked at chronic marital and domestic violence in any detail, nor done justice to the way in which people with learning difficulties and physical handicaps and disabilities might deal differently with traumatic events. We have not discussed emotional processing, nor have dissociative disorders been described. We have also not tackled the subject of unintended traumatisation by those whose aim is to help (i.e. the medical profession): the effects on children of enduring painful, disfiguring and distressing treatments for life-threatening disease, often with the added burden of knowing that their parents are condoning such "assaults". These subjects certainly deserve consideration and may well be dealt with in future editions.

After a serious physical injury, appropriate treatment is regarded as essential, irrespective of the cause of the injury. We believe that the same principle applies to serious psychological injury. It may be that avoidance of, and refusal to confront the trauma is behaviour which is adaptive for some individuals and should not automatically be pathologised. However, there is a danger that individuals may be revisited by earlier distress as they grow older and defence mechanisms become less effective. Psychological traumatisation is an under-recognised risk to the health of individuals and societies (Davidson *et al*, 1991). Untreated post-traumatic stress and related morbidity costs money, spoils lives, and hinders the effective functioning of individuals and the wider society of which they are part.

Definitions

The concept of PTSD fits better with certain stages of development and certain kinds of trauma than with others. Our language for describing these experiences must become more precise, be open to critical evaluation and modifiable over time, to facilitate the provision of effective, continually evaluated treatment services. The terms which we use must take account of age, gender, culture, language, politics and socio-economic status, as well as of personal history, suffering and coping strategies.

William Parry-Jones (chapter 14) emphasises the need for further work on clarification and a clearer definition of the language used in describing such experiences. He outlines this task in relation to concepts such as "stress", "grief" and "trauma" so as more clearly "to identify distinctive features and meaning". For example, the word "depression" may be used to describe a symptom, a state of mind or a nosological category of illness. There is need more precisely to identify the range of normal responses to catastrophe and disaster and the threshold criteria for 'caseness'. Concepts such as 'coping' and 'resilience' also deserve critical debate.

Classification

Colin Murray Parkes (chapter 7) delineates the spectrum of responses to stress and provides a framework for classifying disasters. Our hope is that readers who wish to consider particular disasters within specific age ranges will bear in mind this wider frame.

Future editions of the *International Classification of Diseases* and the *American Diagnostic and Statistical Manual* will require revision of the concept of PTSD, particularly concerning children, adolescents and the elderly.

Diagnosis must be considered in the context of multiaxial classifications and the existence of comorbidity. Variations must be identified, not just in relation to age and sex, but also to developmental levels, coping skills, personal psychosocial circumstances, culture, religion and the nature of the traumatic event. The subjective meaning of the traumatic event, that is, the meaning of the trauma to the individual in his/her inner world, is important.

In the light of clinical experience (as, for example, Feinstein & Dolan, 1991; Scott & Stradling, 1994), there were important changes in the stressor criterion from DSM–III (American Psychiatric Association, 1980) and DSM–III–R (American Psychiatric Association, 1987) to DSM–IV (American Psychiatric Association, 1994). These are discussed in chapter 3 and chapter 8. The stressor criterion remains an area of specific focus, particularly in the light of the apparent PTSD-type symptoms in the general population (Breslau *et al*, 1991; Davidson *et al*, 1991; Weiss *et al*, 1992). Further changes may be necessary in the future. In addition, there may be difficulties with a diagnostic definition which might include almost anyone who has been subjected to a major stressor.

The designation of the conflict or disaster (e.g. man-made or natural disasters, or just or unjust conflicts), as seen in the conflicts of Vietnam or former Yugoslavia, may affect both the assigned meaning and the outcome for individuals and society.

Diagnosis

Care is needed in the assessment of psychological morbidity after a traumatic event. There is a need to consider comorbidity. For example, there is a higher incidence of coexisting major depression in the elderly (chapter 12).

Richman (chapter 25) reminds us to be aware of the possibility of the "medicalisation of distress". The establishment of a diagnostic category of PTSD within disease classification systems could be regarded as an attempt to extend medical and psychiatric domains. Is there any evidence that the application of a label such as PTSD results in a better outcome for those who receive it, than for traumatised individuals who, prior to 1980, had no such term to describe their condition? We need research studies to help us answer such questions.

Cultural issues

This book has been written from a 'Western' viewpoint. Most of the contributors are working in the UK. Reference has been made to the importance of considering cultural and ethnic factors (see chapters 10 and 25). Even within a single country there may be many different cultures, religions and social groups, each with their own norms and expectations.

Currently, researchers from a variety of disciplines in developed countries are attempting to measure the effects of massive trauma on impoverished or developing societies, and as yet there is insufficient understanding or knowledge about how responses to trauma may be expressed differently according to prevailing sociocultural norms.

Summerfield points out in chapter 10 that Western debates about experiences like torture or rape have focused on the psychological effects of what is seen as an extreme violation of individual integrity and identity. Non-Western people have different notions of the self in relation to others. Therefore, those who work with individuals need to be aware of, and sensitive to, their client's cultural, social and religious beliefs, and to consider the social and cultural norms of the society within which they are working. Where possible, local professionals should be facilitated in their work by visiting professionals, rather than be supplanted by them. In the future, it is to be hoped that there will be a wider awareness and understanding of differing cultural and religious beliefs and philosophies.

Political issues may affect individual and communal vulnerability. Thus, as discussed in chapter 25, the effect of an earthquake on a community and the individuals in it depends substantially upon the economic level of the society in which it occurs.

Treatment

The chapters on treatment (Part III) present a number of different approaches, including behavioural and cognitive approaches, psycho-therapeutic techniques, and the use of drugs. Treatment outcome studies have, on the whole, been disappointing (Solomon *et al*, 1992). Possible therapeutic interventions require careful evaluation. Most studies of drug treatments of PTSD are limited. Studies of drug treatments may be hindered by a tendency to resist prescribing drugs for survivors of catastrophes, on the theoretical grounds that they are not 'ill', a debate initiated by those who consider that a diagnosis 'medicalises' the responses to trauma, humiliating trauma survivors by defining them as patients or victims. In our view, such important and strongly felt arguments should not deter us, as clinicians and researchers, from continuing our attempts to explore the diversity of individual and group reactions to traumatic events and seeking to alleviate their suffering.

The few studies of early intervention have failed to establish that they are effective in reducing the rate of PTSD. For example, no randomised controlled trials on the effectiveness of critical incident stress debriefing as yet exist. Those debriefed value the experience, and therapists are impressed by its effectiveness, yet independent assessment provides no evidence that debriefing had any measurable beneficial effect upon outcome.

It is important to note that a diagnosis of PTSD is poorly predictive of capacity to function, nor a reliable indicator of a need for psychological treatment (chapter 10).

At present, therapists need to be eclectic and flexible in their approach. Multiple treatment models may be appropriate. The survivor of trauma may need to learn new coping strategies to deal with heightened arousal, while at the same time receiving an anxiolytic or antidepressant drug. In addition, he/she may require more in-depth understanding of the reason why the present trauma and loss resonates with earlier life experiences, such as may be achieved by psychodynamic psychotherapy. In the future, an increased understanding of the neurophysiological changes that occur in PTSD may lead to the development of new psychopharmacological and other treatments.

Research

The need for further research has been commented on throughout this book, and elsewhere. Research into PTSD is still at a relatively early stage. Much of the work has been on combat veterans. Many of the studies in the literature are small in scale and limited in their design. There is a need for clinically defined, ethically approved evaluation schemata. It is difficult to set these up, given that disasters in general are sudden, unpredictable and very often overwhelming. However, what can be predicted is that disasters will occur. For example, prospective studies, studies with proper controls, careful clinical evaluation with consideration of all relevant factors, epidemiological studies in different societies, and re-evaluation of retrospective studies, would all be helpful. These can be planned in advance and would need to be adequately funded. Plans for community responses to future disasters (chapter 26) should routinely include a research component.

A developmental approach to the evaluation of the impact of trauma on individuals involves not only consideration of the individual's personal and psychosocial development, but the conceptualisation of specific sequences of traumatic experiences. Davidson *et al* (1991) suggested that adverse effects in childhood may serve either as predisposing risk factors or as traumata themselves. Thus, developmental studies are required and epidemiological studies concerning the incidence and prevalence of traumatic stress responses are needed in developed and developing nations, under conditions of peace, civil disturbance and war.

Population screening should take account of concepts of vulnerability and resilience, and subsequent outcome studies should use the variables discussed in this volume. Currently available retrospective studies, such as those of Holocaust survivors and Second World War veterans, could be re-evaluated in the light of developing knowledge and of opportunities for study of reactivated trauma – for example, in relation to anniversaries of the ending of wars and conflicts.

Prospective comparative treatment studies, complex in structure and dependent at least in part upon individual interviews with survivors, utilising random allocation of individuals to different treatments, are costly to fund, staff and maintain over time, but are essential. These may have to be multicentre and international in some cases. Research on how to tailor therapeutic interventions to individual sufferers with differing profiles would aid therapists to select the most effective treatment.

It has been argued that comparison or control groups may be unethical, given that there is at least partial knowledge concerning the effectiveness of some disaster response programmes, as described in Part III. The hard reality is that disasters at all levels are so common throughout the world that untreated comparison groups are readily available. Moreover, we are only at the start of initiating randomised controlled treatment studies, and it would be unethical to continue to use treatments without evaluating them.

Children

Throughout this book are descriptions of events in which children have been involved. For very young children, witnessing or being caught up in horrific experiences, without understanding or being able to fit what they are witnessing into any pre-existing schema, may leave them with more lasting and treatment-resistant post-traumatic symptomatology than if the same phenomena occurred to older people (see chapter 5). This may be made worse for them by the fact that the people to whom they would usually turn for help to make sense of their experiences may themselves be the victims of the horror and have died, or may be too traumatised themselves to be properly available to them. Children, too, suffer from the scotomata of adults, who wish to believe that they were "too young" to be affected by events, or that by not talking about them with the children, they will forget more rapidly.

As they develop, children may find traumatic images recurring, of which they can make little sense, since they were not properly processed at the time they were first received. They may bring to mind new questions and new understanding of events previously processed with the understanding of a child at an earlier stage of development. Children have to be helped repeatedly as they reach new developmental stages, to review the traumatic events in the light of their more mature cognitive abilities and greater understanding of emotional reactions.

Many of the research diagnostic instruments are designed for the assessment of adults. Although they are sometimes used for studies of children or adolescents, this is often unsatisfactory. Young children may more often express post-traumatic stress through bodily symptoms or disturbed behaviour when compared with older children, adolescents or adults, as young children cannot always articulate their thoughts or feelings. Hence, attempts to record and measure the responses to trauma more accurately in young children are required. This is discussed in chapter 14.

We need to understand what factors may protect children from developing PTSD after they have experienced a traumatic event or events and to understand better what interventions for children are most helpful, and what the possible long-term effects of experiencing psychological trauma in early childhood may be.

Pynoos *et al* (1995) recently published a model based on systems theory. Their model is designed for research in child and adolescent trauma but, in our view, it has relevance across the whole age range. It incorporates a complex tripartite model for understanding the aetiology of post-traumatic distress deriving from the nature of the traumatic experience and the subsequent traumatic reminders and secondary stresses. Resistance and vulnerability, which directly mediate distress, are differentiated from resilience, which refers to early attempts at adjustment and recovery, effective for the survivor. The authors tackle the difficult conceptual problems of the effect of new or repeated traumatic exposures on developing individuals who are dependent on carers, who may be at differing stages of their own life-cycles, and whose own responses to the traumatic event(s) are dependent on their individual experiences and constitution. The model attempts to integrate family, peer, community and societal influences with the child's continuing growth and development which bring its own challenges and changes. They point out that as children grow older, the chances increase that they may be involved in a potentially traumatic event without the support of their parents, and that some intrafamilial disasters, such as one parent killing the other, leave even very young children without that support and protection. They point out that there is "an enhanced appreciation of the extent to which children are exposed to terrorism, war, atrocities against civilians, ethnic or religious violence and political oppression and torture".

Traumatic reminders for children may differ from those for adults and need to be appreciated by those caring for them; for example, a young child may become terrified when she sees an expression on her mother's face which triggers a reminder of the disaster in which they were both involved. Secondary stresses and adversities will also differ for children who will, for example, be more profoundly affected by malnutrition at certain stages of their development than others. Lack of schooling following a massive community disruption, such as occurs in war or civil conflict, may have permanent effects on children who are at a crucial stage in their educational progress. Bereavement is known to affect children differentially, and loss of parents may have effects on their subsequent mental health (see chapter 16).

Pynoos *et al* consider that a developmental model has heuristic value for clinical assessment and intervention and the definition of new avenues for future research. Their model "clearly indicates the need for more defined and rigorous typologies of traumatic exposures, traumatic reminders and secondary stresses" and repays close study.

The elderly

It seems from Hyman's review (chapter 12) that the elderly too are considered not to suffer from psychological stress from trauma, and very little research has been carried out on this age group. The elderly find themselves revisiting traumatic events, the memory of which they have been able to suppress or repress until the losses and psychological changes of old age render these defences inoperable.

Education

Politicians, planners and managers must be helped to conceptualise and provide responses to psychological traumas where they exist, and to recognise that appropriate planning and early interventions may prevent adverse mental health consequences. Arguments for the provision and funding of such measures will be stronger if supported by research findings. Chapters 20 and 21 on service provision and effective outcomes stress the importance of continuing education across the range of providers.

Chapter 26 outlines early, incomplete and mainly under-regarded recommendations for local authority planning for disaster. Advance planning for disasters is an essential component of health and social resources, and any society which attempts to establish a resource network available at the point of need should include the concept of psychological traumatisation when developing, funding and evaluating a range of services to be resourced. Comprehensive mental health and educational programmes require preparation and effective inter-agency liaison, as described also in chapters 7, 14 and 25.

Legal issues

These issues are discussed in detail in Part IV. This area of law continues to develop. There has been an increasing recognition that psychiatric morbidity may be associated with experiencing traumatic events. Claims for compensation after a disaster can be expected. Care needs to be taken when preparing legal reports (Neal, 1994), as discussed in chapter 14. Those involved in clinical and legal work need to be aware of the latest clinical work, research findings and legal decisions. Doctors need to be wary about criminalising sickness or medicalising crime. They cannot reduce the complexity of an individual's very personal response to trauma to a single diagnosis, simply to fit in with legal requirements. Anger is discussed in the chapter on PTSD and crime: however, anger is a response to trauma that is often overlooked and dismissed. Excessive and unpredictable anger may be the source of some considerable distress and social dysfunction, particularly with male survivors, although not recognised in diagnostic classification.

The helpers

Many different professionals may become involved in disasters and in helping those affected by a disaster (for example, military personnel, police, healthcare workers, social workers, teachers, legal advisors and volunteers). One of the recurring messages of this book is the need to ensure that such people are properly selected, trained and supported.

It is in this context that the issue of protectiveness, which excludes outside help (adults who take responsibility for legal minors or the frail elderly; professionals who wish to retain responsibility), must be balanced with concepts of helpful service provision (finance, specialist knowledge and manpower via national or international sources) and inappropriate intrusiveness.

All clinical work and research lays strong ethical obligations upon those who undertake it, but disaster work in particular has hidden, yet increasingly recognised, ethical dimensions. Thus study of the interface between law, medicine, psychiatry and disaster services, as indicated in Andrew Sims' Foreword, must be an area of continuing, increasing concern to all workers within this developing field of knowledge.

New developments

Research into memory (chapter 5) and the neurophysiological changes in response to stress (chapter 6D) may provide new and important understandings. Future work must emphasise the continuity of responses to trauma. Traumatic stress may recur in the next generation or in the individual's old age. Traumatic memories, repressed for many years, may suddenly re-emerge in later years. The abused child may grow up to become an abusive adult. The traumatised adult, emotionally cut off and numbed as a result of early trauma, may be incapable of responding to the emotional needs of his or her children.

As yet, psychological traumatisation is under-recognised as a risk to health and social well-being. We hope that this book will be perceived as a contribution to the establishment of improved health and social functioning for survivors of disaster.

References

American Psychiatric Association (1980) *Diagnostic and Statistical Manual of Mental Disorders* (3rd edn) (DSM–III). Washington, DC: APA.
—— (1987) *Diagnostic and Statistical Manual of Mental Disorders* (3rd edn, revised) (DSM–III–R). Washington, DC: APA.
—— (1994) *Diagnostic and Statistical Manual of Mental Disorders* (4th edn) (DSM–IV). Washington, DC: APA.
Breslau, N., Davis, G. C., Andreski, P., *et al* (1991) Traumatic events and post-traumatic stress disorder in an urban population of young adults. *Archives of General Psychiatry*, **48**, 216–222.
Burke, J. D., Moccia, P., Borus, J. F., *et al* (1986) Emotional distress in fifth-grade children ten months after a natural disaster. *Journal of the American Academy of Child and Adolescent Psychiatry*, **25**, 536–541.
Davidson, J. R. T., Hughes, D., Blazer, D. G., *et al* (1991) Post-traumatic stress disorder in the community: an epidemiological study. *Psychological Medicine*, **21**, 713–721.

Feinstein, A. & Dolan, R. (1991) Predictors of post-traumatic stress disorder following physical trauma: an examination of the stressor criterion. *Psychological Medicine*, **21**, 85–91.

Green, B. L., Korol, M., Grace, M. C., *et al* (1991) Children and disaster: age, gender, and parental effects on PTSD symptoms. *Journal of the American Academy of Child and Adolescent Psychiatry*, **30**, 945–951.

Kuterovac, G., Dyregrov, A. & Stuvland, R. (1994) Children in war: a silent majority under stress. *British Journal of Medical Psychology*, **67**, 363–375.

Neal, L. A. (1994) The pitfalls of making a categorical diagnosis of post traumatic stress disorder in personal injury litigation. *Medicine, Science and the Law*, **34**, 117–122.

Pynoos, R. S., Steinberg, A. M. & Wraith, R. (1995) A developmental model of childhood traumatic stress. In *Manual of Developmental Psychopathology* (eds D. Cicchetti & D. Cohen), pp. 72–95. New York: John Wiley.

Raphael, B., Meldrum, L. & McFarlane, A. C. (1995) Does debriefing after psychological trauma work? *British Medical Journal*, **310**, 1479–1480.

Scott, M. J. & Stradling, S. G. (1994) Post-traumatic stress disorder without the trauma. *British Journal of Clinical Psychology*, **33**, 71–74.

Solomon, S. D., Gerrity, E. T. & Muff, A. M. (1992) Efficacy of treatments for posttraumatic stress disorder. *Journal of the American Medical Association*, **268**, 633–638.

Weiss, D. S., Marmar, C. R., Schlenger, W. E., *et al* (1992) The prevalence of lifetime and partial stress disorder in Vietnam theater veterans. *Journal of Traumatic Stress*, **5**, 365–376.

Index

Compiled by CAROLINE SHEARD

Aberfan disaster 86–7
abreaction 7, 50
accommodation 70
accountability, professional 375
ACTH, response to CRF 57–8
acute combat stress reaction 138–40
acute reaction to stress 19
acute stress disorder 26, 221
acute stress reaction 19, 23, 346
adaptation and memory 48
adenylate cyclase 55
adjustment disorder 23, 220
adjustment reaction 19, 232
adolescents
    intervention with 234, 285
    psychopharmacological treatment 285
'adrenal exhaustion' 12
adrenaline 55
adrenocorticotrophic hormone, response to CRF 57–8
Advanced Link Line Network 308
advocacy 155, 212, 378
aggression and television violence 189–91
aggressor, identification with 275
AIDS workers 333
air disasters 85, 108–10
    see also Lockerbie air disaster
Air Safety Action Group 109
alcohol abuse and crime 353
Allen Report 383–8
alprazolam 298, 299
American Civil War 135
amitriptyline 296
amygdala 44, 46–7, 56, 60
anger 352
anticonvulsants 56
antidepressants, tricyclic 56, 295–7, 301

antisocial behaviour 352–3
anxiety and bereavement 34, 35
anxiety disorders 31, 298
    comorbidity with PTSD 27
anxiety management 16, 269–70
anxiety neurosis 20
anxiolytics 298–9
armed services 328, 329
Armenian earthquake 91, 202, 379
arousal theory 189
ASD 26, 221
assessment
    adults 223–5
    children 225–8
    medico-legal 363–72
assimilation 70
assumptive world 12–13, 14
asylum-seekers 206
attachment 12, 63, 162
    anxious–ambivalent 15
    avoidant 45
    detached 15
    inconsistent 15
    in infancy 14–15
    insecure 15–16, 186
    and memory 45
    secure 14–15
automatism 145, 355–6
autonomic function in PTSD 55–6, 294
avoidance 64–5, 98, 127–8, 244
    criteria for 21

basal ganglia 44
battered woman syndrome 181–2, 355, 357
battleshock 138–40
behaviour modification in childhood 282–5
behavioural models 64–6

benzodiazepines 298, 299
bereavement 12, 31, 83, 250
  and anxiety 34, 35
  cultural 168
  and curriculum planning 318–19
  and depressive disorders 34, 35
  outcomes 40–1
  risk factors 254
  and separation anxiety 34
  studies 33–5
  support services 260–1
  traumatic 35–42
  and traumatic stress 32
Bereavement Care 321
bereavement counselling
  achieving satisfactory termination
    255
  assessment for 253–4
  children 256–7
  common features 254
  common issues 254–5
  and culture 258
  efficacy 259–60
  general aims 252–3
  and pathological grief 257–8
  practical aspects 253–6
  and practical support 254–5
  realising the loss 255
  resolving the lost relationship 255
  techniques 255–6
  theoretical foundations 250–2
  therapeutic alliance 254
  voluntary services 320–1
beta-endorphins 58–9
bibliotherapy 256
bicultural workers 212
biological models of PTSD 55–60
Birleson Depression Inventory 226
bodies
  photographs of 105–7
  right to view 104–7
bombing incidents 310, 311
borderline personality disorder 327,
  357
Bradford fire 246, 309
breach of contract 341
breach of duty 343–4
breathing, controlled 269
Briquet's syndrome 28
British Airways information unit 85
Buffalo Creek disaster 130
bullying 193

burnout 86, 333
  prevention 334–5
buspirone 298, 299
buspirone/prolactin test 58
bystanders 83, 345, 346

CAPS 128–9, 224–5
carbamazepine 56, 299, 300, 301
casualty bureau 307
casualty clearing station 306
catastrophic stress 19
catharsis 7
causation 230
  legal implications 369–71
Center for Epidemiological Studies of
    Depression, depression scale 34
central government departments 387
CESD depression scale 34
change, response to 12–13
Charcot, Jean-Martin 5–6, 7
Cheddar/Axbridge air crash 85
child abuse 191–2
  effects in adulthood 359
  transgenerational transmission 181
child mental health services 319
Child Post Traumatic Stress Reaction
    Index 226
child sexual abuse 191, 192–3
  adult survivors 180
children 281, 397–8
  Allen Report recommendations 385–6
  assessment 225–8
  bereavement counselling 256–7
  cognitive–behavioural therapies
    282–5
  as combatants 163
  concept of death 225
  coping and adjustment 163–4
  debriefing 246
  effects of bullying 193
  effects of conflict 150, 161–4
  effects of inter-parental violence
    184–8
  effects of television violence 189–91
  family therapy 285–6
  group therapy 286
  informed consent 375
  intervention with 234
  psychiatric morbidity following RTAs
    127
  psychodynamic psychotherapy 287–
    92

psychopharmacological treatment 285
psychotherapy 288–92
PTSD criteria in DSM–III–R 21–3
questionnaires 226–7
risk factors 315
torture and mutilation 162–3
treatment approaches 281–6
under four 227–8
as victims of violence 191–3
as witnesses
    to homicide 188
    to random violence 189
    to rape 188–9
    to violence 184–91
Children's Manifest Anxiety Scale 226
chronic grief syndrome 15, 41
CISD 239–41, 323, 324
civil law
    faults of system 347–8
    and psychiatric injury 341–50
civil violence 156–60
civilian populations
    and civil violence 156–60
    effect of conflict on 135–6, 148–64
Clapham train crash 84–5
clarification 255
classification 19–29, 221, 393–4
client-centred methods 251
Clinical Interview Schedule 126
Clinician Administered Post-traumatic
    Stress Scale 128–9, 224–5
clomipramine 297
clonazepam 299, 301
clonidine 56, 298–9
cognitive appraisal 67, 243
cognitive–behavioural models 64–70
cognitive–behavioural therapies 233,
    264–70
    case studies 270–2, 273
    in childhood 282–5
    efficacy 272–3
cognitive deficiency 284
cognitive distortion 284
cognitive models 64–5, 66–7, 268
cognitive–perceptual deficits and crime
    352
cognitive processing 50–1, 208
    model 69–70
    therapy 69–70, 268
cognitive restructuring 213, 256
cognitive schemata 64, 69–70, 208

cognitive therapy 267–9
    in childhood 284–5
combat fatigue 19
combatants
    children as 163
    effect of conflict on 134–45
comorbidity 26–8, 144–5, 220–1
    and psychopharmacological treat-
        ment 295
compassion fatigue 327
Compassionate Friends 322
compensation 28–9
    for criminal injuries 372
    for psychiatric injury 347
    and road traffic accidents 127, 130
competence, professional 376–7
completion tendency 243–4
compulsive self-reliance 15, 16
conditioning
    classical 65–6
    instrumental 66
conflict
    collective experience of trauma 151–3
    effect on children 150, 161–4
    effect on civilian populations 135–6,
        148–64
    effect on combatants 134–45
    epidemiology 148–9
conscription 138
containment 287
contingency plans in schools 315
control 17–18
coping 393
    in childhood 163–4
    and debriefing 245–6
    fostering skills 16–18
    techniques 71
Coping with a Major Personal Crisis 97
coroners 388
corticoid hormones 11
corticotropin–releasing factor, response
    of ACTH to 57–8
cortisol
    basal plasma 57
    in dexamethasone suppression test
        57
    ratio to noradrenaline 57
    urinary free 56–7
counselling 233
    see also bereavement counselling
counsellors 232, 234
counterdisaster syndrome 326–7

countertransference 211, 276, 327
court appearances 335
CPTSRI 226
CRF, response of ACTH to 57–8
crime 360
  and childhood trauma 359
  and cognitive–perceptual deficits
    352
  and drug and alcohol abuse 353
  and re-experiencing phenomena
    352
  and social and interpersonal dys-
    function 353
  and war trauma 351–2
criminal injuries compensation 372
criminal investigations 349
criminal law 351
  expert witnesses 358–9
  prosecution evidence 358
  psychiatric defences 354–8
  and PTSD 353–8
Criminal Procedures: Insanity and
    Unfitness to Plead Act 1991 354
criminal violence, responses to 177–8
crisis intervention 233, 238–9, 247
  research on 242–3
critical care nurses 333
critical incident stress debriefing 239–
    41, 323, 324
cross-cultural psychiatry 153
crowd problems 306
Cruse Bereavement Care 260, 320–1
CSR 138–40
culture 234, 394–5
  and bereavement counselling 258
  and displacement 152, 168, 169–70
  and normality 10
  and therapy 153–5
  and torture 152, 212
*Current Provision and Recommendations for
    the Management of Psychosocial
    Morbidity following disasters in
    England* 388–90
curriculum, death and bereavement
    issues 318–19

Davey, Audrey 86, 87
death
  children's concepts of 225
  and curriculum planning 318–19
  fear of 63

debriefing 239–41, 247, 317
  and aetiological models of PTSD
    243–6
  children 246
  cognitive factors 244–5
  and coping 245–6
  elderly 246
  group 244
  innovations 241–2
  on-scene/near scene 240
  research on 242–3
defence mechanisms 62, 64–5, 246,
    274–5
definitions 393
  disaster 82–3
  major incident 383–4
  refugee 165
  trauma 61
déjà vu 328
delusions 221
denial 107, 245, 274
Department of Health Report 388–90
depersonalisation 328
depressive disorders 232
  and bereavement 34, 35
  comorbidity with PTSD 27–8
  following torture 208–9
  in victims of child sexual abuse 192
DES 26
desensitisation 51, 190, 282–3
desipramine 296
desipramine/growth hormone test 58
dexamethasone suppression test 57, 58
diagnosis 219–22, 231–2, 368–9, 394
*Diagnostic and Statistical Manual of
    Mental Disorders see* DSM–I; DSM–
    II; DSM–III; DSM–III–R; DSM–IV
diazepam 298
Dickens, Charles 4
differential diagnosis 220–1, 231–2
diminished responsibility 355
Directors of Social Services 85
disaster planning 336
disaster studies 32–3, 81–2
disasters 81–2
  community 94–130
  definition 82–3
  international
    large-scale 91–2
    medium-scale 89
    small 85

legal processes following 349–50
local
    large-scale 89–90
    medium-scale 85–7
    small 84
national
    large-scale 90–1
    medium-scale 87–9
    small 84–5
organising psychosocial responses
    383–91
and psychiatric injury 349–50
scale 83
in schools 314–19
service provision 305–25
site of 88
and social systems 82
spread 83
typology 83–92
Disasters Working Party 383–8
disavowal 107, 245, 274
disorders of extreme stress 26
displacement *see* refugees
dissociative states 48, 145, 274, 354,
    356–7
distancing techniques 71
domestic violence 176, 181–3
    effect on children 184–8
Donkin, Horatio 7
dopamine 55, 56
drug abuse 59
    and civil violence 157
    and crime 353
DSM–I 135
DSM–II 135
DSM–III 20–1, 135, 394
DSM–III–R 21–3, 377, 394
DSM–IV 23–6, 221, 346, 365, 366, 394
DST 57, 58
duty of care 341–2

education 399
eggshell personality principle 365
elderly 398–9
    acute PTSD 202
    chronic/reactivated PTSD 199–201
    debriefing 246
    effect of conflict on 150
    treatment 202–3
emotional processing 64, 68
    and torture 207–8
employers, role of 323–5, 388

encephalins 58–9
endogenous opioids and PTSD 58–9
EPQ 224
Erichsen, John 5
ethical committees 379–80
ethics 374–81
evacuation 377
exhaustion delirium 19
expert witnesses 335, 354, 358–9
exposure 266–7
eye movement desensitisation 278
Eysenck Personality Questionnaire 224

falaka 152
Falklands conflict 91–2, 142
    veterans 153
family help unit 84
family therapy 277, 282, 285–6
fatigue 11–12
fear
    in combat 138
    conditioned 46–7
    learned 14
    structures 68–9
fight or flight response 11, 56
fire service 329
First World War 7–8, 135, 136–7
flashbacks 46, 50, 221, 274, 354
flooding 282–3
fluoxetine 297–8, 301
foreseeability 365
    and negligence 342–3
forward control post 306
Freud, Sigmund 6, 7, 61
funerals 250

General Health Questionnaire 126, 224
general practitioners 100–3, 386
genocide 149
GHQ–28 126, 224
glucocorticoid receptors 57
glucose 11
glycogen 11
Government investigations 349
GPs 100–3, 386
grief 18, 31, 230
    counselling 253
    interaction with trauma 31–42
    measurement 226
    pathological 253, 257–8, 346
    and psychological trauma 258
    resolution 251

therapy 253
Grief Reaction Inventory 33
gross stress reaction 20, 135
group therapy 276–7
  in childhood 286
guided self–dialogue 269
guilt 23
Gulf War 142–3, 243
Gulf War syndrome 143

hallucinations 221, 328
health authorities 386, 388–90
help-lines 84
helpers 84, 232, 399–400
  effects of disasters on 326–36
helplessness 287
Herald of Free Enterprise 88, 97–8, 283, 286, 346
Hillsborough disaster 307, 345, 346
hippocampus 44 5, 17, 56, 60
historical perspective 3–8
history taking, medico-legal 366–8
Hogan Sibling Inventory of Bereavement 227
Holocaust survivors 151, 154, 199–201, 202–3
  transgenerational effects 151, 214
homicide 37, 177
  children as witnesses 188
  following domestic violence 183, 188
Homicide Act 1957 355
hospital services 330
HPA axis 56–7
human rights
  and social justice 155
  therapist commitment to 211
Hungerford Massacre 84, 116–20
hypothalamic-pituitary-adrenal axis 56–7
hysteria, male 6, 7, 8

ICD–9 19
ICD–10 23, 24, 221, 346, 365, 366
ideology 152
IES *see* Impact of Event Scale
illusion of centrality 90
imaginal exposure 266
imipramine 295–6, 297, 299
immune response 11
Impact of Event Scale (IES) 33, 36, 40, 126, 223–4
  use with children 226

incident control post 306
Index of Bereavement Risk 254
individual protective equipment 138
individual psychotherapy 275–6
Indochinese Psychiatric Clinic 211
industry, emergency planning 323–5, 388
information and referral centre 84
information processing models 67–9, 243–4, 268
informed consent 375
initial defusing 240
inner cordon 306
inquests 105, 349
inquiries 349, 388
insanity, temporary 355
insanity defence 354–5
internal inquiries 349
international agencies, services for refugees 171
International Classification of Diseases see
  ICD–9; ICD–10
International Rehabilitation and Research Centre for Torture Victims 211
International Society for the Study of Traumatic Stress 115
inter-parental violence 184–8
interpersonal dysfunction and crime 353
interpersonal violence
  responses of adults 176–83
  responses of children 184–93
interpreters 212, 221–2
intervention 230–1
  and age 234
  community level 234–5
  crisis 233, 238–9, 242–3, 247
  differentiation and selection of models 232–3
  fantasies 246
  long-term 233–4
  rationale for 232
  stages and strategies 232–5
interventionists 232
interviews
  medico-legal purposes 363, 366–8
  semistructured 224
  structured 224
intrusion 64–5, 98, 244
IPE 138
irritable heart syndrome 135

Jacobs Separation Anxiety Scale 40
jamais vu 328
judicial review 349
Jupiter disaster 94–6, 226, 286
Just World Hypothesis 176

K–SADS–Present Episode 227
Kegworth air disaster 108–10
KIDDIE–SADS 227
kindling phenomenon 56
King's Cross Events Schedule 224
King's Cross fire 111–15
Korean War 20, 140, 141

learned helplessness 15–16, 56, 66–7,
    181–2
learning
    classical 65
    instrumental 65
    state-dependent 45
Lebanon 158
Leeds Permanent Building Society,
    employee education and support
    323–5
legal issues 399
    civil law 341–50
    criminal law 351–60
    psychiatric assessment 363–72
liability 341
lithium 299, 301
litigation 28–9
local authorities 386
Lockerbie air disaster 29, 89, 99–103,
    202, 246, 332
locus coeruleus 56, 59, 60, 294
log 305
long-term potentiation 44
loss 13
    differentiation from threat 39–40
    as stressor 31
    and traumatic stress 32–3
Low Moor explosion 332–3
lymphocyte glucocorticoid receptors 57

McCarthy, John 331
McNaughton rules 354
major incident, definition 383–4
malignant memories 157
malingering 221, 357
Managua earthquake 90
MAOIs 297

Marchioness riverboat disaster 104–7,
    349–50
Maslach Inventory 333
massed practice 283
meaning 68
media 307, 331, 380–1
medial hypothalamic nuclei 56
Medical Foundation for the Care of
    Victims of Torture 322
medical neutrality, violations of 148
medico-legal interview 363, 366–8
medico-legal report 368–71
memorial services 385
memory 44
    and attachment 45
    development 45
    explicit/declarative 44–5
    false 49
    implicit/procedural 44–5
    and narrative 45
    traumatic 46–8
        therapeutic interventions 49–51
memory talk 45
mens rea, effect of psychiatric illness on
    353–4
mental health services, impact of civil
    violence on 156–7
mental state examination 368
metacognition 45–6
metamemory 45–6
Mickle, Julius 6
monoamine oxidase inhibitors 297
monsterisation 13
morale in combat 139
mortuary facilities, temporary 307
mother–child interaction as predictor
    of response to stress 14–16
motor vehicle accidents *see* road traffic
    accidents
mourning 10, 31, 250, 251
    basic tasks 251
    in childhood 257
    facilitation 252–3
    guided 258
multiple personality disorder 274, 357

naloxone 58
naltrexone 300
narrative
    coherence 50
    and memory 45
narrativisation 51

National Association of Bereavement
  Services 321
National Vietnam Veterans Readjust
  ment Study 141
negative thinking 267–8
negligence 341–4, 347–8
neighbour principle 342
nervous shock 344, 363, 365–6
neurasthenia 135
neuroendocrine abnormalities in PTSD
  56–8
neuroleptics 300
neuroses 19
neurotransmitters 55, 56, 60
non-governmental organisations,
  services for refugees 171
noradrenaline 11, 55, 56, 57
normal distress reactions 231
normality and culture 10
Northern Ireland 29, 156, 157 8, 159,
  310, 311–12
  ceasefire 312–13
Northfield experiments 136
nostalgia 135

object relations 63
obsessive–compulsive disorder 221
operant conditioning in childhood
  283–4
Operation Desert Storm *see* Gulf War
opiates 59
organised state violence 205, 206
Ormeau Road bombing 310
Orvaschel Questionnaire 227
oustees 165
outer cordon 306
outreach 88–9
over-accommodation 70

Page, Herbert 5, 7
pain, sensation in emergencies 11
Pan Am disaster 29, 89, 99–103, 202,
  246, 332
panic anxiety disorder 27
panic disorder 71
parenting
  good enough 16
  as predictor of response to stress 14–
  16
Parents of Murdered Children 322
Pavlovian conditioning in childhood
  282–3
PD 329

peace-keeping operations 144
phenelzine 296, 297
phobic anxiety states 27
physiological models of PTSD 55–60,
  294–5
pining *see* separation anxiety
Piper Alpha oil platform disaster 121–
  5, 242, 345, 346
police 305–8, 329, 387
population displacement *see* refugees
post-event dialogue 45
post-traumatic stress disorder (PTSD)
  acute 295
  chronic 295
  classification 19–29, 221, 393–4
  and criminal law 353–8
  diagnosis 219–22, 231–2, 368–9, 394
  diagnostic criteria 20, 22–3, 24, 25,
  221
  in the elderly 199 203
  legal recognition 346
  models 54–72, 243–6, 294–5
  origins 3–8
  prognosis 228–9, 369
  screening 228, 231
  treatment 395–6
    adults 264–78
    children and families 281–92
    pharmacological 285, 294–302,
    324
    see also specific therapies
POWs 143–4, 201
pre-trauma training for incidents at
  work 323–4
Press Council 387
prisoners of war 143–4, 201
problem-solving 269
professional bodies 387
prognosis 228–9, 369
projection 275
projective identification 275
propranolol 298, 301
provocation, as defence 357–8
proximity 342
pseudo-dementia 328
PST 13
psychiatric defences 354–8
psychiatric illness, effect on *mens rea*
  353–4
psychiatric injury
  causative event 344–5
  and civil law 341–50
  and disasters 349–50

fear for oneself 345
fear for others 345–6
level of compensation for 347
recognised 346–7
psychiatrists as expert witnesses 358–9
psychoanalytical models 61–3
psychodynamic psychotherapy 274–7
  in childhood 287–92
psychological debriefing 239
psychopharmacological treatment 234,
    294, 295–300, 302
  in childhood 285
  and comorbidity 295
  future research directions 301–2
  goals for 295
  and physiological changes in PTSD
    294–5
  recommendations for use 300–1
psychosocial response organisation
    383–91
psychosocial transition 13
psychotherapy 233–4
  child 288–92
  and memory 49–51
PTSD Reaction Index 33
public inquiries 349

quantum of damages 371
questionnaires 223–4
  for children 226–7
  translation 222
  use of 223

racially motivated violence 179
railway accidents 4–5
railway spine 5
rape 179–80
  acquaintance/stranger 178
  children as witnesses 188–9
  effect on older women 202
  trauma syndrome 358
  victims 21, 176
rapid eye movement latency 59
real-life exposure 267
reality testing 268
reflecting back 255
reflective self-function 287
refugees 148, 149, 165–6
  and culture 152
  definition 165
  development 165
  identification and diagnosis of
    mental disorder 169

intervention 169–71
  mental health 167–8
  process of displacement 166–7
  role of international agencies and
    non-governmental organisations
    171
  services in resettlement countries
    170–1
  social support in camps 170
  specialised mental health prog-
    rammes for 171–2
  and torture 206
relaxation 16, 269
religious leaders 331
REM latency 59
repetition compulsion 61, 64–5, 180,
    275, 276
reports, medico-legal 368–71
repression 8, 48
rescue fantasies 125, 186
rescuers 84
  effects of disasters on 326–36
research 222–3, 396–7
  and accountability 375–6
  on children and conflict 164
  and competence 376–7
  on debriefing 242–3
  ethics 374–7, 378–9
  and scientific integrity 378–9
resilience 393, 398
resistance 398
response prevention 283–4
responsiveness, numbing of 59
retrieval inhibition 48
rewards 283
rewind and hold 266
rituals 256
Rivers, William 7–8
road traffic accidents (RTAs) 21, 38–9
  and compensation 127, 130
  elderly victims 202
  physical injury in 129
  psychological consequences 126–30
role-playing 270, 285
RTAs *see* road traffic accidents
Ryan, Michael 116

Saigh Children's Post-Traumatic Stress
    Disorder Inventory 226–7
SAMM 322
satiation 283
Schedule for Affective Disorders and
    Schizophrenia 227

schizophrenia 221
school phobia 193
schools 234, 314–19
SCL–90 224
screening 228, 231
Second World War 91, 136–7, 141
    veterans 201, 352
security 306
selective serotonin reuptake inhibitors
    297–8, 301
self-defence 357–8
self-exposure 266
self-help groups 331
self-reflection 51
senior managers 330
separation anxiety 12, 162
    and bereavement 34, 35
serotonin 56
service provision
    by employers 323–5
    by volunteers 320–2
    police 305–8
    schools 314–19
    social workers 309–13
service veterans 137
sexual assault 179–80
    in conflicts 148
    see also rape
sexual harassment 179
shaping behaviour 283
shell-shock 7–8, 135, 136–7
shock 310
SIA 58–9
SIDS 36–7
sleep disturbance 59, 294
sleepwalking 355, 356
social dysfunction and crime 353
social justice and human rights 155
social learning theory 186, 190
social services in disasters 309–13
social skills training in childhood 285
social support 71–2, 98
social systems 82
somatisation disorders 28, 149
somatoform pain disorder 127
source monitoring 45–6
Special Psychiatric Rapid Intervention
    Teams 241
splitting 274–5
SPRINT 241
Standardized Assessment of Personality
    126

startle response 11, 14, 282
state control and torture 205
stimuli
    conditioned 65–6
    unconditioned 65
Strange Situations Test 14
stress 230
    inoculation 200–1, 270
    preparation for 16–18
    responses to 10–13
    developmental aspects 14–16
Stress Clinic 114
stress-induced analgesia 58–9
stress response syndromes 31, 32, 238,
    244
sudden infant death syndrome 36–7
suicide 37, 38
    and civil violence 159
    risk of 234
summarising 255
Support after Murder and Manslaughter
    322
survival mode 68
survivor guilt 23, 98, 109, 122, 189, 246
    in rescuers 328
survivors 83
symbolism 63
Symptom Checklist 224
systematic exposure 70

T stage 311
telephone services 307–8
television violence, effects on children
    189–91
terrorism 156–60, 310, 311–12
testimony 213, 214
testosterone 58
Texas Grief Inventory 34, 40
therapeutic alliance 49, 254
therapeutic neutrality 378
therapists 232, 330–1
    experience of trauma 331–2
    prevention of burnout 334–5
    and torture victims 211
    welfare 234
thought-stopping 269
threat 32–3
    differentiation from loss 39–40
    response to 11–12
thyroid stimulating hormone 58
tortious liability 341

torture 148, 152, 205–6, 213–14
  of children 162–3
  depressive reactions 208–9
  existential dilemma 209–10
  and incomplete emotional proc-
    essing 207–8
  individual psychological reactions
    207–10
  somatic symptoms 209
  treatment 210–13
traffic control 306
transference 274, 276
transgenerational effects 151, 154, 181,
    214, 332–3
transient situational disturbance 20
translators 212
transport workers 328, 329
trauma 230
  definition 61
  interaction with grief 31–42
traumatic bonding 182
traumatic experience
  collective 151–3
  processing and storage 46–7
  retrieval, re-enactment and recall 47–
    8, 352
traumatic neuroses 6, 7, 32
traumatic stress
  and conflict 134–5
  disaster studies 32–3
  psychoanalytical models 61–3
  reaction to 31, 40–1
traumatisation
  psychological 230–1
  vicarious 26
tricyclic antidepressants 56, 295–7, 301

Tuke, D.H., *Dictionary of Psychological
    Medicine* 6–7

UFC 56–7
unconsciousness 127
United Nations Convention Relating to
    the Status of Refugees 165
urinary free cortisol 56–7

valproate 56, 299–300
Victim Support 321–2
victimisation 63, 70
victims 83
  innocent/deserving 176
  self-help groups 331
Victims of Pan Am Flight 103 99
Victorian psychiatry 3–4
Vietnam war 20, 21, 92, 140–1
  veterans 153, 201
    comorbidity 27
    criminal acts 351
    divorce 352
violence
  cycle of 180–1, 359
  interpersonal 176–93
voluntary agencies 260, 320–2, 387
vulnerability 398

Waite, Terry 331
war *see* conflict
war graves, pilgrimage to 92
war neurosis 137

yearning *see* separation anxiety
yohimbine 55
Zeebrugge disaster 88, 97–8, 283, 286, 346